PERGAMON INTERNATIONAL LIBRARY
of Science, Technology, Engineering and Social Studies

*The 1000-volume original paperback library in aid of education,
industrial training and the enjoyment of leisure*

Publisher: Robert Maxwell, M.C.

The Newly Industrializing Countries in the World Economy

THE PERGAMON TEXTBOOK
INSPECTION COPY SERVICE

An inspection copy of any book published in the Pergamon International Library
will gladly be sent to academic staff without obligation for their consideration for
course adoption or recommendation. Copies may be retained for a period of 60 days
from receipt and returned if not suitable. When a particular title is adopted or
recommended for adoption for class use and the recommendation results in a sale
of 12 or more copies the inspection copy may be retained with our compliments.
The Publishers will be pleased to receive suggestions for revised editions and new
titles to be published in this important international Library.

Pergamon Titles of Related Interest

Dell/Lawrence   THE BALANCE OF PAYMENTS ADJUSTMENT
  PROCESS IN DEVELOPING COUNTRIES
Renninger   MULTINATIONAL COOPERATION FOR DEVELOPMENT
  IN WEST AFRICA
Solís   ECONOMIC POLICY REFORM IN MEXICO
Stepanek   BANGLADESH – EQUITABLE GROWTH?
Wionczek   SOME KEY ISSUES FOR THE WORLD PERIPHERY

Related Journals*

COMPUTERS AND INDUSTRIAL ENGINEERING
DESIGN ABSTRACTS INTERNATIONAL
HABITAT INTERNATIONAL
LONG RANGE PLANNING
TECHNOLOGY IN SOCIETY
URBAN SYSTEMS
WORLD DEVELOPMENT

*Free specimen copies available upon request.

The Newly Industrializing Countries in the World Economy

Bela Balassa

Pergamon Press

New York • Oxford • Toronto • Sydney • Paris • Frankfurt

Pergamon Press Offices:

U.S.A.	Pergamon Press Inc., Maxwell House, Fairview Park, Elmsford, New York 10523, U.S.A.
U.K.	Pergamon Press Ltd., Headington Hill Hall, Oxford OX3 0BW, England
CANADA	Pergamon Press Canada Ltd., Suite 104, 150 Consumers Road, Willowdale, Ontario M2J 1P9, Canada
AUSTRALIA	Pergamon Press (Aust.) Pty. Ltd., P.O. Box 544, Potts Point, NSW 2011, Australia
FRANCE	Pergamon Press SARL, 24 rue des Ecoles, 75240 Paris, Cedex 05, France
FEDERAL REPUBLIC OF GERMANY	Pergamon Press GmbH, Hammerweg 6, Postfach 1305, 6242 Kronberg/Taunus, Federal Republic of Germany

Copyright © 1981 Pergamon Press Inc.

Library of Congress Cataloging in Publication Data

Balassa, Bela A
  The newly industrializing countries in the world
economy.

  (Pergamon policy studies on international
development)
  1. Underdeveloped areas – Commerce – Addresses,
essays, lectures. I. Title. II. Series.
HF1413.B345 1980   330.9172′4   80-20787
ISBN 0-08-026336-4
ISBN 0-08-026335-6 (pbk.)

Cover Illustration WORLD BANK PHOTO by Keum Yong Choi

All Rights reserved. No part of this publication may be reproduced, stored in a retrieval system or transmitted in any form or by any means: electronic, electrostatic, magnetic tape, mechanical, photocopying, recording or otherwise, without permission in writing from the publishers.

Printed in the United States of America

330.9172
B17

83-4812

Contents

PART II

Contents

LIST OF TABLES

Essay 2

Essay 3

Essay 6

Essay 7

Essay 8

Essay 9

Preface

The existence of considerable diversity among developing economies has been increasingly recognized. Within this group, the newly-industrializing countries have assumed considerable importance in the world economy over the last fifteen years. In several industries, they have become competitors of the developed countries in the markets of these countries as well as in other markets.

This volume of essays places the newly-industrializing countries in the context of the changing patterns of industrial development and world trade. The essays examine the economic interdependence of countries at different levels of development, evaluate the policies followed, and consider policy measures that may be taken to more fully exploit the benefits of international specialization for rapid economic growth.

The introductory essay provides an overview of the process of industrial development and alternative development strategies. It is followed by the essays of Part I that analyze the external shocks suffered by the newly-industrializing developing countries after 1973 and their policy responses to these shocks; examine the implications of the trade policies of the developed countries and of the Tokyo Round of Multilateral Trade Negotiations for the developing countries; investigate the changing pattern of comparative advantage in manufactured goods and the effects of these changes on employment in the developed countries; and review recent and prospective future trends in trade in manufactured goods between developed and developing countries.

The essays of Part II evaluate the policies applied by selected newly-industrializing countries following the oil crisis and the world recession, and review their economic plans and projections. Recommendations are further made on economic policies for the future.

The essay on Greece and two essays each on Korea and Taiwan were prepared as policy advisory reports for the governments concerned and are published with their concurrence. The essays on Brazil, Portugal, Turkey, and Hungary were written in response to invitations by national institutions; they were originally published in conference volumes or academic journals. The essays of Part I also first appeared in academic journals while the introductory essay was published in the Princeton *Essays of International Finance*. Permission for publication to all concerned is gratefully acknowledged.

The author further wishes to express his appreciation to government officials and economists in the individual countries for their interest and support and to the World Bank under whose auspices all the essays of the volume, except the one on Greece, were prepared. However, the essays express the opinions of the author and should not be interpreted to reflect the views of particular governments or the World Bank.

Bela Balassa

A Reader's Guide

This volume is a sequel to the author's *Policy Reform in Developing Countries* that examined the principles of desirable policy reforms and provided applications of these principles to practical situations in countries that have already established an industrial base.[1] The essays of the present volume focus on the process of industrial development and the changing pattern of comparative advantage and examine appropriate policies for trade and economic growth in countries at different levels of development. Nine essays of the volume are devoted to general issues relating to development and trade, with attention given to the place of the newly industrializing countries in the world economy, while the remaining nine analyze the policies of selected newly-industrializing countries.

Newly-industrializing countries have been defined as countries that had per capita incomes between $1100 and $3500 in 1978, and where the share of the manufacturing sector in the gross domestic product was 20 percent or higher in 1977. The group includes Argentina, Brazil, Chile, Hong Kong, Israel, Korea, Mexico, Singapore, Taiwan, Uruguay, and Yugoslavia that are customarily classified as developing countries; Greece, Portugal, Spain and Turkey among the member countries of the OECD, the international economic organization of developed countries; and Hungary, Bulgaria, and Romania among socialist countries.[2]

The introductory essay of the volume was first presented as the Frank Graham Memorial Lecture at Princeton University on April 17, 1980.[3] It summarizes the author's ideas on the process of industrial development and on alternative development strategies. Drawing on his research over the last decade, the author examines the determinants of early industrial development, analyzes experience with inward-and outward-oriented strategies at subsequent stages of development, and places the newly-industrializing developing countries in the context of the industrial development process.

In Part I, Essays 2 and 3 use a common analytical framework to investigate policy responses to external shocks by the newly-industrializing developing countries after 1973.[4] The external shocks in question include the deterioration of the terms of trade and the slowdown of world demand while the policy responses comprise additional external financing, export promotion, import substitution, and the deceleration of the rate of economic growth. Essay 2 examines the experience of ten newly-industrializing developing countries and of Colombia and India while Essay 3 analyzes the policies applied in three Latin American countries in greater detail.

In Essay 2, it is shown that the continuation of outward-oriented policies (Korea, Singapore, and Taiwan), and the adoption of such policies in response to external shocks (Chile and Uruguay), permitted surmounting these shocks within a relatively short period, reestablishing or surpassing past rates of economic growth. In turn, maintaining (India) or increasing (Brazil, Colombia, Israel, and Yugoslavia) the bias of the system of incentives in favor of import substitution and against exports had adverse effects on economic performance as did excessively expansionary policies (Argentina and Mexico).

These conclusions are supported by the findings of a detailed investigation of three Latin American countries, Brazil, Mexico, and Uruguay, in Essay 3. After long stagnation, policy changes in Uruguay led to a rise in per capita incomes surpassing that of Brazil, which again turned towards import substitution. At the same time, Brazil became increasingly indebted as the proceeds of foreign loans were in large part used for raising consumption levels and for investment in high-cost import substituting industries. Finally, continued expansionary policies, financed largely by foreign borrowing, adversely affected the non-oil sectors of the Mexican economy.

Essays 4 and 5 examine the trade policies applied by the developed countries.[5] Following an analysis of the favorable effects of postwar trade liberalization on world trade and economic growth, benefiting in particular the newly-industrializing countries, Essay 4 describes the emergence of protectionist pressures in the developed countries in the wake of the oil crisis and the world recession. It further analyzes the adverse economic effects of the measures of "new protectionism," including non-tariff restrictions, government subsidies, and cartelization, for developed and developing countries alike and makes recommendations for policy changes.

Essay 5 reports that the trend towards increased protection in the developed countries has not continued further and, in some respects, it has been reversed. A major event has been the successful completion of the Tokyo Round of Multilateral Trade Negotiations. The essay evaluates the tariff reductions and the new non-tariff codes adopted in the Tokyo Round from the point-of-view of the developing countries and concludes that it is in the interest of these countries to subscribe to the codes. The conclusion applies in particular to the newly-industrializing developing countries that account for about 85 percent of the manufactured exports of the developing countries.

Essay 6 analyzes the changing pattern of comparative advantage in the process of economic development. The estimates obtained for eighteen developed and eighteen developing countries demonstrate that inter-country differences in the structure of exports are largely explained by differences in physical and human capital endowments. These results lend support to the 'stages' approach to comparative advantage, according to which the structure of exports changes with the accumulation of physical and human capital. With countries progressing on the comparative advantage scale, then, their exports will supplant the exports of countries that graduate to a higher level. To the extent that one developing country replaces another in exporting particular commodities to the markets of the developed countries, the problem of adjustment in the latter group of countries does not arise.

The estimates of Essay 6 on the physical and the human capital intensity of trade, together with data on labor coefficients, are utilized in Essay 7 to indicate the extent to which developed countries exchange physical and human capital for labor in trading manufactured goods with the developing countries.[6] Nevertheless, the employment effects of this trade are, on balance, favorable for the developed countries. This is because the excess of exports over imports more than compensates for the higher labor intensity of imports.

In reviewing the experience of the 1973–1978 period, Essay 8 provides further evidence on the changing pattern of comparative advantage, with the newly-industrializing countries increasingly exporting skill-intensive commodities, and the less developed countries embarking on the exportation of unskilled labor intensive products. The review of recent trends in trade in manufactured goods in the essay is further complemented by projections of this trade in Essay 9.[7]

The growth of manufactured exports of the industrial countries accelerated during the 1973–1978 period, reflecting the spending of oil earnings by OPEC and the increase of foreign borrowing by non-OPEC developing countries. In turn, while the slowdown of economic expansion in the industrial countries contributed to a decline in the rate of growth of their imports of manufactured goods from the developing countries, the data do not provide evidence of the effects of increased protectionism.

Essay 9 projects rapid increases in trade in manufactured goods between the industrial and the developing countries between 1978 and 1990, on the assumption that present trade policies continue. Increases in this trade will provide benefits to all concerned through resource allocation according to comparative advantage, economies of scale, and increased competition.

Further gains may be obtained through trade liberalization by the industrial countries that would lead to more rapid increases in their imports than projected under the continuation of present policies, with consequent increases in their exports. This could be accomplished without involving excessively large adjustment costs if the liberalization of trade proceeded over a ten-year horizon.

The newly-industrializing countries, too, would obtain additional benefits if they liberalized their system of protection. The essays of Part II of the volume, written between September 1977 and September 1979, analyze incentive policies and economic plans in selected newly-industrializing countries and offer recommendations for future policies.

Following a review of reforms introduced in second half of the sixties, Essay 10 analyzes measures taken in Brazil in response to the oil crisis and the world recession.[8] While Brazil avoided substantial reductions in rates of economic growth, this was done at the cost of rising foreign indebtedness. At the same time, the cost of economic expansion increased with rise in the level and dispersion of rates of import protection and of fiscal and credit subsidies, and the increased use of discretionary measures. The essay makes recommendations for reducing protection and subsidy rates and replacing discretionary decision-making by the application of automatic rules. Certain reform measures have subsequently been taken but only limited progress has been made towards the above objectives.

In Portugal, the effects of the oil crisis and the world recession were aggravated by the policies adopted in the aftermath of the April 1974 Revolution. After reviewing the policy improvements made between 1976 and 1979, Essay 11 makes recommendations for agricultural and industrial policies that would prepare Portugal for entry into the European Common Market.[9] The policy recommendations aim at modernizing agriculture, exploiting Portugal's comparative advantages within the manufacturing sector, increasing the rate of investment, and reducing unproductive expenditures in the public sector. Various steps in these directions have since been taken, particularly after the October 1980 elections.

Essay 12 provides a critical appraisal of projections made in the preliminary plan document for the 1978–1982 period in Greece.[10] It further examines the economic perspectives for Greece following entry in the European Common Market and makes recommendations for reducing labor costs, encouraging savings and investment, and undertaking structural reforms so as to ensure that the potential advantages of participation in the EEC are fully realized. While Greece has since become member of the Common Market, few policy changes have in fact been made.

Rather than domestic adjustment, Turkey's response to the oil price increase and the world recession was borrowing abroad that brought the economy to a crisis. Essay 13 makes recommendations for the adoption of an outward-oriented strategy that would make increased use of market signals and serve simultaneously short-term and medium-term objectives.[11] Far-reaching reforms were introduced in January 1980 and further liberalization measures have subsequently been taken.

Apart from foreign borrowing, Hungary sought to alleviate the consequences of increases in oil prices and the world recession by loosening its ties with the world economy. Essay 14 describes the adverse effects of the actions taken and makes recommendations for restoring and further extending the Hungarian economic reform of 1968 that entailed decentralizing decision-making in the framework of an open economy.[12] This objective has been served by reforms undertaken since, in particular the price reform of January 1, 1980.

In reviewing the 15-year Social and Economic Development Plan (1976–

81) for Korea, Essay 15 takes a position in favor of continued export orientation and against a strategy emphasizing import substitution. It further makes recommendations for corresponding changes in the plan projections.

Essay 16 comments on the subsequent revision of the plan projections for Korea.[13] It notes that, in raising export projections and reducing the extent of import substitution, the revised projections reflect a greater degree of outward orientation, although less than proposed by the author. In reaffirming the need for increased outward orientation, the essay focuses on policy measures that may contribute to the twin objectives of lowering the rate of inflation and maintaining high rates of economic growth. In the event, large capital-intensive investments in intermediate products and heavy machinery have reduced the availability of funds for investments in export industries and have contributed to inflation, with adverse effects on the competitiveness of Korean exports and on economic growth after 1978.

Essay 17 makes recommendations for modifying the original targets of the Six Year Plan (1975–1981) for Taiwan, with a view to maintaining the strategy of outward orientation.[14] The essay calls for upgrading traditional manufactured exports, developing the exports of machinery and equipment, and reducing investment targets for highly capital-intensive intermediate goods industries.

As noted in Essay 18, the revised Six Year Plan presents a realistic and consistent set of projections that reflect the need for exports to continue their leading role in Taiwan's industrial development. The essay makes recommendations on incentive policies that would contribute to continued rapid growth. Various steps have since been taken to reinforce Taiwan's outward orientation.

ESSAY 1

The Process of Industrial Development and Alternative Development Strategies*

I. Introduction

The Subject Matter

In the title of the essay, the use of the expression "industrial development" rather than "industrialization" is meant to convey the idea that the development of manufacturing industries is part and parcel of overall economic development. At its earlier stages, industrial development is contingent on demand and savings generated in the primary sector; subsequently, intersectoral flows assume importance and protection and other incentives to manufacturing will affect the profitability of primary activities.

The expression "process" in the title emphasizes the element of continuity in industrial development as well as the idea that countries may proceed through similar stages in the course of their industrialization. While the concept of "stages" has fallen into disuse, and even disrepute, it is a convenient way to characterize the pattern of industrial development until countries become full-fledged industrial nations.

The use of the expression "process" does not mean to convey the idea that, once begun, industrial development would continue uninterrupted. There are, in fact, "accidents de parcours" that may halt or reverse the process. Such

* The invitation to present the Graham Memorial Lecture at Princeton University provided me with the welcome opportunity to review and to summarize my ideas on the process of industrial development and on industrial development strategies. This essay retains the format of the lecture and it eschews footnote references. A list of my publications, from which the empirical evidence cited in the essay is derived, is contained in the Appendix.

accidents may be due to external causes, such as the theft of a few specimens of the Hevea plant at the start of the century, leading to the production of rubber in the South East Asia, that cut short the export boom in Brazil and reduced thereby demand for industrial products.

But, more often than not, the "accident de parcours" are due to inappropriate policies. More generally, the results obtained will depend on the policies applied. This will be the case, in particular, after the completion of the first stage of import substitution. The reference to "alternative development strategies" in the title of the essay reflects my view as to the importance of the choice of policies for industrial and economic development.

The Role of Objective Factors

This is not to deny the role of objective factors, such as country size, natural resource endowment, location, preferential ties, foreign investment, foreign aid, education, and political and social conditions, in the process of industrial development. At the same time, the importance of these factors should not be exaggerated.

The size of the country will influence the scope for the exploitation of economies of scale and the extent of domestic competition, and hence the degree to which inward-oriented industrial development may proceed without incurring excessive costs. But a large country may unduly postpone policy reform while a small country will be under greater pressure to carry out reforms.

In this connection, reference may be made to the positive correlation observed between the size of domestic markets and tariffs in the present-day industrial countries at their early stages of industrial development. While the United States and Russia had the highest rates of protection at the time of their early industrial development, the small countries of the Benelux and Scandinavia were traditionally free traders.

The correlation between country size and protection is far from perfect in the developing countries of today, indicating the importance of policy choices. Thus, Brazil, the developing country with the largest domestic market, turned towards promoting manufactured exports in the mid-sixties as continued import substitution encountered market limitations and led to a slowdown of industrial and economic growth. In turn, a large developing country, India, a medium-size country, Chile, and a small country, Uruguay, continued with inward-oriented policies during the period preceding the oil crisis.

Also, contrary to the oft-expressed view that seeks to explain the adoption of an outward-oriented development strategy by Far Eastern developing countries in terms of market size, these countries are hardly small as far as developing countries are concerned. Thus, Korea may be considered a large developing country, having a population nearly one-half larger than Argentina;

Taiwan has a population more than one-half larger than Chile; and Hong Kong more than one-half larger than Uruguay, with Singapore not far behind.

The availability of natural resources will benefit industrial development by providing domestic markets and investible funds for manufacturing industries as well as materials for further transformation. It is, however, a mixed blessing as the availability of primary exports may lead to the postponement of domestic policy change; high wages in natural resource industries raise wages and hence production costs in manufacturing industries; and natural resource exports give rise to an unfavorable exchange rate for industrial activities. While the Kuwait syndrome represents a rather special case, oil earnings have adversely affected the international competitiveness of manufacturing industries in Venezuela and, more recently, in Mexico.

In reference to the success of Denmark and Norway in transforming their export structure, it has been suggested that these countries have benefited from their favorable geographical location, with nearby markets for manufactured goods in Western Europe. However, Japan did well in exporting manufactures notwithstanding its distant location as did subsequently Korea and Taiwan that had more success in exporting to the United States than to the nearby Japanese market.

Location will be relevant for regional economic integration. But regional integration may lead to the establishment of a high cost area as it happened in Central America; at any rate, integration efforts have met with little success in developing countries. And, countries as different as Brazil and Ivory Coast see the large markets of the industrial countries to be more promising than regional markets. Finally, Korea and Taiwan have reached high growth rates of exports and GNP without having access to regional markets.

Preferential ties to industrial countries, too, are said to provide advantages for exporting manufactured goods. A better formulation would be to speak of potential advantages as the Philippines in the first half of the century and, more recently, the former French territories participating in the Lome convention have not been successful in exploiting the opportunities provided by preferential access. In turn, contrary to popular misconceptions, Korea and Taiwan have not enjoyed preferential access to the U.S. market.

Also, foreign direct investment has been of much greater importance in Latin America than in the Far East. With the exception of Singapore, Far Eastern developing countries have by-and-large followed the Japanese pattern in relying on indigenous entrepreneurship. At any rate, it is not only the volume but the direction of foreign direct investment that matters. While investment in export industries will contribute to economic growth, foreign direct investment in industries operating behind high protection may entail a net loss of foreign exchange for the host country. This will be the case if the foreign exchange cost of materials and machinery, augmented by the repatriation of profits, exceeds the cif import value of the product.

In the case of Korea and Taiwan, foreign aid should be set against defense spending it was to a large degree destined to finance. In fact, since the late fifties in Taiwan, and since the mid-sixties in Korea, defense spending has exceeded foreign aid by an increasing margin. At the same time, the contribution of foreign aid to economic development will depend on the form it takes as the tying of aid tends to raise industrial costs and food aid may hinder agricultural development.

Education has further been cited as a major factor contributing to the economic success of the Far Eastern countries. But, measured by the Harbison-Myers index, Chile and Uruguay had high education levels in the nineteen-sixties and nevertheless exhibited poor economic performance. At any rate, the level of education is the result of investment in human capital, which is affected by government policies.

Political and social conditions may also assist or hinder industrial development. At the same time, there are successful, as well as unsuccessful, economic performers among both dictatorships and democracies. Furthermore, references to social conditions often become ex-post rationalizations. Thus, while the growth successes of Korea and Taiwan have come to be attributed to the Confucian ethic, twenty years ago AID administrators ridiculed the notion that the commercial-minded Taiwanese would become successful producers and exporters of manufactured goods and only fifteen years ago Korea was considered a hopeless case.

II. Early Stages of Industrial Development

The Generation of a Surplus in the Primary Sector

Industrial development generally begins in response to domestic demand generated in the primary sector that also provides investible funds for manufacturing industries. Demand for industrial products and investible savings represent possible uses of the surplus generated in agriculture, understood in a larger sense to include crops, livestock, fisheries, and forestry, or in mining. The surplus is generated as primary output comes to exceed subsistence needs and, more often than not, it is associated with export expansion.

At the same time, the effects of primary exports on industrial development depend to a considerable extent on input-output relationships and on the disposition of incomes generated in the export sector. Infrastructure in the form of ports, railways, and roads are often important inputs for primary exports, and their availability may contribute to the development of industrial activities.

The disposition of incomes generated in the export sector is affected by ownership conditions. In the case of foreign ownership, a substantial part of the surplus may repatriated, albeit taxing the earnings of foreign capital does add to domestic incomes. There are leakages in the form of investing and spending abroad, as well as consuming imported luxuries, in the case of domestic ownership in a system of plantation-type agriculture and large-scale mining, too. And, as Douglas North noted, plantation owners have little incentive to finance human investment in the form of general education.

By contrast, in cases when family-size farms predominate, demand is generated for the necessities and the conveniences of life as well as for education. Such demand contributes to the development of domestic industry that enjoys "natural" protection from imports in the form of transportation costs. It further contributes to be the accumulation of human capital that finds use in manufacturing industries.

The process of industrial development may be accelerated if natural protection is complemented by tariff or quota protection. This last point, in turn, leads me to the discussion of the next step in the industrialization process: the first, or "easy" stage of import substitution.

The First Stage of Import Substitution

With the exception of Britain at the time of the Industrial Revolution, and, more recently, Hong Kong, all present-day industrial and developing countries protected their incipient manufacturing industries producing for domestic markets. There were differences, however, as regards the rate and the form of protection. While the industrial countries of today relied on relatively low tariffs, a number of present-day developing countries applied high tariffs or quantitative restrictions that limited or even excluded, competition from imports.

At the same time, high protection discriminates against exports through the explicit or implicit taxation of export activities. Explicit taxation may take the form of export taxes while implicit taxation occurs as a result of the effects of protection on the exchange rate. The higher the rate of protection, the lower will be the exchange rate necessary to ensure equilibrium in the balance of payments, and the lower the amount of domestic currency exporters receive per unit of foreign exchange earned.

The adverse effects of high protection are exemplified in the case of Ghana, where import prohibitions encouraged inefficient, high-cost production in manufacturing industries; taxes on the main export crop, cocoa, discouraged its production; and other crops were adversely affected by the unfavorable exchange rate. Ghana's neighbor, the Ivory Coast, in turn, followed a policy encouraging the development of both primary and manufacturing activities. As a result, it increased its share in cocoa exports, developed new primary exports, and expanded manufacturing industries.

Differences in the policies applied may largely explain that, between 1960 and 1978, per capita incomes fell from $430 to $390 in Ghana, in terms of 1978 prices, as compared to an increase from $540 to $840 in the Ivory Coast.

This has occurred notwithstanding the fact that the two countries have similar natural resource endowments and, at the time of independence, Ghana had the advantage of a higher educational level and an indigenous civil service corps.

Indeed, there is no need for high protection at the first stage of import substitution, entailing the replacement of the imports of nondurable consumer goods, such as clothing, shoes, and household goods, and of their inputs, such as textile fabrics, leather and wood, by domestic production, since these commodities suit the conditions existing in developing countries that are at the beginning of the industrialization process. The commodities in question are intensive in unskilled labor; the efficient scale of output is relatively low and costs do not rise substantially at lower output levels; production does not involve the use of sophisticated technology; and a network of suppliers of parts, components, and accessories is not required for efficient operations.

The relative advantages of developing countries in these commodities explain the frequent references made to the "easy" stage of import substitution. At the same time, to the extent that the domestic production of these commodities generates external economies in the form of labor training, the development of entrepreneurship, and the spread of technology, there is an argument for moderate infant industry protection or promotion.

III. Inward-Oriented Industrial Development Strategies

The Choice of Second-Stage Import Substitution

In the course of first-stage import substitution, domestic production will rise more rapidly than domestic consumption, since it not only provides for increases in consumption but also replaces replaces imports. The rate of growth of output will however decline to that of consumption, once the process of import substitution has been completed.

Maintaining high industrial growth rates, then, necessitates turning to the exportation of manufactured goods or moving to second-stage import substitution. This choice, in fact, represents alternative industrial development strategies that may be applied after the completion of the first stage of import substitution. I will first consider second-stage import substitution, representing the application of an inward-looking industrial development strategy, and will subsequently examine an outward-oriented strategy that does not discriminate against exports, with favorable effects on the exporting of manufactured goods.

Second-stage import substitution was undertaken in the postwar period in several Latin American countries, some South Asian countries, in particular India, as well as in the European Socialist coutries. In Latin America, it responded to the ideas of Raul Prebisch, in whose view adverse foreign market conditions for primary exports and lack of competitiveness in manufactured exports would not permit developing countries to attain high rates of economic growth by relying on export production. Rather, Prebisch suggested that these countries should expand their manufacturing industries oriented towards domestic markets. This purpose was to be served by industrial protection that was said to bring additional benefits through improvements in the terms of trade.

Similar ideas were expressed by Gunnar Myrdal. Myrdal influenced the policies followed by India, which were also affected by the example of the Soviet Union that chose an autarchical pattern of industrial development. And, the European socialist countries faithfully imitated the Soviet example; they attempted to reproduce the Soviet pattern in the framework of much smaller domestic markets and also lacking the natural resource base of the Soviet Union.

Second-stage import substitution involves the replacement of the imports of intermediate goods and producer and consumer durables by domestic production. These commodities have rather different characteristics from those replaced at the first stage. Intermediate goods, such as petrochemicals and steel, tend to be highly capital-intensive. They are also subject to important economies of scale, with efficient plant size being large compared to the domestic needs of most developing countries and costs rising rapidly at lower output levels. Moreover, the margin of processing is relatively small and organizational and technical inefficiencies may contribute to high costs.

Producer durables, such as machinery, and consumer durables, such as automobiles and refrigerators, are also subject to economies of scale. But, in these industries, economies of scale relate not so much to plant size as to horizontal and to vertical specialization, entailing reductions in product variety and the manufacture of parts, components, and accessories on an efficient scale in separate plants.

Reducing product variety will permit longer production runs that lower production costs through improvements in manufacturing efficiency along the "learning curve," savings in expenses incurred in moving from one operation to another, and the use of special-purpose machinery. Horizontal specialization is however limited by the smallness of domestic markets in the developing countries. Similar conclusions apply to vertical specialization that leads to cost reductions through the subdivision of the production process among plants of efficient size.

In this connection, reference may be made to General Motors that has ten thousands of subcontractors, each producing a part or component. This extended division of the production process has permitted General Motors to produce at a substantially lower cost than its U.S. competitors. Some years ago, Martin Shubik reached the conclusion that, without antitrust legislation, only General Motors will survive in the United States and predicted the disappearance of several small American car producers. This has in fact occurred since and, without federal support, Chrysler would have met a similar fate.

At the same time, the production of parts, components, and accessories has to be done to precision for consumer durables and, in particular, for machinery. This, in turn, requires the availability of skilled and technical labor and, to a greater or lesser extent, the application of sophisticated technology.

Given the relative scarcity of physical and human capital in developing countries that completed the first stage of import substitution, they are at a disadvantage in the manufacture of highly physical-capital intensive intermediate goods and skill-intensive producer and consumer durables. In limiting the scope for the exploitation of economics of scale, the relatively small size of their national markets also contributes to high domestic costs in these countries. At the same time, net foreign exchange savings tend to be small because of the need for importing materials and machinery.

The domestic resource cost ratio relates the domestic resource cost of production, in terms of the labor, capital, and natural resources utilized, to net foreign exchange savings (in the case of import substitution) or net foreign exchange earnings (in the case of exports). In the absence of serious distortions in factor markets, the domestic resource cost (DRC) ratio will be low for exported commodities. It is also relatively low for consumer nondurables and their inputs, in the production of which developing countries have a comparative advantage. However, for the reasons noted beforehand, DRC ratios tend to be high in the manufacture of intermediate goods and producer and consumer durables.

Correspondingly, the establishment of these industries to serve narrow domestic markets is predicated on high protection. Also, rates of protection may need to be raised as countries "travel up the staircase," represented by DRC ratios, in embarking on the production of commodities that less and less conform to their comparative advantage. This will occur as goods produced at earlier stages have come to saturate domestic markets. High protection, in turn, discriminates against manufactured and primary exports and against primary activities in general.

Characteristics of Inward-Oriented Development Strategies

In the postwar period, several capitalist countries in Latin America and in South Asia and the socialist countries of Central and Eastern Europe adopted inward-oriented industrial development strategies, entailing second-stage import substitution. Capitalist countries generally utilized a mixture of tariffs and import controls to protect their industries whereas socialist countries relied on import prohibitions and on industry level planning.

Notwithstanding differences in the measures applied, the principal characteristics of the industrial development strategies applied in the two groups of countries show considerable similarities. To begin with, while the infant industry argument calls for temporary protection until industries become internationally competitive, in both groups of countries protection was regarded as permanent. Also, in all the countries concerned, there was a tendency towards what a Latin American economist aptly described as "import substitution at any cost."

Furthermore, in all the countries concerned, there were considerable variations in rates of explicit and implicit protection among industrial activities. This was the case, first of all, as continued import substitution involved undertaking activities with increasingly high domestic costs per unit of foreign exchange saved. In capitalist countries, the generally uncritical acceptance of demands for protection contributed to this result, when, in the absence of price comparisons, the protective effects of quantitative restrictions could not even be established. In socialist countries, the stated objective was to limit imports to commodities that could not be produced domestically, or were not available in sufficient quantities, and no attempt was made to examine the implicit protection the pursuit of this objective entailed.

In both groups of countries, the neglect of intraindustry relationships further increased the dispersion of protection rates on value added in processing, or effective protection, with adverse effects on economic efficiency. In Argentina, high tariffs imposed on caustic soda at the request of a would-be producer made the theretofore thriving soap exports unprofitable. In Hungary, the high cost of domestic steel, based largely on imported iron ore and coking coals, raised costs for steel-using industries and large investments in the steel industry delayed the substitution of aluminum for steel, although Hungary had considerable bauxite reserves.

Countries applying inward-oriented industrial development strategies were further characterized by the prevalence of sellers' markets. In capitalist countries, the size of national markets limited the possibilities for domestic competition in industries established at the second stage of import substitution while import competition was practically excluded by high protection. In socialist countries, the system of central planning applied did not permit competition among domestic firms or from imports and buyers had no choice among domestic producers or access to imported commodities.

The existence of sellers' markets provides little inducement for catering to the users' needs. In the case of industrial users, it led to backward integration as producers undertook the manufacture of parts, components, and accessories in order to minimize supply difficulties. This outcome, observed in capitalist as well as in socialist countries, led to higher costs, since economies of scale were foregone.

Also, in sellers' markets, firms had little incentive to improve productivity. In capitalist countries, monopolies and oligopolies assumed importance, and the oligopolists often aimed at the maintenance of market shares while refraining from actions that would invoke retaliation. In socialist countries, the existence of assured outlets and the emphasis on short-term objectives on the part of managers discouraged technological change.

The managers' emphasis on short-term objectives in socialist countries had to do with uncertainty as to the planners' future intentions. In capitalist countries, fluctuations in real exchange rates (nominal exchange rates, adjusted for changes in inflation rates at home and abroad) created uncertainty for business decisions. These fluctuations, resulting from intermittent devaluations in the face of rapid domestic inflation, aggravated the existing bias against exports as the domestic currency equivalent of export earnings varied with the devaluations, the timing of which was uncertian.

In countries engaging in second-stage import substitution, distortions were further apparent in the valuation of time. In capitalist countries, negative real interest rates adversely affected domestic savings, encouraged self-investment, including inventory accumulation, at low returns, and provided inducements for the transfer of funds abroad. Negative interest rates also necessitated credit rationing that generally favored import-substituting investments, whether it was done by the banks or by the government. In the first case, the lower risk of investments in production for domestic as compared to export markets gave rise to such a result; in the second case, it reflected government priorities. Finally, in socialist countries, ideological considerations led to the exclusion of interest rates as a charge for capital and as an element in the evaluation of investment projects.

There was also a tendency to underprice public utilities in countries following an inward-oriented strategy, either because of low interest charges in these capital-intensive activities or as a result of a conscious decision. The under-pricing of utilities benefited, in particular, energy-intensive industries and promoted the use of capital.

In general, in moving to the second stage of import substitution, countries applying inward-oriented development strategies de-emphasized the role of prices. In socialist countries, resources were in large part allocated centrally in physical terms; in capitalist countries, output and input prices were distorted and reliance was placed on non-price measures of import restrictions and credit allocation.

Effects on Exports and on Economic Growth

The discrimination in favor of import substitution and against exports did not permit the development of manufactured exports in countries engaging in second-stage import substitution behind high protection. There were also adverse developments in primary exports as low prices for producers and for consumers reduced the exportable surplus by discouraging production and encouraging consumption.

In fact, rather than improvements in the external terms of trade that were supposed to result, turning the internal terms of trade against primary activities led to a decline in export market shares in the countries in question. Decreases in market shares were especially pronounced in cereals, meat, oilseeds, and nonferrous metals, benefiting developed countries, in particular, the United States, Canada, and Australia.

The volume of Argentina's principal primary exports, chiefly beef and wheat, remained, on the average, unchanged between 1934-38 and 1964-66 while the world exports of these commodities doubled. In the same period, Chile's share fell from 28 percent to 22 percent in the world exports of copper, which accounts for three-fifths of the country's export earnings.

Similar developments occurred in socialist countries where the allocation of investment favored industry at the expense of agriculture. In Hungary, the exports of several agricultural commodities, such as goose liver, fodder seeds, and beans, declined in absolute terms and slow increases in production necessitated the imports of cereals and meat that were earlier major export products.

The slowdown in the growth of primary exports and the lack of emergence of manufactured exports did not provide the foreign exchange necessary for rapid economic growth in countries pursuing inward-oriented industrial development strategies. The situation was aggravated as net import savings declined because of the increased need for foreign materials, machinery, and technological know-how. As a result, economic growth was increasingly constrained by limitations in the availability of foreign exchange, and intermittent foreign exchange crises occurred as attempts were made to expand the economy at rates exceeding that permitted by the growth of export earnings.

Also, the savings constraint became increasingly binding as high-cost, capital intensive production at second-stage import substitution raised capital-output ratios, requiring ever-increasing savings ratios to maintain rates of economic growth at earlier levels. At the same time, the loss of incomes due to the high cost of protection reduced the volume of available savings and, in capitalist countries, negative interest rates contributed to the outflow of funds.

In several developing countries, the cost of protection is estimated to have reached 6-7 percent of the gross national product. At the same time, there is evidence that the rate of growth of total factor productivity was lower in countries engaging in second-stage import substitution than in the industrial countries. Rather then reducing the economic distance vis-à-vis the industrial countries that infant industry protection was supposed to promote, then, there was a tendency for this lag to increase over time.

IV. Outward-Oriented Industrial Development Strategies

The Choice of Outward Orientation

The slowdown in economic growth that eventually resulted from the pursuit of an inward-oriented development strategy led to policy reform in several of the countries applying such a strategy. Among capitalist countries, policy reforms were undertaken in the mid-sixties in Argentina, Brazil and Colombia, and in subsequent years in Mexico. The reforms generally involved providing subsidies to manufactued exports, reducing import protection, applying a system of crawling pegs, adopting positive real interest rates, and introducing greater realism in the pricing of public utilities.

Among socialist countries, central resource allocation and price determination gave place to the decentralization of decision making in Hungary. This involved introducing market relations among firms and linking domestic prices to world market prices through the exchange rate, with adjustment made for import tariffs and for export subsidies.

The policy reforms undertaken by countries that engaged in second-stage import substitution thus involved making increased use of the price mechanism and reducing price distortions, in particular in foreign trade. The incentive systems that emerged as a result of the reforms in the period preceding the 1973 oil crisis may be compared with the incentive systems applied in countries that adopted an outward-oriented industrial development strategy immediately following the completion of first-stage import substitution.

An outward-oriented development strategy should not be interpreted to mean favoring exports over import substitution. Rather, it is characterized by providing similar incentives to production for domestic and for export markets. Thus, the definitions of inward- and outward- oriented development strategies are not symmetrical. At the same time, these definitions reflect reality as few countries gave incentives to any of their exports appreciably in excess of incentives to sales in domestic markets.

Apart from the lack of a bias against exports, countries applying outward-oriented development strategies generally had positive real interest rates, adopted realistic prices for public utilities, reduced inter-industry differences in incentives, and provided for automaticity and stability in the incentive system. On the whole, these countries minimized price distortions and relied on the market mechanism for efficient resource allocation and rapid economic growth.

Among present-day industrial countries, an outward-oriented development strategy was adopted by Denmark and Norway in the years immediately following the Second World War. In Southern Europe and, with certain limitations, in Japan, this occurred starting in the mid-fifties. Finally, in Korea, Singapore and Taiwan, an outward-oriented strategy has been pursued since the early sixties.

In comparing the incentive systems applied by the three Far Eastern countries and those adopted in the four Latin American countries following second-stage import substitution, several features deserve attention. These relate to the treatment of the export sector, relative incentives to exports and import substitution, the variability of incentive rates among particular activities, relative incentives to manufacturing and to primary production, and the automaticity and stability of the incentive system.

In the three Far Eastern countries, a free trade regime was applied to exports. Exporters were free to choose between domestic and imported inputs; they were exempted from indirect taxes on their output and inputs; and they paid no duty on imported inputs. The same privileges were extended to the producers of domestic inputs used in export production.

The application of these rules provided equal treatment to all exports. And while some additional export incentives were granted, they did not introduce much differentiation among individual export commodities. At the same time, these incentives ensured that in the manufacturing sector, on the average, exports received similar treatment as import substitution. Furthermore, there was little discrimination against primary exports and against primary activities in general; incentives were on the whole provided automatically; and the incentive system underwent few modifications over time.

Latin American countries (Argentina, Brazil, Colombia, and Mexico) that reformed their incentive system after engaging in second-stage import substitution granted subsidies to their nontraditional exports. They also reduced the extent of import protection, both directly through tariff cuts and import liberalization, and indirectly as the growth of exports in response to the subsidies provided diminished the need for exchange rate depreciation and thereby reduced the protective effects of tariffs.

The four Latin American countries did not, however, provide exporters with a free choice between domestic and imported inputs. Rather, in order to safeguard existing industries, exporters were required to use domestic inputs produced under protection. To compensate exporters for the resulting excess cost, as well as for the effects of import protection on the exchange rate, the countries in question provided explicit export subsidies.

These subsidies did not suffice, however, to provide producers with export incentives comparable to the protection of domestic markets. Thus, there continued to be a bias in favor of import substitution and against exports, albeit at a reduced rate. The extent of discrimination was especially pronounced against traditional primary exports that did not receive export subsidies and, in some instances, continued to be subject to export taxes.

Furthermore, with export subsidies and the protection of inputs used in export industries varying among industries, there was considerable variation in the extent of export subsidies to value added in the production process. Considerable intercommodity variations were observed also in regard to effective rates of protection on sales in domestic markets. At the same time, some of the incentives were subject to discretionary decision-making.

Nevertheless, with the adoption of the crawling peg, the policy reforms undertaken in the four Latin American countries imparted considerable stability to the incentive system. Also, discrimination against exports and against primary activities was reduced to a considerable extent while such discrimination persisted in countries that continued to apply policies of import substitution during the period until the oil crisis of 1973. Such was the case in India, Chile and Uruguay.

In India, the introduction of selected export subsidies in the mid-sixties was far overshadowed by the continued use of import prohibitions and the controls imposed on investment; subsidies were also subject to complex regulations and discretionary decision making. Chile traditionally had the highest level of import protection in Latin America and, after brief experimentation with import liberalization, import restrictions were reimposed in the early seventies. Protection levels were also high in Uruguay and little effort was made to promote exports.

Incentives and Export Performance

There is evidence that the system of incentives applied affects the country's export performance. Econometric estimates made for a number of countries show that increases in export prices due to export incentives are associated with a rise in the volume of exports. In the case of Korea, it has also been shown that export incentives are positively correlated with the share of exports in domestic output and with the contribution of exports to increases in output in an interindustry framework.

These results are confirmed by a comparison of the export performance of countries applying different incentive schemes. The comparisons have been made for three groups of countries: countries that adopted an outward-oriented industrial development strategy following the completion of the first stage of import substitution (Korea, Singapore, and Taiwan); countries that moved to the second stage of import substitution but subsequently reformed their systems of incentives (Argentina, Brazil, Colombia, and Mexico); and countries that continued to apply an inward-oriented development strategy during the period until the 1973 oil crisis (India, Chile, and Uruguay).

Export performance may be indicated in a variety of ways. For purposes of the comparison, I have made use of the rate of growth of exports and changes in export-output ratios. In the case of the ten developing countries I have considered, the results obtained by the use of the two measures gave broadly similar results.

Increases in manufactured exports and in export-output ratios during the 1960-66 period were the most rapid in the three Far Eastern countries, which adopted an outward-oriented strategy in the early sixties. These countries further improved their export performance in the 1966-73 period, when they intensified their export promotion efforts. As a result, the share of exports in manufactured output rose from 1 percent in 1960 to 14 percent in 1966 and to 41 percent in 1973 in Korea, from 11 percent to 20 percent and to 43 percent in Singapore, and from 9 percent to 19 percent and to 50 percent in Taiwan. Notwithstanding their poor natural resource endowment, the three countries also had the highest growth rates of primary exports, and hence of total exports, among the ten countries.

Between 1966 and 1973, the growth of manufactured exports accelerated in the four Latin American countries that reformed their system of incentives during this period. In particular, the share of exports in manufactured output rose from 1 percent in 1966 to 4 percent in 1973 in both Argentina and Brazil. Nevertheless, this share remained much lower than in the Far East and the countries in question experienced a continued erosion in their traditional primary exports, although they made gains in nontraditional primary exports that received subsidies. Correspondingly, the countries in question experienced an acceleration in the rate of growth of their total exports but they were far surpassed by the three Far Eastern countries.

India, Chile and Uruguay, which continued with an inward-looking development strategy, did poorly in primary as well as in manufactured exports and showed a decline in the share of exports in manufactured output between 1960 and 1973. India lost ground in textiles, its traditional export, and was slow to develop new manufactured exports. As a result, its share in the combined exports of manufactured goods of the ten countries declined from 69 percent in 1960 to 12 percent in 1973. In the same period, Chile's share fell from 4 percent to 1 percent, while in Uruguay it never reached one-fifth of one percent of the total.

Exports, Employment, and Economic Growth

Continued import substitution behind high protection in narrow domestic markets involves "travelling up the staircase" by undertaking the production of commodities that involve increasingly higher domestic costs per unit of foreign exchange saved. By contrast, exporting involves "extending a lower step on the staircase" by increasing the production of commodities in which the country has a comparative advantage, with low domestic resource costs per unit of foreign exchange. Exporting further permits the fuller use of capacity and allows reductions in unit costs through the exploitation of economies of scale contributing thereby to efficient import substitution. Finally, exposure to foreign competition provides stimulus for technological change.

Resource allocation according to comparative advantage, higher capacity utilization, and the exploitation of economies of scale lower capital-output ratios in export activities, and the resulting savings in capital may be used to increase output and employment elsewhere in the economy in countries where labor is not fully employed. This will occur through the indirect effects of export expansion that creates demand for domestic inputs and generates higher incomes which are in part spent on domestic goods.

The higher incomes made possible through export expansion will give rise to increased savings, and there is some evidence that a greater than average proportion of incomes generated in the export sector is saved. Lower capital-output ratios and higher savings ratios, then, will ease the savings constraint to economic growth. Export expansion will also ease the foreign exchange constraint, permitting thereby increases in the importation of materials and machinery.

The experience of individual countries provides evidence of the direct and indirect effects of exports during the period preceding the 1973 oil crisis. In countries for which data are available, capital-labor ratios were substantially lower in export industries than in import-substituting industries. At the same time, there was a shift toward labor-intensive export industries in countries following an outward-oriented development strategy, such as Korea, while a shift in the opposite direction occurred in countries pursuing inward-oriented strategies, such as India.

Available data also indicate that the rate of capacity utilization increased to a considerable extent during the sixties in Korea and Taiwan, and after 1965 in Brazil. The shift towards labor-intensive industries and increased capacity utilization, in turn, led to higher employment and lower incremental capital-output ratios in the countries concerned.

Manufacturing employment increased by 10-12 percent a year in Korea and Taiwan, leading to reductions in unemployment rates. *Pari passu* with the decline in unemployment, real wages increased rapidly as the rate of growth of the demand for labor on the part of the manufacturing sector exceeded the rate at which labor was released by the primary sector. After the 1966 policy reforms of the mid-sixties, real wages increased also in Brazil. By contrast, real wages declined in India, Chile, and Uruguay.

Furthermore, income increments were achieved at a considerably lower cost in terms of investment in countries that consistently followed an outward-oriented strategy. Thus, in the 1960-73 period, incremental capital output ratios were 1.8 in Singapore, 2.1 in Korea, and 2.4 in Taiwan. At the other extreme, these ratios were 5.5 in Chile, 5.7 in India, and 9.1 in Uruguay. The four Latin American countries that undertook policy reforms represent an intermediate group, with incremental capital-output ratios declining after the institution of policy reforms. In Brazil, where the rate of capacity utilization increased to a considerable extent, the ratio fell from 3.8 in 1960-66 to 2.1 in 1966-73.

Outward orientation also appears to have been associated with higher domestic savings ratios and it attracted foreign investment. Increased export and the inflow of foreign capital, in turn, permitted increasing the imports of materials and machinery. A case in point is Brazil where the ratio of imports to the gross national product rose from 6.1 percent in 1966 to 11.1 percent in 1973.

The operation of these factors gave rise to a positive correlation between exports and economic growth. The three Far Eastern countries had the highest GNP growth rates throughout the period; the four Latin American countries that undertook policy reforms improved their growth performance to a considerable extent after the reforms were instituted; while India, Chile, and Uruguay remained at the bottom of the growth league.

V. The Choice of a Development Strategy: Lessons and Prospects

Inward vs. Outward Oriented Development Strategies

The evidence is quite conclusive: countries applying outward-oriented development strategies had a superior performance in terms of exports, economic growth, and employment whereas countries with continued inward orientation encountered increasing economic difficulties. At the same time, policy reforms aimed at greater outward orientation brought considerable improvements in the economic performance of countries that had earlier applied inward-oriented policies.

It has been suggested, however, that import substitution was a necessary precondition for the development of manufactured exports in present-day developing countries. In attempting to provide an answer to this question, distinction needs to be made between first-stage and second-stage import substitution.

I have noted that, apart from Britain and Hong Kong, the exportation of nondurable consumer goods and their inputs was preceded by an import subsitution phase. At the same time, there have been differences among the countries concerned as regards the length of this phase and the level of protection applied. First-stage import substitution was of relatively short duration in the present-day industrial countries and in the three Far Eastern developing countries that subsequently adopted an outward-oriented strategy; it was longer in most other developing countries that also generally had higher levels of protection.

Nor did all nondurable consumer goods and their inputs go through an import-substitution phase before their exportation was undertaken by the Far Eastern countries. In the textile, clothing, and shoe industries, examples are synthetic textiles in Korea, plastic shoes in Taiwan, and fashion clothing in Singapore, all of which began to be produced largely for export markets. Plywood and wigs, that were Korea's leading exports in the late sixties and early seventies, did not go through an import substitution phase either.

Wigs provide a particularly interesting example as they reflect the responses of entrepreneurs to incentives. Korea originally exported human hair to the industrial countries, in particular the United States. Recognizing that human hair was made into wigs by the use of a labor-intensive process, entrepreneurs subsequently came to exploit what appeared to be a profitable opportunity to export wigs, given the favorable treatment of exports in Korea and the limitations imposed on wigs originating from Hong Kong in the United States. The supply of human hair soon proved to be insufficient, however, and firms turned to exporting wigs made of synthetic hair, that became Korea's second-largest single export commodity following plywood.

The example indicates that entrepreneurs will export commodities which correspond to the country's comparative advantage if the system of incentives does not discriminate against exports. It also points to the need to leave the choice of exports to private initiative. Thus, one can hardly assume that government planners would have chosen wigs as a major potential export and that they would have effected a switch from human hair to synthetic hair in making wigs. And even if a product group, such as toys, were identified, the choice of particular products had to be made by the entrepreneur who has to take the risks and reap the rewards of his actions. At the same time, providing similar incentives to all export commodities other than those facing market limitations abroad, and avoiding a bias against exports will ensure that private profitability corresponds to social profitability as was, by and large, the case in countries following outward-oriented strategy.

These considerations may explain that Singapore and Taiwan did not need a planning or targeting system for exports. Export targets were in effect in Korea, but the fulfilment of these targets was not a precondition of the application of the free trade regime to exports or the provision of export incentives. And while successful exporters were said to enjoy advantageous treatment in pending tax cases and the existence of export targets may have exerted pressure on some firms, these pressures merely served to enhance the effects of export incentives without introducing discrimination among export products. At any rate, most firms continually exceeded their targets. A case in point is the increase of Korean exports by two-thirds between the second quarter of 1975 and the second quarter of 1976, exceeding the targets by a very large margin.

The reliance on private initiative in countries which adopted an outward-oriented development strategy can be understood if we consider that exporters require flexibility to respond to changing world market conditions. Nor can the government take responsibility for success and failure in exporting that will affect the profitability of the firm. For these reasons, among socialist countries, Hungary gave firms the freedom to determine the product composition of their exports following the 1968 economic reform and, in particular, after 1977.

Nor was the expansion of manufactured exports predicated on export targets in Latin American countries that reformed their system of incentives in the period preceding the 1973 oil crisis. The question remains, however, if the development of exports was helped by the fact that these countries had undertaken second-stage import substitution.

The question may be answered in the negative as far as nondurable consumer goods and their inputs are concerned. Had appropriate incentives been provided, these commodities could have been exported once first-stage import substitution had been completed as was the case in the Far Eastern countries. In fact, to the extent that the products in question had to use some domestic inputs produced at higher than world market costs, exporters were at a disadvantage in foreign markets. It may also be assumed that the inability to fully exploit economies of scale and the lack of sufficient specialization in the production of parts, components, and accessories in the confines of the protected domestic markets retarded the development of the exports of intermediate products and producer and consumer durables.

More generally, as a Hungarian economist pointed out, there is the danger that second-stage import substitution leads to the establishment of an industrial structure that is "prematurely old," in the sense that it is based on small-scale production with inadequate specialization and outdated machinery. Should this be the case, moving subsequently towards outward orientation will encounter difficulties.

Such difficulties were apparent in the case of Hungary and may also explain that, while exports grew rapidly from a low base, their share in manufacturing output remained small in the Latin American countries that moved towards an outward orientation from the second stage of import substitution. In turn, in the period following the oil crisis, the Far Eastern countries increasingly upgraded their exports of nondurable consumer goods and began exporting machinery, electronics and transparent equipment.

For several of these products, including shipbuilding in Korea, photographic equipment in Singapore, and other electronic products in Taiwan, exporting was not preceded by an import substitution phase. There are even examples, such as color television sets in Korea, where the entire production was destined for foreign markets.

Intermediate goods, machinery, and automobiles require special attention, given the importance of economies of scale on the plant level in the case of the first; the need for product (horizontal) specialization for the second; and the desirability of vertical specialization in the form of the production of parts, components, and accessories on an efficient scale for the third. In all these cases, production in protected domestic markets will involve high costs in most developing countries and the establishment of small-scale and insufficiently specialized firms will make the transition to exportation difficult. This contrasts with the case of nondurable consumer goods and their inputs, where efficient production did not require large plants or horizontal and vertical specialization.

It follows that, rather than entering into second-stage import substitution as a prelude to subsequent exports, it is preferable to undertake the manufacture of intermediate goods and producer and consumer durables for domestic as well as for foreign markets. This will permit the exploitation of economies of scale and ensure efficient import substitution in some products, while others continue to be imported. At the same time, it will require providing equal incentives to exports and to import substitution in the place of import protection that discriminates against exports.

Vulnerability and Policy Response to External Shocks

Outward orientation involves increasing the share of exports in the gross national product. The high share of exports, in turn, has been said to increase the vulnerability of the national economies of countries undertaking such a strategy to foreign events. In assessing the validity of this claim, the experience of the 1973 oil crisis and the subsequent 1974-75 world recession offers an interest.

Available evidence indicates that the Far Eastern countries applying an outward-oriented strategy weathered the effects of the quadrupling of oil prices

and the world recession better than countries with continued inward orientation. This may be explained by differences in the "compressibility" of imports
and in the flexibility of the national economies of countries applying different
strategies. Outward orientation is associated with high export *and* import
shares that permit reductions in nonessential imports without serious adverse
effects on the functioning of the economy. By contrast, continued inward
orientation involves limiting imports to an unavoidable minimum such that any
further reduction will have a considerable cost in terms of regional growth.
Also, the greater flexibility of the national economies of countries pursuing an
outward-oriented strategy, where firms learn to live with foreign competition,
makes it possible to change the product composition of exports in response to
changes in world market conditions whereas inward òrientation entails
establishing a more rigid economic structure.

I come next to policy responses to external shocks. While there were
pressures for a shift towards inward orientation in the immediate aftermath of
the oil crisis and the world recession, the Far Eastern countries continued with
an outward-oriented development strategy that permitted maintaining high
rates of growth of exports and GNP. Thus, taking the 1973-79 period as a
whole, per capita GNP rose at average annual rates of 8.3 percent in Korea,
6.1 percent in Singapore, and 5.5 percent in Taiwan. Growth rates declined,
however, after 1978 in Korea as the exchange rate became increasingly
overvalued and some large, capital-intensive investments were undertaken.

Brazil attempted to maintain past rates of economic growth by relying on
foreign borrowing and on increased import protection. The high capital-
intensity of import substitution projects, however, raised capital-output ratios
and led to a decline in the rate of economic growth, with per capita incomes rising 5.2 percent a year in 1966–73, 4.5 percent in 1973–76, and 2.4 percent in
1976-79. At the same time, the servicing of foreign loans imposed an increasing
burden on Brazil's balance of payments.

Policy changes in the opposite direction occurred in Chile and in Uruguay
that had applied an inward-oriented strategy until the 1973 oil crisis. These
countries responded to the deterioration of their terms of trade and the
slowdown in the growth of foreign demand for their export products by
reforming the system of incentives. The reforms involved eliminating quantitative restrictions, reducing the bias against exports, liberalizing financial
markets, and adopting positive real interest rates.

In Uruguay that had a stagnant economy in the previous decade, the reform
of the system of incentives led to rapid increases in exports and in the gross
national product, with per capita GNP rising 3.1 percent a year between 1973
and 1976 and 4.3 percent between 1976 and 1979. The growth of exports and
GNP accelerated also in Chile, following a period of dislocation due to the
application of a severe deflationary policy aggravated by rapid reductions in
tariffs.

Argentina and Colombia rely on domestically produced oil and hence were not affected by the quadrupling of petroleum prices. Colombia also enjoyed higher coffee prices that more than offset the shortfall in exports due to the slowdown in the growth of foreign demand. But, it reduced incentives to nontraditional exports, with attendant losses in export market shares, and was not able to translate increases in foreign exchange earnings from traditional exports into higher GNP growth rates. Finally, the distortions caused by rapid inflation were largely responsible for low GNP growth rate in Agrentina.

Mexico lost export market shares in both traditional and nontraditional exports following the adoption of domestic expansionary policies, financed in large part by the inflow of foreign capital. And while the discovery of large oil deposits benefited Mexico's balance of payments, it increased the overvaluation of the currency that discriminated against agricultural and manufacturing activities. Finally, substantive policy changes did not occur in India, that continued to lose export market shares.

Policy Prescriptions and Prospects for the Future

The experience of developing countries in the postwar period leads to certain policy prescriptions. First, while infant industry considerations call for the the preferential treatment of manufacturing activities, this should be done on a moderate scale, both to avoid the establishment and the maintenance of inefficient industries and to ensure the continued expansion of primary production for domestic and for foreign markets.

Second, one should provide equal treatment to exports and to import substitution in the manufacturing sector, in order to ensure resource allocation according to comparative advantage and the exploitation of economies of scale. This is of particular importance in the case of intermediate goods and producer and consumer durables, where the advantages of large plant size and horizontal and vertical specialization are considerable, and import substitution in the framework of small domestic markets makes the subsequent development of exports difficult. In turn, providing equal incentives will contribute to efficient exportation and import substitution through specialization in particular products and in their parts, components and accessories.

Third, infant industry considerations apart, variations in incentive rates within the manufacturing sector should be kept to a minimum. This amounts to the application of the "market principle" in allowing firms to decide on the activities to be undertaken. In particular, firms should be free to choose their export composition in response to changing world market conditions.

Fourth, in order to minimize uncertainty for the firm, the system of incenives should possess stability and automaticity. This purpose would also be served if the reform of the system of incentives necessary to apply the principles just described was carried out according to a timetable made public in advance.

It has been suggested, however, that the practical application of these principles—characteristic of an outward-oriented development strategy—would encounter market limitations in the industrial countries, which are aggravated by protectionist policies followed in these countries. In addressing this issue, one needs to examine recent and prospective trends in trade in manufactured goods between the industrial and the developing countries.

Notwithstanding protectionist pressures in the industrial countries, their imports of manufactured goods from the developing countries rose at a rapid rate during the period following the oil crisis, averaging 10.2 percent a year in volume terms between 1973 and 1978. Moreover, the "apparent" income elasticity of demand for these imports, calculated as the ratio of the growth rate of imports to that of the gross domestic product, increased from 3.6 in 1963-73 to 4.1 in 1973-78.

Given the increased volume of manufactured imports from the developing countries, one may expect the "apparent" income elasticity of demand for manufactured goods originating in these countries to decline in the future. Assuming an elasticity of 3.2 and an GDP growth rate of 3.9 percent in the industrial countries, I have projected their manufactured imports from the developing countries to rise at an average annual rate of 12.5 percent between 1978 and 1990. The projections reflect the assumption of unchanged policies in the industrial countries, including the maintenance of the Multifiber Arrangement.

As a result of these projected changes, the share of the developing countries in the consumption of manufactured goods in the industrial countries would rise from 1.5 percent in 1978 to 4.0 percent in 1990, with an incremental share of 8.9 percent. Incremental shares would be the highest in clothing, 28.1 percent; they would be 7.2 percent in textiles and 6.6 percent in other consumer goods. Nonetheless, the production of textiles and clothing would rise at an average annual rate of 2 percent in the industrial countries. And, these countries would have a rising export surplus in trade in manufactured goods with the developing countries that would contribute to the growth of their manufacturing sector.

At the same time, in accordance with the "stages" approach to comparative advantage, changes would occur in the product composition of the manu-factured exports of the developing countries as they proceed to higher stages of industrial development. This process is exemplified by Japan that shifted from unskilled-labor intensive exports to skill-intensive and to physical-capital intensive exports and is increasingly expanding its technology-intensive exports.

Shifts in export composition are now occurring in the newly-industrializing developing countries, including the Far Eastern countries and Latin American countries that carried out policy reforms after the mid-sixties. The Far Eastern countries that have a relatively high educational level may increasingly take the place of Japan in exporting skill-intensive products while Latin American countries may expand the exports of relatively capital-intensive products.

Countries at lower stages of industrial development, in turn, may take the place of the newly-industrializing countries in exporting products that require chiefly unskilled labor.

To the extent that the newly-industrializing countries replace Japanese exports, and their exports are in turn replaced by countries at lower stages of industrial development, the threat to the manufacturing industries of the industrial countries is reduced. Nor does the upgrading and the diversification of manufactured exports by the newly-industrializing countries represent a serious threat, inasmuch as the exports of individual commodities would account for a relatively small proportion of the consumption and production of the commodities in question in the industrial countries. This conclusion also applies to the international division of the production process, which is exemplified by the development of Ford's "world car" that will entail manufacturing in nineteen countries.

It follows that it is in the interest of the newly-industrializing developing countries to upgrade and to diversify their exports in line with their changing comparative advantage. This is further in the interest of countries at lower stages of industrial development, since they can replace the exports of unskilled-labor intensive commodities from the newly-industrializing countries in industrial country markets.

There are also considerable possibilities to expand trade in manufactured goods among the developing countries themselves. First of all, with increases in oil earnings, the largely open markets of the OPEC countries will experience rapid growth. Furthermore, the newly-industrializing countries may trade skill-intensive and physical-capital intensive goods among themselves and exchange these commodities for the unskilled-labor intensive products of countries at lower stages of industrial development.

The expansion of this trade is predicated on the pursuit of outward-oriented strategies by the newly-industrializing countries, so as to provide appropriate incentives to exports and to allow imports from other developing countries. The pursuit of such a strategy would also contributed to efficient import substitution by ensuring low-cost manufacture through international specialization and the international division of the production process. Similar conclusions apply to countries at lower stages of industrial development.

Finally, lowering protection in the industrial countries would lead to increases in their manufactured imports from the developing countries over and above projected levels. This also corresponds to the well-conceived interests of the industrial countries that would benefit from shifts to high-technology products within a manufactured sector as higher export earnings would permit the developing countries to increase their imports of these products.

Trade liberalization in the industrial countries could proceed over a ten-year horizon without involving excessively large adjustment costs. One may accept, for example, a decline in the production of textiles and clothing over time by not replacing the normal attrition of workers and depreciated equipment in branches that utilize largely unskilled labor. In turn, new entrants into the industrial labor force may increasingly enter technologically advanced industries where productivity levels are substantially higher.

Apart from expanding the volume of trade, then, the pursuit of appropriate policies by developed and by developing countries would permit shifts in the pattern of international specialization in response to the changing structure of comparative advantage in countries at different levels of industrial development. As a result, the efficiency of resource allocation would improve, and rates of economic growth accelerate, with benefits to all concerned.

Appendix

Selected Publications*
Bela Balassa

"The Economic Reform in Hungary," *Economica,* 37, (1970), 1–22.

"Growth Strategies in Semi-Industrial Countries," *Quarterly Journal of Economics,* 84 (1970), 24–47.

"Growth Performance of Eastern European Economies and Comparable Western European Countries" (with Trent Bertrand), *American Economic Review, Papers and Proceedings,* 60 (1970), 314–20.

"Industrial Policies in Taiwan and Korea," *Weltwirtschaftliches Archiv,* Band 106 (1971), 55–77.

"Trade Policies in Developing Countries," *American Economic Review, Papers and Proceedings,* 61 (1971), 178–87.

"Effective Protection in Developing Countries," in *Trade, Balance of Payments and Growth: Essays in International Economics in Honor of Charles P. Kindleberger* (J. Bhagwati, R. Jones, R. A. Mundell, and J. Vanek, eds.), Amsterdam, North Holland, 1971, 300–23.

The Structure of Protection in Developing Countries, Baltimore, Md., The Johns Hopkins University Press, 1971.

"Indicators of Protection and of Other Incentive Measures" (with D. M. Schydlowsky) in *The Role of the Computer in Economic and Social Research in Latin America* (Nancy D. Ruggles, ed.) Proceedings of a Conference on The Role of the Computer in Latin America held in Cuernavaca, Mexico, in September 1971. New York, National Bureau for Economic Research, 1974, 331–46.

"Reforming the System of Incentives in Developing Countries," *World Development,* 3 (1975), 365–82.

"Latin American Trade Policies in the 1970s: A Comment," *Quarterly Journal of Economics,* 89 (1975), 483–86.

"Trade, Protection, and Domestic Production: A Comment," in *International*

*These publications provide empirical evidence in support of the propositions advanced in the Essay.

Trade and Finance: Frontiers for Research (Peter B. Kenen, ed.) Proceedings of a Conference on Research in International Trade and Finance held at Princeton University in March 1973. Cambridge, Cambridge University Press, 1975, 154–63.

"Korea's Development Strategy for the Fourth Five-Year Plan Period (1977-81)," *Discussion Papers on the Guidelines for the Fourth Five Year Plan,* Seoul, Economic Planning Board, 1975, 21–62.

"Effects of Commercial Policy on International Trade, the Location of Production, and Factor Movements" in *The International Allocation of Economic Activity,* (Bertil Ohlin, Per-Ove Hesselborn, and Per Magnus Wijkman, eds.) Proceedings of a Nobel Symposium held in Stockholm in June 1976, Macmillan, London, 1977, 230–58.

Policy Reform in Developing Countries, Oxford, Pergamon Press, 1977.

"Export Incentives and Export Performance in Developing Countries: A Comparative Analysis," *Weltwirtschaftliches Archiv,* 114 (1978), 24-61.

"Exports and Economic Growth: Further Evidence," *Journal of Development Economics,* 5 (1978), 181–89.

"The 'New Protectionism' and the International Economy," *Journal of World Trade Law,* 12 (1978), 409-36. Republished as Essay 4 in this volume.

"The Economic Reform in Hungary Ten Years After," *European Economic Review,* 11 (1978), 245–268. Republished as Essay 14 in this volume.

"The Changing Pattern of Comparative Advantage in Manufactured Goods," *Review of Economics and Statistics,* 61 (1979), 259–66.

"Incentive Policies in Brazil," *World Development,* 7 (1979), 1023–42. Republished as Essay 10 in this volume.

"Barriers to Development: Discussion" in *Economic Growth and Resources,* Volume 1. The Major Issues (Edmond Malinvaud, ed.) Proceedings of the Fifth World Congress of the International Economic Association held in Tokyo in September, 1977. London, Macmillan, 1979, 169–76.

"A 'Stages' Approach to Comparative Advantage" *Ibid.* Volume 5, National and International Issues (Irma Adelman, ed.). London, Macmillan, 1979, 121–56. Republished as Essay 6 in this volume.

"The Changing International Division of Labor in Manufactured Goods," *Banca Nazionale del Lavoro, Quarterly Review,* 32 (1979), 243–85. Republished as Essay 7 in this volume.

"The Tokyo Round and the Developing Countries," *Journal of World Trade Law,* 14 (1980), 93–118. Republished as Essay 5 in this volume.

"Prospects for Trade in Manufactured Goods between Industrial and Developing Countries, 1978–1990," *Journal of Policy Modeling,* 3 (1980), 437–55. Republished as Essay 9 in this volume.

"Policy Responses to External Shocks in Selected Latin American Countries." Proceedings at the NBER/FIPE/BEBR Conference on Trade Prospects among the Americas: Latin American Diversification and the New

Protectionism, held in Sao Paulo, Brazil in March 1980, *Quarterly Review of Economics and Business,* 21 (1981). Republished as Essay 3 in this volume.

"The Newly-Industrializing Developing Countries after the Oil Crisis" *Weltwirtschaftliches Archiv,* 117 (1981). Republished as Essay 2 in this volume.

"Trade in Manufactured Goods: Patterns of Change," *World Development,* 9 (1981). Republished as Essay 8 in this volume.

Development Strategies in Semi-Industrial Countries, Baltimore, Md., The Johns Hopkins University Press, 1981.

Part I

ESSAY 2

The Newly-Industrializing Developing Countries After The Oil Crisis

Introduction

In recent years, much attention has been given to the emergence of the newly-industrializing countries on the world scene.[1] This essay will examine the experience of the newly-industrializing developing countries during the period following the quadrupling of oil prices in 1973–74 and the world recession of 1974–75. It will focus on the policy responses of these countries to external shocks and analyze the economic effects of the policies applied.

As an introduction to the discussion, Section I will briefly review the incentive policies followed by the newly-industrializing developing countries during the 1960-73 period and the effects of these policies on exports and on economic growth. Next, the methods employed to estimate the balance-of-payments effects of external shocks, and of policy responses to these shocks, will be described (Section II).

In Section III, estimates will be presented on the balance-of-payments effects of external shocks, in the form of the deterioration of the terms of trade and the slowdown of world demand for the exports of the newly-industrializing developing countries. Section IV will analyze policy responses to external shocks in the individual countries, including increased reliance on foreign financing, export promotion, import substitution, and lowering the rate of economic growth, and provide estimates on the balance-of-payments effects of these policies. In the conclusion, the policies followed by the newly-industrializing developing countries during the 1973–78 period will be evaluated in a comparative framework.

I. The Newly-Industrializing Developing Countries in the 1960–73 Period

For purposes of the analysis, the newly-industrializing developing countries

29

have been defined to include developing countries that had per capita incomes in excess of $1100 in 1978 and where the share of the manufacturing sector in the gross domestic product was 20 percent or higher in 1977.[2] The countries in question are Argentina, Brazil, Chile, Mexico, and Uruguay in Latin America; Israel and Yugoslavia in the Europe-Middle East area; and Hong Kong, Korea, Singapore, and Taiwan in the Far East.

With the exception of Hong Kong and Uruguay, these countries were the subject of an earlier study by the author of incentive policies, exports, and economic performance which dealt with the period preceding the 1973 oil crisis.[3] The study also covered Colombia that is on the borderline of becoming a newly-industrializing country and India that has an industrial sector larger than any developing country other than Brazil and Mexico, which co-exists with a very large and backward agricultural sector.

For comparability with the earlier study, Colombia and India have been retained in the present investigation. Also, the earlier study has been extended to include Uruguay but not Hong Kong that offers characteristics little different from those of Singapore, another city-state.

Correspondingly, the analysis of the pre-1973 and post-1973 periods in this essay will cover altogether twelve countries. In accordance with the scheme of classification applied in the earlier study, the countries have been divided into four groups on the basis of the policies applied in the period preceding the oil crisis.

The countries of the first group, Korea, Singapore, and Taiwan, adopted outward-oriented strategies, providing similar incentives to sales in domestic and in foreign markets, after the completion of the first stage of import substitution that entailed replacing the imports of nondurable consumer goods and their inputs by domestic production. The second group, Argentina, Brazil, Colombia, and Mexico, moved to the second stage of import substitution, involving the replacement of the imports of intermediate goods and producer and consumer durables by domestic production, but subsequently reformed their incentive system by reducing the bias against exports. In turn, the countries of the third group, Israel and Yugoslavia, started export promotion at an early date but their efforts slackened somewhat afterwards. Finally, India, Chile, and Uruguay, classified in the fourth group, continued to pursue inward-oriented strategies throughout the period preceding the 1973 oil crisis.

Incentives and Export Performance

The first group of Far Eastern countries established a free trade regime for exports and their domestic inputs. Some additional subsidies were also provided, equalizing the treatment of exports and import substitution in the manufacturing sector, without introducing substantial interindustry differences in export incentives. At the same time, there was little discrimination against primary activities; incentives were granted by-and-large automatically; realistic exchange rates were established; and stability in the system of incentives was ensured over time.

The early application of outward-oriented policies explains that, in the 1960–66 period, the countries of the first group experienced more rapid increases in manufactured exports than any of the other nine countries and had the highest share of exports in manufacturing output. They also showed the best export performance in the 1966–73 period, when their export promotion efforts intensified. Increases in manufactured exports were accompanied by the rapid growth of primary exports, again surpassing all the other countries under consideration in 1960–66 as well as in 1966–73.

Unlike the first group, the second group of countries began their export-promoting efforts after having embarked on second-stage import substitution. They also differed from the first group in that, with few exceptions, the use of imported inputs in export production was limited to cases when comparable domestic products were not available. To compensate exporters for the resulting high costs, and for the effects of continued import protection on the exchange rate, the countries of the second group provided subsidies to nontraditional exports. Export subsidies lessened, but did not eliminate, the bias against exports, which remained particularly pronounced in the case of traditional primary products. And, while the adoption of the crawling peg imparted considerable stability to the system of incentives, incentives to value added continued to vary greatly among industries and several of the incentive measures were subject to discretionary decision making.

Within this group of Latin American countries in the 1966–73 period manufactured export growth rates were the highest in Argentina and Brazil that introduced considerable export incentives in the mid-sixties. As a result, between 1966 and 1973, the share of exports in manufactured output rose from 0.9 percent to 3.6 percent in Argentina and from 1.3 percent to 4.4 percent in Brazil. Nevertheless, this share remained substantially lower than in the countries of the first group; in 1973, Korea exported 40.5 percent, Singapore 42.6 percent, and Taiwan 49.9 percent of its manufacturing output.

Having extended to a considerable extent the scope of export-promoting measures in the mid-sixties, Colombia increased the share of exports in its manufacturing output from 3.0 percent in 1966 to 7.5 percent in 1973. The corresponding figures were 2.9 percent and 4.4 percent in Mexico that benefited from the proximity of the United States but, apart from the establishment of a free trade zone in the border area, did not provide export incentives until early 1971.

With continued discrimination against traditional primary exports, the four Latin American countries saw their world market shares dwindle in practically all of these commodities. Three of these countries, Argentina, Brazil, and Colombia, however, experienced gains in nontraditional primary exports that benefited from export subsidies, thereby raising the rate of growth of primary exports after 1966.

As a result of their early export promotion efforts, Israel and Yugoslavia surpassed the second group of countries, while falling behind the first, in terms of the share of exports in manufacturing output in 1966. But, as their export promotion efforts slackended, this share increased relatively little, from 12.8 percent to 14.1 percent in Israel and from 13.8 percent to 16.9 percent in Yugoslavia, between 1966 and 1973. In the same period, the share of exports in the increment of manufacturing output declined in Israel and hardly changed in Yugoslavia. Israel, however, gained in both traditional and nontraditional primary exports which suffered little discrimination while smaller increases were observed in Yugoslavia where a bias against primary exports existed.

The fourth group of countries continued to apply an inward-oriented strategy, entailing considerable discrimination against primary as well as manufactured exports, during the period under consideration. As a result, they lost market shares in traditional primary exports, did poorly in nontraditional primary exports, and also suffered losses of market shares in manufactured exports. India's share in the combined exports of manufactured goods of the twelve countries under consideration decreased from 50.4 percent in 1960 to 31.0 percent in 1966 and to 10.7 percent 1973; Chile's share declined from 1.9 percent to 1.5 percent and, again, to 0.5 percent; while Uruguay's share never reached 0.5 percent of the total.

Exports and the Growth of Output

Exportation provides advantages over import substitution by contributing to resource allocation according to comparative advantage, greater capacity utilization, the exploitation of economies of scale, and improvements in technology stimulated by competition in foreign markets. To the extent that exports give rise to more rapid increases in output than import substitution, the indirect effects of export growth, too, will be larger in countries where resources are not full utilized.

These considerations explain that exports and output are highly correlated in an intercountry context. In the 1960–73 period, the Spearman rank correlation coefficient between the growth of exports and that of output was 0.67 for agriculture, 0.71 for manufacturing, and 0.89 for the national economy taken as a whole. In the same period, the coefficients obtained in correlating exports with output net of exports were 0.74 in the case of manufacturing and 0.77 for the gross national product, presumably reflecting the indirect effects of exports.[4]

Alternatively, one may introduce exports, in addition to labor and (domestic and foreign) capital, as an explanatory variable in a regression equation designed to explain intercountry differences in GNP growth rates. The inclusion of exports in such a production function-type relationship reflects the assumption that outward-orientation enhances the productivity of labor and capital. In estimates made by pooling data for the 1960–66 and

1966–73 periods that were available for ten out of the twelve countries (excepting Singapore and Uruguay), adding the export variable to the regression equation raised the coefficient of determination from 0.58 to 0.77. The export variable was significant at the 1 percent level; all other variables (labor, domestic capital and foreign capital) were significant at the 5 percent level.

At the same time, the method applied tends to underestimate the effects of export growth on the growth of output by failing to account for the impact of exports on other variables in the equation. Yet, there is evidence that exports and domestic savings are positively correlated. Also, the improved balance-of-payments situation attendant on the expansion of exports increases the attractiveness of the country concerned for foreign capital.

II. Estimating the Balance-of-Payments Effects of External Shocks and of Policy Responses to these Shocks

The Analytical Framework

The world economic situation changed with the quadrupling of oil prices in 1973–74 and the world recession of 1974–75. In examining the policy responses of the newly-industrializing developing countries to these external shocks, the following analysis will consider reliance on foreign financing and the use of macroeconomic policy measures aimed at reducing the rate of economic growth, together with incentives to exports and to import substitution.

The balance-of-payments effects of external shocks in the form of the deterioration of the terms of trade and the slowdown of world demand for the exports of the newly-industrializing developing countries will be estimated by postulating a situation that would have obtained in the absence of external shocks. The same procedure will be applied in estimating the effects of policy responses to external shocks.

In developing the analytical framework, designed to estimate the effects of external shocks, and of policy responses to these shocks, the point of departure is the balance-of-payments identity. This is defined in terms of the resource gap that equals the deficit in merchandise trade, non-factor services and private transfers combined; the resource gap is financed by the net flow of external financing.

The resource gap is shown in equations (1) and (2) for years 0 and 1, respectively. In the equations, M and X denote merchandise imports and exports valued in base year (0) prices; P_{01}^m and P_{01}^x represent percentage changes in import and export prices between years 0 and 1; and S and R refer to the balance of non-factor services and private transfers and to the resource gap, respectively, valued in terms of current prices.

(1) $R_0 = M_0 - X_0 - S_0$

(2) $R_1 = M_1(1 + P_{01}{}^m) - X_1(1 + P_{01}{}^x) - S_1$

Taking the difference between equations (2) and (1) and rearranging terms, we express changes in the resource gap between years 0 and 1 in equation (3) in terms of changes in import and export prices for the volume of imports and exports in period 1 $(P_{01}{}^m M_1 - P_{01}{}^x X_1)$; changes in the volume of imports $(M_1 - M_0)$; changes in the volume of exports $(X_1 - X_0)$; and changes in the balance of non-factor services and private transfers $(S_1 - S_0)$.

(3) $R_1 - R_0 = (P_{01}{}^m M_1 - P_{01}{}^x X_1) + (M_1 - M_0) - (X_1 - X_0) - (S_1 - S_0)$

Equation (3) is modified if we examine the effects of policy actions taken at home and abroad. As a first step, we introduce hypothetical exports $(X_1{}^h)$ that would be reached if the country in question maintained its base-period share in world markets. Now, differences between actual and hypothetical exports $(X_1 - X_1{}^h)$, shown on the left-hand side of equation (4), are taken to have resulted from domestic policy actions as regards exports.

(4) $(R_1 - R_0) + (X_1 - X_1{}^h) = (P_{01}{}^m M_1 - P_{01}{}^x X_1)$
    $+ (M_1 - M_0) - (X_1{}^h - X_0) - (S_1 - S_0)$

Next, we introduce the effects of changes in foreign demand. For this purpose, we calculate the trend value of exports $(X_1{}^t)$ on the assumptions that the trend of foreign export demand remained the same as in the base period and that the country under consideration maintained its export share unchanged. The difference between trend and hypothetical values $(X_1{}^t - X_1{}^h)$, shown on the right-hand side of equation (5), thus represents the effects of the external shock due to changes in foreign demand for the country's export products. (Since this export shortfall adds to the deficit, it is shown with a positive sign.)

(5) $(R_1 - R_0) + (X_1 - X_1{}^h) = (P_{01}{}^m M_1 - P_{01}{}^x X_1)$
    $+ (X_1{}^t - X_1{}^h) + (M_1 - M_0) - (X_1{}^t - X_0) - (S_1 - S_0)$

In turn, hypothetical imports $(M_1{}^h)$ are calculated for the actual growth rate of GNP in the country concerned on the assumption that the income elasticity of import demand remained the same as in the base period. Differences between hypothetical imports $(M_1{}^h)$ and actual imports (M_1), shown on the left-hand side of equation (6), are taken to reflect the effects of import-substituting policies.

(6) $(R_1 - R_0) + (X_1 - X_1{}^h) + (M_1{}^h - M_1) = (P_{01}{}^m M_1 - P_{01}{}^x X_1)$
    $+ (X_1{}^t - X_1{}^h) + (M_1{}^h - M_0) - (X_1{}^t - X_0) - (S_1 - S_0)$

Furthermore, we calculate the trend value of imports on the assumptions that the income elasticity of import demand and the rate of growth of GNP remained the same as in the base period (i.e. no change in the rate of growth of imports). Differences between the trend value of imports and hypothetical imports $(M_1 - M_1{}^h)$, shown on the left-hand side of equation (7), are assumed to reflect the effects of changes in the rate of growth of GNP on imports.

$$(7) \quad (R_1 - R_0) + (X_1 - X_1^h) + (M_1^h - M_1) + (M_1^t - M_1^h) =$$
$$(P_{01}^m M_1 - P_{01}^x X_1) + (X_1^t - X_1^h) +$$
$$(M_1^t - M_0) - (X_1^t - X_0) - (S_1 - S_0)$$

The difference between the trend values for imports and exports, adjusted for the actual balance of nonfactor services and private transfers, equals the amount of net external financing that would have been necessary in the absence of external shocks and policy reactions to these shocks (the trend value of the resource, R_1^t). In turn, the sum of the differences between trend values and actual values of imports and exports equals the difference between the trend value of the resource gap and its actual value in the base year.

Introducing the trend value of the resource gap and rearranging terms, we show the excess of the actual resource gap over its trend value on the left-hand side of equation (8). This is taken to represent the additional inflow of external funds associated with the balance-of-payments effects of external shocks (additional net external financing).

$$(8) \qquad (R_1 - R_1^t) + (X_1 - X_1^h) + (M_1^h - M_1) +$$
$$(M_1^t - M_1^h) = (P_{01}^m M_1 - P_{01}^x X_1) +$$
$$(X_1^t - X_1^h) + (M_1^t - M_0) - (X_1^t - X_0) -$$
$$(S_1 - S_0) - (R_1^t - R_0)$$

The last term on the right-hand side of equation (8) equals the sum of the previous three terms and indicates the amount of additional net external financing that would have been necessary in the absence of external shocks if past trends continued, over and above the inflow of external funds in the base year. The term is shown with a negative sign, so that the last four terms add up to zero and can be omitted.

Under the assumption that the country in question is a price-taker in world markets, the right-hand side of equation (8) is taken to indicate the effects of external shocks on the balance of payments. This is decomposed into effects on the terms of trade $(P_{01}^m M_1 - P_{01}^x X_1)$ and on export volume $(X_1^t - X_1^h)$. The former is further decomposed into a pure terms of trade effect calculated on the assumption of balanced trade in base year prices, $(P_{01}^m - P_{01}^x) X_1$, and the effects of increased import prices on unbalanced trade, $(M_1 - X_1) P_{01}^m$.

In turn, the left-hand side of equation (8) consists of terms representing policy responses to external shocks, including additional net external financing $(R_1 - R_1^t)$, increases in the country's export share in world markets $(X_1 - X_1^h)$, import substitution $(M_1^h - M_1)$, and the effects of lower GNP growth rates on the country's imports $(M_1^t - M_1^h)$.

In the case of manufactured exports, the effects of lower growth rates of GNP abroad and the effects of changes in the foreign income elasticity of demand for these exports have further been distinguished. This has involved calculating the constant-income-elasticity exports of manufactured goods from developing countries to developed countries, developing countries, and centrally planned economies that would have been obtained if the income elasticities of import demand in the base period were combined with the actual GNP growth rates (X_{ml}^c).

Assuming further that the country in question maintained its share in the manufactured exports of the developing countries unchanged, the difference between the trend value of manufactured exports and the constant-income-elasticity exports of manufactured goods ($X_{ml}^t - X_{ml}^c$) is taken to reflect the effects of changes in GNP growth rates abroad. In turn, the difference between constant-income-elasticity exports and hypothetical exports ($X_{ml}^c - X_{ml}^h$) represents the effects of changes in foreign income elasticities of demand for the manufactured exports of the developing countries. Again, a positive sign denotes an export shortfall.

Estimating the Effects of External Shocks

In the practical application of the analytical framework, the average for the years 1971–73 (for short, "1972") has been taken as the basis for estimating terms of trade effects. It may be objected that, due to the effects of the world boom of 1972–73, the terms of trade of the developing countries were particularly favorable in 1971–73. However, the differences as compared to the nineteen-sixties are small, and the terms of trade of the developing countries in 1971–73 were in fact slightly less favorable than in the nineteen-sixties[5] if we exclude fuel, the price of which started to rise in late 1973.

Changes in the terms of trade as compared to the 1971–73 base period have been attributed to external shocks. The underlying assumption is that the country in question is a price-taker in world markets. Such an assumption applies *grosso modo* to the principal exports of countries under study, the principal exception being coffee in Brazil and in Colombia. Nevertheless, in the absence of the explicit modelling of the world coffee market, the assumption has been retained in this case also.

Terms of trade effects have been decomposed into a pure terms of trade effect, calculated on the assumption of balanced trade in terms of "1972" prices, and the effects of the rise in import prices on unbalanced trade (the deficit or surplus in the balance of merchandise trade) expressed in "1972" prices. In the event of unbalanced trade, then, the expressed terms of trade effects include the impact of increases in import prices on the trade deficit (surplus). This estimate reflects the assumption that, in the absence of external shocks, import prices would have remained unchanged during the period under consideration. The assumption of unchanged import prices has the following rationale.

While primary product prices were rising rapidly during the 1971–73 world boom, historical experience indicates that such price increases were followed by a decline or, at the least, by a flat price trend. Primary product prices, in turn, influence the prices of manufactured goods and it may not be unreasonable to assume that the world economy would have experienced a return to the noninflationary situation of the nineteen-sixties if the quadrupling of petroleum prices did not occur. At any rate, the rapid rise in petroleum prices accounts for a substantial part of the increase in import prices during this period.

In order to indicate the impact of the quadrupling of petroleum prices on the terms of trade, the balance of payments effects of changes in the prices of fuel and nonfuel imports are separately shown. On the export side, distinction has been made between traditional primary exports[6], taken individually, fuels, nontraditional primary exports other than fuels, and manufactured goods.

The trend value of exports that would have occurred in the absence of external shocks has been estimated on the assumptions that the world exports of the country's traditional primary export products, taken individually, and the developing countries' exports of fuels, nontraditional primary products other than fuels, and manufactured goods grew at the same rate as in the 1963–73 period and that the country concerned maintained its "1972" market share in these exports. The underlying assumption is that a developing country competes against all suppliers in the world market for its traditional primary exports while its nontraditional exports compete against those of other developing countries.

The effects of changes in foreign demand in the country's exports have been derived as the difference between trend and hypothetical values of exports, both expressed in "1972" prices. Hypothetical exports have been estimated on the assumptions that the country's exports of traditional primary products rose at the same rate as world exports and that its exports of fuels, nontraditional primary products other than fuels, and manufactured goods increased at the same rate as developing country exports, from a "1972" basis. It thus again reflects the assumption that the country maintained its "1972" market share during the period under consideration.

Estimating the Effects of Policy Responses to External Shocks

Among policy measures taken in response to external shocks, the amount of additional net external financing has been estimated as the difference between the actual resource gap or net external financing and the trend value of the resource gap. The latter has been calculated on the assumption that the country's imports and exports, expressed in "1972" prices, rose at the same rate as in the 1963–73 period, taking further the actual net balance of nonfactor services and private transfers as a datum. In turn, total external financing has been defined as the sum of actual net external financing, interest payments, and dividends.

The effects of export promotion have been represented by increases (decreases) in exports, expressed in "1972" prices, that were associated with changes in the country's "1972" market shares. Separate calculations have been made for traditional primary products, taken individually, fuels, nontraditional primary products other than fuels, and manufactured goods.

Import substitution has been defined as savings in imports associated with a decrease in the country's income elasticity of import demand as compared to the 1963–73 period, again expressed in "1972" prices. Separate calculations have been made for fuel and for nonfuel imports.

The effects on imports of lower economic growth rates in the country concerned have been derived by applying income elasticities of import demand for the 1963–73 period to GNP growth rates observed in the 1963–73 period and to actual GNP growth rates during the period under consideration. Again, separate calculations have been made for fuel and for nonfuel imports.

It should be noted, however, that changes in export market shares and in the rate of economic growth may have been due to circumstances outside the country's control. A decrease (increase) in the country's export market share may have occurred because of an acceleration (deceleration) of the growth of exports by competing suppliers. In turn, a fall in foreign demand for the country's export products may have contributed to a decline in its rate of economic growth.

Changes in export market shares, in import demand, and in the rate of economic growth may also have been due to internal events. In particular, domestic policy changes may have occurred independently of external shocks and may themselves constitute an "internal" shock. The methodology applied does not permit separating the balance-of-payments effects of policy changes taken in response to external shocks from the effects of autonomous domestic policy changes; such distinctions become a matter of interpretation.

The estimates reported in this essay have been made for the years 1974 to 1978, taken individually.[7] Averages for the 1974–78 period are also shown. This permits considering changes over time and indicating the results for the entire period.

III. The Balance-of-Payments Effects of External Shocks

This section will present empirical evidence on the balance-of-payments impact of external shocks, in the form of terms of trade effects and export volume effects, in the twelve newly-industrializing developing countries. Under each heading, the discussion will proceed by separating countries into four groups according to the scheme of classification described in Section I. This will be followed by a comparative analysis of the relative importance of the sources of external shocks in the twelve countries.

Table 2.1 reports the estimated terms of trade effects and export volume effects on the balance of payments of the newly-industrializing developing countries. Table 2.2 relates terms of trade effects to the average of exports and imports (average trade) and to the gross national product, and export volume effects to exports and to the gross national product, all expressed in "1972" prices.[8]

Terms of Trade Effects

Among the first group of Far Eastern countries, Korea suffered the largest terms of trade loss in 1974, equivalent to one-half of the average value of its exports and imports. The quadrupling of petroleum prices accounted for two-thirds of this loss. Higher petroleum prices adversely affected also Taiwan, where the terms of trade loss equalled one-third of the average value of trade in 1974.

In the same year, the terms of trade loss amounted to one-sixth of the average of exports and imports in Singapore, where the export value of petroleum products nearly equalled the import value of petroleum. Nevertheless, with the average value of trade exceeding its gross national product, the ratio of the terms of trade loss to GNP was the highest in Singapore; 18 percent in 1974. It was followed by Taiwan (10 percent) that also had a relatively high trade share and by Korea (8 percent).

In Korea and in Taiwan, the terms of trade improved in subsequent years when the rise of petroleum prices decelerated. In Korea, the terms of trade loss was equivalent to 4 percent of GNP in 1978, with the pure terms of trade effect accounting for two-thirds of the total. In Taiwan, the terms of trade effects turned positive in 1978 as the gain from higher import prices on its large trade surplus in terms of "1972" prices more than compensated for the loss due to the negative pure terms of trade effect. In turn, the unfavorable impact of higher import prices on its trade deficit was offset only in part by the favorable pure terms of trade effect in Singapore, resulting in a terms of trade loss equivalent to one-fifth of GNP in 1978.

In 1974, the terms of trade loss equalled one half of the average value of exports and imports in Brazil that was the only major petroleum importer in the second group of Latin American countries. The corresponding ratio was one-fifth in Mexico that experienced unfavorable trends in the prices of its traditional primary exports; it was 4 percent in Colombia and −8 percent in Argentina that gained from increases in cereal prices. Expressed as a proportion of GNP the terms of trade loss was 3 percent in Brazil, 1 percent in Mexico, and practically zero in Colombia and in Argentina.

Owing largely to increases in coffee prices, Brazil and Colombia experienced considerable improvements in their terms of trade in subsequent years. By 1978, the terms of trade loss declined to 2 percent of GNP in Brazil, with the pure terms of trade effect accounting for three-fourths of the total, while Colombia had a terms of trade gain amounting to 3 percent of its GNP.

As a result of higher prices on its rising petroleum exports, Mexico's terms of trade loss disappeared by 1977, with the favorable pure terms of trade effect compensating for the adverse impact of higher import prices on the trade

TABLE 2.1
Balance of Payments Effects of External Shocks and of Policy Responses to These Shocks: Absolute Values (U.S. $ million)

Balance of Payments Effects	1974	1975	1976	1977	1978	Average 1974-78
I.						
			ARGENTINA			
I. *External Shocks*						
(1) Terms of Trade Effects	−180	622	194	193	−524	61
(2) Export Volume Effects	18	113	−59	38	54	33
(3) Together	−161	735	135	231	−470	94
II. *Policy Responses*						
(4) Additional Net External Financing	156	1523	−241	−732	−1680	−195
(5) Increase in Export Market Share	−209	−739	−386	565	327	−89
(6) Import Substition	90	32	710	350	631	363
(7) Import Effects of Lower GNP Growth Rate	−198	−81	52	49	252	15
(8) Together	−161	735	135	231	−470	94
			COLOMBIA			
I. *External Shocks*						
(1) Terms of Trade Effects	47	159	−139	−710	−511	−231
(2) Export Volume Effects	62	101	82	230	205	136
(3) Together	109	260	−58	−479	−306	−95
II. *Policy Responses*						
(4) Additional Net External Financing	213	108	93	−227	122	62
(5) Increase in Export Market Share	39	110	−126	−118	4	−18
(6) Import Substitution	−133	46	−23	−134	−417	−132
(7) Import Effects of Lower GNP Growth Rate	−10	4	−1	−1	−15	−6
(8) Together	109	260	−58	−479	−306	−95
			INDIA			
I. *External Shocks*						
(1) Terms of Trade Effects	1116	1919	872	396	962	1053
(2) Export Volume Effects	34	342	322	595	852	429
(3) Together	1150	2260	1194	991	1815	1482
II. *Policy Responses*						
(4) Additional Net External Financing	1587	2529	994	1723	3128	1992
(5) Increase in Export Market Share	−328	−79	1	−362	−677	−289
(6) Import Substitution	−173	−165	202	−302	−546	−197
(7) Import Effects of Lower GNP Growth Rate	63	−25	−3	−68	−91	−25
(8) Together	1150	2260	1194	991	1815	1482
			KOREA			
I. *External Shocks*						
(1) Terms of Trade Effects	1712	1806	1203	623	1247	1318
(2) Export Volume Effects	45	493	254	673	791	451
(3) Together	1757	2299	1456	1296	2038	1769
II. *Policy Responses*						
(4) Additional Net External Financing	486	−296	−2141	−3291	−2906	−1630
(5) Increase in Export Market Share	445	934	1658	2211	2625	1575
(6) Import Substitution	795	1412	2272	3395	4082	2391
(7) Import Effects of Lower GNP Growth Rate	31	248	−333	−1019	−1762	−567
(8) Together	1757	2299	1456	1296	2038	1769

Sources: International and national trade statistics; gross national product—World Bank data bank.

Note: Numbers may not add up due to rounding.

TABLE 2.1 (continued)

	1974	1975	1976	1977	1978	Average 1974-78	1974	1975	1976	1977	1978	Average 1974-78
	BRAZIL						**CHILE**					
	3143	3306	2635	805	1977	2373	45	710	478	932	1130	659
	168	529	341	787	793	523	−52	87	74	98	175	76
	3311	3835	2976	1592	2770	2897	7	797	552	1030	1304	735
	4568	2749	823	−2327	−1857	791	−563	225	−430	50	505	−43
	108	793	341	524	445	442	288	249	447	462	538	397
	−742	675	2335	3491	3945	1941	202	18	218	248	84	154
	−624	−381	−524	−95	237	−278	66	309	318	270	177	227
	3311	3835	2976	1592	2770	2897	−7	797	552	1030	1304	735
	MEXICO						**URUGUAY**					
	662	1073	525	−114	90	447	117	183	176	213	176	173
	95	247	179	363	402	257	31	31	10	11	18	20
	758	1320	704	249	492	705	148	214	186	224	194	193
	1979	2508	1533	336	856	1442	121	196	71	161	135	137
	−93	−235	−507	−301	148	−198	11	48	124	81	86	70
	−1136	−1031	−533	−80	−813	−719	17	−18	8	11	16	7
	8	78	211	293	302	178	−1	−11	−17	−29	−43	−20
	758	1320	704	249	492	705	148	214	186	224	194	193
	ISRAEL						**YUGOSLAVIA**					
	1054	1079	745	757	1116	950	1653	2009	1479	2387	2159	2009
	12	217	119	318	409	215	134	443	608	800	1247	646
	1066	1296	864	1075	1525	1165	1787	2452	2087	3187	3765	2655
	1209	952	362	338	459	664	2044	1817	518	1979	2072	1686
	−278	−206	−321	−205	−161	−234	−321	−28	73	−580	−440	−259
	49	282	287	86	180	177	−216	−28	573	933	1166	486
	87	267	535	856	1047	558	279	691	923	855	968	743
	1066	1296	864	1075	1525	1165	1787	2452	2087	3187	3765	2655
	SINGAPORE						**TAIWAN**					
	678	911	602	433	997	724	1208	836	191	−72	−348	363
	3	297	163	398	557	284	−14	581	237	813	992	522
	681	1208	765	832	1554	1008	1194	1416	428	742	644	885
	1011	1042	587	139	630	682	1556	520	−987	−1499	−2955	−673
	211	−15	4	300	636	227	−343	−302	243	199	666	93
	−742	−193	−402	−304	−524	−433	−509	107	−7	523	1432	309
	202	374	576	697	812	532	491	1093	1179	1520	1501	1157
	681	1208	765	832	1554	1008	1194	1416	428	742	644	885

TABLE 2.2
Balance of Payments Effects of External Shocks and Policy Responses
to These Shocks: Ratios (per cent)

	1974	1975	1976	1977	1978	1974-78
ARGENTINA						
I. *External Shocks*						
(13) Terms of Trade Effects/Avg. Trade	−7.7	29.1	9.0	6.6	−19.3	2.5
(14) Terms of Trade Effects/GNP	−0.4	1.3	0.4	0.4	−1.1	0.1
(15) Export Volume Effects/Exports	0.8	5.7	−2.2	1.0	1.4	1.1
(16) Export Volume Effects/GNP	0.0	0.2	−0.1	0.1	0.1	0.1
(17) External Shocks/GNP	−0.3	1.5	0.3	0.5	−1.0	0.2
II. *Policy Responses*						
(18) Addl. Net External Financing/Avg. Trade	6.7	71.2	−11.3	−25.1	−61.9	−8.0
(19) Addl. Net External Financing/GNP	0.3	3.2	−0.5	−1.5	−3.5	−0.4
(20) Increase in Export Market Shares/Export	−8.7	−37.8	−14.4	15.1	8.8	−3.0
(21) Import Substitution/Imports	4.0	1.4	44.2	16.9	37.2	18.2
(22) Import Effects of Lower GNP Growth/Imports	−8.7	−3.5	3.2	2.4	14.9	0.7
COLOMBIA						
I. *External Shocks*						
(13) Terms of Trade Effects/Avg. Trade	4.4	15.5	−14.0	−69.1	−39.2	−21.3
(14) Terms of Trade Effects/GNP	0.4	1.2	−1.0	−5.1	−3.4	−1.7
(15) Export Volume Effects/Exports	6.2	9.3	8.7	26.2	18.4	13.5
(16) Export Volume Effects/GNP	0.5	0.8	0.6	1.6	1.3	1.0
(17) External Shocks/GNP	0.9	2.0	−0.4	−3.5	−2.0	−0.7
II. *Policy Responses*						
(18) Addl. Net External Financing/Avg. Trade	20.1	10.5	9.4	−22.1	9.3	5.7
(19) Addl. Net External Financing/GNP	1.7	0.9	0.7	−1.6	0.8	0.5
(20) Increase in Export Market Shares/Export	3.9	10.1	−13.4	−13.4	0.4	−1.8
(21) Import Substitution/Imports	−11.8	4.8	−2.2	−11.4	−28.0	−11.4
(22) Import Effects of Lower GNP Growth/Imports	−0.9	−0.4	−0.1	−0.1	−1.0	−0.5
INDIA						
I. *External Shocks*						
(13) Terms of Trade Effects/Avg. Trade	40.9	65.5	29.1	12.4	29.0	34.7
(14) Terms of Trade Effects/GNP	1.8	2.8	1.3	0.5	1.2	1.5
(15) Export Volume Effects/Exports	1.3	11.7	9.5	18.7	27.6	14.1
(16) Export Volume Effects/GNP	0.1	0.5	0.5	0.8	1.1	0.6
(17) External Shocks/GNP	1.9	3.3	1.7	1.3	2.3	2.1
II. *Policy Responses*						
(18) Addl. Net External Financing/Avg. Trade	58.1	86.3	33.2	53.8	94.3	65.6
(19) Addl. Net External Financing/GNP	2.6	3.7	1.4	2.3	4.0	2.8
(20) Increase in Export Market Shares/Export	−12.3	−2.7	0.0	−11.4	−21.9	−9.5
(21) Import Substitution/Imports	−6.2	−5.6	7.8	−9.1	−15.4	−6.5
(22) Import Effects of Lower GNP Growth/Imports	2.3	−0.9	−0.1	−2.1	−2.6	−0.8
KOREA						
I. *External Shocks*						
(13) Terms of Trade Effects/Avg. Trade	51.8	50.6	25.6	11.3	18.4	27.6
(14) Terms of Trade Effects/GNP	8.3	8.2	4.8	2.2	3.9	5.1
(15) Export Volume Effects/Exports	1.5	14.6	5.3	12.5	12.6	9.9
(16) Export Volume Effects/GNP	0.2	2.2	1.0	2.4	2.5	1.8
(17) External Shocks/GNP	8.5	10.4	5.8	4.5	6.4	6.9
II. *Policy Responses*						
(18) Addl. Net External Financing/Avg. Trade	14.7	−8.3	−45.6	−60.0	−42.8	−34.2
(19) Addl. Net External Financing/GNP	2.3	−1.3	−8.5	−11.5	−9.1	−6.3
(20) Increase in Export Market Shares/Export	15.0	27.7	34.8	41.0	41.9	34.6
(21) Import Substitution/Imports	21.8	37.5	49.1	60.8	55.7	47.9
(22) Import Effects of Lower GNP Growth/Imports	0.8	6.6	−7.2	−18.3	−24.1	−11.4

Sources: Table 2.1 and World Bank data bank.

TABLE 2.2 (Continued)

1974	1975	1976	1977	1978	1974-78	1974	1975	1976	1977	1978	1974-78
		BRAZIL						CHILE			
49.0	52.2	43.2	13.6	31.3	38.2	3.9	65.2	41.6	76.6	80.0	54.8
3.3	3.3	2.4	0.7	1.7	2.2	0.5	8.6	5.5	10.0	11.0	7.2
3.4	9.6	6.1	13.7	13.0	9.4	−3.6	6.5	4.6	5.9	10.1	4.9
0.2	0.5	0.3	0.7	0.7	0.5	−0.5	1.0	0.9	1.0	1.7	0.8
3.5	3.9	2.8	1.4	2.3	2.7	−0.1	9.6	6.4	11.0	12.7	8.0
71.3	43.4	13.5	−39.3	−29.4	12.7	−49.0	20.7	−37.5	4.1	35.7	−3.6
4.8	2.8	0.8	−2.1	−1.6	0.7	−6.0	2.7	−5.0	5.0	4.9	−0.5
2.2	14.4	6.1	9.1	7.3	7.9	19.8	18.7	27.9	27.9	31.3	25.5
−9.3	9.5	35.5	57.3	60.4	28.3	24.0	2.1	31.4	31.9	7.6	18.1
−7.9	−5.3	−8.0	−1.6	3.6	−4.0	7.9	36.1	45.7	34.7	16.1	26.7
		MEXICO						URUGUAY			
21.5	35.6	18.9	−4.2	2.6	14.8	48.2	62.6	51.8	64.1	51.0	55.7
1.3	2.0	1.0	−0.2	0.1	0.8	3.9	5.9	5.6	6.5	5.2	5.4
5.3	14.6	10.6	18.9	15.5	13.3	12.6	10.5	2.5	2.9	4.6	5.9
0.2	0.5	0.3	0.6	0.7	0.5	1.1	1.0	0.3	0.3	0.5	0.6
1.4	2.4	1.3	0.4	0.8	1.3	5.0	6.9	5.9	6.8	5.7	6.1
64.3	83.3	55.2	12.4	24.4	47.8	50.0	66.9	21.0	48.4	39.0	44.0
3.8	4.6	2.8	0.6	1.4	2.6	4.1	6.3	2.2	4.9	3.9	4.3
−5.2	−13.9	−30.2	−15.6	5.7	−10.2	4.3	16.2	30.4	21.5	22.0	20.4
−26.1	−23.8	−13.8	−2.3	−18.4	−17.5	7.1	−6.4	2.8	3.7	5.4	2.4
0.2	1.8	5.5	8.3	6.8	4.4	−0.3	−3.9	−6.2	−10.1	−14.1	−7.3
		ISRAEL						YUGOSLAVIA			
55.1	57.6	37.4	34.7	47.7	46.1	47.4	56.1	41.3	68.0	67.3	561.
11.1	11.0	7.7	7.8	11.0	9.7	5.3	6.4	4.5	6.7	6.7	5.9
0.9	16.7	7.9	19.0	21.2	14.1	5.5	16.0	19.7	30.0	43.8	23.4
0.1	2.2	1.2	3.3	4.0	2.2	0.4	1.4	1.8	2.2	3.3	1.9
11.2	13.2	8.9	11.1	15.0	11.9	5.7	7.8	6.3	8.9	10.0	7.8
63.2	50.9	18.2	15.5	19.6	32.2	58.6	50.7	14.5	56.4	55.4	47.1
12.7	9.7	3.7	3.5	4.5	6.8	6.5	5.7	1.6	5.6	5.5	5.0
−22.6	−15.9	−21.4	−12.2	−8.4	−15.3	−13.1	−1.0	2.4	−21.8	−15.5	−9.4
1.9	11.5	11.6	3.2	6.5	6.8	−4.8	−0.6	14.1	21.4	25.1	11.0
3.3	10.9	21.6	31.9	38.0	21.6	6.2	15.7	22.6	19.6	20.9	16.9
		SINGAPORE						TAIWAN			
16.8	23.5	13.8	9.2	18.6	16.1	31.9	23.4	4.0	−1.4	−6.0	7.9
18.1	22.8	14.2	9.4	19.8	16.7	10.4	7.0	1.4	−0.5	−2.1	2.7
0.1	0.1	4.8	10.4	12.7	8.0	−0.4	15.9	4.6	15.4	15.5	10.8
0.1	7.4	3.8	8.6	11.0	6.6	−0.1	4.9	1.8	5.6	6.1	3.9
18.2	30.3	18.0	18.0	30.8	23.3	10.2	11.9	3.2	5.1	4.0	6.5
24.4	26.9	13.5	2.9	11.8	15.2	41.1	14.6	−20.5	−30.1	−51.1	−14.7
27.0	26.1	13.8	3.0	12.5	15.8	13.3	4.4	−7.4	−10.4	−18.1	−5.0
6.6	−0.5	0.1	7.8	14.5	6.4	−9.4	−8.3	4.7	3.8	10.4	1.9
−14.6	−4.0	−7.6	−5.4	−8.3	−8.0	−13.0	3.1	−0.2	11.1	27.9	7.1
4.0	7.8	10.9	12.4	12.9	9.8	12.5	31.4	26.6	32.4	29.2	26.7

deficit. In turn, the favorable impact of higher import prices on its trade surplus slightly exceeded the unfavorable pure terms of trade effects in Argentina.

In the third group, Israel and Yugoslavia suffered the consequences of the quadrupling of petroleum prices that resulted in a terms of trade loss equivalent to one-half of the average value of their trade in 1974. Given differences in trade shares, the corresponding ratio with respect to GNP was 11 percent in Israel and 5 percent in Yugoslavia. These figures changed little in subsequent years. At the same time, in both countries, the effects of higher import prices on the trade deficit expressed in "1972" prices exceeded the pure terms of trade effect by a large margin.

The quadrupling of petroleum prices adversely affected the balance of payments of all three countries of the fourth group, although Chile benefited from high copper prices that continued during much of 1974. The terms of trade loss expressed as a proportion of average trade and the gross national product, respectively, was 48 percent and 4 percent in Uruguay, 41 percent and 2 percent in India, and 4 percent and 1 percent in Chile in 1974.

Subsequently, however, copper prices declined precipitiously, leading to a terms of trade loss equivalent to 11 percent of Chile's GNP in 1978. In the same year, the fall in beef prices contributed to a terms of trade loss equal to 5 percent of GNP in Uruguay. Finally, increases in tea prices contributed to a decline in India's terms of trade loss that amounted to one percent of GNP in 1978.

Export Volume Effects

Export volume effects were negligible in the first group of Far Eastern countries in 1974 as foreign demand continued to be strong during much of the year. These effects increased in subsequent years, however, with year-to-year changes paralleling the world business cycle. By 1978, the shortfall in exports due to the slow growth of world demand reached 13 to 16 percent of export value in the three countries. With differences in export shares, the ratio of the export shortfall to GNP was 11 percent in Singapore, 6 percent in Taiwan, and 3 percent in Korea in 1978.

A similar pattern was observed in Brazil, Colombia, and Mexico, with the export shortfall reaching 18 percent of the value of exports in Colombia, 16 percent in Mexico, and 13 percent in Brazil in 1978. Given the relatively low share of exports in the gross national product, the ratio of the export shortfall to GNP did not exceed one percent in any of the three countries, however. And, this ratio was practically zero in Argentina that benefited from the rise in world demand for beef and maize.

Israel followed the time pattern observed in the above mentioned countries, with the ratio of the export shortfall to export value exceeding 21 percent in 1978. In turn, the export shortfall rose uninterruptedly in Yugoslavia, reaching the highest level (44 percent of the value of exports) among all the countries under study in 1978, largely because of unfavorable developments in centrally planned economies whose 1978 imports from the developing countries were below the "1972" level. Finally, the export shortfall, expressed as a proportion of GNP, increased from practically nil in 1974 to 3 percent in Yugoslavia and to 4 percent in Israel in 1978.

India also exhibited the pattern observed in most other countries, with the ratio of the export shortfall to export value rising from 1 percent in 1974 to 28 percent in 1978, and that calculated with respect to GNP increasing from nil in 1974 to 1 percent in 1978. The pattern was similar in Chile, except that strong demand for copper gave rise to a gain in 1974; the export shortfall equalled 10 percent of Chile's exports and 2 percent of its GNP in 1978. By contrast, owing to the rise in world demand for beef and wool, the ratio of the export shortfall to export value declined from 12 percent in 1974 to 5 percent in 1978 in Uruguay, with a parallel decline shown with respect to GNP.

Terms of Trade vs. Export Volume Effects

The results indicate the relative importance of terms of trade effects in newly-industrializing developing countries that rely on imported petroleum. In 1974 and 1975, on the average, the ratio of the terms of trade loss to the export shortfall ranged between 4 and 6 in Taiwan, Singapore, Uruguay, Yugoslavia and Korea; it was between 8 and 10 in India, Brazil and Israel; and it reached 22 in Chile. The corresponding ratios for the remaining countries were 1 in Colombia, 3 in Argentina, and 5 in Mexico.

With the exception of Chile and Uruguay, the ratio of terms of trade effects to export volume effects declined during the period under consideration. For one thing, apart from Chile and Uruguay that experienced unfavorable changes in the prices of their principal traditional exports, there was a tendency for terms of trade losses as a percentage of GNP to decline over time due largely to the slowdown in the rise of petroleum prices. For another thing, export volume effects showed an increasing trend, with fluctuations around the trend parallelling the business cycle, except that Uruguay benefited from increased world demand for beef and wool.

Still, terms of trade effects continued to exceed export volume effects by a considerable margin in all the petroleum importing countries other than India where increases in the price of tea reduced terms of trade losses towards the end of the period and Taiwan where high import prices on its trade surplus measured in "1972" prices gave rise to a terms of trade gain. In 1978, the ratio of these effects was 2 in Brazil, Korea, Singapore and Yugoslavia, and 3 in Israel; it was 6 in Chile, and 10 in Uruguay. In the same year, terms of trade effects were negative in Argentina and Colombia and practically nil in Mexico.

The results show the importance of the quadrupling in petroleum prices in 1973–74, the effects of which were fully felt by January 1974. They conflict with conventional wisdom that gives emphasis to the unfavorable effects of the world recession and the subsequent slow recovery in the developed countries on the balance of payments of the developing countries. Also, the results do not support the view that the exports of manufactured goods from the developing countries were adversely affected by increased protectionism in the developed countries.

Thus, data available in a geographical breakdown show an increase in the "apparent" income elasticity of demand for the imports of manufactured goods in the developed countries, calculated as the ratio of the rate of growth of their imports to that of the gross national product. For the period as a whole, increases in the income elasticity of demand offset one-fifth of the export shortfall due to lower GNP growth rates in the developed countries.

At the same time, in intra-LDC trade, the favorable effects of higher GNP growth rates and income elasticity of import demand cumulated, with favorable effects for countries, such as those of the second group, where a large share of manufactured exports was sold in developing country markets. By contrast, in centrally planned economies, the decline in the income elasticity of demand aggravated the adverse effects of lower GNP growth rates, importantly contributing to the large export shortfall observed in Yugoslavia.

IV. The Policies Applied and their Balance-of-Payments Effects

Section III of the essay analyzed the impact of external shocks, in the form of terms of trade and export volume effects, on the balance of payments of the newly-industrializing developing countries classified into four groups. Section IV will examine the policies applied in the four groups of countries and indicate the balance-of-payments effects of these policies.

The balance-of-payments effects of the policies applied are shown in Table 2.1 while Table 2.2 relates the results to the value of exports, imports, average trade, and the gross national product, as the case may be, all expressed in "1972" prices. In turn, Table 2.3 provides information on the financing of the resource gap, Table 2.4 on nominal and real interest rates, the government budget and the money supply, Table 2.5 on nominal and real exchange rates vis-à-vis the U.S. dollar, Table 2.6 on debt service and the external debt, and Table 2.7 on expenditure shares, incremental capital-output ratios, and rates of economic growth.

Korea, Singapore, and Taiwan

In 1974, the combined balance-of-payments effects of external shocks equalled·18 percent of the gross national product in Singapore, 10 percent in Taiwan, and 9 percent in Korea. The effects of these shocks increased in subsequent years in Singapore, reaching 31 percent of GNP in 1978. After a small increase in 1975, the ratio declined to 6 percent in Korea and to 4 percent in Taiwan in 1978.

All three countries continued with outward-oriented policies in the years following the quadrupling of petroleum prices and the world recession. In Korea, quantitative import restrictions were liberalized and tariffs were lowered in 1973 and in 1977. The resulting reductions in import protection appear to have been greater than reductions in export subsidies which occurred through the elimination of tax benefits on income derived from exports and decreases in wastage allowances on imported inputs used in export production. Also, new facilities were established for medium-term and long-term export credits.[9]

Import liberalization proceeded more rapidly in Taiwan than in Korea while reductions in tariffs were smaller in magnitude. In turn, Singapore had practically no import restrictions and further reduced its already low tariffs. And, both Singapore and Taiwan instituted new facilities for medium-term and long-term export credit.

At the same time, there are differences among the three countries in regard to the macro-economic policies followed as well as the course of the real exchange rate. *Korea* increased reliance on foreign borrowing in order to overcome the adverse effects of external shocks it suffered in 1974. At the same time, it ensured that the incremental inflow of capital was invested rather than consumed by providing investment incentives, reducing the government deficit, and re-establishing positive real interest rates. These measures contributed to the increase in the share of investment in aggregate expenditure from 23 percent in 1971–73 and to 27 percent in 1974–76.

With the rapid rise of investment, Korea expanded production for export as well as for domestic markets. Notwithstanding the appreciation of the exchange rate vis-à-vis the U.S. dollar from its undervalued "1972" level, increases in exports and import substitution, taken together, offset the adverse effects of external shocks on Korea's balance of payments in 1975, eliminating the need for additional net external financing.

Following the liberalization of imports, export expansion assumed increased importance relative to import substitution while the two effects combined came to exceed the adverse balance-of-payments effects of external shocks by more than four times in 1977. Although higher GNP growth rates added $1.0 billion to the import bill, and Korea continued to suffer the effects of adverse external shocks, additional net external financing reached $−3.3 billion as a result.

The increase in the share of investment in aggregate expenditure from 27 percent in 1974–76 to 30 percent in 1977–79 importantly contributed to the acceleration of economic growth in Korea. Notwithstanding the increased investment effort, however, export shares did not rise further and negative import substitution (i.e. an increase in import shares) occurred in 1978, largely as a result of the continued appreciation of the real exchange rate and the domestic expansionary measures applied that maintained rapid rates of economic growth at the cost of increased inflationary pressures.[10] These

TABLE 2.3
Financing the External Resource Gap (in millions of current U.S. $)

	1971	1972	1973	"1972"	1974	1975	1976	1977	1978	Average 1974-78
ARGENTINA										
Interest Receipts	16	7	26	16	128	55	50	128	333	139
Interest Payments	−226	−279	−343	−283	−425	−467	−515	−500	−719	−525
Dividends	−46	−61	−77	−61	−36	−16	−25	−211	−324	−122
Other Factor Payments	−33	−8	−33	−25	−59	−15	−5	−27	−143	−50
Official Transfers	−3	−4	11	1	0	−1	−5	0	0	−1
Direct Investment	11	10	10	10	10	0	0	82	273	73
Portfolio Capital	−94	112	56	25	−78	203	−221	137	−503	−92
Errors and Omissions	29	40	69	46	26	4	486	324	297	227
Changes in Reserves	444	65	−845	−112	−76	1080	−921	−1837	−2269	−805
Net External Financing	98	−118	−1126	−382	−510	843	−1156	−1904	−3055	−1156
Total External Financing	370	220	−706	−38	−49	1326	−616	−1193	−2012	−509
COLOMBIA										
Interest Receipts	9	18	24	17	65	56	65	65	123	75
Interest Payments	−114	−135	−168	−139	−201	−250	−269	−252	−269	−248
Dividends	−71	−70	−70	−70	−55	−68	−109	−86	−114	−86
Other Factor Payments	−32	−33	−25	−30	−23	−18	−17	−2	−3	−13
Official Transfers	31	24	23	26	32	17	13	6	6	15
Direct Investment	43	18	24	28	41	40	25	64	75	49
Portfolio Capital	303	228	123	218	231	142	171	−91	149	120
Errors and Omissions	90	103	69	87	−17	10	211	159	138	100
Changes in Reserves	1	−178	−161	−113	95	−112	−633	−586	−528	−353
Net External Financing	260	−25	−161	25	168	−183	−543	−723	−423	−341
Total External Financing	445	180	77	234	424	135	−165	−385	−40	−6
INDIA										
Interest Receipts	48	43	51	47	94	130	195	274	468	232
Interest Payments	−350	−350	−391	−364	−304	−386	−347	−413	−338	−358
Dividends	0	0	0	0	0	0	0	0	0	0
Other Factor Payments	8	10	13	10	45	79	−29	−67	0	6
Official Transfers	144	163	110	139	2094	194	401	394	993	815
Direct Investment	−1	3	−13	−4	−6	−11	−8	0	0	−5
Portfolio Capital	757	275	482	505	−937	958	921	437	0	276
Errors and Omissions	−95	−254	−42	−130	−290	−455	−296	−134	199	−195
Changes in Reserves	−22	129	108	72	20	−362	−2214	−2425	−1692	1335
Net External Financing	489	19	318	275	716	147	−1377	−1934	−370	−564
Total External Financing	839	369	709	639	1020	533	−1030	−1521	−32	−206
KOREA										
Interest Receipts	23	21	41	28	82	47	70	134	282	123
Interest Payments	−109	−150	−192	−150	−294	−424	−480	−675	−968	−568
Dividends	−3	−25	−10	−13	−30	−25	−37	−51	−50	−39
Other Factor Payments	236	229	176	214	150	125	182	310	328	219
Official Transfers	63	50	36	50	67	67	152	53	38	75
Direct Investment	42	64	95	67	119	57	81	93	89	88
Portfolio Capital	741	425	509	558	1624	2398	1782	1305	2006	1823
Errors and Omissions	26	21	45	31	107	−226	−232	−63	−327	−148
Changes in Reserves	39	−141	−348	−150	171	−376	−1314	−1372	−707	−720
Net External Financing	1058	494	352	635	1996	1643	204	−266	691	854
Total External Financing	1170	669	554	798	2320	2092	721	460	1709	1461

TABLE 2.3 (Continued)

1971	1972	1973	"1972"	1974	1975	1976	1977	1978	Average 1974-78
				BRAZIL					
43	131	327	167	718	364	282	358	640	472
−374	−544	−908	−609	−1448	−1861	−2091	−2460	−3334	−2239
−412	−310	−530	−417	−554	−532	−790	−1330	−1538	−949
8	8	10	9	−1	−75	−120	−33	−44	−55
20	23	16	20	−2	−10	−4	5	3	−2
536	570	1341	816	1268	1090	1212	1678	1880	1426
1595	3115	2768	2493	5371	4956	6988	4540	9486	6268
−9	438	355	261	−64	−35	1024	−614	298	122
−483	−2431	−2307	−1740	989	1016	−2683	−495	−4646	−1164
924	1000	1072	999	6277	4913	3818	1649	2745	3880
1710	1854	2510	2025	8279	7306	6699	5439	7617	7068
				MEXICO					
65	80	97	81	153	117	124	168	245	161
−309	−345	−513	−389	−806	−1094	−1675	−1978	−2550	−1621
−359	−435	−581	−458	−794	−840	−666	−400	−480	−636
133	149	157	146	182	186	253	260	279	232
7	10	8	8	22	27	27	16	18	22
307	301	457	355	678	610	628	556	532	601
629	154	1524	769	3122	4872	5233	1616	2956	3560
34	651	−411	91	−845	−1249	−3046	53	−557	−1129
−134	−190	−154	−159	−79	−178	595	−375	−428	−93
373	375	584	444	1633	2451	1473	84	15	1098
1041	1155	1678	1291	3233	4385	3814	2294	3045	3354
				ISRAEL					
120	137	238	165	335	322	363	370	496	377
−177	−240	−334	−250	−526	−652	−663	−715	−939	−699
−29	−20	−42	−30	−53	−49	−38	−46	−48	−47
−68	−114	−198	−127	−235	−242	−222	−193	−218	−222
240	344	1050	545	990	1002	1436	1277	1560	1253
57	113	148	106	81	45	47	81	134	78
533	411	835	593	985	1901	1024	232	1345	1097
58	53	−4	36	−183	149	22	430	391	162
−224	−519	−532	−425	815	197	−44	−237	−860	−26
510	165	1161	612	2209	2673	1925	1199	1861	1973
716	425	1537	893	2788	3374	2626	1960	2848	2719
				SINGAPORE					
83	96	137	105	182	211	208	273	383	251
−30	−128	−298	−152	−371	−295	−349	−374	−454	−369
0	0	0	0	0	0	0	0	0	0
117	61	80	86	82	69	32	32	38	51
11	4	11	9	1	0	−3	−3	−4	−2
116	191	389	232	597	611	651	335	517	542
171	205	334	237	−99	−32	199	272	274	123
755	451	262	489	902	433	152	180	630	459
−319	−337	−411	−356	−295	−408	−298	−313	−665	−396
904	543	504	650	999	589	592	402	719	660
934	671	802	802	1370	884	941	776	1173	1029

TABLE 2.3 (Continued)

	1971	1972	1973	"1972"	1974	1975	1976	1977	1978	Average 1974-78
CHILE										
Interest Receipts	12	1	5	6	24	5	10	18	39	19
Interest Payments	−100	−124	−114	−113	−286	−282	−320	−360	−454	−340
Dividends	−30	−25	0	−18	−8	−7	−2	−23	−30	−14
Other Factor Payments	−13	5	12	1	−26	−11	−47	−54	−34	−34
Official Transfers	4	2	10	5	8	13	16	16	0	11
Direct Investment	−66	−1	−5	−24	−557	50	−1	21	182	−61
Portfolio Capital	134	342	470	316	761	257	167	776	1496	691
Errors and Omissions	−109	0	−86	−65	−117	−19	−3	−33	−68	−48
Changes in Reserves	239	130	−100	90	90	277	−333	−210	−720	−179
Net External Financing	71	330	192	198	−111	283	−513	151	411	44
Total External Financing	201	479	306	329	183	572	−191	534	895	399
URUGUAY										
Interest Receipts	1	1	6	3	5	4	7	12	18	9
Interest Payments	−22	−25	−31	−26	−45	−71	−79	−77	−95	−73
Dividends	0	0	0	0	−4	−4	0	−2	0	−2
Other Factor Payments	−1	−1	−1	−1	−4	−5	−3	−10	−6	−6
Official Transfers	8	8	7	8	17	5	0	0	0	4
Direct Investment	0	0	0	0	0	0	0	66	129	39
Portfolio Capital	102	40	20	54	160	165	160	238	−31	138
Errors and Omissions	−51	−62	−30	−48	−82	−38	−13	35	158	12
Changes in Reserves	13	−36	−27	−17	40	62	−73	−179	−129	−56
Net External Financing	50	−75	−56	−27	89	118	−1	83	44	67
Total External Financing	72	−50	−25	−1	136	193	78	165	139	142
YUGOSLAVIA										
Interest Receipts	17	17	50	28	93	62	90	123	150	104
Interest Payments	−147	−165	−222	−178	−285	−343	−364	−381	−455	−366
Dividends	0	0	0	0	0	0	0	0	0	0
Other Factor Payments	0	0	0	0	0	0	0	0	0	0
Official Transfers	−1	−1	14	4	1	−1	0	−1	0	0
Direct Investment	0	0	0	0	0	0	0	0	0	0
Portfolio Capital	428	147	168	248	947	1067	900	1544	1267	1145
Errors and Omissions	0	0	0	0	0	0	0	0	0	0
Changes in Reserves	−70	−566	−646	−427	243	−63	−1065	−11	−250	−229
Net External Financing	227	−568	−636	−326	999	722	−439	1274	712	654
Total External Financing	374	−403	−414	−148	1284	1065	−75	1655	1167	1019
TAIWAN										
Interest Receipts	40	46	111	66	164	149	154	212	376	211
Interest Payments	−56	−24	−43	−41	−82	−142	−261	−313	−400	−240
Dividends	−21	−25	−49	−32	−65	−90	−61	−67	−75	−72
Other Factor Payments	20	48	−2	22	11	11	−51	−19	−104	−30
Official Transfers	2	2	−5	0	−2	−6	−1	−2	−7	−4
Direct Investment	53	27	62	47	83	15	72	49	114	67
Portfolio Capital	−162	−29	−485	−225	1019	552	266	−1080	1633	−175
Errors and Omissions	−24	−25	−116	−55	13	−5	−243	−141	−135	−102
Changes in Reserves	−41	−514	−60	−205	−41	−12	−413	246	−6	−45
Net External Financing	−189	−494	−587	−423	1100	472	−538	−1115	−1870	−390
Total External Financing	−112	−445	−495	−351	1247	704	−216	−735	−1395	−79

Sources: International Monetary Fund, *Balance of Payments Yearbook, International Financing Statistics,* various issues. Yugoslavian data from World Bank Report. For India, 1978/79 fiscal year was used for 1978, from World Bank Report.

Note: Total external financing is the sum of net external financing, interest payments and dividends.

influences, combined with credit allocation favoring large, capital-intensive investments in intermediate products, led to a decline in the volume of exports in 1979.

Additional net external financing was nearly offset by the trend value of the resource gap in 1977,[11] so that actual net external financing was practically nil. With unfavorable developments in trade, net external financing reached $0.7 billion in 1978 while total external financing was $1.7 billion. Also, Korea's gross debt service ratio (interest payments and amortization expressed as a proportion of the value of merchandise exports) increased from 17 percent in 1973 to 20 percent in 1978 while the ratio of the (gross) external debt to GNP rose from 18 percent to 25 percent.[12]

Taiwan let its real exchange rate appreciate by 23 percent in 1974 as compared to its "1972" level, leading to a decline in export market shares and to negative import substitution. These unfavorable changes in trade flows aggravated the effects on economic growth of the deflationary policies applied, involving a decline in the real value of the money supply by 24 percent in 1974. As a result, economic growth came practically to a halt whereas the 41 percent increase in wholesale prices in 1974 was followed by a 5 percent decline in 1975.

Savings in imports associated with the decline in the rate of economic growth did not fully offset the adverse balance-of-payments effects of losses in export market shares and negative import substitution in 1974. Correspondingly, Taiwan's additional net external financing requirements exceeded the negative effects of external shocks, necessitating large foreign borrowing. The situation changed in subsequent years as the policies applied encouraged new investment and improved Taiwan's competitive position.

To begin with, real interest rates rose to 19 percent in 1975 when wholesale prices declined and it remained in the 7–9 percent range in the following years. Also, increased investment incentives were provided through amendments to the Statute for Encouragement of Investment and there was a surplus in the government budget. Finally, Taiwan's real exchange rate depreciated from year to year, exceeding the 1973 level, and approaching the "1972" average, towards the end of the period.

As a result, the share of gross domestic investment in aggregate expenditure increased from 28 percent in 1971–73 to 33 percent in 1974–76, with a decline to 31 percent in 1977–79 due largely to the decline in the rate of inventory accumulation. The rise in the rate of investment and improvements in its competitive position, in turn, contributed to increases in export shares and import substitution in Taiwan. At the same time, in conjunction with the liberalization of imports, export promotion assumed greater importance vis-à-vis import substitution.

These influences contributed to the acceleration of economic growth in Taiwan. Its gross national product grew at an average annual rate of 10 percent after 1975 while it hardly changed in the previous two years. Still, due to the slowdown in earlier years, Taiwan continued to experience import savings. All in all, the balance of payments impact of domestic economic policies affecting exports, import substitution, and the rate of economic growth exceeded the adverse effects of external shocks more than five times in 1978.

Correspondingly, additional net external financing became increasingly negative and amounted to -3.0 billion in 1978. Adjusted for the trend value of the resource gap, actual net external financing was -1.9 billion, and total external financing -1.4 billion, representing largely the repayment of foreign debt. In the same year, the gross debt service ratio was 7 percent, only slightly exceeding the 6 percent ratio in 1973 while the gross external debt ratio was 16 percent as compared to 11 percent in 1973.

The real exchange rate in *Singapore* fell by 20 percent between "1972" and 1974 and increased only slightly in 1975. While exports continued to benefit from subsidies, reductions in import tariffs aggravated the effects of the appreciation of the real exchange rate giving rise to negative import substitution, and a slowdown in economic growth. Growth was further slowed by deflationary policies, although these were much less far-reaching than in Taiwan, with the real value of the money supply declining by 11 percent in 1974.

In 1974 and 1975, taken together, the net balance-of-payments effects of domestic economic policies added slightly to the adverse effects of external shocks in Singapore, thus raising external financing requirements. Financing took the form of the acceleration of the growth of foreign direct investment and the clandestine inflow of portfolio capital that shows up in the errors and omissions item. Political stability in Singapore was attractive to foreign investors and direct investment was further motivated by increased incentives through the extension of the tax-exempt status of pioneer industries from five to ten years and the establishment of the Capital Assistance Scheme to furnish capital to skill-intensive industries. At the same time, the inflow of foreign capital permitted maintaining gross investment at over one-third of aggregate expenditure.

The real exchange rate depreciated in subsequent years, surpassing the 1973 level by one-tenth, although falling short of the "1972" average in about the same proportion. Improvements in Singapore's competitive position were translated into rising export shares while negative import substitution continued during the period under consideration as tariffs were further reduced. With the effects of export promotion exceeding negative import substitutions, and high investment shares being maintained, the rate of economic growth accelerated. Nevertheless, Singapore continued to experience import savings due to the slowdown in the rate of economic growth in the early part of the period.

Given the positive net balance-of-payments effects of domestic economic policies, additional net external financing requirements were considerably lower than the balance-of-payments effects of external shocks. With the trend value of the resource gap being small, actual net external financing was $0.7 billion while interest and dividend payments raised total external financing to

TABLE 2.4
Nominal and Real Interest Rates, the Government Budget and the Money Supply

	1971	1972	1973	"1972"	1974	1975	1976	1977	1978
ARGENTINA									
Nominal Interest Rate[a]	23.2	30.1	26.2	26.5	26.5	94.5	115.3	121.8	142.8
Real Interest Rates[b]	−11.3	−24.7	−17.3	−17.8	7.9	−33.9	−64.1	−11.1	−1.3
Government Revenue[c]	6.6	5.7	5.2	5.8	6.0	3.9	5.3	6.2	—
Government Expenditure[c]	8.9	8.5	10.7	9.4	12.3	16.1	13.8	10.4	—
Budget Surplus (Deficit)[c]	−2.3	−2.8	−5.5	3.5	−6.3	−12.2	−8.5	−4.2	—
Change in the Money Supply – Nominal[d]	35.9	67.0	103.6	68.8	71.6	196.5	297.7	148.7	133.3
– Real[b]	−2.2	−5.5	32.7	8.3	46.4	0.8	−33.6	−0.3	−5.2
COLOMBIA									
Nominal Interest Rate[a]	14.0	14.0	14.0	14.0	16.0	16.0	20.0	20.0	22.0
Real Interest Rate[b]	2.2	−3.7	−10.9	4.1	−14.7	−7.5	−2.4	−5.3	3.7
Government Revenue[c]	9.7	8.9	8.4	9.1	8.1	9.5	9.3	9.0	9.5
Government Expenditure[c]	10.5	10.9	9.4	10.3	9.0	9.8	8.5	8.1	8.8
Budget Surplus (Deficit)[c]	−0.8	−2.0	−1.0	−1.3	−0.9	−0.3	0.9	0.8	0.7
Change in the Money Supply – Nominal[d]	11.9	27.1	30.7	23.2	17.8	20.1	34.7	30.4	25.0
– Real[b]	0.3	7.4	2.2	3.3	−13.4	−4.3	9.6	2.9	6.3
INDIA									
Nominal Interest Rate[a]	6.0	6.0	7.0	6.3	9.0	9.0	9.0	9.0	9.0
Real Interest Rate[b]	0.9	−3.3	−7.3	−3.2	−15.2	4.5	7.3	3.0	10.1
Government Revenue[c]	9.9	9.6	8.4	9.3	9.0	10.3	10.6	10.6	—
Government Expenditure[c]	12.1	11.6	9.9	11.2	10.6	12.5	13.4	13.2	—
Budget Surplus (Deficit)[c]	−2.2	−2.0	−1.5	1.9	−1.6	−2.2	−2.8	2.6	—
Change in the Money Supply – Nominal[d]	13.6	12.8	16.9	14.4	10.2	9.3	24.9	16.8	21.6
– Real[b]	8.1	2.9	1.3	4.1	−14.3	4.8	22.9	10.4	22.9
KOREA									
Nominal Interest Rate[a]	16.0	11.0	11.0	12.7	11.0	14.0	14.0	14.0	15.0
Real Interest Rate[b]	6.9	−2.4	3.8	2.8	−21.9	−9.9	1.7	4.6	3.0
Government Revenue[c]	17.2	15.6	15.4	16.1	16.0	17.7	20.7	19.7	20.3
Government Expenditure[c]	17.8	20.1	16.6	18.2	17.8	19.4	20.3	19.4	19.8
Budget Surplus (Deficit)[c]	−0.6	−4.5	−1.2	−2.1	−1.8	−1.7	0.4	0.3	0.5
Change in the Money Supply – Nominal[d]	16.4	45.1	40.6	34.1	29.5	25.0	30.7,	40.7	24.9
– Real[b]	7.2	27.5	31.5	22.1	−8.9	−1.3	16.6	29.1	11.8

$1.2 billion. Much of external financing continued to take the form of direct investments, and the gross debt service ratio declined from 9 percent in 1973 to 7 percent in 1978. And while the ratio of the gross external debt to GNP rose from 13 percent to 15 percent, Singapore's net reserves continued to exceed its gross external debt nearly three times.

Argentina, Brazil, Colombia, and Mexico

In 1974, the balance-of-payments effects of external shocks represented 4 percent of GNP in Brazil, 1 percent in Mexico and Colombia, and practically nil in Argentina. After increases in 1975, when adverse changes in the terms of trade reinforced the impact of the world recession, these ratios declined until 1977, with a small deterioration occurring in 1978, Argentina excepted. The

TABLE 2.4 (Continued)

	1971	1972	1973	"1972"	1974	1975	1976	1977	1978
				BRAZIL					
Nominal Interest Rate[a]	20.0	20.0	18.0	19.3	18.0	18.0	28.0	30.0	33.0
Real Interest Rate[b]	0.0	1.2	1.1	0.8	−8.6	−7.3	−10.7	−8.7	−3.3
Government Revenue[c]	9.8	10.5	10.7	10.3	10.8	9.6	10.8	10.6	10.4
Government Expenditure[c]	10.1	10.6	10.6	10.4	10.2	9.6	10.8	10.6	10.3
Budget Surplus (Deficit)[c]	−0.2	−0.1	0.1	−0.1	0.6	0.0	0.0	0.0	0.1
Change in the Money Supply – Nominal[d]	29.2	40.0	49.1	39.4	33.6	39.2	38.5	36.6	41.0
– Real[b]	7.7	18.1	27.7	17.8	3.5	9.4	−3.3	−4.1	2.5
				MEXICO					
Nominal Interest Rate[a]	4.5	4.5	4.5	4.5	4.5	4.5	4.5	4.5	4.5
Real Interest Rate[b]	0.6	1.7	−8.8	−2.2	−14.7	−5.4	−14.6	−26.0	−9.7
Government Revenue[c]	8.5	9.7	10.9	9.7	11.4	13.2	13.1	11.6	19.4
Government Expenditure[c]	9.3	11.6	14.1	11.7	15.0	16.7	16.5	14.9	24.1
Budget Surplus (Deficit)[c]	−0.8	−1.9	−3.2	−2.0	−3.6	−3.5	−3.4	−3.3	−4.7
Change in the Money Supply – Nominal[d]	7.6	17.9	22.4	16.0	20.7	21.4	29.1	26.0	31.1
– Real[b]	3.6	14.7	5.7	8.0	−1.5	9.9	5.6	−10.7	13.2
				ISRAEL					
Nominal Interest Rate[a]	—	—	—	—	—	—	—	—	—
Real Interest Rate[b]	—	—	—	—	—	—	—	—	—
Government Revenue[c]	39.6	34.3	38.5	37.5	42.4	49.2	55.5	57.5	—
Government Expenditure[c]	55.0	47.2	67.3	56.5	66.1	70.3	76.6	78.5	—
Budget Surplus (Deficit)[c]	−15.4	−12.9	−28.8	−19.0	−23.7	−21.1	−21.1	−21.0	—
Change in the Money Supply – Nominal[d]	28.2	28.7	32.3	29.7	18.0	21.7	27.1	38.8	45.0
– Real[b]	16.3	16.3	11.2	14.6	−22.1	−13.6	−2.8	0.2	−5.3
				SINGAPORE					
Nominal Interest Rate[a]	8.0	7.5	9.0	8.2	10.3	7.1	6.8	7.0	7.7
Real Interest Rate[b]	6.0	5.3	−13.7	−0.8	−9.9	4.3	9.0	3.6	2.8
Government Revenue[c]	22.3	23.1	21.5	22.3	22.2	25.5	24.2	23.5	23.7
Government Expenditure[c]	18.1	16.3	15.1	16.5	15.2	17.3	18.8	19.6	20.5
Budget Surplus (Deficit)[c]	4.2	6.8	6.4	5.8	7.0	8.2	5.4	3.9	2.2
Change in the Money Supply – Nominal[d]	7.9	35.5	10.4	17.9	8.6	21.5	15.2	10.3	11.7
– Real[b]	6.0	32.7	−12.7	8.7	−11.3	18.3	17.6	6.8	6.6

relevant ratios for 1978 were: Brazil, 2 percent; Mexico, 1 percent; Argentina, −1 percent; and Colombia, −2 percent.

The four Latin American countries did not continue with reforms towards greater outward orientation during the period under consideration. Brazil and Colombia, in fact, increased the bias against exports through greater import protection and reduced export subsidies, respectively. Furthermore, Colombia let its real exchange rate to increasingly appreciate vis-à-vis the U.S. dollar. In the early part of the period, the exchange rate was overvalued also in Argentina and Mexico while there was little change in relative incentives to exports and to import substitution in the two countries.

At the same time, there were differences among the countries of the second group in regard to the macro-economic policies applied. In *Brazil*, the immediate response to external shocks was to increase foreign borrowing for the sake of maintaining a high rate of economic growth. In the years 1974 and

TABLE 2.4 (Continued)

1971	1972	1973	"1972"	1974	1975	1976	1977	1978

CHILE

15.0	20.0	50.0	28.3	—	267.3	197.9	93.8	63.2
−14.7	−51.1	−73.3	−46.4	—	−22.7	−4.5	1.1	16.5
18.2	15.9	16.9	17.0	24.3	18.9	—	—	—
26.1	26.1	24.8	25.7	34.9	17.8	—	—	—
−7.9	−10.2	−7.9	−8.7	−10.6	1.1	—	—	—
120.0	145.3	316.7	194.1	272.4	257.4	193.7	108.2	68.6
63.1	0.0	−25.8	12.4	−15.2	−24.8	−5.9	8.7	20.4

URUGUAY

—	—	—	—	—	—	45.6	65.2	59.7
—	—	—	—	—	—	−3.3	9.9	7.5
—	—	21.9	—	20.1	18.5	20.9	22.0	23.2
—	—	23.1	—	23.8	22.9	23.1	22.9	23.6
—	—	−1.2	—	−3.7	−4.4	−2.2	−0.9	−0.4
53.9	46.9	80.0	60.3	64.2	64.0	66.1	38.1	79.7
27.5	−22.6	−16.3	−3.8	−8.1	−4.8	10.3	−8.2	20.9

YUGOSLAVIA

—	—	—	—	—	—	—	—	—
—	—	—	—	—	—	—	—	—
20.9	23.8	20.3	21.7	22.2	22.1	22.4	23.4	—
25.3	24.1	20.7	23.4	24.9	24.2	24.3	25.1	—
−4.4	−0.3	−0.4	−1.7	−2.7	−2.1	−1.9	−1.7	—
15.9	41.7	38.4	32.0	25.2	32.8	60.2	16.8	20.4
2.0	26.5	23.1	17.2	−3.8	8.9	51.2	5.8	12.7

TAIWAN

12.0	11.3	13.3	12.2	14.8	13.3	12.0	10.8	10.8
11.8	6.6	−7.7	3.6	−18.3	19.3	8.9	7.9	7.0
—	—	—	—	14.4	16.4	16.1	16.5	16.8
—	—	—	—	10.0	12.1	12.4	13.2	12.9
—	—	—	—	4.4	4.3	3.7	3.2	3.9
24.6	37.9	49.3	37.3	7.0	26.9	23.1	29.1	34.1
24.4	32.1	21.6	26.0	−23.9	33.6	19.7	25.7	29.5

Source: International Monetary Fund, *International Financial Statistics.*

Notes: (a) Discount rate, except for countries noted below; (b) Deflated by the wholesale price index; (c) Expressed as a proportion of the gross national product, the data do not include grants, lending, and repayments; (d) Sum of private sector demand deposits and currency outside the banks (M1).

For Argentina, the nominal interest rate, Singapore and Uruguay, the prime rate, and for Chile 30 day time deposits rates at commercial banks were used.

1975, taken together, the deterioration of the balance of payments resulting from external shocks was fully financed from abroad; increases in export market shares were offset by the rise in imports associated with higher GNP growth rates; and import substitution was practically nil.

Apart from permitting continued increases in domestic consumption, the amounts borrowed were employed to finance large investments in infrastructure and in highly capital-intensive industries producing intermediate goods for the domestic market. In turn, private investments in machinery industries were promoted through the increased application of credit preferences while real interest rates turned negative.

Measures aimed at reducing imports included increases in tariffs, advance deposit requirements, and import restrictions. Notwithstanding the introduction of some new export incentives, the net effects of the measures applied was to increase the bias against exports and in favor of import substitution. At the same time, the real value of the cruzeiro in terms of the U.S. dollar changed relatively little.

The application of these measures led to considerable import substitution that came to exceed the combined balance-of-payments effects of external shocks after 1976, when additional net external financing turned negative. This result should, however, be considered in the light of the increased burden of interest payments and dividends that rose from $1.0 billion in "1972" to $2 billion in 1974, approached $3 billion in 1976 and was nearly $5 billion in 1978, raising total external financing requirements to $7.6 billion.

With the amortization of foreign loans adding to the debt service burden, the gross debt service ratio rose from 43 percent in 1973 to 68 percent in 1978 whereas the gross debt service ratio rose from 43 percent in 1973 to 68 percent in 1978 whereas the gross external debt ratio increased from 14 percent to 24 percent. In turn, the rate of growth of GNP declined after 1976, reflecting the effects of investments in capital intensive industries, the decline in the rate of domestic saving associated with the maintenance of negative interest rates, the distortions due to accelerating inflation brought about by expansionary policies, and the deflationary policies followed between mid-1977 and mid-1978.

In *Mexico*, additional net external financing exceeded the balance-of-payments effects of external shocks by a considerable margin throughout the period under consideration. This result obtained as savings in imports associated with lower GNP growth rates did not suffice to offset the deterioration of the balance of payments resulting from losses in export market shares and negative import substitution.

Decreases in export market shares and negative import substitution show the direct and indirect effects of expansionary policies followed by the Echeverria Administration from 1972. These policies entailed rapid increases in government expenditures without corresponding increases in revenues. As a result, the budget deficit, expressed as a proportion of GNP, increased from 1 percent in 1971 to 4 percent in 1974; it was between 3 and 4 percent of GNP in the following two years.

The budget deficit was financed by money creation[13] and by foreign borrowing. Money creation gave rise to rapid inflation and to the deterioration of Mexico's competitiveness that is not fully reflected by real exchange rates calculated by reference to relative prices. This is because, in Mexico's relatively open economy, increases in wages could not be fully translated into higher prices.

The decline in Mexico's competitiveness was not offset by a devaluation until September 1976. The devaluation, and the restrictive monetary policies adopted by the Administration of Lopez Portillo in 1977, with the real value of the money supply decreasing by 11 percent, led to reductions in import shares. However, increases in fuel exports apart, there was little improvement in export performance as the abolition of export subsidies largely offset the effects of the devaluation.

Expansionary policies were adopted again in 1978, when the real value of the money supply increased by 13 percent and the budget deficit approached 5 percent of GNP. With pressures on domestic capacity and the appreciation of the real exchange rate, the extent of negative import substitution increased to a considerable extent in 1978. This increase was only partly offset by the rise of petroleum exports and improvements in market shares for manufactured exports, reflecting the effects of the re-introduction of export subsidies.

As a result of these changes, Mexico's additional net external financial requirements increased again in 1978. This increase was largely offset by the rise in tourist earnings and private transfers, so that actual net external financing was practically zero in 1978. Interest payments on debt contracted after 1971 and, to a lesser extent, dividend payments, however, gave rise to total external financing of $3.0 billion that was largely met by additional foreign borrowing.

With continued foreign borrowing, Mexico's gross external debt ratio increased from 16 percent in 1973 to 36 percent in 1978. In the same period, the gross debt service ratio rose from 67 percent to 113 percent. And while adding tourist revenue to merchandise exports would lower the latter ratio to 72 percent, tourist revenue in Mexico is in large part offset by tourist expenditures abroad.

In *Colombia*, the adverse effects of external shocks were aggravated by negative import substitution in 1974 as the real exchange rate appreciated by 4 percent as compared to the "1972" average. In the following year, however, import shares declined in response to the deflationary policies followed, with the real value of the money supply falling by 13 percent in 1974 and by 4 percent in 1975. Colombia also experienced increases in export market shares in 1975, due to the release of coffee from stockpiles as coffee prices rose towards the end of the year.

With the rapid rise of coffee prices, the balance-of-payments effects of external shocks turned positive in 1976 and increased further in 1977, with a small decline in 1978. The opportunities provided by improvements in the balance of payments were not utilized, however, to accelerate the rate of economic growth in Colombia. Rather, the policy measures applied adversely affected the competitiveness of the noncoffee sector.

To begin with, the authorities limited the rate of crawl of the exchange rate, notwithstanding the acceleration of inflation occasioned by the rise in the money supply as the credit measures taken did not suffice to offset the effects of

TABLE 2.5
Nominal and Real Exchange Rates, 1971–1978

	1971	1972	1973	"1972"	1974	1975	1976	1977	1978
ARGENTINA									
Exchange Rate, National Currency per US dollar	4.6	8.2	9.4	7.4	8.9	36.6	140.0	407.6	795.8
Index of Exchange Rates	62.2	110.8	127.0	100.0	120.3	494.6	1891.9	5508.2	10754.1
Domestic Wholesale Price Index	53.8	95.1	143.5	100.0	171.2	503.4	3015.5	7520.9	18505.3
Index of Relative Prices vis-à-vis the US	60.6	102.6	136.8	100.0	137.3	369.5	2117.2	4973.1	11368.9
Index of Real Exchange Rate vis-à-vis the US dollar	102.6	108.0	92.8	100.0	87.6	133.9	89.4	110.8	94.6
COLOMBIA									
Exchange Rate, National Currency per US dollar	20.080	22.018	23.813	21.970	27.109	31.202	34.976	36.923	39.252
Index of Exchange Rates	91.4	100.2	108.4	100.0	123.4	142.0	159.2	160.1	178.7
Domestic Wholesale Price Index	81.1	96.1	122.9	100.0	167.1	209.6	257.6	326.5	384.0
Index of Relative Prices vis-à-vis the US	87.7	99.7	112.6	100.0	128.9	147.9	173.9	207.5	226.8
Index of Real Exchange Rate vis-à-vis the US dollar	104.2	100.5	96.3	100.0	95.7	96.0	91.5	77.2	78.8
INDIA									
Exchange Rate, National Currency per US dollar	7.501	7.594	7.742	7.612	8.102	8.376	8.960	8.739	8.193
Index of Exchange Rates	98.5	99.8	101.7	100.0	106.4	110.0	117.7	114.8	107.6
Domestic Wholesale Price Index	89.3	97.8	112.9	100.0	145.2	151.4	153.8	162.8	161.1
Index of Relative Prices vis-à-vis the US	96.0	100.7	102.8	100.0	111.3	106.2	103.1	102.8	94.3
Index of Real Exchange Rate vis-à-vis the US dollar	102.6	99.1	98.9	100.0	95.6	103.6	114.2	111.7	114.1
KOREA									
Exchange Rate, National Currency per US dollar	350.80	393.97	398.32	381.03	405.97	484.00	484.00	484.00	484.00
Index of Exchange Rates	92.1	103.4	104.5	100.0	106.5	127.0	127.0	127.0	127.0
Domestic Wholesale Price Index	90.0	101.5	108.5	100.0	154.3	195.4	218.9	238.7	266.6
Index of Relative Prices vis-à-vis the US	96.7	104.5	98.8	100.0	118.2	137.0	146.7	150.6	156.3
Index of Real Exchange Rate vis-à-vis the US dollar	95.2	98.9	105.8	100.0	90.1	92.7	86.6	84.3	81.3

TABLE 2.5 (Continued)

	1971	1972	1973	"1972"	1974	1975	1976	1977	1978
BRAZIL									
Exchange Rate, National Currency per US dollar	5.288	5.934	6.126	5.783	6.790	8.129	10.675	14.144	18.070
Index of Exchange Rates	91.4	102.6	105.9	100.0	117.4	140.6	184.6	244.6	312.5
Domestic Wholesale Price Index	84.1	99.7	116.4	100.0	150.4	191.3	274.3	390.6	537.3
Index of Relative Prices vis-à-vis the US	90.6	103.1	106.4	100.0	115.7	134.6	184.3	247.6	316.4
Index of Real Exchange Rate vis-à-vis the US dollar	100.9	99.5	99.5	100.0	101.5	104.5	100.2	98.8	98.8
MEXICO									
Exchange Rate, National Currency per US dollar	12.500	12.500	12.500	12.500	12.500	12.498	15.426	22.573	22.767
Index of Exchange Rates	100.0	100.0	100.0	100.0	100.0	100.0	123.4	180.6	182.1
Domestic Wholesale Price Index	93.2	95.8	111.0	100.0	136.0	150.2	183.7	259.3	300.1
Index of Relative Prices vis-à-vis the US	100.3	98.7	101.1	100.0	104.2	105.4	123.3	163.8	176.1
Index of Real Exchange Rate vis-à-vis the US dollar	99.7	101.3	98.9	100.0	96.0	94.9	100.1	110.3	103.4
ISRAEL									
Exchange Rate, National Currency per US dollar	0.373	0.420	0.420	0.404	0.450	0.639	0.798	1.046	1.747
Index of Exchange Rates	92.3	103.9	103.9	100.0	111.3	158.0	197.4	258.7	432.1
Domestic Wholesale Price Index	93.1	97.1	109.9	100.0	130.5	142.7	149.2	158.5	170.5
Index of Relative Prices vis-à-vis the US	94.4	100.1	105.4	100.0	134.2	172.9	216.4	282.3	401.8
Index of Real Exchange Rate vis-à-vis the US dollar	97.8	103.8	98.6	100.0	82.9	91.4	91.2	91.6	107.5
SINGAPORE									
Exchange Rate, National Currency per US dollar	3.0478	2.8092	2.4436	2.7669	2.4369	2.3713	2.4708	2.4394	2.2740
Index of Exchange Rates	110.2	101.5	88.3	100.0	88.1	85.7	89.3	88.2	82.2
Domestic Wholesale Price Index	90.5	92.4	117.0	100.0	143.0	146.8	144.0	148.7	155.7
Index of Relative Prices vis-à-vis the US	97.6	95.5	106.8	100.0	110.0	103.2	96.8	94.1	91.7
Index of Real Exchange Rate vis-à-vis the US dollar	112.9	106.3	82.7	100.0	80.1	83.0	92.3	93.7	89.6

TABLE 2.5 Continued

	1971	1972	1973	"1972"	1974	1975	1976	1977	1978
CHILE									
Exchange Rate, National Currency per US dollar	0.012	0.020	0.111	0.048	0.832	4.911	13.054	21.529	31.656
Index of Exchange Rates	25.2	42.0	232.9	100.0	1746.0	10303.0	27386.0	45166.0	66411.0
Domestic Wholesale Price Index	17.4	42.7	239.9	100.0	1054.0	5008.0	15623.0	29945.0	41938.0
Index of Relative Prices vis-à-vis the US	18.7	44.0	218.5	100.0	808.0	3837.0	10471.0	18916.0	24554.0
Index of Real Exchange Rate vis-a-vis the US dollar	134.8	95.5	106.6	100.0	216.1	268.5	261.5	238.8	270.5
URUGUAY									
Exchange Rate, National Currency per US dollar	0.260	0.563	0.875	0.566	1.216	2.299	3.395	4.750	6.125
Index of Exchange Rates	45.9	99.5	154.6	100.0	214.8	406.2	599.8	839.2	1082.2
Domestic Wholesale Price Index	43.0	81.6	175.4	100.0	313.5	540.4	813.7	1223.2	1817.4
Index of Relative Prices vis-à-vis the US	47.8	86.9	165.3	100.0	248.6	391.9	564.5	799.2	1103.3
Index of Real Exchange Rate vis-a-vis the US dollar	96.0	114.5	93.5	100.0	86.4	103.6	106.3	105.0	98.1
YUGOSLAVIA									
Exchange Rate, National Currency per US dollar	14.958	17.000	16.189	16.049	15.913	17.386	18.193	18.298	18.644
Index of Exchange Rates	93.2	105.9	100.9	100.0	99.2	108.3	113.4	114.0	116.2
Domestic Wholesale Price Index	88.8	99.4	111.9	100.0	145.6	177.5	188.3	207.7	221.9
Index of Relative Prices vis-à-vis the US	95.5	102.5	101.9	100.0	111.7	124.6	126.3	131.3	130.3
Index of Real Exchange Rate vis-a-vis the US dollar	97.6	103.3	99.0	100.0	88.8	91.0	89.8	86.8	89.2
TAIWAN									
Exchange Rate, National Currency per US dollar	40.000	40.033	38.263	39.432	38.000	38.000	38.000	38.000	37.054
Index of Exchange Rates	101.4	101.5	97.0	100.0	96.4	96.4	96.4	96.4	94.0
Domestic Wholesale Price Index	90.2	94.1	115.6	100.0	162.5	154.3	158.6	163.0	168.7
Index of Relative Prices vis-à-vis the US	97.3	97.3	105.6	100.0	124.9	108.6	106.7	103.3	99.3
Index of Real Exchange Rate vis-a-vis the US dollar	104.2	104.2	91.9	100.0	77.2	88.8	90.3	93.3	94.7

Source: International Monetary Fund, *International Financial Statistics*, various issues, World Bank Reports.

Note: For Chile and Singapore the consumer price index was used.

the increase in foreign exchange reserves on domestic money holdings.[14] After remaining unchanged in 1975, the real exchange rate appreciated vis-à-vis the U.S. dollar by 5 percent in 1976, 11 percent in 1977, and 2 percent in 1978, bringing it one-fifth below the "1972" level.

The adverse effects on exports of the appreciation of the exchange rate were aggravated by reductions in subsidies while only modest measures of import liberalization were taken. With the increased bias against exports, Colombia's export market share in manufactured goods declined by nearly one-half. Furthermore, fuel exports increasingly gave place to imports, reflecting the effects of the policies applied in earlier years that were inimical to new exploration. At the same time, little change was shown in traditional and in nontraditional primary exports except that releases from stockpiles raised the volume of coffee exports again in 1978.

The appreciation of the real exchange rate also led to negative import substitution in Colombia after 1975. The adverse balance-of-payments effects of declines in export shares and negative import substitution offset the favorable effects of external shocks in the years 1976 to 1978, on the average, while the maintenance of past GNP growth rates did not have differential effects on imports.

Correspondingly, additional net external financing was practically zero in Colombia in the years 1976 to 1978 combined. Due largely to smuggling that is included under non-factor services, there was nevertheless a surplus in the actual resource gap that was only partly offset by interest and dividend payments. With continued small borrowing abroad, Colombia accumulated nearly $2 billion of reserves between 1975 and 1978, reducing its net external debt ratio from 13 percent to 4 percent. In the same period, the gross external debt ratio decreased from 17 percent to 15 percent while the gross debt service ratio fell from 32 percent to 18 percent (there was little change in these ratios between 1973 and 1975).

In *Argentina*, internal shocks predominated during the period under consideration. As a result of the expansionary monetary and fiscal policies followed, the real value of the money supply rose 33 percent in 1973 and by 46 percent in 1974 while the budget deficit increased from 2 to 3 percent of GNP in the early seventies to 5 percent in 1973 and to 6 percent in 1974. The government attempted to offset the inflationary effects of these policies on the trade balance by successive devaluations, but it only succeeded to accelerate the wage-price spiral as labor unions and other interest groups were able to maintain, and even to increase, their real incomes. Correspondingly, the real exchange rate appreciated by 14 percent in 1973 and 6 percent in 1974; it was 12 percent below its "1972" level in the latter year.

Further devaluations in 1975 were accompanied by price and wage controls, giving rise to the depreciation of the real exchange rate in that year. This proved temporary, however, as prices and wages rebounded once the controls were lifted. The increase in the ratio of the governmental budget deficit to 12 percent of GNP in 1975 further contributed to inflation, with the wholesale price index rising at an average annual rate of 300 percent between the fourth quarters of 1974 and 1975 and approaching 1000 percent in early 1976.

Rapid inflation caused considerable dislocation, leading to the fall of GNP in 1975 and, again, in the first quarter of 1976. With declines in export market shares aggravating the effects of external shocks, Argentina also suffered large losses in foreign exchange reserves that raised question about its creditworthiness. The new government, which came to power in March 1976, attempted to remedy the situation by introducing a policy package including deflationary monetary measures, increases in interest rates, reductions in the deficit in the government budget, wage control, and devaluation accompanied by reductions in export taxes on traditional primary exports.

Reductions in export taxes and the depreciation of the real exchange rate, attendant on the doubling of the peso-dollar rate in the last quarter of 1976, had their full impact on exports only in 1977. The expansion of exports was concentrated in traditional and nontraditional primary commodities, while Argentina continued to lose market shares in manufactured goods where export incentives were below their pre-1973 level. It also experienced continued import substitution as reductions in tariffs had little effect, given the high level of tariff redundancy.

Increases in exports and import substitution, together with the rise of investment activity reflecting greater confidence, contributed to economic expansion in 1977. But, the government was unable to restrain wages and it continued to run a budget deficit, albeit at a reduced rate. Following a four-month "price truce," in which the largest industrial firms participated, prices responded to the rising cost of labor. While earlier rates of inflation were not again reached, wholesale prices rose at an average annual rate of 150 percent in both 1977 and 1978.

The distortions caused by high rates of inflation contributed to the fall of GNP in 1978, thereby lessening import requirements. With reduced pressure on domestic capacity, import shares also declined but this was offset by a fall in export shares as the real exchange rate appreciated again. At the same time, Argentina benefited from favorable external shocks in the form of improvements in its terms of trade and increases in foreign demand for its traditional exports. As a result of these influences, additional net external financing increasingly turned negative. With the negative trend value of the resource gap, reflecting the assumption that earlier trade surpluses continued, actual net external financing became even more negative, giving rise to considerable reserve accumulation and the repayment of loans.

Loan repayments explain the high gross debt service ratio in 1978 (49 percent) that followed a decline from the peak reached in 1975 (34 percent) to 23 percent in 1977, when it equalled the 1973 figure. In turn, the gross external debt ratio increased from 7 percent in 1973 to 10 percent in 1978 while the net external debt ratio declined from 5 percent to 3 percent, reflecting the accumulation of reserves.

The accumulation of reserves facilitated the task of the government to introduce a new economic program. This was done at the end of December 1978, involving a slowdown in increases in wages, public utility prices, money creation, and the depreciation of the exchange rate, together with the opening of capital markets to foreign transactions and a five-year tariff reduction plan. The effects of this program were not apparent, however, until the end of 1979.

Israel and Yugoslavia

In 1974, the combined balance-of-payments effects of external shocks amounted to 11 percent of GNP in Israel and 6 percent in Yugoslavia. In both countries, the adverse effects of these shocks increased in 1975, declined in 1976, and increased again afterwards. In 1978, they equalled 15 percent of the gross national product in Israel and 10 percent in Yugoslavia.

The Israeli economy further suffered the shock of the 1973 Yom Kippur war that was followed by increases in the importation of military equipment from $0.5 billion in 1972 to $1.9 billion in 1975, approaching one-half of nonmilitary imports in that year. Military imports represented about one-half of total defense expenditures that amounted to three-tenths of the gross national product in 1975.

Israel as well as Yugoslavia raised the level of import protection, thereby increasing the bias against exports, and let the real exchange rate appreciate. In Israel, the real exchange rate vis-à-vis the U.S. dollar declined to 83 percent of the "1972" level in 1974 and stabilized at 91 percent in subsequent years. In Yugoslavia, a 10 percent appreciation occurred.

Israel also adopted deflationary policies in response to the shocks it experienced. Following increases of 16 percent in 1972 and 11 percent in 1973, the real value of the money supply fell by 22 percent in 1974 and by 14 percent in 1975, declining further by 3 percent in 1976. And, after increases from 13 percent in 1972 to 29 percent in 1975, the government budget deficit, expressed as a proportion of the gross national product, declined to 24 percent in 1975 and to 21 percent in 1975 and 1976.

The policies applied led to losses in exports, a fall in the rate of investment, and the deceleration of economic growth. Israel's export market shares decreased by 21 percent between "1972" and 1976; the share of investment in aggregate expenditure declined from 26 percent in 1971–73 to 23 percent in 1974–76; and the growth rate of GNP fell from 8.2 percent in 1963–73 to 2.6 percent in 1973–76. Lower GNP growth rates, in turn, resulted in import savings amounting to 3 percent of total imports in 1974, increasing to 11 percent in 1975 and to 22 percent in 1976.

Savings in imports permitted reducing additional net external financing from 13 percent of GNP in 1974 to 10 percent in 1975 and 4 percent in 1976.

TABLE 2.6
Debt Service and the External Debt (in US $ millions, current prices)

ARGENTINA

	1971	1972	1973	"1972"	1974	1975	1976	1977	1978
Gross Debt Service	502	538	744	595	1000	1011	1223	1284	3161
Net Debt Service	486	531	718	578	872	956	1173	1156	2828
Merchandise Exports	1740	1941	3266	2316	3931	2961	3912	5642	6403
Gross Debt Service Ratio	28.9	27.7	22.8	25.7	25.4	34.1	31.3	22.8	49.4
Net Debt Service Ratio	27.9	27.4	22.0	25.0	22.2	32.3	30.3	20.5	44.2
Gross External Debt	—	—	3323	—	3641	3450	5055	5890	7290
Net External Debt	—	—	2215	—	2406	3286	3970	2977	2143
Gross National Product	37907	43400	48130	43145	56115	60839	62947	70018	72752
Gross External Debt Ratio	—	—	6.9	—	6.5	5.7	8.0	8.4	10.0
Net External Debt Ratio	—	—	4.6	—	4.3	5.4	6.3	4.3	2.9

BRAZIL

	1971	1972	1973	"1972"	1974	1975	1976	1977	1978
Gross Debt Service	1467	1942	2654	2021	3371	4031	5084	6511	8608
Net Debt Service	1424	1811	2327	1854	2653	3665	4802	6153	7966
Merchandise Exports	2904	3991	6199	4365	7951	8670	10128	12120	12659
Gross Debt Service Ratio	50.5	48.7	42.8	46.3	42.4	46.5	50.2	53.7	68.0
Net Debt Service Ratio	49.0	45.4	37.5	42.5	33.4	42.3	47.4	50.8	62.9
Gross External Debt	6622	9521	12572	9572	17165	21171	25985	32000	43500
Net External Debt	4899	5338	6156	5465	11893	17135	19441	24744	31606
Gross National Product	64340	74871	90227	76479	108864	125212	143198	158556	180024
Gross External Debt Ratio	10.3	12.7	13.9	12.5	15.8	16.9	18.1	20.2	24.2
Net External Debt Ratio	7.6	7.1	6.8	7.1	10.9	13.7	13.6	15.6	17.6

CHILE

	1971	1972	1973	"1972"	1974	1975	1976	1977	1978
Gross Debt Service	283	391	522	399	888	805	985	1153	1416
Net Debt Service	271	390	517	393	864	800	975	1135	1377
Merchandise Exports	961	855	1249	1022	2481	1552	2083	2190	2408
Gross Debt Service Ratio	29.4	45.7	41.8	39.0	35.8	51.9	47.3	52.6	58.8
Net Debt Service Ratio	28.2	45.6	41.4	38.4	34.8	51.5	46.8	51.8	57.2
Gross External Debt	—	—	4048	—	4774	5263	5195	5434	6911
Net External Debt	—	—	3964	—	4868	5540	5201	5315	6109
Gross National Product	9275	9708	9851	9611	11398	10980	12010	13819	16442
Gross External Debt Ratio	—	—	41.1	—	41.9	47.9	43.3	39.3	42.0
Net External Debt Ratio	—	—	40.2	—	42.7	50.5	43.3	38.5	37.2

TABLE 2.6 (Continued)

COLOMBIA

	1971	1972	1973	"1972"	1974	1975	1976	1977	1978
Gross Debt Service	285	315	358	319	465	471	486	484	551
Net Debt Service	276	297	334	302	400	415	421	419	428
Merchandise Exports	689	863	1176	909	1417	1465	1745	2443	3010
Gross Debt Service Ratio	41.4	36.5	30.4	35.1	32.8	32.2	27.9	19.8	18.3
Net Debt Service Ratio	40.1	34.4	28.4	33.2	28.2	28.3	24.1	17.2	14.2
Gross External Debt	—	—	2102	—	2370	2693	2806	3019	3361
Net External Debt	—	—	1568	—	1921	2172	1648	1198	905
Gross National Product	9447	10613	12078	10713	14124	16030	17615	19645	22993
Gross External Debt Ratio	—	—	17.4	—	16.8	16.8	15.9	15.4	14.6
Net External Debt Ratio	—	—	13.0	—	13.6	13.5	9.4	6.1	3.9

MEXICO

	1971	1972	1973	"1972"	1974	1975	1976	1977	1978
Gross Debt Service	788	876	1390	1018	1398	1929	2933	4398	7040
Net Debt Service	723	796	1293	937	1245	1812	2809	4230	6795
Merchandise Exports	1363	1665	2071	1700	2850	2861	3316	4418	6217
Gross Debt Service Ratio	57.8	52.6	67.1	59.9	49.1	67.4	88.4	99.5	113.2
Net Debt Service Ratio	53.0	47.8	62.4	55.1	43.7	63.3	84.7	95.7	109.3
Gross External Debt	—	—	8310	—	12389	17263	22000	26785	32622
Net External Debt	—	—	6955	—	10996	15724	20973	25366	30675
Gross National Product	41284	46102	52391	46592	60478	68624	73159	80402	91914
Gross External Debt Ratio	—	—	15.9	—	20.5	25.2	30.1	33.3	35.5
Net External Debt Ratio	—	—	13.3	—	18.2	22.9	28.7	31.5	33.4

URUGUAY

	1971	1972	1973	"1972"	1974	1975	1976	1977	1978
Gross Debt Service	46	71	106	74	63	138	140	149	207
Net Debt Service	45	70	100	72	58	134	133	137	189
Merchandise Exports	206	214	322	247	382	384	547	608	688
Gross Debt Service Ratio	22.3	33.2	32.9	30.1	16.5	35.9	25.6	24.5	30.1
Net Debt Service Ratio	21.8	32.7	31.1	29.0	15.2	34.9	24.3	22.5	27.5
Gross External Debt	—	—	369	—	557	667	750	791	866
Net External Debt	—	—	168	—	403	392	405	168	17
Gross National Product	2823	2829	3027	2893	3430	3906	4212	4629	5157
Gross External Debt Ratio	—	—	12.2	—	16.2	17.1	17.8	17.1	16.8
Net External Debt Ratio	—	—	5.6	—	11.7	10.0	9.6	3.6	0.3

TABLE 2.6 (Continued)

	1971	1972	1973	"1972"	1974	1975	1976	1977	1978
INDIA									
Gross Debt Service	644	605	784	678	2717	789	769	961	908
Net Debt Service	596	562	733	630	2623	659	574	687	440
Merchandise Exports	2037	2415	2961	2471	3899	4355	5323	5980	6252
Gross Debt Service Ratio	31.6	25.1	26.5	27.4	69.7	18.1	14.4	16.1	14.5
Net Debt Service Ratio	29.3	23.3	24.8	25.5	67.3	15.3	10.8	11.5	7.0
Gross External Debt	—	—	11252	—	12386	13178	14263	15534	16432
Net External Debt	—	—	10181	—	11743	12703	11738	10579	9744
Gross National Product	57001	58930	64766	60232	71374	85327	91516	104389	117520
Gross External Debt Ratio	—	—	17.4	—	17.4	15.4	15.6	14.9	14.0
Net External Debt Ratio	—	—	15.7	—	16.5	14.9	12.8	10.1	8.3
ISRAEL									
Gross Debt Service	403	557	612	524	797	838	1102	1141	1449
Net Debt Service	283	420	374	359	462	516	739	771	953
Merchandise Exports	960	1149	1509	1206	1825	1941	2416	3083	3924
Gross Debt Service Ratio	42.0	48.5	40.6	43.4	43.7	43.2	45.6	37.0	36.9
Net Debt Service Ratio	29.5	36.6	24.8	29.8	25.3	26.6	30.6	25.0	24.3
Gross External Debt	3395	4081	5093	4190	6210	7373	9040	10760	12529
Net External Debt	2698	2862	3278	2946	5049	6435	7998	9535	10204
Gross National Product	7307	8559	9412	8426	10968	12340	12856	13652	15332
Gross External Debt Ratio	46.5	47.7	54.1	49.7	56.6	59.7	70.3	78.8	81.7
Net External Debt Ratio	36.9	33.4	34.8	34.9	46.0	52.1	62.2	69.8	66.6
YUGOSLAVIA									
Gross Debt Service	485	672	838	665	1014	1358	1267	1431	1855
Net Debt Service	468	655	788	637	921	1296	1177	1308	1705
Merchandise Exports	1836	2237	3020	2364	3805	4072	4896	4896	5668
Gross Debt Service Ratio	26.4	30.0	27.7	28.1	26.6	33.3	25.9	29.2	32.7
Net Debt Service Ratio	25.5	29.3	26.1	26.9	24.2	31.8	24.0	26.7	30.1
Gross External Debt	—	—	2443	—	3193	5476	6896	8589	10323
Net External Debt	—	—	1131	—	2216	4784	5215	6740	8104
Gross National Product	24392	26595	29226	26738	36100	39882	43679	50137	57032
Gross External Debt Ratio	—	—	8.4	—	8.8	13.7	15.8	17.1	18.1
Net External Debt Ratio	—	—	3.9	—	6.1	12.0	11.9	13.4	14.2

TABLE 2.6 (Continued)

KOREA

	1971	1972	1973	"1972"	1974	1975	1976	1977	1978
Gross Debt Service	332	401	531	421	751	958	1359	1848	2561
Net Debt Service	309	380	490	393	669	911	1289	1714	2278
Merchandise Exports	1060	1616	3215	1964	4453	5071	7693	9986	12654
Gross Debt Service Ratio	31.3	24.8	16.5	21.5	16.9	18.9	17.7	18.5	20.2
Net Debt Service Ratio	29.2	23.5	15.2	20.0	15.0	18.0	16.8	17.2	18.0
Gross External Debt	—	—	3556	—	4693	6047	7370	8622	11992
Net External Debt	—	—	2667	—	4546	5515	5746	5989	9461
Gross National Product	15089	16616	20159	17288	23775	27894	33516	40070	47996
Gross External Debt Ratio	—	—	17.6	—	19.7	21.7	22.0	21.5	25.0
Net External Debt Ratio	—	—	13.2	—	19.1	19.8	17.1	14.9	19.7

SINGAPORE

	1971	1972	1973	"1972"	1974	1975	1976	1977	1978
Gross Debt Service	44	156	316	172	389	322	377	406	711
Net Debt Service	−39	60	179	67	207	111	169	133	328
Merchandise Exports	1755	2181	3610	2515	5785	5377	6586	8242	10134
Gross Debt Service Ratio	2.5	7.2	8.8	6.8	6.7	6.0	5.7	4.9	7.0
Net Debt Service Ratio	−2.2	2.8	5.0	2.7	3.6	2.1	2.6	1.6	3.2
Gross External Debt	—	—	459	—	558	600	772	1089	1120
Net External Debt	—	—	−1827	—	−2254	−2407	−2592	−2769	−4183
Gross National Product	2739	3209	3686	3211	4304	5028	5620	6478	7597
Gross External Debt Ratio	—	—	12.5	—	13.0	11.9	13.7	16.8	14.7
Net External Debt Ratio	—	—	−49.6	—	−52.4	−47.9	−46.1	−42.7	−55.1

TAIWAN

	1971	1972	1973	"1972"	1974	1975	1976	1977	1978
Gross Debt Service	138	176	250	188	256	360	624	659	855
Net Debt Service	98	130	139	122	92	211	470	447	479
Merchandise Exports	1998	2914	4375	3095	5518	5302	8156	9349	12644
Gross Debt Service Ratio	6.9	6.0	5.7	6.1	4.6	6.8	7.7	7.0	6.8
Net Debt Service Ratio	4.9	4.5	3.2	4.0	1.7	4.0	5.8	4.8	3.8
Gross External Debt	—	—	1281	—	1535	2252	3030	3521	3903
Net External Debt	—	—	158	—	346	1083	1420	2074	2394
Gross National Product	8793	10250	12138	10394	13391	15033	17636	20266	24527
Gross External Debt Ratio	—	—	10.6	—	11.5	15.0	17.2	17.4	15.9
Net External Debt Ratio	—	—	1.3	—	2.6	7.2	8.1	10.2	9.8

Sources: Exports, Interest Payments and Receipts: Table 1. Amortization Reserve Holdings: International Monetary Fund, *International Financial Statistics,* various issues. GNP in Current Prices: World Bank data base. Gross External Debt: National Foreign Assessment Center, *Non-OPEC LDC's; External Debt Positions,* Washington, D.C., January 1980. Israel Gross External Debt, Bank of Israel.

Note: Gross external debt includes public as well as private debt; net reserves are defined as the sum of foreign exchange holdings, gold reserves as valued by national authorities, SDR holdings, reserve position with the International Monetary Fund, less use of Fund credit.

Actual net external financing was substantially higher, however, because of increases in military imports that have not been included in the trade figures. Although about one-half of the financing took the form of official grants, Israel's gross external debt increased from $5.1 billion in 1973 to $9.0 billion in 1976, equalling 70 percent of GNP in that year.

In response to the slowdown of economic growth, an expansionary monetary policy was adopted in 1977, with the nominal money supply rising by 39 percent in 1977 as compared to increases of 22 percent in 1975 and 27 percent in 1976. Given the indexing of wage and other incomes, monetary expansion was translated into higher prices, however, so that the real value of the money supply and the real exchange rate remained unchanged. With constant real exchange rates, export and import shares, on balance, did not vary and GNP stagnated.

A substantial devaluation was undertaken in the third quarter of 1977, followed by further devaluations in 1978, resulting in a depreciation of the real exchange rate by 17 percent. The depreciation was only partly offset by reductions in export subsidies and in import tariffs, so that net incentives to exports and to import replacing activities increased. Greater incentives in turn, led to increases in export market shares and to import substitution.

The resulting expansion in the production of traded goods contributed to economic growth in 1978. This was, however, accomplished at the cost of accelerating inflation, with the wholesale price index rising by 53 percent in 1978, following increases of 35–40 percent in previous years. Also, the uncertainty created by rapid inflation led to a further decline in the rate of investment while the resulting distortions raised incremental capital-output ratios.

With the gross national product remaining substantially below the level it would have reached if earlier trends continued, import savings amounted to nearly two-fifths of actual imports in 1978. Increased import savings, together with higher export shares and import substitution, offset in large part the increase in the balance-of-payments effects of adverse external shocks in that year. But, with military imports more than doubling between 1977 and 1978, actual net external financing reached $1.9 billion in that year while total external financing was $2.8 billion. Furthermore, with increased indebtedness, the gross external debt ratio rose from 54 percent in 1973 to 82 percent in 1978. In turn, the gross debt service ratio was maintained below 40 percent only because Israel could obtain long-term loans in the United States.

Yugoslavia responded to the external shocks it suffered in 1974 by adopting deflationary monetary policies that gave rise to a 4 percent decline in the real value of the money supply in 1974 after increases of over 20 percent in the preceding two years. However, the external shocks were not met by a devaluation; rather, the nominal exchange rate appreciated vis-à-vis the U.S. dollar and the real exchange rate fell by 11 percent.

The appreciation of the real exchange rate led to losses in export market shares and to negative import substitution in Yugoslavia. The adverse impact of these changes on the balance of payments was not fully offset by import savings associated with the decline in the rate of economic growth resulting from the application of deflationary policies. Correspondingly, additional net external financial requirements exceeded the balance-of-payments effects of external shocks in 1974 and, despite increases in workers' remittances, Yugoslavia had to borrow $1.0 billion to finance its resource gap. Borrowing requirements changed little in 1975, when import savings at low GNP growth rates and reductions in import shares due to the application of import restrictions approximately offset the increase in the adverse balance-of-payments effects of external shocks.

In response to the slowdown of economic growth, expansionary policies were adopted in 1976, entailing a 51 percent rise in the real value of the money supply. These policies were accompanied by further restrictions on imports. The resulting decline in import shares, together with decreases in the adverse balance-of-payments effects of external shocks, lowered additional net external financial requirements to a considerable extent and Yugoslavia accumulated reserves in 1976.

Reserve accumulation remained temporary, however, and Yugoslavia had to borrow $1.5 billion in 1977 and $1.3 billion in 1978 as the adverse balance-of-payments effects of external shocks increased. At the same time, with the acceleration of the rate of economic growth, further import savings did not occur while import substitution due to import restrictions was offset by declines in export market shares. These declines occurred as the exchange rate remained overvalued and there was increased discrimination against export activities through import protection and preferential credit allocation to import-substituting industries.

The loss in market shares occurred in traditional primary exports as well as in manufactured goods. Within the latter category, the losses were concentrated in developed country markets where Yugoslavia's export share declined by one-half between "1972" and 1978. This compares with a gain in market shares in exports to the centrally planned economies.

Yugoslavia's poor performance in developed country markets led to increased indebtedness in convertible currencies. The gross external debt ratio rose from 8 percent in 1973 to 18 percent in 1978 while the gross debt service ratio increased from 28 percent to 33 percent. The gross debt service ratio is raised further if it is compared to merchandise exports in terms of convertible currencies alone while it is reduced if workers' remittances are added to merchandise exports. With these adjustments, the gross debt service ratio was 30 percent in 1978. At the same time, a substantial part of foreign borrowing went into investment, increasing its share in aggregate expenditure from 29 percent in 1971–73 to 30 percent in 1974–76 and 33 percent in 1977–79.

TABLE 2.7
Domestic Expenditure Shares, Incremental Capital-Output Ratios, and GNP Growth Rates

	1963-73	1970-73	1973-76	1976-79	1973-79
ARGENTINA[a]					
Domestic Expenditure Shares (in current prices)[b]					
Private Consumption	65.5	52.5	48.6	45.4	47.4
Public Consumption	13.7	22.9	28.5	27.4	28.1
Total Consumption	79.2	75.5	77.2	72.8	75.5
Gross Domestic Fixed Investment	20.3	24.0	22.7	27.4	24.5
Increases in Stock	0.5	0.5	0.1	−0.2	0.0
Gross Domestic Investment	20.8	24.5	22.8	27.2	24.5
Incremental Capital-Output Ratios[c]	*4.3*	*5.5*	*20.4*	*9.9*	*13.0*
Growth Rates (constant prices)[d]					
Gross National Product	4.7	4.8	0.9	1.9	1.2
Population	1.4	1.3	1.3	1.3	1.3
Per Capita GNP	3.3	3.5	−0.4	0.6	−0.1
COLOMBIA					
Domestic Expenditure Shares (in current prices)[b]					
Private Consumption	73.2	72.3	72.3	68.9	70.6
Public Consumption	7.2	8.1	7.2	7.1	7.2
Total Consumption	80.4	80.3	79.5	76.0	77.8
Gross Domestic Fixed Investment	18.0	18.7	18.9	20.5	19.7
Increases in Stock	1.6	1.0	2.6	3.5	3.0
Gross Domestic Investment	19.6	19.7	20.5	24.0	22.2
Incremental Capital-Output Ratios[c]	*3.6*	*2.8*	*3.8*	*2.9*	*3.2*
Growth Rates (constant prices)[d]					
Gross National Product	5.6	7.0	4.6	6.6	5.5
Population	2.7	2.3	2.3	2.2	2.3
Per Capita GNP	2.9	4.7	2.3	4.4	3.2
INDIA					
Domestic Expenditure Shares (in current prices)[b]					
Private Consumption	73.1	72.7	69.6	68.0	68.8
Public Consumption	9.2	9.4	9.4	9.7	9.5
Total Consumption	82.3	82.1	78.9	77.7	78.4
Gross Domestic Fixed Investment	17.7	15.3	17.0	20.0	18.2
Increases in Stock	n/a	2.6	4.2	2.3	3.5
Gross Domestic Investment	17.7	17.9	21.1	22.3	21.6
Incremental Capital-Output Ratios[c]	*5.8*	*8.9*	*4.4*	*5.3*	*4.9*
Growth Rates (constant prices)[d]					
Gross National Product	3.4	1.5	4.2	3.7	4.3
Population	2.3	2.1	2.0	2.0	2.0
Per Capita GNP	1.1	−0.6	2.2	1.7	2.3
KOREA					
Domestic Expenditure Shares (in current prices)[b]					
Private Consumption	69.8	67.2	63.3	59.1	61.2
Public Consumption	9.2	9.8	10.0	10.9	10.4
Total Consumption	79.0	77.0	73.2	70.1	71.6
Gross Domestic Fixed Investment	19.4	21.2	23.6	28.0	25.7
Increases in Stock	1.6	1.8	3.2	1.9	2.6
Gross Domestic Investment	21.0	23.0	26.8	29.9	28.4
Incremental Capital-Output Ratios[c]	*2.1*	*2.4*	*2.7*	*3.1*	*2.9*
Growth Rates (constant prices)[d]					
Gross National Product	9.1	8.9	8.9	10.1	10.1
Population	2.2	2.0	1.9	1.8	1.9
Per Capita GNP	6.9	6.8	7.0	8.3	8.3

Source: World Bank data base.

Notes: [a]1979 data not available on expenditure shares. [b]Expenditure shares exclude data for the first year of each period. [c]Incremental capital output ratios have been calculated by assuming a

TABLE 2.7 (Continued)

1963-73	1970-73	1973-76	1976-79	1973-79	1963-73	1970-73	1973-76	1976-79	1973-79
	BRAZIL					CHILE			
71.4	67.8	67.2	68.5	67.9	73.6	73.5	78.5	77.6	78.2
10.6	9.6	9.3	9.5	9.3	12.2	14.1	13.2	12.4	12.8
82.0	77.4	76.6	77.9	77.2	86.0	87.6	91.6	89.9	90.9
18.0	22.6	23.4	22.1	22.8	14.0	12.4	10.4	10.1	9.1
n/a	n/a	n/a	n/a	n/a	n/a	n/a	n/a	n/a	n/a
18.0	22.6	23.4	22.1	22.8	14.0	12.4	10.4	10.1	9.1
2.3	*1.7*	*3.1*	*4.3*	*3.6*	*6.2*	*6.7*	*−15.3*	*1.2*	*2.8*
8.0	12.1	7.3	5.3	6.3	3.7	1.6	−2.4	9.0	3.6
2.9	2.8	2.8	2.8	2.8	1.9	1.7	1.7	1.7	1.7
5.2	9.2	4.5	2.4	3.4	1.8	−0.1	−4.1	7.3	1.9
	MEXICO[a]					URUGUAY[a]			
72.3	72.1	65.1	64.5	64.9	75.5	73.5	73.6	73.3	73.4
7.8	8.5	10.6	11.6	11.0	13.7	14.2	14.2	12.6	13.5
80.1	80.6	75.7	76.1	75.9	89.2	87.7	87.7	85.9	87.0
19.9	19.0	21.3	21.2	21.3	10.8	10.0	12.1	14.2	12.9
n/a	0.4	2.9	2.7	2.9	n/a	2.3	0.2	−0.1	0.1
19.9	19.4	24.3	23.9	24.1	10.8	12.3	12.3	14.1	13.0
3.1	*3.0*	*3.8*	*5.5*	*4.1*	*9.6*	*−11.0*	*3.6*	*3.3*	*3.4*
6.4	6.0	3.3	5.8	4.2	1.2	−1.5	3.3	5.0	3.9
3.2	3.2	3.3	3.3	3.3	0.8	0.2	0.2	0.7	0.5
3.2	2.7	0.0	2.5	0.9	0.4	−1.6	3.1	4.3	3.4
	ISRAEL					YUGOSLAVIA[a]			
52.8	45.6	45.7	49.7	47.6	53.2	55.5	53.6	50.0	52.2
24.4	28.5	31.3	29.5	30.5	16.9	15.9	16.6	16.6	16.6
77.2	74.0	77.1	79.1	78.1	70.1	71.4	70.2	66.6	68.7
22.8	24.8	21.9	19.5	20.8	29.9	26.7	27.7	31.4	29.2
n/a	1.3	1.0	1.4	1.2	n/a	1.9	2.3	2.2	2.2
22.8	26.0	22.9	20.9	21.9	29.9	28.6	29.8	33.4	31.3
2.7	*3.3*	*11.0*	*7.1*	*8.8*	*5.3*	*5.9*	*4.3*	*4.4*	*4.4*
8.2	8.9	2.6	3.3	2.3	6.2	5.8	5.1	6.5	5.7
3.1	3.2	2.5	2.2	2.3	1.0	1.0	0.9	0.9	0.9
5.1	5.7	0.1	1.2	0.0	5.2	4.9	4.2	5.6	4.7
	SINGAPORE					TAIWAN			
68.9	55.4	54.9	56.6	55.7	57.9	54.6	52.9	52.6	52.8
10.8	10.2	9.4	10.1	9.7	17.5	16.9	14.5	16.2	15.3
79.7	65.6	64.3	66.8	65.5	75.4	71.5	67.3	68.9	68.1
20.3	30.9	32.1	31.4	31.7	24.6	25.3	28.6	27.9	28.2
n/a	3.4	3.6	1.9	2.7	n/a	3.4	4.2	3.3	3.8
20.3	34.4	35.7	33.2	34.5	24.6	28.5	32.7	31.1	31.9
1.8	*2.6*	*5.5*	*3.4*	*4.2*	*2.5*	*1.8*	*4.1*	*2.7*	*3.2*
10.5	10.4	6.3	8.8	7.5	9.6	11.2	4.4	9.6	7.6
1.9	1.7	1.5	1.1	1.3	2.3	2.1	1.9	1.9	2.0
8.6	8.6	4.8	7.6	6.1	7.3	9.1	2.5	7.7	5.5

one year lag between investment and output; the ratio for 1970–73, for example, has been derived by dividing the sum of gross fixed capital formation in 1970, 1971, 1972 by the increment in GNP between 1970 and 1973, both measured in constant prices. [d]Growth rates have been calculated by regression analysis.

India, Chile, and Uruguay

Among countries that followed inward-looking policies during the preceding decade, the combined balance-of-payments effects of external shocks equalled 2 percent of the gross national product in India, and 5 percent in Uruguay in 1974, it was practically nil in Chile. In India, the ratio increased in 1975, declined in 1976 and 1977, and returned to approximately the 1974 level in 1978. These adverse effects were more than offset, however, by increases in workers' remittances from the Middle East and in tourist receipts.

In turn, adverse balance-of-payments effects of external shocks increased to a considerable extent in Chile and in Uruguay. The ratio of these effects on GNP reached 10 percent in 1975 in Chile and, after a slight decline in 1976, increased further in subsequent years, reaching 13 percent in 1978. The increase was smaller in Uruguay, where the ratio fluctuated between 6 percent and 7 percent, with the former figure applying in 1978.

India and the two Latin American countries of the group also had contrasting experiences as far as incentive policies are concerned. While substantive changes in the system of incentives were not made in India, Chile and Uruguay introduced major reforms during the period under consideration. These reforms involved substantially reducing the bias against exports, raising real exchange rates and real interest rates, reducing budget deficits and increasing the role of market forces in general.

In response to the external shocks suffered in 1974, *India* adopted deflationary policies, with the real value of the money supply falling by 14 percent in that year. Nevertheless, inflation continued at a higher rate than in the United States and it was not fully offset by a devaluation. The appreciation of the real exchange rate vis-à-vis the U.S. dollar contributed to losses in export market shares and to negative import substitution, the adverse balance-of-payments effects of which were offset only in part by the import savings associated with the decline in the rate of economic growth resulting from the deflationary policies applied. Correspondingly, additional net external financing requirements exceeded the adverse balance-of-payments of external shocks by a considerable margin.

This situation continued in subsequent years, except for 1976 when a substantial devaluation in real terms led to import substitution in India. However, the actual resource gap was much smaller and it turned into a surplus of $1.4 billion in 1976 and $1.9 billion in 1977, largely because of the rise in workers' remittances and tourist receipts. The surplus was translated into reserve accumulation in 1976 ($2.2 billion) as well as in 1977 ($2.4 billion) that continued at a slightly reduced rate (1.7 billion) in 1978. Although preliminary data indicate that the surplus in India's resource gap declined to $0.4 billion in that year, this was in part offset by increases in official grants. With the accumulation of reserves, the net external debt ratio declined from 16 percent in 1973 to 8 percent in 1978; in the same period, the gross external debt ratio decreased from 17 percent to 14 percent and the gross debt service ratio from 27 percent to 15 percent.

The conservative policies of reserve accumulation were not conducive to the acceleration of economic growth. Nevertheless, GNP growth rates rose somewhat compared to the 1963–73 period as the performance of agriculture improved and the rate of domestic savings increased in response to the rise of real interest rates. There was also negative import substitution in response to the trade liberalization measures introduced towards the end of the period.

Import liberalization was, however, limited to noncompeting imports. This benefited, in particular, production for domestic markets through the easier availability of imported inputs while exporters already had such privileges beforehand. Also, the practical application of export promotion measures continued to be plagued by administrative difficulties and the incentives actually granted fell far short of the rates of import protection as domestically-produced goods faced practically no foreign competition. In particular, labor-intensive manufactures received few export incentives, although they conform to India's comparative advantage. Correspondingly, India continued to lose export market shares, especially in manufactured goods, where actual exports fell to 70 percent of hypothetical exports, calculated on the assumption of unchanged market shares, in 1978.

Chile, in turn, abandoned its inward-oriented strategy in favor of outward orientation. It abolished all import restrictions and reduced tariffs over a five-year period to 10 percent in June 1979, the only exception being the automobile industry. Tariff reductions were part of a package of economic policies that included a substantial devaluation in real terms, the abolition of price control, the establishment of realistic prices for public utilities, the elimination of budget deficits, the establishment of positive real interest rates, and the liberalization of financial markets.

The course of the economy in the years immediately following the fall of Allende in September 1973 was, however, determined by the deflationary policies of the newly-installed Pinochet government. These policies aimed at lowering the rate of inflation that reached 500 percent a year; they became even more severe in 1975 in response to the terms-of-trade loss Chile suffered in that year.

The policies applied led to a decline in the real value of the money supply by 15 percent in 1974 and by 25 percent in 1975 while the government budget deficit gave place to a surplus. The continued indexing of wages held back the decline in the rate of inflation, however. As measured by the adjusted consumer price index prepared by the World Bank, December-to-December price increases were 405 percent in 1973, 376 percent in 1974 and 341 percent in 1975.

With the indexing of wages, the brunt of the adjustment fell on the unemployed. In conjunction with the 7 percent fall of GNP between 1973 and 1975, unemployment rose from 5 percent of the labor force in December 1973 to 14 percent in December 1975 in the Greater Santiago area. Unemployment rates fell to 10 percent in December 1976 but declined slowly afterwards as much of the subsequent rise in the gross national product was attained through increases in the productivity of labor and capital.

The gross national product rose by 13 percent between 1975 and 1977 and by 20 percent between 1977 and 1978, although investment rates remained unchanged, reflecting a decline in incremental capital-output ratios. At the same time, inflation rates, measured from December to December, fell from 341 percent in 1975 to 174 percent in 1976, 63 percent in 1977, and 30 percent in 1978. The decrease in the rate of growth of the money supply was smaller, so that real money balances held by firms and individuals were replenished.

The policies applied further involved substantial increases in the real exchange rate, although the extent of appreciation is overstated by the use of the (adjusted) consumer price index used in the calculations, by reason of declines in retail margins. Still, this index has been utilized because it incorporates adjustments for suppressed inflation in the early seventies that have not been made in the wholesale price index.

The depreciation of the real exchange rate led to rapid increases in export market shares, with the resulting expansion representing 31 percent of total exports in 1978. Increases in market shares were particularly pronounced in manufactured goods; in 1978 these exports reached three times the level that would have been attained if Chile maintained its "1972" market shares. There was also considerable import substitution in response to the depreciation of the real exchange rate, but this came to a standstill in 1977, and declined afterwards, as tariff reductions increasingly weighed upon import-substituting industries. Import savings associated with lower GNP growth rates also declined as economic growth accelerated.

At the same time, the balance-of-payments effects of external shocks increased to a considerable extent, necessitating additional net external financing. Nevertheless, with rapid increases in GNP, the gross external debt ratio hardly surpassed the 1973 level in 1978 (42 percent) while its peak level was 48 percent in 1975. The improvement was even greater in terms of the net external debt ratio as Chile accumulated reserves. The rise in the gross debt service ratio from 42 percent in 1973 to 59 percent in 1978, in turn, is fully explained by increased loan repayments that are included under amortization.

In response to the quadrupling of oil prices, deflationary monetary policies were adopted in *Uruguay*, with the real value of the money supply falling by 8 percent between 1973 and 1974. The high rate of inflation also led to reductions in the real value of government revenues, however, and the budget deficit increased. Also, Uruguay failed to devalue *pari passu* with inflation, and the real exchange rate vis-à-vis the U.S. dollar appreciated by 8 percent.

With the fall in the real exchange rate, there was little change in export shares and in import substitution, so that Uruguay had to rely on foreign borrowing, complemented by reductions in reserves, to finance its rising resource gap. Rather than attempting to remedy its external situation by deflating further the economy, however, the government opted for a "fuite en avant" by introducing reforms that represented a break with the policies followed in the preceding decades.

The policy changes introduced in July 1974 included decontrolling domestic prices, eliminating import restrictions, reducing tariffs, and abolishing minimum foreign financing requirements for imports, with exceptions made for capital goods in the latter case. Also, interest rates were raised, foreign capital movements liberalized, and the system of minidevaluations adjusted so as to depreciate the peso in real terms.

The real exchange rate increased by 20 percent in 1975, rose further in 1976 and 1977 and, notwithstanding a decline in 1978, it remained 5 percent above the 1973 level and only slightly below the "1972" average. And while tariff reductions remained limited in scope, nontraditional exports received tax and tariff rebates, preferential credits, and tax relief, thereby reducing the longstanding bias against exports.

The measures applied gave impetus to the rapid expansion of exports. Increases were especially large in manufactured exports that exceeded the hypothetical level, calculated on the assumption of unchanged market shares, more than three times in 1978. Improvements in the system of incentives, together with the establishment of positive real interest rates and reductions in the budget deficit, further contributed to decreases in incremental capital-output ratios, a rise in the share of investment in GNP, and ultimately to the acceleration of economic growth. The gross national product increased at an average annual rate of 3.3 percent between 1973 and 1976 and 5.0 percent between 1976 and 1979, following a decline in the early seventies and virtual stagnation in the previous decades.

While the rise in imports associated with the acceleration of economic growth in part offset increases in export shares, and there was little import substitution, the net effect of domestic economic policies was to reduce external financial requirements attendant upon external shocks. Correspondingly, the rise in the gross debt service ratio from 33 percent in 1973 to 36 percent in 1975 was followed by a decline to 25 percent in 1977. And while increases in external shocks and the fall in beef exports due to the imposition of restrictions in the Common Market[15] occasioned a rise in this ratio to 30 percent in 1978, the 1973 level was not again reached.

Uruguay's external debt increased to a considerable extent following the oil crisis, with the gross external debt ratio reaching 16 percent in 1974. It remained at this level afterwards while the net external debt ratio declined from 6 percent in 1973 to nil in 1978. The latter figure takes account of increases in the national valuation of gold holdings; the ratio was 6 percent if such an adjustment is not made.

TABLE 2.8

Representative Ratios of Balance of Payments Effects of
External Shocks and of Policy Responses to These Shocks
(average for years 1974 to 1978)

	External Shocks		Terms of Trade Effects	Export Volume Effects	Additional Net External Financing	Increase in Export Market Shares	Import Substitution
	as a percentage of				as a percentage of		
	GNP	Average Trade			External Shocks[a]		
Argentina	0.2	3.8	65	35	−207	−95	386
Brazil	2.7	46.6	82	18	27	15	67
Chile	8.0	61.1	89	11	−6	54	21
Colombia	−0.7	−8.8	−243	143	65	−19	−139
Mexico	1.3	23.4	63	37	205	−28	−102
Uruguay	6.1	62.2	90	10	71	36	4
India	2.1	48.8	71	29	134	−20	11
Israel	11.9	56.6	82	18	57	−20	15
Yugoslavia	7.8	74.2	76	24	64	−10	18
Korea	6.9	37.1	74	26	−92	89	135
Singapore	23.3	22.5	72	28	68	23	−43
Taiwan	6.5	19.3	41	59	−76	10	35

Source: See Tables 2.1, 2.6, and 2.7.

Conclusions and Evaluation

Among newly-industrializing developing countries in the years 1974 to 1978, on the average, the ratio of the balance-of-payments effects of external shocks to the gross national product was the highest in Singapore (23 percent). The same ratio is obtained in relating the effects of external shocks to the average value of exports and imports, which provides an indication of the adjustment in trade flows necessary to offset the adverse balance-of-payments impact of external shocks. The corresponding ratios were 7 percent and 37 percent in Korea and 7 percent and 19 percent in Taiwan (Table 2.8).[16]

The three Far Eastern countries did not modify their outward-oriented strategies in response to external shocks and, correspondingly, experienced further increases in export market shares during the period under consideration. These countries also provided increased investment incentives and re-established positive real interest rates, leading to a rise in the rate of domestic saving and investment.

The policies applied enabled the three Far Eastern countries to maintain rates of economic growth higher than any other newly-industrializing developing country. This was the case notwithstanding the fact that Taiwan and, to a lesser extent, Singapore accepted reductions in the rate of economic growth in the years 1974 and 1975 for the sake of limiting their foreign indebtedness and lowering the rate of inflation.

Korea, in turn, increased reliance on foreign capital so as to maintain rapid rates of economic growth following the external shocks it suffered in 1974. Correspondingly, Korea's external debt reached 25 percent of GNP in 1978, although rapid increases in exports made it possible to limit the gross debt service ratio to 20 percent, substantially below the levels observed in the early

Effects of Lower GDP Growth Rate	Gross Debt Service Ratio	Growth Rate of GNP		Incremental Capital Output Ratio		Overall Savings Ratio	
		1973-79	1975-79	1973-79	1975-79	1973-79	1975-79
├─────────────┤	├────── percent ──────┤					├────── percent ──────┤	
16	33.6	1.2	1.3	13.0	16.6	24.6	26.9
−10	53.6	6.3	5.8	3.6	3.9	20.9	21.4
31	49.0	3.6	8.0	2.8	1.4	10.3	8.9
−7	24.4	5.5	6.1	3.2	3.1	22.1	23.2
25	90.0	4.2	4.7	4.1	4.0	22.2	22.7
−11	26.7	3.9	4.3	3.4	3.6	12.1	12.5
−2	23.8	4.3	3.7	4.9	5.7	20.9	21.9
48	40.4	2.3	2.2	8.8	10.8	6.6	6.1
28	29.7	5.7	6.1	4.4	4.7	26.5	28.3
−32	18.8	10.1	11.0	2.9	2.8	23.6	24.0
53	6.1	7.5	8.2	4.2	3.6	27.6	28.2
131	6.7	7.6	9.8	3.2	2.6	32.6	32.3

Note: aSigns have been reversed in the case of Colombia.

seventies. The situation deteriorated in 1979, when exports declined as the exchange rate became increasingly overvalued and some large, capital-intensive investments were undertaken.

In the second group of Latin American countries, the balance-of-payments effects of external shocks were negligible in Argentina and in Colombia, which did not suffer from increases in petroleum prices. Colombia further enjoyed the favorable effects of increased coffee prices. The opportunities provided by improvements in the balance of payments were not utilized, however, to accelerate the rate of economic growth. Rather, Colombia let its real exchange rate appreciate and reduced export subsidies, with adverse effects on exports as well as on import substitution.

Brazil also increased the bias against exports by raising the level of import protection and favoring import-substituting industries in the allocation of credits. Furthermore, it substantially increased foreign borrowing, with a view to maintaining high rates of economic expansion in the face of the adverse balance-of-payments effects of external shocks that equalled 3 percent of GNP and 47 percent of the average value of trade in the 1974–78 period. Given the high capital intensity of import-substituting industries, however, incremental capital-output ratios increased to a considerable extent, leading to a slowdown in economic growth as Brazil failed to utilize the proceeds of foreign credits to raise the share of investment in GNP. At the same time, the gross debt service ratio increased from 43 percent to 68 percent, and the ratio of external indebtedness to GNP from 14 percent to 24 percent, between 1973 and 1978.

The application of expansionary fiscal policies led to the deterioration of Mexico's competitive position, necessitating foreign borrowing far in excess of the balance-of-payments effects of external shocks that averaged 1 percent of

GNP and 23 percent of the average value of trade during the period under consideration. As a result, Mexico's gross external debt reached 35 percent of its GNP in 1978, notwithstanding large increases in oil earnings, and the gross debt service ratio surpassed 100 percent. At the same time, with decreases in (non-oil) export shares and negative import substitution, the rate of economic growth did not reach the levels observed in the 1963–73 period and growth involved a high cost in terms of investment inasmuch as the incremental capital-output ratio nearly doubled after 1973.

In Argentina, expansionary policies led to rapid inflation as resistance to a decline in real incomes on the part of labor unions and other groups generated a wage-price spiral. Rapid inflation, in turn, caused considerable dislocation and the rate of economic growth declined from 4.7 percent in 1963–73 to 1.2 percent in 1973–79. But, import savings at lower GNP growth rates and favorable external shocks at the end of the period led to reserve accumulation that facilitated the introduction of economic reforms in December 1978.

In the third group of countries, the balance-of-payments effects of external shocks averaged 12 percent of GNP in the years 1974 to 1978 in Israel and 8 percent in Yugoslavia; the corresponding ratios with respect to the average value of trade were 57 percent and 74 percent, respectively. In response to these shocks, Israel and, in particular, Yugoslavia increased the bias against exports through higher import protection, resulting in losses in export market shares.

During much of the period under consideration, Israel applied deflationary policies and let the exchange rate appreciate, resulting in a decline in the rate of economic growth from 8.2 percent in 1963–73 to 2.3 percent in 1973–79. And while the devaluation of the exchange rate towards the end of the period led to the expansion of exports and GNP, this was accomplished at the cost of accelerating inflation. Also, the ratio of the gross external debt to GNP increased from 54 percent in 1973 to 82 percent in 1978, and the gross debt service ratio was maintained below 40 percent only because Israel was able to obtain long-term loans in the United States.

In Yugoslavia, the gross external debt ratio rose from 8 percent to 18 percent, and the gross debt service ratio from 28 percent to 33 percent, between 1973 and 1978. Much of the inflow of capital went into investment, permitting the maintenance of relatively high GNP growth rates (5.7 percent between 1973 and 1979). Yugoslavia's poor export performance in developed country markets, however, creates dangers for the future, and the efficiency of some of the capital-intensive import-substituting investments is open to doubt.

The average balance-of-payments effects of external shocks equalled 2 percent of India's GNP and 49 percent of the average value of its trade during the 1974–78 period, but these effects were largely offset by earnings derived from workers' remittances and tourism. By contrast, the balance-of-payments effects of adverse external shocks equalled 8 percent of GNP and 61 percent of the average value of trade in Chile and 6 percent and 62 percent in Uruguay.

And, whereas the two Latin American countries adopted outward-oriented policies in response to these shocks, India did not substantially modify the system of incentives and chose to accumulate reserves. As a result, India experienced further losses in export market shares and its GNP growth rate did not substantially rise above the level experienced in the previous decade, notwithstanding the improved performance of agriculture and increases in the rate of domestic savings.

The turn towards outward orientation was accompanied by severe deflationary policies in Chile that was not the case in Uruguay where tariff reductions also proceeded at a slower rate. The effects of the differences in the policies applied are apparent in the pattern of economic growth in the two countries. In Chile, an average rate of GNP growth of 1.6 percent between 1971 and 1973 was followed by a decline of 2.4 percent between 1973 and 1976 and an increase of 9.0 percent between 1976 and 1979; in Uruguay, the corresponding growth rates were −1.5 percent, 3.3 percent, and 5.0 percent, respectively.

The acceleration of economic growth in the two countries was associated with a substantial decline in incremental capital-output ratios. They also experienced a fall in the ratio of external debt, net of reserve accumulation, to GNP. Finally, the debt service ratio fell in Uruguay while the increase in this ratio in Chile is explained by the repayment of foreign loans that is included under amortization.

The findings point to the advantages of outward-oriented policies for export performance and for economic growth in the face of external shocks. Countries applying such policies experienced increases in their export market shares while losses in market shares occurred in countries characterized by inward orientation (Table 2.8).[17] Reliance on export promotion in response to external shocks under an outward-oriented strategy, in turn, favorably affected economic growth.

In the group of twelve newly-industrializing developing countries, the rank correlation coefficient between the extent of reliance on export promotion in response to external shocks, defined as the ratio of the increment in exports associated with increases in market shares to the balance-of-payments effects of external shocks, and the rate of growth of GNP was 0.50 during the 1973-79 period.[18] This result is statistically significant at the one percent level.[19]

The extent of correlation between the two variables is reduced by reason of the fact that in the two countries, Chile and Uruguay, which adopted outward-oriented policies during the period under consideration, the favorable effects of these policies on economic growth were observable with a time lag. To allow for this lag, the extent of reliance on export promotion in response to external shocks was also correlated with the rate of GNP growth in the period 1975-79; a Spearman rank correlation coefficient of 0.72 was obtained in this case.

The favorable experience of countries applying an outward-oriented development strategy may be explained by the efficient use of resources and rapid technological change under such a strategy that provides similar incentives to exports and to import substitution. This proposition receives support from the observed high correlation between the extent of reliance on export promotion and the incremental capital-output ratio. Using the reciprocal of the incremental capital-output ratio in the calculations, the Spearman rank correlation coefficient between the two variables was 0.75 in the 1973-79 period. Practically the same result, a coefficient of 0.77, is obtained if incremental capital-output ratios for the 1975-79 period are used in the calculations, in order to allow for the possibility of lags in the adjustment.

The introduction of lags will affect the results, however, in attempting to explain intercountry differences in GNP growth rates in terms of the incremental capital-output ratio and the domestic savings ratio. Thus, in replacing data for 1973-79 by data for 1975-79, the Spearman rank correlation coefficient increases from 0.43 to 0.82 if the reciprocal of the incremental capital-output ratio, and it declines from 0.59 to 0.46 if the domestic savings ratio, is correlated with the rate of growth of GNP.[20] The results obtained for the years 1975-79 closely correspond to estimates for the 1960-73 period in a 113 country sample where rank correlation coefficients of 0.72 and 0.40 were obtained in the two cases, respectively.[21]

In order to separate the effects of the incremental capital-output ratio and of the domestic savings ratio on economic growth, multiple regression techniques have further been applied. The results shown in equations (1) and (2) indicate that the rate of economic growth is affected by both variables, which are highly significant statistically and explain about four-fifths of intercountry variations in GNP growth rates.[22] It is also apparent that, in an intercountry context, a 10 percent increase in the reciprocal of the incremental capital-output ratio is associated with a 9-10 percent increase in the GNP growth rate and a 10 percent increase in the domestic savings ratio is associated with a 3-4 percent increase in the GNP growth rate.

(1) 1973-79: $\log y = 1.806 + 0.972 \log \triangle Y/I + 0.385 \log S/Y$ $R^2 = 0.782$
         (2.594) (4.866)   (1.973)

(2) 1975-79: $\log y = 1.935 + 0.852 \log \triangle Y/I + 0.311 \log S/Y$ $R^2 = 0.872$
         (4.145) (7.454)   (2.157)

The importance of policy choices is further indicated by the lack of a negative correlation between the balance-of-payments effects of external shocks, expressed as a proportion of GNP, and the rate of economic growth. In fact, the correlation between the two variables was slightly positive, 0.19, statistically significant at the 10 percent level. This result is compatible with the hypothesis that external shocks provided inducement for policy improvements as was the case in Chile and Uruguay.

There was no significant statistical relationship between reliance on additional net external financing in response to external shocks and the rate of growth of GNP, with the Spearman correlation coefficient between the two variables being -0.09. The result reflects the fact that the effects of foreign borrowing on economic growth depend on the uses to which the proceeds of foreign loans are put. In Brazil, for example, where the proceeds were used largely for raising consumption levels and for investment in high-cost import-substituting industries, the rate of economic growth declined while foreign debt increased.

At the same time, servicing the foreign debt entails a cost for the national economy, lowering the rate of economic growth under *ceteris paribus* assumption. In fact, in the twelve newly-industrializing developing countries, the correlation between the gross debt service ratio and the rate of growth of GNP, as measured by the Spearman rank correlation coefficient, was -0.60 during the 1973-79 period.

The experience of the newly-industrializing developing countries during the period under consideration also provides evidence on the responsiveness of exports and of import substitution to changes in real exchange rates as well as on the effects of changes in real interest rates and investment incentives on domestic savings and investment. It further appears that overvalued exchange rates and negative real interest rates, as well as large budget deficits and the resulting rapid inflation, tend to depress the rate of economic activity.

These findings have implications for the policy measures that may be taken in response to recent increases in oil prices. They indicate, first of all, the need to lessen the bias in the system of incentives against exports and in favor of import substitution. They further point to the need to maintain realistic exchange rates and interest rates, limit the budget deficit, and avoid using the proceeds of foreign borrowing to increase consumption and to carry out investments in industries that do not correspond to the country's comparative advantage. More generally, the findings suggest the need to reduce distortions in product and factor markets and to increase reliance on the market mechanism.

ESSAY 3

Policy Responses to External Shocks in Selected Latin American Countries

Introduction

The non-OPEC developing countries suffered external shocks of considerable magnitude after 1973. In the 1973–78 period, these shocks included the quadrupling of petroleum prices, which took full effect in 1974, and the world recession of 1974–75, which was followed by a relatively slow recovery. The external shocks adversely affected the balance-of-payments of the countries in question through the deterioration of their terms of trade and through the slowdown in the growth of foreign demand for their export products.

The non-OPEC developing countries adopted various policy measures in response to these external shocks. Depending on the country concerned, the policy responses involved additional external financing, export promotion, import substitution, and lowering the rate of economic growth.

This essay will examine the economic effects of external shocks, and of the policy measures taken in response to these shocks, in three Latin American countries (Brazil, Mexico, and Uruguay) during the 1973–78 period. Brazil and Uruguay are representative of countries that suffered the consequences of increased petroleum prices, but they differ in the policies adopted. The terms of trade deteriorated to a much lesser extent in Mexico, which started exporting substantial quantities of petroleum in 1977. At the same time, the choice of 1978 as the terminal year permits us to separate the effects of the two oil shocks, the second being the approximate doubling of petroleum prices in 1979.

Sections I and II will present estimates of the balance-of-payments effects of external shocks, and of policy measures taken in response to these shocks, respectively. Section III will describe the policies applied in some detail, relating them to changes observed in the individual countries. In the conclusions, a comparative analysis of the findings will be provided.

The methodology applied in deriving the estimated balance-of-payments effects is described in "The Newly Industrializing Developing Countries after the Oil Crisis," Essay 2 in this volume, where some of the results cited in the following sections are also reported. The estimates have been made for the years 1974 to 1978, taken individually.[1] Averages for the 1974–78 period are also shown in the tables. This permits considering changes over time and indicating the results for the entire period.

I. The Balance-of-Payments Effects of External Shocks

This section will present empirical evidence on the balance-of-payments effects of external shocks, in the form of terms of trade effects and export volume effects, in the three countries under consideration.[2] The relevant estimates are reported in Table 3.1. Summary estimates are further shown in Table 2.1 while Table 2.2 relates terms of trade effects to the average of export and import (average trade) and to the gross national product, and export volume effects to exports and to the gross national product, all expressed in the average prices of the years 1971 to 1973 (for short, "1972" prices). Table 3.2 disaggregates the foreign demand effects on the manufactured exports of Brazil. Tables 3.3 and 3.4 show the extent of export shortfalls due to the deceleration of the growth of foreign demand for the various commodity categories and for individual traditional primary exports, respectively.

Terms of Trade Effects

Among the three countries under study, Brazil and Uruguay suffered a substantial deterioration of their terms of trade in 1974, amounting to about 50 percent of the average value of their exports and imports in that year. The quadrupling of petroleum prices was the principal factor contributing to these changes while increases in the prices of non-oil imports and exports were nearly in balance.

At the same time, given its higher trade share, the ratio of the terms of trade loss to GNP was greater in Uruguay (3.9 percent) than in Brazil (3.3 percent). And, with the price of its principal traditional export, beef, declining after 1974, Uruguay's terms of trade deteriorated further in subsequent years. The terms of trade loss reached a peak, amounting to 64.1 percent of the average value of exports and imports and 6.5 percent of GNP in 1977; the corresponding ratios were 55.7 percent and 5.4 percent in the 1974–78 period, on the average. As shown in Table 3.1, the estimated terms of trade loss was even larger if it is calculated under the assumption of balanced trade in "1972" prices as Uruguay had a rising trade surplus in terms of these prices.

Brazil benefited from increases in the prices of its coffee and soybean exports after 1974. Export prices were the most favorable in 1977, when the terms of trade loss as compared to "1972" was 13.3 percent of the average value of exports and imports and 0.7 percent of GNP. The terms of trade deteriorated again in 1978, with the resulting loss amounting to 31.3 percent of the average value of exports and imports and 1.7 percent of GNP; these ratios averaged 38.2 percent and 2.2 percent, respectively, in the entire 1974–78 period. About one-half of the loss due to the terms of trade effects reflects the impact of increased import prices on Brazil's trade deficit, estimated in "1972" prices.

Mexico imported only a small quantity of petroleum even before the discovery of large oil-deposits in the mid-seventies. Correspondingly, it suffered a smaller terms of trade loss than Brazil and Uruguay in 1974, amounting to 21.5 percent of the average value of exports and imports and 1.3 percent of GNP. Following a temporary deterioration in 1975, the situation improved in subsequent years, largely as a result of the benefits Mexico derived from higher prices on its rising petroleum exports. By 1977, Mexico enjoyed a net gain from terms of trade changes, although this gave rise to a small loss in 1978 when import prices rose rapidly. The terms of trade loss was 14.8 percent of the value of trade and 0.8 of GNP in 1974–78, on the average. This loss was due to the impact of increased import prices on Mexico's trade deficit, estimated in "1972" prices, as the "pure" terms of trade effect, calculated on the assumption of balanced trade in terms of "1972" prices, was favorable.

Export Volume Effects

In 1974, export volume effects, calculated in "1972" prices, were much smaller than the terms of trade effects in all three countries. Assuming unchanged export market shares, the export shortfall due to the slowdown in the growth of foreign demand equalled 3.4 percent of the value of exports in Brazil, 5.3 percent in Mexico, and 12.6 percent in Uruguay. In the same year, the ratio of the export shortfall to GNP was 0.2 percent in Brazil and in Mexico and 1.1 percent in Uruguay.

The observed intercountry differences in export shortfalls are explained by differences in the commodity composition of exports. Brazil and, in particular, Mexico benefited from the relatively high export share of manufactured goods (18 percent and 41 percent in "1972"), for which foreign demand continued to rise in 1974. But, while Mexico was adversely affected by a decline in the world exports of cattle, the unfavorable effects of the world recession on Brazil's exports were attenuated by relatively strong demand for oilcake, oilseeds, and iron ore. Finally, manufactured goods accounted for a small share of Uruguay's exports (9 percent), which also suffered the adverse consequences of a decline in foreign demand for wool.

In subsequent years, demand for the exports of Brazil and Mexico by-and-large paralleled the world business cycle, with a shortfall in export volume experienced in 1975 and 1977 and gains in 1976.[2] At the same time, in both

TABLE 3.1

Balance of Payments Effects of External Shocks and of Policy Responses to These Shocks: Related Data ($ millions)

	BRAZIL				
	1974	1975	1976	1977	1978	1974-78 Average
I *External Shocks*						
Effects of Increased Import Prices	6222	6453	7143	7170	8523	7102
of which, Fuels	2611	2743	3400	3588	3943	3257
Non-fuels	3611	3710	3743	3582	4580	3845
Effects of Increased Export Prices	3079	3149	4508	6365	6546	4729
of which, Traditional Primary Products	1668	1571	2522	3367	2597	2345
Fuels	82	151	192	171	154	150
Nontraditional Primary Products Other than Fuels	725	727	938	1484	1691	1113
Manufactured Goods	604	699	855	1343	2104	1121
Difference (Terms of Trade Effects)	3143	3306	2635	805	1977	2373
of which: Pure terms of trade effect	736	1845	1590	414	1431	1203
Unbalanced trade effect	2407	1461	1045	391	546	1170
Trend Value of Exports, in "1972" Prices	4932	5259	5619	6018	6461	5658
Hypothetical Exports, in "1972" Prices	4764	4730	5279	5231	5668	5134
Difference (Export Volume Effects of Changes in Foreign Demand)	168	529	341	787	793	523
of which, Traditional Primary Products	138	324	237	498	421	324
Fuels	2	13	12	17	25	14
Nontraditional Primary Products Other than Fuels	68	83	65	111	138	93
Manufactured Goods	−40	109	26	161	210	93
of which, Growth Effects	41	175	186	240	318	192
Income Elasticity Effects	−81	−66	−160	−80	−108	−99
II *Policy Reactions*						
Actual Resource Gap, in Current Prices	6277	4913	3818	1649	2745	3880
Trend Value of Resource Gap, in "1972" Prices	1709	2164	2995	3976	4599	3089
Difference (Additional Net External Financing)	4568	2749	823	−2327	−1857	791
Actual Exports, in "1972" Prices	4872	5523	5620	5755	6113	5577
Hypothetical Exports, in "1972" Prices	4764	4730	4279	5231	5668	5134
Difference (Increase in Export Market Shares)	108	793	341	524	445	442
of which, Traditional Primary Products	−253	94	−76	−122	−481	−168
Fuels	−27	1	4	−9	−11	−8
Nontraditional Primary Products Other than Fuels	170	312	309	400	467	332
Manufactured Goods	218	386	105	254	470	287
Hypothetical Imports, in "1972" Prices	7205	7813	8918	9577	10476	8798
Actual Imports, in "1972" Prices	7946	7139	6583	6087	6531	6857
Difference (Import Substitution)	−742	675	2335	3491	3945	1941
of which, Fuels	205	224	214	299	308	250
Non-fuels	−947	451	2121	3192	3637	1691
Trend Value of Imports, in "1972" Prices	6581	7432	8394	9482	10713	8520
Hypothetical Imports, in "1972" Prices	7205	7813	8918	9577	10476	8798
Difference (Import Effects of Lower GDP Growth Rate)	−624	−381	−524	−95	237	−278
of which, Fuels	−71	−47	−63	−21	9	−39
Non-fuels	−553	−335	−461	−74	228	−239

countries, the ratio of the export shortfall to the value of exports was considerably higher in 1978 (13.0 percent in Brazil and 15.5 percent in Mexico) than it had been in 1974. For the period as a whole, this ratio averaged 9.4 percent in Brazil and 13.3 percent in Mexico, equalling 0.5 percent of GNP in both cases.

Different developments are shown in Uruguay. While the ratio of the export shortfall to the value of exports remained relatively high in 1975 (10.5 percent), it fell to a considerable extent in subsequent years. The ratio averaged 2.7 percent in 1976–77, when the rise in world demand for beef and wool led to positive export-volume effects for traditional exports. With some deterioration in 1978, the foreign demand-induced losses in export volume

TABLE 3.1 (Continued)

	MEXICO						URUGUAY				
1974	1975	1976	1977	1978	1974-78 Average	1974	1975	1976	1977	1978	1974-78 Average
1706	2245	2160	2378	3720	2442	251	270	316	443	474	351
301	235	239	106	170	210	102	122	122	145	180	134
1405	2011	1921	2272	3551	2232	149	148	194	298	294	217
1044	1173	1637	2492	3630	1995	134	87	140	230	298	178
288	271	575	631	606	473	71	2	−4	40	44	31
92	348	425	809	1411	617	0	0	0	0	0	0
275	215	207	353	269	264	41	49	77	87	109	73
388	338	429	700	1344	640	22	36	67	104	144	75
662	1073	523	−114	90	447	117	183	176	213	176	173
−335	−298	−699	−1188	−1454	−794	129	193	332	353	318	265
998	1371	1222	1074	1544	1242	−12	−9	−157	−141	−142	−92
1995	2171	2368	2591	2841	2393	268	280	293	307	323	294
1900	1923	2189	2227	2439	2136	237	249	283	296	305	274
95	247	179	363	402	257	31	31	10	11	18	20
83	95	93	141	114	105	26	20	3	−5	−2	9
1	7	6	9	13	7	0	0	0	0	0	0
30	36	28	48	60	41	6	7	6	10	12	8
−18	109	51	165	215	105	−1	4	2	6	8	4
53	193	195	242	291	195	2	7	7	9	10	7
−70	−83	−144	−78	−76	−90	−3	−3	−5	−3	−3	−3
1633	2451	1473	−84	15	1098	89	118	−1	83	44	67
−346	−57	−60	−420	−841	−345	−32	−78	−72	−78	−91	−70
1979	2508	1533	336	856	1442	121	196	71	161	135	137
1807	1688	1680	1926	2587	1938	248	297	407	378	391	344
1900	1923	2189	2227	2439	2136	237	249	283	296	305	274
−93	−235	−509	−301	148	−198	11	48	124	81	86	70
−110	−169	−179	−183	−129	−154	6	−6	28	−15	−28	−3
3	89	101	192	354	148	0	0	0	0	0	0
14	−31	−122	−90	−176	−80	−14	6	18	4	13	5
−1	−124	−309	−220	99	−111	18	48	78	92	101	68
3215	3303	3338	3433	3610	3380	253	269	280	298	317	283
4351	4335	3870	3512	4424	4098	236	287	272	287	301	277
−1136	−1031	−533	−80	−813	−719	17	−18	8	11	16	7
82	117	125	167	176	134	1	3	11	16	14	9
−1218	−1149	−657	−247	−990	−852	16	−22	−4	−5	2	−3
3223	3382	3549	3726	3912	3558	252	258	263	268	274	263
3215	3303	3338	3433	3610	3380	253	269	280	298	317	283
8	78	211	293	302	178	−1	−11	−17	−29	−43	−20
2	10	27	38	42	24	−2	−6	−9	−15	−22	−11
6	68	185	255	259	155	1	−5	−8	−14	−21	−9

Sources: International and national statistics.

averaged 5.9 percent of export value, and 0.6 percent of GNP, in the 1974–78 period, on the average.

Comparative Analysis

The results indicate the relative importance of terms of trade effects and, within these effects, that of the loss suffered due to increases in petroleum prices, in Brazil and in Uruguay in the 1974–78 period. On the average, the loss due to terms of trade effects amounted to 2.2 percent of GNP in Brazil and 5.4 percent in Uruguay during this period whereas export volume effects were

0.5 percent and 0.6 percent in the two countries, respectively. Terms of trade effects averaged 0.8 percent of GNP in Mexico, which imported little petroleum even before the discoveries in the mid-seventies, while export volume effects were 0.5 percent of GNP.

These conclusions conflict with the conventional wisdom that gives emphasis to the unfavorable effects of the 1974–75 world recession and the subsequent slow recovery in the developed countries on the balance-of-payments of the developing countries. Nor does one find evidence of the alleged adverse effects of increased protectionism on the exports of manufactured goods by the developing countries. As is apparent from Table 3.1, the average foreign income elasticity of demand for the manufactured exports of these countries rose during the period under consideration, offsetting in part the unfavorable effects of lower GNP growth rates.[3]

Table 3.2 reports estimates of growth effects and income elasticity effects on Brazil's exports in a geographical disaggregation. The data show that only the centrally planned economies experienced a decline in their income elasticity of demand for the manufactured exports of the developing countries during the period under consideration. In the developed countries, which continued to provide markets for the bulk of the developing countries' exports of manufactured goods, increases in the income elasticity of demand for these exports offset one-fifth of the export shortfall due to their lower GNP growth rates. And, increases in the income elasticity of demand enhanced the favorable effects of higher GNP growth rates on intra-LDC trade in manufactured goods.[4]

II. The Balance-of-Payments Effects of Policy Responses to External Shocks

In the 1974–78 period, on the average, the balance-of-payments effects of external shocks were estimated at 2.7 percent of GNP in Brazil, 1.3 percent in Mexico and 6.1 percent in Uruguay. In absolute terms, the relevant magnitudes are $2.9 billion in Brazil, $0.7 billion in Mexico, and $0.2 billion in Uruguay.

This section will present estimates of the balance-of-payments effects of policy responses to external shocks in the form of additional net external financing, export promotion, import substitution, and lowering economic growth rates in the years 1974–78, on the average. Subsequently, in Section III, the policy measures employed by the individual countries will be discussed and the effects of these policies on the time pattern of the results indicated.

The estimates are reported in Tables 2.1 and 3.1 while Table 2.2 relates the results to the volume of exports, imports, average trade, and GNP as the case may be, all expressed in "1972" prices. Changes in the amount and the sources of external financing are reported in Table 2.3 while Tables 3.3 and 3.4 show the gains (losses) due to increases (decreases) in export market shares for various commodity categories and for individual traditional primary

TABLE 3.2
Foreign Demand Induced Changes in Exports of Manufactured Goods in Brazil
(U.S. $ million in "1972" Prices)

	Export Growth Rates "1972"–1977	"1972"	1974	1975	1976	1977	1978	1974-78 Average
Hypothetical Value of Exports								
DC		490	649	610	815	822	956	770
LDC		297	430	477	541	603	667	544
CPE		17	20	21	16	21	16	19
World		804	1099	1107	1372	1446	1638	1332
Trend Value of Exports								
DC	16.6	490	666	777	906	1056	1231	927
LDC	11.8	297	371	415	464	519	580	470
CPE	13.5	17	22	25	28	32	36	29
World		804	1059	1217	1398	1607	1848	1426
Constant Income Elasticity Value of Exports								
DC		490	609	598	710	805	917	728
LDC		297	387	419	475	533	581	479
CPE		17	22	24	27	29	32	27
World		804	1018	1041	1212	1367	1530	1233
Constant Income Elasticity less Hypothetical Value of Exports (Income Elasticity Effects)								
DC		0	-40	-11	-105	-18	-38	-42
LDC		0	-43	-58	-66	-70	-86	-65
CPE		0	2	3	11	8	16	8
World		0	-81	-66	-160	-80	-108	-99
Trend less Constant Income Elasticity Value of Exports (Growth Effects)								
DC		0	57	179	196	252	314	199
LDC		0	-16	-4	-11	-14	-1	-9
CPE		0	0	1	2	3	5	2
World		0	41	175	186	240	318	192
Trend less Hypothetical Value of Exports (Foreign Demand Effects, total)								
DC		0	17	167	91	234	276	157
LDC		0	-59	-62	-77	-84	-87	-74
CPE		0	-2	4	12	11	21	10
World		0	-40	109	26	161	210	93

Source: See text.

Notes: DC—developed countries; LDC—less developed countries; CPE—centrally planned economies.

Numbers may not add up because of rounding.

TABLE 3.3
Trade Effects of External Shocks and of Policy Responses
to These Shocks: Commodity Groups

			BRAZIL			
	1974	1975	1976	1977	1978	1974-78 Average
Exports						
Traditional Primary Products						
Hypothetical/Trend	95.3	89.4	92.6	85.1	88.0	89.9
Actual/Hypothetical	90.9	103.4	97.4	95.7	84.5	94.2
Fuels						
Hypothetical/Trend	97.4	78.6	82.0	76.3	68.1	79.6
Actual/Hypothetical	52.0	102.3	106.9	84.5	78.8	84.4
Nontraditional Primary Products Other Than Fuels						
Hypothetical/Trend	92.3	90.9	93.1	88.7	86.5	90.2
Actual/Hypothetical	120.9	137.5	134.9	145.8	152.9	138.7
Manufacturing Goods						
Hypothetical/Trend	103.8	91.0	98.1	90.0	88.6	93.5
Actual/Hypothetical	119.8	134.9	107.6	117.6	128.7	121.5
Total						
Hypothetical/Trend	96.6	89.9	93.9	86.9	87.7	90.7
Actual/Hypothetical	102.3	116.8	106.5	110.0	107.9	108.6
Imports						
Fuels						
Hypothetical/Trend	107.9	104.7	105.8	101.8	99.3	103.5
Actual/Hypothetical	78.8	78.3	81.3	75.4	76.3	77.9
Nonfuels						
Hypothetical/Trend	109.7	105.2	106.3	100.9	97.6	103.2
Actual/Hypothetical	115.2	93.3	72.7	61.8	60.4	77.9
Total						
Hypothetical/Trend	109.5	105.1	106.2	101.0	97.8	103.3
Actual/Hypothetical	110.3	91.4	73.8	63.6	62.3	77.9

exports, respectively. Table 3.3 also provides information on the extent of import substitution, and on the decline of imports due to the deceleration of the rate of economic growth, for fuel and for non-fuel imports.

It is apparent that there are considerable differences among the three countries as far as policy responses to external shocks are concerned. In Brazil, additional net external financing ($791 million) provided about one-fourth, and import substitution ($1941 million) two-thirds, of balance-of-payments requirements attendant upon the external shocks. At the same time, the gain from increased export market shares ($442 million) was in large part offset by the rise in imports resulting from high GNP growth rates in Brazil ($278 million).[5]

The contribution of additional net external financing surpassed two-thirds of the total in Uruguay, amounting to $137 million in 1974–78, on the average. Increased export market shares ($70 million) was another important factor in attenuating the effects of external shocks. But, the acceleration of economic growth added $20 million to Uruguay's import bill and import substitution amounted to only $7 million. Nonetheless, the net effects of the domestic policy measures (i.e. excluding external financing) on Uruguay's balance of payments were strongly positive.

TABLE 3.3 (Continued)

	MEXICO					URUGUAY				
1974	1975	1976	1977	1978	1974-78 Average	1974	1975	1976	1977	1978	1974-78 Average
89.0	87.9	88.7	83.4	87.2	87.2	83.9	87.9	98.5	102.7	100.9	95.1
83.5	75.5	75.3	72.2	83.4	78.4	104.7	96.2	116.4	91.9	84.7	98.2
97.4	78.6	82.0	76.3	68.1	79.6	—	—	—	—	—	—
110.6	447.6	448.5	760.8	1369.7	624.3	—	—	—	—	—	—
92.3	90.9	93.1	88.7	86.5	90.2	92.3	90.9	93.1	88.7	86.5	90.2
104.2	91.5	68.9	76.4	54.5	78.5	80.7	108.0	123.0	104.8	117.0	107.1
102.1	88.6	95.3	87.0	85.3	90.7	102.1	88.6	95.3	87.0	85.3	90.7
99.9	85.3	70.6	80.1	107.9	89.1	160.9	260.7	312.0	337.9	329.7	288.3
95.2	88.6	92.4	86.0	85.8	89.2	88.3	88.8	96.6	96.5	94.4	93.1
95.1	87.8	76.8	86.5	106.1	90.7	104.5	119.4	143.8	127.5	128.2	125.6
98.9	94.5	86.9	83.1	83.2	88.5	104.1	115.7	122.6	135.8	150.5	126.5
49.8	32.5	29.8	11.3	15.9	26.9	97.7	92.9	77.1	72.6	78.6	82.5
99.8	97.9	94.5	92.7	92.9	95.4	99.6	102.4	103.4	106.2	109.0	104.2
139.9	136.7	120.8	107.6	129.1	126.6	92.6	109.7	101.6	102.0	99.1	101.1
99.8	97.7	94.0	92.1	92.3	95.0	100.3	104.4	106.4	110.8	115.5	107.6
135.3	131.2	116.0	102.3	122.5	121.3	93.4	106.9	97.3	96.4	94.9	97.7

Sources: International and national statistics. For explanation, see text.

Different conclusions apply to Mexico where decreases in export market shares ($198 million) and negative import substitution ($719 million) were offset only in part by the favorable balance-of-payments effects of lower GNP growth rates ($178 million). Correspondingly, average net external financing in 1974–78 ($1442 million) was more than double the balance-of-payments effects of external shocks in Mexico.

Additional Net External Financing

In the 1974–78 period, on the average, additional net external financing amounted to 12.7 percent of the average value of exports and imports in Brazil, 47.8 percent in Mexico, and 44.0 percent in Uruguay. But, given its larger trade share in GNP, the ratio of additional net external financing to GNP was higher in Uruguay (4.3 percent) than in Mexico (2.6 percent), with Brazil (0.7 percent) occupying third place.

It will be recalled that additional net external financing has been estimated as the difference between the actual resource gap (the balance for goods, nonfactor services and private transfers) and its trend value (the difference between the trend values of imports and exports), both expressed in "1972" prices, adjusted for the actual net balance of non-factor services and private transfers. In Brazil, the trend value of the resource gap was 2.9 percent of GNP in 1974–78, on the average; the comparable figures are −0.6 percent in Mexico and −2.2 percent in Uruguay.

In the case of Brazil, the relatively high trend value of the resource gap reflects the fact that its "1972" trade deficit would have increased further if export and import trends observed in the preceding decade continued. In turn, improvements in its service balance and increases in private transfers would have eliminated Mexico's resource gap, had past trends in exports and imports continued. Finally, the continuation of export and import trends would have led to further increases in the surplus in the balance for goods, nonfactor services, and private transfers which Uruguay experienced in "1972."

In the 1974–78 period, the actual resource gap (net external financing) averaged 3.6 percent of GNP in Brazil, 2.0 percent in Mexico, and 2.1 percent in Uruguay. In absolute terms, the relevant figures are: Brazil, $3880 million, Mexico $1098 million, and Uruguay $67 million. In the same period, interest payments and dividends amounted to $3188 million, $2257 million, and $75 million in the three countries, respectively.[6] As a result, total external financing averaged $7068 million in Brazil, $3355 million in Mexico, and $142 million in Uruguay.

There are some differences among the three countries as far as the sources of total external financing are concerned. If we combine errors and omissions (mostly unreported short-term capital flows) with portfolio capital, we find that the latter accounted for 90 percent of total external financing in Brazil, 72 percent in Mexico, and 106 percent in Uruguay. Foreign direct investment accounted for another 20 percent of external financing in Brazil, 18 percent in Mexico and 27 percent in Uruguay. In turn, Uruguay devoted 27 percent of total external financing to accumulate reserves during the period; the comparable figures are 16 percent for Brazil and 3 percent for Mexico.

Export Promotion

Uruguay showed the best export performance during the 1974–78 period, with increases in its export market shares accounting for more than one-fifth of its exports, on the average. This gain came almost exclusively from manufactured exports, in particular leather, clothing, and shoes.

Manufactured exports averaged $103 million in 1974–78 as compared to hypothetical exports of $35 million, calculated under the assumption that Uruguay maintained its "1972" share in developing country exports of manufactured goods. A slight gain is also shown in nontraditional primary exports other than fuels and a small loss in traditional primary exports. In the latter case, the gain in market shares in wool, with actual exports exceeding hypothetical exports by 15 percent, more than offset the 6 percent loss in beef, with practically no change shown in the case of wool tops.

Brazil also increased its average export market share, albeit to a much lesser extent than Uruguay, representing a gain of less than one-thirteenth of exports. This result reflects gains obtained in regard to nontraditional exports other than fuels, where actual exports exceeded hypothetical exports by 39 percent, as well as in regard to manufactured goods, where this ratio was 21 percent. In the first case, fruits and vegetables and vegetable oils (in particular, soybean oil, representing the domestic transformation of soybeans); in the second, nonelectrical machinery, transport equipment, iron and steel, textiles, electrical machinery, footwear, and clothing, in this order, were largely responsible for the outcome.

In turn, a small loss is shown for traditional primary exports and for fuels which represent an insignificant part of Brazil's exports. Among traditional primary exports, there is a wide divergence among individual commodities. Gains in actual as compared to hypothetical exports are shown for oilseed cake (90 percent), iron ore (63 percent), cocoa beans (43 percent), and soybeans (12 percent) as against losses of 78 percent for cotton, 71 percent for coniferous sawnwood, 53 percent for meat, 34 percent for sugar, and 32 percent for coffee, with practically no change for castor oil.

Finally, losses in market shares were responsible for a decline in the exports of Mexico by one-tenth. The losses were the largest in traditional primary exports, amounting to 22 percent of hypothetical exports. Mexico experienced a gain in its world market share only in the case of coffee, where actual exports exceeded hypothetical exports by 23 percent, with no change shown for tomatoes. Losses for the other products were sugar, 79 percent; beef, 46 percent; cattle, 33 percent; crustaceans and molluscs, 25 percent; and cotton, 6 percent.

Mexico also experienced a loss in its market share for nontraditional exports other than fuels (21 percent) and manufactured goods (11 percent). By contrast, actual exports of fuels exceeded hypothetical exports more than six times. The resulting gain in fuel exports equalled one-third of the loss in the other commodity groups.

Import Substitution

Brazil leads in terms of import substitution in the period 1974–78, with actual imports being 22 percent smaller than hypothetical imports, calculated on the assumption of unchanged income elasticity of import demand for total imports, on the average. The same result is obtained for fuel and for nonfuel imports taken separately.

Uruguay also experienced considerable import substitution in fuels (18 percent) that was in part offset by negative import substitution in other products (1 percent). As a result of these changes, Uruguay showed a small

TABLE 3.4
Ratios of Hypothetical, Trend, and Actual Exports:
Traditional Primary Products

SITC Code		1974	1975	1976	1977	1978	1974-78 Average
	Brazil						
011	Meat, Fresh, Chilled, Frozen						
	Hypothetical/Trend	88.2	88.0	95.7	99.4	99.1	94.2
	Actual/Hypothetical	43.6	37.0	47.1	54.5	49.1	46.8
0611	Sugar, Raw, Centrifugal						
	Hypothetical/Trend	99.0	84.8	85.6	107.2	88.5	93.0
	Actual/Hypothetical	96.7	73.3	37.3	65.4	56.4	66.0
0711	Coffee, Green, Roasted						
	Hypothetical/Trend	90.8	93.3	93.3	72.6	82.1	68.2
	Actual/Hypothetical	68.3	74.2	74.6	59.6	62.4	86.4
0721	Cocoa Beans						
	Hypothetical/Trend	99.3	95.3	94.4	77.8	88.7	91.1
	Actual/Hypothetical	127.5	179.5	131.4	132.4	143.7	143.2
0813	Oilseed Cake						
	Hypothetical/Trend	99.9	93.0	110.1	104.9	114.0	104.4
	Actual/Hypothetical	122.8	176.9	194.6	231.6	202.3	189.5
2214	Soybeans						
	Hypothetical/Trend	101.6	87.9	95.6	87.7	95.5	93.7
	Actual/Hypothetical	133.4	170.4	155.0	108.8	23.0	111.8
2432	Sawnwood (Coniferous)						
	Hypothetical/Trend	85.6	69.0	86.8	91.8	87.8	84.2
	Actual/Hypothetical	49.7	47.8	21.2	20.8	12.4	28.7
2631	Cotton, Raw						
	Hypothetical/Trend	86.4	89.6	89.0	85.5	93.4	88.8
	Actual/Hypothetical	35.4	43.4	2.2	14.3	16.6	22.1
2813	Iron Ore						
	Hypothetical/Trend	105.4	91.1	82.5	72.6	65.9	83.5
	Actual/Hypothetical	135.1	174.1	171.0	156.2	180.0	162.7
4225	Castor Oil						
	Hypothetical/Trend	102.8	64.8	90.9	68.2	92.6	83.9
	Actual/Hypothetical	107.0	99.2	101.5	93.5	92.3	98.9
	Mexico						
0011	Bovine Cattle						
	Hypothetical/Trend	72.9	78.6	72.8	67.0	68.3	71.9
	Actual/Hypothetical	57.3	30.9	64.8	74.8	104.2	67.1
0111	Bovine Meat, Fresh, etc.						
	Hypothetical/Trend	89.3	88.0	94.5	100.0	102.2	94.8
	Actual/Hypothetical	40.8	12.9	35.7	68.4	96.3	54.2
036	Crustaceans and Mulluscs						
	Hypothetical/Trend	91.3	90.6	95.3	84.0	86.4	89.5
	Actual/Hypothetical	82.7	91.3	71.3	73.5	59.7	74.7
0544	Tomatoes, Fresh						
	Hypothetical/Trend	93.9	89.8	93.1	93.3	97.6	93.6
	Actual/Hypothetical	85.4	95.1	95.7	112.4	110.6	100.3
0611	Sugar, Raw, Centrifugal						
	Hypothetical/Trend	99.0	84.8	85.6	107.2	88.5	93.0
	Actual/Hypothetical	69.9	29.7	0.2	0.0	11.2	21.4
0711	Coffee, Green, Roasted						
	Hypothetical/Trend	90.8	93.3	93.3	72.6	82.1	86.4
	Actual/Hypothetical	113.1	128.1	146.7	117.0	106.1	122.8
2631	Cotton, Raw						
	Hypothetical/Trend	86.4	89.6	89.0	72.4	93.5	86.2
	Actual/Hypothetical	102.4	91.8	82.9	92.1	101.0	94.2
	Uruguay						
0111	Bovine Meat, Fresh, etc.						
	Hypothetical/Trend	89.3	88.0	94.5	100.0	102.2	94.8
	Actual/Hypothetical	106.2	80.7	129.9	87.4	70.4	93.8
2621	Wool, Greasy						
	Hypothetical/Trend	73.5	76.1	91.6	100.6	81.8	84.7
	Actual/Hypothetical	133.0	154.5	76.4	96.9	126.5	114.9
2628	Wool, Tops						
	Hypothetical/Trend	76.3	102.1	124.6	118.0	118.4	107.9
	Actual/Hypothetical	64.9	97.1	108.5	104.1	110.2	99.3

Sources: International and national statistics. For explanation, see text.

degree of net import substitution, with the difference between actual and hypothetical imports being 2 percent.

In turn, Mexico experienced negative net import substitution, raising its import bill by about one-fifth. With the discovery of new deposits leading to positive import substitution in fuels, where actual import hardly exceeded one-fourth of hypothetical imports, the extent of negative import substitution in nonfuel imports was even larger (27 percent).

Lowering Economic Growth Rates

The import saving resulting from the decline in the rate of growth of GNP amounted to 4 percent of the total imports of Mexico in the 1974–78 period on the average. By contrast, the acceleration of the rate of economic growth raised the import bill by 3 percent in Brazil and 8 percent in Uruguay. However, as noted above, the Brazilian result is affected by the choice of the base year.

III. The Policies Applied

This section will consider the policy measures applied in the three countries under study, relate them to the time pattern of the estimates, and examine their economic effects. Apart from Tables 2.1, 2.2, 2.3 and 3.1 referred to earlier, use will be made of information on nominal and real interest rates, the money supply, government revenue and expenditures (Tables 2.4 and 3.5), changes in real exchange rates (Table 3.6), and foreign debt and debt servicing (Table 2.6); other data cited originate in the World Bank data bank. The discussion will proceed by taking the three countries individually; a brief comparative evaluation will be made in the conclusion.

Brazil

Brazil's resource gap increased from $1.0 billion in "1972" to $6.3 billion in 1974. The principal factors contributing to this increase were the deterioration of the terms of trade (3.1 billion, of which the rise in fuel prices represented $2.4 billion) and the acceleration of imports, reflecting in part the effects of high GNP growth rates ($0.6 billion) and in part negative import substitution ($0.7 billion), due largely to stock-building. Interest payments and dividends further raised Brazil's total external financing requirements to $8.3 billion. This deficit was financed by foreign borrowing ($5.4 billion), direct investment ($1.3 billion), reductions in reserve holdings ($1.0 billion), and interest receipts on foreign holdings ($0.7 billion).

The increase in the resource gap and the uncertainties associated with the installation of the new government gave rise to a relatively restrictive monetary and fiscal policy stance from mid-1974. With the acceleration of inflation (the wholesale price index rose by 29 percent in 1974 as compared to 17 percent in

TABLE 3.5
Money Supply, Government Revenue, and Expenditure
(in domestic currency)

In Nominal Terms

Year	Money Supply[a]		Government Revenue		Government Expenditure		Deficit or Surplus Billions
	Billions	Percent Change	Billions	Percent Change	Billions	Percent Change	
Brazil (cruzeiros)							
1970	34.75	26.7	19.19	37.6	19.93	35.5	−0.74
1971	44.91	29.3	26.98	40.6	27.65	38.7	−0.67
1972	62.89	40.0	37.74	39.9	38.25	38.3	−0.52
1973	93.78	49.1	52.86	40.1	52.57	37.4	0.30
1974	125.33	33.6	76.81	45.3	72.93	38.7	3.88
1975	174.51	39.2	95.45	24.3	95.37	30.8	0.07
1976	241.71	38.5	166.22	74.2	165.80	73.8	0.42
1977	330.29	36.6	242.89	46.1	241.85	45.9	1.04
1978	465.62	41.0	349.22	43.8	344.35	42.4	4.87
Mexico (pesos)							
1970	53.80	10.7	42.48	12.2	48.56	3.5	−6.08
1971	57.89	7.6	47.49	11.8	51.65	6.4	−4.16
1972	68.24	17.9	57.49	21.1	68.61	33.2	−11.32
1973	83.52	22.4	67.58	17.6	87.58	27.3	−20.00
1974	100.77	20.7	92.64	37.1	122.01	39.3	−29.37
1975	122.36	21.4	130.71	41.1	165.12	35.3	−34.41
1976	157.97	29.1	161.40	23.5	203.15	23.0	−42.4
1977	199.04	26.0	193.54	19.9	248.8	22.5	−55.26
1978	260.86	31.1	407.32	110.5	506.70	103.6	−99.38
Uruguay[b] (pesos)							
1970	87.8	14.5	n.a	n.a	n.a	n.a	n.a
1971	135.1	53.9	n.a	n.a	n.a	n.a	n.a
1972	198.4	46.9	n.a	n.a	n.a	n.a	n.a
1973	357.1	80.0	552.0	n.a	580.0	n.a	−28.0
1974	586.2	64.2	914.0	65.6	1084.0	86.9	−170.0
1975	961.5	64.0	1519.0	66.2	1877.0	73.2	−358.0
1976	1597.4	66.1	2669.0	75.7	2952.0	57.3	−283.0
1977	2205.3	38.1	4313.0	61.6	4486.0	52.0	−173.0
1978	3962.2	79.7	6923.0	60.5	7044.0	57.0	−121.0

Source: International Monetary Fund, *International Financial Statistics,* various issues.

Notes: (a) End-year data. (b) Data are expressed in millions.

1973), the real value of the money supply increased by only 3 percent in 1974 as compared to 28 percent in 1973. The relevant figures are 7 and 18 percent for government expenditures and 12 and 20 percent for government revenues, resulting in a surplus in the budget.

The restrictive monetary and fiscal stance had its effect on economic activity with a time lag, and the rate of growth of GNP declined from 9.8 percent in 1974 to 5.1 percent in 1975. The deceleration of economic growth was concentrated in manufacturing industries. The slowdown in industrial expansion and the strong showing of the Opposition in the November 1974 elections led to the adoption of a more expansionary monetary policy in the second

Wholesale Price Index	In Real Terms						
	Money[a]		Government Revenue		Government Expenditure		Deficit or Surplus
(1973 = 100)	Billions	Percent Change	Billions	Percent Change	Billions	Percent Change	Billions
60.2	57.58	3.6	31.82	12.5	30.04	10.8	−1.22
72.2	62.04	7.7	37.27	17.1	38.20	15.6	−0.93
85.6	73.26	18.0	43.96	17.9	44.56	16.7	−0.60
100.0	93.75	28.0	52.86	20.0	52.57	18.0	0.29
129.1	96.80	3.2	59.33	12.2	56.33	7.2	3.00
164.2	105.93	9.4	57.94	−2.3	57.89	2.8	0.04
235.3	102.41	−3.3	70.42	21.6	70.24	21.3	0.18
335.1	98.24	−4.1	72.24	2.6	71.93	2.4	0.31
461.1	100.65	2.4	75.48	4.5	74.43	3.5	1.05
80.9	66.50	4.6	52.51	—	60.02	—	−7.52
84.0	68.92	3.6	56.54	8.4	61.49	2.4	−4.95
86.3	79.07	14.7	66.62	17.8	79.73	29.7	−13.12
100.0	83.52	5.7	67.58	1.4	87.58	9.8	−20.00
122.5	82.29	−1.5	75.48	11.7	99.60	13.7	−23.98
135.3	90.42	9.9	96.61	28.0	122.04	22.5	−25.43
165.5	95.45	5.6	97.52	0.9	122.75	0.6	−25.62
233.6	85.22	−10.7	82.85	−15.0	106.51	−13.2	−23.66
270.4	96.48	13.2	150.64	81.8	187.39	80.7	−36.75
20.3	432.5	− 0.6	n.a	n.a	n.a	n.a	n.a
24.5	551.4	27.5	n.a	n.a	n.a	n.a	n.a
46.5	426.7	−22.6	n.a	n.a	n.a	n.a	n.a
100.0	357.1	−16.3	552.0	n.a	580.0	n.a	−28.0
178.5	328.0	−8.1	512.0	7.3	607.3	4.7	−95.2
307.7	312.2	−4.8	493.7	3.6	610.0	0.4	−116.3
463.4	344.4	10.3	576.0	16.7	637.0	4.4	−61.1
696.5	316.3	−8.2	619.2	7.5	644.1	1.1	−24.8
1034.6	382.5	20.9	669.1	8.1	680.8	5.7	−11.7

quarter of 1975, with the real value of the money supply rising by 9 percent for the year as a whole. Also, the budget surplus disappeared and the government undertook considerable expenditures outside the budget.

These expenditures were in large part designed to develop import-substituting industries producing intermediate products in the framework of the Second National Development Plan. The Plan called for large investments in pulp and paper, petrochemicals, fertilizer, steel, and nonferrous metals, with the objective to reach—or to approach—levels of selfsufficiency by 1979.

Investments in intermediate products were accompanied by measures taken to promote capital goods industries, utilizing a combination of import restrictions, fiscal incentives, and credit preferences. Additional measures that aimed at reducing imports in general included increases in tariffs, advance

TABLE 3.6
Real Exchange Rates, 1970–1978

	1970	1971	1972	1973	1974	1975	1976	1977	1978
Brazil									
Exchange Rate, Cruzeiro/U.S. Dollar	4.593	5.288	5.934	6.126	6.790	8.129	10.675	14.144	18.070
Index of Exchange Rate	75.0	86.3	96.9	100.0	110.8	132.7	174.3	230.9	295.0
Index of Relative Prices vis-à-vis									
the United States	73.5	85.2	96.8	100.0	108.8	126.5	173.5	232.7	297.4
Brazil's Trading Partners	79.7	91.1	100.6	100.0	106.6	126.3	173.1	229.6	288.0
Index of the Real Exchange Rate vis-à-vis									
the United States Dollar	102.0	101.3	100.1	100.0	101.8	104.9	100.5	99.2	99.2
the Currencies of Brazil's Trading Partners	94.1	94.7	96.3	100.0	103.9	105.1	100.7	100.6	102.4
Mexico									
Exchange Rate, Peso/U.S. Dollar	12.500	12.500	12.500	12.500	12.500	12.498	15.426	22.573	22.767
Index of Exchange Rate	100.0	100.0	100.0	100.0	100.0	100.0	123.4	180.6	182.1
Index of Relative Prices vis-à-vis									
the United States	98.8	99.2	97.6	100.0	103.1	104.2	121.9	162.0	174.2
Mexico's Trading Partners	103.0	103.1	99.7	100.0	103.0	104.7	122.6	161.7	170.8
Index of the Real Exchange Rate vis-à-vis									
the United States Dollar	101.2	100.8	102.5	100.0	97.0	96.0	101.2	111.5	104.5
the Currencies of Mexico's Trading Partners	97.1	97.0	100.3	100.0	97.1	95.5	100.6	111.7	106.6
Uruguay									
Exchange Rate, Peso/U.S. Dollar	0.250	0.260	0.563	0.875	1.216	2.299	3.395	4.750	6.125
Index of Exchange Rate	28.6	29.7	64.3	100.0	139.0	262.7	388.0	542.9	700.0
Index of Relative Prices vis-à-vis									
the United States	24.8	28.9	52.6	100.0	150.4	237.1	341.5	483.5	667.5
Uruguay's Trading Partners	27.9	31.7	55.7	99.9	149.1	264.4	346.4	504.4	646.8
Index of the Real Exchange Rate vis-à-vis									
the United States Dollar	115.3	102.8	122.2	100.0	92.4	110.8	113.6	112.3	104.9
the Currencies of Uruguay's Trading Partners	102.5	93.7	115.5	100.0	93.2	99.4	112.0	107.6	108.2

Sources: International Monetary Fund, *International Financial Statistics, Direction of Trade,* various issues.

deposit requirements, restrictions on private imports, and limitations on imports by public institutions and firms.

Measures were also taken to increase incentives to exports by the use of credit preferences and, subsequently, the so-called BEFIEX scheme, under which additional subsidies are provided to firms that undertake long-term export commitments. The extent of these measures was, however, substantially less than that of the measures of import protection, thereby increasing the bias against exports that had existed already in 1973. At the same time, the cruzeiro was devalued but little in real terms.

The measures taken gave rise to considerable import substitution, equalling 36 percent of import value by 1976, increasing further to 57 percent in 1977 and to 60 percent in 1978.[7] In turn, while Brazil increased its export shares in 1975, it suffered a substantial decline in 1976 and, notwithstanding subsequent increases, it reached only one-half of the gain experienced in 1975, as a proportion of exports, in 1978. Changes after 1975 may be explained by the increased emphasis given to import substitution as well as by the appreciation of the cruzeiro in real terms.

Import substitution, higher export shares, and the fall in the rate of growth of GNP in 1975 led to a reduction in Brazil's resource gap from $6.3 billion in 1974 to $4.9 billion in 1975. Total external financing declined to a lesser extent (from $8.3 billion to $7.3 billion), reflecting increased interest charges on existing debt. It was financed by foreign borrowing ($5.0 billion), foreign direct investment ($1.1 billion), and reductions in reserve holdings ($1.0 billion).

The adoption of expansionary monetary policies contributed to the acceleration of economic growth in 1976, with GNP rising by 8.7 percent. Increased import substitution, however, more than offset the higher imports attendant on the acceleration of growth and the decline in export market shares. Correspondingly, Brazil's resource gap declined from $4.9 billion in 1975 to $3.8 billion in 1976 and total external financing fell from $7.3 billion to $6.7 billion. Foreign borrowing ($7.0 billion, to which $1.0 billion of errors and omissions should be added), however, exceeded this amount as Brazil accumulated foreign exchange reserves ($2.7 billion).

In response to the acceleration of inflation, with the wholesale price index rising at an annual rate in excess of 40 percent, restrictive monetary policies were again adopted in the second half of 1976 and were maintained until mid-1977. These policies were reflected in the decline in the real value of the money supply by 3 percent in 1976 and by 4 percent in 1977. However, in 1976, government expenditures rose by 22 percent in real terms and only in 1977 did the rate of growth of these expenditures decline to 3 percent. At the same time, the growth of extra–budgetary expenditures accelerated, leading to considerable financing in domestic and in foreign capital markets.

Restrictive monetary policies contributed to a slowdown in economic expansion, with GNP rising by 4.5 percent in 1977. The resulting decline in import requirements, together with increased import substitution and the rise in export market shares, led to a further decrease in Brazil's resource gap to $1.6 billion in 1977. Total external financing requirements fell to $5.4 billion, notwithstanding the growing burden of interest payments and dividends ($3.8 billion). Foreign borrowing decreased also, from $7.0 billion in 1976 to $4.5 billion in 1977, and the decline was even greater if the $0.6 negative adjustment for errors and omissions is taken into account.

In response to the slowdown of economic activity, monetary policy became more expansionary in mid-1977, with the money supply rising at an average annual rate of 4 percent in real terms until mid-1978, when a restrictive policy was again adopted. The gross domestic product rose by 5.8 percent, while the resource gap increased to $2.7 billion and total external financing to $7.6 billion. Reserve accumulation of $4.6 billion further contributed to foreign borrowing of $9.5 billion in that year.

Data on external financing have been expressed in net terms. But, with the accumulation of foreign debt, amortization charges increased rapidly, raising Brazil's gross external financing requirements. As shown in Table 2.6, gross debt service (interest payments and amortization), expressed as a proportion of exports, increased from 42.8 percent in 1973 to 68.0 percent in 1978. In the same period, the net debt service ratio, derived by adjusting for interest receipts, rose from 37.5 percent to 63.0 percent.

With increased borrowing, the stock of foreign debt increased from $12.6 billion on December 31, 1973 to $43.5 billion at the end of 1978, representing 13.9 percent and 24.2 percent of GNP respectively. Deducting the value of net reserve holdings from these data, the relevant figures are $6.2 billion and $31.6 billion, with an increase in the ratio to GNP from 6.8 percent to 17.6 percent.[8]

Mexico

As noted above, the effects of external shocks on Mexico's balance of payments were substantially smaller than in the other two countries under study (1.4 percent of GNP in 1974 as compared to 3.5 percent in Brazil and 5.0 percent in Uruguay). At the same time, Mexico experienced substantial increases in import shares or negative import substitution, representing a loss of $1136 million which exceeded the balance-of-payments effects of external shocks ($758 million) by a substantial margin. With the decline in export market shares, giving rise to a loss of $93 million in "1972" prices, and an import saving of $8 million due to the deceleration of the growth of GNP, the resource gap increased from $0.4 billion in "1972" to $1.6 billion in 1974.

In the same period, interest payments and dividends increased from $0.8 billion to $1.6 billion, bringing total external financing requirements to $3.2 billion in 1974. The principal source of financing was foreign borrowing which rose from $0.8 billion in "1972" to $3.1 billion in 1974. The differences are smaller if adjustment is made for errors and omissions; the adjusted figures are $0.7 billion and $2.3 billion.

Negative import substitution and decreases in export market shares show the direct and indirect effects of expansionary fiscal policies followed by the Echeverria Administration from 1972. These policies involved rapid increases in government expenditures without commensurate increases in revenues. In terms of current prices, the deficit in the government budget increased from 5 billion pesos in 1971 to 17 billion pesos in 1972, 27 billion pesos in 1973, and 33 billion pesos in 1974, reaching 3.6 percent of GNP in that year. The deficit was financed in part by money creation and in part by borrowing in domestic and in foreign capital markets. The money supply rose by 18 percent in nominal terms in 1972, 22 percent in 1973, and 21 percent in 1974.

Expansionary fiscal policies contributed to inflation with a time lag. The wholesale price index rose by 16 percent in 1973 and 23 percent in 1974 as compared to an average of 3 percent in the preceding two years. With the peso-dollar exchange rate remaining at 12.50, the real exchange rate appreciated by 3 percent in both 1973 and in 1974 vis-à-vis the U.S. dollar, although the extent of appreciation was less vis-à-vis other currencies.

However, changes in wholesale prices and in the real exchange rate did not fully reflect the effects of the expansionary policies, since Mexico's close trading relationships with the United States limited the rise in domestic prices. Correspondingly, producers could not fully translate increases in wages averaging 28 percent in 1974 into higher prices, and profit margins declined, adversely affecting domestic production and hence the balance of trade. Also, expansionary policies directly affected the trade balance by reducing exportable supplies through increases in domestic demand as well as through "leaks" into higher imports.

In 1975, the budget deficit increased further in real terms. At the same time, with the continued maintenance of fixed parities, the real exchange rate appreciated by an additional one percent vis-à-vis the United States and by 2 percent vis-à-vis Mexico's major trading partners. Finally, uncertainties relating to rumored changes in Echeverria's policies and the fall of the peso in forward markets contributed to a decline in the rate of growth of GNP from 5.3 percent in 1974 to 3.5 percent in 1975.

The favorable balance-of-payments effects of lower growth rates were much overshadowed, however, by the decline in Mexico's export market shares, representing a loss of $235 million in 1975 in terms of "1972" prices. Exports were also adversely affected by the world recession while there was little change in import substitution.

The net effect of these changes was to increase Mexico's resource gap from $1.6 billion in 1974 to $2.5 billion in 1975. With interest payments and dividends of $1.9 billion, Mexico's total external financial requirements reached $4.4 billion in 1975. In the same year, foreign borrowing amounted to

$4.9 billion, or $3.6 billion if we adjust for errors and omissions, while foreign direct investment was $0.6 billion.

The budgetary deficit increased again in real terms in 1976, inflation accelerated, and the balance of payments deteriorated further. In response to these changes, on September 1, 1976 the Echeverria Administration abandoned the fixed parity of the peso. Simultaneously, however, export subsidies were eliminated and, coupled with rapid inflation in the wake of the depreciation of the peso, the competitiveness of Mexican exports declined again.

Correspondingly, Mexico's position in export markets deteriorated further. At the same time, imports fell in absolute terms in part because of import substitution in response to the depreciation of the peso, and in part because of the deceleration of economic expansion. The rate of growth of GNP declined to 1.3 percent in 1976 as unsettled conditions in financial markets, labor unrest, and land seizures undermined business confidence.

Notwithstanding the loss in export market shares, the fall in imports, together with favorable changes in the terms of trade and improvements in foreign business conditions, resulted in a decline in net external financial requirements from $2.5 billion in 1975 to $1.5 billion in 1976. The decline was only partly offset by increases in interest payments and dividends from $1.9 billion to $2.3 billion. For the first time in the seventies, Mexico reduced its foreign exchange reserves, by $0.6 billion, to finance its deficit while unsettled conditions in financial markets were reflected in errors and omissions of −$3.0 billion that partly offset foreign borrowing of $5.2 billion.

The peso reached its lowest point, with 28 pesos to the dollar, shortly before the inauguration of the Administration of Lopez Portillo in January 1977. It stabilized afterwards and remained in the 22–23 range during the next two years. The new Administration also lowered the budgetary deficit, and let the money supply decline, in real terms. And, although inflationary pressures were aggravated, the depreciation of the peso was sufficient to raise its real value in 1977 by over 10 percent above the 1976 level, irrespective of whether comparisons were made with the U.S. dollar or with the currencies of Mexico's major trading partners.

The depreciation of the real exchange rate had its principal effect on import substitution, resulting in a further decline in the constant-price value of imports, notwithstanding the increase in the growth rate of GNP from 1.3 percent in 1976 to 3.7 percent in 1977. It had less of an impact on exports as the effects of the devaluation were largely offset by the abolition of export subsidies, except that increases in the exports of petroleum added $1.0 billion to Mexico's foreign exchange earnings in 1977.

As a result of these changes, Mexico's resource gap turned into a small surplus in 1977. However, interest payments and dividends gave rise to total external financial requirements of $2.3 billion. Gross financial requirements were raised further by the amortization of Mexico's foreign debt. The gross debt service ratio was 100 percent in 1977 as compared to 67 percent in 1973.[9] Net debt service ratios were only slightly lower.[10]

The *deus ex machina* of petroleum exports added $1.8 billion to Mexico's foreign exchange earnings in 1978 and an improvement was also shown in market shares for nonfuel exports, largely reflecting the effects of the re-introduction of export subsidies. But, the return to expansionary policies, with the budget deficit increasing by one-half and the money supply by one-sixth in real terms, led to a deterioration in Mexico's balance of trade. Apart from increases in imports as a result of the 6.5 percent rise in GNP, pressures on domestic capacity and the appreciation of the real exchange rate greatly increased the extent of negative import substitution.

The ensuing deterioration in Mexico's trade balance was nearly offset by improvements in non-factor services. Nevertheless, as a result of increases in interest payments and dividends, total external financial requirements came to amount to $3.0 billion in 1978. This was largely financed by foreign borrowing ($3.0 billion), adjusted for a negative balance on errors and omissions ($0.6 billion).

With increased foreign borrowing, Mexico's gross external debt increased from $26.8 billion at the end of 1977 to $32.6 billion at the end of 1978; the corresponding figure was $8.3 billion at the end of 1973. Deducting the value of net reserve holdings, the relevant figures are $7.0 billion in 1973, $25.4 billion in 1977, and $30.7 billion in 1978, representing 13.3 percent, 31.5 percent, and 33.4 percent of the gross domestic product, respectively. The gross debt service ratio reached 113 percent, and the net debt service ratio attained 109 percent, in 1978.

Uruguay

Among the three countries under study, Uruguay suffered the largest external shocks in 1974, amounting to 5.0 percent of its GNP, largely on account of the deterioration of its terms of trade. In response to this situation, the government reduced the rate of growth of the money supply from 80 percent in 1973 to 64 percent in 1974. With rapid inflation, the real value of the money supply fell by 8 percent.

But the high rate of inflation also led to reductions in the real value of government revenue and increases in the budget deficit. Furthermore, Uruguay failed to devalue *pari passu* with inflation, so that the real exchange rate appreciated by 7 percent between 1973 and 1974, irrespective of whether comparisons are made with the United States or with Uruguay's principal trading partners.

With the fall in the real exchange rate changes in export shares and in import substitution were small. Correspondingly, the government relied on foreign borrowing to finance its resource gap. Foreign borrowing reportedly amounted to $160 million, as compared to total external financing of $136 million, of which interest payments and dividends represented $47 million. With negative errors and omissions of $82 million partly compensating for reported foreign borrowing, Uruguay also drew on its reserves in the amount of $40 million.

Important policy changes were made in July 1974. They included decontrolling domestic prices, eliminating import quotas, and abolishing minimum foreign financing requirments for imports, with exceptions made for capital goods in the latter case. Also, the indexing of financial obligations was introduced and interest rates raised so as to stimulate domestic savings, and foreign capital movements were liberalized. Finally, the system of mini-devaluations was adjusted so as to depreciate the peso in real terms.

In 1975, the depreciation of the real exchange rate approximately offset its appreciation in 1974 vis-à-vis the currencies of Uruguay's principal trading partners, and a devaluation of 11 percent occurred vis-à-vis the U.S. dollar. Also, tariffs were lowered while nontraditional exports received tax and tariff rebates, preferential credits, and tax relief. As a result of the imposition of these measures, the longstanding bias against exports and in favor of import substitution was reduced to a considerable extent.

The liberalization of the economy led to an acceleration of economic growth in late 1974 and in 1975, with GNP rising by 3.4 percent in 1974 and 3.9 percent in 1975, following a decline in the early seventies. Higher growth rates, and reductions in protection, in turn, led to greater imports, although these changes were overshadowed by increases in export market shares that represented a response to improved export incentives.

But, with the continued deterioration in its terms of trade, due largely to a fall in beef and wool prices, Uruguay's resource gap increased from $89 million in 1974 to $118 million in 1975. Total financial requirements were raised further by interest payments and dividends of $75 million and Uruguay again relied on foreign borrowing ($165 million, reduced by negative errors and omissions of $38 million) and on reductions in reserve holdings ($62 billion) to provide the necessary financing.

Monetary policies became increasingly restrictive in mid-1975 and government expenditures were reduced at the same time, although the budget deficit did not decline until the following year. These measures contributed to a slowdown in the rate of economic expansion, with GNP rising by 2.5 percent in 1976. At the same time, the measures taken earlier, together with the further depreciation of the real exchange rate, led to explosive increases in exports, in particular manufactured exports. In 1976, three-tenths of exports represented increases in export market shares over "1972." Expressed differently, actual exports were 44 percent higher than hypothetical exports, calculated under the assumption of unchanged market shares. The corresponding figure was 212 percent for manufactured exports, 16 percent for traditional exports, and 23 percent for nontraditional primary exports.

The resulting increase in exports by $124 million in terms of "1972" prices was responsible for the net positive effects of domestic policy measures that amounted to $115 million in 1976, again expressed in "1972" prices. Correspondingly, Uruguay's resource gap was eliminated in 1976 although interest payments and dividends gave rise to total financial requirements of $78 million. With the rebuilding of reserves ($73 million) and a small negative balance on errors and omission ($13 million), foreign borrowing was $160 million in 1976.

Foreign borrowing increased in 1977, amounting to $238 million, to which $35 million for errors and omissions should be added. Much of the proceeds of foreign loans went into increases in reserves ($179 million), while the resource gap was $83 million and interest payments and dividends $79 million. An important factor contributing to the increase in the resource gap was the decline in beef exports that resulted from the application of protectionist policies in the European Common Market. Manufactured exports continued their favorable performance while a decline in the export shares of nontraditional primary exports is shown.

At the same time, the acceleration of economic growth, with GNP rising by 3.7 percent in 1977, contributed to increased imports while there was little import substitution. All in all, the net positive balance-of-payments effects of domestic policy measures are estimated at $63 million as compared to $115 million a year earlier. Note, however, that under the methodology utilized, the effects of Common Market protection on Uruguay's beef imports are represented as a decline in export market shares.

Beef exports declined further in 1978, but gains in the exports of nontraditional primary products and manufactured goods more than compensated for the resulting loss in export market shares. There was also some import substitution in 1978 that was more than offset by higher imports associated with a GNP growth rate of 3.8 percent.

With domestic policies leading to improvements in the balance of payments throughout the 1974–78 period and the growth of exports accelerating, the rise in the gross debt service ratio from 32.9 percent in 1973 to 35.9 in 1975 was followed by decreases to 25.6 percent in 1976 and 24.5 percent in 1977. And, notwithstanding an increase to 30.1 percent in 1978, the 1973 level was not exceeded in that year.[11]

Uruguay's external debt increased from $369 million at the end of 1973 to $866 million at the end of 1978, with its ratio to GNP rising from 12.2 percent to 16.8 percent during this period. Adjusting for net reserves, the relevant figures were $168 million and $17 million, representing 5.6 percent and 0.3 percent of the gross national product, respectively.[12]

Conclusions

This essay has examined the impact of external shocks in the form of the quadrupling of oil prices in 1973–74 and the world recession of 1974–75, followed by a slow recovery, on three Latin American countries, Brazil, Mexico, and Uruguay. In so doing, separate consideration has been given to terms of trade effects and to export volume effects. The essay has further analyzed policy responses to these shocks, involving additional net external financing, export promotion, import substitution, and lowering the rate of economic growth.

It has been shown that, in the 1974–78 period, terms of trade effects were far more important than export volume effects in Brazil and Uruguay, which import much of their energy requirements. On the average, export volume effects were exceeded by terms of trade effects even in Mexico that benefited from the high price of petroleum, the exports of which assumed importance from 1977. At the same time, the adverse export volume effects of lower economic growth rates in the developed countries were partly offset by increases in their propensity to import manufactured goods from the developing countries.

Among the countries under study, Brazil did not follow consistent macro-economic policies during the period under consideration but, on the whole, aimed at maintaining rapid effects of external shocks. At the same time, it oriented public investment largely towards import substitution in intermediate products, increased the protection of domestic industry, and favored import-substituting industries in the allocation of preferential credits.

The measures applied led to a considerable degree of import substitution in Brazil where, after increases in 1975, export shares declined again. At the same time, import substitution proved to be increasingly costly, leading to a rise of incremental capital-output ratios from 2.3 in 1963–73 to 3.1 in 1973–76 and 4.3 in 1976–79; the ratio was 1.7 in the 1970–73 period, when growth was especially rapid (Table 2.7).

With small increases in the share of gross fixed capital formation in GDP, expressed in terms of constant prices, the rise in incremental capital-output ratios resulted in a decline in the rate of economic growth in Brazil. At the same time, data expressed in terms of current prices indicate that the inflow of capital did not modify the allocation of resources between consumption and investment.

It would appear, then, that a substantial part of foreign borrowing went into consumption, while the remainder, together with domestic savings, was invested in activities that bring lower returns than had been the case in the past. This finding suggests the need for improving the efficiency of the allocation of investment funds. This objective would be served by reducing the scope of government investment, making this more responsive to efficiency criteria, lessening the anti-export bias in the incentive system, and reducing the scope of preferential credits while adopting positive real interest rates.

Some steps in this direction were taken in 1979 and in the first half of 1980 under successive Planning Ministers, Mario Henrique Simonsen and Antonio

Delfin Netto, reducing the size of the public investment budget and modifying the system of incentives. Still, more needs to be done in introducing rigorous project evaluation in the public sector and improving incentives to exports vis-à-vis import substitution. Furthermore, given Brazil's large indebtedness and the 120 percent rise in petroleum prices between 1978 and mid-1980, a reduction in the rate of economic growth could not be foregone. This conclusion is strengthened if we consider the need to lower the rate of inflation that reached 100 percent in the first half of 1980.

In Mexico, an internal shock—the ambitious public expenditure program of President Echeverria, undertaken without adequate financing—dominated external shocks. With the exchange rate maintained unchanged until nearly the end of the Echeverria Administration, unsustainable balance-of-payments deficits emerged while labor unrest and land seizures undermined business confidence.

Confidence was re-established in the first year of Lopez Portillo's Administration, which also limited money creation and the expansion of government expenditure. Monetary expansion accelerated, however, in the following year and the budget deficit increased again, approaching 5 percent of GNP. The budget deficit, in turn, led to rapid increases in the real value of the money supply.

As a result, the rate of inflation accelerated, exceeding 30 percent in the first half of 1980 and there was a considerable spillover into higher imports. Also, notwithstanding the rapid rise in oil earnings, Mexico continued to borrow abroad, thereby avoiding the depreciation of the peso. At the same time, with the exchange rate remaining in the narrow range of 22.5–23.0 pesos to the dollar in the face of rapid inflation, the competitive position of Mexican exports again deteriorated. Finally, while some import liberalization occurred in 1977, the appreciation of the peso in real terms led to increased demands for protection.

These considerations point to the need to reduce reliance on foreign borrowing and to accept exchange rate changes for the sake of improving the competitiveness of the non-oil sector in Mexico. This could require, first of all, lowering the budget deficit. It would further be necessary to introduce rigorous project evaluation for public investment.

Apart from increasing the competitiveness of Mexican agriculture and industry, the proposed measures would reduce inflationary pressures and contribute to the efficiency of investment. As shown in Table 2.7, incremental capital-output ratios rose from 3.0 in 1963–73 to 4.1 in 1973–79; the ratio was 3.1 in 1970–73.

Among the three countries under study, Uruguay suffered by far the greatest external shocks, the effects of which continued throughout the period under consideration. The government used the occasion of the external shocks to undertake long overdue reforms of the incentive system and to shift resources from the public to the private sector, by reducing the budget deficit from about four percent of GNP in 1974 and 1975 to less than one percent in 1977 and 1978.

These reforms led to the rapid expansion of exports and decreases in incremental capital-output ratios from 9.6 in 1963–73 to 3.6 in 1973–76 and 3.3 in 1976–79 (the ratio was negative in 1971–73 when Uruguay's GNP declined). With the rise in the share of gross domestic capital formation in GNP, expressed in constant prices, from 10.4 percent in 1964–73 to 13.6 percent in 1974–76 and 18.5 percent in 1977–79, after near-stagnation in the decade preceding the quadrupling of petroleum prices, Uruguay experienced rapid economic growth. The average annual rate of growth of GNP was 3.3 percent between 1973 and 1976; it rose to 5.0 percent between 1976 and 1979, with a rate of growth of 8.4 percent in 1979.

As a result of greater export orientation, rapid economic growth was attained with only a temporary increase in Uruguay's indebtedness. Thus, external debt, adjusted for net reserves other than gold, accounted for the same proportion of GNP at the end of 1978 as five years earlier; the ratio declined to a considerable extent if account is taken of the revaluation of gold holdings that is included in the value of net reserves reported in Table 2.6.

The case of Uruguay shows that incentive reforms may permit surmounting the effects of sizable external shocks. At the same time, further reforms would be necessary in order to fully utilize the country's growth potential. These would involve additional reductions in tariffs and the rationalization of agricultural interventions. Also, there is need to avoid an appreciation of the currency in real terms that is said to be desired for the sake of reducing the rate of inflation.

The results further show the contrast between the policies followed by Uruguay and Brazil, the two countries that experienced external shocks of considerable magnitude after 1973. Uruguay was able to surmount these shocks without a rise in its external debt ratio by turning towards outward-orientation and increasing reliance on the private sector. In turn, Brazil increased the bias in the incentive system in favor of import substitution and against exports, it further promoted import substitution through public investments, and accepted a considerable increase in its external debt for the purpose of maintaining rapid economic growth.

Nonetheless, with increases in incremental capital-output ratios, the rate of growth of GNP declined in Brazil while the opposite was the case in Uruguay. As a result, in the 1976–79 period, the growth rate of GNP of Uruguay came to exceed that of Brazil, with an acceleration shown in the former and a deceleration in the latter during this period. The differences are even larger in per capita terms; 4.3 percent in Uruguay and 2.4 percent in Brazil between 1976 and 1979. The corresponding figure was 2.5 percent in Mexico, where this result was attained at the expense of rapid increases in the external debt.

ESSAY 4

The "New Protectionism" and the International Economy

I. Trade Liberalization in the Postwar Period

The Progress of Trade Liberalization

The postwar period saw steady progress in trade liberalization until the oil crisis and the world recession of 1974–75. Apart from liberalizing quantitative restrictions imposed on imports during the depression of the nineteen-thirties and the Second World War, efforts were concentrated on lowering tariffs. Reductions in tariffs originally aimed at reversing the increases effectuated during the depression, but they were subsequently lowered much below pre-1930 levels.[1]

Tariff reductions were undertaken in the framework of the General Agreements on Tariffs and Trade (GATT) on the basis of the dual principles of nondiscrimination and reciprocity. Nondiscrimination means that, customs unions and free trade areas apart, reductions in tariff barriers extended to all participating countries under the application of the most-favored-nation (MFN) clause. In turn, reciprocity means that, in negotiating tariff concessions, an attempt is made to balance the interests of the participating countries.

During the nineteen-fifties, trade liberalization proceeded on the basis of item-by-item negotiations, with the participating countries making offers to each other to lower tariffs in exchange for tariff reductions on items of export interest to them. After initial successes, this procedure became increasingly cumbersome and was superseded by across-the-board tariff reductions, first in the Dillon round and subsequently in the Kennedy round of negotiations, with exceptions made for so-called sensitive items.

Although most developing countries did not actively participate in trade negotiations in the framework of GATT, they enjoyed the benefits of tariff reductions being automatically extended to them under the application of the

MFN clause. Indeed, it appears that the benefits of multilateral trade liberalization for the developing countries far exceeded the benefits they have derived from the application of the Generalized System of Preferences which, despite its name, has remained limited in scope.[2] And while the elimination of tariffs on the intra-area trade in the framework of the European Economic Community and the European Free Trade Association favored imports from the partner countries over imports from outsiders, including the developing countries, tariffs on these imports were reduced on the average by one-half during the nineteen-sixties. At the same time, the developing countries benefited from increased demand for their exports that accompanied the acceleration of economic growth in Western Europe following the success of integration efforts.[3]

Trade liberalization pertained largely to raw materials and to manufactured goods while food imports remained subject to barriers. As tariffs on most raw materials were reduced to low levels by the mid-fifties, in this essay emphasis will be given to trade in manufactured goods.[4] This choice is also warranted by reason of the fact that trade in manufactured products had to bear the brunt of the "new protectionism" since 1973 and that prospective changes in the international division of labor between developed and developing countries affect primarily these commodities.

International Trade and Economic Growth

As noted above, the elimination of barriers to intra-area trade contributed to the acceleration of economic growth in Western Europe. More generally, the expansion of international trade has favorable effects on economic growth. Apart from improvements in resource allocation according to comparative advantage, these effects find their origin in the exploitation of large-scale economies through the construction of larger plants (the traditional form of economies of scale), reductions in product variety in individual plants (horizontal specialization), and greater specialization in the production of parts, components, and accessories (vertical specialization), as well as in technological change that is stimulated by foreign competition. Rapid economic growth, in turn, contributes to increased imports, thereby extending the gains to other countries.

Ragnar Nurkse suggested that the effects of trade on economic growth are indicated not by "the *average* ratio of world trade to world production [but by] the *incremental* relationship between trade and production . . ."[5] He noted that such a relationship was observed during the nineteenth century, when the expansion of international trade at a rate much exceeding that of domestic production importantly contributed to economic growth in the industrial countries. Economic growth was, in turn, transmitted to other countries of the world as the industrial countries' imports of primary products rose at a substantially higher rate than their national income.

Nurkse claimed, however, that "the world's industrial centers in the mid-twentieth century are not 'exporting' their own rate of growth to the primary-producing countries through a corresponding expansion of demand for primary products"[6] and that the developing countries face difficulties in exporting manufactured goods to the industrial countries. According to Nurkse, "Industrialization for export markets may encounter . . . difficulties on the supply side. In the scale of comparative advantage there may be a wide gap, or at any rate a certain discontinuity, between the traditional primary products and the new manufactured goods which a country would seek to export . . . Equally serious are the obstacles which industrialization for export is liable to encounter on the side of external demand"[7] due to protection in the industrial countries.

These pessimistic views, subsequently given increased emphasis by writers such as Gunnar Myrdal[8] and Raul Prebisch[9], were not borne out by the facts. To begin with, an "incremental relationship" between exports and production in the industrial countries was obtained also during the postwar period as their exports rose much more rapidly than their gross national product. Between 1953, the first "normal" postwar year, and 1960, when the effects of tariff reductions in the EEC and EFTA began to be felt, the export volume of the industrial countries increased at an average annual rate of 7.0 percent while their combined GNP rose 3.6 percent a year.[10]

The industrial countries' imports of primary products from the developing countries also increased more rapidly than their combined GNP. These imports rose at an average annual rate of 5.1 percent between 1953 and 1960, exceeding the GNP growth of the industrial countries by about one-half, with even larger increases shown in regard to manufactured goods.[11] At the same time, the export performance of a number of developing countries was adversely affected by their own policies: the bias against exports in countries pursuing import substitution policies led to a loss in their world shares in primary exports[12] and forestalled the emergence of manufactured exports.

Developments Until the Oil Crisis

The observed trends in trade and growth continued and even accelerated after 1960 when trade liberalization in the framework of the Dillon and the Kennedy rounds, integration in Western Europe, and the adoption of export-oriented policies in several developing countries gave added impetus to world trade. The exports of the developed countries rose at an average annual rate of 8.8 percent between 1960 and 1973,[13] the last year before the quadrupling of oil prices and the world recession, exceeding the growth of their combined GNP, estimated at 4.8 percent a year, by a considerable margin.

Economic growth in the developed nations led to a rapid rise of their imports from the developing countries, with increases averaging 7.2 percent a year between 1960 and 1973. The imports of manufactured goods rose especially rapidly, far exceeding earlier projections. Thus, while the United Nations foresaw an increase of only 60 percent during the sixties, these imports increased fivefold between 1960 and 1970 and their rate of growth averaged 18.3 percent between 1960 and 1973.[14] But, the imports of primary commodities from the developing countries also rose at an average annual rate of 7.2 percent, during the 1960–1973 period, notwithstanding losses in market shares in some of those countries that continued to follow policies biased against imports.

Policy differences were of particular importance for trade in manufactured goods. Within the developing country group, the largest export increases were experienced in countries that applied export-oriented policies and liberalized their imports. Thus, Korea, Singapore, and Taiwan, which first adopted such policies, increased their share in the combined exports of manufactured goods by developing countries from 2.7 percent in 1960 to 32.7 percent in 1973. By contrast, the share of India, a country that continued with protectionist policies throughout the period, fell from 24.6 percent in 1960 to 6.6 percent in 1973.[15]

The rise in their foreign exchange earnings allowed the developing countries to increase their imports from the developed nations at a rapid rate. These imports rose 6.2 percent a year between 1960 and 1973, with manufactured imports growing at an average annual rate of 6.5 percent. As a result, by 1973, the developing countries provided markets for 37.7 percent of the manufactured exports of the developed nations, excluding trade between the United States and Canada as well as within the European free trade area in manufactured goods.[16]

II. Oil Crisis, World Recession, and Protectionist Pressures

The Post-1973 Situation

It has been shown that the rapid expansion of foreign trade contributed to economic growth in the developed countries during the postwar period. Growth in the developed countries, in turn, was transmitted to the developing countries through trade. At the same time, imports by the developing countries provided an important market for the manufactured exports of the developed countries.

These changes occurred in an atmosphere marked by progressive trade liberalization on the part of the developed nations and by the adoption of export-oriented policies, accompanied by reduced protection, in several developing countries. The atmosphere was marred only by quantitative import restrictions, pertaining chiefly to Japanese exports, and by the adoption of the International Cotton Textiles and, subsequently, Multifiber Arrangement. Nevertheless, the Multifiber Arrangement provided for an annual growth of 6 percent in the exports of textiles and clothing and, as a result of increases in their quota allocation and the upgrading of their export products, the volume of the developing countries' exports of textiles and clothing rose substantially faster.[17]

The situation changed as the quadrupling of oil prices aggravated the recession that followed the 1972–73 world economic boom. In adding to inflationary pressures, the oil price increase led to stronger anti-inflationary measures on the part of the developed countries than would have been otherwise the case. The recession was further aggravated by policy reactions on the part of the developed countries to the increase in their combined balance-of-trade deficit vis-à-vis OPEC from $17.2 billion in 1973 to $66.6 billion in 1974.[18] And, while the United States has maintained a steady rate of expansion since mid-1975 without regard to its balance-of-payments consequences, in the other developed countries the desire to lower inflation rates and/or to reduce balance-of-payments deficits has not permitted economic expansion to proceed at a rate approaching capacity growth following the recession. As a result, unemployment has continued to increase in Western Europe and Japan, while it has not yet declined to pre-1973 levels following the deep recession in the United States.

High unemployment and unused capacity in a number of industries of the developed countries have contributed to the emergence of protectionist pressures, which have been intensified by reason of the continued existence of trade deficits in most developed countries. The protectionist measures proposed and actually applied, if not the extent of their application, have a certain resemblance to those observed during the depression of the nineteen-thirties.[19] They may be subsumed under the heading "new protectionism" and include various forms of non-tariff restrictions on trade, government aids under the aegis of the "rationalization of industry," as well as attempts made at the establishment of worldwide market-sharing arrangments.

Non-tariff Restrictions

As noted above, the Multifiber Arrangement, the principal case outside agriculture where non-tariff measures were applied prior to the oil crisis, provided for a 6 percent annual rate of growth in textiles and clothing exports to the developed countries. The new agreement, pertaining to the 1978–82 period, is more restrictive. While notionally setting a 6 percent annual rate of growth for the exporting countries, taken together, it leaves considerable scope for the importing countries to set lower limits through bilateral negotiations.

In fact, the European Common Market that forced the adoption of the revised rules at the behest of France and the United Kingdom, required that the largest developing country exporters reduce their 1978 exports of textiles and clothing to the EEC below the 1976 level (the relevant figures are −9 percent for Hong Kong, −7 percent for Korea, and −25 percent for Taiwan). And while better overall terms are provided to very poor countries, the total imports of eight sensitive products, accounting for 62 percent of EEC imports of textiles and clothing from developing countries, will decline below the 1976 level in 1978 and will increase slowly afterwards, with growth rates in the 1978–82 period ranging from 0.3 percent a year for cotton yarn to 4.1 percent a year for sweaters.[20] Import growth rates were also set at less than 6 percent a year for another important group of clothing products, so that the rate of growth of the imports of textiles and clothing into the EEC will remain much below 6 percent.

The United States reached agreements with Hong Kong, Korea, and Taiwan to freeze their 1978 exports of textiles and clothing to the U.S. at the 1977 level and to increase the exports of a number of sensitive items, accounting for about 70 percent of exports in the case of Korea, at a rate substantially less than 6 percent afterwards. Taking further account of bilateral agreements negotiated with other countries, it is apparent that the 6 percent annual rate of growth of the imports of textiles and clothing under the Multifiber Arrangement will not be attained in the United States either.

In regard to steel, the European Common Market established guideline prices for five product groups and a mandatory minimum price for reinforcing bars in 1976. As of January 1978, basic or reference prices were set for all products based on the lowest foreign (i.e., Japanese) production costs adjusted for transport costs. Imports below the reference price come under anti-dumping rules, with a levy imposed in the amount of the price difference. This scheme is assumed to be temporary, to be replaced by bilateral agreements negotiated with steel exporting countries. The Commission subsequently negotiated agreements with some 20 countries to accept the same share in the EEC market in 1978 as they had in 1976, implying an average cut in steel imports by 8 percent from the 1977 level.[21] The cuts would be larger for the new developing country exporters that increased their steel exports to a considerable extent between 1976 and 1977.

In establishing reference prices for steel, the EEC Commission drew on the Solomon-plan in the United States that came into effect in February 1978. Under the plan, the reference or trigger prices were set on the basis of assumed Japanese production costs and the cost of shipping to U.S. markets. Correspondingly, the reference prices rise, and the chance of effective import competition declines, as one moves from West to East.[22]

The adoption of import restrictions in regard to textiles and steel is a manifestation of protectionist tendencies that have emerged in recent years. In the United States, the practical application of the provisions of the 1974 Trade Act also points in this direction. Under the Act, the U.S. Treasury has to reach a decision within one year after petitions are filed requesting the imposition of countervailing duties on exports that are allegedly subsidized by foreign countries, and countervailing action was extended to duty free imports, including those entering under the generalized preference scheme. In turn, dumping was redefined as selling at less than full production cost, including a margin for profit, rather than at less than the domestic sales price as beforehand.

The Trade Act also weakened the conditions for escape-clause action by requiring only that imports are "a substantial cause of serious injury, or the threat thereof" while previously such action could be taken only if imports were "the major cause" of serious injury *and* the increase in imports causing or threatening the injury was the result of previous trade concessions. Furthermore, "orderly marketing agreements," representing negotiated restrictions on exports to the United States, were introduced in the arsenal of protectionist measures. Finally, the two houses of Congress can overrule the President if he rejects recommendations made by the International Trade Commission on anti-dumping and escape clause action.

While the Trade Act of 1974 also liberalized the conditions for granting adjustment assistance to help domestic industries adversely affected by imports, it is the possibilities provided for the use of protective measures that have come to be increasingly utilized. To begin with, there was a substantial increase in positive findings in countervailing duty cases; there were thirty-four positive findings in the years 1974–77 as compared to thirteen in the preceding 11 years. And, at least in one case, the criteria for imposing countervailing duties were modified to the detriment of foreign exporters.[23]

The number of anti-dumping cases also increased after 1974 and the recent interpretation of production costs in the exporting countries may give impetus to further increases in the future. Thus, the Treasury established a formula for steel based on the "constructed value" of Japanese production costs plus an arbitrary markup of 10 percent for general expenses and another 8 percent for profits, both of which are far above the industry average.[24]

At the same time, the International Trade Commission became active in its investigation of complaints that imports are harming domestic industries— even if this may involve encroaching on the territory of other governmental organizations.[25] It issued 42 decisions in 1976 as compared to 15 in 1975, with the amount of imports affected rising from $248 million in 1975 to $1.9 billion in 1976, and surpassing $5 billion in 1977.[26] Finally, although President Carter overruled ITC recommendations in several cases, some important decisions favored protectionist interests.

Apart from steel and textiles, particular instances are orderly marketing agreements with Japan on color television sets and with Korea and Taiwan on footwear, both in 1977. In the first case, imports were limited to 1.75 million sets a year until 1980, representing a 40 percent reduction from the 1976 level. In the second case, import limitations apply until 1981 and, despite annual increases in quotas, the 1976 level would not be reached by the end of the four-year period of the agreement. The application of protectionist measures in these well-publicized cases, in turn, contributed to demands for protection in industries such as citizen-band radios, electric ovens, railroad equipment, bicycle tires and tubes, copper, and zinc.

The taking of protectionist measures by the Carter Administration was rationalized on the grounds that these help to forestall more drastic action by Congress. At the same time, according to *The Wall Street Journal* "the sentiment in Congress for protectionism is rising again." This reflects increased protectionist pressures emanating largely from labor,[28] with labor and industry joining forces whenever they perceive a common interest.[29]

It should be emphasized that, whatever the outcome, protectionist demands create uncertainty for exporters. Thus, demands for countervailing or anti-dumping action may induce foreign producers to limit exports to the United States for fear of a financial loss in the form of the payment of additional duties for which they have to put up a bond.[30] More generally, even if they ultimately prove unsuccessful, protectionist demands are reportedly initiated in the expectation that foreign producers will cut back their expansion plans for the U.S. market.[31]

Protectionist pressures also increased in Western Europe, in particular in Britain and France. In Britain, the Cambridge Group provided theoretical justification for the protectionist attitude taken by the Labor government[32] while in France protectionism has political backing from the right as well as from the left. Notwithstanding the generally liberal attitudes in Germany and Italy,[33] the position taken by these two countries apparently influenced the Common Market Commission, as evidenced by the imposition of strict limits on the importation of textiles and clothing as well as the increased reliance on countervailing and anti-dumping legislation.[34]

At the same time, while the application of protectionist measures in the United States is circumscribed by legislation, in Western Europe as well as in Japan, protectionism often takes the form of discretionary measures by national governments. Such "occult" measures, which do not find their origin in legislation, present a particular danger for foreign countries, and especially for developing countries, both because legal recourse is lacking and because they create additional uncertainty.

Limiting attention to protectionist measures actually taken by the industrial countries, one may cite an estimate by the GATT Secretariat, according to which the application of these measures over the last two years has led to restrictions on 3 to 5 percent of world trade flows, amounting to $30–50 billion a year.[35] Reference may further be made to a list prepared by the Taiwanese government on restrictions affecting manufactured exports. The list includes one item for 1975, nine items for 1976, and 33 items for 1977, of which seven are still under investigation.

Government Aids to Industry

Prior to the oil crisis, government aids were used in the major European countries as well as in the United States principally in favor of the shipbuilding industry. Furthermore, regional aids provided in Western Europe benefited certain industries that are concentrated in depressed regions.

Government aids, often granted under the heading "rationalization", came into greater use after the 1974–75 recession. They take a variety of forms, including direct subsidies as well as preferential tax and credit treatment. These aids provide indirect protection to domestic industry by reducing its production or sales costs.

The German government provides 75 to 90 percent of the difference between the full-time wage and the wage earned by workers who had to be put on a part-time basis because of unfavorable business conditions. This scheme subsidizes weak industries indirectly as they are likely to have proportionately more part-time workers. In turn, other European countries have directly or indirectly subsidized employment. These measures, together with the introduction of regulations making it difficult to fire workers, contributed to labor hoarding.

A case in point is the British Temporary Employment Subsidy Scheme that compensates firms for keeping workers on the job who would otherwise be no longer needed. In 1977, about one-half of benefits under this scheme accrued to textiles, clothing, and footwear industries that reportedly received a subsidy equivalent to about 5-10 percent of their total production cost. At the same time, as *The Economist*[36] notes, little effort was made to put pressure on subsidized companies to rationalize their operations. It would appear, then, that the subsidy provides an additional protection to the three industries without contributing to adjustment.

While employment schemes are not industry-specific, they tend to benefit labor-intensive industries which have higher than average unemployment rates. In several countries, government aids were also provided to specific industries. This is the case in particular in France where the automobile, data-processing, pulp and paper, steel, and watch industries received various forms of government aids. Whatever their avowed purpose, these aids will shore up, and hence protect, weak industries that find it difficult to face foreign competition. The takeover of insolvent firms by the government, and the financing of their deficits as well as the deficits of other state-owned firms from public funds, had similar effect in Italy.

Government aids applied by the individual Common Market countries discriminate against imports from member as well as from non-member countries. In turn, in several instances, actions were proposed, or were actually taken, on the Common Market level. To begin with, the EEC steel industry has a legalized cartel, Eurofer, which ensures compliance with minimum prices and also sets quotas for market sharing among producers. Furthermore, the Common Market provided financial aid to the steel industry under the Treaty establishing the Coal and Steel Community; the regional fund will reportedly be doubled between 1974 and 1981, in large part to provide assistance to the steel industry; and the EEC Commission is preparing a sectoral policy for steel.[37]

The Common Market countries also contemplate taking joint action on shipbuilding and synthetic fibers. For one thing, the EEC Commission demanded that Japan cut back its exports of ships[38] and proposals were made for establishing a credit scheme aimed at financing domestic shipbuilding. For another thing, it was proposed to establish a production cartel for synthetic fibers, and "a common market plan to ease the financial pain of redundancies"[39] is reportedly in preparation.

Apart from shipbuilding where subsidies have long been used, under the Solomon-plan the United States will use a variety of measures, including loan guarantees, accelerated depreciation provisions, and subsidies to research, to aid the domestic steel industry. Also, a variety of export promotion measures are reportedly under consideration.[40]

In Japan, a bill containing special measures for aiding certain industries in difficulties was introduced in February 1978. The bill aims at providing assistance to the aluminum, shipbuilding, steel, and synthetic fiber industries, formalizing and extending aids that have been provided in the past. Its application may also be extended to other industries, some of which have been beneficiaries of government assistance in the past.[41]

International Cartels and Market-Sharing

While government aids under the guise of the rationalization of domestic industries led to moves aimed at cartelization in the steel, shipbuilding, and synthetic fiber industries in the European Common Market, proposals were further advanced for cartelization on the world level. In this connection, reference may be made to statements by Raymond Barre, the French Prime Minister, "to define collective rules for an orderly growth of international trade . . . "[42] in the framework of "a genuine organization of international trade" and "organized liberalism".[43] It was proposed that the definition of "collectively defined and applied rules which will generate conditions for growth security and dependability in trade . . . should be one of the main objectives of the international negotiations to be held in the coming months; they must not simply repeat the negotiations of the last 20 years."[44]

Negotiations on the organization of international trade would cover a variety of industries, including steel and shipbuilding that have experienced worldwide overcapacity; some sophisticated industries, such as aircraft and computers, where the United States is in a particularly strong position and infant industry arguments are invoked in favor of European producers; 45 as well as industries such as textiles, shoes and electronics, where competition on the part of developing countries and Japan is feared.[46]

While the purpose of the French government's proposals may have been to take the wind out of the sails of the domestic opposition and were not again voiced since the parliamentary elections held in March 1978, moves toward the establishment of world-wide cartels were made in the shipbuilding and steel industries. In the shipbuilding inudstry, market sharing arrangements were proposed in the framework of the Organisation for Economic Co-operation and Development (OECD) entailing a division of new orders between the

European countries, Japan, and the developing countries, together with increases in the prices charged by Japanese producers (*Business Week,* December 5, 1977). In the steel industry, earlier reports that a steel working-group established in the framework of the OECD is "planning to unveil a model for an international system to monitor prices, trade, and structural changes in steel industries in the member countries [that] could provide the basis for 'sectoral' talks on steel..."[48] have been given credence by meetings of United States, Common Market, and Japanese officials allegedly aiming to establish a "world steel agreement."[49]

The Effects of the Measures Applied

The preceding section of the essay examined the emergence of the "new protectionism" in the developed countries following the oil crisis and the 1974–75 recession. It was noted that the "new protectionism" is characterized by the employment of non-tariff restrictions on trade, the granting of government aids to domestic industries, as well as attempts made at organizing world trade. This contrasts with the "old protectionism" that involves placing reliance primarily on tariffs. At the same time, various considerations indicate the superiority of tariffs over the measures employed, or proposed to be used, under the aegis of the "new protectionism".

To begin with, tariffs are instruments of the market economy. Consumers make their choice between domestic and imported goods and among alternative foreign suppliers on the basis of price, quality, delivery dates, and other product characteristics, and domestic as well as foreign producers compete in the market without government interference or quantitative limitations. Also, tariffs do not inhibit shifts in trade patterns in response to changes in comparative advantage that are reflected by changes in relative costs.

In turn, non-tariff measures interfere with the operation of the market mechanism by restricting consumer choice and limiting competition between domestic and foreign producers. The use of non-tariff measures also involves administrative discretion that introduces arbitrariness in the decision-making process, when the decisions actually taken are affected by the relative power position of various groups. With consumer groups generally having less influence on decision making than pressure groups representing various segments of labor and business, then, the "new protectionism" involves a bias towards restrictive measures.

At the same time, limiting imports in quantitative terms increases the market power of domestic producers, thus enabling them to raise prices, when restrictions applied to raw materials and intermediate products may spread forward as users seek to offset the higher prices of their inputs.[50] Also, incentives for improvements in productivity are reduced as a result and there is a tendency to freeze production patterns, thereby obstructing changes in international specialization according to shifts in comparative advantage.

Quantitative limitations on trade interfere with the market mechanism in the exporting countries, too. With allowed exports falling short of the amount producers would like to sell at the going price, they may collude or the government may apportion among them the amount that can be exported. This, in turn, may entail discriminatory pricing, with higher prices charged in export than in domestic markets. Foreign firms may also attempt to evade the restrictions through additional processing (e.g. steel), changing the basic material used (e.g. textiles), or shifting the place of production to countries which enjoy preferential treatment (e.g. television sets).

Apportioning quotas among exporting countries also involves interference with the market mechanism. Maintaining historical market shares in the allocation process discriminates against new exporters while changing market shares is subject to discretionary decision-making. At the same time, the decisions taken will be influenced by the bargaining power of the importing country and that of actual and potential exporters, generally favoring larger countries over smaller ones.

In cases where both parties can inflict damage, the possibility of retaliation will arise. An example is Australia threatening to impose embargo on uranium in retaliation to European restrictions on steel imports. A retaliatory motive is also apparent in the imposition of antidumping duties by the Common Market on kraftliner-paper imported from the United States in early 1978 as the U.S. had used similar measures against European steel products.

There is further the danger of a cumulative process. Thus, while George Meany, the Secretary General of the AFL-CIO called for "fair trade—do unto others as they do to us, barrier for barrier, closed door for closed door,"[51] measures taken by the United States for alleged offenses by others are bound to elicit foreign reactions. Apart from retaliation, this may take the form of imitative action as in the case of the imposition of trigger prices in the framework of the so-called Davignon Plan for the Common Market steel industry.

International trade is also affected by government aids to domestic industry, which came into increased use in recent years. Apart from distorting competition among the firms located in different countries, these aids represent a futher increase in the role of the state in economic life and extend the scope of bargaining. Thus, the government may wish to obtain a *quid pro quo* for its aid in the form of stipulated levels of employment, the regional allocation of production etc. At the same time, within particular industries, inducements are provided for collusive action to divide up the "spoils" and to increase bargaining power vis-à-vis the government.

Moreover, government aids become the subject of policy competition in the international arena. This first occurred in the case of shipbuilding as, Japan excepted, substantial subsidies were provided to the industry in all producing countries. Policy competition was further extended to new technologically advanced industries, such as computers and integrated circuits and, more recently, to some "old" industries, such as steel and textiles.

Note may further be taken of implicit subsidies provided in the form of preferential export credits where, despite the efforts made, the coordination of policies was not accomplished. In fact, export promotion measures are coming into increasing use, as evidenced by a statement made by K. H. Beyen, State Secretary for Economic Affairs in the Netherlands: "Rather reluctantly, we have been forced to give a certain amount of assistance to our exporting industry when it is threatened with distortion of competition by measures taken in other countries."[52]

The dangers of policy competition were first recognized by Richard Cooper in the mid-sixties, when this existed only in an embryonic form.[53] More recently, Assar Lindbeck pointed to the dangers of the trend towards greater government intervention and policy competition. In Lindbeck's view, "It could be reasonably argued that future conferences on international trade should perhaps concentrate on reducing various selective subsidies rather than cutting tariffs. That would have the additional advantage of perhaps stopping, or even reversing, the enormous concentration of economic powers to central planning administration and politicians, which is perhaps the major consequence for our societies of selective interventions."[54]

The international organization of trade was proposed, in part, in order to limit policy competition. It also represents a response to collusive action on the national level, inasmuch as national cartels would have limited power in an international economy characterized by strong trade ties among the countries concerned. Orderly marketing arrangements and other forms of quantitative restrictions, entailing the division of markets among exporting countries also gave an impetus to the international organization of trade.

These developments are apparent in the European Common Market, where measures taken on the national level to provide financial aid to particular industries and to limit imports gave rise to efforts at cartelization and trade restrictions on the Common Market level. Proposals for cartelization came from the EEC Commission in the guise of the rationalization of industry as well as from industries that expect to benefit from cartelization. Apart from the shipbuilding, steel, and synthetic fibers industries, such proposals have been put forward in regard to automobiles, chemicals, and shoes and subsequently for zinc, pulp and paper, and even hosiery.[55]

The Common Market experience points to the tendency of cartelization to spread among industries. This may occur along the chain of input-output relationships as the cartelization of an input-producing industry affects the costs of the input-using industry, or, in the form of imitative behavior. At the same time, cartelization tends to engender price increases[56] while hindering long-run improvements in productivity that may have been its raison d'être in the first place. This is because, under market-sharing arrangements, producers would derive little benefit from improving productivity as they are enjoined from expanding their sales, whereas higher-cost firms can continue their operations without having to fear competition from lower-cost rivals.[57]

An oft-cited example is the limitation imposed on the sales of small and medium-scale steel producers in Italy's Brescia region, who produce reinforcing rods and various other steel products in the framework of the EEC steel cartel. In an effort to maintain market shares, larger firms in the EEC countries that had higher production costs objected to sales by the Bresciani producer at low prices. The process of bargaining was affected by political considerations, in part because several of the high-cost firms are state-owned and in part because the governments of the individual countries wish to defend the interests of their national industries.

The difficulties multiply if the organization of trade or production is attempted on the world level, where the decisions concern not only the division of markets among the producers of a single country or of the European Common Market but among producers of the major developed and developing countries. Bargaining and international politics will now increasingly take the place of market forces, with a tendency to freeze existing patterns, thereby discriminating against new producers, obstructing changes in comparative advantage, and foregoing the benefits that may be obtained from shifts to lower-cost sources.

Finally, reference may be made to the complications introduced when the organization of trade is undertaken in industries characterized by product differentiation. Thus, in making comparisons with the Multifiber Arrangement, the view has been expressed that for an international agreement on steel "to be foolproof, the list of alloys and specifications would be so vast that any deal might well sink under a sea of paper."[58]

III. Conclusions and Policy Recommendations

The Risks of Protectionism

In Section I of this Essay it has been shown that considerable progress was made in trade liberalization during the postwar period until the oil crisis and the recession of 1974-75. The developed countries eliminated quantitative import restrictions imposed during the Second World War and substantially reduced tariffs on raw materials and on manufactured goods. Furthermore, an increasing number of developing countries adopted export-oriented policies, accompanied by reduced protection.

Trade liberalization led to the rapid growth of world trade. The expansion of world trade, in turn, contributed to economic growth in developed and developing countries alike. For one thing, export expansion favorably affected the growth performance of the developed nations. For another thing, economic growth in the developed nations was transmitted to the developing countries through trade and provided opportunities to these countries to successfully carry out export-oriented policies.

The experience of the first three postwar decades contrasts with that of the depression in the nineteen-thirties, when the imposition of non-tariff barriers, the "rationalization" of production, and the establishment of international cartels contributed to the decline in world trade.[59] The non-tariff barriers employed during the depression included increased reliance on countervailing and anti-dumping duties, as well as formal and informal (or "voluntary") quotas.[60] Governments also provided aid to their industries in the guise of rationalization and a number of international cartels were formed.[61]

It was estimated that 42 percent of world trade between 1929 and 1937 was cartelized or was subject to cartel-like arrangements.[62] The League of Nations reports that "international cartels have actually been established in all branches of industry and at practically all stages of production, from industrial raw materials to different types of producers' and consumers' finished goods; minerals and metals and their products; wood, wood-pulp and different kinds of paper; textiles; chemical and pharmaceutical products; glass, earthenware and porcelain; electrical goods, etc. Among the products covered by international cartels, manufactures are preponderant."[63]

Non-tariff measures and government aids again came into increased use after 1974 and efforts were also made to establish international cartels and cartel-like arrangements. The employment of these measures has, in turn, contributed to a slowdown in world trade. In particular, while world trade rose by 11 percent in 1976, the increase was only 4 percent in 1977 when protectionist actions increased.

The comparisons with the nineteen-thirties should not be interpreted to mean that the measures applied in recent years would be comparable in magnitude. Also, there is hope that the Tokyo-round of Multilateral Trade negotiations will suceed. At the same time, the experience of the nineteen-thirties indicates the economic costs involved in the application of these measures and the danger that they will multiply through retaliation and imitation.[64]

Policies for Long-Term Growth

Just as in the nineteen-thirties, protectionist measures have been invoked on the grounds that imports are responsible for the loss of jobs. This argument is obviously incorrect as far as trade among the developed countries is concerned as the expansion of this trade does not lead, on balance, to a decrease in employment opportunities in the developed world.

Nor is the argument valid as far as trade with the developing countries is concerned. Between 1973 and 1976, the exports of manufactured goods from the developed nations to the oil-importing developing countries increased substantially more than their imports of manufactured goods from these countries.[65] It would appear, then, that manufactured trade with the developing countries is likely to have favorable, rather than unfavorable, effects on employment in the developed nations.[66]

The high rate of unemployment in the developed nations, then, cannot be attributed to international trade. Rather, unemployment has been the result of the policies applied by these countries, which have unfavorably affected domestic production and investment in particular in Western Europe and Japan.[67] Nor can one expect that protection would reduce unemployment; it will only shift unemployment from lower-skilled labor used in import-competing industries to higher-skilled labor used in export industries.

Apart from employment considerations, the desire on the part of the individual countries to improve their balance-of-payments position created pressures for the application of protectionist measures. We find a "fallacy of composition" here as protectionist actions taken by any one country can improve its position only temporarily as the OPEC surplus must be matched by the colletive deficit of the non-oil countries.

At the same time, the taking of protectionist actions by a number of countries simultaneously cannot fail to be detrimental to all. National incomes will be lower as a result since resources are not used to best advantage and potential economies of scale obtainable in export industries are not exploited. Furthermore, protection reduces the pressure for productivity improvements in import-competing industries whereas possible improvements in export industries are foregone.

The application of protective measures is also likely to adversely affect investment activity in the developed nations. While protection may not lead to increased investment in high-cost import-competing activities which have a precarious existence, it may discourage investment in low-cost export activities which suffer discrimination under protection. The direct subsidization of high-cost activities from government funds will have similar effects by syphoning off funds that could have otherwise been used for investment in low-cost activities.

While protections tends to lower the rate of economic growth through its adverse effects on national income and investment activity, measures aimed at accelerating economic growth would reduce pressures for protection. Such measures, involving increased inducement to investment and lessening the rigidities introduced through government measures and labor legislation, would have to be carried out with special vigor in the surplus countries, particularly Germany and Japan, both to offset the deflationary effects of the appreciation of their currencies and to reduce asymmetries in the balance-of-payments of the developed countries.[68] At the same time, it should be recognized that the deficit vis-à-vis OPEC is not immutable as there are possibilities for reducing the imports of energy. This would require, in particular, the adoption of appropriate policies in the United States to lower consumption, and to increase the production, of energy.

Problems of Adjustment

It has been concluded that, in leading to higher incomes and employment, growth-oriented policies would reduce protectionist pressures in the developed countries. In turn, the avoidance of protectionism would contribute to economic growth that requires a continuing transformation of the industrial structure, entailing shifts from lower to higher productivity activities.[69] This conclusion also applies to the developing countries whose economic growth depends to a considerable extent on the availability of trade opportunities in the developed countries as well as on their own policies for making use of these opportunities.

More generally, trade permits economic growth to proceed in the world economy through shifts in product composition. This entails the developed countries increasingly specializing in research and technology intensive products; the newly-industrializing developing countries upgrading their exports which are now based largely on unskilled labor; and the less developed countries proceeding to export unskilled-labor intensive manufactures.[70]

Structural transformation cannot proceed smoothly and creates problems of adjustment in industries that decline in absolute or in relative terms. Adjustment problems, in turn, have often given rise to efforts to reduce the speed of adjustment. This has been the case, in particular, when adjustment in developed countries was presumed to have been triggered by increased imports.

The objective of reducing the speed of adjustment has been pursued by the measures of the "new protectionism" as well as by adjustment assistance as it has been applied in practice in most developed countries. Thus, in reporting the results of a comparative study, Goran Ohlin concludes that "adjustment assistance seems in practice often designed to bolster the defences against imports rather than to clear the ground for them [and] public policy has sought to delay the transfer of resources."[71]

In this connection, several questions need to be raised, including the appropriate purpose of adjustment policies, the choice between import restrictions and adjustment assistance, as well as the choice of the particular measures to be employed. These questions will be taken up briefly in the context of the industrial transformation of the developed countries.

As to the first question, adjustment policies that artificially bolster employment and raise profitability in high-cost industries by reducing the cost of labor and other inputs or by increasing the price received by producers, run counter to the process of industrial transformation that is necessary for continued growth. Rather, policies should aim at promoting the movement of resources from lower to higher productivity activities.

Nor should one single out imports as being the cause of reduced employment and profitability as, more often that not, this has been the result of technological change. Also, it is incorrect to argue that losses suffered by domestic nationals due to increased imports require different treatment than losses due to technological change on the grounds that the beneficiaries are foreign nationals in the first case and domestic nationals in the second. In fact, with higher imports leading to increased exports in the process of adjustment, the beneficiaries will be domestic nationals in the first case, too.

In view of these considerations, it is preferable to use adjustment assistance rather than import restrictions to ease the problems of adjustment to changing conditions in domestic industry. The question remains, however, what kind of adjustment measures, and government aids in general, should be utilized for this purpose.

It has been suggested that the measures applied should promote the movement of resources from lower-productivity to higher-productivity industries. This is in the interest of the developed countries as it contributes to improved resource allocation and rapid economic growth. It is also in the interest of the developing countries because of the gains they can obtain through international specialization. The community of interests is further enhanced by reason of the fact that, in contributing to the foreign exchange earnings of the developing countries, the application of the proposed measures would permit them to avoid high-cost import substitution policies that would have adverse effects for all.

The described objectives would be served if, rather than subsidizing production and employment in high-cost industries, the developed countries were to encourage the expansion of efficient activities and ensure the transfer of resources to these activities. Appropriate measures include reducing government-induced rigidities in labor markets, retraining workers, and promoting research and development.

But, adjustment assistance may not carry the entire burden, especially if sudden changes in trade flows occur, necessitating the use of safeguard measures to temporarily restrain the growth of imports. At the same time, the application of safeguard measures should be made subject to internationally-agreed upon rules with special attention given to the needs of the developing countries.[72]

ESSAY 5
The Tokyo Round And The Developing Countries

Introduction

This essay will review the results of the Tokyo Round of Multilateral Trade Negotiations (MTN) from the point of view of the developing countries. It will further make recommendations for actions that may be taken in order to ensure that the developing countries can fully exploit the opportunities the international trade framework provides following the completion of the Tokyo Round.

As an introduction to the discussion, Section I will examine recent trends in protectionism in the developed nations as they concern the developing countries. This will be followed by an evaluation of tariff reductions in the MTN on export products of interest to the developing countries, with attention given to the erosion of preferences these countries now receive under the Generalized Systems of Preferences or GSP (Section II). In Section III, the implications for the developing countries of the codes on non-tariff measures, established in the framework of the MTN, will be reviewed.

Section IV will examine the texts formulated by the so-called framework group and recommendations will be made for policies that may be applied by developing and by developed countries in matters of trade interest to the former group of countries.

I. Recent Trends in Protectionism in the Developed Countries

In the years following the oil crisis of 1973, protectionist actions by the developed countries multiplied. They included various forms of non-tariff restrictions, government aids to industry, as well as efforts made to establish international cartels. The actions taken until early 1978 were reviewed in the author's "The 'New Protectionism' and the International Economy."[1] In the same article, it was stated that the continuation of protectionist trends presents grave dangers for both the developing and the developed countries.

Since early 1978, however, there have been some favorable signs. Of particular importance is the completion of the Multilateral Trade Negotiations carried out in the framework of the Tokyo Round. This has followed earlier, rather pessimistic, forecasts about the prospective failure of the negotiations that had been given wide coverage.[2]

At the same time, fears that too much has been given away by the U.S. government to protectionist interests in exchange for their support for the MTN[3] have proved to be exaggerated. To begin .with, while the U.S. Administration promised the domestic textile industry to "tighten controls for the remaining life" of the Multifiber Arrangement and to hold 1979 textile imports at 1978 levels "where necessary to preclude further disruption," the limitations actually imposed on the subsequent use of partially-filled quotas and on quota transfers among categories do not appear to have materially affected textile imports from the developing countries. Also, the House of Representatives has defeated legislation to raise domestic sugar prices, and the quota on stainless steel and other specialty steel products has been extended for only eight months and has, at the same time, been increased by 24 percent. And, the removal of a major stumbling block in Congress through the continued preferential treatment to small-scale and minority-owned firms in government procurement will have limited impact on imports.[4]

Furthermore, since early 1978, the United States had made less use of *nontariff restrictions* that are particularly objectionable from the point of view of the developing countries. Thus, a review of the measures applied has led to the conclusion that "the earlier reliance on OMA's [orderly marketing agreements] appears to have given way to a preference for the traditional remedy of tariff measures. The change constitutes a return to reliance on the price system (as opposed to quantitative restrictions under OMAs) and to the principal of non-discrimination in commerical policy."[5]

In fact, in the seven affirmative "escape clause" decisions taken by President Carter between January 1978 and October 1979, four have entailed raising tariffs on a temporary basis and on a degressive scale and only three have involved limited imports in quantitative terms. At the same time, the latter decisions have affected developing countries only in the case of quotas on clothespins imported from Taiwan and the OMAs on color television sets originating in Korea and Taiwan, accounting for less than one percent of U.S. imports from the two countries.

In the same period, the President has rejected recommendations for escape clause action by the International Trade Commission in six cases, all of which would have affected developing country exports. And, after an upsurge in 1976, the total number of recommendations on escape-clause actions by the ITC has declined from fourteen in that year to twelve in 1977, ten in 1978, and one in the first three quarters of 1979.[6]

Furthermore, few of the applications for countervailing action against developing country exports have been positively acted upon. Thus, while the

Amalgamated Clothing and Textile Workers Union initiated countervailing duty procedures against Argentina, Colombia, India, Korea, the Philippines, Taiwan and Uruguay, the Treasury made a positive finding in the case of Uruguay only and countervailing duties have subsequently been eliminated in the latter case also.[7] More recently, the U.S. Customs Service has revoked an earlier finding that certain Mexican textile exports are subsidized by the Mexican government,[8] and the U.S. Treasury has rejected a petition by Florida growers who alleged that Mexico was selling tomatoes and other produce at unfairly low prices.[9] However, a positive finding has been made on the existence of subsidies to pig iron in Brazil.[10]

Following bilateral agreements on textiles and steel, negotiated in the framework of the Multifiber Arrangement and of the Community's steel program, there have been few cases of the application of safeguard measures in the European Common Market and none of them have involved developing countries.[11] And, although the practice of "occult" import restrictions by national authorities has continued, there are indications of an easing on the part of the two countries, France and the United Kingdom, where protectionist actions had been the most prevalent. In this condition, reference may be made to the liberal attitude taken in regard to trade with the developing countries in the orientations of the VIIIth Plan in France[12] and to the turn toward liberalism in the United Kingdom following the advent of the conservative government of Margaret Thatcher.

At the same time, the International Monetary Fund has concluded that Japan significantly liberalized imports in 1978, involving the elimination of import quotas, tariff reductions in advance of the conclusion of the Tokyo Round negotiations, as well as the expansion of credit availabilities and improvements in credit conditions for imports.[13] The process of liberalization has continued in 1979, contributing to the rapid expansion of Japanese imports from the developing countries, albeit from a relatively low base.[14]

After the proliferation of *government aids to industry* in the years following the oil crisis, changes in the opposite direction have occured in this regard also. In France, decisions have been reached to reduce the number of workers in its high-cost steel industry and to lower industrial subsidies in general,[15] while the Conservative Government of Margaret Thatcher has embarked on a program of denationalization and has announced a cutback in regional aids from $1.4 billion to $0.9 billion over a period of three years.[16] Also, in conjunction with the increased opening of its economy, government intervention in industry is on the decline in Japan. Finally, apart from shipbuilding, government intervention in industry has not been prevalent in the United States.

As far as the estalishment of *cartels* is concerned, the refusal of the EEC Commission to accept the cartel for synthetic fibers proposed by Commissioner Etienne Davignon[17] has implications beyond this industry. The decision has discouraged other industries, such as automobiles, chemicals, shoes, zinc, pulp and paper, and hosiery, from proposing the establishment of cartels they had reportedly contemplated in the event that the establishment of the synthetic fiber cartel had been countenanced.[18] Also, France has ceased to promote its earlier proposals for world-wide "organized trade" and efforts made to establish cartels on shipbuilding and steel in the framework of the OECD have not met with success.

All in all, available information on non-tariff restrictions, government aids to industry, and attempts at cartelization point to the conclusion that, since early 1978, the trend toward increased protectionism in the developed countries has not continued further and, in some respects, it has even been reversed. These changes have, in turn, contributed to an upswing in the exports of manufactured goods from the developing countries to the developed countries. While the volume of these exports grew by only 7-8 percent in 1977,[19] the increase was 15-16 percent in 1978.[20]

Increases were especially pronounced in engineering products, where the value of the exports of the developing countries to the developed countries rose by 24 percent in 1977 and by 37 percent in 1978, corresponding to a volume increase of about 15 percent in the first year and 30 percent in the second. And, notwithstanding the restrictions applied, the textile and clothing exports of the developing countries to the developed countries rose by 24 percent in value terms and by 8-9 percent in volume terms in 1978. This followed a near-stagnation in volume in the previous year,[21] and compares with increases of 2-3 percent in the consumption of textiles and clothing in the developed countries.

These relatively favorable changes should not give rise to complacency. To begin with, import restrictions on textiles and clothing, steel, and several other products of interest to the developing countries remain in effect. Also, while recent events appear to reflect an increased understanding of the adverse effects of protectionism, the time-period elapsed is too short to speak of a durable reversal of protectionist trends. Thus, economic changes, in particular the U.S. recession, as well as political developments, will influence actions that may be taken in the future, and sectoral interests continue to push for protection.

At the same time, in years to come, trade policy actions will be influenced by the rules established in the framework of the MTN. In the following, we will review the results of the Tokyo Round of negotiations from the point of view of the developing countries, examining actions related to tariffs first and the codes on non-tariff measures afterwards.

II. Tariff Reductions Under the Tokyo Round

The United States originally proposed a tariff cut of 60 percent on industrial products, whereas the European Common Market put forward a harmonization formula that would have reduced higher tariffs to a greater extent. After protracted negotiations, the Swiss formula has been accepted, under which the rate of tariff reduction is calculated as the ratio of the old tariff to itself plus 14 percent. This formula provides for less tariff harmonization than proposed by the Common Market, and it results in a smaller average tariff cut than recommended by the United States. Under the formula, a 20 percent duty will be reduced by 59 percent, a 10 percent duty by 42 percent, and a 5 percent duty by 26 percent. These tariff cuts are extended to developing countries under the most-favored-nation (MFN) clause.

Preliminary estimates show an average tariff reduction on industrial products of 38 or 33 percent, depending on whether simple or import-weighted averages are calculated. Tariff reductions are smaller on industrial products of interest to the developing countries, for which the simple average of tariff reductions is 37 percent and their weighted average 26 percent.[22]

At the same time, developing countries would experience an erosion of preferences for products that receive GSP treatment. According to an UNCTAD report,

"Practically all industrial products covered by GSP will be subject to MFN tariff cuts and there will be a significant erosion of existing GSP margins. And, in contrast to the GSP-covered products, there would be a less radical shift in the structure of tariffs affecting the bulk of the value of non-GSP-covered imports from the developing countries in the post-Tokyo period."[23]

The same UNCTAD Report presents estimates on the effect of tariff reductions in the MTN on the industrial exports of the developing countries. According to the estimates, the $1.7 billion expansion in these exports due to tariff reductions on non-GSP products, or trade creation, would be more than offset by the $2.1 billion decline in exports due to the erosion of preferences under GSP, representing a decrease in trade diversion in the markets of the preference-granting countries vis-à-vis competing developed country exporters.[24]

The UNCTAD Report does not give an indication of the methodology utilized in arriving at these results. The methodology is described in a subsequent study that has updated the UNCTAD estimates.[25] It involves utilizing estimates of price elasticities of import demand derived in an earlier Brookings study,[26] together with data on reductions in preference margins on the GSP exports, and reductions in tariffs on the non-GSP exports, of the developing countries, and relating these to the value of imports from competing developed countries in the first case and from developing countries in the second.[27] The authors estimate the decline in exports due to the partial loss of preference margins in GSP products at $1.8 billion, and the increase in industrial exports due to tarrif reductions on non-GSP products at $0.9 billion, giving rise to a net decline of $0.9 billion in the industrial exports of the developing countries to the developed countries.

The methodology used in arriving at the estimates seriously biases the results, however. This is because the decline in the exports of GSP-products due to the partial loss of preferences is calculated with respect to the *exports of the competing developed countries* while the new trade created is estimated with respect to *the exports of the developing countries* in non-GSP products. Under the assumption of identical import demand elasticities and calculating with similar percentage rates of preference reduction and tariff reduction for GSP-and and non-GSP products, respectively, the estimate decline in developing country exports of GSP goods exceeds the increase in their non-GSP exports since the exports of GSP-products by the competing developed countries is much greater than the exports of non-GSP products by the developing countries.

The trouble lies in the authors' failure to follow their own approach to its logical conclusion. Thus, they note that "the assumption underlying this approach is that the degree of substitutability between domestic products and those from all sources of imports (i.e. both developed and developing countries) embodied in elasticities for trade creation estimates holds as well for the trade diversion estimates.[28] Now, while in the case of GSP products there is *substitution against imports from competing suppliers,* in the case of non-GSP products *substitution* takes place *against domestic production in the importing countries.* With the latter exceeding the former several times, it follows that the expansion of developing country exports in non-GSP products in response to tariff reductions in the MTN will much exceed the decline in their exports in GSP-products due to reductions in their preference margin.[29]

An additional shortcoming of the estimates is that the authors fail to allow for the limitations imposed on imports from developing countries under GSP. In the United States, the imports of a particular product from a beneficiary country cannot exceed $35 million or 50 percent of total U.S. imports of the product under the so-called "competitive need" formula. In turn, in Western Europe and Japan, imports under GSP are limited by tariff quotas.

In estimating the effects of a 50 percent across-the-board tariff cut, Baldwin and Murray related imports from both beneficiaries and non-beneficiaries to domestic demand and took account of the limitations imposed on imports under GSP in the developed countries. According to their results, the $32 million decline in the developing countries' 1971 industrial exports due to the partial loss of preference margins would be far exceeded in increases in exports due to tariff reductions on non-GSP products ($27 million) and the absence of limitations on the exports of GSP-products ($106 million), to which increases in the exports of developing countries that do not enjoy GSP-treatment ($268 million) should be added.[30] At the same time, Baldwin and Murray under-estimate potential increases in the exports of non-GSP products by excluding textiles and shoes from the calculations.

Using the same methodology, but including textiles and shoes in the calculations, Murray has subsequently estimated the effects of the Tokyo Round of U.S. imports of industrial goods from Latin America. According to his results, U.S. imports of non-GSP products from Latin American countries would rise by $52 million from their 1978 level while the decline in GSP exports due to the partial loss of preferential margins would be only $10 million. The latter figure is smaller than the $24 million fall in GSP exports due to the loss of preferences on products that have been reclassified from the GSP to the non-GSP category on the basis of the "competitive need" formula in 1979. And, the expansion of Latin American exports due to the reduction of tariffs on these, recently reclassified, products has been estimated at $64 million.[31]

These results are supported by Birnberg's estimates of the effects of a 60 percent across-the-board tariff undertaken by the developed countries. The results show a $866 million increase in the 1974-75 industrial exports of the developing countries, even though textiles have been excluded from the calculations, as against a $83 million decline in their exports due to the partial loss of preferential margins. And, manufactured exports to the United States have been estimated to increase by another $111 million as a result of the application of tariff reductions to items that have been excluded from GSP under the "competitive need" formula. Estimates of export expansion for products whose exports under GSP are limited by tariff quotas have not been made for European countries and Japan.[32]

We may conclude that the opposition expressed to MFN-type tariff reductions on the grounds that the partial loss of preference margins would more than offset the increased exports of the developing countries resulting from these tariff reductions is misguided. Under reasonable assumptions, the latter will exceed the former several times. Further gains will be obtained by reason of the fact that MFN-type tariff reductions apply to products that have lost their GSP status in the United States as well as to products whose imports are limited by tariff-quotas in Western Europe and Japan.

An additional consideration is the fragility of the concessions under GSP as evidenced by the substantial shift from the GSP to the non-GSP category in the United States and by recent reductions in tariff quotas in the European Common Market. By contrast, tariff reductions in the framework of the Tokyo Round are "bound" in the sense that tariffs cannot be unilaterally raised again under GATT rules. Finally, while developing countries that "graduate" will lose GSP status, they will continue to benefit from MFN-type tariff reductions undertaken in the framework of the Tokyo Round.

III. The Codes of Non-tariff Measures

In the postwar period, trade negotiations conducted in the GATT framework concentrated on reductions in tariff barriers.[33] With reductions in tariff levels, the restrictive effects of existing non-tariff barriers became increasingly apparent (the usual simile is with the iceberg emerging as the sea level recedes). Also, increases in imports resulting from tariff reductions gave rise to the application of new non-tariff measures in favor of some adversely affected industries. Finally, in the years following the oil crisis, the desire to improve the balance of payments and to increase employment led to the use of various non-tariff measures.[34]

The Tokyo Round represents an effort to limit the use and misuse of non-tariff measures and to establish an international machinery of conflict resolution on their application. This has been done in the framework of codes dealing with subsidies and countervailing measures, customs valuation, import licensing, technical barriers to trade, and government procurement. The provisions of the individual codes will be discussed in the following, with emphasis given to their implications for developing countries.[35]

Code on Subsidies and Countervailing Measures

Section B of Article XVI of GATT, added in 1955, contains the provision that "contracting parties shall cease to grant either directly or indirectly any form of subsidies on the export of any product other than a primary product." This provision has been subscribed to by the developed countries only and it has been honored in its breach as evidenced by the number of countervailing actions since taken. Countervailing actions, involving the imposition of duties not exceeding the rate of the subsidy, may be taken under Article VI of GATT, whenever subsidies "cause or threaten material injury to an established domestic industry, or . . . retard materially the establishment of a domestic industry." Under a grandfather clause in GATT, however, the United States has not applied the injury test;[36] in fact, once the existence of foreign subsidization was established, the imposition of countervailing duties by the Treasury has been mandatory.

The Agreement of Interpretation and Application of Articles VI, XVI, and XXIII[37] of the General Agreement on Tariffs and Trade (for short, the Code on Subsidies and Countervailing Measures) reaffirms the prohibition on *export subsidies* on industrial products, further extending this to mineral products. The Annex to the Code also provides an illustrative list of export subsidy measures.

The prohibition does not apply to *domestic subsidies,* although the signatories are exhorted to attempt avoiding the adverse effects of such subsidies on foreign industries. Thus, according to the Code,

"Signatories recognize that subsidies other than export subsidies are widely used as important instruments for the promotion of social and economic policy objectives and do not intend to restrict the right of signatories to use such subsidies to achieve these and other important policy objectives . . . Signatories recognize, however, that subsidies other than export subsidies . . . may cause or threaten to cause injury to a domestic industry of another signatory or serious prejudice to the interests of another signatory or may nullify or impair benefits accruing to another signatory under the General Agreement . . . Signatories shall therefore seek to avoid causing such efforts through the use of subsidies . . ." (Article 11, Paras. 1 and 2).

The Code further provides for dispute settlement procedures concerning the use of export as well as domestic subsidies:

"Whenever a signatory has reason to believe that an export subsidy is being granted or maintained by another signatory in a manner inconsistent with the provisions of this Agreement [or] that any subsidy is being granted or maintained by another signatory and that such subsidy either causes injury to its domestic industry, nullification or impairment of benefits accruing to it under the General Agreement, or serious prejudice to its interests, such signatory may request consultations with such other signatory" (Article 12, Paras. 1 and 3).

If a mutually acceptable solution is not reached, the matter may be referred to the Committee of Signatories that will made recommendations to the parties concerned and, "in the event the recommendations are not followed, it may authorize such countermeasures as may be appropriate, taking into account the degree and nature of the adverse effects found to exist" (Article 13, Para. 4). This authorization is expressed in discretionary language; thus, the Code does not allow for unilateral retaliation by signatories in the event that the Committee has not authorized countermeasures. Correspondingly, the use of countermeasures under Section 301 of the 1974 Trade Act would put the United States in violation of its obligation under the Code.[38]

Developing countries are exempted from the obligation to forego the use of export subsidies and hence are not subject to any action by reason of the granting of export subsidies *per se.* Nor are developing countries subject to countervailing action in the event that their use of subsidies lead to the displacement of the exports of another signatory in third-country markets.

Article 14 of the Code further recognizes that "subsidies are an integral part of economic development programmes of developing countries" (Para. 1) and states that various measures of government intervention in the developing countries, such as government grants, loans, and guarantees, "shall not, *per se,* be considered subsidies" (Para. 7). And while "developing country signatories agree that export subsidies on their industrial products shall not be used in a manner which causes serious prejudice to the trade or production of another signatory" (Para. 3) and "a developing country signatory should agree or enter into a commitment to reduce or eliminate export subsidies when the use of such export subsidies is inconsistent with its competitive needs" (Para. 5), these are hortatory rather than mandatory provisions and do not create obligations for the developing countries. Finally, the provision of Para. 8 that "the Committee shall, upon the request by an interested signatory, undertake a review of a specific export subsidy practice of a developing country signatory to examine the extent to which the practice is in conformity with the obligations of this Agreement" is balanced by the provision of Para 9 allowing for "periodic reviews of measures maintained or taken by developed country signatories under the provisions of this Agreement which affect interest of a developing country signatory."

Developing countries, too, are subject to countervailing action, however, if their subsidized exports cause "material injury to a domestic industry, threat of material injury to a domestic industry or material retardation of the establishment of such an industry" (Article 2, Para. 1, footnote 2). At the same time, through the adoption of this provision, the United States has agreed to apply an injury test as a pre-condition for taking countervailing action. Also, in limiting the application of the injury test to a "like product" (Article 6, Para. 2), the condition for the application of countervailing duties are more stringent under the Code than under present U.S. law applied in the event of the subsidization of products that enter duty free.[39]

From the point of view of the developing countries, the principal benefit to be obtained from the Code on Subsidies and Countervailing Measures is the application of the injury test by United States, in the absence of which producers and labor unions have repeatedly petitioned for countervailing action in the past. It should be added, however, that the United States may not apply the injury test with respect to countries that are not signatories to the Code and the latter could not participate in the dispute mechanism of the Committee of Signatories.[40]

As noted above, the developing countries also enjoy "special and differential" treatment through the codification of their right to grant export subsidies, the exclusion of actions against them in the event that their subsidies adversely effect the exports of other signatories in third country markets, and the exclusion of certain measures they may apply from the subsidy category. In turn, the obligations taken by the developing countries in exchange for special and differential treatment under the Code remain rather vague.

Finally, developing countries may utilize the Committee procedure against developed countries if these provide export subsidies, utilize subsidies that are prejudicial to their interests, or take unilateral retaliatory measures. For example, they may request the Committee to consider the case of subsidies to shipbuilding by developed countries. The developing countries may also air their grievances during the course of the annual review of the implementation and operation of the Code. And, as in the case of all other Codes, possibilities are provided for amending the Code "having regard, *inter alia,* to the experience gained in its implementation" (Article 19, Para. 7).

Code on Customs Valuation

As stated in its preamble, the Agreement on Implementation of Article VII of the General Agreement of Tariffs and Trade (the Code on Customs Valuation) reflects the recognition of "the need for a fair, uniform, and neutral system for the valuation of goods for customs purposes that precludes the use of arbitrary or fictitious customs values." According to a Congressional document, it "was prompted, in large part, by longstanding complaints about U.S. valuation practices and by the desire to establish an international valuation system which would be used by all of the world's major trading countries."[41]

The Code provides a primary valuation standard based on the transaction value of imported goods and several alternative standards that are resorted to in a prescribed order whenever customs value cannot be determined under the higher ranking standard. The application of these standards will affect the valuation of about one-fifth of United States imports, including items, such as benzenoid chemicals, rubber and plastic shoes, and wool knit gloves, the customs valuation of which is presently based on the American Selling Price (ASP), as well as items on the so-called Final List, among which ball and roller bearings and certain pneumatic tires are said to be valued materially higher for customs purposes than transaction value.[42] The application of the Code will also represent a substantial reduction of Canadian and New Zealand tariffs that use a different valuation standard. It will, however, make little difference for tariffs levied by the EEC and by other countries applying the Brussels Definition of Value.

At the same time, the application of the new standards will have beneficial effects overall by ensuring consistency, transparency, and simplicity in the valuation of imports. It will also permit avoiding abuses that have involved the national authorities arbitrarily raising customs values in the past.

In order to ensure that national practices conform to the Code, a Committee on Customs Valuation, assisted by a Technical Committee on Customs Valuation, is established to handle disputes. The Committee may authorize adversely affected parties to suspend the application of the Code to parties that have not ceased to follow actions contrary to the Code. Provisions have further been made for an annual review of the implementation and operation of the Code.

For the reasons noted, the application of the developed countries will benefit the developing countries. Furthermore, these countries are to receive technical assistance in implementing the Code; they may postpone implementation for five years; and they may delay the application of provisions pertaining to trade between related parties for another three years.

Developing countries do not consider the delays provided in the proposed Code sufficiently long and have submitted an alternative text, proposing a ten-year extension instead. The alternative text also gives greater latitude to national customs authorities to value transactions by related parties (mainly transactions between multinational corporations and their subsidiaries).

Code on Import Licensing

Recognizing that "the inappropriate use of import licensing procedures may impede the flow of international trade," the stated aim of the Agreement on Import Licensing Procedures is "to simplify, and bring transparency to, the administrative procedures and practices used in international trade, and to ensure the fair and equitable application and administration of such procedures and practices." The Code requires that "the rules for import licensing procedures shall be neutral in application and administered in a fair and equitable manner" (Article 3). It also calls for transparency and simplicity in regard to import licensing procedures and for the avoidance of practices used by some countries, where minor documentation errors or significant variations in value or quantity led to the refusal of applications for licenses. The Code does not, however, affect the existence of import licensing whether automatic or non-automatic.

Automatic licensing (i.e. import licensing where approval of application is freely granted) "shall not be administered in a manner so as to have restricting effects on imports subject to automatic licensing," and "any person, firm or institution which fulfils the legal requirements of the importing country . . . shall be equally eligible to apply for and to obtain import licenses," which "shall be approved immediately upon receipt, to the extent administratively feasible, but within a maximum of ten working days" (Article 13).

The Code further calls for transparency and simplicity in the administration of non-automatic import licenses and for their equitable distribution. In the allocation of these licenses "special consideration should be given to those importers importing products originating in developing countries and, in particular, the least developed countries" (Article 14.1). Developing countries will also benefit from the simplification and greater domestic transparency of procedures applied in the administration of import licenses that has been used to protective effect by European countries and Japan.

The developing countries may make use of the dispute settlement mechanism operated by the Committee of Signatories to ensure that they receive special consideration in the allocation of non-automatic import licenses to developed countries. They may also attempt to bring under the Code the so-called "voluntary export restraints" that generally require export licenses or visas as the condition of importation.[43]

In the event that the Committee's recommendations are not followed, it may authorize the suspension of obligations under the Code or the adversely affected parties may resort to Article XXIII of GATT. Finally, the Committee will review as necessary, but at least once every two years, the implementation and the operation of the Code.

Code on Technical Barriers to Trade

According to Robert Baldwin, "the customs valuation and import licensing problems faced by exporters and importers are often child's play when compared with those arising from the many product standards with which these traders must contend."[44] In fact, there is a bewildering array of technical regulations and standards, and governments have recently added new standards concerning energy efficiency and the environment to the traditional health, sanitary, and product-safety standards.

Technical regulations and standards, as well as procedures pertaining to testing and codification, constitute barriers to international trade in the event that they are used with a protectionist intent as well as in cases when the cost of compliance is greater for imported than for domestically produced goods. The cost of compliance is particularly burdensome for developing countries, given their more limited information-gathering, engineering, and marketing capabilities.[45] And, to the extent that this cost does not increase proportionally with volume, developing countries with smaller export volumes will bear a greater burden.

According to its Preamble, the Agreement of Technical Barriers to Trade aims "to ensure that technical regulations and standards, including packaging, marketing, and labelling requirements, and methods for certifying conformity with technical regulations and standards do not create unnecessary obstacles to international trade." For this purpose, the Code calls on the signatories to adopt existing international technical regulations and standards and to contribute to the development of such regulations and standards. In the absence of international regulations and standards, the signatories should frame their national regulations and standards in terms of performance rather than design or descriptive characteristics that have been used to protective effect and should provide information on these standards and regulations to interested parties. Futhermore, imported products should be accepted for testing under conditions not less favorable than domestic products and certification systems should not be formulated or applied with a view to creating obstacles to international trade. In all these regards, national governments should ensure compliance by local government and non-governmental bodies as well.

The Code makes exceptions for developing countries that "should not be expected to use international standards as a basis for their technical regulations or standards, including test methods, which are not appropriate to their development, financial and trade needs" (Article 12, Para. 4). "It is further recognized that the special development and trade needs of developing countries, as well as their stage of technological development, may hinder their ability to discharge fully their obligations under this Agreement" (Article 12, Para. 8). Correspondingly, these countries may receive "specified, time-limited exceptions in whole or in part from obligations under this Agreement" (*Ibid*). Finally, the developed countries should "provide technical assistance to developing countries to ensure that the preparation and application of technical regulations, standards, test methods, and certification systems do not create unnecessary obstacles to the expansion and diversification of exports from developing countries" (Article 12, Para. 7).

The application of the Code on Technical Barriers to Trade by the developed countries will provide benefits to the developing countries, the exports of which have been adversely affected by the existence of such barriers. Apart from increased information and technical assistance they are to receive under the Code, the developing countries are to benefit through the introduction of rules that aim at avoiding the use of technical regulations, standards, test methods, and certification system to protective effect. At the same time, they may use the grievance procedure under the Code, involving resort to Article XXIII of GATT, in order to ensure that its provisions are applied in practice. Finally, in subscribing to the Code, developing countries would take part in the annual reviews of its operation and implementation, in the periodical reviews of the special and differential treatment they are to receive under the Code, as well as in the tri-annual reviews that permit adjusting the rights and obligations "where necessary to ensure mutual economic advantage and balance of rights and obligations" (Article 15, Para. 8).

Code on Government Procurement

Government procurement — the purchase of goods and services by governmental entities for their own consumption — is expressly excluded from the application of GATT rules, under which foreign suppliers receive national and nondiscriminatory treatment. With the rising share of governmental expenditure in GNP and the important role of publicly-owned transportation and communication facilities and utilities in most countries, this exception to GATT rules has increasingly become a limiting factor in international trade.

The United States discriminates against foreign suppliers under the Buy American Act that presently provides a 6 percent price advantage to domestic suppliers (12 percent to suppliers in depressed areas) while the Defense Department gives U.S. producers a 50 percent preference. In turn, other developed countries tend to rely on administrative action to favor domestic over foreign suppliers and may even limit tenders to domestic firms.

The Agreement on Government Procurement aims at liberalizing formal as well as informal methods of government procurement. Its Preamble states that "laws, regulations, procedures and practices regarding government procurement should not be [applied] so as to afford protection to domestic products or suppliers and should not discriminate among foreign products or suppliers.[46] These objectives are to be served by providing national treatment and applying the MFN clause of foreign suppliers of products purchased by governmental entities subject to the Code above a limit of SDR 150 thousand (approximately US $200 thousand).

The Code calls upon the signatories to state technical specifications in terms of performance rather than design, to use international standards whenever available, and to provide for open tendering procedures. It provides detailed rules to how tenders should be invited and how choice among bidders should be made. Furthermore, information requirements are specified, with the aim of ensuring the transparency of the process of public procurement.

The Code sets up machinery for consultation and for the resolution of disputes on government procurement. Whenever a mutually satisfactory solution is not reached, the Committee of Signatories will make recommendations for actions to be taken. If the Committee's recommendations are not accepted, it may authorize retaliation by the adversely affected party. The Code also provides for the annual review of its implementation and operation as well as for a tri-annual review "with a view to broadening and improving the Agreement on the basis of mutual reciprocity having regard to the provisions . . . relating to developing countries." (Part IX, Article 6(b)).

The provisions in question aim to "facilitate increased imports from developing countries, bearing in mind the special problems of the least developed countries and those at low stages of economic development" (Part III, Article 3). Under the application of MFN rules, this does not however entail granting preferential margins, unless the commodities in question are GSP products. Rather, it involves providing technical assistance and setting up information centers "to respond to reasonable requests from developing country parties for information relating to, *inter alia,* laws, regulations, procedures and practices regarding government procurement . . . " (Article 10). These provisions also apply to suppliers in least-developed countries that are not signatories of the Code.

The Code further limits the obligations taken by developing countries. These countries may negotiate exclusions from the rule on national treatment with respect to particular governmental entities or products and may request the Committee to grant such exclusions once the Code comes into effect.

IV. Policy Actions by Developing and by Developed Countries

The Codes on Non-tariff Measures and the Developing Countries

The Codes on non-tariff measures establish rules for permissible and nonpermissible behavior, determine information requirements for ensuring the transparency of the regulations applied, and provide for dispute settlement and surveillance procedures. They also call for periodical, mostly annual, reviews of the implementation and the operation of the Codes. Furthermore, the Codes on Technical Barriers to Trade and on Government Procurement envisage holding tri-annual reviews with the aim of effecting modifications in the Codes. And, every Code contains a provision for possible future amendments, "having regard, *inter alia,* to the experience gained in its implementation."

The dispute settlement and surveillance procedures have the objective of avoiding violations and assuring the application of the Codes. While the dispute settlement mechanism was not working well in GATT, the establishment of a Committee of Signatories for each of the Codes, and the care taken in defining the procedures to be applied, provide possibilities for its efficient operation in the future. In this regard, the agreement reached by the United States and the European Economic Community to settle their dispute on the alleged subsidization of synthetic fibers by the United States in the framework of GATT is a favorable sign.[47]

The developing countries may make an important contribution to the successful operation of the Codes in general, and the policing of the actions taken by the developed countries in particular, by participating in the dispute settlement and surveillance procedures. Such participation, in turn, presupposes that developing countries subscribe to the Codes. This is also a precondition for participation in the periodical reviews that provide a forum to examine the practical implementation of the Codes and, in the cases indicated, to effect revisions. And, subscribing to the Codes will allow the developing countries to invoke the provisions for future amendments in the Codes.

Participation in dispute settlement procedures and in the review of the operation of the Codes is of interest to the developing countries even in cases such as the Code on Customs Valuation, where the benefits by-and-large accrue to participants and non-participants alike. At the same time, in most instances, the benefits of the Codes are restricted to the signatories. Subscribing to the Codes is also a pre-condition for enjoying the special and differential treatment available to developing countries, the only exception being the Code on Government Procurement which includes the least developed countries among its beneficiaries even if they do not subscribe to the Code.

Among the individual Codes, the Code on Subsidies and Countervailing Measures is of particular interest to the developing countries. This is not only because they are excepted from particular obligations but also because the United States government interprets the Code so that the material injury clause applies solely to countries that subscribe to it. And, the developing countries may utilize the Committee procedure to bring up the question of subsidies to shipbuilding, and of industrial subsidies in general, by developed country governments.

Developing country signatories may further utilize the procedures established under the Code on Import Licensing to initiate action in the so-called voluntary export restraint cases. At the same time, developing country signatories can exert pressure on the developed countries to ensure that they do not use technical regulations and standards to protective effect and provide information on their application. Finally, while the provisions of the Code on Government Procurement extend to non-signatory least-developed countries, it is the industrializing developing countries that have the best chance to benefit from the Code.

The Framework Group

The benefits to be derived from the general provisions of the Codes, from special and differential treatment, and from participation in dispute settlement and surveillance procedures point to the desirability for the developing countries to subscribe to the Codes on non-tariff measures. This conclusion is strengthened if we consider that participation will make it possible for the developing countries to contribute to shaping the Codes in the process of their practical application and modifying them through future revisions and amendments.

Similar considerations apply to the statements and declarations formulated by the so-called "framework group." These statements and declarations, drafted at the behest of Brazil,[48] establish a legal basis for providing preferential treatment to developing countries and specifically deal with trade measures taken for balance-of-payment purposes and with safeguard actions for development purposes.[49]

To begin with, the so-called "enabling clause" in the settlement on Differential and More Favorable Treatment; Reciprocity and Fuller Participation of Developing Countries provides a legal basis for "differential and more favorable treatment" of developing countries. Apart from special and differential treatment in the framework of the Codes on non-tariff measures, this clause pertains to tariff preferences granted by developed countries, preferential arrangements among developing countries, and the special treatment of the least developed countries.

The statement also recognizes the "particular situation and problems" (Para. 6) of the least developed countries as well as the lack of applicability of the principle of reciprocity to relationships between developed and developing countries. Thus,

> "The developed countries do not expect reciprocity for commitments made by them in trade negotiations to reduce or remove tariff and other barriers to the trade of developing countries . . . Developed contracting parties shall therefore not seek, neither shall less-developed contracting parties be required to make, concessions that are inconsistent with the latter's development, financial, and trade needs" (Para. 5).

Developing countries are to receive special and differential treatment under the declaration of Trade Measures Taken for Balance-of-Payment Purposes, too. In applying such measures, a developed country signatory should "take into account the export interests of the less-developed contracting parties and may exempt from its measures products of export interest to those contracting parties" (Para. 2). Furthermore, in the course of its consultations, the Committee on Balance-of-Payments Restrictions should "give particular attention to the possibilities for alleviating and correcting the balance-of-payments problems" (Para. 12) of developing countries through measures taken by other (in practice, developed) countries to facilitate the expansion of export earnings.

In turn, the declaration of Safeguard Action for Development Purposes extends the scope of applications of such actions by the developing countries — previously limited to the establishment of particular industries — to "the development of new or the modification or extension of existing production structures with a view to achieving fuller and more efficient use of resources in accordance with the priorities of their economic development" (Para. 1). "Difficulties in the application of . . . programmes and policies of economic development" (Para. 2) are also given as possible grounds for the developing countries to take actions that conflict with the obligations they have assumed in GATT.

The "Graduation" Clause

The statements and declarations drafted by the framework group recognize the need for developing countries to receive special and differentiated treatment and provide a legal basis for such treatment. At the same time, the relevant provisions remain rather vague and their practical application will importantly depend on the effectiveness of the procedures of consultation and dispute settlement.

According to the Understanding Regarding Notification, Consultation, Dispute Settlement and Surveillance, "contracting parties reaffirm their resolve to strengthen and improve the effectiveness of consultative procedures." It is further stated that "during consultations, contracting parties should give special attention to the particular problems and interests of less-developed contracting parties." Developing countries may also request the intervention of the Director-General of GATT in the event that a complaint they have brought against a developed country has not been otherwise resolved. Finally, the statement on Differential and More Favorable Treatment; Reciprocity and Fuller Participation of Developing Countries envisages a "review of the operation of these provisions, bearing in mind the need for individual and just efforts by contracting parties to meet the development needs of developing countries and the objectives of the General Agreement" (Para. 9).

At the same time, questions have been raised concerning the "principle of graduation" contained in the statement dealing with the "enabling clause."

> "Less-developed contracting parties expect that their capacity to make contributions or negotiated concessions or take other mutually agreed action under the provisions and procedures of the General Agreement would improve with the progressive development of their economies and improvement in their trade situation and they would accordingly expect to participate more fully in the framework of rights and obligations under the General Agreement through participation in the operation of the GATT System" (Para. 7).

According to the UNCTAD Report, "the developing countries are seriously concerned with the acceptance of this principle and reject its application. Not only are there no universally accepted criteria for such categorization, but the principle would permit developed countries to discriminate among developing countries in an arbitrary and unilateral measure."[50] Such a negative view is not warranted, however.

To begin with, the provision in question does not allow for unilateral and discriminatory actions on the part of the developed countries. Nor do signatory developing countries make any commitments as regards "graduation." They only "expect to participate more fully" in GATT, once their economic development so warrants without taking any obligations as to when and how this will happen.[51] This provision will need to be interpreted by the signatories, when the participation of the developing countries in the relevant Committee is again of importance.

Last but not least, the idea underlying the rejection of the principle of graduation is that a two-tier system in the world economy, with corresponding rights and obligations, is an immutable fact. Yet, history tells us that countries do graduate from developing to developed country status. In the postwar period, Japan, Israel, and Ireland have made the transition and Greece, Portugal, and Spain are in the process of doing so in conjunction with their entry into the European Common Market.

More generally, it should be recognized that in the process of development the economic conditions of the individual countries change, and so does the need for particular policies. For example, while the preferential treatment of the manufacturing sector may be desirable at earlier stages of development on infant industry grounds, successful industrialization will progressively reduce the economic justification of such treatment. Adopting a more open trade system will then be in the well-conceived interest of the newly-industrializing developing countries.

The less-developed countries, too, have an interest in the newly-industrializing developing countries adopting an increasingly open trade system. For one thing, in contributing to shifts in export composition towards more sophisticated and skill or capital-intensive products in line with their changing comparative advantage, the adoption of such a system by the newly-industrializing countries would provide opportunities for the expansion of the exportation of simpler and unskilled-labor intensive products by the least-developed countries.[52] For another thing, trade liberalization by the newly-industrializing countries would permit the less developed countries to sell on the markets of these countries.

Finally, the political decision-making process in the developed countries is not favorable to the maintenance of unilateral concessions in regard to countries that have established strong positions in world trade. A refusal of such countries to take any steps towards the establishment of a more open trade system may then lead to protectionist pressures in the developed countries, with adverse effects for all concerned.[53]

Policies by the Developed Countries

The next question concerns the actions developed countries may take in regard to the international trade system. Proposals for a new round of negotiations in the framework of UNCTAD[54] or elsewhere are hardly practical. Such an effort, occupying decision-makers and a large technical staff over several years, could not be mounted immediately following the completion of the Tokyo Round of negotiations that began in the wake of the September 1973 Tokyo Declaration.

Rather, at this juncture, one should impress upon the developed countries to abide by the obligations they have taken, to ensure the functioning of the dispute settlement and surveillance mechanism, and to accept the resolution of disputes that concern them. And, as various provisions of the individual Codes and the texts prepared by the framework group involve considerable ambiguity, the developed countries should be induced to accept interpretations that are favorable to the developing countries.

Apart from being open to different interpretations, the individual Codes and the texts prepared by the framework group are not immutable. Thus, all the Codes are subject to periodical reviews, two of them specifically provide for revisions and every Code is open to subsequent amendments. As noted above, the statement on Differential and More Favorable Treatment; Reciprocity and Fuller Participation of Developing Countries also calls for a review of its provisions "bearing in mind" the need "to meet the development needs of developing countries." Furthermore, in the Understanding Regarding Notification, Consultation, Dispute Settlement, and Surveillance, "the Contracting Parties agreed to conduct a regular and systematic review of development in the trading system," again with special reference to "matters affecting the interests of less-developed contracting parties." Such reviews provide an opportunity to safeguard the interests of the developing countries, and to exert pressure for trade liberalization by the developed countries.

The Draft Code on Safeguard Measures

The developed countries also have a responsibility to work towards the establishment of equitable safeguard procedures. The application of safeguard measures is presently regulated by Article XIX of GATT. Article XIX has rarely been utilized, however, in part because the country invoking it risks retaliation and in part because it does not permit discrimination among exporters. Instead, countries have employed protective measures in the form of Orderly Marketing Agreements and Voluntary Export Restraint programs.

The draft Code on Safeguard Measures, formulated in the framework of the Tokyo Round negotiations, was to bring all types of safeguard actions back into the GATT framework. It defined the criteria that would have to be met to justify safeguard action; stated the procedures to be followed in taking such action; and provided for a consultation and dispute settlement mechanism.

In fact, an agreement on the Safeguard Code has not been reached. While this has largely been due to the differences in the positions of the EEC and of the developing countries on the question of selectivity, there are other issues left to be settled. They include the need for a multinational forum to countenance the application of safeguard measures; the length of the time period of application of these measures; and the taking of domestic measures of adjustment by developed countries.

An agreement on the application of safeguard measures is a task of great importance. Since the failure of the negotiating parties to agree on the

Safeguard Code in the MTN, a step in this direction has been taken by the creation of a Committee in GATT that is charged to evolve a safeguard code. From the point of view of the developing countries such a code should fulfill certain requirements.

The principal requirement for a system of safeguards should be their temporary nature. This would require setting time limits for the application of safeguards. Also, in order to ensure that adjustment does take place, the extent of the safeguards should diminish over the period of their application according to a pre-determined time table.

If time limits are set for the application of safeguards, one may forego the requirements that a multinational forum countenance their imposition. An extension of the time period of their application should, however, be subject to approval by such a forum. Extensions should be granted only in exceptional circumstances and be dependent on a plan for domestic adjustment. They should not be repeated.

Imposing time limits on the application of safeguards would also reduce objections to selectivity that, at any rate, have been practiced by by developed countries. At the same time, selectivity should be made dependent on the fulfillment of well-defined conditions. It should be applied, in the first place to developed country exporters and it should under no circumstance be invoked against least-developed countries. As far as other developing countries are concerned, selectivity should be subject to the requirement that their share in the domestic consumption of the product in question in the importing countries does not decline.

Conclusions

After reviewing recent developments in the trade policies of the developed countries, this essay has set out to evaluate the results of the Tokyo Round of Multilateral Trade Negotiations from the point of view of the developing countries. It has been shown that the tariff reductions undertaken by the developed countries, and extended to the developing countries, will benefit the exports of the latter group of countries and these benefits will be offset only in part by the erosion of preferences provided under GSP.

The developing countries also stand to benefit from the application of the texts formulated by the so-called "framework group" that provide a legal basis for their "special and differentiated treatment" and allow these countries to apply trade measures for balance of payments purposes and safeguard actions for development purposes. For reasons noted above, these conclusions are not affected by the eventual introduction of a "graduation" procedure.

In November 1979, the Contracting Parties to GATT adopted the tariff reductions negotiated in the Tokyo Round and accepted the text of the statements and declarations drawn up by the framework group, which thus became part of GATT. Few developing countries have so far subscribed to the

Codes on non-tariff measures, however. Yet, as shown above, it is in the interest of the developing countries to subscribe to the Codes, the benefits of which are generally restricted to the signatories as is special and differential treatment for the developing countries.

One should not interpret these conclusions to imply that the Codes on non-tariff measures would be without shortcomings. But, just as it would serve no useful purpose to speculate that the Codes could have been more favorable to the developing countries had they more effectively participated in the negotiations, from the point of view of these countries it would be counter-productive to forego participation on the grounds that the Codes have not lived up to their expectations. At any rate, while the Codes cannot be modified at the present time, the signatory developing countries can contribute to shaping them in the process of their practical application and can utilize the possibilities provided for future revisions and amendments. In fact, it would be desirable that a substantial number of developing countries subscribe to the individual Codes, so that they can act as a pressure group both to ensure the implementation of the provisions which are of interest to them and to contribute to the favorable interpretation and modification of the Codes.

In turn, the developed countries should abide by the obligations they have taken, should ensure the functioning of the dispute settlement and surveillance mechanism, and accept the resolution of disputes that concern them. And most importantly, these countries should make an effort towards the establishment of equitable safeguard procedures.

ESSAY 6
A 'Stages' Approach to Comparative Advantage

Introduction

This essay analyzes the changing pattern of comparative advantage in manufactured goods in the process of accumulation of physical and human capital that characterizes economic development. The investigation will be limited to exports, since the commodity pattern of imports is greatly influenced by the system of protection in the importing countries. And, as trade in natural resource products depends to a considerable extent on the country's resource endowment, we will deal with comparative advantage in manufactured goods alone. Section I of the essay describes the product classification schemes and country characteristics used to evaluate comparative advantage. The empirical results on the changing pattern of comparative advantage are presented in Section II; they are further analyzed in Section III. Section IV examines the policy implications of the results.

I. Product Classification Schemes and Country Characteristics

In investigating the determinants of trade between developed and developing countries, Lary, Kojima, Fels, and Mahfuzer Rahman considered developing countries as a group.[1] In turn, Hufbauer attempted to explain differences in the average product characteristics of the exports of individual countries in an inter-country framework, but his sample of 24 countries included only 9 countries that may be considered developing and they were all at the upper end of the distribution in terms of per capita incomes.[2]

Herman and Tinbergen, and subsequently Herman suggested a scheme of "ideal" export composition allegedly reflecting the physical and human capital endowments of countries classified into 11 groups, but did not subject their scheme to statistical testing.[3] Finally, Hirsch correlated export performance and value-added per worker in the nonagricultural sector in an intercountry framework for each of 18 industry groups and also correlated export-output ratios with the average product characteristics of the 18 industry groups for each of 29 countries, without, however, attempting to establish a statistical relationship between the two sets of estimates.

149

A different approach has been followed in the present investigation. Thirty-six countries have been chosen for the investigation, of which 18 are developed and 18 developing. For each country, regression equations have been estimated relating their "revealed" comparative advantage in 184 manufacturing product categories to the relative capital intensity (capital-labor ratio) of the individual categories. The regression coefficients thus obtained have in turn been correlated with particular country characteristics in an inter-country framework. In this way, results obtained in "commodity space" have been transposed into "country space," so as to indicate the effects of country characteristics on international specialization in manufactured goods.

The first question concerns the choice of product characteristics for the investigation. Harry Johnson has suggested that the concept of capital be extended to include human capital as well as intellectual capital in the form of production knowledge, noting that, "such an extension is fully consistent with Irving Fisher's approach to the relation between capital and income."[5] However, as Branson observes, the aggregation of various forms of capital assumes that they are perfect complements or perfect substitutes in production.[6]

We have experimented with an aggregate measure of capital as well as with separate variables for physical and human capital.[7] Technological variables used in recent work on U.S. comparative advantage have not been introduced in the analysis because of their limited relevance to developing countries that engage in research and development to a small extent, if at all.[8] Rather, investment in research and development has been assumed to be part of physical capital (e.g. laboratories) or human capital (e.g., scientists and engineers engaged in R&D).

Capital intensity may be defined in terms of flows (Lary's measure of value added per worker) or stocks (the value of the capital stock plus the discounted value of the difference between average wages and the unskilled wage, divided by number of workers). The latter approach was used by Kenen and recently by Fels and Branson.[9]

The stock measures of capital intensity (k^s) is expressed in (1)

$$(1) \quad k_i^s = p_i^s + h_i^s = + \frac{\overline{w}_i - w_i^u}{r^h}$$

for industry i, where p_i and h_i respectively, refer to physical and human capital per man, $\overline{w}_i$ is the average wage rate, w_i^u the wage of unskilled labor, and r^h the discount rate used in calculating the stock of human capital. This approach implicitly assumes that the rental price of physical capital, i.e. the risk-free rate of return and the rate of depreciation, is the same in all industries. The assumption is made explicit in expressing the flow equivalent (FE) of the stock measure of capital intensity as in (2), where r^p is the

$$(2) \quad (FE) \, k_i^s = p_i^s \, (r^p + d) + (\overline{w}_i - w_i^u)$$

discount rate for physical capital and d is the rate of depreciation.

In turn, the flow measures of capital intensity (k^f) is expressed in (3) where va refers to value added per man. Now, nonwage value added

$$(3) \quad k_i^f = va_i = p_i^f + h_i^f = (va_i - \overline{w}_i) + \overline{w}_i \, (va_i - \overline{w}_i) + [(\overline{w}_i - w_i^u) + w_i^u]$$

per man $(va_i - \overline{w}_i)$ is taken to represent physical capital intensity and wage value added per man $(\overline{w}_i)$ human capital intensity.

As far as physical capital intensity is concerned, the two measures would give the same result in risk free equilibrium, provided that product, capital, and labor markets were perfect, and nonwage value added did not include any items other than capital remuneration. However, production is subject to risks that vary among industries and, assuming risk aversion, profit rates will include a risk premium that will differ from industry to industry. Also, the situation in a particular year will not represent an equilibrium position and this fact, as well as imperfections in product, capital, and labor markets, will further contribute to interindustry variations in profits. Moreover, nonwage value added may include items other than capital's remuneration, such as advertising.

Finally, while the stock measure imputes differences between average wages and the unskilled wage to human capital, the flow measure includes the entire wage value added under this heading, thus overestimating human capital intensity by the amount of the unskilled wage. This would not give rise to problems if the unskilled wages were the same in every industry. However, unskilled wages may differ among industries due to factors such as disutility of work and the power of labor unions.

The existence of interindustry differences in risk, market imperfections, the inclusion of items other than capital's remuneration in non-wage value added, and the inclusion of unskilled wages in wage value added represent deficiencies of the flow measures of capital intensity. In turn, the lack of consideration given to interindustry differences in depreciation rates and in the extent of obsolescence of existing equipment, as well as the use of historical rather than replacement values for physical capital, represent disadvantages of the stock measure.

The implications of the described shortcomings of the two measures of capital intensity for the results will depend on the particular circumstances of the situation. The usefulness of the stock measure would be greatly impaired in an inflationary situation where historical values of physical capital shown in the account differ from replacement values and the magnitude of these differences varies with the age of equipment. This is not the case in the present study since the benchmark years used for estimating capital intensity (1969 and 1970) are part of a long noninflationary period. By contrast, the usefulness of the flow measure is limited by reason of the fact that profit rates show considerable variation over time and interindustry differences in profit rates cannot be fully explained by reference to risk factors.

These considerations tend to favor the use of the stock measure of capital intensity. Nevertheless, given the error possibilities involved, interest attaches to making estimates by the use of both measures[10], which also permits us to examine the stability of the results derived under alternative assumptions. This has been done in the present investigation, with emphasis given to the estimates obtained by the use of the stock measure in evaluating the results.

For purposes of the calculations, we have attempted to obtain data on the capital intensity of the production process for Japan, the factor intensities of which may be presumed to lie in between the relevant magnitudes for highly-developed and less-developed countries. However, for lack of information on physical capital and on unskilled wages in a sufficiently detailed breakdown, this attempt had to be abandoned and we have had to have recourse to U.S. data.

The use of U.S. data in the investigation will be appropriate if factor substitution elasticities are zero or they are identical for every product category. While these assumptions are not fulfilled in practice, Lary has shown variations in capital intensity to be small in U.S.-U.K., U.S.-Japan, and U.S.-India comparisons as regards the flow measure of capital.[11] For lack of information, similar comparisons could not be made for the stock measure and the further investigation of this question had to be left for future research.

In defining the manufacturing sector for purposes of the present investigation, we have taken the concept used in the U.S. Standard Industrial Classification (SIC) as our point of departure. From this category (SIC 19 to 39), we have excluded foods and beverages (SIC 20) and tobacco (SIC 21), where the high cost of transportation and the perishability of the basic material give an advantage to primary-producing countries. We have further excluded primary nonferrous metals (SIC 333), where transportation costs account for a high proportion of delivered price of the basic material, and ordnance (SIC 19) for which comparable trade data are not available. In turn, given the relatively low cost of transporting the raw material[12] and the prevalence of production for exports based on imported materials, we have retained petroleum products and wood products in the manufactured product category. We have also retained nonmetallic mineral products by reason of the ubiquity of the basic materials.

Defining the manufacturing sector as SIC industry groups 22 to 39 less 333, the product classification scheme used in this investigation has been established on the basis of the 4-digit SIC categories. Particular 4-digit categories have been merged in cases when the economic characteristics of the products in question were judged to be very similar and when comparable data did not exist according to the U.N. Standard International Trade Classification, which has been used to collect trade figures.[13]

Data on the capital stock, employment, value added, and wages used in calculating capital intensity originate from the U.S. Census of Manufacturing. In turn, the data for unskilled wages have been taken from the *Monthly Labor Review,* published by the U.S. Bureau of Labor Statistics; they relate to 2-digit industries, thus involving the assumption that unskilled wages are equalized at this level.

In order to reduce the effects of variations due to the business cycle and nonrecurring events, we have used simple averages of data for the two latest years (1969 and 1970) for which information was available. Finally, we have estimated the value of human capital under the stock measure by discounting differences between the average wage and the unskilled wage for the individual product categories at a rate of 10 percent.[14]

As noted earlier, the investigation covers altogether 36 countries. The sample is evenly divided between developed and developing countries; the countries in the first group had per capita incomes above $1800 in 1972; incomes per head did not exceed $1400 (more exactly, $1407) in the second group. The variability of per capita incomes is 1:3 in the developed country subsample, 1:13 in the developing country subsample, and 1:56 in the entire sample. Thus, the sample, and, in particular the developing country subsample, exhibits considerable variability, which permits indicating the changing pattern of comparative advantage in the process of economic development.

The distinction between developed and developing countries has been introduced in the econometric analysis through the use of a dummy variable for developed countries. At the same time, we have used continuous variables to denote country characteristics, including physical and human capital endowment. These are shown in Table 6.1 together with per capita incomes.[15]

In the absence of data on the physical capital stock in the individual countries, we have taken the sum of gross fixed investment over the period 1955-71, estimated in constant prices and converted into U.S. dollars at 1963 exchange rates, as a proxy for physical capital endowment. The data have been derived from the *World Tables, 1976,* published by the World Bank; they have been expressed in per capita terms.

A similar procedure has been employed by Hufbauer, except that he used data for the period 1953-64 and included manufacturing investment only.[16] The choice of a longer period in the present study reflects the fact that capital equipment is used beyond eleven years; also, we have considered all capital, and not only that used in the manufacturing sector. In turn, in using value added per worker as a proxy for capital endowment, Hirsch does not separate physical and human capital and neglects intercountry differences in profit rates and in unskilled wages.[18]

Hufbauer has taken the ratio of professional, technical and related workers to the labor force in manufacturing as a proxy for human capital endowment.[19] The use of this measure is objectionable, because the group of professional, technical, and related workers includes various liberal occupations, such as, jurists, preachers, artists, and athletes, and excludes production supervisors, foremen, and skilled workers that are of considerable importance in the developing countries.

A more appropriate procedure appears to be to make use of the Harbison-

TABLE 6.1
Country Characteristics and Regression Coefficients Obtained in Estimates for Individual Countries

	Country Characteristics					Regression Coefficients					
	DUMMY	GNPCAP	GDICAP	HMIND	SKILLS	β_j^s	β_j^f	β_j^{sp}	β_j^{sh}	β_j^{fp}	β_j^{fh}
Argentina	0	1139.65	2013.68	122.0	8.76	0.32	0.19	0.25	-0.04	0.60	-1.49
Australia	1	3271.69	6675.24	183.3	10.93	0.34**	0.78*	0.23	0.12	0.50*	0.09
Austria	1	2741.26	5129.79	112.9	10.08	-0.31*	-0.93*	-0.33*	0.04	-0.64*	0.03
Belgium	1	3701.15	5441.70	140.5	11.62	0.11	0.04	0.24*	-0.11	0.51*	-1.30*
Brazil	0	511.27	1016.00	29.3	8.57	-0.69*	-1.48*	-0.35	-0.42	-0.74**	-0.80
Canada	1	4691.51	7970.65	179.9	14.92	0.75*	0.87*	0.46*	0.25	-0.22	2.25*
Colombia	0	357.08	751.59	32.3	7.41	-1.31*	-2.48*	-0.06	-1.31*	-0.33	-3.82*
Denmark	0	4187.67	6259.56	139.2	13.63	-0.40*	-0.12	-0.44*	0.05	-0.15	0.08
Finland	1	2877.73	6999.27	109.9	14.89	-0.26	-0.62*	0.08	-0.37**	-0.32	-0.34
France	1	3841.68	7211.24	138.8	13.46	-0.07	-0.08	-0.06	-0.00	0.11	-0.50**
Germany	1	4218.84	7102.15	114.3	10.71	0.20*	0.43*	-0.05	0.26*	0.05	0.69*
Greece	0	1407.20	2196.43	93.7	9.60	-0.27	-1.05*	0.11	-0.49	-0.08	-1.90*
Hong Kong	0	1048.88	1370.61	60.7	5.09	-2.30*	-2.84*	-1.83*	-0.52**	-0.94*	-3.15*
India	0	102.03	214.25	50.2	9.64	-1.10*	-2.30*	-0.93*	-0.09	-0.19	-4.58*
Ireland	1	1840.20	2701.89	110.7	12.53	-0.48*	-0.80*	-0.44*	-0.04	-0.39**	-0.66
Israel	1	2416.28	4280.96	148.9	19.19	-0.37**	-0.70*	-0.02	-0.41**	0.27	-2.02*
Italy	1	2176.52	3366.47	91.3	7.05	-0.33*	-0.46*	-0.20**	-0.12	-0.29**	-0.06
Japan	1	2740.95	4765.11	146.2	8.26	-0.31**	-0.52*	-0.42*	0.11	-0.70*	0.86**
Korea	0	301.03	402.89	66.7	6.15	-1.67*	-3.02*	-0.46	-1.24*	-0.69**	-3.91*
Malaysia	0	408.62	494.56	34.5	9.53	-0.88*	-2.32*	-0.26	-0.63**	-0.56	-3.65*
Mexico	0	745.41	1067.02	41.1	9.22	-0.91*	-1.48*	-0.17	-0.80*	-0.40	-2.38*
Morocco	0	279.13	293.08	27.9	8.23	-1.18*	-2.95*	-0.18	-1.06*	-0.23	-6.10*

TABLE 6.1 (Cont'd.)
Country Characteristics and Regression Coefficients Obtained in Estimates for Individual Countries

| | Country Characteristics | | | | | Regression Coefficients | | | | | |
	DUMMY	GNPCAP	GDICAP	HMIND	SKILLS	β_j^s	β_j^f	β_j^{sp}	β_j^{sh}	β_j^{fp}	β_j^{fh}
Netherlands	1	3466.90	5375.15	158.6	11.62	0.28*	0.44*	0.22*	0.07	0.55*	−0.67*
Norway	1	3786.91	7806.11	107.4	13.91	0.22	0.01	0.44*	−0.25	−0.05	0.18
Pakistan	0	104.11	197.76	33.1	4.63	−1.56*	−3.11*	−0.93*	−0.63	−0.51	−5.78*
Philippines	0	223.50	448.72	134.2	10.98	−1.34*	−2.28*	−0.07	−1.39*	−0.53	−3.03*
Portugal	0	1084.26	1154.43	68.1	5.09	−0.81*	−2.09*	−0.01	−0.90*	−0.82*	−1.80*
Singapore	0	1354.41	1189.84	97.6	8.00	−1.47*	−2.35*	−1.11*	−0.38	−1.03*	−2.01*
Spain	0	1333.76	2049.09	63.4	7.28	−0.43*	−0.56*	−0.03	−0.42*	−0.12	−0.82**
Sweden	1	5141.10	9452.90	129.6	20.87	0.21	0.15	−0.16	0.39*	−0.44*	1.50*
Switzerland	1	4810.02	8852.63	112.6	13.13	0.04	−0.10	−0.44*	0.50*	0.08	−0.23
Taiwan	0	481.94	629.88	103.5	7.06	−1.56*	−2.61*	−0.68*	−0.87*	−0.98*	−2.45*
Turkey	0	431.16	581.22	37.5	10.32	−0.42	−1.62*	−0.06	−0.42	−0.36	−2.01*
U.K.	1	2765.25	4844.68	136.2	11.44	0.13	0.46*	−0.18**	0.34*	0.19	0.31
U.S.A.	1	5679.47	7616.20	325.0	14.21	0.84*	1.47*	0.24*	0.62*	0.23	2.22*
Yugoslavia	0	798.30	1162.06	110.0	13.73	−0.47**	−1.41*	−0.29	−0.20	−0.81*	−0.60

Country Characteristics: DUMMY = 1 for developed, 0 for developing countries; GNPCAP = GNP per capita in 1972, $US; GDICAP = Cumulated gross fixed investment per capita, 1955–71, $US; HMIND = Harbison-Myers index; SKILLS = share of professional, technical and related workers in the total non-agricultural labor force.

Regression Coefficients have been obtained by regressing for each country the ratio of 'revealed' comparative advantage, estimated for 184 product categories, on measures of capital intensity. The coefficient β^s has been estimated by regressing the comparative advantage ratio on the stock measure of total capital intensity as in (4), while β_j^{sp} and β_j^{sh} have been obtained by regressing this ratio on physical and human capital intensity, introduced simultaneously in the estimating equation as in (5), again using the stock measure of capital. β_j^f, β_j^{fp}, and β_j^{fh} are the corresponding regression coefficients estimated by substituting the flow measure of capital for the stock measure in (4) and (5).

Regression coefficients that are significant at the 5 percent level have been denoted by * and those significant at the 10 percent level by **.

Myers index of human resource development.[20] While this index is a flow measure,[21] the use of estimates pertaining to 1965[22] permits us to provide an indication of a country's general educational level, and thus its human capital base, in 1972, the year for which trade data have been obtained. Nevertheless, we have also experimented with the skill ratio employed by Hufbauer, utilizing the data reported in the ILO *Yearbook of Labor Statistics.*

II. The Empirical Results

As noted in the introduction, the investigation is limited to exports since the commodity pattern of imports is greatly influenced by the system of protection. Following earlier work by the author,[23] a country's relative export performance in the individual product categories has been taken as an indication of its "revealed" comparative advantage.

For this purpose, we have calculated the ratio of a country's share in the world exports of a particular commodity category to its share in the world exports of all manufactured goods. Thus, a ratio of 1.10 (.90) means that the country's share in the particular product category is 10 percent higher (lower) than its share in all manufactured exports.[24] These ratios can be considered to express a country's comparative advantage in manufactured goods that are characterized by product differentiation and are hence exported by a variety of countries.

For each of the 36 countries, the ratio of "revealed" comparative advantage, calculated for the individual product categories, has been regressed on variables representing the capital intensity of the individual product categories. Separate equations have been estimated using the stock and the flow measures of (total) capital intensity, as well as by simultaneously introducing physical and human capital under the two definitions of capital intensity.

The estimating equation is shown in (4) for total capital intensity

(4) $\log x_{ij} = \log \alpha_j + \beta_j{}^s \log k_i{}^s$

and in (5) for physical and human capital intensity taken individually. The equations have been estimated in a double-logarithmic form,

(5) $\log x_{ij} = \log \alpha_j + \beta_j{}^p \log p_i + \beta_j{}^h \log h_i$

so that the value of the β coefficient for country j indicates the percentage change in the country's comparative advantage ratio (x_{ij}) associated with a one percent change in capital intensity.[25] A positive (negative) β coefficient thus shows that a country has a comparative advantage in capital (labor) intensive products while the numerical magnitude of the β coefficient indicates the extent of the country's comparative advantage in capital (labor) intensive commodities.[26] The estimated β coefficients are reported in Table 6.1.

In the regression equations utilizing the stock measure of (total) capital intensity, the β coefficient is statistically significant at the 5 percent level for 22 countries and at the 10 percent level for 26 countries. In turn, in regression equations utilizing the flow measure, the β coefficient is significant at the 5 percent level in the case of 29 countries, with no additional countries included at the 10 percent level. In interpreting the results, it should be noted that the β coefficients that have values near to zero have an economic interpretation even if they are not significantly different from zero; they indicate that a country is at the dividing line as far as comparative advantage in capital and labor-intensive products is concerned.

The β coefficients estimated by using the stock and the flow measures of capital intensity are highly correlated, with a Spearman rank correlation coefficient of 0.96. This finding is in part explained by the relatively high degree of correspondence in the ranking of product categories by the two measures of capital intensity. The Spearman rank correlation coefficient between the two is 0.78.

In turn, in estimates obtained by disaggregating capital into its physical and human capital components, a high degree of correspondence has been obtained in regard to the β coefficients pertaining to human capital intensity (Spearman rank correlation coefficient of 0.84) but not for physical capital intensity (Spearman rank correlation coefficient of 0.65). These differences are explained if we consider that human capital intensity was defined in a similar way under the stock and the flow measure of capital while this was not the case for physical capital intensity.

The level of statistical significance of the coefficients, too, is lower if we disaggregate capital into its physical and human capital components. The β coefficients are significant at the 5 (10) percent confidence level in 14 (17) cases for the physical capital intensity variable and in 13 (17) cases for the human capital intensity variable if we use a stock measure of capital. The corresponding figures are 11 (15) for the physical capital intensity variable and 21 (24) for the human capital intensity variable under the flow measure.[27]

Next, we have tested the hypothesis that intercountry differences in the β coefficients can be explained by differences in country characteristics that determine the pattern of comparative advantage. This test has been carried out by regressing the β coefficients estimated for the individual countries on variables representing their physical and human capital endowments in an intercountry framework. (6) shows the estimating equation for the case when

(6) $\beta j = f(GDICAP_j, HMIND_j)$

per capita physical capital endowments (GDICAP) and human capital endowments (HMIND) are introduced simultaneously in the equation.[28]

In estimating equation (6) statistically significant results have been obtained for both the physical and the human capital endowment variables, regardless of whether the dependent variable originated in country regressions utilizing the stock or the flow measure of capital intensity. In both regressions, the physical as well as the human capital endowment variables are significant at the 5 percent confidence level, while the coefficient of determination is 0.65

using the stock measure and 0.78 using the flow measure of capital intensity (equations 1.3 and 2.3 in Table 6.2).[29]

The level of statistical significance of the regression coefficients for the physical and human capital endowment variables is hardly affected if we introduce a dummy variable (DUMMY) representing the level of economic development. In turn, the dummy variable is not statistically significant if used in combination with either or both capital endowment variables, and its introduction does not increase the coefficient of determination.

We have also experimented with the ratio of professional, technical, and related workers to the labor force in the place of, and together with, the Harbison-Myers index. This variable (SKILLS) is not statistically significant at even the 10 percent level. Nor does it appreciably affect the statistical significance of the other variables in the regression equation or raise the coefficient of determination. It can thus be rejected as an unsuitable alternative for the Harbison-Myers index.

It will be recalled that the level of statistical significance of the β coefficients for the physical capital intensity variable in the country regressions has been generally low. Statistically poor results have also been obtained in regressing these coefficients on variables representing physical and human capital endowment in an intercountry framework as in (6). The explanatory power of the regressions is low as is the level of statistical significance of the coefficients in cases when the physical and the human capital endowment variables are introduced simultaneously in the estimating equations. However, the coefficients are statistically significant when these variables are introduced separately (Table 6.3).

The explanatory power of the regressions is relatively high in cases when the β coefficients obtained in regard to the flow measure of human capital intensity are used as the dependent variable in equation (6). Also, both the physical and the human capital endowment variables are highly significant when introduced simultaneously in the equations. The level of significance is lower in cases when the stock measure of capital intensity is employed instead of the flow measure.

III. The Analysis of the Results

We have further examined deviations from the relationships estimated in an intercountry context. Upward deviations from the regression line are shown with respect to the physical capital endowment—but not with regard to the human capital endowment—of Argentina and the United States. The results indicate that the actual capital intensity of the exports of these countries much exceeded expected values based on their physical and human capital endowments.

The results for Argentina are explained if we consider that, during the period under study, this country represented an extreme case among the

TABLE 6.2
Intercountry Regression Equations for the Total Capital Intensity Measure

Dependent Variable	Equation Number	Coefficient of Determination	Explanatory Variables				
			GDICAP	HMIND	DUMMY	SKILLS	CONSTANT
β_j^s	1.1	0.61	1.90 (7.28)				-1.17 (-9.60)
	1.2	0.46		0.85 (5.35)			-1.38 (-7.25)
	1.3	0.65	1.46 (4.24)	0.34 (1.92)			-1.37 (-8.78)
	1.4	0.61	1.66 (2.87)		0.16 (0.48)		-1.16 (-9.38)
	1.5	0.59		0.45 (2.37)	0.69 (3.19)		-1.30 (-7.64)
	1.6	0.65	1.39 (2.40)	1.34 (1.83)	0.05 (0.15)		-1.36 (-8.44)
	1.7	0.62	1.63 (4.42)			0.03 (1.06)	-1.41 (-5.51)
	1.8	0.62	1.40 (2.23)		0.15 (0.45)	0.03 (1.04)	-1.40 (-5.39)
	1.9	0.66	1.27 (3.09)	0.32 (1.78)		0.02 (0.85)	-1.54 (-5.96)
	1.10	0.66	1.20 (1.93)	0.31 (1.70)	0.05 (0.15)	0.02 (0.84)	-1.54 (-5.80)
β_j^f	2.1	0.71	3.59 (9.12)				-2.27 (-12.43)
	2.2	0.58		1.67 (6.84)			-2.74 (-9.39)
	2.3	0.78	2.57 (5.37)	0.77 (3.12)			-2.72 (-12.54)
	2.4	0.72	2.72 (3.19)		0.57 (1.14)		-2.25 (-12.29)
	2.5	0.73		0.91 (3.42)	1.30 (4.30)		-2.60 (-10.83)
	2.6	0.78	2.11 (2.66)	0.74 (2.91)	0.33 (0.71)		-2.69 (-12.05)
	2.7	0.71	3.45 (6.14)			0.02 (0.34)	-2.39 (-6.13)
	2.8	0.72	2.60 (2.76)		0.57 (1.12)	0.01 (0.32)	-2.36 (-6.05)
	2.9	0.78	2.50 (4.46)	0.77 (3.05)		-0.001 (-0.03)	-2.71 (-7.44)
	2.10	0.78	2.12 (2.45)	0.74 (2.84)	0.32 (0.70)	-0.001 (-0.03)	-2.68 (-7.24)

Note: For explanation of symbols, see Table 6.1. In the estimating equations, GDICAP has been expressed in units of 10,000 dollars and HMIND in units of 100.

TABLE 6.3
Regression Equations For Physical and Human Capital Intensity Measures

Dependent Variable	Equation Number	Coefficient of Determination	Explanatory Variables			
			GDICAP	HMIND	DUMMY	CONSTANT
β_j^{sp}	3.1	0.17		0.32 (2.64)		−0.56 (−3.81)
	3.2	0.19	0.67 (2.86)			−0.46 (−4.22)
	3.3	0.22	0.45 (1.42)	0.16 (1.00)		−0.55 (−3.83)
	3.4	0.23	0.55 (1.03)	0.17 (1.01)	−0.07 (−0.23)	−0.56 (−3.75)
β_j^{fp}	4.1	0.25		0.37 (3.16)		−0.65 (−4.66)
	4.2	0.29	0.75 (3.39)			−0.53 (−5.17)
	4.3	0.30	0.50 (1.67)	0.19 (1.24)		−0.64 (−4.74)
	4.4	0.40	0.21 (0.43)	0.17 (1.08)	0.21 (0.72)	−0.62 (−4.46)
β_j^{sh}	5.1	0.59		0.55 (4.74)		−0.87 (−6.23)
	5.2	0.61	1.30 (6.99)			−0.75 (−8.73)
	5.3	0.62	1.07 (4.27)	0.17 (1.36)		−0.86 (−7.55)
	5.4	0.50	0.81 (1.95)	0.16 (1.18)	0.19 (0.78)	−0.84 (−7.19)
β_j^{fh}	6.1	0.64		2.45 (5.87)		−3.91 (−7.81)
	6.2	0.69	5.36 (7.77)			−3.25 (−10.13)
	6.3	0.69	3.96 (4.96)	1.07 (2.33)		−3.87 (−9.65)
	6.4	0.69	3.83 (2.58)	1.06 (2.24)	0.09 (0.10)	−3.86 (−9.29)

Note: For explanation of symbols, see Tables 6.1 and 6.2.

developing countries as far as distortions due to the application of protective measures are concerned. The distortions, in turn, have affected the pattern of exports and imports; in particular, with the implicit subsidy to capital goods through the overvaluation of the exchange rate associated with high protection, exports have been biased in a capital-intensive direction.

The results for the United States are somewhat of a puzzle as the findings of other authors would have led us to expect that actual U.S. exports are less, rather than more, physical-capital intensive than the hypothetical exports derived from intercountry relationships. And while the solution to the puzzle may well be that the ratio of physical to human capital intensity is even higher for the imports than for the exports of the United States, our results conflict with those of Hufbauer which show the U.S. to be below the regression line.[30] Note, however, that Hufbauer's results pertain to an earlier year and he provides evidence that U.S. exports have become increasingly physical-capital intensive over time. Finally, our calculations using direct input coefficients are preferable to earlier estimates derived by the use of direct plus indirect coefficients once we admit international trade in intermediate products.

In turn, the exports of Hong Kong are less capital-intensive than expected on the basis of its physical capital endowment. It would appear that Hong Kong's export structure does not yet fully reflect the large investments in physical capital carried out during the period under consideration. Finally, deviations from the regression line are relatively small in regard to human capital endowment.

Next we have estimated a matrix of Spearman rank correlation coefficients for pairs of country characteristics in the 36 country sample. From Table 6.4 it is apparent that the extent of the correlation is the weakest in regard to the skill ratio, reinforcing our conclusion as to the inappropriateness of this variable.

In turn, the correlations between per capita, GDI and the Harbison-Myers index, on the one hand, and per capita GDP on the other, indicate the effects of investment in physical and in human capital on incomes per head. The existence of this correlation also explains that the inclusion of all three variables in the regression equation raises the standard error of the coefficients to a considerable extent.[31] Nevertheless, the fact that the level of statistical significance of the physical and human capital endowment variables much exceeds that for incomes per head may be taken as an indication of the "primacy" of the former.

We have seen that the intercountry regressions provide the same general results, irrespective of whether we use a stock or a flow measure of capital intensity. This finding may be explained by the relatively high degree of correspondence in the ranking of the product categories by the two measures of capital intensity that is shown by the estimated Spearman rank correlation coefficient of 0.78 (Table 6.5).[32]

The rankings of the 18 two-digit industry groups, are also rather similar under the two measures of capital intensity. Among the individual industry

TABLE 6.4
Spearman Rank Correlation Coefficients for Country
Characteristics in the 36 Country Sample

	GNPCAP	GDICAP	HMIND	SKILLS
GNPCAP	1.000	0.984	0.754	0.674
GDICAP	0.984	1.000	0.730	0.697
HMIND	0.754	0.730	1.000	0.660
SKILLS	0.674	0.697	0.660	1.000

Note: For explanation of symbols, see Table 6.1. All coefficients
are statistically significant at the 1 percent level.

TABLE 6.5
Spearman Rank Correlation Coefficients for Alternative Measures
of Capital Intensity

	(PC+HC)/L	VA/L	PC/L	HC/L	(VA−W)/L	W/L
(PC+HC)/L	1.000	0.782	0.758	0.907	0.680	0.835
VA/L	0.782	1.000	0.636	0.685	0.951	0.809
PC/L	0.758	0.636	1.000	0.488	0.604	0.562
HC/L	0.907	0.685	0.488	1.000	0.565	0.839
(VA−W)/L	0.680	0.951	0.604	0.565	1.000	0.631
W/L	0.835	0.809	0.562	0.839	0.631	1.000

Note: For explanation of symbols see Table 6.1.

All coefficients are statistically significant at the 1 percent level.

groups, apparel and other textile products, leather and leather products, and
stone, clay and glass products are relatively labor intensive while petroleum
and coal products, chemicals, and paper and paper products are relatively
capital intensive (Table 6.6). In turn, considerable differences are shown
between the two sets of industry groups, with the capital per worker ratio under
the stock measure (expressed in tens of thousand U.S. dollars) ranging
between 14.0 and 22.1 in the three labor-intensive, and between 74.4 and
191.7 in the three capital-intensive industry groups, with the overall average
being 48.8.

At the same time, the results vary to a considerable extent within each
industry group. For example, fur goods are very capital intensive although they
belong to the highly labor-intensive apparel and other textile products industry
group. In turn, explosives are relatively labor intensive although they belong to
the capital-intensive chemicals industry group.

Moreover, substantial differences are observed among individual product
categories in terms of their factor intensity. At one extreme, we find woolen
yarn and thread with (total) capital per worker of 3.2 followed by earthenware
food utensils (3.5), footwear (3.8), leather bags and gloves (5.5), vitreous
china food utensils (7.2), costume jewelry (8.6), and games and toys (8.7),

TABLE 6.6
Average Factor Intensities for 18 Aggregated Product Categories (Dollars)

No.	SIC No.	Product Category	p_i^s	h_i^s	k_i^s	p_i^f	h_i^f	k_i^f
1.	22.	Textile mill products	9404	17814	27219	3885	5919	9804
2.	23.	Apparel & other textile products	2024	11967	13991	3583	5165	8748
3.	24.	Lumber & wood products	11266	12184	23449	4452	6431	10883
4.	25.	Furniture & fixtures	4520	21698	26198	4431	6669	11100
5.	26.	Paper & allied products	57609	40126	97735	11467	10397	21864
6.	27.	Printing & publishing	8417	36191	44607	8962	8941	17903
7.	28.	Chemical & allied products	41417	33031	74448	19485	9882	29367
8.	29.	Petroleum & coal products	126110	65629	191739	31310	11910	43220
9.	30.	Rubber & plastic products	10188	18579	28766	6406	7784	14190
10.	31.	Leather & leather products	5860	17281	23142	4420	6824	11244
11.	32.	Stone, clay & glass products	11843	10003	21846	5571	6742	12313
12.	33.	Primary metal & allied products	32937	30130	63066	6774	10385	17159
13.	34.	Fabricated metal products	9073	27860	36933	7330	8715	16045
14.	35.	Nonelectrical machinery	10045	29011	39056	7326	9704	17030
15.	36.	Electrical equipment & supplies	7122	30836	37958	5808	8916	14724
16.	37.	Transportation equipment	11602	27067	38669	11090	10824	21914
17.	38.	Instruments & related products	11147	41230	52376	13530	9619	23150
18.	39.	Misc. manufactured products	5667	17761	23428	6228	9319	15547
		All categories	20518	28278	48796	9645	9308	18953

Source: See text.

Note: For explanation of the definitions and symbols used, see equation (1) to (3) in the text.

which are the most labor intensive among the 184 product categories. At the other end of the spectrum, petroleum products (191.7), wood pulp (135.5), organic chemicals (124.2) synthetic rubber (120.6), carbon black (101.2), inorganic chemicals (92.8), and paper (89.1) are the most capital intensive.[33]

There is less of a correspondence in the rankings of product categories by their physical and their human capital intensity. The Spearman rank correlation coefficient between these indicators is 0.49 under the stock measure of capital and 0.63 under the flow measure. In turn, the correlation coefficient is 0.60 between the two measures of physical capital intensity and 0.84 between the two measures of human capital intensity. These differences are explained by the fact that the flow measure of capital intensity is sensitive to inter-industry differences in profits that do not affect the stock measure whereas both measures of human capital intensity are affected by average wages in the various product categories.

Among the individual product categories, organic chemicals, cellulosic man-made fibers, dyeing and tanning extracts, fertilizers, carbon black, and petroleum refining and products have relatively high physical as compared to human capital intensity, regardless of whether we use the stock or the flow measure of capital. The opposite result has been obtained for canvas products, radio and TV equipment, aircraft, ships and boats, and scientific instruments and control equipment. The first group includes product categories where the ratio of physical to human capital was between 1.5 and 5 using the stock measure of capital intensity and exceeded 1.2 using the flow measure. In turn, product categories in the second group had a ratio of physical to human capital of between 0.1 and 0.2 under the stock measure of capital and less than 0.6 under the flow measure.

IV. The Implications of the Findings

This paper has investigated the changing pattern of comparative advantage in the process of the accumulation of physical and human capital that characterizes economic development. Comparative advantage has been defined in terms of relative export performance, thus neglecting the composition of imports which is greatly affected by the structure of protection.

For each country, export performance has been related to the capital intensity of the individual product categories, using a stock as well as a flow measure of capital, with further distinction made between physical and human capital. Next, the regression coefficients thus obtained have been correlated with country characteristics, such as physical and human capital endowment and the level of economic development in an intercountry framework..

The empirical estimates show that intercountry differences in the structure of exports are in a large part explained by differences in physical and human capital endowments. The results lend support to the 'stages' approach to comparative advantage, according to which the structure of exports changes with the accumulation of physical and human capital.[34] This approach is also supported by intertemporal comparisons for Japan, which indicate that Japanese exports have become increasingly physical capital and human capital intensive over time.[35]

These findings have important policy implications for the developing countries. To being with, they warn against distorting the system of incentives in favor of products in which the country has a comparative disadvantage. The large differences shown among product categories in terms of their capital intensity point to the fact that there is a substantial penalty for such distortions in the form of the misallocation of productive factors. This will be the case in particular when the system of incentives is biased in favor of import substitution in capital-intensive products and against exports in labor-intensive products.

Possible magnitudes of the economic cost of distortions are indicated in Table 6.7. The table provides comparisons for seven capital-intensive and seven labor-intensive product categories between production costs in the United States, and in a hypothetical developing country where unskilled wages are one-third of U.S. wages[36] and the cost of capital is commensurately higher.[37] In the latter country, the estimated cost of capital-intensive products is 15 to 32 percent higher, and that of labor-intensive products 38 to 52 percent lower, than in the United States, so that differences in relative costs between capital and labor-intensive products range from 1.87 to 2.76.[38]

The results can further be utilized to gauge the direction in which a country's comparative advantage is moving. This may be done by substituting projected future values of a country's physical and human capital endowments in the intercountry regressions, so as to estimate the prospective values of the β coefficients.[39] In turn, these coefficients can be used to derive the hypothetical structure of exports corresponding to the country's future physical and human capital endowments. Comparing the projected export structure with the actual structure of exports, one can then indicate prospective changes in export flows.[40]

The stages approach to comparative advantage also permits one to dispel certain misapprehensions as regards the foreign demand constraint under which developing countries are said to operate. With countries progressing on the comparative advantage scale, their exports can supplant the exports of countries that graduate to a higher level. Now, to the extent that one developing country replaces another in the imports of particular commodities by the developed countries, the problem of adjustment in the latter group of countries does not arise. Rather, the brunt of adjustment will be borne in industries where the products of newly graduating developing countries compete with the products of the developed countries.

A case in point is Japan whose comparative advantage has shifted towards highly capital-intensive exports. In turn, developing countries with a relatively high human capital endowment, such as Korea and Taiwan, can take Japan's

TABLE 6.7
Hypothetical Production Costs Calculated under Alternative Assumptions (U.S. Dollars)

Product Category	United States				Developing Country				Ratio of Total Costs
	Physical Capital	Human Capital	Unskilled Labor	Total Costs	Physical Capital	Human Capital	Unskilled Labor	Total Costs	
Capital-Intensive									
1. Petroleum refining & products	37833	6563	5342	49738	54215	9405	1781	65401	1.315
2. Wood pulp	26400	4747	6382	37529	37831	6802	2127	46760	1.246
3. Organic chemicals	22635	4875	6632	34142	32436	6986	2211	41633	1.219
4. Synthetic rubber	20826	5121	6632	32579	29844	7338	2211	39393	1.209
5. Carbon black	18669	3893	6632	29194	26753	5579	2211	34543	1.183
6. Inorganic chemicals	16044	3928	6632	26604	22991	5629	2211	30831	1.159
7. Paper	14778	3983	6382	25143	21177	5707	2127	29011	1.154
Labor-Intensive									
8. Games & toys	1521	359	5436	7316	2180	514	1812	4506	0.616
9. Vitreous china food utensils	1608	186	6082	7876	2304	267	2027	4598	0.584
10. Costume jewelry	978	533	5436	6947	1401	764	1812	3977	0.572
11. Leather bags & purses	711	311	5096	6118	1019	446	1699	3164	0.517
12. Earthenware food utensils	1056	0	6082	7138	1513	0	2027	3540	0.496
13. Woollen yarn & thread	486	160	4228	4874	696	229	1409	2334	0.479
14. Footwear	660	156	5450	6266	946	224	1817	2987	0.477
All Categories	6155	2828	5831	14815	8818	4052	1944	14815	1.000

Note: U.S. production costs have been calculated by adding 30 percent of the gross value of physical capital, assumed to reflect pre-tax earnings and depreciation, to observed labor costs. In turn, for the hypothetical developing country it has been assumed that unskilled wages are one-third of U.S. wages and the cost of capital is correspondingly higher. The latter has been estimated to exceed U.S. costs by 43.3 percent under the assumption that value added in the entire manufacturing sector is the same in the two cases. All data are expressed per worker.

place in exporting relatively human capital-intensive products, and countries with a relatively high physical capital endowment, such as Brazil and Mexico, can take Japan's place in exporting relatively physical capital-intensive products. Finally, countries at lower levels of development can supplant the middle-level countries in exporting unskilled labor-intensive commodities.

The prospects of economic growth through exports thus appear brighter once we understand the character of the changing pattern of comparative advantage. Further work on the experience of individual countries over time would be necessary, however, in order to study this process in greater depth.

ESSAY 7

The Changing International Division of Labor In Manufactured Goods

Introduction

This essay will examine the employment effects for the developed countries of their trade in manufactured goods with the developing countries. Section I will analyze the employment effects of existing trade flows with consideration given to the skill-composition of employment and to the physical and the human capital intensity of trade. In turn, section II will indicate the employment effects of possible future changes in the trade of manufactured goods between the developed and the developing countries and examine the policy implications of the findings.

I. The Employment Effects of Trade in Manufactured Goods between Developed and Developing Countries[1]

The Available Evidence

In recent years, there has been much discussion on the employment effects of trade liberalization undertaken by the developed countries. As far as trade with the developing countries is concerned, the emphasis has been on the employment implications of imports from these countries. In the present investigation, we will focus on the effects of the mutual trade of the two groups of countries on manufacturing employment in the developed countries. Following a review of earlier results, estimates of the employment effects of actual and prospective trade in manufactured goods between developed and developing countries will be presented.

To begin with, reference may be made to the findings of studies on the employment effects of multilateral trade liberalization. These studies have

169

concluded that net changes in trade and employment in the developed countries resulting from multilateral trade liberalization would be negligible. Baldwin finds, for example, that—for his preferred set of elasticities—a 50 percent multilateral across-the-board tariff cut in all commodities, excluding textiles in U.S. exports and imports, petroleum in U.S. imports, and agricultural products in U.S. exports to the EEC, would have practically no effect on the U.S. trade balance and would represent a net employment loss of only 15 thousand in the United States.[2] Thus, "the main conclusion emerging from the study is that the United States can participate in a substantial tariff-cutting negotiation without causing significant adverse trade and employment effects in the country."[3]

Baldwin's calculation refers to direct plus indirect changes in employment, the latter being derived by utilizing the 367 sector U.S. input-output table for 1967. Cline et al. provide estimates of direct and indirect employment effects for twelve alternative tariff-cutting formulas, all of which exclude petroleum products and textiles. Labor-input coefficients have been available in a 92 sector breakdown in the United States, a 160 sector breakdown for Japan, and a 10 to 30 sector breakdown for the Common Market countries. For Canada, U.S. coefficients have been used.[4]

Under formula (1), representing a 60 percent multilateral across-the-board tariff cut that approximately corresponds to the median of the twelve alternative estimates, a net direct employment gain of 18.8 thousand and a direct plus indirect employment gain of 28.9 thousand is shown for the United States while the corresponding figures are −25.7 and −50.6 thousand for Canada, 2.7 and 23.9 thousand in Japan, and −112.2 thousand (direct effects only) for the EEC; in the latter case, it is estimated that total exports would decline as the decrease in intra-EEC trade would outweigh the increase in extra-EEC exports.[5] Correspondingly, Cline concludes that "those who fear serious employment dislocation from liberalizing imports are without empirical support".[6]

It is not possible, however, to derive any conclusions from the results of these studies on the employment effects of increased trade between developed and developing countries, in part because the estimates include trade among the developed countries that far outweighs trade between developed and developing countries, and in part because textiles, an important export product of the developing countries, has been excluded.[7] In the following, we will concentrate on the employment effects of trade in manufactured goods between developed and developing countries.

In a paper entitled "Impact of LDC Exports on Employment in American Industry," Anne Krueger has estimated the direct employment effects of changes in the share of imports in domestic consumption and in the net trade balance of the United States for the 1970–76 period in the two-digit breakdown of the U.S. Standard Industrial Classification, encompassing 20 manufacturing sectors. While additional estimates are provided on the employment effects of imports in some four-digit categories where import competition has been especially strong, the employment effects of imports from, and exports to, the developing countries are not separately examined. Krueger thus relies on data on total imports in rejecting "the belief that the underlying cause of the difficulties of industries seeking protection is competition from abroad, especially from the LDCs."[8]

In turn, Grinols and Thorbecke have estimated the direct plus indirect employment effects of changes in the U.S. trade balance with developing countries between 1963 and 1975 for a sample of 22 industries among the 157 sectors of the 1972 input-output table, where changes in the net trade balance exceeded $175 million. The authors find that there has been a net gain of 219 thousand jobs in the United States, which is reduced to 147 thousand jobs if the four food processing industries are excluded.[9] Having further examined "the effects on U.S. employment of a hypothetical 10% change in the prevailing US-LDC trade pattern for every year of the sample period" they conclude that "protectionistic measures as they relate to US-LDC trade are more likely to reduce domestic employment than increase it."[10]

The results obtained by Grinols and Thorbecke are explained by the growing export surplus of the United States in manufactured trade with the developing countries. Thus, between 1963 and 1975, the sum of positive increments in the U.S. trade balance in manufactured goods with the developing countries in the 18 manufacturing industries (excluding food processing) exceeded the sum of negative increments about three-and-a-half times. If we adjust for differences in the absolute increment in trade flows, and calculate the average number of jobs per $1 million of exports and imports, the conclusions reaches by Grinols and Thorbecke are reversed: an increase in exports of $1 million would entail a gain of 34.7 jobs in industries of the first group as compared to a loss of 56.3 jobs resulting from a $1 milion increase in imports in the second group, i.e., a ratio of 0.62.[11] At the same time, to the extent that the application of protectionist measures would lead to decreases in imports and exports by equal amounts, it is these latter results that indicate the employment implications of such measures.

Estimates of the employment effects of increased trade with the developing countries have also been made for Belgium and Germany. In the first case, the ratio of direct plus indirect employment for BF 1 billion worth of exports to that for imports has been estimated at .84 for 1970 by utilizing a 27 sector input-output table, of which 20 sectors produce manufactured goods.[12] In the second case, two sets of estimates are available.

Utilizing a 47 sector input-output table, with 28 sectors producing manufactured commodities, Schumacher has estimated the ratio of the direct plus indirect employment effects of a balanced increase of German trade in manufactured goods with the developing countries at 0.96 while a net employment gain is shown only if direct effects in the manufacturing sector are considered.[13] The latter estimate contrasts with more recent calculations by

Hiemenz and Schatz who projected a gain of 400 thousand jobs through increased exports and a loss of 846 thousand jobs through increased imports in trade in manufactured goods with the developing countries for 1985, assuming that recent trends continue and utilizing the same industrial breakdown as Schumacher.[14]

In turn, Lydall has utilized a 20 sector input-output table, of which 10 sectors produce manufactured goods, to estimate the direct plus indirect employment effects of trade liberalization in selected industries of the developed countries, matched by the re-spending of increased export proceeds by the developing countries in the country of importation. Results obtained for the United States, France, Germany, and the United Kingdom show net losses in employment if trade in textiles and clothing is liberalized; there is a net gain if trade liberalization occurs in wood products, paper and printing, and ferrous and nonferrous metals; and net employment effects are approximately nil for machinery and other manufactured goods.[15]

Lydall has compared employment changes in selected import-competing industries with across-the-board export proceeds by the developing countries. The re-spending assumption has also been made by Birnberg, who has compared the direct employment effects of a 60 percent across-the-board tariff cut for U.S. imports of manufactured goods other than textiles from the developing countries with the employment effects of the increase in U.S. exports that would result from the spending of the increment in the foreign exchange earnings of the developing countries in the United States. Birnberg's results show a gain of 31.5 jobs for a $1 million increase in the exports and a loss of 37.1 jobs for a $1 million increase in the imports of the United States, i.e. a ratio of 0.85.[16] The results for imports from the developing countries originate from Cline's study while exports have been estimated in a framework of a 21 sector input-output table, with 16 sectors producing manufactured commodities.

These estimates of the employment effects of trade in manufactured goods between developed and developing countries are subject to various limitations. Lydall and Birnberg make different assumptions as regards exports and imports; they as well as de Grauwe *et al.,* Schumacher, and Hiemenz and Schatz are highly-aggregated commodity classification schemes that include products of varying labor intensity in the individual categories; while Grinols and Thorbecke, who employ a more detailed classification scheme, cover only selected commodity categories.

Employment Effects in the Developed Countries Resulting from the Expansion of Their Trade in Manufactured Goods with the Developing Countries

Underlying Assumptions. In the present investigation, a detailed commodity framework has been used to estimate the employment effects for the developed countries of the simultaneous expansion of manufactured exports and imports in their trade with the developing countries. For this purpose, use has been made of a 184 commodity category breakdown of the manufacturing sector that was earlier employed in a study of the changing pattern of comparative advantage.[17] Each commodity category includes products that have similar economic characteristics, including labor intensity.

The labor-input coefficients used in the calculations originate from the U.S. Census of Manufacturing for the year 1975. The Census provides data for the four-digit categories of the Standard Industrial Classification, which have been combined whenever considered necessary in arriving at the 184 commodity category classification scheme. This classification scheme has further been matched against the UN Standard International Trade Classification that is used in reporting trade statistics.

The U.S. labor-input coefficients have been utilized for the other developed countries as well. While Lydall shows that labor-input coefficients are negatively correlated with per capita incomes, the differences in the coefficients are considerably smaller at the higher income levels of the developed countries.[18] At any rate, by 1975 most developed countries had approached —and some may have exceeded—U.S. incomes per head.

At the same time, the choice of U.S. coefficients has been made necessary by reason of the lack of labor-input coefficients in a comparable commodity breakdown for the other developed countries. In the only other country, Japan, that has a detailed industrial classification scheme, rapid increases of labor productivity have rendered the 1970 coefficients used by Cline out of date, and comparability with the 184 commodity category classification scheme could not be assured. Note further that unpublished calculations by Robert E. Baldwin show that the use of Japanese input-output coefficients give results very close to those obtained by Grinols and Thorbecke for the sectors covered by the latter.

The coefficients pertain to labor inputs used directly in the production process. In the absence of an input-output table in the appropriate breakdown, estimating the indirect employment effects of trade in manufactured goods would have involved a very substantial effort. At the same time, for reasons noted below, such an effort did not appear warranted.

To begin with, calculating indirect effects on the basis of historical coefficients assumes unchanged proportions of domestically produced and imported inputs that would not be appropriate for estimating the employment effects of an *expansion* of trade. This is because product market equilibrium requires that the marginal cost of domestically produced inputs equals the world market price plus the tariff, so that the increased demand for inputs at higher export levels would be satisfied from abroad.

Nontraded inputs by definition originate from domestic sources and should ideally be included in the calculations. Such inputs are, however, of limited importance, averaging 8–12 percent of the product price, and their omission is not likely to bias the results. This is because, other things being equal, nontraded inputs used in import-substituting industries can be expected to be more labor intensive than nontraded inputs used in export industries.

At any rate, available estimates indicate that the use of direct, as opposed to direct plus indirect, labor-input coefficients make little difference for the results. Cline's estimates of the employment effects of multilateral trade liberalization, reported above, show small differences between the two alternatives in relation to the total trade of developed countries. The same conclusion applies to Schumacher's estimates of the employment effects of increased trade in manufactured goods between Germany and the developing countries.

Employment Effects of a Balanced Expansion of Trade. The employment effects in the developed countries that would result from a *balanced* expansion of their trade in manufactured goods with the developing countries (i.e. with exports and imports rising by equal amounts) have been estimated on the assumption of the unchanged composition of exports and of imports. Under this assumption, comparisons of average labor-input coefficients for exports and for goods competing with imports will indicate the employment effects of balanced trade expansion.

Average labor-input coefficients for the exports and the imports of manufactured goods in trade between developed and developing countries are reported for eighteen industry groups in Table 7.1. The estimates have been derived by averaging labor-input data obtained in the 184 industry breakdown, using the value of exports and imports in trade between developed and developing countries in the year 1976 as weights. The table provides estimates for the OECD as a whole, the United States, the EEC and Japan.[19]

The estimates show the existence of considerable differences in average labor-input coefficients for the exports and for the imports of manufactured goods of the developed countries in trade with the developing countries. For the OECD, taken as a whole, the average number of jobs for $1 million of output is 18.4 for exports to, and 28.5 for imports from, the developing countries, the ratio of the two being 0.65. The corresponding ratios are 0.61 for the United States, 0.65 for the EEC, and 0.73 for Japan. Thus, among the developed countries, the average ratio of labor-input coefficients for exports and imports appears to be negatively correlated with per capita incomes as the Heckscher-Ohlin theory would lead us to expect.

These estimates conflict with the by-now popular view, according to which trade in manufactured goods between the developed and the developing countries has negligible net employment effects. At the same time, they confirm the results reached in the author's cited study on the stages approach to comparative advantage, according to which developing countries tend to specialize in labor-intensive commodities.

Comparisons with the results obtained by other authors in regard to the employment effects of trade with the developing countries offer further

TABLE 7.1

Average Labor Input Coefficients in Manufactured Trade between Developed and Developing Countries
(Jobs per $ million of output)

	OECD		USA		EEC		JAPAN	
	Export	Import	Export	Import	Export	Import	Export	Import
1. Textile Mill Products	28.66	32.73	29.28	34.34	28.30	32.05	28.46	31.55
2. Apparel & Other Textile Products	40.13	43.12	40.69	40.78	41.38	43.14	39.08	40.53
3. Lumber & Wood Products	25.12	25.62	25.45	25.80	23.92	25.30	27.63	26.09
4. Furniture & Fixtures	32.68	32.68	32.68	32.68	32.68	32.68	32.68	32.68
5. Paper & Allied Products	11.80	12.48	11.00	14.36	12.83	12.40	11.92	10.81
6. Printing & Publishing	26.66	24.58	26.64	24.59	27.27	25.02	28.20	27.73
7. Chemicals & Allied Products	10.67	11.37	10.29	13.07	10.96	10.37	11.37	10.53
8. Petroleum Products	10.30	10.30	10.30	10.30	10.30	10.30	10.30	10.30
9. Rubber & Plastic Products	22.87	43.27	22.46	43.96	25.13	42.30	18.13	40.41
10. Leather & Leather Products	28.21	30.93	30.06	35.93	33.26	26.69	22.25	28.13
11. Stone, Clay & Glass Products	24.44	30.82	25.51	34.91	25.89	29.81	24.69	31.64
12. Primary Metal & Allied Products	13.59	13.35	15.56	13.63	14.29	13.11	12.59	13.07
13. Fabricated Metal Products	21.27	22.93	21.37	23.20	21.35	23.29	21.30	22.31
14. Nonelectrical Machinery	19.73	20.42	18.75	20.39	20.00	20.88	20.20	20.43
15. Electrical Equipment & Supplies	24.59	24.68	25.05	24.75	24.46	24.69	24.50	25.30
16. Transportation Equipment	15.86	18.90	13.85	12.29	13.42	19.14	20.25	26.88
17. Instruments & Related Products	22.15	23.23	21.27	24.81	21.39	20.32	21.04	23.18
18. Misc. Manufactured Products	23.44	23.65	23.44	25.63	22.28	21.77	29.05	21.39
Total	18.44	28.53	17.77	29.12	18.50	28.40	19.30	26.32

Source: See text.

interest. As shown above, the average ratio of direct plus indirect employment coefficients for U.S. exports and imports of manufactured goods in trade with the developing countries was .62 for selected industries in the Grinols-Thorbecke study. Thus, the differences between the direct employment effects estimated in this investigation and the direct plus indirect employment effects estimated by Grinols and Thorbecke is small, although the comparability of the results is reduced by differences in industry coverage.

In turn, de Grauwe's results for Belgium and Schumacher's estimates for Germany refer to earlier years, and shifts have since occurred in favor of the importation of labor-intensive goods, such as clothing and electronics, from the developing countries at the expense of capital-intensive iron and steel and chemicals. In fact, Schumacher's results show increases in the relative labor-intensity of imports after 1972, although the ratio of estimated average direct plus indirect labor-input coefficients for German exports and imports of manufactured goods was only 0.94 for changes in the composition of this trade between 1972 and 1976.[20] Furthermore, as we have seen, projections made by Hiemenz and Schatz indicate a considerable employment loss for German trade in manufactured goods with the developing countries.

The Belgian and the German estimates are based on the assumption that labor-input coefficients are the same for exports and for imports in each industry group. The present estimates, however, show the existence of considerable differences in the coefficients as between the developed countries' exports and imports in trade with the developing countries *within* most industry groups. This is indicated by a comparison of average labor-input coefficients for exports and for imports in the 18 industry group breakdown. (Table 7.1).

To being with, there are large differences in average labor-input coefficients for exports and imports in the case of rubber and plastic products; stone, clay and glass products; and transportation equipment. In these industry groups, the ratios of the average labor-input coefficients for exports as compared to imports are 0.53, 0.79, and 0.84, respectively, for the OECD taken as a whole.

The results for these industry groups are explained by the dominant role played by highly labor-intensive rubber footwear in the developed countries' imports, and by the relative importance of highly capital-intensive tires and tubes in their exports, of rubber and plastic products; by the high share of relatively labor-intensive glass containers in the imports, and the high share of relatively capital intensive exports of cement in the exports, of stone, clay and glass products by the developed countries; and by the high share of relatively labor-intensive ships and boats in the imports, and the high share of relatively capital-intensive motor vehicles in the exports, of transportation equipment by these countries.

Labor-input coefficients are higher for imports than for exports in the trade of the OECD countries with the developing countries in most other industry groups, too. The opposite result is shown only for printing and publishing and for primary metals. But, in these cases, the differences are small; the ratio of labor-input coefficients in export-import relationships is 1.08 in the first case and 1.02 in the second. At the same time, printing and publishing is a relatively unimportant item in trade between developed and developing countries.[21]

There are a few additional exceptions for individual developed countries and country groups but the differences exceed 10 percent only for transportation equipment in the United States (a ratio of 1.13), leather and leather products in the EEC (a ratio of 1.25), and miscellaneous manufactured products in Japan (a ratio of 1.36). In the United States, this result is due to the relatively high share of the imports of automobile parts and accessories that are combined with capital-intensive motor vehicles; in the EEC, the high export share of capital-intensive leather has contributed to the outcome; while in Japan the exportation of relatively labor-intensive toys and sports goods is largely responsible for the result obtained in regard to miscellaneous manufactured products.

The numerical magnitudes of *between* and *within* industry group differences in labor-input coefficients are of further interest. These can be shown by comparing the ratios of average labor-input coefficients for exports and imports reported above with the ratios derived on the assumption that labor-input coefficients are invariant within each of the eighteen industry groups. The relevant results are .65 and .71 for the OECD, taken as a whole, .61 and .66 for the United States, .65 and .70 for the EEC, and .73 and .81 for Japan. It appears, then, that within-industry group differences in labor-input coefficients account for about one-sixth of the difference in average labor-input coefficients for exports and imports, estimated in a 184 commodity category breakdown. It may be suggested that additional disaggregation would further increase differences in the coefficients.

Thus far, we have compared average labor-input coefficients for manufactured goods traded between developed and developing countries. These coefficients will be relevant in the event of a *balanced* expansion of manufactured trade between the two groups of countries. In such an eventuality, the number of jobs lost through increased imports would be about one-half higher than the number of jobs gained through exporting, for the OECD taken as a whole.

Employment Effects of a Proportional Expansion of Trade. An alternative hypothesis postulates equi-proportionate increases in the exports and imports of manufactured goods in trade between developed and developing countries (i.e. identical rates of change for exports and imports) or a *proportional* expansion of trade. Assuming further unchanged export and import structures as beforehand, the employment effects of a proportional expansion of trade are indicated in Table 7.2 that provides information on the labor content of manufactured exports, and of products competing with manufactured imports, in the trade of the developed countries with the developing countries. The estimates have been derived by multiplying export and import values for 1976 by the labor-input coefficients estimated in the 184 industry breakdown.

TABLE 7.2
Total Employment Effects of Manufactured Trade Between Developed and Developing Countries, 1976
(thousand jobs)

	OECD			USA			EEC			JAPAN		
	Export	Import	Balance	Export	Import	Balance	Export	Import	Balance	Export	Import	Balance
1. Textile Mill Products	138.9	192.2	-53.3	15.4	62.5	-47.1	48.7	74.3	-25.6	61.7	18.8	42.9
2. Apparel & Other Textile Products	40.8	218.2	-177.4	13.0	81.5	-68.5	19.8	90.1	-70.3	3.4	13.7	-10.3
3. Lumber & Wood Products	10.4	26.3	-15.9	2.0	11.5	-9.5	5.2	8.9	-3.7	0.3	2.2	-1.9
4. Furniture & Fixtures	19.7	10.6	9.1	3.4	4.1	-0.7	12.8	3.4	9.4	1.7	1.6	0.1
5. Paper & Allied Products	33.3	2.8	30.5	8.6	1.0	7.6	6.5	1.2	5.3	3.6	0.1	3.5
6. Printing & Publishing	25.0	2.7	22.3	4.5	0.8	3.7	15.3	0.8	14.5	1.4	0.2	1.2
7. Chemical & Allied Products	163.4	23.4	140.0	37.5	10.4	27.1	73.8	6.6	67.2	28.8	2.8	26.0
8. Petroleum Products	1.1	0.0	1.1	0.0	0.0	0.0	0.7	0.0	0.7	0.0	0.0	0.0
9. Rubber & Plastic Products	32.2	63.1	-30.9	4.4	41.8	-37.4	16.0	11.5	4.5	8.1	3.2	4.9
10. Leather & Leather Products	10.1	36.2	-26.2	2.5	15.1	-12.6	3.7	13.7	-10.0	3.1	2.0	1.1
11. Stone, Clay & Glass Products	51.6	10.9	40.7	6.6	4.5	2.1	25.7	3.2	22.5	11.0	1.3	9.7
12. Primary Metal & Allied Products	194.2	27.7	166.5	25.7	11.9	13.8	77.4	9.8	67.6	73.1	2.8	70.3
13. Fabricated Metal Products	91.9	7.3	84.5	15.9	2.8	13.1	49.5	2.2	47.3	13.5	0.3	13.2
14. Nonelectrical Machinery	527.4	18.7	508.7	142.7	6.4	136.3	261.7	6.6	255.1	71.5	1.6	69.9
15. Electrical Equipment & Supplies	417.3	122.7	294.6	106.3	77.9	28.4	187.1	29.9	157.2	88.6	10.8	77.8
16. Transportation Equipment	486.2	13.7	472.5	108.0	2.6	105.4	145.1	5.0	140.1	177.4	3.0	174.4
17. Instruments & Related Products	72.7	17.8	54.9	16.3	9.5	6.8	22.3	4.5	17.8	17.2	1.5	15.7
18. Misc. Manufactured Products	47.7	58.0	-10.3	9.1	27.2	-18.1	25.3	18.3	7.0	9.4	6.3	3.1
Total	2363.8	852.5	1511.3	521.9	371.5	150.4	996.7	289.9	706.8	573.8	72.3	501.6
of which sum of positive balances			1825.4			344.3			816.3			513.8
negative balances			314.1			193.9			109.5			12.2

Source: See text.

The results show substantial positive employment effects for the OECD countries in their trade in manufactured goods with the developing countries. Similar conclusions apply to the United States, the EEC, and Japan. Thus, in the event of a proportional expansion of trade, the ratio of jobs gained through exports to jobs lost through imports would be 2.8 in the OECD taken as whole, 1.4 in the United States, 3.4 in the EEC, and 7.9 in Japan. It is apparent that differences in the results shown in Tables 7.1 and 7.2 are explained by intercountry variations in export-import ratios in manufactured trade with the developing countries.

The proportional expansion of manufactured trade between developed and developing countries would create new jobs in most industry groups in the developed countries. Exceptions are textiles, clothing, lumber and wood products, rubber and plastic products, leather and leather products, and miscellaneous manufactures. For the OECD countries, taken together, a 10 percent proportional increase in trade flows would entail the loss of altogether 31 thousand jobs in these industries as compared to a total gain of 183 thousand jobs in the other industry groups. Comparable figures are 19 thousand and 34 thousand for the United States and 11 thousand and 82 thousand for the EEC. Finally, Japan would experience a gain of 51 thousand jobs in its export industries, with practically no loss of jobs elsewhere.[22]

The Skill-Intensity of Trade

We have seen that average labor input-coefficients are about one-half greater for the manufactured imports of the developed countries from the developing countries than for their exports to these countries. The opposite conclusion is reached if we consider professional and technical labor alone. In this occupational group, the ratio of labor-input coefficients for exports as compared to imports is 1.20 in the OECD taken as a whole, 1.20 in the United States, 1.29 in the EEC, and 1.12 in Japan (Table 7.3A). Thus, there would be a gain in the employment of professional and technical labor in the developed countries, even if one assumed a balanced expansion of their trade in manufactured goods with the developing countries. On the OECD level, as well as for the EEC and Japan, there would also be gains in the employment of foremen and skilled workers, under this assumption while a small loss is shown for the United States. In turn, the largest losses would be incurred in regard to semi-skilled and unskilled production workers, where the ratio of labor-input coefficients for exports as compared to imports is 0.44 for the OECD taken as a whole, 0.42 for the United States, 0.45 for the EEC, and 0.50 for Japan.[23]

The results cited in Table 7.3A point to the existence of considerable differences in the occupational structure of production for exports and for import substitution in the trade of the developed countries with the developing countries. These differences are put into focus in Table 7.3B that provides

TABLE 7.3

Employment Effects of Trade in Manufactured Products between Developed and Developing Countries According to Occupational Categories

	OECD		USA		EEC		JAPAN	
	Export	Import	Export	Import	Export	Import	Export	Import
A. *Labor-Input Coefficients* (No. of Jobs per $ Million of Output)								
1. Professional & Technical Workers	2.07	1.72	2.36	1.97	2.03	1.57	1.93	1.72
2. Managers & Administrators	1.03	1.40	1.06	1.47	1.08	1.36	0.91	1.32
3. Sales Workers	0.28	0.50	0.28	0.51	0.37	0.51	0.22	0.47
4. Clerical Workers	2.29	2.93	2.35	3.08	2.32	2.85	2.23	2.72
5. Foremen & Skilled Workers (Craftsmen)	4.28	3.84	3.69	3.89	4.08	3.69	5.26	3.94
6. Production Workers, Unskilled and Semi-skilled (Operators)	7.32	16.57	7.08	16.68	7.53	16.81	7.36	14.63
7. Workers in Construction, Transportation, Material Handling, etc.	0.39	0.50	0.36	0.50	0.38	0.50	0.42	0.48
8. Laborers	0.78	1.06	0.60	1.02	0.76	1.11	0.99	1.04
Total	18.44	28.53	17.77	29.12	18.50	28.40	19.30	26.32
B. *Employment Shares* (percent)								
1. Professional & Technical Workers	11.22	6.04	13.26	6.77	10.98	5.52	9.99	6.53
2. Managers & Administrators	5.57	4.91	5.96	5.04	5.83	4.80	4.73	5.01
3. Sales Workers	1.54	1.76	1.56	1.75	1.72	1.78	1.14	1.78
4. Clerical Workers	12.43	10.27	13.20	10.59	12.55	10.03	11.53	10.32
5. Foremen & Skilled Workers								

TABLE 7.3 (Cont'd.)
Employment Effects of Trade in Manufactured Products between Developed and Developing Countries According to Occupational Categories

	OECD		USA		EEC		JAPAN	
	Export	Import	Export	Import	Export	Import	Export	Import
(Craftsmen)	23.23	13.45	20.76	13.37	22.07	12.99	27.25	14.96
6. Production Workers, Unskilled & Semi-skilled (Operators)	39.71	58.08	39.84	57.27	40.58	59.19	38.11	55.60
7. Workers in Construction, Transportation, Material Handling, etc.	2.09	1.76	2.04	1.73	2.07	1.77	2.15	1.84
8. Laborers	4.23	3.73	3.39	3.49	4.11	3.92	5.14	3.95
Total	100.00	100.00	100.00	100.00	100.00	100.00	100.00	100.00
C. *Employment Effects of Trade in 1976* *(Thousands of Jobs)*								
1. Professional & Technical Workers	265.2	51.5	69.2	25.2	109.4	16.0	57.3	4.7
2. Managers & Administrators	131.8	41.9	31.1	18.7	58.2	13.9	27.1	3.6
3. Sales Workers	36.4	15.0	8.1	6.5	17.2	5.2	6.5	1.3
4. Clerical Workers	294.0	87.6	68.9	39.3	125.1	29.1	66.2	7.5
5. Foremen & Skilled Workers (Craftsmen)	549.0	114.7	108.4	49.7	220.0	37.7	156.3	10.8
6. Production Workers, Unskilled & Semi-skilled (Operators)	938.6	495.1	207.9	212.7	405.5	171.6	218.7	40.2
7. Workers in Construction, Transportation, Material Handling, etc.	49.4	15.0	10.6	6.4	20.6	5.1	12.4	1.3
8. Laborers	99.8	31.8	17.6	13.0	40.9	11.4	29.5	2.9
Total	2363.8	852.5	521.9	371.5	996.7	289.9	573.8	72.2

Source: Table 7.1 and text.

information on the average employment shares of the various occupational categories in the manufactured exports and imports of the OECD countries, taken together, the United States, the EEC, and Japan.

Among occupational categories, the share of professional and technical workers in total employment is nearly double for the exports than for the imports of manufactured goods in the OECD countries' trade with the developed country manufactured exports to the developing countries is about one-third lower than that of their imports, with little variation shown among the OECD countries.

Also, the share of foremen and skilled workers in total employment is about three-fourths higher for the exports than for the imports of the OECD countries in their manufactured trade with the developing countries, with Japan at the top (1.82) and the United States (1.55) at the bottom of the range. The differences go in the same direction,[24] but they are numerically smaller, for managers and administrators, clerical workers, service workers, and for workers in construction, transportation, and material handling.

Differences in the opposite direction are observed in regard to sales workers and, in particular, for the largest category, unskilled and and semi-skilled production workers. In the latter case, the average employment share of developed country manufactured exports to the developing countries is about one-third lower than that of their imports, with little variation shown among the OECD countries. Again, these results conform to the Heckscher-Ohlin theory of international specialization.

By comparison, Keesing found that in 1957 the exports of the United States, Germany, Sweden, and the United Kingdom were relatively skill-intensive while skill intensity was higher for imports than for exports in the Netherlands, Belgium, Italy, France, and Japan.[25] In interpreting Keesing's estimates, it should be recalled, however, that they pertain to a relatively early postwar year and concern the total manufactured trade of the countries in question that was dominated by trade among the developed countries themselves.

In turn, Baldwin and Lewis estimate that a 50 percent multilateral tariff cut in manufacturing (textiles excluded) would provide a net employment gain in the professional and technical labor and in the management and administration categories, as against losses in all other labor categories, in the United States.[26] A comparison of the Baldwin-Lewis estimates with those reported in Table 7.3C shows that, as expected, increased trade with the developing countries would lead to a larger shift from low-skill to high-skill occupations than that resulting from an increase in U.S. overall trade.

While the estimates reported in Table 7.3A indicate the employment effects of a *balanced* expansion of manufactured trade between developed and developing countries in the various occupational categories, the estimates of Table 7.3C show the effects of *proportional* change in this trade. It is apparent that an equi-proportionate increase in OECD exports and imports in trade in manufactured goods with the developing countries would have a net employ-ment-creating effect in all eight occupational categories. The same results have been obtained for the EEC and Japan and, with the exception of unskilled and semi-skilled production workers, for the United States.

The Human and the Physical Capital Intensity of Trade

We have considered the effects of trade in manufactured goods between developed and developing countries on employment in the former group of countries for various skill classes. In order to express the skill intensity of trade in a single number, Keesing (1965, 1968, 1971)[27] has calculated ratios of jobs in high-skilled to low-skill occupations. Given the arbitrariness involved in making such a distinction, we have instead followed Kenen in estimating the human-capital intensity of trade. This procedure also permits making com-parisons between the physical and the human capital intensity of the exports and imports of the developed countries.

Physical capital and human capital coefficients have been taken from "A 'Stages Approach' to Comparative Advantage," referred to earlier, where the derivation of these coefficients is described in detail. Two sets of coefficients have been calculated: "stock" and "flow" coefficients. The former have been defined as the value of fixed capital per worker (physical capital) and the discounted value of the difference between the average wage and the unskilled wage (human capital), and the latter as nonwage value added per worker (physical capital) and the average wage (human capital).

Table 7.4 provides information on average physical and human capital coefficients for exports and imports of manufactured goods in the trade of developed countries with the developing countries. As is apparent from the table, for the OECD taken as a whole, capital coefficients for exports are substantially higher than for imports. The average ratios of the coefficients for exports and for imports are 1.58 for physical capital and 1.44 for human capital utilizing the stock measure, and 1.48 and 1.28, respectively, utilizing the flow measure.

Similar results have been obtained for the United States and the EEC, except that, in the latter case, the stock measure shows the same ratios for physical and for human capital. Note further that in the EEC the ratio for human capital under the flow measure (1.28) is roughly the same as that obtained for Belgium, where this was estimated at 1.26 for 1970.[29]

The ratios of physical and human capital coefficients for exports and for imports are, however, substantially lower for Japan than for the other developed countries. This result may be taken to reflect the fact that capital accumulation in Japan has not been commensurate with incomes per head that have rising very rapidly in recent years.

The cited estimates indicate the relatively high physical capital and skill-intensity of the manufactured exports of the developed countries to the

TABLE 7.4
Physical and Human Capital Coefficients of Manufactured Exports and Imports of Developed Countries
(thousand dollars per worker)

	OECD			USA			EEC			JAPAN		
	Export	Import	Ratio	Export	Import	Ratio	Export	Import	Ratio	Export	Import	Ratio
Stock Measures												
Physical Capital	16.6	10.5	1.58	15.6	9.2	1.68	15.3	11.0	1.39	14.1	11.9	1.18
Human Capital	29.7	20.6	1.44	30.6	19.9	1.54	29.1	21.0	1.39	24.8	22.0	1.13
Together	46.3	31.1	1.49	46.2	29.2	1.58	44.4	32.0	1.39	38.9	33.9	1.15
Flow Measures												
Physical Capital	8.6	5.8	1.48	8.8	5.5	1.60	9.0	5.9	1.53	8.1	6.7	1.21
Human Capital	9.6	7.5	1.28	9.8	7.6	1.29	9.5	7.4	1.28	8.4	7.6	1.10
Together	18.2	13.4	1.36	18.7	13.1	1.42	18.5	13.3	1.39	16.5	14.3	1.15

Source: See text.

developing countries as compared to their imports from these countries. It is thus apparent that, in their manufactured trade with the developing countries, the developed countries exchange physical and human capital for labor.

II. Employment Implications of Prospective Trends in Trade In Manufactured Goods between Developed and Developing Countries.[30]

Projections of Growth and Trade

In the preceding section, we have examined the employment implications for the developed countries of a *balanced* and a *proportional* expansion of their trade in manufactured goods with the developing countries. Consideration has further been given to the occupational structure and to the physical and human capital-intensity of this trade.

Neither a balanced nor a proportional expansion of trade in manufactured goods between developed and developing countries is a likely occurrence. Rather, these alternatives represent extreme cases, assuming a zero trade balance in manufactured goods *on the margin* in the first case, and an equi-proportionate expansion of *all* manufactured trade flows in the second.

Correspondingly, in order to evaluate the employment implications of future trade in manufactured goods between the developed and the developing countries, projections of trade flows have to be made. In projecting trade flows, we have taken the estimates of the *World Development Report, 1978*[31] as a point of departure.

WDR I forecasts the following growth rates of the total exports of manufactured goods from the developing countries between 1975 and 1985: textiles, 6.2 percent; clothing, 8.3 percent; chemicals, 13.0 percent; iron and steel, 14.5 percent; machinery and transport equipment, 17.3 percent; and other manufactures 10.0 percent; averaging 12.2 percent.[32] The same estimates are employed in regard to the developing countries' exports to the developed countries, which account for about three-fourths of the total.

We have applied the export growth rates assumed in the *World Development Report, 1978* for 1975–85 to project the future exports of the developing countries to the developed countries in individual industry groups for the 1976–86 period. The resulting estimates, reported in Table 7.5, entail an average growth rate for manufactured exports of 12.6 percent, slightly higher than the 12.2 percent shown in the Report.[33] The difference is largely due to the fact that nonelectrical and electrical machinery and transport equipment, which have the highest projected growth rate, had a larger share in the developing countries exports of manufactured goods in 1976 than in 1975.

Our estimates for textiles and clothing, however, represent a departure from the WDR II projections that call for developing country exports to rise at an annual average rate of 4.5 percent in the first case, and 5.5 percent in the

TABLE 7.5

Projected Expansion of Exports and Imports in Manufactured Goods between the Developed and Developing Countries
($ million; percent)

	Exports 1976	Annual Growth Rate	Projected Exports, 1986	Increment in Exports, 1976-86	Imports 1976	Annual Growth Rate	Projected Imports, 1986	Increment in Imports, 1976-86
1. Textile Mill Products	4846	3.4	6770	1924	5874	6.2	10719	4845
2. Apparel & Other Textile Products	1016	3.4	1419	403	5060	8.3	11231	6171
3. Lumber & Wood Products	414	3.4	578	164	1025	10.0	2659	1634
4. Furniture & Fixtures	601	3.4	840	239	324	10.0	839	515
5. Paper & Allied Products	2819	6.8	5443	2624	228	10.0	592	364
6. Printing & Publishing	937	6.8	1809	872	110	10.0	285	175
7. Chemical & Allied Products	15316	6.8	29570	14254	2058	13.0	6986	4928
8. Petroleum Products	107	3.4	149	42	4	10.0	9	5
9. Rubber & Plastic Products	1407	3.4	1966	559	1458	10.0	3782	2324
10. Leather & Leather Products	357	3.4	499	142	1171	10.0	3036	1865
11. Stone, Clay & Glass Products	2112	3.4	2950	838	344	10.0	892	548
12. Primary Metal & Allied Products	14289	6.3	26323	12034	2076	10.7	5736	3660
13. Fabricated Metal Products	4318	6.3	7954	3636	320	10.7	884	564
14. Nonelectrical Machinery	26731	9.1	63865	37134	916	20.3	5812	4896
15. Electrical Equipment & Supplies	16971	9.1	40546	23575	4970	20.3	31550	26580
16. Transportation Equipment	30652	6.8	59179	28527	725	20.3	4601	3876
17. Instruments & Related Products	3281	9.1	7839	4558	768	10.0	1991	1223
18. Misc. Manufactured Products	2036	6.8	3931	1895	2454	10.0	6365	3911
Total	128210	7.4	261630	133420	29881	12.6	97968	68087

Source: See text.

second, between 1976 and 1986.[34] The latter figures appear overly low. For one thing, they assume no change in the market share of the developing countries in the domestic consumption of textiles and clothing in the developed countries, although the developing countries may further increase their share at the expense of developed country exporters such as Japan. For another thing, the estimates do not take account of the continuous upgrading of the exports of textiles and clothing from the developing countries that has raised the unit value of these exports at a rate much exceeding average prices in world trade.[35]

In estimating the future exports of manufactured goods from the developed countries to the developing countries, we have applied the GDP growth rate of 5.7 percent projected in *World Development Report, 1978* for the developing countries in the 1975–85 period[36] to the 1976–86 period. Next, we have assumed varying income elasticities of demand in the developing countries for different groups of manufactures, constrained to an average of 1.3 for all manufactured goods combined. The latter figure equals the income elasticity of import demand for manufactured imports estimated for the period 1963–73.[37] In conformity with the experience of this period, it has further been assumed that the share of the developed countries in the manufactured imports of the developing countries would remain unchanged during the period of projection.

An income elasticity of import demand of 1.6 has been assumed for nonelectrical and electrical machinery and for instruments and related products that are required by the investment effort developing countries would have to make in order to reach high rates of economic growth. In turn, an income elasticity of import demand of 1.2 has been assumed for paper and paper products, printing and publishing, chemicals, transport equipment, and miscellaneous manufactured products where a high income elasticity of domestic demand is partially counter-balanced by import substitution. Finally, an elasticity of import demand of 1.1 has been postulated for metals and metal products where import substitution efforts are likely to be more important and an elasticity of 0.6 has been assumed for all other industry groups, where income elasticities of domestic demand are relatively low and the import substitution effort tends to be considerable.

These estimates would give rise to an average rate of growth of 7.4 percent for the exports of manufactured goods from the developed countries to the developing countries between 1976 and 1986 as compared to the projected growth rate of 12.6 percent for their imports. Expressed in 1976 prices, there would be an absolute increment of $133 billion in the exports, and $68 billion in the imports, of manufactured goods by the OECD countries in their trade with the developing countries during the 1976–86 period (Table 7.5). The ratio of exports to imports would correspondingly decline from 4.3 in 1976 to 2.7 in 1986, with the incremental ratio being 2.0.

The Employment Effects of Projected Trade Flows

The employment implications of projected trade in manufactured goods between developed and developing countries will be considered in the following for the OECD taken as a whole. The estimates have been made on the assumption that labor-input coefficients would remain unchanged during the 1976–86 period. Correspondingly, changes in employment resulting from trade flows have been overestimated by neglecting future increases in labor productivity and the substitution of capital for labor in response to increases in real wages.

As shown in Table 7.6A the projected expansion of trade in manufactured goods between the developed and the developing countries would have a positive effect on manufacturing employment in the former group of countries. The increase of employment in exports is estimated at 2478 thousand and the decline of employment in imports at 1736 thousand, with net increases shown in all labor categories.

The average labor-input coefficients for increases in exports and in imports are estimated at 18.6 and 25.5, respectively, with their ratio being 0.73. It is thus apparent that the projections would entail a slight reduction in the labor-intensity of imports from the developing countries that would result from changes in the commodity composition of this trade. Similar considerations apply to the capital coefficients shown in Table 7.6C.

Nevertheless, substantial differences in labor-input coefficients and in capital intensity remain as between projected exports and imports in manufactured trade between developed and developing countries. Also, there are considerable differences in projected increases in employment among occupational categories. The incremental export-import ratio is the lowest, 1.10 in the unskilled and semi-skilled production workers as opposed to an overall average of 1.43. These results are not surprising, given the occupational distribution of labor in production for exports and for imports in the developed countries.

Prima facie, it is surprising, however, that the largest projected gain among the skilled and technical labor categories is shown for foremen and skilled workers, with an incremental export-import ratio of 2.18, rather than for professional and technical workers, where the incremental ratio is 1.65. This result is explained by the fact that in electrical and equipment, the industry group with the highest professional and technical labor coefficients, imports from developing countries are projected to rise at a rapid rate, with the absolute increment in imports exceeding the increment in the exports of these commodities between 1976 and 1986.

At the same time, future increases of imports of electrical equipment from the developing countries are likely to involve the increased importation of parts, components, and accessories, coupled with the eventual dominance of these countries in the world export of radios, television sets, automotive electrical equipment, and simple electronics. The products in question have

TABLE 7.6
Employment Implications and Capital Coefficients for Increase in Manufactured Trade between Developed and Developing Countries, 1976-86

	Increment in Exports	Increment in Imports	Incremental Balance	Ratios
A. *Employment Effects by Occupational* Category (thousands of jobs)				
1. Professional & Technical Workers	300.6	182.2	118.4	1.65
2. Managers & Administrators	143.8	94.0	49.8	1.53
3. Sales Workers	38.6	28.3	10.3	1.36
4. Clerical Workers	320.5	206.5	114.0	1.55
5. Foremen and Skilled Workers (Craftsmen)	571.5	261.9	309.6	2.18
6. Production Workers, Unskilled & Semi-Skilled (Operators	960.9	874.4	86.2	1.10
7. Workers in Construction, Transportation, Material Handling, etc.	50.9	31.4	19.5	1.62
8. Laborers	92.7	58.0	34.7	1.60
Total	2478.4	1736.0	742.4	1.43
of which sum of positive balance			742.4	
negative balance			0.0	
B. *Employment Effects by Industrial* Groups (thousands of jobs)				
1. Textile Mill Products	55.1	158.6	−103.5	0.35
2. Apparel & Other Textile Products	16.2	266.1	−249.9	0.06
3. Lumber & Wood Products	4.1	41.9	−27.8	0.10
4. Furniture & Fixtures	7.8	16.8	−9.0	0.46
5. Paper & Allied Products	31.0	4.5	26.5	6.89
6. Printing & Publishing	23.3	4.3	19.0	5.42
7. Chemicals & Allied Products	152.1	56.0	96.1	2.72
8. Petroleum Products	0.4	0.1	0.3	4.00
9. Rubber & Plastic Products	12.8	100.6	−87.8	0.13
10. Leather & Leather Products	4.0	57.7	−53.7	0.07
11. Stone, Clay & Glass Products	20.5	17.4	3.1	1.18
12. Primary Metal & Allied Products	163.5	48.9	114.6	3.34
13. Fabricated Metal Products	77.4	12.9	64.5	6.00
14. Nonelectrical Machinery	732.6	100.0	632.6	7.33
15. Electrical Equipment & Supplies	579.7	656.1	−76.4	0.88
16. Transportation Equipment	452.4	73.2	379.2	6.18
17. Instruments & Related Products	101.0	28.4	72.6	3.56
18. Miscellaneous Manufactured Products	44.4	92.5	−48.1	0.48
Total	2478.4	1736.0	742.4	1.43
of which positive balance			1408.6	
negative balance			666.2	
C. *Capital Coefficients* (thousand dollars per job)				
Stock Measures				
Physical Capital	15.2	10.6	—	1.43
Human Capital	30.2	25.3	—	1.19
Together	45.3	35.9	—	1.26
Flow Measures				
Physical Capital	8.7	6.3	—	1.38
Human Capital	9.6	8.4	—	1.14
Together	18.4	14.7	—	1.25

Sources: Tables 7.3–7.5 and Text.

lower professional and technical labor requirements than electrical machinery and equipment in general. This is not shown by the results, however, because the occupational statistics were not available in sufficient detail, and a distinction between the two groups of electrical machinery and equipment could therefore not be made.

It follows that the results shown in Table 7.6A understate the gain in professional and technical employment in the developed countries that would result from increased trade in manufactured goods with the developing countries. The same conclusion is likely to apply to other skilled categories, all of which show a net employment gain. Thus, the shift from low-skill to high-skill occupations in the developed countries, resulting from their increased trade in manufactured goods with the developing countries, would be greater than estimated here.

Total employment in the developed countries would rise in 10 out of the 18 industry groups with the largest gains experienced in nonelectrical machinery, transportation equipment, and instruments and related products (Table 7.6B). In turn, there would be employment losses in textiles, clothing, lumber and wood products, furniture, rubber and plastic products, leather and leather products, electrical equipment, and miscellaneous manufactures.

Conclusions and Policy Implications

In this essay, we have examined the employment implications for the developed countries of their manufactured trade with the developing countries. The employment effects of a *balanced* expansion of trade have been indicated by the use of labor-input coefficients that are, on the average, one-half larger for the imports than for the exports of manufactured goods in the developed countries. In turn, due to differences in trade volume, the ratio of jobs gained through exports to jobs lost through imports in the OECD countries would be 2.8 in the event of *proportional* increase in their manufactured exports and imports in trade with the developing countries, taking 1976 trade flows as a basis.

Neither a balanced increase nor a proportionate increase in manufactured trade between developed and developing countries is a likely occurrence, however. We have, therefore, estimated the employment implications of the expected expansion of this trade in the period 1976–86 by taking the projections of the *World Development Report, 1978* as a starting point. The results show positive employment effects for the OECD countries together with an upgrading of the labor force in these countries. Particular interest attaches to the effects of trade in manufactured goods on the skill-composition of labor, since one should look to general economic policies rather than trade policies to ensure a satisfactory level of overall employment.

The upgrading of the labor force, as well as the exchange of physical and human capital for unskilled labor, would have favorable effects on resource allocation and on economic growth in the developed countries.[38] At the same time, welfare gains are not limited to the exchange of productive factors through trade, and additional gains would be forthcoming as a result of increased competition which provides inducements to technological change.

The upgrading of the labor force would be associated with a shift of labor from unskilled-labor intensive to skill-and physical capital-intensive industries. The sum of job losses in the former group of industries in the OECD countries is estimated at 666 thousand accounting for a small proportion of employment in these industries. In the case of textiles, clothing, leather and leather products, the estimated net job loss of 407 thousand compares with total employment of 9213 thousand in this sector in the OECD countries, taken together, in 1976. For the miscellaneous manufacturing product group, the comparable figures are 48 thousand and 1421 thousand respectively.[39]

Note further that the ten-year time period considered in this study may permit adjustments to take place among industries and allow sufficient time for the upgrading of labor. In fact, one may envisage larger increases in the imports of manufactured goods by the developed countries from the developing countries than projected in the *World Development Report, 1978* without appreciable adverse effects on employment in import-competing industries. For one thing, WDR I foresees a decline in the incremental share of manufactured goods imported from the developing countries in developed country markets from 7.1 percent in 1970–75 to 5.4 percent in 1975–85,[40] despite the large increase in this share that occurred between 1975 and 1976. For another thing, there are possibilities for additional increases in the share of exports to the developing countries in the manufactured output of the developed countries, which is projected to rise only slightly from the 1975 level in WDR I.[41]

The above considerations indicate the advantages of liberal trade policies for the developed countries. This conclusion is strengthened if we consider that, under the projections reported in this essay, the import-competing industries of the developed countries may not experience job losses in the absolute terms inasmuch as increased demand associated with economic growth leads to higher domestic consumption and production. Furthermore, increased imports of labor-intensive products may be a substitute for the immigration of unskilled and semi-skilled labor, whether legal or illegal.[42] By disregarding labor migration, the above calculations overestimate job losses to the nationals of the developed countries in import-competing industries.

ESSAY 8

Trade In Manufactured Goods: Patterns of Change

Introduction

This essay will examine the changing pattern of trade in manufactured goods between the developed industrial (for short, industrial) and the developing countries. Section I of the essay will review recent changes in this trade and the policies applied. In Section II, the comparative advantages of the industrial and the developing countries in manufactured goods will be analyzed and changes in the commodity composition of this trade indicated. In the conclusion, the implications of the results will be drawn with reference to the benefits of trade in manufactured goods for the participants.

I. Trade in Manufactured Goods Between Industrial and Developing Countries

This section reports on changes in trade in manufactured goods between the industrial countries and the developing countries during the 1973–78 period. The former group is defined to include the United States, Canada, the European Common Market (EEC),[1] the European Free Trade Association (EFTA),[2] and Japan; within the latter group, data for OPEC[3] and for the non-OPEC developing countries[4] are separately shown. The two groupings exclude the countries of Southern Europe (other than Portugal); Australia, New Zealand, and South Africa; and the centrally planned economies. While the countries of Southern Europe may be appropriately included in the developing country group, this has not been done in the present paper because the future trade prospects of these countries are intimately linked with their accession to the Common Market, to take place during the eighties.

Manufactured goods are defined as commodity classes 5 to 8 in the UN Standard International Trade Classification less nonferrous metals (68). Trade in manufactured goods will be examined first in value terms, indicating changes in the balance of trade, and subsequently in volume terms. Changes in trade volumes will further be related to the rate of economic growth, and the

193

results will be evaluated with reference to the trade policies followed by individual countries and country groups.

Changes in the Balance of Trade in Manufactured Goods

The value of the manufactured exports of the industrial countries to the OPEC countries increased slightly more than fivefold between 1973 and 1978 while the reverse flow of these commodities remained at very low levels. As a result, the industrial countries' trade surplus in manufactured goods with OPEC rose from $12.3 billion in 1973 to $63.5 billion in 1978. This increase covered 69 percent of the rise in the oil import bill of the industrial countries with OPEC, from $28.7 billion in 1973 to $102.9 billion in 1978.[5]

The extent of coverage of the increase in oil imports by manufactured exports to OPEC, however, varies to a considerable extent among the industrial countries and country groups. The relevant ratios for 1978 are: the United States, 38 percent; Canada, 56 percent; the European Common Market, 99 percent; the European Free Trade Association, 119 percent; and Japan, 65 percent. The observed differences in these ratios are largely explained by intercountry differences in the rate of growth of oil imports and in the initial coverage of oil imports by manufactured exports to OPEC, while the rate of expansion of the exports of manufactured goods to OPEC has varied little among the industrial countries.

Thus, the ratio of 1978 to 1973 oil imports ranged from 7.5 in the United States to 2.6 in the European Common Market and the 1973 coverage of oil imports by manufactured exports to OPEC varied from 68 percent in EFTA to 21 percent in Canada. In turn, the ratio of 1978 to 1973 exports of manufactured goods to OPEC was between 5.0 and 5.5 in the major industrial countries and country groups; it was 6.1 in Canada.

Intercountry differences in the rate of expansion of manufactured exports from the industrial countries to the non-OPEC developing countries have also been rather small. Japan occupies first place, with a ratio of 1978 to 1973 exports of 2.7, followed by the European Free Trade Association (2.4), the European Common Market and the United States (2.3), and Canada (2.2). The differences are larger as regards the growth of manufactured imports from the non-OPEC developing countries; the ratios of 1978 to 1973 imports are 3.0 in the European Common Market, 2.9 in the United States, 2.6 in the European Free Trade Association, 2.4 in Canada, and 1.9 in Japan.

Changes in the industrial countries' trade balance in manufactured goods with the non-OPEC developing countries have been further affected by their initial position in this trade, as expressed by the ratio of manufactured exports to imports in 1973. This ratio was the highest in Japan (4.4), followed by the European Common Market (3.4), the European Free Trade Association (3.2), with the United States (1.4) and Canada (1.1) far behind.

Given its high initial trade position, slightly above-average export expansion, and substantially below-average import growth, Japan experienced by far the largest increase in its trade surplus in manufactured goods with the non-OPEC developing countries. This increase, from $7.5 billion in 1973 to $21.4 billion in 1978, accounted for fully one-half of the rise in the combined manufactured trade surplus of the industrial countries with the non-OPEC developing countries.

The EEC and EFTA also increased their trade surplus in manufactured goods with the non-OPEC developing countries; the increase was from $11.2 billion to $23.2 billion in the first case and from $1.7 billion to $4.0 billion in the second. In the same period, the U.S. trade surplus with these countries declined from $2.8 billion to $2.6 billion. With very similar export and import trends, differences in the 1973 trade position of the EEC and EFTA, on the one hand, and the United States, on the other, explain the observed differences in the results.

Changes in the Volume of Manufactured Trade and in the Gross Domestic Product

Table 8.1 provides data on changes in the volume of trade in manufactured goods between the industrial and the developing countries in the 1973–78 period. Information is also provided on the rate of growth of GDP in the industrial countries and on their "apparent" income elasticities of import demand for manufactured goods originating in the developing countries, derived by dividing the rate of growth of these imports by that of GDP.

The table shows an apparent income elasticity of import demand of 4.1 for the industrial countries in the 1973–78 period; their combined manufactured imports from the developing countries rose at an average annual rate of 10.2 percent in volume terms as compared to an average rate of growth of GDP of 2.5 percent. The volume of manufactured imports from the developing countries increased more rapidly in the preceding decade (16.5 percent a year), when considerably higher rates of GDP growth (4.6 percent) were associated with a lower apparent income elasticity of import demand (3.6).

The results for the 1973–78 period were affected to a considerable extent by the 1974–75 recession. In 1975, the industrial countries' GDP was slightly below the 1973 level and the volume of their imports of manufactured goods from the developing countries was only 3 percent higher. In the following three years, growth rates averaged 4.3 percent for GDP and 16.5 percent for the volume of manufactured imports, i.e. an apparent income elasticity of 3.8. The relevant results are 3.8 percent and 11.5 percent, corresponding to an apparent income elasticity of import demand of 3.0, if we limit our attention to the last two years on the grounds that the results for 1976 represented a "rebound from the recession."

At the same time, substantial differences are observed among industrial countries and country groups in regard to both their GDP growth rate and the rate of increase of their imports of manufactured goods from the developing countries. Japan leads in terms of the rate of GDP growth (3.6 percent) but

TABLE 8.1
The Rate of Growth of Manufactured Trade between Industrial and Developing Countries and that of the Industrial Countries' Gross Domestic Product (percent)

	Exports			Imports		Apparent Income Elasticity
	OPEC	Non-OPEC	All LDC	All LDC	GDP	
1963–1973[a/], Industrial Countries	—	—	8.2	16.5	4.6	3.6
1973–1978						
United States	23.7	6.3	10.6	11.1	2.5	4.4
Canada	33.7	8.8	16.5	6.8	3.4	2.0
EEC	23.3	6.2	12.5	12.1	2.1	5.8
EFTA	23.8	5.4	10.7	8.4	1.5	5.6
Japan	26.4	9.9	14.2	3.0	3.6	0.8
Industrial Countries, total	24.2	7.2	12.5	10.2	2.5	4.1
of which 1974	45.3	24.5	29.7	4.2	0.4	10.5
1975	52.8	-4.5	11.5	-1.5	-0.8	1.9
1976	16.4	0.7	6.7	27.3	5.2	5.3
1977	12.9	7.8	9.9	7.6	3.6	2.1
1978	1.1	9.6	6.0	15.5	4.0	3.9

Sources:

1963–1973: United Nations, *Monthly Bulletin of Statistics* and *Yearbook of National Accounts Statistics*, various issues.

1973–1978: Value of Trade—GATT, *International Trade*, 1978/79. Unit Values—GATT, *Network of World Trade by Areas and Commodity Classes*, 1955–1976, Geneva, 1978 and *International Trade*, 1977/78 and 1978/79 and United Nations, *Monthly Bulletin of Statistics*. Gross Domestic Product—Organization for Economic Co-operation and Development, *National Accounts of OECD Countries*, 1979, and *Economic Outlook*, December, 1979, United Nations, *Yearbook of National Accounts Statictics*, 1978. Gross Domestic Product—Organization for Economic Co-operation and Development, *National Accounts of OECD Countries*, 1979, and *Economic Outlook*, December, 1979, United Nations, *Yearbook of National Accounts Statistics*, 1978.

trails the other industrial countries by a considerable margin as far as the growth of the volume of manufactured imports from the developing countries is concerned (3.0 percent a year), with an apparent income elasticity of import demand of 0.8 for the 1973–78 period. Canada was second to Japan in terms of GDP growth rates (3.4 percent a year), and had the second-lowest growth rate of manufactured imports originating in the developing countries (6.8 percent), with an apparent income elasticity of 2.0.

The European Common Market and the European Free Trade Association had the lowest GDP growth rates (2.1 percent and 1.5 percent) and the highest apparent income elasticities of import demand (5.8 and 5.6), with the volume of manufactured imports from the developing countries rising at average annual rates of 12.1 percent and 8.4 percent, respectively. GDP growth rates in the United States equalled the average for the industrial countries in the period 1973–78 (2.5 percent) while the rate of growth of imports (11.1 percent) and the apparent income elasticity of import demand (4.4) were slightly above the average.

Table 8.2 further shows that the volume of manufactured exports of the industrial countries to the developing countries increased at an average annual rate of 12.5 percent between 1973 and 1978, the relevant results being 24.2 percent to OPEC, and 7.2 percent to non-OPEC, countries. Relative rates of growth of exports and imports in value terms show identical results as the terms of trade in manufactured goods did not change between the two groups of countries.[6]

The time pattern of exports and imports, however, exhibited substantial variations. The volume of manufactured exports from the industrial countries to the OPEC countries grew by nearly one-half in 1974 and by more than one-half in 1975, reflecting the tripling of OPEC export earnings in 1974 and the adjustment to the higher level of earnings in 1975. But the rate of growth of manufactured imports to the OPEC countries declined rapidly in subsequent years, with practically no change shown in volume terms in 1978. The results are explained by the slowdown in the rise of oil earnings in 1976 and in 1977 and the absolute decline of these earnings in 1978.

The volume of manufactured exports to the non-OPEC developing countries increased by one-fourth in 1974, declined slightly in 1975, and remained practically unchanged in 1976. The relevant growth rates are 7.8 percent and 9.6 percent in 1977 and in 1978, respectively. For the 1973–78 period as a whole, these exports rose at an average annual rate of 7.2 percent, corresponding to an apparent income elasticity of import demand of 1.8 as the GDP of the non-OPEC developing countries grew 4.1 percent a year. The apparent income elasticity is 3.0 for the OPEC countries whose gross domestic product rose by 8.2 percent a year between 1973 and 1978.[7]

The combined GDP of the developing countries increased at an average annual rate of 5.3 percent between 1973 and 1978 as compared to a rise of 12.5 percent a year in the volume of their manufactured imports from the

TABLE 8.2
Imports of Manufactured Goods by Industrial Countries

	1973			1978			Incremental Ratios (1973–1978)		
	M/GDP	M_{LDC}/GDP	M_{LDC}/M	M/GDP	M_{LDC}/GDP	M_{LDC}/M	$\Delta M/\Delta GDP$	$\Delta M_{LDC}/\Delta GDP$	$\Delta M_{LDC}/\Delta M$
United States	3.28	0.57	17.37	4.60	1.00	21.74	6.71	1.69	25.17
excluding Canada	2.49	0.57	22.90	3.65	1.00	27.42	5.50	1.69	30.70
Canada	14.83	0.43	2.90	15.29	0.61	3.99	16.05	0.87	5.42
excluding United States	3.43	0.43	12.53	3.51	0.61	17.37	3.64	0.87	23.89
EEC	11.32	0.48	4.24	13.44	0.77	5.73	15.93	1.11	6.97
excluding Intra EEC Trade	3.86	0.48	12.45	4.89	0.77	15.74	6.09	1.11	18.23
excluding Intra European Trade	2.65	0.48	18.08	3.31	0.77	23.26	4.08	1.11	27.20
EFTA	18.82	0.48	2.55	18.34	0.62	3.38	13.15	0.56	4.26
excluding Intra EFTA Trade	15.38	0.48	3.12	15.38	0.62	4.03	11.36	0.56	4.93
excluding Intra European Trade	3.32	0.48	14.44	3.48	0.62	17.84	2.67	0.56	20.98
Japan	2.38	0.53	22.57	1.80	0.44	24.43	1.38	0.37	26.80
Industrial Countries	7.19	0.52	7.23	8.39	0.78	9.30	9.61	1.07	11.13
excluding U.S.–Canada & Intra European Trade	2.60	0.52	20.03	3.17	0.78	24.58	3.78	1.07	28.27

Sources: GATT, *International Trade, 1978/79*, OECD, *Economic Outlook, December 1979* and *National Accounts of OECD Countries*, and United Nations, *Yearbook of National Accounts Statistics, 1978*.

Notes: M = total imports of manufactured goods. M_{LDC} = manufactured imports from developing countries. GDP = gross domestic product.

industrial countries, corresponding to an average apparent income elasticity of import demand of 2.4. The rate of growth of GDP was higher (6.2 percent) and that of manufactured imports from the industrial countries lower (8.2 percent) in the 1963–73 period, when the apparent income elasticity of import demand as 1.3.[8] However, during the earlier period, the income and the import shares of the OPEC countries were much smaller.

The Policies Applied

Following the quadrupling of oil prices, the OPEC countries attempted to increase their absorption of manufactured imports at a rapid rate. While in 1974 these countries had an export surplus of $84 billion, the suplus fell to $53 billion in 1975 and to $43 billion by 1978.[9] Apart from the rising imports of the capital-surplus oil exporters, foreign borrowing on the part of the other OPEC countries contributed to this result.

Foreign borrowing also contributed to the high rate of growth of the manufactured imports of the non-OPEC developing countries from the industrial countries. The net overall trade deficit of these countries rose from $15 billion in 1973 to $37 billion by 1978, with much of the increase being financed by borrowing abroad. Foreign borrowing permitted the non-OPEC developing countries to increase their import surplus in manufactured goods vis-à-vis the industrial countries from $23 billion in 1973 to $51 billion in 1978, notwithstanding their higher oil bill.

Foreign borrowing represented a policy response on the part of the non-OPEC developing countries to the oil crisis and the 1974–75 world recession. The promotion of exports, to be discussed below, was another form of policy response. At the same time, the high and rising apparent income elasticity of import demand does not give evidence of overall import substitution in manufactured goods during this period.[10]

The rapid growth of their exports of manufactured goods to the non-OPEC developing countries favorably affected economic activity in the industrial countries. Such effects were of particular importance in 1974, when the volume of these exports rose by one-fourth while the industrial countries were sliding into recession. In recent years, too, the increase in the export surplus of the industrial countries in manufactured trade with the non-OPEC developing countries had a multiplier effect on their national economies as it was not fully offset by higher primary imports.

Notwithstanding the rise in their export surplus, the industrial countries' imports of manufactured goods from the developing countries grew rapidly, with the apparent income elasticity of import demand rising from 3.6 in 1963–73 to 4.1 in 1973–78. These results do not provide evidence of increased protectionism on the part of the industrial countries. While the effects of the "new protectionism" were noticeable in 1977 when the volume of manufactured imports from the developing countries increased by only 9 percent, the rise was

16 percent in 1978 when improvements were made on the protection front.[11] And, available information points to further rapid increases in 1979.[12]

The observed changes could not, however, be explained on the basis of demand considerations alone. While access to industrial country markets has provided opportunities for export expansion, the exports of manufactured goods from the developing countries had responded to the policies followed by these countries. A number of developing countries adopted an export-oriented strategy during the sixties and have continued with this strategy since 1973. Available evidence suggests that countries following an export-oriented strategy were better able to surmount the adverse effects of the quadrupling of oil prices and the 1974–75 world recession than countries with an import-substitution orientation.[13]

Although supply factors have had a crucial role in determining the overall rate of expansion of manufactured exports by the developing countries, the allocation of these exports among the industrial countries has been affected by the trade policies followed by these countries. It has often been said that the United States has traditionally been more open to imports from developing countries than the other industrial nations. Data for 1973 offer only weak evidence in support of this proposition. Thus, excluding trade between the United States and Canada that takes place largely in the framework of multinational corporations and one-third of which is subject to free trade treatment under the U.S.-Canada automotive agreement, as well as trade within the European free trade area in manufactured goods encompassing the EEC and EFTA, the ratios of imports from developing countries to the total imports of manufactures and to the gross domestic product were not substantially higher in the United States than in the EEC and Japan (Table 8.2).[14]

The increased opening of the American economy, together with the deterioration of its competitive position, contributed to rapid increases in U.S. imports of manufactured goods between 1973 and 1978, with the developing countries increasing their share in the total. Thus, the incremental ratio of manufactured imports originating in the developing countries to the gross domestic product was substantially higher during this period in the United States (1.69) than in the European Common Market (1.11), although the differences are smaller as far as the incremental share of the developing countries in their manufactured imports (30.7 percent and 27.2 percent, respectively) is concerned.

The contrast with Japan is much more pronounced. With an apparent income elasticity of import demand of only 0.8, the ratio of Japan's manufactured imports from the developing countries to its GDP fell from 0.53 in 1973 to 0.44 in 1978, corresponding to an incremental ratio of 0.37 between 1973 and 1978. In the same period, the incremental share of imports from developing countries in the total imports of manufactured goods was 28.3 percent in Japan.

instances, physical capital-labor ratios are substantially lower than for average, although relatively high human capital intensity raises their rall capital-labor ratio. At the same time, within the first category, eloping countries exported chiefly electronic components that are highly or intensive while a large share of exports in the second category were ios that are produced by relatively simple techniques.

We have further calculated weighted averages of capital-labor ratios for the orts and the imports of the industrial countries in their trade in manufactured ds with the non-OPEC developing countries, the weights being the value of orts and imports in the eleven commodity-group breakdown. In 1973, the vant ratios for exports (expressed in thousand U.S. dollars per worker) e 13.8 for physical capital and 27.5 for human capital, totalling 41.3. In , average capital-labor ratios for the manufactured imports of the industrial ntries from the non-OPEC developing countries were 9.8, 25.1, and 34.8, ectively.

The results indicate the comparative advantages of the industrial countries apital-intensive commodities vis-à-vis the non-OPEC developing countries. is conclusion applies also to the industrial countries and country groups, en individually, with percentage differences in average capital-labor ratios their exports and imports in trade in manufactured goods with the non-EC developing countries ranging between 18 percent in the United States 36 percent in Canada. At the same time, for the industrial countries, taken gether, as well as for the individual countries and country groups, the extent comparative advantage vis-à-vis the non-OPEC developing countries pears to be greater in regard to physical than for human capital.

hanges in the Commodity Composition of Trade, 1973–1978

Industrial Country Exports. In the exports of the industrial countries to EC in the 1973–1978 period, above-average increases are shown for nsumer goods; the ratio of 1978 to 1973 exports was 5.3 for motor vehicles, 4 for household appliances, 5.9 for clothing and 7.2 for other consumer ods as against an overall average of 5.0.[21] In turn, the lowest ratios are served in the case of iron and steel (3.5), chemicals (3.4), and textiles (2.5). inally, machinery and equipment exhibited average ratios (5.0 to 5.1), cept for the high ratio shown for the "other machinery and transport quipment" category (6.8) where aircraft and other military equipment are of nportance.

Given the limited domestic production of manufactured goods in most of e OPEC countries, these results tend to reflect patterns of domestic use. It ould then appear that, on the whole, increases in oil earnings were used more increase consumption and military expenditure than to raise investment vels.

Iron and steel, chemicals, and textiles also experienced smaller than aver- ge increases in industrial country exports of manufactured goods to the non-

Japan used a variety of formal and informal measures to limit the imports of manufactured goods, in particular from developing countries. These measures were liberalized in 1978.[15] As a result, the volume of manufactured imports from the developing countries increased by more than one-fourth between 1977 and 1978,[16] following a decline in the 1973–77 period.

A consideration of the imports of all manufactured goods originating in the developing countries does not suffice, however, to appraise the effects of the trade policies followed by the industrial countries. For this purpose, it is further necessary to examine the commodity composition of imports, since some products encounter non-tariff barriers in the industrial countries while others are subject only to tariffs. This question will be taken up in Section II below.

II. Comparative Advantage and the Commodity Composition of Trade in Manufactured Goods

In an earlier paper,[17] the author has shown that the pattern of world exports of manufactured goods can be explained in terms of intercommodity differences in capital-labor ratios and intercountry differences in capital endowments. The indicators of comparative advantage derived in that paper will be utilized in the following to analyze the pattern of export-import ratios in manufactured trade between the industrial and the non-OPEC developing countries in 1973. Subsequent changes in the commodity composition of this trade will further be examined, with consideration given to the factors that influenced the observed results. Finally, the role of the newly-industrializing countries in the exports of manufactured goods from the developing countries will be noted.

The Structure of Comparative Advantage

In order to examine the comparative advantages of the industrial and the developing countries in their mutual trade in manufactured goods, the capital-labor ratios reported in the earlier paper have been averaged in the eleven commodity category breakdown employed in GATT statistics, using U.S. production data as weights.[18] The estimated ratios pertain to physical as well as to human capital. The former has been obtained as the ratio of the (physical) capital stock to employment; the latter has been estimated as the discounted value of the difference between the average and the unskilled wage, taken to represent the return on investment in human capital. The relevant data are shown in Table 8.3.[19]

Although the eleven commodity category scheme involves a considerable degree of aggregation, substantial differences are observed in capital-labor ratios among the individual categories. The ratio of physical capital per worker (expressed in thousand U.S. dollars per worker) is the highest for iron and steel (27.7) and for chemicals (21.4); it is the lowest for clothing (2.4) and for other

TABLE 8.3
Comparative Advantage Ratios and Trade in Manufactured Goods between Industrial and Developing Countries

	Capital per Worker ($ thousand)			Export Surplus² ($ billion)		Export-Import Ratio³		Ratio of 1978 to 1973 Trade^b			Ratio of NICs^c in imports from non-OPEC LDCs
	Physical	Human	Total	1973	1978	1973	1978	Export non-OPEC LDC	Import non-OPEC LDC	Export OPEC	
Iron & Steel	27.71	28.15	55.85	3.00	5.73	6.45	5.82	1.95	2.16	3.45	76
Chemicals	21.37	25.51	46.88	5.43	12.02	6.90	7.91	2.26	2.53	3.38	47
Other Semimanufactures	19.59	24.21	43.80	-0.11	0.58	1.00	1.10	2.57	2.34	5.17	58
Engineering Products, subtotal	9.61	29.38	38.99	18.52	45.16	6.01	4.61	2.59	3.38	5.74	83
Machinery for Specialized Industries	9.44	28.34	37.79	6.81	16.79	53.98	29.46	2.50	4.54	5.01	90
Office & Telecommunication Equipment	7.91	35.22	43.15	1.13	2.31	1.88	1.62	2.50	2.91	5.09	75
Road Motor Vehicles	12.89	25.40	38.39	3.39	8.76	38.67	21.37	2.64	4.78	5.31	91
Other Machinery & Transport Equipment	9.66	30.27	39.93	6.62	16.80	7.07	5.20	2.70	3.67	6.81	77
Household Appliances	8.29	39.09	47.38	0.47	0.31	1.42	1.08	2.56	3.36	5.43	95
Textiles	10.00	16.62	26.62	0.32	0.05	1.16	1.01	1.58	1.81	2.50	55
Clothing	2.37	11.00	13.37	-3.03	-8.75	0.11	0.09	2.18	2.81	5.88	81
Other Consumer Goods	6.73	25.99	32.72	-0.86	-3.70	0.80	0.49	2.55	3.22	7.24	90
Manufactured Goods, total	11.89	26.11	38.00	23.29	51.14	2.50	2.20	2.41	2.74	5.04	75

Sources: Capital per Worker: Bela Balassa, "A 'Stages' Approach to Comparative Advantage" *op. cit.* Exports and Imports: GATT, *International Trade 1978/79* and GATT tapes.

Notes: (a) Industrial countries' exports to, and imports from, the non-OPEC developing countries. (b) Ratio of the industrial countries' exports and imports, respectively, in trade with developing countries. (c) Newly industrializing countries, defined to include Argentina, Brazil, Chile, Mexico, Uruguay, Israel, Hong Kong, Korea, Singapore and Taiwan.

consumer goods (6.7). The ratio of human capital per worke
for clothing (11.0), followed by textiles (16.6); it is the high
appliances (39.1) and for office and telecommunication e
Combining physical and human capital, iron and steel (
appliances (47.4) and chemicals (46.9) are at the upper
textiles (26.6) and other consumer goods (32.7) at the lowe
(Table 8.3).

If engineering products are considered as a single grou
import ratios in trade between the industrial countries and
developing countries largely correspond to the pattern
advantage as represented by capital-labor ratios, the only
semimanufactures.[20] As shown in Table 8.4, iron and steel an
the highest overall capital-labor ratios also had the highe
ratios (6.5 and 6.9 respectively) in 1973. Apart from se
engineering products placed next in terms of overall capi
(39.0) as well as export-import ratios (6.0).

At the other extreme, the exports of the industrial count
OPEC developing countries hardly reached one-tenth of the
case of clothing that exhibits by far the lowest capital-labor
lowest export-import ratio (0.8) is shown for the other c
category, including shoes, travel goods, toys, sports goods,
miscellaneous products, which exhibit the second-lowest ca

A seemingly aberrant result is observed in the case
manufactures that had an export-import ratio of 1.0 in 1973,
their relatively high capital-labor ratio (43.8). However,
commodities included in this category are natural resource pro
fact provides an advantage to developing countries that posses
in question. Also, the category is rather heterogeneous as it in
intensive products, such as pulp and paper, as well as labor-inte
such as leather and rubber manufactures, when weighting by U
imparts an upward bias to the estimated average capital-labo
group as a whole.

Apart from their above-average capital intensity, the sophis
production process and the need for the availability of precisi
parts, components, and accessories limited the export possi
developing countries in a variety of engineering products. Th
large part explain the very high export-import ratios in the
industrial countries with the non-OPEC developing countries
machinery for specialized industries (54.0) and road motor vehi
turn, the export-import ratio was 7.1 for the other machinery
equipment category, which also includes some relatively sim
such as bicycles.

Finally, 1973 export-import ratios were relatively low fo
telecommunication equipment (1.9) and for household applian

OPEC developing countries. In these three commodity categories, the ratios of 1978 to 1973 exports were 2.0, 2.3, and 1.6, respectively, as compared to an overall average of 2.4. The relevant ratio is 2.6 for the consumer goods categories, the only exception being clothing (2.2). Finally, the ratio of 1978 to 1973 imports of machinery and equipment was 2.5, except that the imports of military equipment raised this ratio to 2.7 for the other machinery and transport equipment category.

These results conflict with the popular image, which has found its way into economic models, that the non-OPEC developing countries would limit their consumer goods imports in favor of the imports of machinery and equipment. In fact, with clothing imports being small in absolute terms, the imports of consumer goods appear to have increased somewhat more than the imports of capital goods, and increases in the imports of military equipment were even larger.

Industrial Country Imports. In the imports of the industrial countries from the non-OPEC developing countries, the largest increases are observed in the specialized machinery and the road motor vehicles categories; the ratios of 1978 to 1973 exports are 4.5 and 4.8, respectively, as compared to an overall average of 2.7. But this result was achieved from a very small base; in fact, between 1973 and 1978, the trade surplus of the industrial countries with the non-OPEC developing countries increased from $6.8 billion to $16.8 billion in specialized machinery and from $6.6 billion to $16.8 billion in motor vehicles.

The next largest increases, with the ratio of 1978 to 1973 imports being 3.7 and 3.4, took place in the other machinery and transport equipment and the household appliances categories. Shipbuilding and the exportation of parts and components of machinery and transport equipment importantly contributed to the growth of imports originating in the non-OPEC developing countries in the first case and radios and T.V. sets in the second. But while the trade surplus of the industrial countries declined in the second category, a substantial increase is shown for the first where aircraft and other military products are of importance.

All in all, the industrial countries' imports of engineering products from the non-OPEC developing countries shows above-average increases, with the ratio of 1978 to 1973 imports being 3.4. As a result of these changes, by 1978 engineering products came to account for 29.4 percent of the manufactured imports of the industrial countries from the non-OPEC developing countries as compared to 23.9 percent in 1973.[22] In absolute terms, the most important categories are other machinery and transport equipment ($4.0 billion in 1978), office and telecommunication equipment ($3.8 billion), and household appliances ($3.7 billion).

The ratio of 1978 to 1973 imports from the non-OPEC developing countries is the lowest for textiles (1.8) that have long been subject to restrictions in the industrial countries. The industrial countries have also benefited from technological change that has led to the application of more capital-intensive techniques. Nevertheless, with textile imports from the non-OPEC developing countries rising more rapidly than exports to these countries, the trade surplus of the industrial countries in textiles declined from $0.3 billion in 1973 to practically zero in 1978.

In the same period, the trade deficit of the industrial countries with the non-OPEC developing countries in clothing rose from $3.0 billion to $8.8 billion. As noted above, the comparative advantage of the non-OPEC developing countries is the strongest in clothing; nor have there been technological changes unfavorable to them in this industry. Thus, notwithstanding the limitations imposed in the framework of the Multifiber Arrangement, the ratio of 1978 to 1973 imports was 2.8 for clothing, exceeding the overall average.

The industrial countries also experienced a rise in their trade deficit in other consumer goods with the non-OPEC developing countries from $0.9 billion in 1973 to $3.7 billion in 1978, with the ratio of 1978 to 1973 exports being 3.2. The commodities included in this category have relatively high unskilled-labor intensity and average skill intensity. With few exceptions, these commodities have not been subject to restrictions in the industrial countries.

Finally, increases in the imports of the industrial countries from the non-OPEC developing countries were below-average in the case of intermediate products, where the relevant ratios are 2.2 for iron and steel, 2.5 for chemicals, and 2.3 for semimanufactures. These products have the highest physical capital-labor ratio, although, as we have seen, the semimanufactures category also includes natural-resource and labor-intensive products.

Some Implications of the Results

It appears that the OPEC as well as the non-OPEC developing countries have utilized increases in foreign exchange availabilities to expand the imports of consumer goods and military equipment more rapidly than the imports of investment goods. Apart from conflicting with popular preconceptions, these results raise questions about the allocation of foreign exchange between current expenditures and investment in these countries.

It further appears that the developing countries have made little headway in exporting commodities that are highly intensive in physical capital, require sophisticated technology, or necessitate the availability of precision-engineered parts, components, and accessories. Several of the developing countries, however, have made progress in exporting skilled-labor intensive commodities, such as ships and T.V. sets, as well as parts, components, and accessories of engineering products to the industrial countries. Also, growth has been rapid in the exports of other consumer goods that have average skill intensity and are relatively intensive in unskilled labor.

A few exceptions apart, products in these commodity categories do not encounter non-tariff barriers in the industrial countries. It should be added, however, that the exports of textiles and clothing, subject to limitations first under the Cotton Textiles and, subsequently, the Multifiber, Arrangement have also experienced a high growth rate. The exports of these commodities increased at an average annual rate of 7.7 percent in volume terms as compared to the average rate of expansion of manufactured exports of 10.2 percent.

The bulk of the manufactured exports of the non-OPEC developing countries to the industrial countries originates in the newly-industrialized developing countries. This group has been defined to include developing countries where per capita incomes exceeded $1100 in 1978 and manufacturing production accounted for at least 20 percent of the gross domestic product. The countries in question are Argentina, Brazil, Chile, Mexico, Uruguay, Israel, Hong Kong, Korea, Singapore, and Taiwan.

As shown in Table 8.3, in 1978 the share of the newly-industrializing countries in the manufactured imports of the industrial countries from the non-OPEC developing countries was 75 percent. This compares with the 46 percent share of these countries in the combined GDP of the non-OPEC developing countries. If comparisons are made with all (OPEC and non-OPEC) developing countries, the relevant shares are 73 percent and 33 percent. And, the four Far Eastern countries in the group, Hong Kong, Korea, Singapore, and Taiwan, accounted for 5 percent of the gross domestic product and 52 percent of the manufactured exports of the developing countries to developed country markets.[23]

Compared to the other non-OPEC developing countries, the newly-industrializing countries tend to export relatively skill-intensive commodities. They have a high export share in engineering products (83 percent) that have higher skill-intensity than any other commodity catagory. Within the engineering group, household appliances with a 95 percent export share of the newly-industrializing countries are the most skill-intensive. The export share of the newly industrializing countries is also high in other consumer goods (90 percent) that have average skill-intensity, and it is the lowest in textiles (55 percent) that have low skill-intensity. They also have low shares in chemicals (47 percent) and in other semimanufactures (58 percent) that are intensive in physical capital and several of which embody natural resources. And while the newly-industrializing countries have an above-average share in clothing exports (81 percent) that are intensive in unskilled labor, more sophisticated items have a higher than average share in their exports of these commodities.

Conclusions

This paper has examined changes in the pattern of trade in manufactured goods in the 1973-78 period. The growth of manufactured exports of the industrial countries to the developing countries accelerated during this period, with an average annual rate of increase of 12.5 percent as compared to 8.2 percent between 1963 and 1973. As the gross domestic product of the developing countries rose 6.2 percent a year in the first period and 5.3 percent in the second, their apparent income elasticity of import demand increased from 1.3 in 1963-73 to 2.4 in 1973-78.

The rise in the apparent income elasticity of import demand in the developing countries reflects both the growth of export earnings of the OPEC countries and the increase of foreign borrowing by the non-OPEC developing countries. In fact, the apparent income elasticity of import demand was 3.0 for the OPEC countries and 1.8 for the non-OPEC developing countries in the 1973-78 period.

Increased exports of manufactured goods to the developing countries favorably affected economic activity in the industrial countries, in particular in 1974 when the volume of these exports rose by one-fourth while the industrial countries were sliding into a recession. At the same time, the developing countries have assumed increased importance as markets for the industrial countries, accounting for 47.3 percent of their exports (excluding U.S.-Canada trade and trade within the European free trade area) and for 5.1 percent of their production of manufactured goods in 1978.[24]

The industrial countries experienced average annual increases of 4.6 percent in their GDP and 16.5 percent in their imports of manufactured goods from the developing countries between 1963 and 1973, corresponding to an apparent income elasticity of import demand of 3.6. The income elasticity increased to 4.1 in the 1973-78 period, when the decline in the rate of growth of GDP (2.5 percent in 1973-78) exceeded that in the rate of growth of imports (10.2 percent).

The results show the effects of the slowdown of economic growth in the industrial countries on their imports from the developing countries, but do not provide evidence of the effects of increased protectionism that would have been expected to lead to a fall in the income elasticity of import demand. Protection, however, appears to have limited the growth of imports into Japan while the imports of textiles and clothing into all the industrial countries have been unfavorably affected by the operation of the Multifiber Arrangement. Nevertheless, these exports rose at an average annual rate of 7.7 percent in the 1973-78 period and came to account for 59.8 percent of the imports (again excluding the U.S.-Canada trade and trade within the European free trade area), and 4.9 percent of the domestic consumption, of textiles and clothing in the industrial countries in 1978. The relevant shares for manufactured imports, taken together, were 24.6 percent and 1.5 percent.[25]

The results further provide evidence of the changing pattern of comparative advantage, with the newly-industrializing countries increasingly exporting skill-intensive commodities and the less-developed countries starting to export unskilled-labor intensive commodities. In turn, the exports of the industrial countries continue to be dominated by products that are intensive in physical capital, require sophisticated technology, or necessitate the availability of precision-engineered parts, components, and accessories.

It would appear, then, that the expansion of manufactured trade between industrial and developing countries has made it possible for these countries to specialize according to their comparative advantage. This pattern of specialization, in turn, has favorable effects on resource allocation and economic growth in the countries participating in international trade.

ESSAY 9

Prospects for Trade In Manufactured Goods Between Industrial And Developing Countries, 1978-1990

Introduction

This essay will examine prospective changes in trade in manufactured goods between the developed industrial (for short, industrial) and the developing countries in the period 1978-1990. The former group is defined to include the United States, Canada, the European Common Market (EEC), the European Free Trade Association (EFTA), and Japan; within the latter group, separate estimates will be made for OPEC and for the non-OPEC developing countries.[1]

Trade in manufactured goods[2] is estimated as a function of the growth of GDP in the two groups of countries. This requires first of all making projections of GDP growth. The projections will be presented in Section I of the paper, drawing on and making comparisons with, estimates of a study prepared for the United Nations by Wassily Leontief and Associates, the second World Development Report of the World Bank, and the Interfutures study of the OECD.

Projections of manufactured trade between the industrial and the developing countries are provided in a seven-commodity group breakdown. The results will be presented in Section II while in Section III the estimated trade flows will be related to the production and the consumption of manufactured goods in the industrial countries. In the conclusion, the increased interdependence of industrial and developing countries through trade in manufactured goods will be noted and suggestions will be made for policies that may contribute to the further expansion of this trade.

211

I. Projections for Economic Growth, 1978-1990

Industrial Countries

The rate of growth of GDP in the industrial countries averaged 2.5 percent between 1973 and 1978 as compared to 4.6 percent in the 1963-73 period. The deceleration of the rate of economic expansion reflects the effects of the 1974-75 recession, aggravated by the quadrupling of oil prices and the subsequent slow recovery. The decline in the growth rate was especially pronounced in the European Free Association, where the 1973-78 growth rate barely exceeded one-third of that in the 1963-73 period; it was the smallest in the United States, where the GDP growth rate declined by less than one-third (Table 9.1).

The base scenario of the second *World Development Report* calls for a GDP growth rate of 4.2 percent for the industrial countries, taken together, in the 1980-90 period; GDP growth rates under the high and the low growth scenarios, respectively, are 4.9 percent and 3.5 percent.[3] For the same period, Wassily Leontief and Associates project a GDP growth rate of 3.8 percent.[4] Finally, Interfutures estimates the average GDP growth rate of the industrial countries at 4.9 percent under the rapid convergent growth, and 3.6 percent under the moderate convergent growth, scenario for the 1975-90 period.[5]

Although these estimates show considerable similarity, there are substantial differences in the projected pattern of growth for the individual countries and country groups. As shown in Table 9.1, WDR II foresees the approximate maintenance of Japan's growth advantage vis-à-vis the other industrial countries, taken as a group, and a slightly higher GDP growth rate for the United States than for the EEC and EFTA. In turn, Leontief expects little difference in the growth performance of Japan and Western Europe but a much lower GDP growth rate for the United States. Interfutures also sees the United States as the laggard while it postulates a substantially higher GDP growth rate for Japan than for the European Common Market.

The estimates by Interfutures are supposedly based on the convergence of productivity levels, with Japan catching up with the United States and the Common Market reaching four-fifths of the U.S. per capita income level by the end of the century.[6] While the convergence hypothesis appears reasonable, the Interfutures estimate is subject to error inasmuch as it expresses data for 1975, and for all subsequent years, in 1970 prices and exchange rates. Yet, the 1970 exchange rates were far from being equilibrium rates and underwent considerable changes in later years, involving in particular the depreciation of the U.S. dollar.

The magnitude of the error can be indicated by comparing ratios of per capita incomes for the year 1975, estimated in 1970 and in 1975 prices and exchange rates. The relevant ratios, expressed as a proportion of U.S. incomes, are .54 and .73 for the European Common Market and .46 and .63

TABLE 9.1
Actual and Projected Growth Rates of the Gross Domestic Product[a] (percent)

	Actual		WDRII	Leontief	Interfutures 1975-90		Present Study
	1963-73	1973-78	1978-90	1980-90	A	B2	1978-90
United States	3.7	2.5	3.8	} 3.1	3.6	2.6	3.5
Canada	5.4	3.4	4.2		4.0	3.1	3.7
EEC	4.6	2.1	3.7	} 4.5	5.3	3.5	3.6
EFTA	4.3	1.5	3.7		n/a	n/a	3.3
Japan	10.4	3.6	6.1	4.7	7.6	6.4	6.0
Industrial Countries, total	4.6	2.5	4.1	3.8	4.9	3.6	3.9
Developing Countries	6.2	5.3	5.6[b]	5.0	6.7[c]	6.0[c]	5.6

Sources: Actual: United Nations, *Yearbook of National Accounts Statistics 1978* and World Bank. Projected: World Bank, *World Development Report, 1979*, Washington, D.C. 1979 and related documents—base variant. Interfutures: *Facing the Future*, Paris, Organization for Economic Co-operation and Development, 1979, 121, 131, and 328. Scenario A: rapid convergent growth. Scenario B2: moderate convergent growth. Leontief, Wassily, Anne P. Carter, and Peter A. Petri, *The Future of the World Economy*, A United Nations Study. New York, Oxford University Press, 1977, Annex VI.

Notes: (a) For definitions, see text. (b) 1980-90. (c) 1975-2000.

for Japan.[7] Correspondingly, utilizing data expressed in 1975 prices and exchange rates, under Interfutures' rapid covergent growth scenario Japan would surpass per capita incomes in the United States by 8 percent in 1990 while the European Common Market would establish approximate parity with the U.S.; furthermore, Japanese and EEC incomes would exceed the U.S. per capita income level by 42 percent and 11 percent, respectively, in 2000.[8]

It appears, then, that the Interfutures estimates would lead to a divergence rather than a convergence of productivity levels and per capita incomes, with the EEC surpassing the United States and Japan surpassing both of them. In the present investigation, GDP growth rates have been estimated by utilizing the labor force estimates of Interfutures and postulating a convergent pattern of productivity levels among the industrial countries with the exception of Japan that has been assumed to get ahead of the European Common Market.

Interfutures projects the labor force to rise at an average annual rate of 1.2 percent in the United States, 0.4 percent in the European Common Market, and 0.8 percent in Japan between 1975 and 1990. At the same time, the higher level of unemployment prevailing in 1975 would permit the United States to increase employment further to an extent greater than the other industrial countries.[9] We have nevertheless assumed that differential productivity growth rates would lead to increases in Common Market GDP (3.6 percent a year) slightly exceeding the U.S. growth rate (3.5 percent) and that a substantially higher growth rate would be experienced in Japan (6.0 percent). Still, substantial differences in per capita incomes would remain, with the EEC reaching 77 percent, and Japan 84 percent, of the U.S. level in 1990.

Assuming further GDP growth rates of 3.7 percent for Canada and 3.3 percent for EFTA, the combined gross domestic product of the industrial countries would rise at an average annual rate of 3.9 percent in the period 1978-90. This projection compares with a 4.1 percent GDP growth rate projected under the base scenario of WDR II for the same period, a growth rate of 3.8 percent estimated by Leontief et. al. for 1980-90, and prospective growth rates of 4.9 percent and 3.6 percent under the two Interfutures scenarios for 1975-90.

Developing Countries

According to WDR II, the gross domestic product of the developing countries[10] would rise at an average annual rate of 5.6 percent under the base scenario and by 6.6 percent and 4.8 percent under the high and low growth scenarios, respectively, between 1980 and 1990. The corresponding projections are 5.0 percent for 1980-90 by Leontief et. al. and 6.7 percent under the rapid convergent growth, and 6.0 percent under the moderate convergent growth, scenario for 1975-2000 by Interfutures (Table 9.1).

The WDR II and Interfutures estimates reflect the assumption that economic growth in the developing countries is linked with growth in the industrial countries. This relationship may be explained by reference to the fact that higher rates of economic growth in the industrial countries entail a more rapid increase of their imports from the developing countries and that growth rates of exports and GDP in the latter group of countries are positively correlated.[11]

A positive correlation between rates of economic growth in the industrial and in the developing countries has been manifest in the past. Thus, GDP growth rates in the two groups of countries were 4.6 percent and 6.2 percent in the 1963-73 period and 2.5 percent and 5.3 percent in the 1973-78 period.[12] At the same time, in the latter period, OPEC and non-OPEC countries need to be separately considered. This is because economic growth in the former group of countries, with an average annual increase of 8.2 percent a year between 1973 and 1978, was largely a function of increases in oil earnings, while the transmission of economic growth from the industrial countries retained its relevance for the latter group, which experienced an average annual GDP growth rate of 4.1 percent between 1973 and 1978. In the following, GDP growth rates for the two groups of developing countries will be separately estimated, with further distinction made between the capital-surplus oil exporters and other OPEC countries.

Under the base scenario of WDR II, the gross domestic product of the capital surplus oil-exporting countries would rise at an average annual rate of 5.0 percent between 1980 and 1990.[13] This estimate reflects the assumption that oil prices would remain unchanged in real terms. We have postulated that, following an increase by about two-thirds between 1978 and 1980, the real price of oil would remain unchanged during the eighties. Assuming further moderate increases in oil output, the real value of the export earnings of the capital surplus oil-exporting countries may double between 1978 and 1990. With increased investment activity, especially in Saudi Arabia which accounts for one-half of the total, the combined gross domestic product of these countries has been projected to rise at an average annual rate of 6.0 percent a year. This figure compares with GDP growth rates averaging 12.8 percent a year in the 1973-78 period,[14] when increases in the real price of oil and in oil production were considerably larger.

The other OPEC countries experienced a rise of GDP of 7.1 percent a year between 1973 and 1978. Continued rapid growth is expected to occur in these countries, the exception being Iran where a long period will be needed to remedy economic dislocation under the Revolution once political conditions stabilize. With Iran accounting for three-tenths of the total, we have projected an average annual rate of growth of 6.0 percent in the other OPEC countries also.

The growth of GDP in the non-OPEC developing countries will be much affected by economic growth in the industrial countries. Assuming the continuation of past relationships, a 3.9 percent rate of growth of GDP in the industrial countries may be accompanied by a 5.5 percent growth rate in the non-

OPEC developing countries. With these countries accounting for nearly three-fourths of the combined gross domestic product of the developing countries, the average GDP growth rate for the developing countries, taken together, would be 5.6 percent.

The 5.6 percent figure equals the estimate of *World Development Report, 1979* which, however, entails a lower projection for the capital-surplus oil exporters and a higher projection for the other developing countries. At the same time, it exceeds the estimate by Leontief et. al. while it is lower than the two Interfutures scenarios that appear to overestimate the growth potential of the developing countries.

II. Trade Projections, 1978-1990

Industrial Country Imports

Under the base scenario of *World Development Report, 1979,* the manufactured exports of the developing countries are projected to rise at an average annual rate of 10.9 percent between 1976 and 1990.[15] This figure barely exceeds the 10.2 percent rate of increase observed in the 1973-78 period,[16] although WDR II expects the rate of growth of GDP in the industrial countries to be two-thirds higher than the actual growth rate of 2.5 percent in 1973-78 (Table 9.1).

WDR II trade projections appear to be overly pessimistic. They seem to have been influenced by the experience of the year 1977, when increased protectionism in the industrial countries led to a slowdown of the growth of their manufactured imports originating in the developing countries. But, with an easing of protectionist trends and a slight increase in the rate of economic growth in the industrial countries the volume of their manufactured imports from the developing countries increased at a rate twice as high in 1978 than in 1977.[17] This compares with the statement made in WDR II: "Preliminary information indicates that developing countries' manufactured exports grew somewhat faster in 1978 than in 1977."[18]

Leontief et. al. are even more pessimistic as they project the GDP of the industrial countries and the total manufactured exports of the developing countries, respectively, to rise at average annual rates of 3.8 percent and 8.5 percent between 1980 and 1990. These estimates correspond to an "apparent" income elasticity of import demand of 2.2 on the assumption that developing country exports to the industrial countries would rise at the same rate as their total manufactured exports. The apparent income elasticity is higher (3.2) for the period 1990-2000, when Leontief et. al. estimate industrial country GDP and the manufactured exports of the developing countries to grow at average annual rates of 2.9 percent and 9.4 percent, respectively.[19]

In turn, the UNIDO projection for the 1974-2000 period assumes a GDP growth rate of 3.0 percent for the industrial countries and an increase of 12.3

percent a year in their imports of manufactured goods from the developing countries, i.e. an apparent income elasticity of import demand of 4.1. At the same time, UNIDO expects the share of the industrial countries in the manufactured exports of the developing countries to decline from 63.4 percent in 1974 to 54.0 percent in 2000, representing increases in the shares of intra-LDC trade and, in particular, of exports to the centrally planned economies.[20]

In estimating future trade flows, an apparent income elasticity of demand of 3.2 has been assumed for the manufactured imports of the industrial countries originating in the developing countries. This compares with an apparent income elasticity of 3.6 in the 1963-73 period and 4.1 in the 1973-78.[21] In postulating a decline in the apparent income elasticity, consideration has been given to the fact that the base year figures of the imports of manufactured goods from the developing countries, and their share in industrial country markets, are considerably higher in the period of projection than in previous periods (Cf. pp. 223-4 below). At the same time, we have assumed the continuation of existing policies in the industrial countries, including the maintenance of the Multifiber Arrangement.

Given the 3.9 percent projected rate of economic growth for the industrial countries and the assumed apparent income elasticity of demand of 3.2, the industrial countries' manufactured imports from the developing countries would rise at an average annual rate of 12.5 percent between 1978 and 1990. At the same time, following WDR II, it has been assumed that the imports of machinery and equipment, and of engineering goods in general, would rise much more rapidly than the average.[22] The projected growth rate for this product group is 17 percent, reflecting expected rapid increases in the imports of consumer electronics, machinery, motor vehicles, and ships from the developing countries, in particular the newly-industrializing countries, as well as the further extension of the international division of the production process, with rising imports of parts, components, and accessories of various engineering products, first from the newly-industrializing, and subsequently from other, developing countries (Table 9.2).

Correspondingly, the share of engineering products in the manufactured imports of the industrial countries from the developing countries would rise from 29.6 percent in 1978 to 47.6 percent in 1990. For the same period, a decline in the combined shares of textiles and clothing from 31.4 percent to 18.1 percent is projected. These estimates reflect the assumption that the continuation of the Multifiber Arrangement would limit the rate of growth of the imports of textiles and clothing from the developing countries to 6 percent and 7 percent, respectively, between 1978 and 1990. The projected growth rates may be on the low side, given the continued upgrading of the quality of developing country exports. At the same time, a shift in the origin of these imports is expected to occur from the newly-industrializing developing countries to countries at lower levels of industrial development.

Below-average increases are projected also for the imports of other semimanufactures (11 percent) and for other consumer goods (11 percent),

TABLE 9.2
Trade in Manufactured Goods between Industrial and Developing Countries (in 1978 prices)

	EXPORTS to									IMPORTS from		
	OPEC			Non-OPEC			Developing Countries			Developing Countries		
	1978 $ billion	1978–90 Growth Rate	1990 $ billion	1978 $ billion	1978–90 Growth Rate	1990 $ billion	1978 $ billion	1978–90 Growth Rate	1990 $ billion	1978 $ billion	1978–90 Growth Rate	1990 $ billion
Iron & Steel	5.00	6.0	10.06	6.92	5.0	12.43	11.92	5.4	22.49	1.25	15.0	6.69
Chemicals	4.87	6.0	9.80	14.35	6.0	28.87	19.22	6.0	38.67	2.43	14.0	11.71
Other Semimanufactures	3.10	9.0	8.72	6.59	6.0	13.26	9.69	7.1	21.98	6.17	11.0	21.59
Engineering Products	46.14	13.3	207.36	57.66	9.0	162.40	103.80	11.2	369.76	12.99	17.0	85.47
Textiles	1.95	8.0	4.91	3.70	4.0	5.92	5.65	5.6	10.83	4.12	6.0	8.28
Clothing	0.47	9.0	1.32	0.85	4.0	1.36	1.32	6.1	2.68	9.64	7.0	21.71
Other Consumer Goods	3.33	10.0	10.45	3.52	5.0	6.32	6.85	7.7	16.77	7.29	11.0	25.50
Manufactured Goods, total	64.84	12.0	252.62	93.62	7.8	230.56	158.46	9.7	483.18	43.88	12.5	180.95

Sources: General Agreements on Tariffs and Trade. *International Trade*, 1978/79 and text.

where the shares of imports originating in the developing countries in the total imports and in the consumption of the industrial countries are relatively high. Finally, above-average increases are postulated for iron and steel (15 percent) and chemicals (14 percent) as some of the newly-industrializing countries can be expected to follow the example of Japan in exporting these commodities. Still, the combined shares of the two product groups in the manufactured imports of the industrial countries from the developing countries would not reach 10 percent in 1990.

While separate projections for the two groups of countries have not been made, the preceding considerations point to changes in the export structure of the newly-industrializing countries and of countries at lower levels of industrial development. In accordance with the stages approach to comparative advantage, developing countries at lower levels of industrialization would increase their market share in unskilled-labor intensive products whereas the newly-industrializing countries would upgrade and diversify their exports.[23]

Industrial Country Exports

The growth of the manufactured imports of the developing countries from the industrial countries will be determined by increases in their gross domestic product and in their foreign exchange earnings, as well as by their import substitution efforts. It is anticipated that increases in industrial capacity in the OPEC countries would lead to a decline in their apparent income elasticity of import demand for manufactured goods originating in the industrial countries. Nevertheless, in view of the expected rapid rise of foreign exchange earnings, an elasticity of 2.0 is projected, giving rise to an average annual increase in manufactured imports of 12.0 percent. This compares to an apparent income elasticity of 3.0 in the period 1973-78.

The OPEC countries are expected to make a considerable effort to expand the production of iron and steel and of chemicals, thereby limiting the growth of imports of these commodities. Increases in domestic capacity are also foreseen in other semimanufactures, textiles, clothing, and some other consumer goods, leading to below-average increases in these imports. In turn, in view of the large investment effort under way in the OPEC countries and their inability to produce investment goods in substantial quantities during the eighties, imports of engineering products are projected to rise relatively rapidly.

In the non-OPEC developing countries, the apparent income elasticity of demand for manufactured goods originating in the industrial countries was 1.8 in the 1973-78 period, representing a considerable increase as compared to an apparent income elasticity of 1.3 in 1963-73. The relatively high elasticity in the more recent period reflects rapid increases in foreign borrowing by the non-OPEC developing countries as well as their increased participation in the international division of the production process, involving in part the importation of manufactured inputs for further processing. The latter, but not the former, tendency is likely to continue during the period of projection. Correspondingly, we have assumed an apparent income elasticity of demand of 1.5 for these countries, resulting in increases of manufactured imports from the industrial countries at an average annual rate of 7.8 percent in the 1978-90 period.

Again, above-average increases are expected for engineering products, in part because of the increased need of the non-OPEC developing countries for sophisticated machinery and transport equipment that the industrial countries can provide, and in part because of the international division of the production process in engineering products. Conversely, increases are expected to be the smallest in relatively labor-intensive textiles, clothing, and other consumer goods. And, import substitution efforts are likely to limit increases in relatively capital-intensive iron and steel, chemicals, and other semimanufactures, too.

These projections would entail an increase of 9.7 percent a year in the manufactured imports of the (OPEC and non-OPEC) developing countries from the industrial countries in the 1978-90 period as compared to the growth of their combined GDP at an average annual rate of 5.6 percent. The resulting apparent income elasticity of demand of 1.7 exceeds the 1.3 figure observed in the 1963-73 period when the relative importance of the OPEC countries was substantially less. It is lower, however, than the apparent income elasticity of 2.4 in the 1973-78 period.

WDR II and Interfutures do not provide estimates of the manufactured imports of the developing countries. In turn, Leontief et. al. project the total manufactured imports of the developing countries to rise at an average annual rate of 7.7 percent between 1980 and 1990, corresponding to an apparent income elasticity of 1.5 on the assumption that their imports from the industrial countries would rise at the same rate as imports from all destinations. The apparent income elasticity is lower (1.3) for the 1990-2000 period, for which GDP and imports are projected to grow at rates of 6.0 percent and 7.9 percent, respectively.

Finally, the UNIDO report estimates that the developing countries would increase their imports of manufactured goods from the industrial countries at an average annual rate of 8.2 percent between 1974 and 2000 but does not provide GDP projections. At the same time, the report expects a decline in the share of the industrial countries in the manufactured imports of the developing countries from 84.0 percent in 1974 to 61.0 percent in 2000, representing increases in intra-LDC trade and in imports from centrally planned economies.[24]

III. The Changing Importance of Trade in Manufactured Goods between Industrial and Developing Countries

Estimated increases of 9.7 percent a year in the industrial countries' exports, and 12.5 percent a year in their imports, of manufactured goods in trade with the developing countries would reduce their export-import ratio in these products from 3.6 in 1978 to 2.7 in 1990. Nevertheless, the export surplus of the industrial countries in manufactured trade with the developing countries would nearly triple, from $115 billion to $303 billion, during this period.

In turn, UNIDO foresees a growth of 8.2 percent a year in the industrial countries' exports, and 12.3 percent a year in their imports, of manufactured goods from the developing countries in the 1974-2000 period. As a result of these changes, the trade surplus of the industrial countries in manufactured goods traded with the developing countries would increase nearly four times between 1974 and 2000 while their export-import ratio would decline from 4.2 to 1.6.[25] In turn, Interfutures projects the export-import ratio to fall from 3.1 in 1970 to 2.0 under the high convergent growth, and to 1.7 under the moderate convergent growth scenario between 1970 and 2000 (p. 332).[26]

Comparable estimates are not available in WDR II while the projections by Leontief et. al. pertain to the total manufactured exports and imports of the developing countries. According to these estimates, the trade deficit of the developing countries in manufactured goods would double between 1980 and 1990 and quadruple between 1980 and 2000 while the ratio of imports to exports would decline from 3.7 in 1980 to 3.5 in 1990 and to 2.9 in 2000.

In turn, we have projected that two-thirds of the increase in the export surplus of the industrial countries in manufactured trade with the developing countries' trade surplus is foreseen also in iron and steel and in chemicals. By contrast, the industrial countries' trade surplus in other semimanufactures and in textiles would decline, and their trade deficit in clothing and in other consumer goods would increase, during the period under consideration.

The next question concerns the share of the developing countries in the industrial countries' exports and imports of manufactured goods. Excluding trade between the United States and Canada and trade within the European free trade area in manufactured goods (to be referred to as partner country trade), the manufactured exports of the industrial countries amounted to $336.3 billion, and their imports to $180.2 billion, in 1978 (Table 9.3). In the same year, exports to, and imports from, the developing countries were $158.5 and $43.9 billion, respectively, while the mutual trade of the industrial countries, excluding trade with the partner countries, was $105.6 billion as reported by the exporting countries, and $110.7 billion as reported by the importing countries.[27] Finally, the industrial countries had manufactured exports of $72.2 billion and imports of $25.6 billion in trade with the rest of the world (Southern Europe, Australia, New Zealand, and South Africa, the centrally planned economies) and with unreported destinations.[28]

In the mutual trade of the industrial countries in manufactured goods, an apparent income elasticity of 2.4 was observed in 1963-73 and an elasticity of 1.9 in 1973-77.[29] We have assumed that the decline in this elasticity will moderate in the future. For the period 1978-90, we have calculated with an

TABLE 9.3

Production, Trade, and Consumption of Manufactured Goods in the Industrial Countries ($ billion in 1978 prices)

	Production (1)	Exports			Imports			Consumption (1) + (5) − (2) (8)
		World (2)	World less Partner Countries (3)	LDCs (4)	World (5)	World less Partner Countries (6)	LDCs (7)	
A. Absolute Values								
1978								
Iron & Steel	429.59	45.45	26.78	11.92	29.35	10.64	1.25	413.49
Chemicals	372.36	84.93	43.30	19.22	62.16	20.70	2.43	349.59
Other Semimanufactures	362.89	49.61	19.17	9.69	48.40	16.33	6.17	361.68
Engineering Products	1143.15	364.31	215.63	103.80	239.25	89.98	12.99	1018.09
Textiles	184.78	27.65	11.47	5.65	24.91	8.97	4.12	182.04
Clothing	85.39	13.32	3.22	1.32	24.11	13.98	9.64	96.18
Other Consumer Goods	532.11	40.90	16.70	6.85	43.81	19.61	7.29	535.02
Manufactured Goods, total	3110.27	626.18	336.27	158.46	471.98	180.20	43.89	2956.07
1990								
Iron & Steel	521.37	82.84	49.23	22.49	57.27	23.59	6.69	495.80
Chemicals	621.22	195.18	96.02	38.67	152.56	53.80	11.71	578.60
Other Semimanufactures	567.69	111.87	43.32	21.98	116.68	44.46	21.59	572.50
Engineering Products	2057.77	983.26	628.68	369.76	611.49	260.46	85.47	1685.00
Textiles	240.08	45.57	21.30	10.83	45.69	17.00	8.28	240.20
Clothing	115.07	24.32	6.14	2.68	48.35	30.12	21.71	139.10
Other Consumer Goods	794.50	93.44	38.94	16.77	106.84	52.34	25.50	808.90
Manufactured Goods, total	4917.70	1536.48	883.63	483.18	1138.88	481.77	180.95	4520.10

Sources: GATT, *International Trade, 1978-79*, Table 9.2 and text.

apparent income elasticity of 1.8, resulting in an average annual rate of growth of 7.0 percent in this trade.

Exports of manufactured goods to the centrally planned economies have been growing rapidly, financed in part by foreign loans. In 1978, these exports amounted to $30.1 billion as compared to imports of $10.2 billion. In view of limitations on their foreign borrowing, the centrally planned economies cannot increase their trade deficit at past rates. Correspondingly, we have assumed a lower rate of growth for the exports (6.0 percent), than for the imports (7.0 percent), of the industrial countries in their trade in manufactured goods with the rest of the world.

In projecting the mutual trade of the industrial countries and their exports to the rest of the world, above-average increases have been assumed for chemicals and engineering products, approximately average increases for other semimanufactures and consumer goods, and below-average increases for iron and steel, textiles, and clothing. In turn, the commodity composition of the industrial countries' imports from the rest of the world is expected to resemble that of imports from the developing countries.

The described changes in trade flows would entail an increase in the share of the developing countries in the industrial countries' exports to non-partner countries from 47.1 percent to 54.7 percent, and an increase in the developing countries' import share from 24.6 percent to 37.6 percent, between 1978 and 1990. The incremental shares of the developing countries would be 59.3 percent for exports and 45.4 percent for imports during this period (Tables 9.3 and 9.4).

The developing countries would assume special importance as markets for the industrial countries in engineering products where they would provide nearly two-thirds of incremental exports, and their incremental share would also exceed 50 percent in the case of other semimanufactures and textiles. In turn, developing countries are expected to account for nearly three-fourths of the increment in clothing imports, and for approximately one-half of the increment in the imports of other semimanufactures, engineering products, textiles, and other consumer goods in the industrial countries.

Further interest attaches to the changing share of exports to the developing countries in the production, and that of imports from the developing countries in the consumption of manufactured goods in the industrial countries. For this purpose, we have estimated prospective changes in the consumption of manufactured goods in the industrial countries in the seven commodity group breakdown. In turn, production estimates for 1990 have been derived by adjusting the consumption forecasts for the projected trade flows.

The consumption of manufactured goods has been projected by utilizing information provided in Landsberg, et. al.[30] and, subsequently, Houthakker and Taylor[31] for the United States, Deaton[32] for the United Kingdom, and Berner[33] for the European Common Market, as well as the projections made by Leontief et. al. for the industrial country groups under consideration.

TABLE 9.4
The Share of the Developing Countries in the Production, Consumption, and Trade of Manufactured Goods in the Industrial Countries

	1978				1990			
	$X_{LDC/X}$	$X_{LDC/P}$	$M_{LDC/M}$	$M_{LDC/C}$	$X_{LDC/X}$	$X_{LDC/P}$	$M_{LDC/M}$	$M_{LDC/C}$
Iron & Steel	44.5	2.8	11.7	0.3	45.7	4.3	28.4	1.3
Chemicals	44.4	5.2	11.7	0.7	40.3	6.2	21.8	2.0
Other Semimanufactures	50.5	2.7	37.8	1.7	50.7	3.9	48.6	3.8
Engineering Products	48.1	9.1	14.4	1.3	58.8	18.0	32.8	5.1
Textiles	49.3	3.1	45.9	2.3	50.8	4.5	48.7	3.4
Clothing	41.0	1.5	69.0	10.0	43.6	2.4	72.1	15.6
Other Consumer Goods	41.0	1.3	37.2	1.4	43.1	2.1	48.7	3.2
Manufactured Goods, total	47.1	5.1	24.6	1.5	54.7	9.8	37.6	4.0

Incremental Shares, 1978–1990

	$\Delta X_{LDC/\Delta X}$	$\Delta X_{LDC/\Delta P}$	$\Delta M_{LDC/\Delta M}$	$\Delta M_{LDC/\Delta C}$
Iron & Steel	47.1	11.5	42.0	6.6
Chemicals	36.9	7.8	28.0	4.1
Other Semimanufactures	50.9	6.0	54.8	7.3
Engineering Products	64.4	29.1	48.2	10.8
Textiles	52.7	9.4	51.8	7.2
Clothing	46.6	5.0	72.9	28.1
Other Consumer Goods	44.6	3.7	55.6	6.6
Manufactured Goods, total	59.3	18.0	45.4	8.9

Source: Table 9.3

Notes: X = exports to non-partner countries; M = imports from non-partner countries. X_{LDC} = exports to developing countries; M_{LDC} = imports from developing countries. P = Production; C = Consumption.

An income elasticity of 0.8 has been assumed for clothing and 0.9 for other consumer goods. Among intermediate products, an income elasticity of 0.6 has been postulated for textiles, reflecting the shift towards higher-quality clothing. The same elasticity has been assumed for iron and steel that are being replaced in several uses by lower-weight materials, some of which belong to the chemical and others in the other semimanufactures categories. Taking account of increased demand at higher income levels, an income elasticity of 1.2 has been postulated for chemicals while an elasticity of 1.0 has been assumed for other semimanufactures.

Engineering products include durable consumer goods as well as investment goods. With increased congestion and high petroleum prices, the sales of passenger cars are expected to rise at a relatively slow rate. The introduction of new products is likely to lead, however, to rapid increases in the demand for household appliances and other durable consumer goods. Finally, with increases in capital-labor ratios, the demand for machinery can be expected to rise at a rate exceeding that of the gross domestic product. All in all, we have calculated with an income elasticity of 1.2 for engineering products.

These estimates correspond to an average income elasticity of demand of 0.9 for manufactured goods, resulting in average annual increases of 3.6 percent in the consumption of manufactured goods between 1976 and 1990. Adjusting for projected values of exports and imports, estimates show manufacturing production to rise by 3.9 percent a year during this period.[34] The difference between the production and the consumption estimates is explained by the increase in the industrial countries' export surplus in manufactured goods from 5.0 percent of their manufacturing production in 1978 to 8.2 percent in 1990. The bulk of this increase would occur in trade with the developing countries, with the relevant ratios being 3.7 percent and 6.2 percent.

The projected growth rate of manufacturing production equals that of GDP in the industrial countries for the 1978-90 period. By comparison, manufacturing production increased at an average annual rate of 2.2 percent and GDP grew 2.5 percent a year, i.e., a ratio of 0.9, between 1973 and 1978 while the ratio was 1.1 in the 1963-73 period.[35]

Table 9.3 indicates the increased share of the developing countries as markets for the manufacturing production of the industrial countries. While exports to the developing countries amounted to 5.1 percent of manufacturing output in 1978, this share is projected to reach 9.3 percent in 1990, with an incremental share of 18.0 percent. Incremental shares are the highest for engineering products (29.1 percent) and vary between 4 percent and 12 percent for the remaining product groups.

In the same period, the share of imports originating in the developing countries in the industrial countries' consumption of manufactured products is projected to rise from 1.5 percent in 1978 to 4.0 percent in 1990, with an incremental share of 8.9 percent. Incremental shares are by far the highest for clothing (28.1 percent). Nevertheless, clothing production in the industrial countries would increase at an average annual rate of 2.3 percent between 1978 and 1990. For the same period, the projected increase is 2.2 percent a year for the production of textiles, where the incremental share of the developing countries (7.2 percent) would be below the overall average.

Conclusions

The projections reported in this paper assume the continuation of existing policies in the industrial countries, including the maintenance of the Multifiber Arrangement. They further assume that the newly-industrializing countries would upgrade and diversity their manufactured exports and that countries at lower levels of industrial development would take their place in exporting unskilled-labor intensive products.

This scenario represents the application of the stages approach to comparative advantage, with changes in export patterns occurring in the process of industrial development. It also points to the interdependence of the industrial and the developing countries through trade in manufactured goods, with benefits accruing to both groups of countries.

To begin with, the estimates indicate that the developing countries will increase in importance as markets for the manufactured exports of the industrial countries. Excluding trade between the United States and Canada and within the European free trade area in manufactured goods, the share of the developing countries in the manufactured exports of the industrial countries is expected to increase from 47 percent in 1978 to 55 percent in 1990, with the developing countries accounting for 59 percent of the increment in exports during this period.

The developing countries would assume increased importance in the total (domestic and foreign) sales of the industrial countries also. While only 5.1 percent of the industrial countries' manufacturing output was sold in the developing countries in 1978, this share is projected to double by 1990, with exports to the developing countries accounting for 18 percent of the increment in output between 1978 and 1990. The incremental share of the developing countries would be particularly high, nearly three-tenths, for engineering production in the industrial countries.

In turn, the share of the developing countries in the imports of manufactured goods by the industrial countries would increase from 25 percent in 1978 to 37 percent in 1990, with an incremental share of 45 percent. In the same period, the ratio of imports from the developing countries to the consumption of manufactured goods in the industrial countries would rise from 1.5 percent to 4.0 percent, with the incremental ratio being 8.7 percent.

Although import growth rates (12.5 percent a year) are expected to exceed the rate of growth of exports (9.7 percent), the increased export surplus of the industrial countries in their trade in manufactured goods with the developing countries would contribute to the growth of their manufacturing output. To the extent that manufactured goods tend to be more skill-intensive than agriculture and services, this trade would make a positive contribution to economic growth in the industrial countries.

The industrial countries stand to obtain further gains as a result of resource allocation according to comparative advantage, involving the exchange of commodities embodying physical and human capital (including research intensive products) for products that have higher unskilled-labor intensity. Furthermore, international specialization permits exploiting economies of scale in the industrial countries, and the growth of imports from the developing countries tends to limit price increases for the consumer.

The developing countries, too, enjoy gains from improved resource allocation and the exploitation of economies of scale through trade in manufactured goods with the industrial countries. They have the further benefit of procuring sophisticated machinery and transport equipment in a world of rapidly changing technology. And, the industrial countries provide markets for the skill-intensive products the newly-industrializing developing countries are increasingly able to manufacture as well as for the incipient manufactured exports of countries at lower levels of industrial development.

At the same time, as we have seen, none of the industries of the industrial countries would experience a decline in output under the projections for the period 1978-90. Thus, production would rise at a rate of over 2 percent a year even in the case of textiles and clothing, the future prospects of which have been of particular concern to the governments of the industrial countries.

These considerations indicate the common interests of the industrial and the developing countries in a liberal trade environment that permits the rapid expansion of their mutual trade. Trade liberalization by the industrial countries could proceed over a ten-year horizon without involving excessively large adjustment costs, even though it would lead to more rapid increases in imports than projected in the present essay under the continuation of existing policies. More rapid increases in the manufactured imports of the industrial countries from the developing countries, in turn, would permit the latter to increase their purchases of manufactured goods, with benefits to all concerned.

The newly-industrializing countries, too, would need to reduce their trade barriers in order to improve economic efficiency and to admit imports from countries at lower levels of industrial development. Efficiency considerations also call for moderate levels of protection in the latter group of countries so as to avoid high-cost import substitution and discrimination against the exportation of manufactured goods. At the same time, in the event that appropriate policies are followed, the newly industrializing as well as the less developed countries could increase their manufactured exports more rapidly than projected in this essay.

Part II

ESSAY 10

Incentive Policies In Brazil

Introduction

The purpose of this essay is to analyze the incentive policies applied in Brazil during the period since the oil crisis and the 1974-75 world recession and to consider possible future policies. For the sake of a better understanding of these measures, the essay will also review the incentive policies employed during the period preceding the oil crisis.

Section I will provide a brief description of the experience of the import substitution era in Brazil, followed by a review of the policy measures introduced in the second half of the sixties and an appraisal of their economic effects. In turn, Section II will describe the measures taken after the oil crisis, examine the performance of the Brazilian economy during this period, and evaluate the policies applied. Finally, Section III will review the policy reform implemented in January 1979 and consider policies that may be employed in the future.

I. Policy Reforms in the Second Half of the Sixties

The Experience of the Import Substitution Era

As is well-known, until the mid-sixties Brazil followed a policy oriented towards import substitution. This policy involved the use of multiple exchange rates; the imposition of high tariffs on imports; and the application of the "Law of Similars," which practically excluded imports by the public sector as well as by private firms that wished to received particular forms of government assistance, whenever a domestic similar existed.

On the basis of available information on tariffs and comparisons of domestic and foreign prices in cases when the existence of domestic similars limited imports, Bergsman and Malan estimated that in 1966 the average nominal protection of Brazilian manufacturing was 99 percent and effective protection 118 or 155 percent, depending on whether the so-called Corden or

231

Balassa formulas were used in the estimation. In the same year, the nominal and the effective protection of primary production other than coffee was slightly above 50 percent.[1]

In its early stages, import substitution led to rapid increases in domestic production. Growth slowed down, however, after 1960 when further import substitution in capital goods and intermediate products encountered increasing difficulties. This was largely because of the high capital and technological requirements of these products and the need for outlets exceeding the size of the domestic market for exploiting economies of scale. Correspondingly, plants were often of less than efficient size or, alternatively, investment involved building ahead of demand, thus creating excess capacity. As a result, the ratio of net to gross foreign exchange savings declined and the domestic resource cost of saving foreign exchange increased. In 1966, the cost of protection in Brazil, including monopoly profits, was estimated at 9.5 percent of GNP.

At the same time, the high protection of domestic markets discriminated against exports, both by lowering the exchange rate and by raising the cost of inputs used in export production. Bergsman and Malan estimate that, assuming no change in government policies in regard to coffee, the exchange rate equivalent of the protective measures applied was 27 percent in 1966. Thus, as a result of the application of protective measures, exporters received about one-fourth less in terms of cruzeiros for dollars earned than what they would have received in the absence of these measures.

Taking further account of the high cost of inputs into export production, the incentive system gave rise to a substantial bias against exports. Even assuming full drawbacks of duties on imported inputs into export production, exporting would have required firms to operate with negative value added in eight out of twenty-one manufacturing industries, and value added obtainable in exporting rarely exceeded one-half of value added in domestic sales in the remaining industries. In fact, imports receiving duty rebates hardly reached 2 percent of manufactured exports in 1966.

Exports were also subject to licensing. It was reported that licenses for primary exports were often refused for the sake of keeping food prices down.[2] And, while licenses to export manufactured goods were rarely refused, these were granted on the condition that at least 70 percent of the value of the product was of domestic origin. The practical administration of this requirement, as well as that of duty rebates, was a deterrent to exports.

Moreover, until the mid-sixties, rebates of indirect taxes were not provided to exporters. Thus, exports suffered additional discrimination as they did not receive the tax rebates that would have been required for tax neutrality under the destination principle, which involves imposing indirect taxes on imports and rebating them on exports.

The observed bias of the incentive system against export production led to a slowdown of exports. For one thing, Brazil was losing market shares in its traditional exports, including coffee, cocoa, and lumber, with an improvement shown only for cotton.[3] For another thing, discrimination against exports hindered the development of new primary and manufactured exports. Correspondingly, between 1960 and 1966, the volume of exports increased by only 3.8 percent a year.

The slow growth of exports, in turn, increasingly "starved" the Brazilian economy of foreign exchange for the purchase of capital goods and intermediate inputs. As a result, the share of imports in the total utilization of manufactured goods declined from 10.8 percent in 1960 to 7.5 percent in 1966; in the same period, the ratio of imports to GNP fell from 7.1 to 6.1 percent.

As Leff[4] notes, a cumulative process occurred, with import protection leading to the slowdown in export growth that, in turn, necessitated further efforts at import substitution, requiring higher protection. As higher protection again had adverse effects on exports, the process continued further, contributing to a slowdown in economic growth. Growth rates of GNP declined from 6.3 percent in the period 1953-60 to 3.8 percent in 1960-66; the corresponding figures for manufacturing were 10.1 and 4.5 percent. These results are not materially affected if we exclude the years of deflationary policies, 1965 and 1966, when the average growth rate of GNP was 3.8 percent.

Reforming Incentive Policies after 1966

The reform of the incentive system, carried out largely in the period 1967-1970, had several facets. First, tax discrimination against the exports of manufactured goods was eliminated and various export subsidies were instituted. Second, rates of import protection were reduced and the exchange rates unified. Third, mini-devaluations were introduced in the place of intermittent changes in the exchange rate. Fourth, the real exchange rate (the nominal exchange rate, adjusted for changes in relative prices at home and abroad) was increased during this period. These measures will be briefly considered in the following.

The profitability of exports was improved first by providing exemptions from federal indirect taxes. Subsequently, exports were exempted from state indirect taxes, taxes on financial operations, and the special tax on fuel and oil. While these measures aimed at eliminating tax discrimination against exports, from 1968 onwards "genuine" export subsidies were also granted in the form of federal and state indirect tax credits, through exempting profits derived in export activities from income taxes, and by providing credits to exporters at preferential rates. Also, duty drawbacks were generalized.

In making comparisons with the situation existing prior to 1967, the combined effect of all the described measures is relevant, since they all improved the profitability of exports. This was estimated to average 45 percent of the fob value of manufactured exports in 1971, of which 27 percent were rebates of indirect taxes and 18 percent "genuine" export subsidies. Within the latter figure, indirect tax credits amounted to 12 percent, income tax exemptions 2 percent, duty drawbacks 1 percent, and credit subsidies 3 percent of fob value.[5]

Subsidies to exports were designed to compensate for the discrimination against exports that resulted from the lower exchange rate and the higher cost of domestic inputs associated with import protection. This contrasts with the situation existing in Far Eastern countries, such as Korea and Taiwan, where import protection rates were lower and exporters were operating virtually under a free trade regime, with only small additional subsidies provided. The contrast is explained by the fact that Brazil, unlike Korea and Taiwan, established relatively high-cost industries producing inputs for exports. Also, in contradistinction with the latter two countries, export subsidy rates exhibited considerable variation in Brazil. The ratio of ";genuine" export subsidies to the fob value of exports ranged from 8 percent on wood products to 37 percent on apparel and footwear.

Export subsidies were limited to manufactured goods and some minerals in Brazil. However, the manufactured goods category was defined to include processed food such as meat and sugar; also, some agricultural products such as soybeans and livestock benefited from promotional measures. Furthermore, with the lowering of import protection on manufactured goods, discrimination against the agricultural sector decreased and licenses for agricultural exports were given practically without limitation.

Parallel with the granting of export subsidies, the protection of imports was reduced. Tariffs on manufactured goods were lowered by about one-half in early 1967, and while tariffs were increased again in 1968, further tariff reductions took place in the following years. In 1973, the average tariff on manufactured goods was estimated at 57 percent as compared to the 99 percent average nominal protection in 1966.[6] With the increasingly liberal implementation of the "Law of Similars," and the unification of exchange rates, the average tariff figure may be taken to be roughly equivalent to the nominal protection of manufactured goods.

It is thus apparent that, as a result of the granting of export subsidies and the lowering of import protection, discrimination against exports decreased to a considerable extent during the period under review. However, discrimination against exports was not eliminated as "genuine" export subsidies did not appreciably increase above the 17 percent average figure shown for 1970 in subsequent years.

Exports were given further impetus by the introduction of the scheme of "mini-devaluations" in 1968 and the depreciation of the real exchange rate. Prior to 1968, the exchange rate had been changed in infrequent intervals, thus giving rise to large variations in real exchange rates and creating uncertainty for exporters as to the cruzeiro equivalent of their foreign exchange earnings. This disincentive to exports largely disappeared as devaluations were undertaken in small steps at frequent intervals, averaging approximately one per month. At the same time, the real exchange rate was increased by devaluing to a greater extent than changes in relative prices would have required.

Finally, exports and economic activities in general benefited from improvements in monetary arrangements that began in the mid-sixties. An important factor contributing to increases in domestic savings and investment was the indexing of financial obligations that gave rise to positive real interest rates averaging 5 percent on Treasury bonds.[7] Forced savings in the form of payroll reductions, channeled through the Housing Bank, also added to total savings while raising the prices of public enterprises increased the availability of savings to the private sector by reducing the public sector deficit. Indexing, together with the establishment of new financial institutions, also improved the structure of financial intermediation in Brazil and increased the efficiency of chanelling savings into investment. Another factor contributing to increased investment activity was the more favorable treatment accorded to the inflow of foreign capital.

Incentives and Economic Performance

Brazil had an excellent economic performance in the 1966-1973 period. To begin with, the volume of total exports grew at an average annual rate of 10.2 percent during this period. With the volume of traditional primary exports (coffee, cocoa, timber, and cotton) rising 0.5 percent a year, export expansion was concentrated in nontraditional primary and manufactured products. Between 1966 and 1973, the volume of nontraditional primary and manufactured exports grew at an average annual rate of 18.0 percent. As a result, the share of these commodities in Brazil's total exports rose from 43.6 percent in 1966 to 73.7 percent in 1973.

In the absence of the relevant price data, a further disaggregation of nontraditional exports is possible only in value terms. The results show the dollar value of nontraditional primary exports rising at an average annual rate of 26.8 percent, with manufactured exports growing at a rate of 38.5 percent between 1966 and 1973. These results compare favorably with results for most other developing countries.

Among eleven newly-industrializing developing countries,[8] Brazil's export performance in nontraditional primary products was exceeded only by Korea (35.5 percent), while its rate of growth of manufactured exports was surpassed by Korea (50.0 percent), Taiwan (47.0 percent), and Singapore (42.0 percent). At the same time, Brazil exceeded the average rate of growth of exports for the eleven countries that was 18.0 percent for nontraditional primary products and 27.1 percent for manufactured goods between 1966 and 1973. In turn, according to UN statistics, the dollar value of manufactured exports from all developing countries, taken together, rose at an average annual rate of 27.3 percent during the same period.

Growth rates are a misleading indicator of export performance if absolute values at the beginning of the period are small. This was not the case in Brazil as far as nontraditional primary exports are concerned. Brazil's nontraditional primary exports amounted to $634 million in 1966, exceeding that of any other newly-industrializing developing country and accounting for 22.6 percent of the combined exports of these products by the eleven countries. By 1973, nontraditional primary exports were $6.2 billion in Brazil, with sugar, soybeans, and animal feedingstuffs each amounting to about one-half of one billion and exports of meat and iron ore for approximately one-third of one billion dollars.

Brazil provided only 4.4 percent of the manufactured exports of the eleven newly-industrializing countries in 1966. With a tenfold increase in its manufactured exports as compared to a fivefold rise for the eleven countries, taken together, Brazil's share nearly doubled between 1966 and 1973, reaching 8.6 percent. At the same time, the importance of exports in Brazil's industrial sector increased to a considerable extent, with the share of exports in manufactured output rising from 1.3 percent in 1966 to 4.4 percent in 1973. In the same period, the ratio of total exports to GNP increased from 6.0 percent in 1966 to 7.7 percent in 1973.

The expansion of exports, together with improvements in the terms of trade, increased Brazil's import capacity. As the volume of exports rose at a rate of 10.2 percent a year and the improvement of terms of trade averaged 2.4 percent a year, Brazil's import capacity increased at an average annual rate of 12.8 percent between 1966 and 1973. With the inflow of foreign capital further adding to foreign exchange availability, the average annual rate of growth of import volume averaged 18.2 percent between 1966 and 1973, whereas the value of imports grew 24.5 percent a year. As a result, the share of imports in Brazilian GNP rose from 5.2 percent in 1966 to 8.7 percent in 1973; in the manufacturing sector, the corresponding ratios are 7.5 and 13.0 percent.

The increased inflow of foreign capital is reflected in the rise in the ratio of foreign savings to gross domestic investment from 0.4 percent in 1966 to 7.7 percent in 1973. During the same period, the share of domestic savings in the gross domestic product increased from 22.2 percent to 25.4 percent. With increases in domestic and in foreign savings, the share of gross domestic investment in GNP rose from 22.3 percent in 1966 to 27.5 percent in 1973.

Rapid export expansion, the increased availability of foreign savings, and the rise of the share of domestic savings in GNP contributed to the economic growth in Brazil. Between 1966 and 1973, the gross national product grew at an average annual rate of 10.0 percent, with agricultural production rising 5.1 percent and manufacturing production 12.6 percent a year. Among the eleven newly-industrializing countries under consideration, Brazil had the best performance in agriculture while it was surpassed by Taiwan (22.0 percent), Korea (21.1 percent), and Singapore (19.8 percent) in regard to the growth of manufacturing production, and by Singapore (11.6 percent), in regard to the growth of GNP, with Taiwan having the same GNP growth rate (10.0 percent).

This, by now "conventional," view of the influences affecting Brazil's economic growth performance, often called the Brazilian "economic miracle," came under criticism in recent years. Edmar Bacha put forward the proposition that "the 1968-74 economic boom conforms to the cyclical growth pattern of the Brazilian economy in the post-war period. There is no 'economic miracle' to be explained despite nearly seven years of unprecedented prosperity in the period."[9] Also, Malan and Bonelli "have attempted to show that the economic boom Brazil experienced from 1968 to 1973 was due to a rather special conjunction of a cyclical upswing with roots in past developments (such as the earlier boom of the late 1950s), with an extremely favorable—and elusively temporary—international situation with respect to both commodity trade and capital movements."[10]

The claims made by Bacha and by Malan and Bonelli as to the cyclical nature of the Brazilian boom during the period under consideration is based on a comparison of potential and actual output in the manufacturing sector. Potential output was derived on the assumption of constant incremental capital-output ratios, utilizing ratios pertaining to the years 1966 and 1972, respectively.[11]

The method applied is open to various objections, however. To begin with, there may be an underlying trend in incremental capital-output ratios due to technological change. In the presence of such a trend, potential output for the end of the period would be underestimated, and the increment in output resulting from increased capacity utilization overestimated. Furthermore, the method applied neglects the effects of policy changes on incremental capital-output ratios. Yet, international comparisons show that these ratios differ to a considerable extent depending on the policies followed. Thus, in the 1960-73 period, incremental capital-output ratios were in the 1.7-2.5 range in Korea, Singapore, and Taiwan, countries that followed outward-oriented policies, while these ratios were 5.5 in Chile and 5.7 in India, where an inward-oriented strategy continued to be applied.

It may be assumed, then, that the increased outward orientation of the Brazilian economy contributed to the decline in Brazil's incremental capital-output ratio from 3.8 in 1960-66 to 2.1 in 1966-73. This conclusion is strengthened if we consider that in 1970 direct plus indirect labor requirements were 78 percent higher for value added in the production of manufactured exports than in that of import-competing goods in Brazil.[12] Moreover, increased outward orientation contributed to higher capacity utilization while, as noted above, import-substitution orientation leads to excess capacity by building ahead of demand under the constraints of the domestic market.

But, higher capacity utilization accounts for a relatively small part of the growth of the Brazilian economy. Data collected by the Vargas Foundation and published in *Conjuntura Economica* show that the average extent of capacity utilization in manufacturing increased only from 83 in the third quarter 1968 to 90 in 1973. This change is rather small as compared to the approximate doubling of the capital stock in the manufacturing sector.[13] At the same time, increased investment was encouraged, on the supply side, by inducements to the inflow of foreign capital and to domestic savings and, on the demand side, by the measures of export promotion. Improved incentives also contributed to the favorable performance of the agricultural sector where we cannot speak of excess capacity in 1966.

Reference may further be made to available evidence on the impact of export incentives—in the form of increases in the real exchange rate for, and subsidies to, exports—on the growth of exports. An export elasticity of 1.1 with respect to the real exchange rate, adjusted for export subsidies, has been obtained for manufactured products by Carvalho and Haddad for the period 1955-1974, using annual data.[14] In turn, Tyler has estimated elasticities of 1.4 and 2.4 with respect to the real exchange rate and export subsidies, taken separately, for manufactured exports during the period 1963-72, using quarterly data and a one-period lag in the estimation.[15]

Additional evidence on the effects of export subsidization is provided in a cross-section framework by Pinto. Relating data for 1971 to data for 1966 (i.e. before export subsidies were introduced) in an 18 industry framework, Pinto has found that export performance is positively correlated with export subsidies expressed as a proportion of value added and negatively correlated with initial export-output ratios.[16]

Further questions arise concerning the claim put forward by Malan and Bonelli that the favorable international environment benefited the Brazilian economy or, as they expressed it, "Ognun sa Navigare a Buon Vento."[17] In this connection, the authors referred to the high rate of economic growth in the developed countries as well as to the availability of foreign capital during the 1966-73 period.

Available data show, however, that the period under consideration was not exceptional as far as the growth of developed economies is concerned. Thus, the combined GDP of the OECD member countries increased at an average annual rate of 4.6 percent between 1966 and 1973 as compared to a growth rate of 5.3 percent in the period 1960-66.[18] At the same time, as we have seen, Brazilian export performance was very different in the two periods. In particular, Brazil nearly doubled its share in the combined exports of manufactured goods by the eleven newly-industrializing developing countries between 1966 and 1973.

Questions arise also concerning the validity of the assertion that the availability of foreign capital would have appreciably changed between 1960-66 and 1966-73. While the Eurodollar market expanded at a rapid rate, one does not observe a tendency for acceleration in foreign direct investment in the developing countries. Rather, the improved climate for foreign capital, as well as increased profitability in a more open economy, were the factors that apparently induced increased foreign investment in Brazil. It should be added that similar changes in foreign investment were observed in few developing countries and no other Latin American country matched Brazil's growth performance.

At the same time, it should be emphasized that export subsidization in Brazil involved superposing a system of export incentives on the system of import protection. Although protection rates were reduced during the period under review, import protection continued at relatively high levels and with large dispersion, necessitating the use of subsidies to offset their adverse effects on exports. Since subsidies to exports also varied to a considerable extent from industry to industry, there were substantial differences in the inter-industry structure of incentives, and hence in the domestic resource costs of saving or earning foreign exchange. As noted in the following section, these differences increased further after 1973.

II. Policy Responses to the Oil Crisis and to the World Recession

Policy Goals and Instruments

As other oil-importing countries, Brazil was affected to a considerable extent by the quadrupling of oil prices and the subsequent world recession. For one thing, the average unit value of Brazil's imports expressed in terms of U.S. dollars, rose by 54 percent between 1973 and 1974 while export unit values increased by only 26 percent.[19] For another, GATT reports that, as a result of the world recession, the volume of world trade in 1975 was about at the same level as in 1973.

Both of these factors contributed to the deterioration of the balance of trade in Brazil. As noted by the former Minister of Planning, João Paulo dos Reis Velloso, in this situation "one of the alternatives was to follow the road of the developed countries: to attempt to resolve the problem of the balance of trade through a recession, which would bring a substantial reduction in imports."[20] Velloso adds that the government rejected this alternative as being "inconvenient" and "inefficient." Rather, it is said to have chosen a "Brazilian alternative," involving a moderate deceleration of economic growth, together with measures aimed at limiting imports, promoting diversified exports, and reducing oil consumption.

The objective of a moderate deceleration of economic growth has not been consistently followed during the period since the oil crisis, however. Rather, considerations of employment and inflation, together with political expediency, have led to the application of policies which to a considerable extent had a stop-and-go character.

To begin with, the substantial loss of foreign exchange reserves, coupled with the uncertainties associated with the installation of the new government, resulted in a relatively restrictive monetary and fiscal policy stance in 1974. End-year figures show that the money supply rose by only 33.6 percent in that year as compared to 49.1 percent in 1973. And, while government expenditures increased at about the same rate (38 percent) as in 1973, a deceleration is shown if adjustment is made for the rate of inflation. Following an increase of 16.8 percent in 1973, the wholesale price index rose by 29.2 percent in 1974, largely reflecting the effects of the quadrupling of oil prices and the delayed price increases following the easing of price controls imposed in 1973.[21]

The deceleration in the expansion of the real money supply and of government expenditures contributed to a slowdown in industrial activity. Bacha reports that the growth rate of the industrial consumption of electricity in the Rio de Janeiro-Saõ Paulo region fell from 16.6 percent in the first quarter of 1974 to 14.7 percent, 11.0 percent, and 4.0 in the second, third, and fourth quarters over the year-earlier quarters.[22] Nevertheless, the slowdown in the growth of monetary and fiscal aggregates continued in the first two quarters of 1975, with the money supply rising less than seasonally (9.7 percent) and government expenditures declining more than seasonally (12.8 percent).

In the aftermath of the strong showing of the Opposition party in the November 1974 Senatorial elections and in response to the further slowdown in the industrial consumption of electricity in the Rio de Janeiro-Saõ Paulo region (1.3 percent in the first quarter of 1975) and the poor harvest prospects, expansionary measures were taken in mid-1975. Between the second quarter of 1975 and the second quarter of 1976, the money supply increased by 43.1 percent and government expenditures rose by 86.1 percent, turning the budget surplus into a deficit.[23]

Both industrial activity and prices responded to the expansionary measures. In particular, after a slight decline in the rate of inflation as measured by the wholesale price index to 27.2 percent in 1975, this rate rose to 43.4 percent between 1975 and 1976. In response to the acceleration of inflation, a more restrictive policy stance was again adopted towards the end of 1976. Between the fourth quarter of 1976 and the fourth quarter of 1977, the money supply increased by 36.6 percent and government expenditure by 41.8 percent. This tendency continued in 1978, with the money supply and government expenditures maintained approximately unchanged in real terms.

Monetary and fiscal policies influence the trade balance indirectly, through their effects on economic activity. The trade balance is further affected by changes in the real exchange rate and by direct measures on exports and imports. With the quadrupling of oil prices and reduced foreign import demand during the 1974-75 world recession, a "maxi-devaluation" appeared to be in store for Brazil. This alternative was, however, rejected by the government, mainly on the grounds that it would exacerbate inflationary pressures, increase the domestic currency equivalent of foreign debt, and undermine the confidence of foreign investors. Rather, the government chose to continue with the system of "mini-devaluations." In this connection, one needs to consider changes in the real exchange rate that have occurred as a result of continued mini-devaluations.

Using the wholesale price index for all commodities, we find that the real exchange rate depreciated between 1973 and 1975 but returned to approximately the 1973 level by mid-1977, irrespective of whether comparisons are made with the U.S. dollar or with an average of the currencies of Brazil's main trading partners. A divergence between the two is shown only from late 1977, when the devaluation of the U.S. dollar exceeded changes in relative prices vis-à-vis other major currencies, so that the cruzeiro appreciated in real terms against the U.S. dollar while depreciating against other major currencies. On a 1973 basis, the index of the real exchange rate vis-à-vis the U.S. dollar was 105.3 in 1975, 98.8 in 1977, and 99.3 in 1978, while the average index vis-à-vis Brazil's trading partners was 106.0 in 1975, 100.6 in 1977, and 102.4 in 1978.[24]

Different conclusions are reached if the wholesale price index for industrial goods is used instead. We then find that the index of the real exchange rate in Brazil continued to rise vis-à-vis both the U.S. dollar and the currencies of Brazil's trading partners, throughout the period. The relevant index numbers for 1978 are 114.2 and 114.0 in the two cases, respectively, again on a 1973 basis.

The differences in the results are explained by the differential behavior of industrial and agricultural prices in Brazil.[1] The divergence between the two indices began in 1976 and continued thereafter. In the year 1978, the wholesale price index for industrial products stood at 428; that for agricultural goods at 542; and that for all commodities at 462, on a 1973 basis. The larger increase of agricultural prices is largely explained by the eight-fold increase in the prices of agricultural exports, fruits and vegetables, and roots and tubers between 1973 and 1978.

Changes in the value of the cruzeiro were accompanied by the application of a variety of measures aimed at limiting imports and promoting exports in Brazil. On the import side, a combination of higher tariffs, advance deposit requirements, quantitative restrictions, and import-substituting investments were used.[25] To begin with, tariffs were increased by 100 percentage points for 1200 items that had tariff rates of between 50 and 105 percent and were raised by 30 percentage points for 800 items that had tariff rates between 40 and 85 percent. Also, a 100 percent one-year deposit was instituted for approximately one-third of imports, representing a duty equivalent of about 50 percent at existing interest rates. At the same time, the importation of about 300 "superfluous" items was prohibited, and the "Law of Similars" came to be applied in a much more restrictive way in the private sector. Finally, limitations were imposed on importation by the government and by public enterprises that had to prepare annual plans providing for import reductions.

It was further envisaged to reduce imports through the increased domestic production of intermediate products and capital goods. The Second National Development Plan (1975-79) called for large investments in pulp and paper, petrochemicals, fertilizers, steel, and non-ferrous metals, with the objective to reach—or to approach—levels of self-sufficiency by the terminal year of the plan, 1979. In turn, capital goods industries were promoted by a combination of import restrictions, fiscal incentives, and credit preferences.

Several measures were instituted to limit oil imports. The quadrupling of oil prices was immediately reflected in the price of gasoline although price increases subsequently fell behind the rate of inflation. Also, the government required that alcohol made chiefly from sugar cane be mixed into all gasoline; it instituted a program aimed at increasing the domestic production of alcohol three-fold by 1980; and it permitted exploration by foreign oil companies.

On the export side, credit limits for manufactured exports were raised and the acceleration of inflation increased the value of credit incentives. The value of duty drawbacks also increased as imports under the drawback scheme were not subject to advance deposit requirements. Finally, under the so-called BEFIEX program, additional subsidies were provided in the form of the duty free entry of machinery and of imported inputs used in production for domestic markets to firms that undertook long-term export commitments.

The measures applied to limit imports and to promote exports did not suffice, however, to re-establish equilibrium in the balance of trade following the oil crisis and the world recession. In order to avoid equilibrating the trade balance through substantial reductions in rates of economic growth, then, Brazil had to have recourse to foreign capital to finance its resource gap (the balance of trade and non-factor services, adjusted for private transfers). This gap rose from $1.1 billion in 1973 to $6.3 billion in 1974. And, the subsequent decline to $1.6 billion in 1977 was followed by an increase to $2.7 billion in 1978 (Table 3.2).

The Brazilian Economic Record, 1973-78

Although it did not attain the growth rates of the preceding seven years, Brazil experienced rapid economic growth in the period following the oil crisis. Between 1973 and 1978, Brazil's GDP rose at an average annual rate of 6.5 percent. This compares favorably with other Latin American newly-industrializing countries whose growth rates were: Argentina, 0.8 percent; Chile, 2.4 percent; Mexico, 3.6 percent; and Colombia, 5.3 percent. Brazil also surpassed the economic growth rates of several other newly-industrializing countries (Israel, 1.9 percent; India, 3.0 percent; and Yugoslavia, 5.6 percent) while falling behind Taiwan (7.0 percent), Singapore (7.1 percent), and Korea (10.4 percent).[26]

Agriculture as well as industry participated in the expansion, with average annual rates of growth of 4.9 and 6.5 percent, respectively, between 1973 and 1978. At the same time, in response to the policies followed, there were considerable year-to-year variations in the growth rate of manufacturing output. The relevant figures are 8.4 percent in 1974, 4.5 percent in 1975, 10.5 percent in 1976, 2.3 percent in 1977, and 7.6 percent in 1978.

During the 1973-78 period, the volume of merchandise exports increased at an average annual rate of 5.2 percent in Brazil whereas imports rose 4.2 percent a year. With coffee exports declining, the volume of non-coffee exports grew substantially more than the overall total, averaging 8.9 percent a year between 1973 and 1978. Within non-coffee exports, average growth rates of export volume were 9.7 percent for minerals and 12.2 percent for manufactured goods including processed food while a decline of 6.9 percent a year is shown for unprocessed products other than minerals.

The volume of Brazil's imports increased at an average annual rate of 5.4 percent between 1973 and 1978 as compared to a 6.5 percent rise in GNP. While these figures indicate a decline in the income elasticity of import demand from 1.6 in 1966-73, the comparisons are misleading, in part because of the operation of noncurrent factors and in part because of the differential behavior of gross fixed domestic investment, capacity utilization, and inventory and accumulation between the two periods.

As noted in Section I, the 1966-73 period followed a period of six years during which the Brazilian economy was "starved" of imports. Notwithstanding a 27 percent increase of GNP, the volume of imports declined by 5 percent between 1960 and 1966—a situation that was not sustainable. The rapid rise of imports between 1966 and 1973, then, in part provided for pent-up import demand. The liberalization of imports during this period also contributed to the growth of imports as did the rise of the share of gross fixed investment in GNP, the increased degree of capacity utilization, and the accumulation of inventories.

To begin with, the share of gross fixed investment in GNP increased from 19.8 percent in 1966 to 23.2 percent in 1973. At the same time, the impact of the increased demand for capital goods on imports was accentuated by the rise in the extent of capacity utilization in the manufacturing sector. Thus, as capacity utilization rates increased from 83 percent in 1968 to 90 percent in 1973, the growth of the volume of capital goods imports (22.0 percent a year) exceeded that of the domestic production of capital goods (16.7 percent a year).[27]

The rise in capacity utilization rates further led to the increased importation of intermediate products and consumer goods as domestic producers could not fully satisfy demand in a variety of industries. At the same time, the importation of raw materials and intermediate products was boosted by the high rate of inventory accumulation that rose from 2.5 percent of GNP in 1966 to 4.3 percent in 1973.

These influences were reversed during the period following the oil crisis. The share of gross fixed investment in GNP measured in current prices, declined from 23.2 percent in 1973 to 22.6 percent in 1978 and the rate of capacity utilization fell from 90 percent in 1973 to an average of 84 percent in 1978. As a result, capital goods imports remained practically unchanged between 1973 and 1978, when the outcome was further affected by import substitution in machinery. Finally, the importation of raw materials and intermediate products, rising 6.0 percent a year in volume terms, was influenced by the decumulation of inventories following precautionary buying in 1973.

While estimates of inventory changes are not available for recent years, it may be surmised that adjusting for inventory changes would result in a rate of import growth of material inputs for domestic transformation exceeding that of GNP.[28] Correspondingly, questions arise about the validity of official claims as regards the magnitude of import savings resulting from the implementation of the plan for the increased production of intermediate goods in Brazil. The official figures calculate import savings in gross terms, thus excluding the increased importation of inputs.

Finally, the import volume of final consumer goods rose at an average annual rate of 6.1 percent between 1973 and 1978. With the decline in the importation of durable consumer goods, even more rapid increases are observed in the importation of nondurables. In the absence of detailed data, however, it is not possible to indicate which commodity groups participated in the expansion.

Brazil After the Oil Crisis: An Evaluation

After the quadrupling of oil prices and the onset of the world recession, the Brazilian authorities made limited use of macro-economic instruments for reducing domestic absorption (aggregate expenditure). And, while the cruzeiro depreciated in terms of the prices of industrial goods, the principal policy measures used for balance-of-payments purposes were import protection, export subsidization, and encouragement of the inflow of foreign capital.

Judging from the relatively high rates of economic growth, Brazil's policies may be considered to have been successful. Further analysis would have to consider, however, the determinants of changes in Brazil's trade balance, the implications of its rising indebtedness, the uses to which foreign borrowing has been put, the impact of the measures applied on inflation, and the effectiveness of the system of incentives and project evaluation.

Brazil's merchandising trade deficit increased from $0.8 billion in 1973 to $6.2 billion in 1974. The quadrupling of oil prices was only partly responsible for this result. Thus, at 1973 import levels, the rise of oil prices represented an increase of $2.3 billion in Brazil's import bill in 1974. And while increases in the prices of other imports added a further $1.5 billion, this was offset by increases in export prices totalling $1.6 billion. The remainder of the deterioration of Brazil's trade balance in 1974 can be found in increased imports at high levels of capacity utilization, the import requirements of investments in intermediate products undertaken according to First National Development Plan (1972-75) and of investments by private firms initiated in previous years, the effects of rapid economic expansion on consumer goods imports, as well as inventory building amounting to 7.4 percent of GNP in 1974 that occurred in response to world-wide shortages of some products and uncertainty as regards government policies, in particular the setting of exchange rates.

The subsequent fall in the rate of capacity utilization, the decrease in the share of gross fixed investment from 24.4 percent of GNP in 1974 to 22.9 percent in 1978, and the decumulation of inventories importantly contributed to the 4 percent decline in the volume of imports between 1974 and 1978. Brazil further benefited from improvements in its terms of trade during this period. While average import prices rose by 13 percent between 1974 and 1977, export prices increased by 26 percent.

Improvements in the terms of trade in part explain the decrease in the merchandise trade deficit from $6.2 billion in 1974 to $2.4 billion in 1978; at constant relative prices, the trade deficit would have been $3.1 billion in 1978. The improvement in the terms of trade was largely due to the 150 percent increase in the price of coffee and the 20 percent increase in the price of soybeans between 1974 and 1978.

Changes in the merchandise trade deficit were nearly matched by changes in the resource gap that declined from $6.3 billion in 1974 to $2.7 billion in 1978. This decline was more than offset, however, by the increasing burden of interest payments, dividends, and the amortization of the debt. These payments rose from $3.4 billion in 1974 to $10.1 billion in 1978; the decrease was from 42.4 percent to 68.0 percent of the value of merchandise exports.

Thus, notwithstanding the decrease in its trade deficit after 1974, Brazil had to borrow increasing amounts in order to service the previously-contracted debt. With continued borrowing, Brazil's total foreign debt rose from $12.6 billion at the end of 1973 to $17.2 billion a year later, and to $43.5 billion at the end of 1978. The increase in the ratio of the foreign debt to GNP was from 13.9 percent in 1973 to 24.2 percent in 1978 (Table 3.5).

The IPEA/INPES report, "A New Option for the Economy," published in the *Diario Comercio & Industria* between February 9 and 17, 1978, suggested that the policy of foreign borrowing followed by Brazil led to excessively high indebtedness. Former Minister of Finance, and subsequently of Planning, Mario Simonsen claimed that this is not the case. In his view, if Brazil succeeds in eliminating its resource gap, the rate of growth of exports and GNP in terms of current dollars would exceed that of interest payments on the external debt, estimated to rise by about 10 percent a year, resulting in a gradual decline in the ratio of debt service payments to exports as well as in the ratio of total indebtedness to GNP.

Simonsen's projections are based on the presumption that Brazil would maintain the 15 percent export growth rate in terms of current dollars it experienced during the period 1973-78. Maintaining past export trends in current prices, however, implicitly assumes the continuation of favorable developments in export prices that rose at an average annual rate of 9 percent during the period, exceeding the rate of world inflation. However, according to available projections, the prices of Brazil's major export products, coffee and soybeans, will decline in real terms in the future, and higher petroleum prices will further contribute to the deterioration of Brazil's terms of trade. Correspondingly, the growth of the volume of exports would need to be stepped up in order to avoid an increase in Brazil's debt-service ratio. We will return to this question in Section III of the essay.

In evaluating the policy of foreign borrowing, the question further needs to be raised if the borrowed funds have been productively used in Brazil. To the extent that borrowing abroad has added to the availability of investment funds without affecting their sectoral allocation, this question may be answered in the affirmative. This is because the marginal productivity of capital in Brazil exceeds the real rate of interest on foreign loans by a considerable margin.[29]

However, foreign borrowing has led to changes in the sectoral allocation of investment. In particular, it has contributed to the implementation of large investments in infrastructure and in intermediate products. Some of the latter projects are of doubtful economic efficiency as noted below, and questions have been raised about several infrastructural projects also. Inefficiences in the allocation of investment funds are reflected in the rise of incremental capital-output ratios from 2.3 in 1964-73 to 3.6 in 1974-78.

Furthermore, it cannot be assumed that the amounts borrowed abroad would have been fully invested. Rather, a substantial part of this borrowing appears to have gone into consumption (private and public) that has slightly increased its share in GNP between 1973 and 1978.[30]

Increases in private consumption have been encouraged by the relatively expansionary policies followed. As noted above, these policies have also contributed to the acceleration of inflation in 1976. With a ratchet-effect operating due to widespread indexing, and rapid increases in food prices, the rate of inflation has remained at about 40 percent a year.

Another factor contributing to inflation has been the imposition of protective measures. Bacha[31] cites a calculation made by Munhoz[32] according to which cost increases brought about by import protection, together with the freeing of interest rates, added 9 percentage points to the rate of inflation in 1976. This conclusion is confirmed by Cline who has show that, along with changes in the rate of growth of the money supply and in that of import prices, increases in import protection have been a major factor contributing to the acceleration of inflation in Brazil.[33]

The conclusions reached by Munhoz and Cline indicate the futility of using protective measures in the place of a devaluation for the sake of avoiding the inflationary effects of the latter. At the same time, substituting the non-neutral measures of import protection and export subsidization for exchange rate changes, which have neutral incentive effects, has increased the dispersion of incentive rates in Brazil.

Interindustry differences in regard to credit preferences have further increased the dispersion of incentive rates. For one thing, the acceleration of inflation has augmented the value of credit preferences to the recipients as nominal interest rates have not been fully adjusted for inflation. For another thing, the scope of credit preferences has increased, in part to pursue particular objectives (e.g. import substitution in intermediate products) and in part to benefit otherwise disadvantaged sectors (e.g. agriculture).

At the same time, the provision of credit preferences has been subject to discretionary decision-making that has created uncertainty and has given rise to divergences in incentive rates among firms within the same industry. Discretionary decision-making in import licensing, investment approvals, fiscal subsidies, and price control, too, has added to these divergences.

The high dispersion of incentive rates, in turn, has interfered with efficient resource allocation by increasing variations in the domestic resource cost of saving and earning foreign exchange. On the export side, industries that produce exports at a high cost by-and-large receive higher subsidies. In 1975, fiscal and credit subsidies to exports averaged 3.0 percent of the fob price in cases where domestic resource cost (DRC) ratio was below 1.25; 28.0 percent in cases where the DRC ratio was between 1.25 and 1.35; and 33.8 in cases where the DRC ratio exceeded 1.35.[34]

Also, increases in tariff rates, the imposition of advance deposit requirements, the selective provision of preferential credits, and the application of import controls have increased the dispersion of incentives to import substitution and have raised their average level as compared to exports. Among industries oriented towards import substitution, capital goods and intermediate products offer particular interest.

Incentives to domestic capital goods industries include import protection as well as production subsidies. In 1977, tariffs averaged 46 percent on electrical and nonelectrical machinery, representing an increase of 7 to 20 percentage points as compared to the situation existing before the oil crisis. In the same period, realized tariffs more than doubled, reaching 17 percent in 1977, as the scope of duty exemption was reduced[35] and machinery imports were generally exempt from advance deposit requirements. The protection of the domestic machinery industry increased further as a result of the generalization of licensing on machinery imports by private firms and the import limitations imposed on public firms.

Domestic machinery producers also receive fiscal and credit subsidies. Fiscal subsidies take the form of tax credits, which are granted to domestic sales on the same basis as to exports, whereas credit subsidies are provided through low-interest loans and the incomplete inflation adjustment of the amount borrowed. Tyler reports that in 1975 the subsidy equivalent of tax credits, and that of credit preferences, amounted to as much as 20 percent and 29 percent, respectively.[36]

Rates of protection and of fiscal and credit subsidies vary among producers, and the imposition of protective measures as well as the granting of subsidies are subject to discretionary decision-making under a number of partly overlapping programs. Users of imported machinery may obtain duty and indirect tax exemptions (reductions) and a waiver of the advance deposit requirements from the Conselho de Desenvolvimento Industrial, from the Ministry of Industry and Commerce in the framework of the BEFIEX program, and from regional and sectoral development institutions. Permission for importation is granted by CACEX on the basis of an examination of the existence of "national similars" and with the aim of increasing the share of domestic machinery in total purchases (the so-called nationalization index). Fiscal incentives to the domestic production of particular types of machinery and equipment are granted by the Ministry of Finance whereas interest rate subsidies are provided through FINAME and other official financing programs.[37]

While in the capital goods industry domestic production has been promoted via import protection and production subsidies, in the case of intermediate products the government itself has promoted, or undertaken, investments under the Second Plan. These investments have not been subject to rigorous economic project appraisal but seem to have reflected the philosophy of import substitution "at any cost."

In the absence of cost data, one cannot provide an economic evaluation of investments in intermediate products. Nevertheless, available information on Brazil's resource endowments and conditions on the world market leads one to doubt the social profitability of investments in petrochemicals. Also, the decline in world market prices has adversely affected the social profitability of investment in fertilizers.

However, Brazil has comparative advantages in the production of pulp and paper, where world market supplies have the tendency to rise at a lower rate than demand. Brazil may also be capable of producing steel competitively. At the same time, some of the new plants reportedly produce at excessively high costs, reflecting to a large extent poor investment planning.

Reference should also be made to the BEFIEX scheme for export promotion under which 23 percent of manufactured exports was carried out in 1977. This scheme is costly for the Brazilian economy as the increased protection of domestic markets permits the implicit subsidization of exports, with the firms charging higher prices on domestic sales while receiving input subsidies. The BEFIEX system thus permits exports to take place at high costs and allows for high profits to exporting firms, in large part multinationals. This last conclusion applies in particular to automobile exports that accounted for two-thirds of exports under the BEFIEX scheme in 1977.

The last point leads to the question of the social profitability of foreign direct investment. In the absence of price distortions, such investment will be profitable to the host country as long as there is profit taxation. This conclusion does not necessarily follow, however, in the presence of price distortions that create a wedge between private and social profitability. In fact, with protection and export subsidization raising profits that are repatriated at the official exchange rate, foreign direct investment in Brazil may lead to losses rather than to gains to the national economy.[38]

We may conclude that the use of the "non-neutral" measures of import protection and of production and export subsidies in lieu of a devaluation have led to inefficiencies in the Brazilian economy by increasing the variability of the domestic resource cost of saving and earning foreign exchange to considerable extent. Furthermore, on the average, incentives to import substitution have risen more than incentives to exports.

The situation has been aggravated by widespread controls that increasingly hamstring business firms and discriminate against small and medium-scale enterprises. Furthermore, controls and, to a large extent, incentives are subject to discretionary decision-making; there are a multiplicity of public agencies exercising controls and granting incentives that have in part overlapping responsibilities; and firms make considerable efforts to obtain favors and to find loopholes in the regulations.

At the same time, with "implicit" exchange rates in the form of import protection and export subsidies exceeding the official exchange rate at which profits are repatriated by a wide margin, foreign direct investment may be socially unprofitable even if profits are taxed. Also, some of the investment in intermediate products may not be socially profitable (e.g. petrochemicals) while other involve excessive costs due to poor investment planning (e.g. steel).

III. Reforming Incentive Policies

Objectives and Instruments

Economic policy in Brazil aims at a variety of objectives. They include rapid economic growth, creating employment, lessening income inequalities, improving the balance of payments, and reducing the rate of inflation. The policy makers have a number of instruments at their disposal that may be used to pursue these objectives, including monetary policy, tax and expenditure policy, credit allocation, direct interventions in the affairs of public firms, contractual relationships with private firms, import controls, import tariffs and advance deposit requirements, export subsidies, and exchange rate adjustments.

In the post-1973 period, policy objectives have often come into conflict as the various instruments used to pursue a particular objective have had adverse repercussions on other objectives. Examples are the effects of expansionary monetary policies on the balance of payments and on inflation; the impact of protective measures on inflation and on the profits of multi-national companies; and the consequences of foregoing a "maxi-devaluation" on the balance of payments, and on the profits of multinational companies.

This is not to underestimate the achievements of the Brazilian economy in the period following the oil crisis, with a high rate of economic growth and the resulting employment creation. However, a high rate of economic growth has been attained at the expense of increased foreign indebtedness, rapid inflation, and economic inefficiencies. Apart from inefficient resource allocation in response to the often bewildering variety of incentives and controls, the task of obtaining incentives and coping with controls have diverted the efforts of firms from productive activities. These adverse consequences, in turn, are potentially damaging for the long-run prospects of the economy.

The 1979 Policy Reforms

The goverment installed in January 1979 has given priority to curbing the excesses of the economy that have led to balance-of-payments deficits, a high rate of inflation, and reduced efficiency. Several measures have been taken to pursue these objectives. They will be reviewed in the following.

On January 24th, 1979, the National Monetary Council adopted changes in the incentive system, involving the abolition of fiscal subsidies to exports, the elimination of advance deposit requirements on imports, and compensating devaluations in the form of accelerated "mini-devaluations." These measures were scheduled to be carried out over a four-year period, ending on June 30, 1983.

The replacement of fiscal subsidies to exports and of advanced deposits on imports by the devaluation of the cruzeiro will simplify the incentive system and contribute to efficient resource allocation through the equalization of these incentives that have hitherto been provided at disparate rates. For one thing, fiscal subsidies have varied to a considerable extent among exports; for another thing, a variety of imports have been exempt from advance deposit obligations.

In 1975, fiscal subsidies to exports varied from practically nil for coffee, sugar, soybeans and iron ore to 35-40 percent on various textile products.[39] In turn, advance deposits were not required on the imports of petroleum, wheat, fertilizers, and agricultural chemicals; the imports of machinery financed from foreign loans; imports by firms receiving various fiscal incentives; the importation of inputs for export production that enter under the drawback or the BEFIEX schemes; and imports from the LAFTA area.

The question arises how various economic activities will be affected by the incentive reform. The additional devaluation of approximately 4.5 percent a year, cumulating to 25 percent by June 30, 1983, equals the average rate of fiscal subsidies to manufactured exports that were 24.9 percent in 1975.[40] There will be a net gain, estimated at 3-4 percent, however, as the receipt of a large fraction of export subsidies has suffered a delay of 4 to 6 months.

At the same time, the cost of imported inputs to the exporter will increase in cases where these inputs were exempted from advance deposit obligations and decline in cases where this was not the case. In 1975, 58 percent of manufactured exports benefited from drawbacks, and inputs imported under drawbacks amounts to one-fourth of these exports.[41] These imports, inputs imported under the BEFIEX scheme, and machinery imported under the BEFIEX and other schemes were exempt from advance deposit obligations.

All in all, approximately three-fourths of manufactured exports were not subject to advance deposit obligations on their imported inputs in 1975. The average cost of these exports will rise by 6 percent as a result of the additional devaluation that will raise the price of imported inputs, representing one-fourth of export value, by 25 percent. This increase will be offset in part by cost reductions for manufactured exports whose imported inputs have been subject to advance deposit obligations, since a cost reduction of equal magnitude (the 50 percent cost of advance deposits less the 25 percent additional devaluation) on imported inputs applies to one-fourth of export value.

It appears then that, on the average, the net effect of changes in the incentive system on manufactured exports will be nil. In turn, the exports of unprocessed primary products, which received no or low fiscal subsidies and were subject to advance deposit requirements on most of their inputs, will be favorably affected. The exports of processed food, too, will derive a benefit, albeit to a lesser extent, inasmuch as they received export subsidies at rates lower than 25 percent and their imported inputs were generally subject to advance deposits. A product with an export subsidy of 10 percent (the approximate average for processed primary commodities), and with imported inputs accounting for 20 percent of export value, will benefit from a 14 percent price increase and a 10 percent reduction in costs, for example.

Initially, about one-third of imports were subject to advance deposits. With the introduction of additional exemptions, this share declined to 21 percent in 1977, and it has been in the 22-24 percent range since. Calculating with an interest rate of 50 percent, the average cost of advance deposits on all imports is estimated at 11-12 percent. This compares to the 25 percent additional devaluation.

Advance deposit obligations generally applied to imports competing with domestic production while their imported inputs often received exemptions. On the average, then, the incentive reform will reduce the protection of import-substituting industries both by lowering the price of competing imports and increasing the cost of imported inputs they use. The dispersion of import protection rates, too, will be lessened by increasing the protection of commodities that compete with imports (e.g. fertilizers) which were not subject to import deposit requirements or use inputs which were subject to such requirements.

From data provided by Tyler[42] it appears that tariffs on manufactured goods averaged 44 percent in 1977, to which the tariff equivalent of advance deposit requirements of 50 percent should be added. Eliminating advance deposit requirements and devaluing the currency by 25 percent will reduce the nominal protection of import-competing goods, calculated at the existing exchange rate, from 94 percent to 80 percent (the 44 percent tariff applied to the cif import price, raised by the 25 percent devaluation). In turn, in the hypothetical case where imported inputs accounted for one-fifth of production value and were exempted from advance deposit requirements, the cost of domestic production of import substitutes will increase by 10 percent.

Putting numerical values on changes in net export subsidies and import protection helps us to evaluate the effects of the incentive reform on resource allocation, the balance-of-payments, and inflation. The resource allocative effects will be favorable; apart from reducing differences in incentives due to differential rates of export subsidies and advance deposit requirements, the measures applied will lessen discrimination in favor of import substitution as against manufactured and, in particular, primary exports. The extension of the export credit system, introduced simultaneously, will further reduce the extent of this bias.

The net effects of the incentive system on the balance of payments are, however, uncertain. Foreign exchange earnings will increase as the exports and imports of primary commodities and processed food expand in response to higher prices in cruzeiros received at the more favorable exchange rate. In turn, imports will rise as a result of the reduced protection of import-competing activities. Finally, the foreign exchange equivalent of the profits of multinationals will fall since these profits will be repatriated at a higher exchange rate.

In increasing the prices received by exporters of primary products and processed food, and raising the cost of imported inputs that were exempted from advance deposit requirements, the incentive reform will contribute to inflationary pressures and these effects will be offset only in part by lower import prices. However, improvements in the government budget, resulting from the increased cruzeiro equivalent of tariffs of actual imports, the duties levied on the increment of imports, and the excess of the budgetary cost of present export subsidies over the interest cost of advance deposits, will permit reducing the rate of money creation.

In fact, the government reportedly plans to use the net increment in revenues to slow down monetary expansion. It further announced its intention to reduce the growth of fiscal expenditures, as well as expenditures by public firms, in order to moderate inflation. Finally, measures have been taken to increase the cost of credit for the purchase of consumer durables.

Policies for the Future

The measures taken, or contemplated to be taken, to reduce public spending and private expenditures on consumer durables would ease inflationary pressures and improve the balance of payments, both directly by reducing expenditures on imports, and indirectly by creating excess capacity in the manufacturing sector that can be used in exporting. The balance of payments would improve further as a result of the increased exports, and the reduced imports, of foodstuffs following the poor harvest years of 1977 and 1978.

Brazil will, however, suffer the consequences of higher petroleum prices; at present import levels, a 50 percent increase in prices would add $2.0 billion to its import bill. Also, indications are that petroleum prices will increase further in real terms over the next four years, while the real prices of coffee and soybeans are projected to decline. It follows that during the 1979-83 period when the incentive reform will be implemented, the cruzeiro will have to depreciate more in real terms than the 25 percent necessary to offset the effects of the elimination of export subsidies and advance deposit obligations.

This conclusion is strengthened if we consider the need to reduce the bias against exports that is clearly manifest under the reform of the incentive system. Following the abolition of fiscal subsidies, only credit subsidies and the BEFIEX scheme will be available to the exporters of manufactured goods while a number of primary exports are burdened by the lack of full reimbursement of indirect taxes.[43] By contrast, tariffs average 44 percent on manufactured goods, which are also often protected by import controls.

Reducing the bias against exports could be accomplished by lowering tariffs, the balance-of-payments effects could be accomplished by lowering additional devaluation. In the process, high tariffs should be reduced proportionately more, so as to lessen interindustry differences in tariff rates. It would further be necessary to liberalize import controls and to limit the scope of credit and fiscal incentives that represent additional elements of import protection.

It should be recognized that tariff reductions would offset the inflationary effects of a devaluation, since the rise in export prices would be compensated by a decline in the prices of imports. Also, the increase in the cruzeiro equivalent of the foreign debt of export industries would be balanced by the rise in the cruzeiro equivalent of their foreign exchange earnings. In turn, import-substituting activities may receive credits to compensate for their higher debt burden.

While steps taken towards equalizing incentives would improve efficiency, it would further be desirable to replace discretionary decision-making by the application of automatic rules. This would reduce the risk of arbitrary actions and the cost to the private sector of coping with a bureaucratic system that increasingly hamstrings business firms. In particular, one would need to liberalize the system of investment approval by the Conselho de Desenvolvimento Industrial and by sectoral and regional development institutions, import control by CACEX, and price control by government agencies, and to phase out the BEFIEX scheme. Finally, one should limit the scope of preferential credits that have provided subsidies to capital-intensive activities and adopt positive real interest rates that would reduce distortions in financial markets and encourage savings.

Greater equality and automaticity in incentives to the private sector would need to be accompanied by improved decision-making in the public sector. This would involve stricter financial control of public agencies and public firms as well as a rigorous economic evaluation of investment projects. As regards the latter, calculations at world market prices are of particular importance.

ESSAY 11
Portugal in Face of the Common Market

Introduction

It is not generally recognized that Portugal was one of the countries with the most favorable growth performance in the decade preceding the oil crisis and the 1974–75 world recession. Per capita incomes in Portugal increased at an average annual rate of 7.4 percent during this period; apart from some oil-exporting countries, exporters and newly-industrializing countries in the Far East, this growth rate was exceeded only in Japan (8.7 percent) and Israel (8.2 percent).[1]

Portugal's growth performance was predicated in large part on the expansion of exports, in particular manufactured exports, after the gradual opening of its national economy and the conclusion of association agreements with the European Free Trade Association (EFTA) and, subsequently, with the European Common Market (EEC). Other important contributing factors were the growth of tourism and of immigrants' remittances. In 1973, merchandise exports amounted to $1843 million, of which 70 percent were manufactured goods; tourist receipts were estimated at $550 million; and private transfers, mainly workers' remittances, were valued at $1097 million.

High GNP growth rates, however, disguised considerable income inequalities in the cities, and, in particular, between the cities and the countryside. Low income levels in the countryside, in turn, reflected the slow progress made in Portuguese agriculture that remained the most backward in Western Europe.

The April 1974 Revolution set out to change institutional arrangements in political as well as in economic life. Section I of the essay will review the experience of the Portuguese economy during the post-Revolutionary period which coincided with the loss of the African colonies, the quadrupling of oil prices, and the 1974–75 world recession, followed by relatively slow growth in the European countries that provide Portugal's principal export markets.

Sections II and III will examine policy measures to be taken in agriculture and industry, respectively, which would prepare Portugal for entry into the

European Common Market. This objective would also be served by measures aimed at encouraging investment and savings and improving the allocation of investment in Portugal. Proposals for the introduction of such measures will be made in Section IV of the essay.

I. The Portuguese Economy in the Post-Revolutionary Period[2]

The Aftermath of the Revolution, 1974–1975

In the South of Portugal (the Alentejo) the Revolution of April 1974 was followed by land reform and, subsequently, by land seizures, leading to the virtual disappearance of latifundia that had earlier characterized the economy of the region. No major changes in ownership relationships occurred in the North, where small- and medium-size farms had been dominant. At the same time, while the events in the Alentejo led to disruptions in production, few measures were taken to increase agricultural productivity in Portugal.

The Revolution further led to the nationalization of banks, insurance companies, public utilities, transportation, and the petrochemical, fertilizer, beer, tobacco, pulp and paper, cement, steel, and shipbuilding industries. Through the nationalization of banks and insurance companies, the state also took over their equity holdings of about thirteen hundred firms in a wide variety of areas. As a result, publicly-owned firms came to account for 10 percent of manufacturing output while firms with partial state ownership accounted for another 5 percent.

The Institute for State Participation (IPE), representing the government's interest in about 300 firms with partial state ownership, declared its intention to exercise close supervision of the activities of these firms. In conjunction with its providing credits to private firms in a situation where rapid wage increases without a commensurate rise in prices led to substantial losses, the government also intervened in the management of about 80 private firms.[3] And, under conditions of political uncertainty, there were fears of further nationalization on the part of private firms.

The workers' commissions established immediately following the Revolution, also, sought to influence management decisions and, in several cases, seized factories from their owners. Furthermore, newly enacted labor legislation made it well-nigh impossible to discharge workers, whatever the circumstances of the case. These regulations contributed to the decline of labor discipline and to the practical cessation of new hiring. Together with uncertainty as regards the treatment of foreign investments, they also hampered the operation of foreign firms in Portugal.

At the same time, increased government interventions, and the desire to find employment for repatriates from the former colonies, led to rapid increases in the size of public administration. As a result, despite substantial reductions in military spending, expenditures on public administration (including defense, health, and education) grew rapidly, with a rise of 14.6 percent in

1974 and 20.8 percent in 1975 in terms of constant prices. In 1974 and 1975, respectively, these increases added 1.4 and 3.1 percentage points to the rate of growth of GDP as measured in national income statistics, without materially augmenting the amount of goods and services available in the economy (Table 11.1).

TABLE 11.1
GDP and Sectoral Growth Rates (Percent)

	1968-73	1974	1975	1976	1977	1978	1973-78
Agriculture	−0.8	−2.1	−6.5	−1.5	−10.0	4.0	−4.1
Industry[a]	10.0	3.7	−8.8	4.3	10.4	3.5	2.2
Construction	12.5	3.5	−15.7	5.0	11.0	5.0	0.9
Public Administration[b]	8.8	14.6	20.8	17.8	7.0	6.0	12.8
Other Services	5.9	−2.4	−5.3	7.9	5.9	1.3	1.9
GDP at factor cost	6.9	2.2	−4.7	6.6	6.5	3.4	2.8
GDP at factor cost without public administration	6.6	0.9	−7.8	4.7	6.4	2.9	1.3

Sources: World Bank, *Portugal: Current and Prospective Economic Trends, November 1978.* *Banco de Portugal, Relatorio do Conselho de Administraçao, Gerencia de 1978,* Vol. 1, 1979.

Notes: [a] Includes manufacturing, mining and electricity, gas and water. [b] Includes defense, health and education.

Correspondingly, the share of public consumption in the current price value of GDP rose from an average of 13.7 percent in 1968–73 to 14.5 percent in 1974 and again to 15.4 percent in 1975. Parallel with these changes, the rise in wages mandated after the Revolution led to increases in the share of private consumption in GDP from 74.5 percent in 1963–73 to 76.1 percent in 1974 and to 80.7 percent in 1975. In 1975, private and public consumption combined totalled 96.1 percent of GDP as compared to 88.2 percent in 1963–73 (Table 11.2).

TABLE 11.2
The Structure of Domestic Expenditure in Portugal (in Current Prices)

	1968-73	1974	1975	1976	1977	1978
Total Consumption (private and public)	88.2	90.6	96.1	92.6	89.8	88.5
Private Consumption	74.5	76.1	80.7	78.5	75.6	74.2
Public Consumption	13.7	14.5	15.4	14.1	14.2	14.3
Gross Investment	18.8	24.9	16.4	20.8	25.4	23.1
Gross Fixed Capital Formation	18.8	19.7	19.7	19.0	20.2	20.0
Variation of Stocks	(0)	5.2	−3.3	1.8	5.2	3.1
Exports of Goods & Services	24.1	25.9	19.7	16.8	17.8	20.0
Imports of Goods & Services	−31.1	−41.4	−32.2	−30.2	−33.0	−31.6
Gross Domestic Product	100.0	100.0	100.0	100.0	100.0	100.0

Sources: Departamento Central de Planeamento, *Situaçao Econòmica Portuguesa,* May 1976 and Banco de Portugal, *Relatorio do Conselho de Administraçao, Gerencia de 1978,* Vol. 1, 1979.

The resulting fall in savings was accentuated by the 7.4 percent decline of GDP, excluding public administration, between 1973 and 1975 (Table 11.1). This decline extended to all productive sectors. It was the largest in the construction industry as a consequence of the 17 percent fall in capital formation, expressed in constant prices, between 1973 and 1975.[4]

In the manufacturing sector, the constraints imposed by the new labor legislation adversely affected production, with labor productivity falling below the 1973 level in 1975. In the same period, rapid increases of nominal wages in the face of price controls led to a 14 percent rise in real wages (Table 11.3) and to a 70 percent increase in wage costs per unit of output (Table 11.4). In turn, profit margins declined; this is indicated by the difference between increases in production costs[5] (48 percent) and in wholesale prices (35 percent), as well as by the difference between increases in wage unit costs and in the GDP deflator for the manufacturing sector, which later rose by 40 percent during the period. And, the data underestimate increases in production costs as they do not include the rise in fringe benefits mandated by law.

The escudo was devalued more-or-less in line with increases in wholesale prices relative to the United States and Portugal's other major trading partners. This comparison, however, gives a misleading indication of changes in Portugal's international competitiveness, since firms were not permitted to raise prices in proportion with cost increases. Using instead an index of production costs in the manufacturing sector, it appears that between 1973 and 1975 Portugal's real exchange rate appreciated by 9.7 percent vis-a-vis the U.S. dollar and by 8.2 percent vis-a-vis the currencies of its main trading partners (Table 11.5).

The deterioration of Portugal's competitive position, together with disruptions in production, led to a decline in Portugal's share in the markets of the developed countries. Between 1973 and 1975, the dollar value of Portuguese manufactured exports to these countries increased by 11 percent as compared to increases of 49 percent for both Greece and Spain. Exports declined in absolute terms to the United States and increases were small also to the EEC and EFTA, with which Portugal has an association agreement. Taking further account of changes in Portuguese exports to the markets of developing countries (other than Portugal's former colonies) and of centrally planned economies, we find that the dollar value of Portuguese manufactured exports (excluding exports to the former colonies) rose by only 15 percent between 1973 and 1975 as compared to increases of 87 percent for Greece and 68 percent for Spain.[6]

If we take the growth of Spanish exports to individual market areas as the "norm," the shortfall in Portugal's manufactured exports due to lower rates of export growth is estimated at $420 million. This compares with an absolute decline of $87 million in manufactured exports to the former Portuguese colonies. Agricultural exports fell, too, while mineral exports increased.

Political uncertainty also led to a decline in tourist receipts, from $550

TABLE 11.3
Nominal and Real Wages in Portugal (1973 = 100)

	1973	1974	1975	1976	1977	1978
Agriculture						
Men						
Nominal Wages	100.0	132.9	165.2	189.1	217.0	255.1
Cost of Living	100.0	126.0	151.7	179.4	227.5	271.7
Real Wages	100.0	105.5	108.9	105.4	95.4	93.9
Women						
Nominal Wages	100.0	140.5	189.3	214.8	255.6	288.3
Cost of Living	100.0	126.0	151.8	179.4	227.4	271.7
Real Wages	100.0	111.5	124.7	119.7	112.4	106.1
Industry and Transportation						
Lisbon						
Nominal Wages	100.0	132.3	157.0	175.7	196.8	218.5
Cost of Living	100.0	125.1	144.2	174.7	216.6	246.9
Real Wages	100.0	105.8	108.9	100.6	90.9	88.5
Porto						
Nominal Wages	100.0	138.5	177.1	197.3	221.4	242.2
Cost of Living	100.0	126.8	149.4	176.4	223.0	263.8
Real Wages	100.0	109.2	118.5	111.8	99.3	91.8
Average for Lisbon and Porto						
Nominal Wages	100.0	135.4	167.1	186.5	209.1	230.4
Cost of Living	100.0	126.0	146.8	175.6	219.8	255.4
Real Wages	100.0	107.5	113.7	106.2	95.1	90.2
Ratio of Average Wages to Per Capita Net National Product	n/a	1.45	1.82	1.83	1.61	1.49
Share of Labor Income in the Net National Product	51.6	56.9	69.3	68.7	60.7	56.4
Per Capital GNP in 1973 prices						
Including Public Administration	100.0	106.8	96.9	103.1	108.7	111.4
Excluding Public Administration	100.0	105.4	92.6	96.7	101.8	103.9

Sources: Unless otherwise indicated, Banco de Portugal, *Relatorio do Conselho de Administraçao.* GNP Data: World Bank data base.

Note: Consumer price index for rural areas calculated by the Bank of Portugal.

million in 1973 to $360 million in 1975, contributing to a fall in the exports of goods and services combined from $3.1 billion in 1973 to $3.0 billion in 1975. In the same period, the imports of goods and services increased from $3.8 billion to $4.8 billion. With immigrants' remittances remaining practically constant at about $1.0 billion, the deficit in the current account of the balance of payments reached $0.8 billion in 1975 as compared to a surplus of $0.3 billion in 1973.

The Period of Normalization, 1976–78

Steps towards normalization were taken in Portugal following the change in the political situation in November 1975. The progress was the slowest in

TABLE 11.4
Cost of Production in Portuguese Manufacturing (1973 = 100)

	1973	1974	1975	1976	1977	1978
(1) Production	100.0	102.3	96.9	102.1	113.4	121.1
(2) Employment	100.0	99.4	98.7	99.3	99.2	98.8
(3) Labor Productivity (1):(2)	100.0	102.9	98.2	102.8	114.3	122.6
(4) Nominal Wages	100.0	135.4	167.1	186.5	209.1	230.4
(5) Wage Costs per Unit of Output (4):(3)	100.0	131.6	170.2	181.4	182.9	187.9
(6) Wholesale Prices (Home and Import Goods)	100.0	129.0	144.9	172.5	223.2	292.8
(7) Prices of Investment Goods	100.0	114.9	139.0	165.2	213.9	265.6
(8) Production Costs	100.0	129.0	149.0	173.8	216.0	274.0
(9) Wholesale Prices for Home-Produced Goods	100.0	125.7	135.1	163.5	210.8	295.9
(10) GDP Deflator for Manufacturing	100.0	124.1	140.2	166.8	216.7	265.0

Sources: Production: 1973–75: *Boletim Mensal de Estatisticas Industriais;* 1976–78: *Boletim Mensal de Estatistica. Employment: Banco de Portugal. Wholesale prices: IMF, International Financial Statistics.* Wages, Prices of Investment Goods and GNP Deflator for Manufacturing: Banco de Portugal, *Relatorio do Conselho de Administraçao.*

Note: The index of production costs has been calculated by weighting the index of wage costs, the index of the prices of purchased inputs, represented by wholesale price index for home and import goods, and the cost of capital goods, represented by a weighted average of price indices for machinery and construction. The relevant weights have been derived from the 1970 input-output table for Portugal: G.E.B.E.I. *Sistema de Matrioes Multisectoriais para o Continente Português, Vol. V, Lisbon, 1975.*

TABLE 11.5
Real Exchange Rates in Portugal, 1973–1978

	1973	1974	1975	1976	1977	1978
Exchange Rate, Escudo/Dollar	24.673	25.408	25.553	30.223	38.277	43.940
Index of the Exchange Rate	100.0	103.0	103.6	122.5	155.1	178.1
Index of Relative Prices vis-à-vis the United States						
(A)	100.0	105.8	103.9	120.4	146.3	190.4
(B)	100.0	108.6	114.7	128.0	149.8	176.2
Index of Relative Prices vis-à-vis Portugal's Trading Partners						
(A)	100.0	105.6	102.2	124.0	145.9	177.4
(B)	100.0	108.4	112.8	131.8	149.4	164.2
Index of the Real Exchange Rate vis-à-vis The US Dollar						
(A)	100.0	97.4	99.7	101.7	106.0	93.5
(B)	100.0	94.8	90.3	95.7	103.5	101.1
The Currencies of Portugal's Main Trading Partners						
(A)	100.0	97.4	101.4	98.8	106.3	100.4
(B)	100.0	95.0	91.8	92.9	103.8	108.5

Sources: Table 11.4 and International Monetary Fund, *International Financial Statistics.*

Notes: The index of the real exchange rate has been calculated by adjusting an index of the nominal exchange rate for changes in wholesale prices at home and abroad (Variant A) and for changes in production costs and the foreign wholesale prices (Variant B). Calculations for Portugal's main trading partners, covering 66.5 percent of Portuguese exports and 70.0 percent of Portuguese imports in 1973. (The United States, Japan, Belgium, France, Germany, Italy, Netherlands, Sweden, Switzerland, United Kingdom and Spain) have been made by weighting with the sum of exports and imports combined in the year 1973.

agriculture, where the situation remained unsettled in the South. After several aborted attempts, a comprehensive agrarian reform law was enacted in September 1977 but its application has been slowed down by political opposition. Moreover, only the beginnings were made in providing support to farmers to raise productivity levels.

More progress was made in the manufacturing sector. Government interventions in private industry practically ceased. Also, labor legislation enacted in February 1977 circumscribed the role of the workers' commissions and provided some, albeit limited, possibilities for employers to lay off workers. In the same year, the scope of the public and the private sectors was delimited by law; the government committed itself not to undertake further nationalizations; it established rules on compensation for nationalized assets; and the foreign investment law was revised, providing greater assurances to foreign investors. Finally, the government imposed ceilings on wage increases and, after mid-1977, the escudo was devalued more rapidly than the rise in production costs and a crawling peg system was introduced in the place of intermittent devaluations that had created considerable uncertainty for exporters.

The policies applied helped to rebuild confidence in the economy. Also, in mid-1978, the government strengthened its anti-inflationary policy. This involved moderating the growth of the money supply and credit, raising interest rates, and slowing down the rate of expansion of public administration. While public administration increased by 17.8 percent in volume terms in 1976, the increases moderated to 7.0 percent in 1977 and 6.0 percent in 1978. And, with wage increases falling behind the rate of inflation, the share of the public consumption in GDP declined from 15.4 percent in 1975 to 14.1 percent in 1976 and remained approximately at this level thereafter (Tables 11.1 and 11.2).

Real wages in industry and transportation fell by 7.7 percent in 1976, 10.5 percent in 1977, and 5.2 percent in 1978, and decreases were not much smaller in agriculture (Table 11.3). Correspondingly, the share of private consumption in GDP declined from 80.7 percent in 1975 to 74.2 percent in 1978. During the same period, the combined share of private and public consumption in GDP fell from 96.1 percent to 88.5 percent, i.e. to approximately the 1968–73 level (Table 11.2).

Increases in nominal wages between 1975 and 1978 (38 percent) exceeded the rise in labor productivity in the manufacturing sector (25 percent) by a relatively small margin,[7] leading to a 10 percent increase in wage costs per unit of output. Taking account of changes in the cost of purchased inputs and capital equipment, production costs in Portuguese manufacturing increased by 84 percent. In the same period, wholesale prices for home-produced goods rose by 119 percent and the GDP deflator for manufacturing by 89 percent, indicating a substantial widening of profit margins (Table 11.4). And while, after the depreciation of the escudo in 1976 and 1977, the real exchange rate calculated in reference to the wholesale price index appreciated again, between 1975–1978 it depreciated by 12.0 percent vis-à-vis the U.S. dollar and 18.2 percent vis-à-vis the currencies in Portugal's trading partners if changes in production costs are used as the benchmark (Table 11.5).

Manufactured exports, however, reacted to improvements in competitiveness with a time lag. Thus, the dollar value of these exports rose by only 3 percent between 1975 and 1977 as compared to increases of 34 percent in both Greece and Spain. In 1978, however, the dollar value of manufactured exports rose by one-fourth, contributing to an increase in the volume of total exports by 13 percent as against 6 percent in 1977. Export growth accelerated again in 1979.

Various reasons may be adduced to explain the slow reaction of Portuguese manufactured exports to the improvement of Portugal's competitive position. Apart from the time needed for expansion, there was reluctance on the part of private industry to increase output because of the continued existence of political uncertainties, so that the expansion entailed utilizing excess capacity. Furthermore, devaluations occurring in discrete intervals until the adoption of the 'crawling peg' in mid-1977 created uncertainty for the exporter. Finally, protected domestic markets provided a profitable outlet until the adoption of an anti-inflationary policy and reductions in import surcharges in 1978.

Increases in tourist receipts were also slow, reaching only $403 million in 1977, as political uncertainty continued to discourage tourism in Portugal. Correspondingly, the share of the exports of goods and services in GDP in 1977 was below the 1975 level, which itself represented a substantial decrease compared to the pre-Revolutionary period (Table 11.2). The share of exports rose again in 1978, however, reflecting increases in merchandise exports as well as in tourism ($592 million in 1978).

After rising in 1977, the share of imports in GDP decreased in 1978 when stronger anti-inflationary measures were applied. In turn, in response to reduced political uncertainty, the adoption of the crawling peg, and higher interest rates, immigrants' remittances increased from $1.1 billion in 1977 to $1.6 billion in 1978. As a result of these changes, the deficit in the current account balance fell by nearly one-half, from $1.5 billion in 1977 to $0.8 billion in 1978.

Portugal in the 1973–78 Period: A Balance Sheet

Along with other oil-importing countries, in 1974 Portugal suffered the shock of a quadrupling of oil prices. Rather than effecting the transfer implicit in the oil price increase, representing about 2 percent of GNP, through an increased export surplus, in the years immediately following the Revolution changes in the opposite direction occurred and the volume of exports declined more than that of imports. With reduced tourist receipts and unchanged workers' remittances, the current account deficit reached $0.8 billion in 1975, equalling 5.1 percent of GNP and much exceeding the cost of increased oil prices in Portugal.

Policy improvements in 1976 and 1977 resulted in only modest increases in exports that remained below their 1973 level in volume terms. In 1977, the shortfall of manufactured exports to destinations other than the former colonies is estimated at $1.0 billion on a 1973 basis if export growth in Spain is taken as the norm. This figure several times exceeds the shortfall of exports to the former Portuguese colonies ($0.3 billion), estimated on the assumption that these would have increased at the same rate as exports to other areas. With slow increases in tourist receipts, the stagnation of workers' remittances, and the continued rapid growth of imports, the share of the current account deficit equalled 7.8 percent of GNP in 1976 and 9.3 percent in 1977.

As confidence was rebuilt and stronger anti-inflationary measures were applied, the current account deficit declined to 4.2 percent of GNP in 1978. Still, in the same year, the volume of exports exceeded the level reached in 1973 by only 5 percent whereas imports were 6 percent higher. Furthermore, although the 1973 level of per capital GNP was regained in 1978, an approximately 6 percent decline in per capita incomes is shown if we exclude public administration. And, while much of this decline was due to the repatriation of Portuguese from the former colonies, in the same period GNP per capita rose by 13 percent in Greece and by 6 percent in Spain.[8]

Nor have the workers enjoyed lasting benefits following the April 1974 Revolution. After temporary increases, by 1978 real wages in industry and transportation were 10 percent below the 1973 level, while in agriculture a decline of 6 percent is shown for men and only women experienced a rise of 6 percent as a result of the application of equal wage provisions (Table 11.3). Thus, although the share of wages and salaries, including fringe benefits, in GNP surpassed the 1973 level (51.6 percent) in 1978 (56.4 percent), with rapid increases in the labor force, the average worker is apparently worse off in Portugal today than he was before the Revolution. By contrast, real wages increased by 47 percent in Greece and by 57 percent in Spain between 1973 and 1978.

In 1978, the share of gross fixed capital formation in GDP exceeded the 1973 level by a small margin (Table 11.2). However, with the price of investment goods rising more rapidly than the average, the volume of investments did not regain the 1973 level by 1978. And, the share of gross fixed investment in Portugal is below the average for the Common Market as well as for Greece and Spain.

In the same period, investment by the private sector declined precipitously and the public sector carried out the bulk of new investments, some which—in particular, the large Sines complex—are of doubtful efficiency. The decline in private investment, in turn, had much to do with the problem of confidence. Although confidence increased after 1976, leading to higher production and exports, this did not suffice to stimulate a substantial volume of private investment. The same conclusion applies to foreign direct investment which showed little change between 1976 and 1978 and is below the pre-Revolution level.

Apart from improving confidence, a variety of measures would need to be taken in order to increase the rate of investment in Portugal. Recommendations to this effect will be made in Section IV below, following an analysis of desirable policy measures in agriculture (Section II) and in industry (Section III). The proposed measures should be considered as part of a development strategy, aimed at increasing Portugal's competitiveness in the European Common Market and reducing the income gap vis-à-vis the present and the prospective future members of the EEC. Estimated at purchasing power parities, real per capita incomes in Portugal are about two-fifths of incomes in France and Germany and two-thirds of incomes in Greece and Spain.[9]

The adoption of the proposals made in this essay would represent a shift from the government's preoccupation with short-term policies to greater emphasis on policies for the medium term. Nevertheless, short-term objectives could not be neglected. In particular, there is need to reduce the deficit of the public sector that rose from 1.4 percent in 1973 to 6.9 percent in 1977 and to 8.7 percent in 1978.[10] This increase occurred, notwithstanding a decline in the rate of growth of public consumption in recent years, as a result of the rapid expansion of subsidies, transfers and public investment. And, the deficit of the public sector appears to have increased again in 1979, thereby contributing to inflationary pressures and reducing the resources available for private investment.

II. Agricultural Policies in Portugal

The Present Situation

As noted in the introduction, agriculture made slow progress in Portugal and it was the most backward in Western Europe prior to the Revolution. In fact, during the postwar period, Portugal increasingly fell behind other European countries as far as agriculture is concerned. Between 1960 and 1975, per capita GDP in Portuguese agriculture declined from 31 percent to 27 percent of the Common Market average. During the same period, this ratio rose from 26 to 43 percent in Greece and from 31 to 44 percent in Spain.[11]

With production rising at an average annual rate of 0.9 percent during the two decades preceding the Revolution,[12] Portuguese agriculture was increasingly less able to satisfy domestic needs. Correspondingly, Portugal's trade balance in agricultural products (defined to include SITC categories 0, 1, 22, and 4) turned negative around 1970 and showed a deficit of $175 million in 1973.

A variety of influences conspired to maintain Portuguese agriculture in a backward state. They included an antiquated tenure system in the South; the fragmentation of holdings in the North; the lack of a coherent agricultural development strategy; a complex and inefficient system of administered prices and subsidies; fragmented agricultural institutions; and the lack of adequate credit facilities and extension services.

In the post-Revolutionary period, the events occurring in the Alentejo have disrupted production while little progress has been made to improve productivity in Portuguese agriculture. These considerations largely explain that agricultural output in 1978 was below the 1973 level and that Portugal experienced a continuing deterioration in its trade balance in agricultural products. Agricultural exports declined from $336 million in 1973 to $315 million in 1977 while imports rose from $511 million to $888 million, giving rise to an agricultural trade deficit of $573 million in 1977.

Much of the increase in the trade deficit in agricultural products occurred in cereals. With grain output stagnant during the period preceding the Revolution, the share of imports in domestic requirements rose from 18 percent in 1963–65 to 44 percent in 1972–74. This share increased further after the Revolution and, if present trends continue, it is expected to reach 60 percent by 1980 and 65 percent in 1985.[13]

Similar considerations apply to livestock. According to World Bank estimates, imports of beef and veal were $32 million in 1977 and are expected to double by 1980 and to triple by 1985. Also, from a net exporter, Portugal became a net importer of dairy products and substantial increases in imports are projected for the decade ahead. The share of imports in domestic requirements is expected to rise in vegetable oils and pulses as well.

It appears, then, that agriculture has increasingly become a drag on the Portuguese economy. At the same time, while Portugal's natural resource endowment is modest, considerable possibilities exist for improving the productivity of land, labor, and capital in agriculture. In particular, if appropriate policies are followed, Portugal should be able to approach yields in cereal production reached in Greece and Spain that have similar agricultural environments,[14] develop its livestock sector, and substantially expand the production of fruits and vegetables. We will consider the policy measures that may contribute to this outcome following a comparison of agriculture in Portugal and in the EEC.

Portuguese Agriculture and the European Common Market

Apart from the period of high world market prices in 1973–74, the variable levies applied in the framework of the Common Agricultural Policy have maintained producer prices in EEC agriculture substantially above world levels. In 1975, the latest year for which comparisons are available, domestic prices exceeded world market prices for maize and beef in Portugal while an approximate equality was maintained for wheat, and prices in Portugal were lower than the world market price for rice and olive oil.[15] At the same time, in view of Portugal's impending entry into the Common Market, comparisons with prices prevailing in the EEC are relevant for evaluating the prospects for Portuguese agriculture. This will be done in the following by utilizing the results of a study prepared by the Instituto Financeiro de Apoio ao Desenvolvimento da Agricultura e Pescas.

Table 11.6 compares prices received by Portuguese producers and the indicative prices[16] established under the Common Agricultural Policy for the years 1972–73 to 1976/77, by utilizing the EEC agricultural unit of account expressed in terms of U.S. dollars and the escudo-dollar exchange rate for conversion. The data show a continuing decline in the ratio of producer prices prevailing in Portugal to the indicative prices of the Community for wheat, beef, veal, red and white wine and, apart from the year 1975/76, milk. In turn, increases in the years 1973/74 and 1974/75 were followed by a decline of the price ratio in the case of barley and maize while pork and olive oil prices in Portugal exhibit an upward trend as compared to the EEC indicative price.

In the latest years for which data are available, producer prices of cereals, beef and veal, olive oil, and wine were all lower in Portugal than the EEC indicative price and only pork and milk prices were higher. Moreover, relative prices in Portugal appear to have declined subsequently by reason of the depreciation of the escudo.

Further interest attaches to comparisons with prices received by producers in Portugal and in the individual Common Market countries.. Prices received by producers in the EEC countries tend to be lower than the indicative price, in part because of transportation costs and in part because the indicative price sets an upper limit to national prices. Producer prices in the individual countries are also affected by national subsidies and by differences between the official exchange rate and the "green rate," derived by adjusting for Monetary Compensation Amounts (MCAs) that represent levies and subsidies applied at the border.[17]

As the data of Table 11.6 indicate, in the latest year for which data are available producer prices in Portugal were substantially below prices in the EEC countries covered (France, Ireland, Italy, and the United Kingdom) for cereals, with the exception of maize, where an approximate price parity was observed. The range of the relevant price ratios was 0.63 to 0.96 for wheat, 0.76 to 0.89 for barley, 0.65 to 0.87 for oats, and 0.58 to 0.63 for rice. However, the prices of milk (1.18 to 1.61) and beef (1.13 to 1.51) were higher in Portugal than in the Common Market countries while for veal the results vary depending on the country concerned (1.33 vis-à-vis Ireland; 0.85 to 0.99 vis-à-vis the other three countries).

The profitability of agricultural production is also affected by the prices of agricultural inputs. The price of fertilizer was generally lower in Portugal than in the Common Market countries under consideration whereas gasoline prices were uniformly higher. And while feed concentrates for livestock were the cheapest in Portugal, chaff was more expensive.

Comparisons of value added, defined as the difference between the producer price and the cost of material inputs, provide an indication of differences in production costs among the countries concerned. Among cereals, the calculations made for alternative production methods show Portugal to be a low-cost producer of rice. In the latest year for which data are available, Portugal also

TABLE 11.6
Ratio of Prices in Portugal to Producer Prices in the Principal Agricultural Producing Countries in the European Common Market for Major Agricultural Products

Country of Comparison	1972/73	1973/74	1974/75	1975/76	1976/77	1977/78
Wheat						
EEC[a]	1.10	1.04	1.04	1.00	.77	
France	1.24	1.35	1.23	1.19	.88	
Italy	1.18	.97	1.09	1.05	.63	
United Kingdom	1.80	1.09	1.34	1.40	.90	
Ireland	1.78	1.15	1.61	1.34	.96	
Barley						
EEC[a]	.82	.95	.99	.84	.72	
France	.93	1.25	1.06	.97	.77	
Italy	.94	1.00	.94	.95	.76	
United Kingdom	1.36	1.01	1.15	1.08	.78	
Ireland	1.45	1.16	1.33	1.16	.89	
Oats						
France	.97	1.10	.98	.90	.65	
Italy	.83	.88	.81	.86	.68	
United Kingdom	1.25	.99	1.04	.99	.72	
Ireland	1.19	1.14	1.24	1.20	.87	
Maize						
EEC[a]	.91	.92	1.19	1.19	.91	
France	1.03	1.11	1.17	1.33	1.01	
Italy	.97	1.05	1.18	1.39	1.02	
Rice						
France	.89	.59	.63	.93	.65	.63
Italy	.93	.73	.83	.88	.71	.58
Milk						
EEC[a]	1.16	1.10	1.10	1.23	1.06	
France	1.22	1.23	1.41	1.42	1.44	
Italy	1.33	1.09	1.05	1.16	1.18	
United Kingdom	1.77	1.56	1.59	1.59	1.61	
Beef						
EEC[b]	.99	.96	.94	.85	.82	
France	.88	.93	1.14	.94	1.16	1.13
Italy	.79	.80	.91	.78	.95	1.21
United Kingdom	1.51	1.29	1.65	1.58	1.67	1.36
Ireland	1.59	1.35	1.85	1.55	1.60	1.51
Veal						
EEC[b]	.96	.93	.93	.86	.81	
France	.65	.66	.89	.75	.83	.85
Italy	.74	.74	.92	.75	.88	.97
United Kingdom	.86	.72	.95	.87	.82	.99
Ireland	1.32	1.11	1.45	1.53	1.04	1.33
Pork						
EEC[c]	1.06	1.16	1.07	1.35	—	
Olive Oil						
EEC[a]	.63	.74	1.03	.83	—	
Red Wine						
EEC[b]	1.32	1.22	.80	.94	—	
White Wine						
EEC[b]	1.39	1.25	.74	.94		

Source: Instituto Financeiro de Apoio ao Desenvolvimento da Agricultura e Pescas, "Análise das Consequências Resultantes da Aplicação de Preços Comunitários à Produção Agrícola Nacional" Lisbon, February 1979 (mimeo).

Notes: (a) indicative price; (b) orientation price; (c) base price.

produced barley and oats at a lower cost that the EEC countries other than Ireland. This conclusion also applies to wheat, except that production costs were about the same as in France and the United Kingdom. Finally, for maize, production costs in Portugal were approximately the same as in France and Italy, the two Common Market countries for which comparable data exist.

The situation is different in regard to livestock products. Portugal is at a considerable disadvantage in milk production vis-à-vis the EEC countries covered in the comparison. In the case of beef and veal, Portugal is at a disadvantage vis-à-vis France and Ireland; it is at par with Italy; and it is at an advantage compared to the United Kingdom. In particular, grain-fed beef would be adversely affected if the subsidies granted through lower input prices were abolished. However, Portugal has good possibilities for exporting lamb and mutton which utilize pasture.

It should be added that there are considerable differences in production costs among farms in Portugal. The results indicate that the least efficient farms often have production costs much exceeding the Common Market level even in the case of cereals where, on the average, Portuguese production appears to be competitive.[18]

Intra-farm differences in production costs indicate the need for improving productivity in Portuguese agriculture. This conclusion is strengthened if we consider that cereal production would have to expand in order to reduce imports following entry into the Common Market and costs in livestock raising would have to be lowered to compete with EEC producers. At the same time, the expansion of the livestock sector would have favorable effects on agricultural employment and provide possibilities for further processing for export.

Increasing cereal yields would also be necessary in order to shift land into the production of fruits and vegetables which are high-value products, generate more income and employment, and serve as a basis for agro-industries. The development of this sector is crucial for the modernization of Portuguese agriculture.

Among fruits and vegetables, price increases in real terms have been projected for the European Common Market up to 1985 for melons, peaches, onions, potatoes, lentils, and dry peas, decreases for apples, apricots, avocados, grapefruit, mandarins and tangerines, asparagus, carrots, cucumber, green pepper, broad beans, and dry beans, and little change for the remainder.[19] At the same time, given its favorable climate, Portugal will benefit from the elimination of the Common Market tariff on a number of these commodities. In particular, Portugal has excellent possibilities for the exportation of citrus fruits, dry fruits, and vegetables, in fresh as well as in processed form.

In its efforts to expand fruit and vegetable exports, Portugal would have to meet competition from Greece and Spain. The same conclusion applies to olive oil and wine where expansion possibilities are excellent in Portugal and prices are lower than in the EEC (Table 11.6), but Greece (olive oil) and Spain (olive oil and wine) are strong competitors. Meeting this competition would again necessitate increasing productivity.

Modernizing Portuguese Agriculture

We may conclude that raising productivity levels in Portuguese agriculture would be necessary in order to improve the unfavorable trade balance of the sector, to exploit the possibilities offered by participation in the European Common Market, and to increase the living standards of a large proportion of the population. At the same time, the expansion of livestock raising and the production of fruits and vegetables would increase employment and provide a basis for agro-industries in Portugal.

A variety of measures may be taken to pursue the objective of raising productivity in Portuguese agriculture. To begin with, there is need to reform the existing system of price supports and agricultural subsidies. As shown in a recent study, "price policies and accompanying subsidies generally did not achieve either the objective or price stabilization, resource allocation toward more efficient production, or income distribution."[20] A particularly undesirable result has been the change in production technology in livestock raising from low-cost pasture to high-cost imported feedgrains sold at subsidized prices. This, in turn, led to the depletion of the breeding herd by providing incentives for fattening young calves to heavy weights at an early age.[21]

The elimination of the subsidy to the use of feedgrains in livestock raising may be considered an urgent task. More generally, in preparation for entry into the EEC, agricultural prices in Portugal should approach Common Market price relationships. This would involve raising the relative prices of cereals other than maize as compared to livestock products. Such a change would also bring Portuguese prices nearer to world market price relations, [22] and contribute to greater efficiency in agricultural resource use.

Additional measures conducive to increases in productivity include regularizing ownership conditions, encouraging the establishment of efficient size farms, increasing agricultural investments, improving credit facilities, expanding agricultural research and extension services, and undertaking various supplementary actions. These measures will be briefly considered in the following.

The agricultural reform law of September 1977 established the conditions under which land may be expropriated in the South and called for the voluntary consolidation of land holdings in the North. As regards the former, the application of the law would entail the return to former owners of land illegally seized. The Assembly has postponed the enactment of implementing legislation, however, thereby lengthening the period of uncertainty in the region that has had adverse effects on agricultural development.

In order to avoid further decapitalization and to restore pre-1974 production levels in the South, it would be necessary to fully implement the provisions of the September 1978 law on expropriation and reform the collective sector. In turn, in the North, measures would need to be taken to encourage the consolidation of fragmented land holdings and land transfers to younger farmers.

It would also be necessary to substantially raise the level of investment in agriculture which has declined to 5 percent of total investment in recent years. This volume of gross investment, equal to about 7 percent of agricultural value added, hardly covers the depreciation of non-land assets and it does not provide for future growth.

Increased investment in agriculture would be required in the public as well as in the private domain. For public investments to be efficient, a project identification and evaluation capability should be established in the Ministry of Agriculture. And, apart from providing appropriate incentives, greater private investment would necessitate improving agricultural credit facilities. This would entail increasing the amount available for agricultural credit, reforming the system of agricultural credit institutions, and redirecting credit towards productive uses.[23]

There is a further need for reforming and expanding agricultural research and extension services. As regards the former, the establishment of a new central research center and the strengthening of regional centers would be desirable, together with the increased involvement of foreign specialists and an expanded training effort. As regards the latter, the newly-established regional agricultural services should be strengthened, with a view to encouraging the application of improved seed and fertilizers, multiple cropping, and modern production methods in general. Further supporting measures include increasing the area under irrigation; improving agricultural marketing and management; setting standards for production and packaging; and expanding facilities for storage and processing, in particular refrigeration and stockyards.

The implementation of these measures would presuppose improvements in the institutional structure and the development of a coherent strategy for agriculture. But, more fundamentally, there is need for a change in governmental attitudes towards agriculture. Thus, it should be recognized that balanced economic expansion in Portugal requires the parallel development of agriculture and manufacturing industries.

III. Policies for the Manufacturing Sector

Prospects for Portuguese Industry in the European Common Market

The current dollar value of Portuguese manufactured exports to the EEC increased by only 18 percent between 1973 and 1977 as compared to an increase of 123 percent for Greece and 141 percent for Spain. This shortfall cannot be explained by the import limitations imposed on a few Portuguese products since Greece and Spain have been subject to similar limitations and

Spain does not even enjoy duty-free treatment in the Common Market. Rather, as noted earlier, the shortfall is related to the economic conditions existing in Portugal following the Revolution of April 1974.

At the same time, Portugal has considerable possibilities for expanding the sales of manufactured goods in the Common Market. For one thing, Portuguese exports of manufactured goods to the EEC are very small, accounting for only 0.3 percent of the imports of manufactures by the Common Market countries. For another thing, Portugal has a considerable wage advantage over these countries.

According to World Bank estimates, in the textile industry for which comparable data are available, the average cost per labor hour in 1976–77 was $1.45 in Portugal as compared to $6.90 in Germany and $5.15 in Italy. Portuguese wages were also substantially lower than in competing countries, such as Ireland ($2.88) and Greece ($2.23). And, with the devaluation of the escudo, since 1976–77 the dollar equivalent of wages has increased less in Portugal than in other European countries.

Portugal's wage advantage is reflected by the pattern of its trade in manufactured goods with the Common Market countries. According to Doenges and Schatz (1978), Portugal's comparative advantage vis-à-vis the EEC, as "revealed" by trade data, was in labor-intensive industries, such as yarn and fabrics, clothing, and footwear. At the same time, industrial development would require increasing value added per man in Portuguese exports that utilize the country's manpower resources.

In the textile industry, efforts may be concentrated on high-quality yarns and fabrics, including mercerized and dyed products, cordurory and velvet. In the case of clothing, the proximity of markets, together with good design capabilities in Portugal, provide possibilities for expansion in fashion clothing, especially for women and children. Fashion items also hold promise in the case of shoes and travel goods.

New exports have been developing or show potential for the future in the engineering industries, where the availability of skilled labor and design capabilities provide advantages to Portugal. Expansion possibilities are particularly favorable in regard to relatively simple metal products (e.g. castings) and machinery (e.g. agricultural and textile machinery) as well as for custom-made items (special purpose machinery and equipment, heavy machine tools).

In machinery production, the lack of Portuguese brand-names points to the need for cooperative arrangements with manufacturers in the more advanced European countries. There are also possibilities for the manufacture of parts, components, and accessories for the foreign assembly of automobiles, machinery, and other equipment, as well as for assembly whenever these operations are relatively labor-intensive.

It would further be desirable to expand the exports of resource-based products. According to results of Doenges and Schatz, Portugal has a "revealed" comparative advantage in wood and cork products and in non-metallic mineral products. As regards the former, design skills and the quality of Portuguese manufacture would permit further transformation in the form of particle board and furniture. As regards the latter, the introduction of new techniques could lead to the expansion of the exports of ceramics, glazed tile, and glass products. Finally, as we have seen, possibilities exist for the exportation of fruits and vegetables in processed form.

In order for these export possibilities to be realized, Portugal would need to follow appropriate policies in regard to the manufacturing sector. The relevant policy measures concern the public and the private sectors as well as investment and savings. They will be considered in the following.

Policies in the Public Sector

As noted earlier, since the 1974 Revolution the bulk of manufacturing investments in Portugal took place in the public sector. This reflects the slow rebuilding of confidence in the private sector as well as the virtual lack of financial control of public investments. Among the latter, the Sines complex, reportedly accounting for 13–14 percent of total gross fixed capital formation in Portugal, deserves separate consideration.

The integrated heavy industrial complex in Sines, comprising a seawater port capable of receiving large vessels, an oil refinery, and plants for the production of petrochemicals, fertilizer, caustic chlorine, steel, railway wagons and for the processing of pyrites, was initiated under Salazar. It was continued after the Revolution, although changing conditions in world markets will hardly permit the exportation of refinery products, petrochemicals, fertilizers and caustic chlorine that had originally been assumed. In particular, investments undertaken or planned in the oil-producing countries of the Middle East, which enjoy the benefits of the availability of both energy and capital, will add to oversupply in the world market. By contrast, Portugal has practically no energy resources and it is scarce in capital. At the same time, capital requirements per job in petroleum refining, petrochemicals, and fertilizers are five to ten times higher than in Portugal's actual and potential export industries.[24]

In May 1977, the establishment of the fertilizer plants, the caustic soda plant, the steel mill, and the second stage of the petrochemical complex was postponed, and doubts were raised about the desirability of proceeding with the pyrite processing plant. Indications are that some of these investments will nevertheless be carried out. Yet, the investments in question have not been subject to rigorous economic project appraisal and the commission appointed in the summer of 1979 to undertake the re-evaluation of the entire Sines complex was subsequently disbanded.

An economic appraisal of proposed investments at Sines in terms of world market prices would be necessary in order to avoid continuing high costs for the Portuguese economy. Other investments in the public sector should also be subject to economic project evaluation. In this way, one may correct the import-substitution bias that has characterized investments by public firms in the recent past and has become increasingly inappropriate as the date of entry into the Common Market approaches.

In this connection, it should be recognized that once Portugal enters into the Common Market, high-cost plants could not compete with imports from other EEC countries and would require large subsidies to survive. In fact, government subsidies have increased rapidly in recent years, reaching 4.0 percent of GNP in 1978 as compared to 1.0 percent in 1973.[25] While these subsidies in part cover the losses of public utilities where prices have not been raised commensurately with costs, a substantial part covers the losses of publicly-owned manufacturing enterprises, including firms located at Sines.

The government has provided benefits to public firms in other ways as well. These include substantial capital transfers (nearly 10 billion escudos in 1978); debt guarantees; delayed payments of social security contributions and indirect taxes; and investment in infrastructure that grew at an average annual rate of 40 percent between 1973 and 1978.[26]

It appears, then, that the public sector involves a considerable cost to the Portuguese economy. In order to reduce this cost, and to ensure that public firms in the manufacturing sector can stand up to competition in the European Common Market, the economic project evaluation of public investments should be complemented by a reform of the management of existing public firms. Such a reform would entail transforming public firms into self-managed units and making them responsible to a supervisory board independent of government administration. At the same time, the firms in question would need to prepare financial plans for phasing out subsidies over a predetermined period.

As regards the establishment of self-managed public firms, reference may be made to the experience of Western European countries. In these countries, successful public firms in the manufacturing sector have generally acted independently from the government. They have operated on the basis of market principles and competed with private firms in the same industry at home and abroad. Public firms also operate in a market setting in Hungary and Yugoslavia, where the profitability of the firm to a considerable extent depends on its ability to compete in foreign markets.[27]

The preceding discussion pertains to publicly-owned firms in manufacturing industries that have been designated by law as being in the public domain. As we have seen, the Portuguese government has also acquired participation in firms outside these industries through the nationalization of banks and insurance companies. These participations range widely across industries and sectors, with the government's share varying from 5 to over 50 percent.

There is little reason to maintain participation in firms where the government is a minority shareholder. And even in cases when the government has a majority share, the task of supervision makes it onerous to retain such, mostly small, firms in the public sector. Apart from the inefficiencies involved, the reprivatization of these firms would increase business confidence in Portugal.

Policies in the Private Sector

The private sector offers excellent possibilities for expansion as it is concentrated in industries where Portugal has a comparative advantage and since successful exporting requires the operation of the profit motive. At the same time, various measures would need to be taken to create appropriate conditions for the further development of the private sector.

To begin with, one would need to ensure that private and public firms receive equal treatment. This applies in particular to the granting of credits and the treatment of tax and social security obligations. As noted above, one should also phase out subsidies that benefit public firms.

Moreover, there is a need to further liberalize regulations on lay-offs that continue to discourage hiring and contribute to uncertainty in firm decision-making. This is of especial importance as Portugal enters the Common Market. For one thing, exporting firms will require flexibility to vary the size of their labor force in response to market conditions. For another thing, competition from imports may necessitate the restructuring of firms, when the alternative to raising productivity through reductions in the labor force may well be bankruptcy.

Existing regulations on wage rates and on income taxes, would also need to be changed, so as to provide adequate remuneration to managers, technicians, and skilled workers. Wage differences among skill classes declined to a considerable extent as minimum and maximum wages were set after the Revolution. Furthermore, the marginal tax rate was raised to 93 percent for annual incomes above 900 thousand escudos, i.e. about $18,000 a year; the marginal tax rate is 50 percent above annual incomes of $12,000.

Low after-tax incomes also discourage the return of expatriate managers and other skilled personnel and provide incentives for emigration. Yet, as noted above, industrial development in Portugal requires the expansion of skill-intensive industries. At the same time, with entry into the Common Market, improved treatment as regards social benefits will make employment in the other EEC countries increasingly attractive.

Confronting competition in the EEC would further require industrial concentration in Portugal, where small, inefficient firms account for a substantial segment of manufacturing industry. On the example of France, Greece and Spain, industrial concentration may be encouraged by the use of fiscal and credit measures.[28] While certain fiscal measures have since been taken, additional measures would be necessary in order to bring about the kind of industrial transformation that occurred in France following the establishment of the Common Market.

Last but not least, there is need to clearly define the role of the government in the Portuguese economy. While proposals have again been made for "indicative" planning, government interference with firm decision-making will become increasingly inadvisable as Portugal becomes a full member of the Common Market. This is because, under free trade conditions within the EEC, firms would need to take the risks and reap the rewards of their actions.

In this connection, reference may be made to the experience of France, where indicative planning had been undertaken prior to the Common Market's establishment. The government had provided production targets to French industry and it could ensure the fulfillment of these targets by imposing restrictions on imports and subsidizing exports. But planning could not be effective once import restrictions were abolished and tariffs were eliminated in the framework of the EEC. In the new situation, firms had to orient their operations towards international competition rather than government-determined production targets. Correspondingly, indicative planning has lost its *raison d'etre* and has been discontinued. Nor has any other EEC country, or the Common Market itself, adopted indicative planning.[29]

At the same time, in order to ensure that private decisions conform to the national interest and to prepare for entry into the Common Market, there is need to reform the system of incentives in Portugal. Such a reform would entail lessening tariff disparities and reducing the bias against exports.

Reforming the system of tariffs would require switching from specific to ad valorem tariffs and rationalizing their structure. In order to avoid having to carry out another full-scale tariff reform a few years later, this should be done by using the EEC common external tariff as a benchmark. But, higher tariffs may apply to products where this is warranted by infant industry considerations. Infant industry tariffs should provide a modest margin, say 10–15 percent, on value added in world market prices (net foreign exchange earnings), with provisions made for their gradual reduction and elimination.

As long as Portuguese industries are protected against imports from the EEC, reducing the bias against exports would require direct or indirect export subsidies. Following the examples of Greece and Spain, one may examine the possibility of granting a subsidy on world market value added in exports (net foreign exchange earnings) during the transitional period of entry into the Common Market. Alternatively, one may extend the scope of preferential credits for export sales and provide such credits for export production and export-oriented investments as well.

Investment incentives as an export promoting device have the advantage of contributing to the creation of new capacity. More generally, increasing the rate of investment is of particular importance in Portugal which has devoted a smaller share of its gross domestic product to fixed capital formation (19.6 percent in 1976–77) than the European Common Market as presently constituted (21.1 percent). The differences are even larger if comparisons are made with Greece (22.2 percent) and Spain (22.8 percent).

The rate of investment may be increased by attracting foreign investment and by increasing domestic investment and savings. The measures that may be taken to pursue these objectives will be considered in Section IV below, with further attention given to the need for improving the allocation of investment funds among economic activities.

IV. The Volume of Investment and Its Allocation

The Treatment of Foreign Direct Investment

The Foreign Investment Code, promulgated in August 1977, represents considerable improvements over the earlier code as it provides increased assurances to foreign investors. Nevertheless, as noted above, there has been little subsequent increase in foreign direct investment in Portugal. Apart from political uncertainty, this may be explained by the continued existence of certain disincentives to such investments. They include the contentious issue of compensation for nationalized foreign assets; the cumbersome legal procedure on lay-offs and the lack of consistency of its application;[30] the delays experienced in the authorization of foreign investments and the bureaucratic procedures applied by the Foreign Investment Institute; and the possibility provided by law that limitations would be imposed on the transfer of dividends, profits, and the proceeds of sale or liquidation in the event of a "serious disequilibrium" in the Portuguese balance of payments.

Apart from removing these sources of disincentives, it would be necessary to provide positive incentives to foreign direct investment so as to make locating in Portugal sufficiently attractive. This is because Portugal has to compete with alternative investment possibilities in the present and the prospective EEC member countries.

In this connection, reference may be made to the experience of Ireland, where incentives provided to foreign investors led to a quadrupling of foreign direct investment between 1973 and 1977. As a result, Ireland was able to take advantage of the opportunities offered by the European Common Market and experienced a 142 percent increase in the dollar value of manufactured exports during this period. With continued increases in the following year, the volume of total exports rose by 53 percent between 1973 and 1978.

As in the case of Ireland, foreign direct investment in Portugal would permit utilizing the opportunities offered by entry in the Common Market. Foreign capital brings technological and managerial know-how as well as marketing expertise that are in short supply in Portugal. Also, the inflow of capital adds to the volume of investment and to foreign exchange receipts, thereby contributing to higher incomes and employment directly as well as indirectly by easing the foreign exchange shortage.

On the example of Ireland and several other countries, tax holidays may be used to attract foreign investment. Tax holidays are preferable to accelerated depreciation provisions that favor capital-intensive industries and production methods. At the same time, tax holidays may be complemented by preferential credits for new investment.

Incentives to Domestic Investment and Savings

In order to encourage investment activity in Portugal, tax holidays and preferential investment credits should be provided to domestic private investment as well. With the equal treatment of foreign and domestic private investment, one may exploit the advantages offered by joint ventures that permit drawing on foreign capital and expertise without 100 percent foreign ownership.

At the same time, savings would need to be generated in order to provide funds for domestic private investment. Private savings may be encouraged through higher real interest rates and the provision of a larger array of financial instruments to savers. These measures would also contribute to the repatriation of the savings of Portuguese workers abroad and discourage the clandestine flow of funds.

The experience of recent years indicates that domestic savings respond to higher real interest rates in Portugal. However, with an acceleration of the rate of inflation since mid-1978, real rates of interest have declined again. Thus, interest rates on time deposits for 90 days and longer vary between 12 and 21 percent while consumer prices rose by 28 percent between the second and third quarter of 1978 and 1979.

Negative real interest rates and the limited choice available among financial investments provide incentives for investment in real estate and in consumer durables as well as for "self-investment" in lower productivity uses.[31] They also discourage the repatriation of the savings of Portuguese workers abroad and give inducement to the clandestine exportation of savings.

Taking account of the depreciation of the escudo, interest rates abroad have exceeded the rate obtainable in Portugal by 10 to 20 percentage points.[32] While the existence of these differences has contributed to the channeling of savings abroad, the imposition of ceilings have led Portuguese firms to borrow abroad at high interest rates. This circular flow of savings, in turn, has entailed a cost to the Portuguese economy.

Real interest rates may be increased by raising nominal rates or by reducing the rate of inflation. In view of the adverse economic effects of a high rate of inflation and Portugal's prospective entry into the Common Market, it would be advisable to reduce inflation rates. As monetary policy cannot alone bear the burden of the fight against inflation, this would necessitate reducing the budgetary deficit. A smaller budgetary deficit would simultaneously decrease the dissaving of the public sector.

The budget deficit may be reduced by curtailing the size of government administration that now accounts for 10 percent of the total labor force, having doubled between 1968 and 1978.[33] And while decreasing the size of government administration will take time, more immediate measures may include reducing the government's investment program and its subsidies to public firms. Also, the introduction of rigorous project evaluation is bound to lead to a reduction in the size of the public investment program in Portugal. At the same time, subsidies to public firms may be reduced by streamlining the operations of these firms and raising the prices of public services.

Improving the Allocation of Investment

Reductions in public investment would increase the availability of funds to the private sector where higher returns may be obtained and more employment is created. Increases in real interest rates would further improve the allocation of investment as one may thereby avoid the "undesired effects from credit rationing, performed under a lot of political and other pressures by slow working, incompetent bureaucracies".[34] At the same time, higher interest rates would lessen existing incentives for capital-intensive industries and processes. The extent of these incentives would further be reduced and the burden of higher interest rates on producers offset, if labor costs were lowered through reductions in social charges.

The application of these measures would tend to encourage labor-intensive production and exports, thereby contributing to the efficient allocation of investment while improving Portugal's competitive position in the Common Market. The described measures would also contribute to increased employment in a situation where the excess supply of labor is not fully reflected in its cost.

At the same time, as noted above, industrial development in Portugal would necessitate the expansion of skill-intensive industries. In order to increase the availability of skilled and technical labor, one may envisage expanding technical education and encouraging in-plant training. As regards the latter, tax benefits to training, provided e.g. in the framework of social security legislation, would reduce the risk to the firm that the workers it has trained move to other firms at home or abroad.

Finally, the efficient allocation of investment would be served through the revitalization of the moribund stock and bond markets and the creation of new financial intermediaries in Portugal. In this connection, particular importance attaches to the enactment of proposed legislation on the establishment of private investment companies, which would be able to issue bonds with one-year maturity or longer.

Apart from improving investment allocation, the revitalization of financial markets would encourage domestic savings and reduce incentives to channel savings abroad. Settling compensation claims for nationalized property would also increase the availability of funds for investment.

Conclusions

In this essay, recommendations have been made for policy measures that may be taken to prepare Portugal for entry into the Common Market. The recommendations aim at raising efficiency in agriculture and industry, increasing investment and savings, and improving the allocation of investment. Their implementation would also have beneficial effects on employment.

In agriculture, there is need for a coherent development strategy. The elements of such a strategy include reforming the system of price supports and agricultural subsidies, regularizing ownership conditions, encouraging the establishment of efficient size farms, increasing agricultural investments, improving credit facilities, expanding agricultural research and extension services, and undertaking various supplementary actions aimed at agricultural modernization.

In the manufacturing industry, public investments should be made subject to economic project evaluation carried out in terms of world market prices. This is of particular importance for the Sines complex, the economic efficiency of which has been queried. There is further need for transforming public enterprises in the manufacturing sector into self-managed units, to be operated on the basis of market principles.

Rigorous project evaluation may be expected to lead to reductions in the size of the public investment program, thereby freeing resources for the private sector that promises higher returns and more employment creation. Furthermore, it should be ensured that public and private firms receive equal treatment as regards credit allocation, taxation and social security. At the same time, there is need to further liberalize legislation on lay-offs, to increase wage differentials according to skills, and to reduce high marginal tax rates.

The successful participation of Portuguese industry in the European Common Market would also necessitate encouraging concentration by the use of credit and fiscal measures. And, it would be desirable to limit government interference in business decisions. One should rely instead on the system of incentives to ensure that private decisions conform to the public interest. This would entail reducing tariff disparities and increasing export incentives.

A variety of measures may be taken to increase the rate of investment and to improve its allocation. Apart from reducing existing disincentives to investment, foreign as well as domestic private firms would need positive incentives in the form of tax holidays and preferential credits. In turn, raising real interest rates and improving the functioning of financial markets would provide inducements to domestic savings and reduce existing incentives to channel savings abroad. Higher real interest rates would also discourage capital-intensive investments while the burden of higher interest costs could be offset by reducing social charges that, too, would favor employment.

Several of the proposed measures, including the actions to be taken in agriculture, the lowering of marginal income tax rates, reductions in social charges, export subsidies, tax holidays for new investment, and the preferential tax treatment of industrial concentration would represent a burden on the government budget. Increasing taxes on consumption would appear to be an appropriate measure to provide the necessary financing, since such taxes do not adversely affect savings. At the same time, reductions in the public investment budget, decreases in governmental subsides, and the curtailment of the size of public administration would permit lowering the budgetary deficit, thus reducing the dissaving of the public sector.

With emphasis on increasing investment at the expense of consumption in general, and reducing unproductive expenditures in the public sector in particular, the policy recommendations made in this essay entail a choice in favor of the second of the two alternatives—restrictive policy measures and a positive, stimulative approach—considered by Lundberg for purposes of short-term stabilization in Portugal.[35] In this way, short-term measures are oriented towards the longer-term objective of preparing Portugal for participation in the Common Market.

ESSAY 12

Planning and Policy Making in Greece

Introduction

Greece was one of the star performers in the world economy prior to the oil crisis and the 1974–75 recession. Between 1960 and 1973, the Greek gross national product increased at an average annual rate of 7.4 percent, with incomes per head rising 6.8 percent a year.[1] By 1973, per capita incomes in Greece reached $1870 as compared to $2450 in Italy, $2150 in Ireland, $1710 in Spain, and $1410 in Portugal.[2]

The described developments indicate the favorable effects of the adoption of policy measures aimed at the "opening" of the Greek economy. The measures in question included granting export incentives, providing relatively low rates of import protection, and entering into an association agreement with the European Common Market. The adoption of an outward-oriented strategy led to the rapid growth of exports, with a sixfold increase in terms of US dollars between 1960 and 1973.

The performance of manufactured exports is particularly noteworthy. The exports of manufactured goods, excluding nonferrous metals, reached $537 million in 1973 as against $20 million in 1960.[3] The rapid rise of exports, in turn, contributed to the fourfold growth of value added in manufacturing between 1960 and 1973 (a growth rate of 10.8 percent per year), raising the share of the manufacturing sector in the gross domestic product from 15.0 to 22.0 percent.[4] In 1973, value added per worker in manufacturing was $7710 in Greece, as compared to $10831 in Italy, $8679 in Ireland, $6198 in Spain, and $3888 in Portugal.[5]

As other countries, the Greek economy was adversely affected by the oil crisis and the world recession, with a decline of GNP by 3.8 percent in 1974.[6] GNP increased again by 5.6 percent in 1975 and 6.4 percent in 1976, but rose only by 3.8 percent in 1977. And, while gross domestic capital formation surpassed the 1974 level by 16 percent in 1977, it fell short of the 1973 level by 14 percent, reflecting a decrease of capital formation in manufacturing and in housing. Manufacturing experienced a continuing decline of investments after the oil crisis; investments in housing increased after 1974 but were still below the 1973 level in 1977.

The relatively poor performance of the Greek economy in 1977 appears to have contributed to the lowering of the sights of the planners for the 1978–82 period. Thus, while the projected growth rate of GNP was 6.5 percent in the provisional plan for 1976–80, alternative projections of 5.0 and 6.0 percent have been put forward in the preliminary plan document for 1978–82.[7]

In the present essay, these projections will be subjected to scrutiny. In so doing, reasons will first be sought for the observed performance in 1977. Subsequently, the growth prospects of the Greek economy will be evaluated and alternative projections will be offered. This will be done by utilizing three approaches, entailing the consideration of the following factors: (1) potential export growth and export elasticities; (2) employment and productivity growth; and (3) marginal capital-output ratios and investment ratios. Finally, the policies necessary for rapid economic growth will be analyzed.

Greek Economic Performance in 1977

The 3.8 percent growth rate of Greek GNP in 1977 compares favorably with growth rates averaging slightly above 2 percent in the European Common Market. The comparison is even more favorable if adjustment is made for the 4.8 percent decline in agricultural output that was due to unfavorable weather conditions. Excluding agriculture, a growth rate of 4.5 percent is obtained for the non-agricultural sectors of the economy; this figure would be further adjusted upwards if consideration was given to the adverse effects of the poor harvest on the demand for trade and transportation services.

The relatively poor performance of the manufacturing sector, with value added rising by only 2.1 percent in 1977, has been attributed to the slow growth of export markets. Slow market growth can provide only partial explanation, however, as Greece also experienced a decline in its export market shares. This decline, in turn, reflects the deterioration of the competitive position of Greek industry.

In 1977 rapid increases in wages, with labor productivity declining by 3 percent, led to a 22 percent rise in unit labor costs in Greece, as compared to an average increase of 10 percent in the principal Common Market countries.[8] These differences were not compensated by exchange rate changes. The value of the Greek drachma in terms of U.S. dollars remained practically unchanged between 1976 and 1977, while in the Common Market the appreciation of the currencies participating in the European snake was approximately offset in depreciation of the French franc, the Italian lira, and the British pound.

Apart from adverse effects on export competitiveness, increases in labor costs contributed to the rise of imports into Greece, with the volume of imports increasing 6.0 percent in 1977 as compared to a decline in exports of 3.6 percent. Also, increases in real wages, averaging 10 percent a year between 1975 and 1977, led to a rise in the share of wage-earners in nonagricultural incomes from 46.2 percent in 1973 to 52.5 percent in 1977,[10] with commensurate reductions in profits, resulting in a decline in the amount of internally-generated funds available for investment. Investment activity in the manufacturing sector was also adversely affected by the lack of information on investment incentives that were to replace these that had come to expire.

Growth Prospects for the Greek Economy and the Role of Exports

With entry into the European Common Market, Greece would have to reduce its economic lag behind the member countries by attaining a rate of growth of per capita incomes in excess of that of the EEC countries. The gross national product would have to increase even more rapidly as population is expected to rise at an average annual rate of 0.9 percent between 1977 and 1982 in Greece while the Common Market is likely to experience little change. In this connection, the question arises as to what the main constraints are to rapid economic growth in Greece.

The preliminary plan document puts emphasis on the export constraint to growth, which is said to be due to foreign demand conditions. Thus, depending on "the trend followed by the level of international demand,"[11] manufacturing exports are projected to rise at average annual rates of 2.5, 5.5, and 10.5 percent, with corresponding rates of growth of manufacturing value added of 5.0, 6.6 and 7.5 percent, respectively. The first of these variants would be associated with a 5.0 percent, the second as well as the third with a 6.0 percent, GDP growth rate; in the second case, more rapid increases in construction, dwellings, and tourism would provide impetus to growth in the place of manufactured exports (Tables 12.1 and 12.2).

These projections appear overly pessimistic. To begin with, references to the limitations of international markets and the high absolute level of Greek manufactured exports in the provisional plan document do not take account of the small share of Greece in the international market in general and in the European Common Market in particular, and fail to consider the advantageous treatment of Greek manufactured exports in the EEC.

In 1977, Greek exports accounted for only about 0.04 percent of the consumption, and 0.2 percent of the imports, of manufactured goods in the developed countries; the corresponding ratios were 0.07 percent and 0.4 percent in the Common Market. In the same year, Greek manufactured exports, excluding nonferrous metals, amounted to $1.2 billion as against approximately $9 billion in Korea and $8 billion in Taiwan, both of which have a smaller manufactured output than Greece. And, manufactured exports accounted for only 4.8 percent of GNP in Greece as compared to 5.3 percent

TABLE 12.1
Value Added, Employment and Productivity in Greece, 1977–1982
(average annual rates of growth in 1970 prices)

	Preliminary Projections			Alternative Projections	
	5.0%	6.0% A	6.0% B	6.0%	6.5%
Agriculture					
Value Added	4.0	4.0	4.0	4.0	4.0
Employment	−2.4	−2.4	−2.4	−2.4	−2.4
Productivity	6.6	6.6	6.6	6.6	6.6
Mining					
Value Added	5.0	6.0	7.0	7.0	7.0
Employment	0.9	0.9	0.9	0.9	0.9
Productivity	4.1	5.1	6.0	6.0	6.0
Manufacturing					
Value Added	5.0	6.6	7.5	7.5	8.3
Employment	1.2	1.6	1.8	1.8	1.9
Productivity	3.8	4.9	5.6	5.6	6.3
Electricity, Gas and Water					
Value Added	8.0	9.5	9.8	9.8	9.8
Employment	3.9	3.9	3.9	3.9	3.9
Productivity	3.9	5.4	5.7	5.7	5.7
Construction					
Value Added	5.9	7.6	6.3	6.3	6.3
Employment	5.4	5.1	4.4	4.4	4.4
Productivity	.5	2.4	1.8	1.8	1.8
Transportation and Communication					
Value Added	5.5	6.5	6.5	6.5	7.0
Employment	2.2	2.9	2.9	2.9	3.2
Productivity	3.2	3.5	3.5	3.5	3.7
Trade and Banking					
Value Added	4.9	5.5	5.5	5.5	6.5
Employment	1.5	1.5	1.7	1.7	2.1
Productivity	3.3	3.9	3.7	3.7	4.3
Other Services					
Value Added	4.9	5.9	5.4	5.4	6.0
Employment	1.0	1.5	1.0	1.0	1.3
Productivity	3.9	4.3	4.4	4.4	4.6
Gross Domestic Product					
Value Added	5.0	6.0	6.0	6.0	6.5
Employment	0.6	0.8	0.7	0.7	0.8
Productivity	4.4	5.2	5.3	5.3	5.7

Sources: KEPE, *Macro-Economic Evaluations* and text.

Note: The estimates shown in this table pertain to assumed 5.0 percent and 6.0 percent GDP growth rates, with further distinction made between variants A and B under the latter, in the preliminary plan projections and to the low and high growth variants (GDP growth rates of 6.0 percent and 6.5 percent, respectively) in the proposed alternative projections.

TABLE 12.2
Primary and Manufactured Export in Greece, 1970–1982
(average annual rates of growth in 1970 price)

		Projections, 1977–82				
		Preliminary 6%			Alternative	
	Actual 1970–77	5.0%	6.0%A	6.0%B	6.0%	6.5%
Primary	4.1	5.7	5.9	6.0	6.0	6.0
Manufacturing	16.9	2.5	5.5	10.5	10.5	15.0
Total	11.7	3.5	5.6	9.2	9.2	12.8

Sources: See Table 12.1

Note: See Table 12.1

in Spain, 9.4 percent in Yugoslavia, and 10.5 percent in Portugal; this ratio was 8.1 percent in Italy at a comparable state of development, in 1961–62.[12]

Finally, its association and prospective membership in the European Common Market puts Greece in a favorable position vis-à-vis newly-industrializing developing countries in general, and Far Eastern countries in particular. Thus, whereas Hong Kong, Korea and Taiwan had to accept an absolute reduction in their exports of textiles and clothing in the European Common Market, Greek exports are not subject to comparable limits.

This is not to say that Greece would not have to develop new exports. The EEC provides a large potential market for these exports and while the difficulties of developing new exports have received emphasis in Greece, it should be recalled that Greek exports of textiles and clothing were practically nil in 1960 and increased rapidly afterwards. In the future, Greece's relatively high educational level and low labor costs would permit expanding skill-intensive exports by upgrading existing exports and developing new export products during the period of the five-year plan.

An indication of the Greek educational level may be provided by utilizing the Harbison-Myers index, which is derived as the sum of the secondary school enrollment rate plus five times the university enrollment rate in the respective age cohorts. Calculations made for 1972 may be taken as an indication of the human resource base of the Greek economy during the period of the five-year plan. According to these results, the educational level of Greece, with a Harbison-Myers index of 140.9, is comparable to that of Ireland (144.7) and Spain (140.6), and exceeds educational levels in Portugal (111.0), and, especially, Turkey (58.3) by a substantial margin.[13]

At the same time, despite rapid increases in wages in recent years, average wages in manufacturing are still much below wages in the Common Market countries. In 1977, hourly wages in manufacturing averaged $1.52 in Greece as compared to $4.75 in Germany and $3.78 in Italy. Greek manufacturing wages are also lower than wages in Ireland ($2.56) and Spain ($2.21), although they exceed wages in Portugal ($0.73).[14]

Apart from upgrading existing exports of textiles and clothing, the availability of relatively cheap skilled labor in Greece would permit expanding the exports of engineering products, including electrical and nonelectrical machinery and equipment.[15] This may take the form of the production of final commodities as well as the manufacture of parts, components and accessories for assembly elsewhere. The latter alternative offers special interest to Greece in the framework of the international division of the production process within the European Common Market.

These considerations point to the opportunities available to Greece for expanding manufactured exports through participation in the European Common Market. Further possibilities exist in the Middle East and in North Africa, where Greece has a transportation cost advantage over most other developing countries. In particular, there are considerable market opportunities in the Middle East that have not been adequately exploited by Greek exporters.

At the same time, the Greek experience as well as the experience of other countries indicates that rapid industrial growth requires exports to rise substantially faster than manufacturing output. In the Far Eastern countries, export elasticities in manufacturing (the rate of growth of manufactured exports divided by that of value added in manufacturing) exceed 2, while these elasticities are in the 1.6 to 2.0 range in the smaller Common Market countries.[16] By contrast, export elasticities of 0.5, 0.8 and 1.4 are assumed in the plan projections (Tables 12.1 and 12.2).

As regards export projections, one may take the World Bank forecast for developing countries as a starting point. According to this forecast, the manufactured exports of the developing countries would rise at an annual average rate of 12.2 percent between 1975 and 1985,[17] corresponding to a growth rate of about 10.5 percent between 1977 and 1985. In view of its prospective membership in the European Common Market, Greece should be able to raise its manufactured exports more rapidly than developing countries on the average. One may then consider 10.5 percent, the upper projection in the provisional plan document as a low estimate. In turn, a consideration of the possibilities open to Greece in exporting to the Common Market and to the Middle East warrant a high estimate of 15.0 percent a year (Table 12.2). And, even the latter figure is below the 16.9 percent growth rate of Greek manufactured exports reached between 1970 and 1977, encompassing periods of the world boom as well as the world recession.

Assuming an export elasticity of 1.4 under the proposed low, and 1.8 under the high, estimate,[18] the rate of growth of value added in manufacturing is estimated at 7.5 percent and 8.3 percent in the two cases. Accepting the preliminary plan projections associated with a 7.5 percent growth of manufacturing for the other sectors of the economy (Assumption B in Table 12.1), the upper projection of the plan, a GDP growth rate of 6.0 percent, may be taken as the low estimate.[19] In turn, the high estimate involves raising projections for service sectors that are linked with manufacturing activities. The corresponding range for the growth of GDP is 6.0 to 6.5 percent for the period 1977–82 as compared to a range of 5.0 to 6.0 percent projected in the preliminary plan document (Table 12.1).

Employment and Productivity Growth

The next question concerns the prospects for employment and productivity growth in the Greek economy. The preliminary plan document projects an increase in the labor force of 140 thousand between 1977 and 1982 and a rise in employment of 90, 120, and 110 thousand under the three variants referred to above, leading to increases in unemployment of 50, 20, and 30 thousand, respectively. Nonagricultural employment would be 20 thousand higher under the proposed high growth alternative, thus erasing the projected rise of unemployment.

Under the proposed high growth alternative, productivity would also increase more rapidly in manufacturing and in several service sectors than envisaged under the preliminary plan projections. Projected rates of growth of labor productivity under this alternative are 6.6 percent for agriculture, 6.0 percent for mining, 6.3 percent for manufacturing, 0.7 percent for electricity, gas, and water, 1.8 percent for construction, 3.7 percent for transportation and communication, 4.3 percent for trade and banking and 4.6 percent for other services. Correspondingly, the average rate of growth of labor productivity under the high growth alternative is 5.7 percent a year. Taken in conjunction with the estimated rate of growth of total employment of 0.7 percent, a GDP growth rate of 6.5 percent is obtained under this alternative (Table 12.1).

While reliable estimates of employment for earlier years are not available, data contained in the preliminary plan document indicate that these projections roughly correspond to productivity growth for the 1970–1977 period. The exception is agriculture, where an acceleration of productivity growth is foreseen. This is explained by the fact that the poor harvest in 1977 greatly reduced agricultural productivity in that year.

Incremental Capital-Output Ratios and Investment Ratios

As in the case of export growth, in this essay the third variant of the preliminary plan projection was taken as the low estimate for employment and productivity. A different procedure is followed in examining the compatibility of projected rates of GNP growth with incremental capital-output ratios (the ratio of gross investment to the increment in value added) and investment ratios (the ratio of gross fixed investment to the gross domestic product).

Sectoral incremental capital-output ratios have been estimated by revising the preliminary plan projections on the basis of data for past periods. Investment ratios, too, have been estimated on the basis of past experience, with account taken of the policies followed that are discussed below. Finally, combining alternative values of incremental capital-output ratios and investment ratios, alternative projections of the growth of GDP have been derived (Table 12.3).

The incremental capital-output ratio of 5.0 assumed for agriculture in the preliminary plan document is on the high side. This ratio was 4.3 in the period 1958–74,[20] and while the inclusion of the poor harvest years of 1976 and 1977 would raise the average to 5.0, the harvest in the base year will reduce incremental capital-output ratio for the 1977–82 period. And although increased expenditure on irrigation will raise this ratio, the expansion of horticulture for exporting to the European Common Market will act in the opposite direction.

On the basis of these considerations, an incremental capital-output ratio of 4.5 has been assumed for agriculture. In turn, estimates of 2.2 and 2.1 have been adopted for manufacturing industries under the proposed low and the high growth alternatives, respectively, as compared to 2.4 in the preliminary plan document (Table 12.3). Various considerations have led to the choice of these alternatives.

To begin with, the incremental capital-output ratio for manufacturing was 2.3 in the 1958–74 period, and it was approximately 2.0 if one excludes the years of the world recession. This ratio did not reach 3 even in 1977, when output growth in manufacturing was only 2 percent. At the same time, the existence of unused capacity in 1977, as well as specialization in labor-intensive products in trade with the Common Market countries, will reduce the incremental capital-output ratio for the plan period.

With adjustments made for some of the other sectors, overall averages of incremental capital-output ratios of 4.2 and 4.0 are obtained under the proposed low and high growth alternatives as against 4.4 under the third variant of the preliminary plan (Table 12.3). By comparison, the average incremental capital-output ratio was 4.2 in the 1958–74 period and 3.8 excluding the years of the world recession.

The next question concerns the share of gross fixed investment in the gross domestic product. Expressed in terms of 1970 prices, this share was 26.1 percent in 1973, it fell to 20.1 percent in 1974 and to 19.1 percent in 1975, rose again to 19.3 percent in 1976 and to 20.1 percent in 1977. Similar changes are observed in terms of current prices except that, in view of the rise in the relative prices of investment goods, the absolute values are higher (27.3 percent in 1973, 20.2 percent in 1975, and 22.7 percent in 1977).

Assuming that the prices of investment goods will not repeat their rapid increase of recent years, a 25 percent share of gross fixed investment in GDP appears realistic under the proposed low growth alternative. In turn, the investment share may reach 26 percent under the high growth alternative,

TABLE 12.3
Incremental Capital-Output Ratios and Gross Fixed Investment in Greece, 1977–1982
(million drachmas, 1970 prices)

| | Incremental Capital-Output Ratios | | | | | Gross Fixed Investment (Average Annual Rate of Change 1977–1982) | | | | |
| | Preliminary Projections | | | Alternative Projections | | Preliminary Projections | | | Alternative Projections | |
	5.0%	6.0%A	6.0%B	6.0%	6.5%	5.0%	6.0%A	6.0%B	6.0%	6.5%
Agriculture	5.0	5.0	5.0	4.5	4.5	10.0	10.0	10.0	5.9	5.9
Mining	7.9	6.7	6.0	6.0	6.0	3.0	5.0	8.0	8.0	8.0
Manufacturing	3.0	2.5	2.4	2.2	2.1	3.0	8.0	11.0	7.4	8.6
Electricity, Gas and Water	9.0	8.5	8.5	8.5	8.5	16.0	22.0	23.7	23.7	23.7
Transport and Communication	9.8	9.0	9.0	8.5	8.1	6.0	8.0	8.0	6.0	7.3
Dwellings	16.8	15.0	15.0	15.0	15.0	2.9	5.2	2.8	2.8	2.8
Rest of Activities	1.8	1.8	1.8	1.7	1.65	4.1	10.0	7.7	5.25	7.9
Total	4.9	4.47	4.40	4.20	3.95	5.3	8.7	8.2	6.6	7.4

Sources: See Table 12.1.

Note: See Table 12.1.

provided that appropriate policies are followed. A 25 percent investment share in conjunction with an overall incremental capital-output ratio of 4.2 would result in a GDP growth rate of 6.0 percent, while an investment ratio of 26 percent and an overall incremental capital-output ratio of 4.0 would give rise to a GDP growth rate of 6.5 percent.

It should be emphasized that the assumed investment and incremental capital-output ratios are on the conservative side. Thus, even during the world recession years, 24 percent of the gross domestic product was devoted to investment in Greece and the ratio was nearly 27 percent in 1977 when the profit squeeze and uncertain business conditions discouraged investment. Also, the projected incremental capital-output ratios are relatively high compared to historical experience in Greece and in other newly-industrializing countries.

The implications of alternative assumptions can be indicated if we consider that an investment ratio of 27 percent and an incremental capital-output ratio of 3.8 would enable Greece to reach a GDP growth rate of 7.1 percent. Lower incremental capital-output and investment ratios, in turn, would bring forth increases in labor productivity that may permit attaining a 7.1 percent growth rate without undue pressure on labor markets.

An Export-Oriented Growth Model

The model underlying the proposed estimates is characterized by export orientation. This is not a choice but a necessity, given the elimination of trade barriers between Greece and the European Common Market countries in the process of Greece becoming a full member of the EEC. At the same time, the option described in the preliminary plan document under the 5 percent GNP growth alternative is not available to Greece, as this growth rate could not be reached if exports increased only at an average annual rate of 3.5 percent. For reasons noted below, neither could the second variant, entailing a 5.6 percent export growth rate and a 6.0 percent rate of growth of GNP, be considered realistic.

Rapid increases in exports are needed, first of all, to pay for higher imports. The preliminary plan projections understate the prospective expansion of imports. Under the two variants referred to above, imports would rise by 5.6 percent (an import elasticity of 1.1)[22] and 7.7 percent (an import elasticity of 1.3) a year. These estimates do not adequately allow for the potential effects of reductions in tariff and non-tariff barriers on imports into Greece. One is reminded here of the experience of France where the Third Plan assumed that imports would remain unchanged during the 1958–61 plan period. Yet, following entry into the Common Market in 1958, imports, as well as exports, increased rapidly.[23]

For goods produced in Greece, tariffs on imports from the European

Common Market are 50 percent of tariffs applying to imports from elsewhere. Reductions in these tariffs will accelerate during the plan period, with their complete elimination foreseen by 1982. Moreover, Greece will have to adopt the Common Market external tariff, which is substantially lower than the Greek tariff, on imports originating from outside the EEC. A case in point is machinery and equipment, where tariffs on goods produced in Greece averaged 23 percent on all imports and 18 percent on imports from the Common Market countries alone, while the common external tariff of the EEC averages 7 percent.[24]

Greece would also have to equalize the indirect tax treatment of imports and domestic goods that presently favors domestic output and eliminate nontariff import restrictions. Finally, while tariffs on goods not produced in Greece and imported from the EEC were eliminated during the sixties, this has only increased the protection of Greek industry that uses such products as inputs. The elimination of tariffs on commodities imported from the Common Market countries and the equalization of tariffs on commodities imported from elsewhere, will thus result in a considerable reduction in the protection of Greek industries.

The rise in investment activity necessary for reaching a high rate of economic growth will also raise the import elasticity for the plan period, because of the high share of imports in investment goods. One may then adopt an import elasticity of 1.4 under the low GDP growth alternative, resulting in an import growth of 8.4 percent. Parallel with more rapid increases in exports, involving an increased need for imported inputs and entailing greater intraindustry specialization, imports would rise even faster under the high GDP growth alternative. Calculating with an elasticity of 1.8, an import growth rate of 11.7 percent is obtained. The assumed elasticities exceed the import elasticity of 1.2 observed in the period 1970–77 but fall short of the import elasticity of 2.0 in 1977, when the effects of the deterioration of the competitive position of Greek manufacturing were felt.

Increases in exports would also be required in conjunction with the shift of labor from low-productivity to high-productivity industries. More generally, the expansion of exports is necessary to promote structural change which is a precondition for the successful integration of the Greek economy into the European Common Market.

It would appear from the foregoing that domestic supply conditions, rather than foreign demand, represent the main constraint to the growth of exports in Greece. In this connection, the question arises what kind of measures would be necessary to ensure rapid increases in exports and to enable Greek producers to confront foreign competition in the European Common Market. In attempting to provide an answer to this question, consideration will be given to the need to reduce the cost of labor, to increase savings and investment, to adopt an industrial policy, and to reform agriculture in Greece.

Policy Measures for Rapid Growth in the Greek Economy

As noted above, the deterioration of the competitiveness of Greek manufacturing in 1977 resulted from rapid increases in unit labor costs unmatched by a devaluation of the drachma.[26] The rise in labor costs, in turn, contributed to the poor performance of Greek exports in 1977 and to the growth of the volume of imports. The ensuing increase in the trade deficit by one-half billion dollars was not fully offset by higher earnings from invisibles, emigrants' remittances, and deposits by Greeks living abroad, thus necessitating increased reliance on foreign loans.[27]

In order to improve the competitive position of Greek industry, it would be necessary to reduce the cost of labor in terms of foreign currency. This could be accomplished if real wages rise at a lower rate than productivity and the drachma depreciates in real terms. An additional depreciation would be required in order to offset the effects of the elimination of export subsidies under Common Market rules, as well as the effects of the elimination and reduction of tariffs on imports originating in EEC and non-EEC countries, respectively.

Improving competitiveness and effecting industrial transformation would further necessitate increased investment. Thus, there is need to reverse the recent tendency of declining investment in the manufacturing sector. The relevant magnitudes, in terms of billion Drachmas at 1970 prices, are 14.5 in 1973, 14.9 in 1974, 13.1 in 1975 and 1976, and 12.1 in 1977.[28]

Investment may be financed from domestic as well as from foreign savings. Domestic savings have declined in recent years in real terms reflecting the adverse impact of negative real interest rates on personal savings[29] and that of decreases in profit margins on corporate savings. Notwithstanding increases in nominal interest rates in mid-1978, real interest rates paid to savers remained negative and further increases in the rates would contribute to higher private savings. In turn, a slowdown in wage increases would contribute to higher corporate savings through a rise in profit shares.

It would further be desirable to encourage the inflow of foreign direct investment, which brings in foreign capital as well as technological know-how and marketing expertise. The promotion of foreign direct investment under Law 2687/53 has met with little success as outflows exceeded inflows over the years 1975–77. Foreign capital will receive improved treatment under legislation enacted in early 1978, which permits reducing taxable profits up to a limit of 25 percent in the case of new investments in the Athens area and from 50 percent upwards for investments in other regions. However, for these measures to be effective, it would be necessary to simplify procedures for the establishment of foreign industries in Greece that presently involve considerable red tape.

The same tax incentives will be provided to domestic investment in the manufacturing sector. The introduction of these measures represents a welcome reversal of the situation existing in previous years, when the expiration of earlier regulations and delays in issuing new regulations created considerable uncertainty, with adverse effects on the investment climate for domestic and foreign investment alike.

The question remains, however, if the new incentives will suffice to generate the volume of investment necessary for rapid increases in exports and the structural transformation in Greek industry. Investment incentives are substantially greater in Ireland, where grants amounting to 40 percent of the investment in the Dublin area and 60 percent in the rest of the country led to substantial foreign direct investment. These investments, in turn, contributed to the rapid growth of employment, output, and exports in Ireland, notwithstanding slow economic growth elsewhere in the EEC. The Irish experience leads one to suggest that the Greek government should contemplate granting additional incentives to investment along with entry into the European Common Market.

The investment incentives applied in Greece do not discriminate among industrial activities. Proposals were put forward, however, for the government to follow a selective policy in providing advantages to firms in industries where "backward" and "forward" linkages with other industries are the most important; to firms that export or replace imports; as well as to investments in some basic industries.

Apart from possible conflicts among these criteria, each of them is open to objections. The linkage measure fails to consider the country's comparative advantages and its application may lead to a situation where the creation of a high-cost industry becomes an obstacle to the establishment of industries which use its products as inputs. In the early postwar period, this was the case in several developing countries, where the establishment of small-scale, high-cost steel plants became an obstacle to the development of steel-using industries that would have otherwise utilized cheap foreign steel.

Furthermore, foreign exchange earnings from exports and foreign exchange savings from import substitution alone could not provide appropriate criteria, since they do not take account of the domestic resource cost of earning (saving) foreign exchange. A more appropriate measure is the domestic resource-cost ratio, which indicates the amount of domestic resources (labor, land, and capital) needed to earn or save a unit of foreign exchange.

The domestic resource cost ratio, or other measures of social profitability, may be used to evaluate projects in basic industries where the government takes a direct or indirect participation. This is of particular importance since the capital-intensive nature of these industries, including steel, petrochemicals, aluminum and paper, raises questions about their suitability to Greece, where capital is relatively scarce.

Project evaluation cannot play much of a role in industries of transformation, however, where the decisions need to be left to private initiative. Governments are hardly capable of foreseeing changes in world market conditions in industries of transformation, which are characterized by product differentiation and rapid changes in technology and tastes. Rather, firms must take the risks and reap the rewards of their own decisions.

It follows that selective intervention on the part of the government in matters relating to private firms in industries of transformation would not be desirable. This conclusion is strengthened if we consider the administrative difficulties of such intervention and its dangers in the form of political influence peddling and corruption.

Industrial Policy

Improving the competitiveness of Greek industry and encouraging structural transformation would necessitate taking various additional measures. Such desirable measures include revising the legal system and simplifying administrative procedures, encouraging industrial concentration, promoting research and development, establishing specialized industrial estates, furthering technical education, providing preferential credits, modifying labor legislation, and promoting exports. They will be considered in turn.

The legal system would require modifications so as to conform to the needs of a modern industrial society. There is further need to simplify existing regulations and administrative procedures. In particular, steps would need to be taken to reduce the amount of paperwork involved in making relatively simple decisions and to limit the scope of permits and licenses that involve discretionary decisions and bureaucratic delays.

The legal system would also need to be modified in order to encourage industrial concentration. At present, almost 50 percent of the industrial labor force is employed in firms with less than ten workers.[30] Industrial concentration is necessary for Greek industry in order to enable it to confront competition in the markets of the other EEC countries as well as in its own domestic market. This was recognized in France and Italy at the time of the establishment of the European Common Market and the industrial policies of the two countries were largely oriented towards encouraging concentration. As a result, in particular in France, the industrial "landscape" has been transformed, with large enterprises taking the place of small firms in a number of industrial branches.[31]

It is of particular importance to modify existing laws in Greece, under which capital gains on the sale of an asset are taxed at the corporate income tax rate. In the case of mergers, firms should be exempted from this tax as long as the proceeds of the sale are used to finance new investments. Following the example of France, additional tax and credit measures could also be used to encourage mergers in Greek industry.

These considerations should not be interpreted to imply that small-and medium-size firms would not have a role to play in the framework of the Common Market. A modern industrial economy needs firms of different sizes to perform a variety of functions involving specialization in the production of parts, components, accessories, and other inputs. But in cases where economies of scale are of importance, firms need to be of sufficient size to confront competition in the EEC.

Apart from economies of scale in production, economies of scale in research and development provide advantages to large firms. At the same time, research and development may be encouraged by providing tax benefits to firms that undertake such activities. The provision of tax benefits is warranted because of the external economies generated by research and development, the effects of which tend to spread to other firms.

Tax incentives to research and development would benefit in particular the engineering industries, which may be considered "infant industries" in Greece. Since tariff protection cannot be provided following entry into the Common Market, Greece would have to find alternative ways to promote these industries in the period of their infancy.

Engineering industries may be promoted by establishing specialized industrial estates and providing various services in these estates. Industrial estates have been used to advantage in the Far East to encourage the parallel establishment of cooperating firms. The engineering industries would also be helped by improvements in the standards, and increases in the scope of technical and managerial education in Greece, as well as through tax concessions for technical training undertaken by the firms themselves.

Another measure of particular interest to the engineering industries include the provision of long-term loans for industrial investment with government guarantees. This would represent a change from the present situation in Greece, where mortgages provide the principal collateral for lending. More generally, the Greek banking system would need to be modernized in order to extend the scope of activities the banks finance.

A case in point is the financing of the indemnities firms will have to pay under existing legislation to workers who will be discharged in conjunction with the industrial transformation necessary to prepare Greece for the Common Market. The need to reduce product variety and to close down inefficient plants would also require modifying existing rules under which firms can discharge only six percent of their labor force in a particular year.

As noted above, export subsidies are not permitted under Common Market rules. There are, however, promotional measures that are permissible under these rules. They include the organization of trade fairs, the collection of market information, and the establishment of specialized trading companies. The implementation of such measures is desirable in order to encourage Greek manufactured exports.

Agricultural Policies

As regards agriculture, linkages with the manufacturing industry need first to be considered. Such linkages are of particular importance in the provision of inputs for food processing, which presently suffers from the uneven quality and the uncertain supply of raw materials, especially in production for export. The government may contribute to improving the situation through its educational effort and by making improved seeds available.

Irrigation and preferential credits for the purchase of farm equipment would also help to increase agricultural productivity. At the same time, it would be desirable to link these schemes to the consolidation of land holdings, given the fragmentation of land holdings in Greece land consolidation can importantly contribute to productivity growth. Finally, as in other countries, extension services may importantly contribute to the goal of high productivity.

Conclusions

In this essay, the proposition has been put forward that Greece has the potential to reach a 6.5 percent, and possibly even 7 percent, rate of economic growth during the period of the 1978–82 five-year plan. The application of various policy measures has been recommended to realize this potential, involving in particular export expansion in the framework of the European Common Market.

To begin with, there is need to slow down increases in real wages in order to improve the competitiveness of Greek industry and to increase profit margins, both of which were adversely affected by the acceleration of wage increases in 1976 and 1977. Having taken the lead in allowing large increases in public sector wages and in the minimum wage in the past two years,[32] it is incumbent on the government to take the lead in moderating wage increases. This would involve limiting increases in minimum wages and in public sector wages, and exerting pressure on private firms to refuse large wage increases.

Apart from higher profit margins, the investment effort would be helped by increasing real interest rates to savers, encouraging the inflow of foreign direct investment, and increasing investment incentives to domestic as well as to foreign investors. Furthermore, a variety of industrial policy measures have been proposed to improve the competitiveness of Greek industry and encourage structural transformation. At the same time, the proposed agricultural policy measures would contribute to agricultural as well as industrial expansion the latter by providing inputs for further processing.

Several of the proposed policy measures involve a budgetary cost. Their financing may be assured, first of all, by reducing public consumption expenditures, which have increased rapidly in recent years. Foregoing the implementation of large capital-intensive projects, such as the proposed petrochemical complex, would represent further budgetary savings. Finally, income tax collection efforts may be improved in Greece.

ESSAY 13

Policies for Stable Economic Growth in Turkey

Introduction

This essay will review Turkey's growth performance during the sixties and the seventies and make recommendations for policies for stable economic growth by taking the policy reforms instituted in the Spring of 1979 as the point of departure. The adjective 'stable' refers to the goal of mitigating the pronounced cyclical pattern that has characterized Turkish economic growth in the past.

Section I will provide the background for the policy recommendations. It will examine Turkey's growth performance in relation to other newly-industrializing countries, and analyze the effects of special factors on economic growth in Turkey. In turn, Section II will describe the Turkish economic situation prior to the policy changes introduced in the Spring of 1979. Comparisons will further be made with the situation existing in Brazil in the mid-sixties, and reference will be made to the economic effects of the policy reform carried out at that time in Brazil. This will be followed by an evaluation of the policy measures adopted in Turkey between March and June 1979.

In Section III, policy recommendations will be put forward for adopting an outward-oriented strategy that would make increased use of market signals. The policy measures under consideration pertain to exchange rates, the system of protection, the allocation of investment funds, the treatment of foreign investment, interest rates and capital markets, the reform of administrative procedures, and reforms in the state enterprise sector.

I. Turkey's Growth Performance in an International Perspective

Economic Growth in Major Semi-Industrial Countries, 1960–78

Table 13.1 shows average annual growth rates of GNP, population, and per capita GNP in the periods 1960–66, 1966–73, 1960–73, 1973–75, 1975–78

TABLE 13.1
GNP, Population and Per Capita GNP Growth Rates in Newly-Industrializing Countries

	1973 (absolute values)	1960–66	1966–73	1960–73	1973–75	1975–78	1973–78
Greece							
Y	19.0	7.2	7.6	7.4	0.8	5.1	4.0
P	8.9	0.5	0.4	0.5	0.7	1.3	1.1
Y/P	2127	7.0	7.2	6.8	0.1	3.8	2.9
Portugal							
Y	12.3	6.3	7.7	7.1	−3.0	4.6	1.6
P	9.1	0.2	0.2	−0.1	1.9	1.2	1.5
Y/P	1348	6.1	7.5	7.2	−4.9	3.4	0.1
Spain							
Y	89.9	8.0	6.3	6.7	3.0	2.3	2.3
P	34.5	1.1	1.0	1.1	1.5	1.4	1.4
Y/P	2603	6.9	5.3	5.7	1.5	0.9	0.9
Turkey							
Y	28.1	5.9	6.5	6.3	7.4	4.8	6.0
P	38.1	2.5	2.5	2.5	2.5	2.1	2.3
Y/P	738	3.4	4.0	3.8	4.9	2.7	3.7
Yugoslavia							
Y	29.2	6.1	7.0	6.2	6.4	6.2	5.6
P	21.0	1.1	0.9	1.0	2.9	0.9	0.9
Y/P	1395	5.0	6.1	5.2	5.4	5.2	5.4
Korea							
Y	20.2	7.1	9.2	8.6	7.0	12.1	10.4
P	33.3	2.5	2.1	2.3	1.9	1.9	1.9
Y/P	605	4.6	7.1	6.3	5.1	10.3	8.5
Taiwan							
Y	12.1	8.6	10.0	9.3	1.5	10.1	7.0
P	15.5	2.9	2.2	2.5	1.9	2.2	2.1
Y/P	782	5.7	7.8	6.8	−0.4	8.0	4.9
Brazil							
Y	90.2	3.8	10.0	6.7	7.2	6.0	6.5
P	103.6	2.9	2.9	2.9	2.8	2.8	2.8
Y/P	870.0	1.0	7.1	3.9	4.4	3.1	3.6

Source: World Bank data bank.

Notes: Y=GNP (in U.S. $ billion); P=Population (in million); Y/P=Per Capita GNP (in U.S. $). Growth rates of GNP population and per capita GNP have been estimated by regressing annual data, expressed in constant domestic prices, on time.

and 1973–78, for selected newly-industrializing countries which may be considered representative of alternative development strategies. They include five Southern European countries: Greece, Portugal, Spain, Turkey and Yugoslavia; two Far Eastern countries: Korea and Taiwan; and a Latin American country: Brazil. In the following, changes in per capita incomes will be used to evaluate the growth performance of these countries.

Among non-European countries, economic growth accelerated in the 1960–66 period in Korea and Taiwan which adopted export-oriented policies in the early sixties (Table 13.1). In turn, continued reliance on import substitution behind high protective barriers encountered limitations in Brazil, contributing to the decline in the rate of economic growth experienced during this period. With subsequent policy changes in the direction of export-orientation, economic growth acelerated in Brazil between 1966 and 1973.[1] In the same period, a further acceleration of growth occurred in the two Far Eastern countries that have provided practically free trade treatment to exports.

In Southern Europe, per capita income growth rates were consistently higher in countries with a greater export-orientation (Greece, Portugal, and Spain) than in Turkey, which—with the partial exception of the devaluation episode of 1970—continued to follow a policy oriented towards import substitution. This conclusion also applies, though differences in growth performance are smaller, if Turkey is compared with Yugoslavia, where a partial reversal of export-oriented policies occurred during the sixties. For the 1960–73 period, taken as a whole, per capital incomes rose at an average annual rate of 6.8 percent in Greece, 6.9 percent in Portugal, 5.7 percent in Spain, 3.8 percent in Turkey, and 5.2 percent in Yugoslavia.

The import substitution-orientation of the Turkish economy is indicated by the relatively low shares of merchandise exports and imports in GNP that averaged 7.8 percent in 1973 (Table 13.2). In the same year, the relevant figures for the other Southern European countries were: Greece, 14.7 percent; Portugal, 21.2 percent; Spain, 10.5 percent; and Yugoslavia, 19.9 percent. Finally, average export and import shares were 28.6 percent in Korea and 40.2 percent in Taiwan and reached 8.2 percent in Brazil, the largest semi-industrial developing country in terms of GNP, having risen from 5.6 percent in 1966 following the policy reform in the mid-sixties.[2]

All the countries under consideration were adversely affected by the quadrupling of oil prices in late 1973 and suffered the effects of the 1974–75 world recession. Policy reactions to these changes, however, varied from country to country. In the Far East, Taiwan accepted a virtual economic standstill in the years 1974–75, followed by the resumption of rapid economic growth based on the continued pursuit of an outward-oriented strategy. The slowdown was of lesser magnitude in Korea, where vigorous export promotion efforts led to the rapid expansion of manufactured exports from mid-1975.[3]

The policies followed by the two Far Eastern countries permitted them to

TABLE 13.2
Export Shares, Export and Import Growth Rates, and Capital Inflow Shares in Newly-Industrializing Countries

	Merchandise Export and Import Shares in GNP, 1973		1973–78 Average Annual Growth Rates of the Volume of Merchandise Trade		Share of Net Capital Inflow in GNP					
	Exports	Imports	Exports	Imports	1973	1974	1975	1976	1977	1978
Greece	8.6	20.7	8.4	1.9	7.1	6.4	4.7	4.7	4.7	3.9
Portugal	16.0	26.4	0.6	1.1	-3.0	6.2	5.1	8.1	9.3	4.4
Spain	7.3	13.6	11.9	1.5	-8.3	3.7	3.4	4.1	2.1	-1.6
Turkey	5.8	9.7	2.5	3.1	-2.8	2.1	5.0	4.7	6.9	2.8
Yugoslavia	15.4	24.3	5.3	2.4	-2.6	4.9	3.7	-0.5	4.0	2.1
Korea	24.7	32.5	19.7	14.8	2.3	11.3	9.5	1.1	0.0	2.4
Taiwan	43.1	37.3	14.5	9.1	-5.6	8.1	4.0	-1.9	-5.0	-7.2
Brazil	7.7	8.7	4.8	2.4	2.7	7.2	5.7	4.6	3.1	3.8

Sources: IMF: *International Financial Statistics*, and World Bank data bank.

Note: Net capital inflow has been equated to the current account deficit; it thus includes changes in foreign exchange reserves. Negative figures refer to a net capital outflow.

rapidly surmount the adverse effects of the world recession on exports, so that between 1973 and 1978 the volume of exports grew at an average annual rate of 14.5 percent in Taiwan and 19.7 percent in Korea. In Southern Europe, the continuation of an export-oriented stance contributed to the maintenance of high export growth rates in Greece (8.4 percent) and Spain (11.9 percent). And while Greece and, to a lesser extent, Spain, supplemented their export earnings by foreign borrowing, they accepted an increase in import volume much smaller (1.9 and 1.5 percent, respectively) than that of exports.

Export growth rates also exceeded the growth of imports in Brazil (4.8 percent and 2.4 percent) and Yugoslavia (5.3 percent and 2.4 percent). At the same time, Brazil and, to a lesser extent, Yugoslavia, relied on foreign borrowing in order to reach high rates of economic growth. Finally, Portugal extensively used foreign loans to offset the economic dislocations attendant upon the April 1974 Revolution. With policy improvements following the stabilization of the political situation, however, the volume of Portuguese exports surpassed the 1973 level in 1978 and the share of foreign borrowing in GNP declined to a considerable extent.

In Turkey, efforts made to maintain high rates of economic expansion through increased foreign borrowing led to an increase in the volume of imports by one-half between 1973 and 1977. Thus, whereas in the other newly-industrializing countries under consideration the share of foreign borrowing in GNP tended to decline over time, it rose in Turkey, reaching 6.9 percent in 1977. With increased difficulties encountered in borrowing abroad, this share decreased in 1978, leading to a substantial fall of imports and a slowdown of economic growth.

Notwithstanding the decline experienced in 1978, the annual average rate of increase of imports in Turkey exceeded that of exports for the period taken as a whole. Exports were adversely affected by the appreciation of the real exchange rate,[4] and their share in GNP fell from 5.8 percent in 1973 to 4.5 percent in 1978, despite the operation of special factors in the latter year, (p. 300) discussed below.

Economic Growth in Turkey: An Evaluation

While the more export-oriented newly-industrializing countries experienced higher rates of economic growth, the 3.9 percent average annual increase of incomes per head in Turkey nonetheless represented a doubling of per capita incomes between 1960 and 1978. In this connection, the question arises what factors explain Turkey's growth performance under policies followed.

As shown in the Appendix, the movement of labor from agriculture to industry and services importantly contributed to economic growth in Turkey during the period under consideration. It is further apparent, that the protection of industry and the disprotection of agriculture gave rise to an overestimation of the rate of productivity growth on the national economic level.

The intersectoral movement of labor and increases in total employment were supported by the high level of investment activity in Turkey. But, new investment brought successively smaller increments of output and created fewer jobs per capital invested. According to estimates based on official Turkish data, the overall incremental capital-output ratio increased from 2.3 in 1963–67 to 2.6 in 1968–72 and to 3.8 in 1973–77, while the amount of investment per job created, expressed in 1976 prices, rose from TL373 thousand to TL522 thousand and, again, to TL722 thousand.

The observed changes are explained in large part by the increasing capital-intensity of the manufacturing sector associated with continuing import-substitution. Thus, the incremental capital-output ratio in manufacturing rose from 1.6 in 1963–67 to 2.4 in 1968–72 and to 4.7 in 1973–77. Parallel with these changes, the amount of investment per job created, again expressed in 1976 prices, increased from TL267 thousand to TL363 thousand and, finally, to TL572 thousand.

The implications of alternatives to import substitution for the growth of the Turkish manufacturing sector have been examined by Anne Krueger, who estimated the hypothetical growth rate of value added in the manufacturing sector for the 1967–72 period on the assumption that a balanced export promotion and import substitution policy was followed. Measured in world market prices, a growth rate of 16.5 percent is obtained under this alternative as compared to 10.3 percent under the plan allocation.[5] The differences are explained by the fact that, due to the capital-intensive nature of import substitution, incremental capital-output ratios under the plan were 48 percent higher than under a balanced policy, which has been defined as one that would have allocated new investment in proportion to each industry's value added in the base year, 1967.[6] At the same time, the method applied underestimates the extent of inefficiencies under the import substitution strategy followed by Turkey, since there were high-cost import substituting industries already in the base year.

It appears, then, that the continued pursuit of the strategy of import substitution gave rise to inefficiencies in Turkey. This conclusion is supported by the fact that while the contribution of import substitution to the growth of the manufacturing sector was positive in the period 1963–68, it turned negative in the period 1968–73,[7] reflecting in part the decline in net foreign exchange savings from import substitution.

At the same time, foreign exchange savings in import-substituting industries were obtained at a high cost to the domestic economy. In 1965, for example, the average ratio of domestic resource costs, estimated at the shadow prices of the factors of production, to net foreign exchange savings (earnings) was 3.4 times higher in ten import-substituting industries than in five export industries.[8]

Notwithstanding the inefficiencies associated with the import substitution strategy, Turkey was able to avoid a decline in the rate of economic growth until 1977 because of increases in the share of gross fixed investment in GDP.

According to official statistics, this share increased from 16.0 percent in 1963–67 to 18.0 percent in 1968–72 and, again, to 22.9 percent in 1973–77. With incremental capital-labor ratios rising more rapidly than incremental capital-output ratios, the rise in the rate of investment did not however suffice to fully absorb increases in the labor force, and unemployment rates as well as the share of "discouraged" workers in the potential labor force showed continuing increases.[9]

The growth of investment, in turn, can be attributed to special factors, viz. increases in workers' remittances[10] and foreign borrowing. Recorded workers' remittances rose from negligible amounts in 1966 to 5.6 percent of GNP in 1973. In the latter year, workers' remittances reached 94 percent of the value of merchandise exports and surpassed by a substantial margin the net value of exports (i.e. exports less the imported inputs used in export production).

Recorded workers' remittances, expressed in terms of U.S. dollars, declined from the peak of $1.7 billion reached in 1974 and did not attain $1.2 billion in recent years. The resulting decline in the ratio of recorded remittances to merchandise exports and GNP appears to have been offset, however, by remittances channeled through the parallel foreign exchange market. By 1977, these 'unofficial' remittances reportedly exceeded recorded remittances by a considerable margin[11], so that the recorded and unrecorded remittances combined may have amounted to 6 percent of GNP.

Moreover, after the oil crisis and the 1974–75 world recession, Turkey borrowed substantial amounts abroad. By 1977, the net capital inflow was nearly double that of export value and approached 7 percent of GNP, as compared to practically nil in the early seventies. As noted above, the subsequent decline in foreign borrowing to 3 percent of GNP is explained by the limited availability of foreign funds.

Apart from contributing to increased investments, workers' remittances and the inflow of foreign capital have had multiplicative effects on Turkey's GDP, due to the existence of foreign exchange stringency that has been aggravated to a considerable extent in recent years. According to one study, in the period 1973–77 the growth rate of GDP would have been 1.2 percentage points lower if net foreign borrowing did not exceed its assumed "normal" level. The corresponding figures are 3.7 percentage points for the growth rate of consumption and 7.5 percentage points for that of investment.[12]

With lower foreign borrowing, then, the rate of growth of domestic investment and consumption would have declined much more than that of GDP as borrowing permitted raising domestic expenditure much above domestic production. At the same time, the estimated figures represent the lower limit of possible values. To begin with, the norm of foreign borrowing chosen much exceeds the average for the period preceding the oil crisis.[13] Moreover, the method applied underestimates the adverse effects of foreign exchange stringency.[14] Finally, the calculations assume that a flexible exchange rate policy would have been followed, with the exchange rate maintained at equilibrium levels throughout the period. In fact, Turkey has not applied such a policy during the period under consideration, and the shortfall in GDP and in domestic expenditure would have been larger under nonoptimal (fixed) exchange rate policies.

Similar considerations apply to workers' remittances. At the same time, there is an important difference between the two, inasmuch as the former but not the latter gives rise to foreign indebtedness. In fact, with much of Turkey's debt being short-term, the servicing of the debt exceeded $1.0 billion in 1978, amounting to 35 percent of the exports of goods and services. This ratio is estimated at 45 percent in 1979.

II. The Turkish Economic Situation and Policy Changes in the First Half of 1979

The Turkish Economic Situation in Early 1979

Debt-service ratios, calculated for a particular year, abstract from the dynamics of economic development. Thus, historical experience shows that large borrowing on a temporary basis will not adversely affect a country's creditworthiness, provided that it is followed by rapid export expansion, which reduces the debt-service ratio over time.

In the post-1973 situation, Korea provides a par excellence case of such a development. After foreign borrowing reached 11.3 percent of GNP in 1974 and 9.5 percent in 1975, exports increased rapidly, reducing the ratio of debt service obligations to previously-contracted debt and eliminating the need for further foreign borrowing. Similar developments occurred in Taiwan, except that the extent of foreign borrowing in 1974 and 1975 had been smaller and this has subsequently given rise to a net inflow of capital.

Similar developments did not occur in Turkey, where the debt-service ratio increased in 1978, notwithstanding the fact that the drawing-down of inventories accumulated previously gave a boost to exports in that year. Also, as noted above, in the years following the oil crisis, imports increased to a considerable extent, surpassing the growth of exports in volume terms. Yet, in view of the deterioration of Turkey's terms of trade due to the quadrupling of oil prices, adding about $0.5 billion (approximately 2 percent of GNP) to Turkey's import bill in 1974, balance of payments equilibrium would have required reducing imports and increasing exports.

Insufficient export increases and the excessive rise of imports may be explained, in large part, by the direct and indirect effects of foreign borrowing. For one thing, the increase in incomes made possible by foreign borrowing syphoned off part of the exportable surplus and led to higher imports. For another thing, the inflow of foreign capital permitted an appreciation of the exchange rate in real terms, with adverse effects on exports and imports.

Compared to the situation existing in 1973, by the first quarter of 1979 the real exchange rate appreciated by 26 or 31 percent vis-à-vis the U.S. dollar and by 18 or 24 percent vis-à-vis the currencies of Turkey's major trading partners, on the average, depending on whether use was made of the wholesale price index compiled by the Business Research and Publications Department of the Ministry of Commerce or by the Istanbul Chamber of Commerce (Table 13.3).

At the same time, the exchange rate applicable in 1973 already represented a considerable appreciation as compared to the situation existing after the large devaluation in 1970. Moreover, the calculations abstract from the fact that Turkey should have devalued more than purchasing power parity relationships, expressed in the real exchange rate calculations, would indicate. According to Dervis and Robinson, the quadrupling of oil prices would have required a devaluation 22 percent greater than that indicated by purchasing power parity relationships. And, according to these authors, increases in the export prices of the developed countries would have required an additional 12 percent devaluation in order to offset the resulting deterioration of Turkey's terms of trade.[15] As the ratio of export to import prices in Turkey declined by 22 percent between 1973 and 1977, these estimates imply that an additional 1.5 percent devaluation would have been needed to offset each one percent deterioration of the terms of trade.

The adverse effects of the appreciation of the real exchange rate on exports was offset only in small part by increases in export rebate rates.[16] At the same time, available evidence points to the existence of a positive correlation between real exchange rates and export performance. Thus, it has been shown that the ratio of exports to value added in agriculture and industry follows changes in the real exchange rate with some time lag.[17] In particular, exports reacted strongly to the 1970 devaluation.

While exporters received the official exchange rate augmented by rebates,[18] "implicit" exchange rates on imports were much higher and varied greatly from product to product. Thus, tariffs were high and show considerable dispersion; advance deposit requirements were in effect on most imports; and, furthermore, the scarcity value of imports varied depending on access to import licenses and to foreign exchange allocation. The situation was aggravated by reason of the fact that, in the past two years, foreign exchange allocations for private imports were practically unavailable. Private importers thus had to obtain foreign exchange on the parallel market while, at the same time, they were obligated to make advance import deposits.

The increased scarcity of foreign exchange is indicated by changes in the ratio of the parallel market rate to the official rate. Taking the price of gold ingots in Turkey as compared to that in the London market to be representative of this difference, the percentage excess of the parallel market rate over the official exchange rate rose from 4 percent in January 1975 to 18 percent in December 1975, fell to 14 percent in December 1976, and increased again to

TABLE 13.3
Real Exchange Rates in Turkey, 1967–1979

Period	Exchange Rate Lira/Dollar	Index of the Exchange Rate	Index of Relative Prices vis-à-vis the United States		Index of Relative Prices vis-à-vis Turkey's Trading Partners		Index of the Real Exchange Rate vis-à-vis the U.S. Dollar		Index of the Real Exchange Rate vis-à-vis the Currencies of Turkey's Trading Partners	
			A	B	A	B	A	B	A	B
1967	9.000	63.6	69.2	68.2	81.4	80.3	91.9	93.3	78.1	79.2
1968	9.000	63.6	69.6	66.6	85.0	81.3	91.4	95.5	74.8	78.2
1969	9.000	63.6	71.9	69.4	88.2	85.1	88.5	91.6	72.1	74.7
1970	11.500	81.3	74.1	73.9	87.9	87.7	109.7	110.0	92.5	92.7
1971	14.917	105.4	83.1	83.2	95.3	95.4	126.8	126.7	110.6	110.5
1972	14.150	100.0	93.8	93.9	100.9	101.3	106.6	106.5	99.1	98.7
1973	14.150	100.0	100.0	100.0	100.0	100.0	100.0	100.0	100.0	100.0
1974	13.927	98.4	109.2	106.7	109.2	106.6	90.1	92.2	90.1	92.3
1975	14.442	102.1	110.0	108.5	108.7	107.1	92.8	94.1	93.9	95.3
1976	16.053	113.4	121.6	121.4	125.6	125.3	93.3	93.4	90.3	90.5
1977	18.002	127.2	142.1	146.5	142.1	146.5	89.5	86.8	89.5	86.8
Q1	17.002	120.2	131.2	133.8	133.2	135.8	91.6	89.8	90.2	88.5
Q2	17.675	124.9	135.8	136.4	137.6	138.4	92.0	91.6	90.8	90.2
Q3	17.889	126.4	142.5	146.0	141.9	145.5	88.7	86.6	89.1	86.9
Q4	19.443	137.4	160.9	165.4	156.9	161.3	85.4	83.1	87.6	85.2
1978	24.282	171.6	201.1	209.3	186.9	194.6	85.3	82.0	91.8	88.1
Q1	21.379	151.1	176.8	180.5	165.7	169.1	85.5	83.7	91.2	89.4
Q2	25.250	178.4	190.5	197.9	181.9	189.0	93.6	90.1	98.1	94.4
Q3	25.250	178.4	206.5	214.8	190.7	198.4	86.4	83.1	93.6	89.9
Q4	25.250	178.4	219.9	238.0	197.9	214.2	81.1	75.0	90.1	83.3

TABLE 13.3 (Cont'd.)
Real Exchange Rates in Turkey, 1967–1979

Period	Exchange Rate Lira/Dollar	Index of the Exchange Rate	Index of Relative Prices vis-à-vis the United States		Index of Relative Prices vis-à-vis Turkey's Trading Partners		Index of the Real Exchange Rate vis-à-vis the U.S. Dollar		Index of the Real Exchange Rate vis-à-vis the Currencies of Turkey's Trading Partners	
			A	B	A	B	A	B	A	B
1979										
Q_1	25.250	178.4	239.7	259.5	216.5	234.4	74.4	68.7	82.4	76.1
Q_2	31.020	219.2	279.5	305.3	258.6	282.5	78.4	71.8	84.8	77.6
As of June 11	47.100	332.9	293.2	320.2	272.2	297.3	113.5	104.0	122.3	112.0
September I	47.100	332.9	321.0	350.6	300.8	328.5	103.7	95.0	110.7	101.3
II	47.100	332.9	330.3	364.3	309.5	341.3	100.8	91.4	107.6	97.5
December I	47.100	332.9	351.4	383.8	332.4	363.1	94.7	86.7	100.2	91.7
II	47.100	332.9	372.1	410.4	352.0	388.2	89.5	81.1	94.6	85.8

Sources: International Monetary Fund, *Direction of Trade*, and *International Financial Statistics*, various issues. Turkey June 1979 exchange rate: Official Gazette, June 11, 1979.

Notes: The index of the real exchange rate has been calculated by adjusting an index of the nominal exchange rate for changes in wholesale prices at home and abroad. Calculations for Turkey's principal trading partners, covering 63.8 percent of Turkish exports and 67.6 percent of Turkish imports in 1973. (the United States, Belgium, France, Germany, Italy, Netherlands, Switzerland, and United Kingdom) have been made by weighting with the sum of exports and imports combined in the year 1973. The sources for Turkish wholesale price indexes are: (A) Business Research and Publications Department of the Department of Commerce, and (B) Chamber of Commerce, Istanbul.

Starting in June 1979, the real exchange rate has been calculated under the assumption that the premium inclusive rate of 47.10 continues to apply in Turkey and that dollar exchange rates for other countries also remain the same. Price indices for Turkey's trading partners have been extrapolated by using the average monthly inflation rate for the preceding twelve months. In the case of Turkey, it has been assumed that the reported price increase of 7.8 percent in April has been followed by increases of 6.0 percent in May and in June. The projections for September and December 1979 have been made under alternative assumptions as to the rate of inflation in Turkey. Variant I assumes increases in wholesale prices of 4 percent, variant II 5 percent, per month.

32 percent in December 1977.[19] By March 1979, the difference between the two rates reached 100 percent.

Estimates on the importance of the parallel foreign exchange market vary. Transaction values in 1976 were estimated at $1.6 billion by the Istanbul Chamber of Commerce and $2.1 billion by the Turkish Industrialists and Businessmen's Association.[20] And, with the increased unavailability of foreign exchange, the importance of the parallel exchange market greatly increased in subsequent years.

Apart from the *level* of the real exchange rate and of the rates of protection, exports and imports are affected by *fluctuations* in these rates. Quarterly data for the years 1977 and 1978 shown in Table 13.3 exhibit considerable variations in real exchange rates. The variations are even greater if we extend the time series backward to 1970 and forward to June 1979.

Fluctuations in real exchange rates associated with intermittent and unforeseen devaluations, as well as changes in rebate rates, create uncertainty for exporters since they cannot foresee future developments in the domestic currency equivalent of export receipts and in the relationship between their revenues and costs. Importers and import-substituting industries protected by tariffs, too, are also subject to uncertainty.[21] And, uncertainty is created for the government itself as shifts take place between the official and the parallel foreign exchange markets in response to changes in the real exchange rate.

Negative real interest rates, also, have adverse effects on economic activity.[22] Thus, there is evidence that the savings rate is positively correlated with the real rate of interest in Turkey.[23] Also, in providing inducements to channel savings into real estate, gold, and foreign assets, highly negative real interest rates reduced the availability of savings for productive uses and contributed to Turkey's balance of payments deficit. Finally, the allocation of savings available for productive uses is subject to inefficiencies, since interest rates cannot fulfill their role as a rationing device.

The described factors adversely affected economic activity in Turkey, leading to disruptions in work and underutilized capacity. According to a recent survey of the Istanbul Chamber of Industry, average capacity utilization in manufacturing was 55.8 percent in 1978, with the ratios being much higher than the average in industries based on domestic inputs, such as mining (80.0 percent), forestry products (71.9 percent) and food processing (76.3 percent), and the ceramics industry (65.2 percent) and below the average in most industries using imported inputs.[24] At the same time, these figures tend to understate the extent of the underutilization of capacity as they take one-shift operations as the norm.

Excluding industries based on domestic inputs, over 50 percent of respondents stated that the shortage of foreign exchange was the principal factor resulting in low capacity utilization. Another one-fifth of respondents indicated insufficient demand, mostly in regard to intermediate products, which is largely related to foreign exchange shortages in user industries.[25]

Finally, one-tenth of the respondents named local material shortages and another one-tenth power outage and shortages as the principal cause of the underutilization of capacity. In the industries in question, shortages of domestic materials were in large part related to the foreign exchange difficulties. The scarcity of foreign exchange also contributed to energy outages and shortages.[26]

While comparable data for earlier periods are not available, it appears that capacity utilization levels in 1978 were substantially lower than on the occasion of previous foreign exchange crises. This fact, together with the existence of higher open and disguised unemployment and the much larger and more enduring current account balance deficits,[27] indicate that the present crisis is much more serious than the previous ones.

The Consequences of Import Substitution Policies

Turkey offers a number of similarities with the economic situation in Brazil prior to the reforms of the mid-sixties. Both countries moved beyond the first "easy" stage of import substitution, involving the replacement of the imports of nondurable consumer goods and their inputs by domestic production, and extended this to intermediate products, and consumer durables that tend to be more capital-intensive, require large-scale operations as well as the availability of parts, components and accessories at a low cost.

Import substitution was carried out behind high protection, entailing considerable discrimination against primary activities and against manufactured exports. The two countries also maintained overvalued exchange rates and adjusted those rates only intermittently, thereby creating an additional burden for exporters. At the same time, the use of tariffs and quantitative controls gave rise to considerable differences in incentives among import-substituting activities as well as among export activities that used protected domestic inputs. Finally, both countries had negative real interest rates and fragmented credit markets, with preferred borrowers (usually in import-substitution industries) benefiting at the expense of others.

The effects of the policies followed in the two countries were also rather similar. After rapid expansion, they experienced a decline in net foreign exchange savings in import substituting activities, a rise in capital-output ratios, and a decrease in rates of export expansion, with adverse repercussions for economic growth. And while in Turkey the effects of workers' remittances and foreign borrowing delayed the decline of the rate of GNP growth until 1977, as noted above growth would have been more rapid if different policies were followed.

Certain differences in the economic situation prevailing in Brazil in the mid-sixties and in Turkey in the late seventies, should however be noted. Turkey enjoys the benefits of proximity to European and Middle Eastern markets and preferential access to the EEC whereas participation in LAFTA provides limited benefits in Brazil. Furthermore, import substitution in Turkey has been less far-reaching than it had been in Brazil in the mid-sixties, although the possibilities for efficient import substitution, too, were greater in the larger Brazilian market. At the same time, the share of exports in GNP was one-third lower in Turkey in 1978 than it was in 1966 in Brazil.

Last but not least, the present economic situation in Turkey may be judged more serious than that of Brazil in the mid-sixties. The foreign exchange shortage, and the resulting distortions in relative prices, are considerably greater, as is the balance of payments deficit and foreign indebtedness, in particular short-term debt. And, unlike Brazil, Turkey has a large state enterprise sector which, after earlier contributions to industrial development, suffers from low efficiency levels and an antiquated system of management.

Notwithstanding these differences, the similarities in the policies followed and in their economic effects lend interest to the policy reform instituted in Brazil in the mid-sixties, and the impact of these measures on the Brazilian economy. These are described in Essay 10 of the present volume.

The success of the policy reform in Brazil provides lessons for Turkey. At the same time, given the differences in the economic situation, in the institutional framework, and in attitudes towards particular policy measures, it cannot be suggested that Turkey applies the same policies as Brazil did in the mid-sixties. These considerations are reflected in the policy recommendations made in Section III of the essay, following an evaluation of recent policy changes in Turkey.

Policy Changes in Turkey, March–June 1979

A variety of measures were taken by the government between March and June 1979 in order to improve the economic situation in Turkey. The measures pertain to exchange rates, prices, the state economic enterprises, the budget deficit, and interest rates. They will be considered in the following.

The Turkish lira was devalued by 6.0 percent on April 5, 1979, bringing the rate to TL 26.50 per U.S. dollar, with an additional premium provided for tourist receipts and workers remittances on a degressive scale. Furthermore, exporters of manufactured goods were permitted to retain one-half of their export receipts for their own use or for transfer to their direct and indirect suppliers who had import licenses.

On June 11, an exchange rate was set of TL 35.00 to the dollar, with a premium of TL 12.10 on all sales of foreign currency except for traditional agricultural exports that are subject to support prices determined by the government,[28] and on all purchases of foreign currency except for the importation of crude oil and its derivates, and the raw materials used in producing fertilizer. At the same time, however, export rebate rates for manufactured exports were reduced by 5 to 15 percentage points and rebates on fruit and vegetable exports were abolished.

Exceptions made for agricultural exports appear to reflect the desire to avoid creating large rents to producers that would otherwise result since the expansion of agricultural output takes time. At the same time, a lower exchange rate was set for imported inputs in fertilizer production so as to prevent increasing production costs in agriculture. However, one may query the decision of applying the TL 35.00 rate to the importation of petroleum and its derivatives as the adoption of a higher rate would be conducive to energy savings.

In turn, the application of the TL 47.10 rate to all other foreign exchange transactions is to be welcomed. The adoption of this rate will give a boost to manufactured exports by increasing their profitability, when the large excess capacity augments the possibilities for export expansion. Furthermore, import savings may be realized as the privileged recipients of import licenses respond to the higher cost of imports.

The experience of May 1979 also indicates that immigrants' remittances respond positively to the exchange rate. Finally, the higher exchange rate will permit the tourist sector to reduce prices in terms of foreign currency, thereby contributing to increased demand on the part of foreign tourists, given the high substitution elasticity in tourism as between different countries.[29]

Table 13.3 provides information on real exchange rates in Turkey following the June 11 devaluation, by taking TL 47.10 as the relevant nominal exchange rate. Compared to the situation existing in 1973, the results show a depreciation of the real exchange rate by 4 to 14 percent vis-à-vis the U.S. dollar and by 12 to 22 percent vis-à-vis the currencies of Turkey's main trading partners. These comparisons do not, however, take account of the depreciation necessary to offset the deterioration of the terms of trade by 33 percent between 1973 and 1978 or that due to the rise of oil prices in 1979. And, an additional depreciation would be warranted if one chose as benchmark the situation existing in 1971 when the exchange rate was particularly favorable to exports.

Furthermore, if recent trends continue, inflationary developments will soon undo the beneficial effects of the devaluation. This could be avoided if the government adopted a sliding peg on the example of Brazil and other Latin American countries, with further devaluations occurring *pari passu* with changes in relative prices. However, decisions have apparently been taken to maintain the adjustable peg system.

The last four rows of Table 13.3 show real exchange rates calculated on the assumption that differential inflationary trends in Turkey and in its major trading partners continue, and that exchange rates are maintained at existing levels. It appears that, even under favorable assumptions as regards the rate of inflation in Turkey, the real exchange rate would return to nearly its 1973 level by September 1979 and it would fall below this level by December 1979. We will return to the policy implications of these results in Section III below.

The calculations shown under Variants I and II are based on the assumptions that wholesale prices in Turkey would rise by 4 and 5 percent a month, respectively, between June and December 1979, representing annual rates of increase of 60 and 80 percent under the two variants. By comparison, wholesale prices rose at an average rate of 4.9 percent per month in the first quarter of 1979 and approximately 6.5 percent per month in the second quarter, when the prices of a variety of commodities and services produced by state economic enterprises (SEEs) were substantially increased. At the same time, keeping inflation below 5 percent a month would require reducing the deficit of the public sector and slowing down increases in wages.

Steps to reduce the public sector deficit were taken in the Spring of 1979, when the prices of SEE products were raised and ceilings were imposed on the expansion of employment in the public sector, on the deficit of the SEEs, on Central Bank credits to the public sector, and on the net domestic assets of the Central Bank. The imposition of these ceilings should have favorable effects on inflation by reducing the rate of money creation that has been associated with the public sector deficit in the past. Increases in minimum wages in the nonagricultural sector, from TL110 to TL180 per day in May 1979, will however add to cost-inflationary pressures, even though almost the entire increase represents compensation for the rise of consumer prices since minimum wages were last determined in January–February 1978. Also, recent wage settlements in the private sector represent annual increases of about 100 percent, and in June 1978 minimum wages for agricultural and forestry workers were raised by 78 percent.

Finally, interest rates on savings deposits were raised in May 1979, with the new rates ranging from 8 percent on savings deposits between 3 and 6 months, to 24 percent on deposits between 3 and 4 years, and a premium of 10 percentage points provided on the repatriated savings of migrant workers. At the same time, interest rates on nonpreferential loans were raised to 20 percent.

Notwithstanding increases in nominal interest rates, real rates of interest remain negative by a substantial margin. Even assuming a rate of inflation of 4 percent a month, real interest rates are between −36 and −52 percent on deposits by domestic savers, −26 and −42 percent on deposits of migrant workers, and −40 percent on nonpreferential loans. Apart from the situation existing prior to the policy reform in Brazil, there are few examples of such high levels of negative real interest rates.

III. Policies for the Future

Towards Greater Export Orientation

We have seen that the continuation of a strategy of import substitution entailed increasing economic costs and only through a combination of workers' remittances and foreign borrowing could Turkey avoid a decline in the rate of economic growth until 1977. Foreign borrowing also made it possible to postpone effecting the "transfer" implicit in the deterioration of the terms of trade which was largely due to the quadrupling of oil prices in late 1973.

Growing foreign indebtedness, however, gave rise to a substantial debt service burden while limiting the possibilities for additional borrowing. As a result, economic growth has decelerated, with per capital incomes rising by about one percent in 1978 and declining at the same rate in 1979; this compares with average increases of 4.1 percent in the years 1975–77. Turkey thus faces the short-term problem of servicing its foreign debt and effecting the transfer implicit in the deterioration of the terms of trade through increased exports and reduced imports as well as the long-term problem of adopting a development strategy for sustained economic growth.

At Turkey's present stage of economic development, the growth objective would be served by a strategy of increased export orientation which contributes to the efficient use of economic resources. This strategy would also contribute to the short-term objective of improving the balance of payments, so that the use of appropriate policy measures would make it possible to avoid a conflict between short-term and long-term objectives.

Increased export orientation, in turn, necessitates placing greater reliance on market forces in both the private and the public sectors. While central decisions may be appropriately taken in regard to a few large import-substituting investments, exporting requires decisions by individual firms that have to continuously adapt to the needs of foreign markets. At the same time, in order to ensure that the decision taken by firms correspond to national economic interests, appropriate incentives need to be provided.

Pursuing these objectives calls for adopting a variety of policy measures that support each other. The measures in question include the provision of appropriate market signals by adopting and maintaining realistic exchange rates and interest rates and reforming the system of protection, as well as changes in institutional arrangements by re-allocating investment funds towards export industries, increasing the efficiency of financial markets, simplifying administrative procedures, and reforming the state enterprise sector. These policy measures will be considered in the following.

Exchange Rate Policy

The devaluation of June 1979 has improved the competitive position of Turkish enterprises to a considerable extent. At the same time, as shown above, competitiveness would decline again over the next few months if the new exchange rate was maintained unchanged in the face of differential inflationary trends at home and abroad. Furthermore, the objectives of reducing uncertainty for exporters and importers and of avoiding economic instability would call for changes in exchange rates to take place in small steps, so as to maintain real exchange rates constant.

While the sliding peg found easy acceptance in Brazil, the exchange rate has become a political issue in Turkey, with every devaluation seen as requiring political courage. It may be difficult, therefore, to envisage the adoption of a sliding peg for the present and, even if it were adopted, there would be a danger that the government may not carry out the devaluation that would be warranted by relative price changes.

In this situation, there is a virtue in automaticity. Correspondingly, it is suggested here that reliance be based on the parallel exchange market for all transactions to which the TL47.10 rate applies at present. This may be accomplished by raising the rate of foreign exchange retention for manufactured exports to 100 percent, allowing for the full transferability of these receipts between exporters and importers, and transferring to the parallel market tourist receipts and expenditures, immigrants' remittances, and all non-governmental imports that are presently subject to the TL47.10 rate.[30]

The proposed transfer of transactions to the parallel foreign exchange market would avoid the re-emergence of the overvaluation of the Turkish lira and fluctuations in its real value, thereby reducing uncertainty for exporters and importers and contributing to stable economic growth. Furthermore, in channeling import transactions by private and by public firms to the parallel exchange market, one would capture the scarcity rent on foreign exchange that presently accrues to the recipients of import licenses and increase the integration of state enterprises in the market economy. This is highly desirable since, in the absence of appropriate price signals, the recent imposition of export targets on state enterprises may be met at a high cost to the national economy.

At the same time, the inflationary effects of the proposed measures should not be exaggerated. With the parallel market rate reportedly used by private and public importers in pricing goods for sale in the domestic market, capturing the scarcity rent in these transactions would not generally result in higher prices. And while the prices of manufacturing and nontraditional agricultural exports would rise, exporters may not adjust their prices to the full extent of the change in the exchange rate in order to improve their competitive position in foreign markets. But, at any rate, increases in export prices would be necessary in order to provide incentives to expand exports.

The above recommendations are given urgency by the rise of oil prices in the first half of 1979. Given the expected geographical composition of Turkish oil imports,[31] increases in oil prices may average about 60 percent for Turkey. At 1978 import levels, the additional cost would be about three-quarter billion dollars, equal to over one-fourth of the value of merchandise exports and 2 percent of GNP.[32] Thus, while Turkey has relied on foreign loans to postpone effecting the "transfer" implicit in the deterioration of the terms of trade after

1973, it now has another "transfer" to cope with. At the same time, foreign borrowing has given rise to substantial financial obligations for the repayment of short-term loans and the servicing of the medium- and long-term debt.[33]

Correspondingly, while an immediate extension of the parallel exchange market to traditional agricultural exports does not appear desirable in order to avoid creating rents for producers, provisions would need to be made for the subsequent integration of the two exchange markets, with commensurate changes in support prices, so as to provide adequate incentives for the expansion of agricultural exports.[34] This conclusion is strengthened if we consider that large differences between the parallel market rate and the official exchange rate would create excessive incentives for exporting agricultural products in processed rather than in crude form.

The proposed measures aim at effecting the transfer implicit in the deterioration of the terms of trade through increased production for export. Given the magnitude of the task involved, it would further be necessary to limit the rise of domestic consumption by reducing the public sector deficit and moderating wage increases. As a result of these actions, inflationary pressures would also be moderated.

Reforming the System of Protection

The proposed extension of the use of the parallel exchange market would represent a first step in the reform of the system of protection. In order to improve the efficiency of resource allocation for sustained economic growth, it would need to be followed by further steps. These should aim at reducing discrimination against primary and manufactured exports and rationalizing the system of tariffs and subsidies.

Except for hazelnuts, in which Turkey has a quasi-monopoly position, it would be desirable to extend the application of the parallel market rate to all primary exports, with corresponding increases in support prices. Increases in agricultural product prices, in turn, should be accompanied by the elimination of various input and credit subsidies to agriculture. It would further be desirable to increase agricultural taxation, preferably in the form of a land tax. Such a tax may be introduced as a *quid pro quo* for raising the exchange rate and agricultural support prices.

Discrimination against the exports of manufactured goods vis-à-vis import substitution is associated with the protection of domestic sales in the form of tariffs, quota restrictions, and import licensing. Tariffs (customs duties) on manufactured goods were generally in the 30–60 percent range in 1973,[35] to which a customs surcharge (15 percent of customs duty), stamp duty (9.0–9.5 percent of cif value) and pier duty (5 percent of the cif value of imports, customs duty, surcharge, and clearance expenses, combined) should be added.[36] At the same time, effective rates of protection, i.e. the protection of value added in the production process, are substantially higher than nominal rates, given that various inputs, e.g. iron and steel, enter duty free.[37]

Customs duties and other charges changed little since 1973. However, with increased foreign exchange stringency, import restrictions have come to be increasingly applied, thus raising the protection of domestic industry and increasing discrimination against exports. Changes in this situation would be necessary, lest exports do not receive adequate incentives.

The bias against manufactured exports may be reduced by offsetting the taxes and tariffs that burden exports and by providing direct or indirect export subsidies. Firstly, on the example of other European countries, one would have to ensure that export rebates provide full compensation for indirect taxes paid at the last and at all previous stages of the manufacturing process. Exporters should also receive rebates for duties paid on direct as well as indirect imported inputs, which is not considered a subsidy under GATT rules. Furthermore, the growth of exports would require the extension of the existing export credit scheme, the implementation of the proposed export insurance scheme and, as discussed below, the increased availability of credits for production and investment in export industries.

Additional incentives to exports may be provided by way of a direct subsidy or indirectly through tariff reductions and the liberalization of imports that reduces incentives to import substitution. A combination of the two alternatives may be appropriate in the case of Turkey. For one thing, subsidies to manufactured exports would provide advantages to manufacturing industries which is desirable at Turkey's present stage of economic development. For another thing, reductions in import protection would avoid excessive discrimination against primary activities and may be linked to a reform of the system of tariffs and import restrictions, with a view to lessening disparities in rates of protection.

Reducing discrimination against exports would have beneficial effects for the national economy as it would permit earning foreign exchange at a lower domestic cost than foreign exchange is save through import substitution and employment would tend to increase. Nevertheless, the proposed changes in the system of protection may be postponed until the effects of the extension of the parallel exchange market and the full rebating of indirect taxes and tariffs on export expansion become apparent.

The Allocation of Investment Funds

Providing incentives to exports is a necessary but not a sufficient condition of export expansion. Channeling resources into export activities would also require the availability of credits for export production as well as for investment in export activities. This may be accomplished by modifying the allocation of investment funds, increasing their volume, and improving the efficiency of financial markets.

Increasing the availability of investment funds for manufactured exports would necessitate modifying the investment allocation for the manufacturing sector in the Fourth Five Year Plan (1978–83), which calls for a 71.5 percent investment share for intermediate products as against a 15.8 percent share for investment goods and durable consumer goods and a 12.7 percent share for nondurable consumer goods. Among intermediate products, petrochemicals and petroleum products, with a planned investment allocation of 13.6 percent, and primary metals, with an allocation of 32.3 percent (iron and steel, 26.0 percent and nonferrous metals, 6.3 percent), would receive the bulk of the total.[38] In turn, among nondurable consumer goods, food processing would receive an allocation of 4.9 percent, and textiles and clothing 5.7 percent.[39]

This allocation appears to conflict with the projected annual average rate of growth of 25 percent for manufactured exports.[40] Also, investments in intermediate products have a long gestation period while the existing foreign exchange stringency in Turkey puts a premium on quick-yielding investments. And, in the situation of capital scarcity observed in Turkey, industries producing intermediate products, on the average, have capital-output and capital-labor ratios several times higher than either nondurable consumer goods or investment goods and durable consumer goods.

According to the data of the Fourth Five Year Plan, incremental capital-output ratios for the 1978–83 period are 54 percent higher in industries producing intermediate products than the overall average for the manufacturing sector. The difference is especially large for iron and steel (199 percent) and for nonferrous metals (55 percent); it is lower for petro-chemicals and petroleum products (10 percent) since the investments undertaken during the previous period will come on stream between 1978 and 1983. By contrast, the incremental capital-output ratio is only 43 percent of the overall average in the case of nondurable consumer goods (of which, 34 percent for food processing and 51 percent for textiles and clothing) and 65 percent for investment goods and durable consumer goods.[41]

Data on incremental capital-output ratios are affected by the length of the period of investment. Such is not the case for capital-labor ratios obtained for a particular year that relate installed capital to actual employment. Data obtained for the United States indicate that capital requirements per job in petroleum refining and products are 6.1 times the overall average for the manufacturing sector while the corresponding ratio for primary metals is 1.6. By contrast, capital requirements per job are 46 percent of the overall average for textiles, 10 percent for clothing, 49 percent on nonelectrical machinery, 35 percent on electrical machinery, and 57 percent for transportation equipment; comparable data for food processing are not available.[42]

High capital-output and capital-labor ratios in petroleum products and primary metals, together with the expected oversupply of petroleum products in the world market and the poor quality of iron ore and coking coal in Turkey, make a *prima facie* case against the further expansion of these industries. This conclusion does not apply to forest products, leather, and ceramics which have relatively low capital-output and capital-labor ratios and make use of domestic materials.

Nondurable consumer goods industries rely largely on domestic materials and utilize Turkey's abundant and relatively cheap manpower. Export possibilities are especially good in nearby Arab markets that presently account for less than 10 percent of Turkish exports. And while the exports of textiles and clothing and of some simple processed food are subject to limitations in the European Common Market, Turkey benefits from its preferential access to the EEC in these commodities and does not encounter barriers for most food preparations.

The availability of low-cost skilled and semi-skilled labor also bestows advantages on Turkey in the production of investment goods and durable consumer goods that are relatively labor-intensive. Also, these goods are rarely subject to quantitative restrictions and bear low tariffs in the Common Market and in other developed countries.

The expansion of industries producing investment goods and durable consumer goods and their inputs may be regarded as the next step in Turkey's industrial development. At the same time, in view of the importance of economies of scale in these industries, the parallel expansion of production for domestic and for export markets would be desirable.

The above considerations point to the need for increasing the amount of investment funds available to consumer goods and investment goods industries and reducing the investment allocation of industries producing intermediate products during the Fourth Plan period. The time thereby gained may be used for the economic project evaluation of the proposed investments in industries producing intermediate goods. Such evaluations should be made in terms of world market prices which represent the alternatives available to Turkey.

Furthermore, the planned 1.2 percent share of tourism in total investment under the Fourth Five Year Plan[43] is not commensurate with Turkey's possibilities for expanding tourism. Given its favorable climate, the natural beauty of the country, and the presence of a large number of archeological sites, tourism has considerable potential in Turkey and could earn foreign exchange at a relatively low cost in terms of domestic resources while contributing to regional development.

The implementation of these recommendations would entail increasing the investment share of the private, as compared to the public, sector. Such a shift would occur as lower investment allocations to state enterprises would increase the availability of investment funds to the private sector by reducing claims on private savings and lowering the "inflation tax" that has adversely affected the real value of these savings in the past.[44]

Increased investments by the private sector would also be desirable for the pursuit of an outward-oriented strategy, since private firms may better respond to the needs of foreign markets and take the risks necessary for successful exporting. In turn, a cutback in the public investment program in manufacturing would permit limiting the inflationary effects of deficit financing that would otherwise be likely to continue, given the overambitious targets for public savings in the Fourth Five Year Plan.

Considering further the substantial delays experienced by state enterprises in implementing investment projects, a moratorium on new public investment projects in manufacturing may seem desirable. This would permit concentrating attention on the completion of ongoing projects and undertaking an economic evaluation of the proposed new investment projects as suggested above. But, ongoing investment projects in the public sectors would also need to be re-evaluated as the investment expenditures necessary for completing them (TL924 million) exceed the entire allocation of the Fourth Five Year Plan to public investments (TL898 million). The differences are even larger for public investments in the manufacturing sector which equal TL199 million in the Plan as compared to TL257 million of the investment needs of ongoing public projects in this sector.[45] At the same time, a number of these investments are at an early stage and can be documented or postponed.

The Treatment of Foreign Investment

We have noted the need for the parallel expansion of the domestic and export sales of industries producing capital goods and durable consumer goods. This is because, in the presence of substantial economies of scale, production for domestic markets alone would lead to small-scale manufacture at a high cost. Such an outcome is in fact observed in the automobile industry, where the average number of cars produced per plant in Turkey is only three percent of that in the European Common Market.[46]

The above considerations also apply to the production of parts, components, and accessories. Government regulations have required firms producing automobiles, buses, and trucks to raise the "national content" of their production to 90 percent, 80 percent, and 75 percent, respectively, by 1978. These targets have been attained in the case of bus manufacture, and national content appear to be about 70 percent for automobiles and 60 percent for trucks.[47] At the same time, increases in national content have entailed the small-scale production of parts, components, and accessories, with consequent high costs.

A more appropriate solution is to concentrate on the production of selected parts, components, and accessories for domestic use and for export and to import others. In this way, the same amount of foreign exchange may be earned at a much lower domestic resource cost since economies of scale can be exploited. Such an alternative also commends itself if the provisions of Turkey's association agreement with the European Common Market are to be implemented.

In the transport equipment industry, aircraft provides another example of the need for Turkey's participation in the international division of the production process. Rather than the local production of aircraft, envisaged in the Annual Programme for 1979, Turkey should carve out for itself a share in the huge world market for aircraft parts and components where duty free entry will be ensured under the Tokyo round of negotiations.

Participation in the international division of the production process in transport equipment would permit Turkey to concentrate on the production of relatively labor-intensive parts, components, and accessories, where it has a comparative advantage. Similar considerations apply to the metal working, machine tool, and electrical and nonelectrical machinery industries. At the same time, subcontracting arrangements in these industries may require the participation of foreign capital. Foreign participation may also contribute to the export-oriented production of capital goods, which are subject to rapid changes in technology. In this connection, reference may be made to the example of Brazil where foreign firms have spearheaded the expansion of the exports of investment goods.

Foreign capital accounts for a small proportion of total industrial investment in Turkey. On December 31, 1977, the total amount of foreign investment was TL2.2 billion as compared to paid-up capital of TL28.4 billion in the hundred largest industrial corporations in 1976.[48] And, the share of foreign investment is even smaller if comparison is made with total capital stock in the manufacturing sector. This is indicated by the fact that foreign capital accounts for only 3 percent of value added in manufacturing.

At the same time, the share of foreign capital in manufacturing investment in Turkey is on the decline. Thus, "there are no recent examples of foreign companies receiving incentives, and there has been little foreign investment activity in Turkey in the past few years."[49] These results reflect the negative attitude towards foreign investment and the bureaucratic difficulties experienced in the course of the approval process. In 1976, for example, while foreign investors made requests for the expansion of capacity in six cases and for new investment in four cases, altogether eight approvals were issued and there were eight cancellations in the same year.[50]

And while a more positive attitude towards foreign investment was expressed by the Ecevit government, the measures actually taken point in the opposite direction. Under the 1978 decree the foreign investor has to take an obligation to increase the national content of its production and to establish "research and development centres" for the advancement of technology. Also, with the exception of investments undertaken exclusively for export, the share of foreign capital may not exceed 50 percent.

These requirements appear overly restrictive. As noted above, increasing national content leads to higher production costs, thus reducing the competitiveness of Turkish industry. Also, greater competition at home and abroad is likely to give more inducement to technological improvements than the formal requirement for establishing "research and development centres." Finally, making exceptions to the 50 percent rule is of particular importance in regard to the investments necessary for the exploitation of Turkey's potential in food processing where foreign marketing is of crucial importance; for the establishment of plants to cater to Middle Eastern markets where delays may lead to the loss of these markets; and for the expansion of tourism where foreign expertise in construction, management, and marketing is needed.

These conclusions are strengthened if we consider that, apart from the apport of technology and marketing know-how, foreign direct investment would add the availability of foreign exchange in Turkey that is necessary to provide a "cushion" during the transitional period, as noted below. Also, it would further add to the availability of investible funds that would permit increased output and employment in Turkey.

Interest Rates and Capital Markets

While foreign investment will add to the availability of investible funds, further efforts would need to be made to increase public and private savings in Turkey. Public savings would rise as a result of measures taken to reduce the deficit of the public sector. In turn, the generation of private savings would require changes in interest rate policy.

Recent increases in interest rates are welcome but they have not fully compensated for the acceleration of inflation. Correspondingly, interest rates are not sufficiently attractive to savers, in particular for longer maturities, severely limiting the availability of long-term finance to private firms. Also, the maximum interest rate on long-term loans by TSKB, the Industrial Development Bank of Turkey, is above the rate it has to pay for funds of similar maturity.

Correspondingly, credit markets and institutions cannot appropriately fulfill their function of generating funds for new investments. In fact, in actual practice, private borrowers are limited to loans of two year maturity. Furthermore, the increase of the withholding tax on dividends led to a practical halt of stock market transactions after April 1978.

In order to increase savings, to channel savings to productive investments, and to ensure stability in the growth process, it would be necessary to raise real interest rates in Turkey and to avoid fluctuations in these rates. In this connection, reference may be made to Fry's estimates cited earlier that show a positive correlation between real interest rates and private savings in Turkey. Similar results were observed in recent years when the decline in real interest rates was associated with a fall in the marginal saving ratio that turned negative as inflation accelerated in 1978.[51] Note further that dramatic increases in private savings occurred in several Asian countries which have established positive real interest rates.[52]

Setting higher real interest rates also improves the allocation of investment funds since the interest rate can again serve as a rationing device. As

McKinnon has noted[53] negative real interest rates lead to the misallocation of investment funds, in part because producers prefer low-return self-investment to negative returns on savings and in part because arbitrariness is introduced as the government and banks make choices among would-be borrowers, whose claims exceed the amount of available investment funds. Last but not least, higher real interest rates would have beneficial effects on Turkey's balance of payments by reducing the desirability of gold purchases, which reportedly amounted to $600 million in 1978, and diminishing the profitability of investment abroad.

As a first step, one may abolish interest rate ceilings on medium-and long-term obligations and loans. Consideration may also be given to the indexing of financial obligations that has been used to good effect in Brazil. Furthermore, there would be need for taking measures to encourage the development of bond and stock markets in Turkey.

Reforming Administrative Procedures

Administrative procedures are notoriously inefficient in Turkey and would need to be simplified in order to ensure the success of an export-oriented strategy. Increasing foreign exchange retention to 100 percent in regard to manufactured exports would serve this objective, as one would avoid the need for foreign exchange allocation to purchase imported inputs, which is a time-consuming and uncertain process. Thus, in the first quarter of 1979, exporters of manufactured goods requested foreign exchange allocation of $14.4 million for projected exports of $176 million and received $9.8 million.

It would further be desirable to abolish export licensing, which has purportedly been used to provide for the needs of domestic users (cement) or to encourage exportation in processed form (synthetic fibers). Such interventions create uncertainty for the exporter, may lead to the loss of export markets, and unduly interfere with the operation of domestic markets.

Also, there would be need for streamlining the system of investment incentives, which take the form of tax exemptions, accelerated depreciation, exemptions from or reductions in customs duties, interest rate rebates, and permission to use external credits. While since 1973 the investment incentives available to sectors that meet certain criteria have been specified in the so-called promotion tables, discretionary decision-making continues in the selection of the recipients and in the choice and the extent of the incentive measures. At the same time, the scope of activities listed in the promotion tables varies, thereby creating uncertainty in firm decision-making.[54] Furthermore, the inclusion of activities in the list and changes over time do not appear to have a clear economic rationale and, with it being a "positive list," it may exclude activities that are socially profitable.

Correspondingly, it would be desirable to replace the "positive list" by a "negative list" that would specify activities which are *not* eligible for investment incentives. The exclusions should be limited in number, comprising activities where foreign markets are restricted or domestic over-capacity exists. All other activities should receive investment incentives automatically.

The handling of applications by potential foreign investors would also need to be streamlined by simplifying existing procedures and concentrating decision-making in a single agency, so as to ensure that decisions are taken expeditiously. Apart from reducing bureaucratic obstacles, a positive policy of attracting foreign direct investment would be needed. In this regard, Turkey may learn from the experience of Ireland which has attracted foreign investment into export industries.

There is further need to reform the system of import allocation that has increasingly become subject to discretionary decision-making as foreign exchange scarcity intensified. In creating uncertainty for the domestic producer, discretionary decision-making interferes with rational operations and it may lead to the interruption of production and low capacity utilization. Following improvements in the balance of payments, it would be desirable to gradually phase out quotas and import licensing, with exceptions made for luxury goods that are not produced domestically.

Reforms in the State Enterprise Sector

State economic enterprises (SEEs) dominate in infrastructure, in the production of intermediate products, and play an important role in textiles, machinery, and electrical equipment in Turkey. While in earlier periods the SEEs had made a substantial contribution to Turkey's industrial development, in recent years, they have been plagued by increasing losses. These losses have contributed to money creation and, in conjunction with the investment requirements of the SEEs, have reduced the availability of funds for private investment as noted above.

Part of the explanation for the large losses of the SEEs lies in the lack of price adjustments for cost increases until the Spring of 1979. An additional factor has been the pressure exerted on these enterprises to increase employment which doubled between 1970 and 1978 as a result. Pressure to increase employment, in turn, represents a manifestation of the prominence given to noneconomic factors in the management of the SEEs. The quality of management has further suffered by reason of the prevalence of political factors in choosing managers and in constituting the Boards of SEEs, the frequent interventions on the part of the ministries, and the low level of managerial compensation.[55]

Regarding the comparative performance of public and private firms in the textile sector, a technical study concludes that the publicly-owned Sümerbank group has been unable to mount a creditable export offensive, its efficiencies are not comparable to those of the best private firms, much of its plant is run down, and some of its recent investments—in the production of rayon, for example—were poorly conceived and poorly executed." Also, "the quality of yarn produced in the private sector was of marked superiority to that of the yarn in the Sümerbank mills. . . . "[56] While similarly detailed comparisons have not been made for other industries, available data show that the state manufacturing enterprises have fallen behind their private counterparts in regard to both the productivity of labor and that of capital.

For one thing, in practically every manufacturing industry, labor productivity is higher in the private than in the public sector, with the unweighted average of the ratio of labor productivities in the two sectors being 1.68 in a 23 industry breakdown.[57] For another thing, increases in the share of the public sector in manufacturing investments from 32.7 percent in 1963–67 to 43.6 percent in 1973–77 were accompanied by a decline in their share in manufacturing value added from 35.8 to 31.4 percent.[58] High-cost production in the state manufacturing enterprises, in turn, has been sustained by protection and by the budgetary financing of losses.

A reform of the state enterprise structure should aim at increasing the contribution of the SEEs to the national economy. In infrastructure, this would require reducing costs while practicing full-cost pricing. In the manufacturing sector, improvements in the international competitiveness of the state enterprises should be the principal objective. Pursuing this objective would, in turn, necessitate increasingly integrating these enterprises in the market economy and providing appropriate incentives to management.

Following the example of Western European countries and, among socialist countries, Hungary,[59] the state enterprises should become self-managed and self-supporting units. Their managers should be chosen by, and be made responsible to, a Board independent from the Government, with the remuneration of management being made dependent on the firm's profits. The latter recommendation assumes the application of market prices to the output and the inputs of state enterprises, and the rationalization of these prices through the adoption of realistic exchange rates and interest rates and, subsequently, the reform of the system of protection.

Conclusions

Following an analysis of the Turkish growth experience in an international context and a review of the economic situation existing in mid-1979, in this essay recommendations have been made for future policy changes in Turkey. The recommendations aim at attaining stable economic growth in the framework of an outward-oriented strategy while contributing to the short-term objective of improving the balance of payments.

The recommendations call for extending the scope of the parallel exchange market, with a view to avoiding the re-emergence of the overvaluation of the Turkish lira and fluctuations in its value. This would initially exclude traditional agricultural exports subject to support prices, which now receive the TL 35.00 rate.

The stated objectives would also be served by reducing discrimination against exports, increasing public and private savings, channeling savings towards export activities, and improving the operation of financial markets. Increases in private savings and the improved operation of financial markets would, in turn, necessitate raising real interest rates. Furthermore, there is a need to improve the treatment of foreign direct investment since it brings technological know-how and contributes to exports.

The proposed measures would represent a shift from direct interventions to greater reliance on markets. Such a shift is overdue, given the increased sophistication of the Turkish economy and the need for greater export orientation which, in turn, requires incentives rather than quantitative targets. At the same time, apart from contributing to economic growth, export orientation would have beneficial effects on employment and hence on the distribution of incomes.

By contrast, import substitution in intermediate products tends to be capital intensive, thus limiting the growth of employment. Also, under present conditions, substantial profits may be made by the recipients of import licenses and by dealers in the parallel foreign exchange market. Finally, large firms associated with banks are at an advantage vis-à-vis medium-size and small firms in obtaining foreign exchange on the parallel market as well as scarce credits.

The proposed policy measures support each other and should be considered a package. Thus, changing exchange rates will have limited effects unless funds are provided for the expansion of export industries. Nor will it suffice to raise real interest rates as long as a substantial part of investment is not subject to economic project evaluation. In fact, for the proposed measures to have their full impact, the state economic enterprises need to be brought more fully into the market economy.

Note further that, apart from providing incentives to export, the described policy measures would contribute to efficient import substitution as well. As we have seen, in the machinery and equipment industries exporting and efficient import substitution go hand in hand. Equalizing rates of import protection will also contribute to efficient import substitution. Finally, this objective would be served by economic project evaluation in state enterprises.

It should be understood that it will take time until the full effects of the proposed measures will be felt. Correspondingly, the government needs a "cushion" to ease the transition from a large balance of payments deficit to an equilibrium position and from an import substitution strategy to an export orientation. Attracting foreign direct investment would help in this regard, but it would further be necessary for the developed countries to provide substantial financial assistance once decisions are reached by the Turkish government on the implementation of the necessary measures.

Appendix

Economic Growth in Turkey: A Statistical Re-appraisal

In examining Turkey's growth performance, one needs to separate the effects of sectoral growth rates of labor productivity (for short, sectoral productivity growth) and those of the intersectoral movement of the labor force. This has been done in Appendix Table 13.1 where hypothetical rates of overall productivity growth have been calculated on the assumption that the sectoral composition of the labor force remained unchanged between 1967 and 1977. The difference between the reported rate of productivity growth, 4.9 percent a year (Variant A), and that calculated on the assumption of the unchanged sectoral composition of the labor force, 2.7 percent a year (Variant B)[60], indicates the impact of the intersectoral movement of the labor force on overall productivity growth.

The movement of labor from low-productivity agriculture to high-productivity industry and services is an integral part of the growth process in a developing economy. There is evidence, however, that intersectoral productivity differences have been overstated in Turkey, thereby leading to an overestimation of overall productivity growth. This question will be considered in the following, utilizing international comparisons and data on protection in Turkey.

In 1967, the base year of the calculations, the ratio of labor productivity in industry to that in agriculture was estimated as 4.23 in Turkey, while the corresponding ratio for services as compared to agriculture was 5.41. These figures much exceed the average ratios estimated by Simon Kuznets[61] for countries with per capita incomes in the $200–574 range in 1958, the group to which Turkey belonged in the base year (1967) of the calculations. The relevant ratios are 2.11 in the industry-agriculture, and 2.61 in the services-agriculture, comparison. The ratios are even smaller for the income group below $200 a year (1.38 and 1.78) and over $574 a year (1.14 and 1.12).

Applying average productivity ratios estimated for the $200–574 income group to Turkey in the year 1967, and taking overall productivity levels in that year as given, the resulting labor productivity figures are shown in column 1967C of Appendix Table 13.1. Applying further actual rates of sectoral productivity growth between 1967 and 1977 to these figures, and calculating with actual employment data in the 1977, we have derived the hypothetical labor productivity figures reproduced in column 1977C of Appendix Table 13.1. The resulting estimates show a 4.1 percent annual average rate of growth of overall productivity between 1967 and 1977 as compared to the reported rate of productivity growth of 4.9 percent.

The application of average sectoral productivity ratios for the $200–574 income group to Turkey may be interpreted as a way to correct for distortions in relative prices resulting from the Turkish system of protection. While intercountry differences in natural resources and in capital-labor ratios also

APPENDIX TABLE 13.1
Gross Domestic Product, Employment, and Productivity in Turkey, 1967–1977[1]

	(absolute figures)							(growth rates)			
	1967	1967C	1967D	1977A	1977B	1977C	1977D	1967-77A	1967-77B	1967-77C	1967-77D
Value Added (TL million, 1968 prices)	93737	93737	93737	183321	148491	169952	174984	6.9	4.7	6.1	6.4
Agriculture	30506	46577	40107	42508	53471	64914	55893	3.4	5.8	3.4	3.4
Industry	24452	18613	14851	55314	42817	42102	33952	8.5	5.8	8.5	8.5
Services	38779	28547	38779	85499	52203	62936	85499	8.2	3.0	8.2	8.2
Employment (thousands)	11621	11621	11621	14151	14151	14151	14151	2.0	2.0	2.0	2.0
Agriculture	8160	8160	8160	7900	9937	1900	7900	-0.3	2.0	-0.3	-0.3
Industry	1545	1545	1545	2430	1881	2430	2430	4.6	2.0	4.6	4.6
Services	1916	1916	1916	3821	2333	3821	3821	7.1	2.0	7.1	7.1
Labor Productivity (TL)	8066	8066	8066	12955	10494	12010	12365	4.9	2.7	4.1	4.4
Agriculture	3738	5708	4915	5381	5381	8217	7075	3.7	3.7	3.7	3.7
Industry	15827	12047	9612	22763	22763	17326	13824	3.7	3.7	3.7	3.7
Services	20240	14899	20240	22376	22376	16471	22376	1.0	1.0	1.0	1.0

Source: Organization for Economic Cooperation and Development, *Turkey*. [1] Paris, OECD Economic Surveys, November 1978. Some of the inconsistent productivity data have been corrected by accepting data on sectoral value added and employment as accurate.

Notes: Variant A: Actual figures. Variant B: Hypothetical figures calculated on the assumption of the unchanged sectoral composition of the labor force between 1967 and 1977. Variant C: Sectoral productivity figures for 1967 calculated on the assumption that productivity ratios in industry-agriculture and services—agriculture comparisons in Turkey were the same in 1967 as in countries with per capita incomes of $200 to $574 in 1958 (Simon Kuznets, *Modern Economic Growth—Rate Structure and Spread*, New Haven, Yale University Press, 1966, pp. 402–3) while taking overall productivity levels in 1967 in Turkey as given and calculating with observed sectoral employment and productivity growth rates. Variant D: Sectoral output and productivity figures re-estimated in terms of world market prices by utilizing ratios between domestic and world market value added of 1.70 for agriculture and 3.68 for industry while taking overall productivity level in 1977 as given and calculating with observed sectoral employment and productivity growth rates.

affect the outcome, it does not appear that these differences would have introduced a bias in the comparisons.

One may also address the issue of relative prices more directly by making adjustments for the price distortions actually observed in Turkey. This has been done on the assumption that, in the absence of price distortions, world market price relations would apply to Turkey. This assumption may be considered realistic as, with the exception of hazelnuts (accounting for 14 percent of exports in recent years) where it has a quasi-monopoly position, Turkey can trade at world market prices. Thus, world market prices will represent the opportunities available to Turkey and may be used to evaluate its rate of economic growth.

According to estimates made by Hasan Olgun in the framework of a 26-sector input-output table, in 1968 the ratios of domestic to world market value added in manufacturing and in agriculture, respectively, were 4.15 and 1.70 at the actual exchange rate.[62] These estimates have been used to derive the sectoral composition of Turkish GNP in 1967 in terms of world market prices, by taking total GDP as given and assuming that value added in the service sector is unaffected by protection.[63] The resulting estimates, shown in Column 1967D of Appendix Table 13.1, have in turn been utilized to re-estimate rates of overall productivity growth in terms of world market prices. This estimate is 4.4 percent a year for the period 1967–77.[64]

These results will overstate, however, the rate of growth of overall labor productivity in Turkey, in part because differences within the manufacturing sector are neglected and in part because no adjustment is made for the overpricing of services. As to the former, Anne Krueger has estimated that in the 1967–72 period the use of domestic prices has entailed an overestimation of the average annual rate of growth of the manufacturing sector under the plan allocation by 0.8 percent as compared to estimation in world market prices.[65] Correspondingly, the above estimates of overall productivity growth in terms of world market prices need to be adjusted downwards.

As regards the service sector, the data appear to overstate the contribution of the large and growing government bureaucracy[66] to economic welfare. This is because, under national accounts conventions, the increase of labor employed in public administration is considered as an addition to GNP, irrespective of its productivity.

ESSAY 14

The Economic Reform
in Hungary Ten Years After

Introduction

On January 1, 1968, Hungary introduced an economic reform; in official parlance, the new economic mechanism. The reform aimed at replacing plan directives by market relations among firms; limiting the scope of central price determination; linking the domestic prices of exports and imports to prices in the world market; and decentralizing a major part of investment decisions.[1]

The economic reform was intended to reverse the apparent deterioration in the efficiency of resource use and the concomitant decline in the rate of economic growth,[2] which occurred under centralized planning as it became more-and-more difficult to make firm-level decisions centrally in an increasingly sophisticated economy. Also, Hungary's small domestic market and poor natural resource endowment called for increased reliance on foreign trade, necessitating the use of prices to ensure that exports and imports conformed to profitability on the national economy level.

At the time of the reform's introduction, a variety of "brakes" were applied, in part to smooth the transition from the old to the new mechanism and in part as a compromise between the supporters of the two. Several of these brakes have been subsequently eased; improvements were made in setting commercial exchange rates, in determining wage increases, and in reducing the scope of quantitative restrictions. In several areas, however, a certain degree of recentralization occurred following the Party[3] resolution of November 1972. For one thing, the supervising ministries to some extent reasserted their power in affecting decision-making by the firm. For another, investment decisions by firms were increasingly influenced through the introduction of various state "preferences".

More importantly, the 1972–73 world boom and increases in oil prices adversely affected the operation of the new economic mechanism, inasmuch as efforts made to limit the effects of inflationary developments in the world market on domestic prices reduced the usefulness of price signals and gave rise to increased central interventions.[4] And, although in 1975 and 1976 domestic prices have again been increasingly aligned to world market prices, differences remain in regard to various commodities, in particular crude oil.

Notwithstanding the shock effect of the world recession, however, the decision has been made to maintain, and to reinforce, the outward-orientation of the Hungarian economy. Thus, whereas several developing countries have contemplated—and a few of them have implemented—changes in policies entailing greater inward-orientation, in Hungary it has been concluded that the cost of inward-orientation would exceed the risk outward-orientation entails.[5] This is expressed by the fact that, for the period of the Fifth Five Year Plan (1976–80), it is planned to increase exports to market economies by 60 percent and to socialist countries by 40 percent.[6] With the net material product projected to rise by 30–32 percent, increases in exports would equal 70 percent of the increment in the net material product during this period as compared to an average ratio of 43 percent in 1975.[7]

Following a short discussion of the achievements of the Hungarian reform, this essay will examine possible policy improvements for ensuring continued rapid growth in an outward-oriented economy. In this connection, consideration will be given to the determination of prices, the setting of exchange rates, export subsidies, and tariffs, the role of profits, and the taking of investment decisions.

I. The Experience with the New Economic Mechanism

Achievements of the Hungarian Reform: 1967–73

Data for the period 1967–73 indicate the success of the new economic mechanism in Hungary. The deceleration of economic growth was reversed, with the net material product increasing at an average annual rate of 6.2 percent between 1967 and 1973. Also, with improvements in incremental capital-output ratios, the rate of growth of consumption (5.7 percent) was only slightly less than that of the net material product.

Even greater improvements are shown if we adjust for changes in both capital and labor inputs. Thus, according to the preliminary results of a study undertaken by Márton Tardos of the Hungarian Institute for Market Research, the growth rate of total factor productivity in Hungary more than doubled between 1962–67 and 1967–72.

These results reflect cost reductions on the firm level that were made in response to profit incentives.[8] National income figures indicate reductions in inventory ratios as firms economized with holdings of stocks. Also, there is evidence—albeit fragmentary and impressionistic—that following the reform firms have come to react more rapidly to domestic and foreign demand and made increased efforts to improve technology.[9]

Manufacturing industry led the expansion, with growth rates averaging 7 percent a year during the entire period. Favorable developments were shown also in agriculture where, following stagnation during the 1958–66 period, production increased at an average annual rate of 2 percent between 1967 and 1973 while Hungary's population remained practically unchanged.

An important factor contributing to the growth of the Hungarian economy was the expansion of the volume of exports at a rate nearly double that of the net material product between 1967 and 1973. The value of exports to developed and developing market economies (including Yugoslavia) increased more than the average, raising their share in the total to 44.1 percent in 1973. However, in volume terms, exports to market economies increased at a lower rate (7.9 percent a year) than to socialist countries (12.4 percent a year), the average being 11.0 percent a year.

Developments During the World Recession and the Structure of Hungarian Exports

During the period 1967–73, Hungary's overall export performance— although not the growth of its exports to market economies—nearly matched that of Austria whose export volume grew at an annual average rate of 11.4 percent. Also, in terms of overall export performance, Hungary was not much behind Greece where the export growth rate was 13.1 percent. In turn, in the Far East, the corresponding figures were Japan, 14.7 percent; Taiwan, 28.7 percent; and Korea, 41.0 percent.[10]

The comparisons are less favorable to Hungary in the period 1973–76. While, after a decline during the world recession, the countries referred to above again substantially increased their exports, Hungarian exports grew at a slower rate. Between 1973 and 1976, the volume of exports rose at an annual average rate of 6.8 percent in Austria, 11.4 percent in Greece, 12.9 percent in Japan, 13.4 percent in Taiwan, and 22.0 percent in Korea. By comparison, an average increase of 3.7 percent a year is shown in the volume of Hungarian exports to market economies and 5.4 percent to the socialist countries.

Various factors may explain these differences, including the macroeconomic policies followed, the slow adaptation of the price structure to changes in the world market, the system of export incentives applied, and the unfavorable commodity structure of exports. These will be considered in the following.

As regards macroeconomic policies, between 1973 and 1975 annual average rates of economic growth were low in Austria (1.0 percent), Greece (0.8 percent), Japan (1.1 percent), and Taiwan (1.5 percent), all of which adopted deflationary policies in order to limit the deterioration of their balance-of-payments resulting from the rise of oil prices and the world recession.[11] In the same period, growth rates averaged 6.1 percent in Hungary which continued to follow an expansionary policy. With total consumption increasing at the same rate, the export surpluses of the preceding two years gave place to deficits amounting to 5.7 percent of the net material product in 1974 and 8.9 percent in 1975, necessitating increased reliance on foreign loans.[12] Only in 1976 were measures taken to limit increases in domestic consumption to 2 percent, with a consequent decline in the import surplus to 5.1 percent of the net material product.

Apart from contributing to an increase in the volume of imports by one-fourth between 1973 and 1975, this policy had adverse effects on exports by channeling output towards domestic markets. Delays in adjusting to changes in world market prices, and the resulting stockpiling of materials and increased central interventions, further contributed to increases in imports and to the relatively slow expansion of exports. Moreover, the system of export incentives applied impeded full participation in the expansion of world trade.[13]

Hungary's exports to market economies were also adversely affected by its relatively unfavorable export structure. During the 1973–76 period, world demand for food and food products increased less rapidly than for manufactured goods, in part due to the world recession and in part as a result of import restrictions imposed by the Common Market countries. These developments were detrimental to Hungary, where food and food products (SITC 0) accounted for 32 percent of the exports to market economies in 1973. The corresponding proportions were 5 percent for Austria, 19 percent for Greece, 2 percent for Japan, 13 percent for Taiwan, and 7 percent for Korea.[14]

Furthermore, despite the improvements made since the introduction of the reform, the structure of Hungary's exports continues to be characterized by a duality as between sales to market economies, largely developed countries, and to socialist countries.[15] Thus, while the respective shares of chemicals and of machinery and transport equipment in Hungarian exports to developed market economies rose from 4.7 to 7.2 percent and from 4.5 to 6.8 percent between 1965 and 1973, manufactured exports to this group of countries continued to be dominated by basic manufactures (24.1 percent). By contrast, machinery and transport equipment accounted for 44.1 percent of Hungary's 1973 exports to the socialist countries (Table 14.1).

With the high share of primary and semimanufactured products, Hungary tends to approximate the export structure of a developing country in its exports to developed market economies. In turn, the higher share of machinery and transport equipment makes the Hungarian export structure in trade with the socialist countries more similar to that of a developed country.[16]

The observed duality in the Hungarian export structure reflects to a large extent differences in the level of technological sophistication between the various groups of countries. These differences are also reflected in the high share of chemicals (22.9 percent) and machinery and equipment (24.8 percent) in Hungarian imports from developed market economies.

Accelerating the growth of Hungary's exports to market economies would require a change in their structure as well as greater adaptability to adjust for changes in world market conditions. In this connection, comparisons with Japan offer particular interest. While in 1960 per capita incomes in the two countries were roughly the same, by 1973 Japan's per capita income was

TABLE 14.1
The Structure of Hungarian Foreign Trade, 1965 and 1973

1965

SITC group	Commodity Group	Socialist Countries Export	Socialist Countries Import	Developed Market Economies Export	Developed Market Economies Import	Developing Economies Export	Developing Economies Import	Total Export	Total Import
0	Food and live animals	12.0	4.8	42.7	11.9	4.2	42.7	18.1	8.2
1	Beverages and tobacco	3.1	0.3	1.6	0.3	0.6	0.2	2.6	0.3
2	Crude materials	2.2	16.6	8.2	15.8	0.1	50.0	3.3	18.0
3	Fuels	1.1	17.0	2.9	0.4	0.2	0.2	1.5	12.1
4	Oils and fats	0.3	0.2	1.4	1.0	0.0	1.1	0.5	0.5
0 to 4	*Primary goods*	*18.7*	*38.9*	*56.8*	*29.4*	*5.1*	*94.2*	*26.0*	*39.1*
5	Chemicals	7.3	5.7	4.7	17.9	6.7	1.5	6.7	8.4
6	Basic Manufactures	15.7	16.4	21.5	27.1	41.8	3.9	13.4	18.4
7	Machinery and transport equipment	43.5	33.8	4.5	20.8	35.6	0.0	34.7	29.0
8	Miscellaneous manufactured goods	14.8	5.2	12.5	4.8	10.8	0.4	14.2	5.1
5 to 8	*Manufactured goods*	*81.3*	*61.1*	*43.2*	*70.6*	*94.9*	*5.8*	*74.0*	*60.9*
	Total	*100.0*	*100.0*	*100.0*	*100.0*	*100.0*	*100.0*	*100.0*	*100.0*

1973

SITC group	Commodity Group	Socialist Countries Export	Socialist Countries Import	Developed Market Economies Export	Developed Market Economies Import	Developing Economies Export	Developing Economies Import	Total Export	Total Import
0	Food and live animals	15.4	2.6	36.2	13.0	8.3	42.0	21.0	8.7
1	Beverages and tobacco	3.2	0.9	1.2	0.8	0.0	1.6	2.5	0.9
2	Crude materials	2.7	11.4	9.8	9.4	0.8	27.2	4.7	11.9
3	Fuels	0.6	14.0	2.6	0.8	0.2	8.7	1.1	9.5
4	Oils and fats	0.1	0.2	1.3	0.4	0.0	0.8	0.4	0.3
0 to 4	*Primary goods*	*22.0*	*29.1*	*51.1*	*24.4*	*9.3*	*80.3*	*29.7*	*31.3*
5	Chemicals	6.9	6.8	7.2	22.9	8.6	3.9	7.1	11.6
6	Basic manufactures	12.1	21.1	24.1	22.0	33.5	13.4	16.7	20.9
7	Machinery and transport equipment	44.1	38.0	6.8	24.8	37.7	0.3	33.0	31.2
8	Miscellaneous manufactured goods	14.9	5.0	10.8	5.9	10.9	2.1	13.5	5.0
5 to 8	*Manufactured goods*	*78.0*	*70.9*	*48.9*	*75.6*	*90.7*	*19.7*	*70.3*	*68.7*
	Total	*100.0*	*100.0*	*100.0*	*100.0*	*100.0*	*100.0*	*100.0*	*100.0*

Sources: United Nations *Commodity Trade Statistics*, and Imre Vajda, "External Equilibrium, Neo-Techniques and Economic Reform," *Acta Oeconomica*, 4 (1967) 291–307.

double that of Hungary.[17] The explanation lies, in large part, in the ability of the Japanese economy to rapidly expand exports while progressively transforming their structure. Thus, between 1960 and 1973, the share of machinery and equipment in Japanese exports to developed market economies rose from 16 to 53 percent.

In recent years, several other countries have made considerable progress in transforming their export structure. In 1973, the share of machinery and transport equipment in exports to developed market economies reached 24 percent in Austria, 17 percent in Spain, 21 percent in Yugoslavia, 12 percent in Korea, and 25 percent in Taiwan. Yet with the exception of Austria, these countries exported very little machinery and transport equipment until the sixties while this product group had already accounted for 7–8 percent of Hungary's exports during the thirties.[18]

At the same time, the rapid expansion of exports to market economies appears necessary to ensure a high rate of economic growth in Hungary. This is particularly the case, given the limitations on increasing the imports of raw materials and fuels from the socialist countries[19] and the need to improve Hungary's balance of trade with market economies.[20] Furthermore, successful exporting requires specialization within manufacturing, thereby necessitating increased imports of manufactured goods that have to be paid for by exports. And, finally, the growth of machinery imports from developed market economies is a precondition for raising the technological level of Hungarian industry.

The need for rapidly increasing exports to market economies has been recognized in the Fifth Five Year Plan, which calls for a 60 percent increase in these exports in the 1976–80 period, noted above. In the following, we will examine possible measures that may be taken to pursue this goal and to contribute to continued rapid economic growth in Hungary.

II. Prices, Exchange Rates, and Protective Measures

Price Determination in the New Economic Mechanism

The new economic mechanism was to replace the central allocation of products by market relationships among firms, with prices equating demand and supply rather than serving a purely accounting function as beforehand. Also, the domestic prices of exports and imports were to be linked to foreign prices by the use of uniform conversion ratios. The continued separation of prices paid by consumers from prices received by producers was however envisaged, with taxes and subsidies used to ensure stability in consumer prices.

The pursuit of stability in consumer prices has meant that increases in producer costs and prices have not been fully transmitted to the consumption sphere, thereby necessitating the increased use of subsidies from the government budget. Excluding luxury taxes, net consumption subsidies reached 10 percent of the total value of consumption in 1976.[21] A wide variety of services and foodstuffs are subsidized whereas industrial products are on the whole taxed, with considerable differences shown within each category.[22] These differences would need to be reduced in order to improve the efficiency of resource allocation.

While the prices of consumer goods and services are in their majority centrally determined, central price setting at the producer level applies to only about one-third of industrial products, chiefly basic materials.[23] But, since 1973, rules established on price calculations and on the interpretation of 'unethical profits'[24] influenced the determination of the so-called free prices also. Finally, prices are affected by differentiated subsidies and taxes on exports and on imports.

The use of import subsidies to hold down the prices of imports reflects a preoccupation with price stability on the part of the Hungarian government. Distinction needs to be made, however, between stability in the overall price level and in relative prices. The former objective can be pursued by revaluing the currency that has in fact been repeatedly done in Hungary, lowering the commercial exchange rate vis-à-vis the U.S. dollar from 60 in 1968 to 41 in 1977.[25] In turn, failing to adjust domestic prices for changes in relative prices on world markets involves either guessing the level of "normal" prices or a conscious decision to postpone adjustments in the case of price changes that are considered permanent.

The latter comment applies especially to the domestic price of crude oil that was one-third of the world market price in 1975[26] and was increased to about 60 percent of the world market level in 1976. And while a lower price is paid to the Soviet Union, Hungary's main supplier, this will eventually approach the world market price, since prices in intra-CMEA trade are now set annually as a five-year moving average of world market prices.

Under the new method of price determination in intra-CMEA trade, one may also question the desirability of setting the domestic prices of imports as a weighted average of prices paid for imports from the CMEA countries and from market economies. This is because the exploitation of Hungary's comparative advantage requires "forward-looking" pricing and prices in intra-CMEA trade follow world market prices with a lag.[27] At any rate, as noted above, much of the increment in Hungary's needs in various raw materials, and particularly crude oil, will have to be supplied from world markets, so that prices paid in these markets will be relevant for determining "marginal" comparative advantage.

It would further be desirable to change the domestic prices of imported goods annually as was done in 1975 and 1976, since returning to the earlier practice of setting prices every five years would give rise to undue rigidities. The question remains, however, if annual variations in world market prices should be fully reflected in the domestic prices of imports.

The answer is in the affirmative as far as imports used in the production of exports to market economies are concerned, since otherwise the profitability of exports on the firm level would not correspond to profitability on the national level. In this way, one can avoid the situation observed in recent years, when "in limiting price adjustments by budgetary action we exclude those informations and impulses that would have forced firms . . . to transform their production structure."[28]

Considerations of efficiency also suggest that the prices of imports destined for domestic use be adjusted to changes in world markets. Exceptions to this rule should be confined to such goods and materials (e.g. sugar), the prices of which show wide fluctuations over time. This is not the case for industrial consumer goods, machinery, and most intermediate products, so that price interventions may run counter to trend-like changes.

Different considerations apply to the prices of imported inputs used in production for export to socialist countries. Since the volume and the prices of these exports are set in the framework of bilateral agreements, a system of taxes and subsidies is necessary to avoid undue profits and losses to producers.

Setting Exchange Rates, Export Subsidies and Tariffs

It has been noted above that, in order to limit the inflationary effects of increases in foreign prices, the forint has been repeatedly revalued. Prior to January 1976, changes in the commercial exchange rate (then called the foreign exchange conversion ratio) were made intermittently and in large steps. As a result, the relationship of the exchange rate and the domestic cost of earning a dollar through exports fluctuated over time.

Beginning January 1976, the commercial exchange rate vis-à-vis the dollar has been changed more frequently. But, at the same time, in conjunction with increases in import prices undertaken in the framework of the price reform of January 1, 1976, the ratio of the commercial exchange rate to the average domestic cost of exports declined.[29] This, in turn, required increases in subsidies to exports to market economies.[30] Since the early seventies subsidy rates have been set on an industry-by-industry basis, the aim being to compensate for differences between average domestic production costs and the export price while ensuring 'normal' profits. This procedure represents an improvement as compared to the situation existing at the time of the introduction of the new economic mechanism, when subsidy rates were set on a firm-by-firm, and even on a product-by-product, basis. However, since 1973, in several industries use has again been made of firm-by-firm subsidies whereas, in other instances, subsidies to exporters showing large profits have been cancelled in short order.

All in all, there are considerable variations in rates of export subsidies among industries and among firms in the same industry. The resulting differences in effective exchange rates for exports (the commercial exchange rate, adjusted for export subsidies) are a source of inefficiencies. Inefficiencies are aggravated by reason of the fact that low tariffs are levied on raw material imports and the share of imported inputs in product prices differ among, as well as within, industries. As a result, variations in the domestic cost of *net* foreign exchange earnings are even greater than differences in export subsidy rates.[31]

One faces a paradox here, inasmuch as the adoption of a low commercial exchange rate can be interpreted to reflect a low valuation of foreign exchange and yet substantial subsidies are provided in cases when domestic production costs are high on the grounds that Hungary needs foreign exchange. At the same time, in attempting to allow for "normal" profits in all exporting industries regardless of cost, little encouragement is given for expanding low-cost exports.

This conclusion applied with particular force to the situation existing in 1974 and 1975, when use was made of taxes levied on individual exporters in order to syphon off what were considered "windfall profits," resulting from the government's decision to hold down the prices of imported goods or from increases in the world market prices of exports. While an adjustment was called for in the former case so as to avoid that exporters benefit by paying world market prices for their imported inputs, taxing away profits that were due to increases in export prices reduced the incentive effects of these prices.[32]

Export taxes were abolished in 1976 but the possibility of cancelling export subsidies remains. Also, recent regulations on selective tax exemptions, production subsidies, and wage preferences, provided to firms that take an obligation to expand exports, introduce an additional element of voluntarism in the decision-making process. At the same time, apart from the disadvantages of treating "old" and "new" exports in a different way, it is difficult to judge the extent to which increases in exports would have taken place even without the additional incentives.

These considerations point to the need for reforming the existing system of export incentives in Hungary. In this connection, interest attaches to the experience of other countries with export promotion measures.

Developing countries in the Far East and in Latin America that have substantially increased their manufactured exports since the early nineteen-sixties have all relied on export incentive measures, such as tax and tariff exemptions and preferential credits, which involve little or no discretionary action on the part of the government and provide practical certainty to the exporter. The most successful exporting countries have extended the application of these measures to the production of domestic inputs for exports; furthermore, they have generally provided similar incentives on a value added basis to exports and to import substitution in manufacturing as well as to individual export activities within the manufacturing sector.[33]

A reform of the Hungarian export incentive system aimed at ensuring the automaticity, certainty, and equality of incentives would also promise benefits. These objectives would be served by unifying effective exchange rates for exports, with exceptions made for high-cost exports on a temporary basis and on a degressive scale.

The implementation of the proposed scheme would lessen arbitrariness in decision-making while improving efficiency in exports. For one thing, reducing differences in effective exchange rates would limit the scope of discretionary actions; for another, low-cost exporters would receive greater incentives through a higher exchange rate. The resulting expansion of exports would, in turn, permit additional reductions in subsidies to high-cost exports.

The proposed scheme could be implemented by increasing the commercial exchange rate vis-à-vis convertible currencies and simultaneously eliminating all export subsidies that were provided at a rate equal to, or lower than, the rate of devaluation. The same results could be achieved without changing the commercial exchange rate in the framework of a reform of the tax system. This would involve reducing direct contributions by producers to the government budget and eliminating production taxes levied on a firm-by-firm basis, replacing these by turnover taxes that would be rebated on exports and imposed on imports.[34] In this way, the destination principle of indirect taxation would be applied, which is also used in the countries of Western Europe.

An explicit or implicit devaluation of the commercial exchange rate has been objected to on the grounds that increases in the domestic prices of imports would be inflationary. However, the inflationary effects of the devaluation could be mitigated by reducing import tariffs on manufactured goods which generally exceed incentives to exports.[35] And while there would be an increase in the domestic prices of raw materials that are subject to low tariffs, this would improve the efficiency of exports and of domestic production in general by eliminating the indirect subsidization of imported inputs and by providing incentives to economize on their use.

Apart from mitigating the domestic inflationary effects of a devaluation, reducing tariffs to a greater extent than export subsidies would also lessen the existing bias against export production. It would thus bring further gains in efficiency through the greater uniformity of incentives to exports and to import substitution.

A devaluation, with compensating reductions in export subsidies and tariffs, which are designed to ensure greater uniformity in incentives, would be a "first-best" solution. In the event that a devaluation was not politically feasible because of the inflationary effects of higher raw material prices, a "second-best" solution would be to provide a uniform export subsidy. Uniformity should be understood by relating subsidies to value added in exports (net foreign exchange earnings) rather than to export value,[36] so as to avoid granting incentives to import-intensive exports that is presently the case. At the same time, additional subsidies could temporarily be provided, again on a value added basis, to high-cost exports on a degressive scale.

Furthermore, as long as average tariffs exceed export subsidies, it would be desirable to extend incentives now given to export production in the form of tariff rebates for imported inputs, rebates of production taxes, and preferential credits to the production of inputs for export. The application of these measures would reduce the implicit taxation of exports through production taxes and tariffs on their inputs and diminish the existing bias of the incentive system in favor of direct as against indirect exports. Also, as the example of the most successful developing country exporters indicates, incentives to industries producing inputs for export can contribute to the deepening of the industrial structure.[37]

A final question concerns the role of trading companies. Under present conditions, trading companies act as intermediaries for the bulk of exports to market economies and also have an importing function. At the same time, these companies have little interest in obtaining better prices abroad since their incomes are not related to the profitability of exports.[38] Also, the monopoly position of the trading companies has created barriers between domestic producers and foreign buyers, thereby reducing the flexibility of response to changing market conditions abroad.

In order that export incentives have their full effects, a transformation of the system of foreign marketing would be necessary. Possible alternatives include increasing indirect marketing by producers or by groups of producers and establishing competing trading firms. In this connection, Hungarian decision-makers would be well advised to review the Japanese experience where trading firms have played an important role in promoting exports.

III. Profits and Investment Decisions

The Role of Profits in the New Economic Mechanism

In the preceding section of this essay, emphasis was given to the need for unifying effective exchange rates. Pursuing this objective would involve accepting increased interfirm differences in profits for the sake of promoting the efficient expansion of exports to market economies. The possibilities are more limited for using profit signals in regard to exports to socialist countries that are determined in the framework of bilateral agreements. Nevertheless, such possibilities exist in this case also.

To begin with, profits can be increased by reducing costs even if prices and the quantities traded are fixed in the agreement. Also, apart from standardized products, the firms have a certain latitude in determining product varieties and their prices.[39] Finally, the further development of the system of inviting competing bids from firms to fill export quotas would contribute to improvements in efficiency.

Greater reliance should also be placed on profit signals in production for domestic markets, while in a number of industries there is effective or potential competition, in other industries competition could be increased by breaking-up firms that encompass several plants often producing identical commodities.[40] At the same time, the break-up of firms would be contrary to the interests of the national economy in cases where this would involve foregoing economies of scale in production, research, or marketing.[41] Exploiting economies of scale is of special importance for exporters that face competition abroad. Now, as long as prices charged in domestic markets do not exceed export prices, profit signals can be relied upon. Furthermore, with the expansion of overall exports, import competition could be increased.

Increased profit differentiation, including also the possibility of losses, was objected to in the past. In particular, it was suggested that differentiation in profits leads to unemployment through the closing down of inefficient plants as well as to increased disparities in personal incomes, neither of which is acceptable in a socialist country. Recent developments, however, have lessened the validity of these objections.

To begin with, while at the time of the introduction of the reform the closing-down of plants was not contemplated on the grounds that it would create unemployment, today there is over-full employment in Hungary so that those losing jobs would find employment elsewhere. At the same time, the closing-down of inefficient plants would be in the interest of the national economy since it would involve a shift of labor to more productive activities.

Greater emphasis on profits would also induce firms to improve labor efficiency and to eliminate unnecessary jobs. Again, the economic effects would be beneficial, since there would be a shift from low-productivity to high-productivity employment. In this connection, note that new investments during the 1976–80 period will create 50,000 jobs while the labor force will hardly change during this period.[42]

In turn, the abolition of the compulsory division of after-tax profits into a distribution fund and an investment fund since 1976 has diminished the possibility that remuneration for equivalent work will diverge. This is because a steeply progressive tax rising to 600 percent is levied on 'above-norm' increases in wages that are payable from the firm's profits while there is no additional tax obligation on reinvested profits which are subject to a flat rate of tax of 36 percent levied on all profits.

The impact of the new regulations is apparent in the fact that the share of reinvested profits increased much beyond expectations. It would further be desirable to use averages of profits for several years rather than profits for a single year for the purpose of wage determination. In this way, one can avoid a situation where existing profit opportunities are not fully exploited for fear that the resulting wage increase creates undue expectations for the future.

Increased reliance on profit signals, in turn, necessitates improvements in the price system. As suggested above, improvements in relative product prices could be attained by increasing price flexibility, reducing the scope of differentiated export subsidies, and lowering tariffs. Efficiency in resource allocation further depends on relative factor prices. Recent reductions in capital charges and increases in taxes and social charges on labor costs reflect the realization of the increased scarcity of labor.

Improvements have also been made in regulations on the determination of allowed (norm) wage increases which are not subject to tax. Thus, in a number of industries the rise of productivity has been introduced as the benchmark for wage increases in the place of the level of average wages in the preceding period. Apart from the service sector where the measurement of productivity increases encounters difficulties, it would be desirable to abolish the latter procedure that "strongly favored expansion by increasing the firm's labor force over measures such as upgrading the labor force or rewarding workers for productivity improvements, [leading] to the creation—or maintenance—of disguised unemployment, the avoidance of quality improvements in the working force, and the practical exclusion of wage incentive schemes aiming at productivity measures".[43] Also, one should set realistic requirements for productivity-linked wage increases, so as to improve the effectiveness of wage setting in contributing to improvements in productivity.[44]

In conjunction with improvements in relative product and factor prices, steps would need to be taken to liberalize the system of regulations, which aimed at mitigating the effects of slow adjustments in domestic prices to prices in the world market. Thus, after a decline from 17 in 1968 to 7 in 1971, the number of products subject to import quotas were increased again to 33 in 1976. Similar changes took place in regard to producers' purchase quotas that declined in number from 28 in 1968 to 7 in 1971 only to increase again to 22 in 1976. Also, seller-buyer relationships were centrally determined in 41 cases in 1976, after a decrease from 50 in 1968 to 9 in 1971.[45]

These regulations have been accompanied by the increased use of subsidies provided under a variety of headings, with their total doubling between 1970 and 1974. Greater use has also been made of production taxes set on a firm-by-firm basis and there have been increased interventions on the part of the ministries in the day-to-day affairs of the firm.

The increased interventions have reduced the role of profit incentives for firm decisions. At the same time, it is increasingly understood that "distorted price relationships will not provide an appropriate measure for central decisions either"[46] leading to a considerable degree of arbitrariness in decisions and the channeling of the productive energies of the firm into bargaining for a "better deal."

The 1976 price reform made an important step to reduce distortions in product prices; the ongoing efforts to reform the price and the tax system further aim at improving the guiding role of prices and profits. These efforts provide a basis for, and their success is also conditioned on, reductions in firm-level interventions on the part of the central authorities.

Investment Decisions

Following the introduction of the new economic mechanism, investment decisions made by firms came to account for about 50 percent of total investments. This proportion increased further in subsequent years, reaching 55 percent in the first half of the seventies. With the bulk of state investments being concentrated in infrastructure and in health, education, and welfare, by 1975 the share of investments subject to firm decision-making reportedly surpassed nine-tenths of the total in agriculture and two-thirds in manufacturing.

These figures, however, overstate the scope for the firm to make its own investment decisions. For one thing, a rising proportion of investments undertaken by firms requires financing by outside sources, chiefly from bank credit and budget support. For another, obtaining bank credit and budget support increasingly requires conforming to the priorities set by the government.

The share of bank credit in investments undertaken by firms was about 20 percent in the early sixties and approached 27 percent in 1975.[47] At the same time, special purpose credits have come to account for much of the total. There are 18–20 separate credit quotas set for particular purposes, and state preferences play a decisive role also for allocation within each quota. In fact, requests for long-term credits can be made only for purposes that correspond to state preferences.

State preferences play an even greater role in the allocation of budget support for investments undertaken by the firm. While at the time of the introduction of the new economic mechanism it was assumed that budget support would be used only for a transitional period, its share in investment financing was increased since, exceeding one-sixth of total investments by firms in the mid-seventies. Moreover, budget support is to serve altogether 59 governmental investment objectives and only one-fourth of the total is subject to competition by firms.

At the same time, the calculation of economic profitability expressed in world market prices has become by-and-large a formality. And, with the great number of requests for funds—between 1971 and 1975, budgetary support was provided in altogether 4000 cases[48]—bargaining has assumed considerable importance in the allocation of investment funds. And while it has been suggested that firms find ways to fit their investments into one or the other "compartments," in practice this has often meant that firms base their decisions to invest on the availability of budget support rather than on the profitability of the new investment.

Until 1976 the role of profitability considerations on the firm level was further reduced by reason of the fact that there was no repayment obligation for the amounts received in the form of budget support. Since 1976 firms are granted a credit in the amount of the budget support, which is repayable from tax reductions provided for this purpose and is subject to interest charges. Furthermore, exceptions aside, budget support is granted only if the investment generates enough profits so that the taxes payable on this profit at least equal the amount of budget support, and the cost of the investment exceeding the projected figure will have to be paid by the firm.

The new regulations represent an improvement compared to the earlier situation, although it is to be seen how many exceptions will be made in practice. Furthermore, there may be a tendency on the part of firms to overstate the possible profits; if the calculations are accepted, budget support will be provided regardless of the amount of actual profits from the new investment that are difficult to separate from profits in existing activities.

In order to increase the efficiency of investments, further changes would need to be made in the system of investment allocation. In conjunction with improvements in the price system and greater differentiation in profits, it would be desirable to increase the share of the firm's profit in investment financing. Also, the scope of competition for external funds would need to be enlarged, with a corresponding reduction in the role of state preferences.

An important step has been taken in this direction by the establishment of a fund, amounting to about 10 percent of industrial investment over the next five years, to provide financing for investments aimed at increasing exports to market economies. The National Bank grants credit on a competitive basis to firms whose net foreign exchange earnings over a period of five years at least equal the amount invested and the exports of which are profitable at the existing exchange rate.

The objectives of efficiency would be served if the principles underlying the allocation of these credits would find more general application. For one thing, competition for credit could be extended to a wider area. For another, use would need to be made of efficiency calculations in terms of world market prices. With the requirements of market economies being the most stringent, products meeting such criteria could be sold in all markets. And, since it is efficient export activities that can replace imports at the lowest cost, there is no conflict between export and import substitution.

Efficiency calculations are of particular importance in regard to the establishment of new factories by the government. In this connection some comments will be made on alternative lines of industrial development in Hungary. For lack of adequate information, agriculture will not be considered, although this sector may offer considerable possibilities for expansion.

To begin with, questions may be raised concerning the desirability of the continued rapid expansion of the chemical industry in Hungary. In the first half of the seventies, this industry (including petroleum and coal derivatives) received about one-fifth of all investment funds destined to the manufacturing sector, more than the light industry or all engineering industries combined.

The chemical industry has the double disadvantage that it intensively uses scarce capital and it requires imported raw materials. Calculations show that the amount of physical capital per man is 126 thousand dollars per worker for petroleum and coal products and 41 thousand per worker for chemicals and allied products as compared to an average of 10 thousand dollars per worker for non-electrical machinery, 7 thousand for electrical equipment and supplies, 12 thousand for transportation equipment, and 11 thousand for instruments and related products.[49]

Also, while petroleum had been available from the Soviet Union at a low price, this will eventually approach the world market price and, at any rate, the increment in Hungary's oil consumption will increasingly come from market economies. Moreover, the oil exporting countries are determined to exploit the advantages they possess in the petrochemical industry due to the abundance of the raw material[50] and the availability of capital. This will then contribute to the worldwide overproduction of petroleum derivatives, enabling Hungary to import these products at a lower cost than it would produce them domestically from imported oil.

In turn, the relative abundance of skilled and technical labor and the low ratio of skilled to unskilled wages as compared to other countries bestows comparative advantages on Hungary in skill-intensive industries. Among these industries, computers, electrical measuring instruments, radio and TV equipment, X-ray apparatus, aircraft, ships and boats, scientific instruments and control equipment, and optical instruments have a ratio of physical to human capital of less than 0.2.[51] The ratio is 0.35 for non-electrical machinery, 0.23 for electrical equipment and supplies, 0.43 for transportation equipment, 0.27 for instruments and related products as against 1.92 for petroleum and coal products and 1.25 for chemicals and allied products.[52]

Production in industries manufacturing non-electrical and electrical machinery, instruments, and transport equipment may be destined for export markets and/or may replace imports in domestic markets. In either case, given the described advantages Hungary possesses in these industries, the domestic cost of earning or saving foreign exchange will be lower than in industries that intensively use physical capital, such as petrochemicals and various other chemical products.[53]

There are several large, well-managed firms producing skill-intensive products in Hungary. These firms could further expand their operations if provided financial resources. Also, there would be need to establish new firms in the industries in question. At the same time, the low-cost production of non-electrical and electrical machinery, instruments, and transport equipment requires large-scale operations as well as the availability of parts, components, and accessories at a low cost. The latter condition is not fulfilled at the present[54] because of the lack of sufficient 'depth' in Hungary's industrial structure, which is associated with an overly high degree of industrial diversification for a country of Hungary's size. Improvements in this regard could be made through increased industrial specialization by providing incentives for the production of inputs for exports as suggested above, and by participation in the international division of the production process through cooperation agreements.

Cooperation agreements have the further advantage of combining Hungary's skilled and technical labor with foreign technology and marketing know-how. Also, such agreements permit narrowing the product composition of firms that is necessary to exploit economies of scale and to abandon unprofitable product lines.

Cooperation agreements may take a number of forms from contractual relationships between domestic and foreign firms to the establishment of joint companies. They may also serve a variety of purposes, including product specialization, the production of parts, components, and accessories in Hungary for assembly elsewhere, the division of manufacturing tasks between the participating companies, and the exchange of products for licenses.[55]

Hungarian firms have entered into cooperation agreements with a number of European companies, including Siemens and Volvo. More recently, agreements have been concluded with International Harvester and Steiger for the production of axles and with Corning Glass for the production of blood analyzers.[56] Still, in this respect Hungary is behind Romania that, following an earlier cooperative agreement on automobile production with Citroen, has concluded an agreement with the West German-Dutch VFW-Fokker aerospace group for setting up an aircraft industry reportedly involving an investment of $600 million.[57]

The government can play a role in the establishment of new companies in cooperation with foreign interests. In turn, existing firms would need to be given considerable freedom to negotiate with foreign producers. Firms would also have to decide on their product composition for exports. Thus, the state cannot determine centrally the type of products to be exported as these will have to respond to changing market conditions, requiring considerable flexibility. The described considerations again put into focus the need to provide appropriate export incentives and to increase direct marketing by producers.

Conclusions

In our discussion of the Hungarian new economic mechanism, distinction has been made between the 1968–73 and the 1973–77 periods. It has been noted that the reform led to improvements in the efficiency of the Hungarian economy that are reflected in the acceleration of productivity growth. Also, while a variety of "brakes" had been applied at the time of the reform's introduction to smooth the transition from the old to the new mechanism and as a compromise between the supporters of the two, the years following the reform saw gradual though slow changes towards liberalization.

This tendency was subsequently reversed, to a large extent in response to the world boom, the subsequent recession, and increases in oil prices. The ensuing changes weakened the link between domestic and world market prices, reduced the scope of application of the profit motive, and increased central interventions. They further contributed to the deterioration in Hungary's export position while the continued expansion of domestic consumption was ensured through foreign borrowing that financed a growing import surplus.

At the same time, it is well recognized that Hungary needs to rapidly expand exports. Apart from the lack of the possibility for continued reliance on foreign loans to finance an import surplus, a small country such as Hungary can best exploit its possibilities for economic growth by participating in the international division of labor.[58] Particular attention is given to increasing exports to the West in order to pay for imports that are necessary for raising the technological level of Hungarian industry.

Responding to the needs of export markets, in turn, requires placing increased reliance on firm-level decision making. This has been acknowledged in the Party resolution of October 25, 1977, which re-emphasized the central role of exports in Hungarian economic growth and pointed to the need for letting firms decide on the product composition of their exports, as well as on changes in their production and export structure.

Placing reliance on firm-level decision making will serve the interests of the national economy if profits were to play a greater role, both as an inducement for improved performance and as a source of investment financing. At the same time, for profits to provide an appropriate signal, there is need to reform the existing system of product and factor prices and exchange rates and to limit the scope of central interventions. After several years characterized by contrary moves, the need for further changes in this direction is increasingly understood.[59] This is reflected in the October 25, 1977 and, in particular, the April 23, 1977 Party resolution that calls for giving increased emphasis to the profit motive, reducing the scope of government preferences and other interventions, and rationalizing the price system. The next few years will show how these guidelines will be implemented.

ESSAY 15
The 15-Year Social and Economic Development Plan for Korea

Introduction

Following the policy reforms undertaken in the early sixties, exports became the engine of economic growth in Korea. The preliminary version of the 15 Year Social and Economic Development Plan for the 1976–91 period has envisaged a certain change in orientation, with a lowering of export growth rates in relation to the rate of growth of GNP and reductions in import shares through import substitution.

This essay will examine the preliminary projections, and the underlying policy assumptions, of the plan. In proposing modifications in the preliminary projections, the 9.4 percent GNP growth rate projected for the 1975–91 period (10.2 percent for 1975–81, and 9.0 percent for 1981–91)[1] will be initially taken as a datum. This projection will be reconsidered at a later point.

As a first step, comparable stages of economic development in Korea and in Japan will be indicated. Next, the preliminary projections for the service, manufacturing, and agricultural sectors will be scrutinized and alternative projections will be offered. This will be followed by a discussion of the implications of the alternative projections for the growth of GNP in Korea. Finally, in the conclusions, the relationship between projections and policy-making will be briefly noted.

Comparisons with Japan

Comparisons with the Japanese economy at similar stages of development offer interest, given the similarities in the natural and human resource endowments of the two countries, the strong Japanese influence on Korean customs, the oft-expressed desire to follow the Japanese example in maintaining high rates of economic growth, and the comparison made with Japan in the preliminary projections themselves. At the same time, account needs to be taken of differences in the size of the two countries, with Japan's population being more than three times that of Korea.

347

One should first consider the question as to when Japan reached Korea's present stage of development. According to the preliminary projections, this occurred in 1955–56 when Japan's per capita GNP was $350 in 1964 prices and exchange rates, equalling the presumed Korean figure for 1975–76. These estimates do not however correspond to official national accounts statistics. In terms of 1964 prices and exchange rates, per capita GNP is estimated at $386 in 1955 and $410 in 1956 in Japan as against $230 in 1975 and $254 in 1976 in Korea.[2] And, in terms of 1975 prices and exchange rates, per capita GNP was $541 in 1975 and $599 in 1976 in Korea as compared to $1003 in 1955 and $1065 in 1956 in Japan.

In fact, we would have to go back to the late forties to get a Japanese per capita income figure equal to that of Korea in 1975–76. But, given the lack of detailed information on industrial and export composition in Japan for earlier years, 1951 may be chosen as the benchmark year for Japan, to be compared with the year 1975 in Korea. In 1951, incomes per head in Japan were $290 in 1964 prices and $753 in 1975 prices.

In turn, the 1951–67 period in Japan will be compared with the 1975–91 period of projection in Korea. Between 1951 and 1967, the average annual rate of growth of GNP was 9.1 percent in Japan, corresponding to increases of GNP per capita of 7.9 percent a year. These figures are comparable with projections of 9.4 percent and 7.8 percent for Korea for the period 1975–91.[3]

The Japanese economy in 1951 was, however, still much affected by the aftermath of the Sino-Japanese War and the Second World War. This largely explains that exports per head were only $16, much below the level reached between the two wars. In fact, the 1935 level of per capita exports was not attained until the mid-fifties.[4] Correspondingly, in making comparisons, use will also be made of Japanese data for the period 1967–75.

Projections for the Service Sectors

The preliminary projections envisage value added in the service sector, taken as a whole, to rise at an average annual rate of 9.3 percent between 1975 and 1991, slightly below the projected rate of growth of GNP.[5] These projections cover considerable differences among subsectors. Public health (14.8 percent), electricity and gas (13.8 percent), communications (13.4 percent), education (12.4 percent), housing (12.1 percent), and transportation (11.4 percent) are projected to rise more rapidly than GNP whereas projected growth rates are 5.8 percent for construction and 7.9 percent for miscellaneous services, including wholesale and retail trade, banking, public administration and private services (Table 15.1).

Comparisons between the growth elasticities for services (the rate of growth of the particular service item divided by the rate of growth of GNP, both expressed in constant prices) in the period 1965–75 and 1975–91 point to the conclusion that the projections for several subsectors are on the low side. To

TABLE 15.1
Industrial Origin of GNP in Korea, 1965–1991

	in Current Prices	in 1975 Prices (percent)				Actual 1965–75		Preliminary Projections 1975–91 (in 1975 Prices)		Alternative Projections 1975–91	
	Actual 1965	Actual 1965	Actual 1975	Preliminary Projections 1991	Alternative Projections 1991	Average Annual Growth Rate	Growth[a] Elasticity	Average Annual Growth Rate	Growth[a] Elasticity	Average Annual Growth Rate	Growth[a] Elasticity
Gross National Product	100.0	100.0	100.0	100.0	100.0	10.4	1.00	9.4	1.00	9.6	1.00
Agriculture, Forestry & Fishery	38.4	46.2	25.4	11.7	9.7	4.0	0.38	4.3	0.46	3.2	0.33
Mining and Manufacturing	19.7	14.3	29.7	44.1	44.6	18.8	1.81	12.2	1.30	12.4	1.29
Mining	1.8	1.9	1.3	1.1	1.1	6.0	0.58	8.6	0.91	8.6	0.90
Manufacturing	17.9	12.4	28.4	43.0	43.5	20.0	1.92	12.3	1.31	12.6	1.31
Light Industry			16.4	16.4				9.4	1.00		
Heavy Industry			12.0	26.6				15.0	1.60		
Services Total[b] I	41.9	39.5	44.9	44.2	45.7	11.9	1.14	9.3	0.99	9.7	1.01
II	41.0	46.7	46.7			10.4	1.00				
Social Overhead	8.7	6.7	11.6	13.2	15.0	15.7	1.51	10.3	1.10	11.4	1.19
Electricity and Gas	1.1	0.4	1.1	2.1	2.0	20.8	2.00	13.8	1.47	13.8	1.44
Water	0.1	0.2	0.2	0.5	0.4	13.8	1.33	13.8	1.47	13.8	1.44
Transportation & Storage	3.4	2.9	4.5	5.9	6.0	15.3	1.47	11.4	1.21	11.7	1.22
Communication	0.6	0.6	1.2	2.1	2.1	17.7	1.70	13.4	1.42	13.7	1.43
Construction	3.4	3.1	4.6	2.6	4.4	14.8	1.42	5.8	0.62	9.4	0.98
Other Services[b] I	33.2	32.3	33.4	31.0	30.7	10.8	1.04	8.9	0.95	9.0	0.94
II	32.3	39.5	35.1			9.2	0.88				
Housing	3.5	2.8	1.8	2.6	2.6	5.6	0.54	12.1	1.29	12.1	1.26
Education	2.0	5.0	3.3	5.0	4.9	5.9	0.57	12.4	1.32	12.4	1.29
Public Health	—	—	0.6	1.2	1.2	—[3]	—	14.8	1.57	14.8	1.54
Miscellaneous Services[b] I	27.8	24.5	27.7	22.2	22.0	11.8	1.13	7.9	0.84	8.1	0.84
II	26.8	31.6	29.5			9.7	0.93				

Sources: Korea Development Institute *Long-Term Social and Economic Development Plan for Korea, 1976–91*, Seoul 1977; *Korea Statistical Yearbook, 1976* and text.

Notes: [a] Growth elasticities have been calculated by dividing the average annual rate of growth of a particular item by the average annual rate of growth of GNP. [b] For the items Total Services, Other Services and Miscellaneous Services, the figures in Row I include and those in Row II exclude the factor income balance with the Rest of the World.[3] For 1965, Public Health is included under Private Services.

begin with, it can hardly be assumed that the growth elasticity for construction would decline from 1.42 to 0.62 between the two periods. Rather, projected increases in the share of gross fixed capital formation in GNP from 25.7 percent to 26.9 percent imply a rise in construction activity at a rate at least equal to that of GNP.

The preliminary projections envisage a fall in growth elasticities for transportation from 1.47 to 1.21 and for communication from 1.70 to 1.42. It is questionable that such reductions could be accomplished given the transportation requirements of the regional decentralization of industry and the need for improved communication in Korea. It is also questionable that the income elasticity of demand for miscellaneous services would decline from 0.93 to 0.84. Thus, while rationalization in commerce should permit reducing the rate of growth of wholesale and retail trade, the relatively low past growth rates of banking and insurance, public administration and defense, and private services may not be maintained in the future.

As a conservative estimate, it may be assumed that the rate of growth of construction activity will approximate that of GNP. Projections of annual growth rates of transportation and communication would further need to be raised by three-tenths of one percentage point, and those for miscellaneous services by two-tenths of one percentage point. Correspondingly, the projected average annual rate of growth of services, taken together, for the period 1975–91 would increase from 9.3 percent to 9.7 percent (Table 15.1).

These projections have been made in terms of constant (1975) prices. At the same time, the share of services in GNP will rise to a greater extent in current shares in constant prices, because of the secular tendency for service prices to increase more rapidly than the general price level. Thus, while the share of services in GNP was the same in 1975 as in 1965 (46.7 percent) in terms of 1975 prices, this share rose from 41.0 percent to 46.7 percent in terms of current prices.

According to the preliminary projections, the share of services in Korea's GNP, including the factor income balance with the rest of the world, would rise from 44.9 percent in 1975 to 48.0 percent in 1991 in terms of current prices, with the constant-price share declining from 44.9 percent to 44.2 percent. Under the alternative projections proposed here, the share of services would reach 45.7 percent of GNP in terms of 1975 prices and 49.5 percent in terms of current prices in 1991.

Japanese data on services are available in current prices only. The share of services in Japan's GNP rose from 44.8 percent in 1951 to 52.5 percent in 1955, 58.9 percent in 1967, and 59.0 percent in 1970, with the largest increases shown in housing and in construction. From available evidence, it appears unlikely that this change would have been due to price increases alone. Thus, the Japanese experience tends to confirm our estimate that the share of services in Korean GNP will rise in terms of constant prices.

Export Projections for the Fifteen-Year Plan Period

The preliminary plan document projects the share of exports in manufacturing output to rise from 21.8 percent in 1975 to 28.5 percent in 1981, and to decline afterwards to 28.2 percent in 1986 and 26.5 percent in 1991. With manufactured goods accounting for 95 percent of commodity exports in 1986, the projected decrease in the share of exports in manufacturing output, coupled with increases in the share of manufacturing in GNP, would give rise to a commodity export growth rate of 9.2 percent in 1986–91.

Given the projected growth rate of 9.0 percent, the estimated growth elasticity for exports (the ratio of export growth rates to the rate of growth in GNP) is 1.0. This would represent a sharp break with Korea's historical experience and it is unprecedented among fast-growing national economies. Thus the Korean export elasticity was 3.08 in 1965–75. And, while the elasticity rose slightly during this period, from 2.87 for 1965–70 to 3.33 for 1970–75, in the preliminary plan document export elasticities are projected to decline to 1.95 in 1975–81, 1.27 in 1981–86, and 1.02 in 1986–91, with an average of 1.47 for the 1975–91 period.

As a result of these changes, the ratio of commodity exports to GNP, measured in terms of 1975 prices, would rise from 27.4 percent in 1975 to 51.1 percent in 1991, with the ratio of the exports of goods and sevices to GNP increasing from 31.4 percent to 57.8 percent. However, with service prices— and the general price level—rising more rapidly than the prices of exports, following an increase from 31.4 percent in 1975 to 44.9 percent in 1981, the ratio of the exports of goods and services to GNP would decline to 42.7 percent in 1986 and to 38.9 percent in 1991 in terms of current prices.

The question arises if it will be possible to maintain the high rates of economic growth projected for the period under consideration in the face of a substantial decline in the rate of growth of exports. This question will be dealt with by considering the experience of developing and developed countries, examining Korea's import needs and comparative advantage, and addressing the issue of vulnerability to foreign events.

Exports and Economic Growth: International Comparisons

Intercountry investigations show that export growth and GNP growth in developing countries are positively correlated.[6] These results have been explained by reference to various factors, including specialization according to comparative advantage, a higher degree of capacity utilization, the exploitation of economics of scale, and improvements in technology stimulated by competition in foreign markets. All these influences appear to have played a role in promoting economic growth through exports in Korea.[7]

Apart from the above-mentioned direct effects of exports, there are also indirect effects operating through input-output relationships and via income changes. The extent of these indirect effects is indicated by the existence of a positive correlation between export growth and the growth of GNP *net* of exports in an intercountry framework.[8] They have also played a role in the Korean context, as increased demand for consumer goods associated with higher incomes and the use of domestic inputs in export production have contributed to the absorption of unemployed and underemployed labor while leading to increased capacity utilization and the exploitation of economies of scale.

Exports also grew much more rapidly than GNP in Japan during its comparable stage of development. In the 1951–67 period, a 9.1 percent average annual rate of growth of GNP was accompanied by a 16.3 percent rate of growth of commodity exports, corresponding to an export elasticity of 1.79. As a result, commodity exports per head increased from $16 in 1951 to $103 in 1967 in terms of current prices and from $22 to $206 in terms of 1975 prices.

The observed relationship between exports and GNP continued in Japan during the 1967–75 period, with average annual growth rates of 13.0 percent and 7.7 percent, respectively, corresponding to an export elasticity of 1.69. As a result, the ratio of commodity exports to GNP, expressed in 1975 prices, increased from 2.9 percent in 1951 to 7.7 percent in 1967 and 11.4 percent in 1975. Nevertheless, this ratio remained substantially below the Korean figure for 1975 (27.4 percent). Also, Korea surpassed Japan's 1967 per capita export level by 1975 and it is projected to exceed the 1975 Japanese figure by nearly four-fifths in 1991.

Apart from the effects of the Sino-Japanese War and the Second World War, leading to considerable decreases in exports, the relatively large size of the Japanese economy may account for these differences between the two countries. In fact, we observe a negative correlation between country size and export shares in an intercountry context. This is apparent from estimates based on a study by Chenery and Syrquin, according to which, for an average country with per capita incomes of $230 in 1964 prices (the Korean figure for the year 1975), the share of commodity exports in GNP would decline by one-half as population size doubled from 35 million to 70 million.[9]

Correspondingly, interest attaches to comparisons with smaller European countries, which have a gross national product comparable to that projected for Korea in 1991. Export elasticities for the period 1960–75 were 1.98 for Belgium and 2.00 for the Netherlands. At the same time, Korea is much behind these countries in terms of commodity exports per head. The relevant figures for 1975 are Belgium, $2941; the Netherlands, $2568; and Korea, $147. According to the preliminary projections, Korea's commodity exports would reach $898 per head in terms of 1975 prices in 1991.

Furthermore, the ratio of the exports of goods and services to GNP in Belgium (45.8 percent) and in the Netherlands (53.5 percent) exceeded the

Korean figure for 1975 (31.4 percent) by a considerable margin.[10] Yet, as noted above, following an increase in the second half of the seventies, the share of the exports of goods and services in Korea's GNP, measured in current prices, is projected to decline from 44.9 percent in 1981 to 38.9 percent in 1991.

Korea is also behind the smaller industrial countries in terms of the share of exports in manufactured output. This share was 21.8 percent in 1975; comparable figures for 1973 were 48.0 percent for Belgium and 36.2 percent for the Netherlands.[11] The relevant ratios exceeded the Korean figure also in some of the larger European countries, such as Germany (23.2 percent) and Italy (24.6). In turn, under the preliminary projections, exports would account for 26.5 percent of Korea's manufactured output in 1991.

At the same time, these comparisons would have to be appraised in the light of the existence of intercountry differences in the import-intensity of exports and of production for domestic use. The import content of manufactured exports is reported to be about 45 percent in Korea, exceeding that of production for domestic use by about one-third. By contrast, in the industrial countries, the import intensity of manufactured output hardly varies between domestic and export markets. Correspondingly, the reported figures tend to overstate export shares in Korea in comparison with the industrial countries.

Finally, the ratio of exports to GNP does not provide an appropriate comparison. With GNP being a value added concept, it should be compared with value added in exports (i.e., exports less direct plus indirect imports) rather than with export value. While firm estimates on the import content of exports are not available for the industrial countries, it may not exceed 30 percent even in the smaller countries,[12] as compared to 45 percent in Korea. In moving to a value added basis, then, a larger downward adjustment needs to be made in Korea's export-GNP ratio than in that of the industrial countries. With this adjustment, the ratio of value added in exports to GNP will be about 17 percent in Korea as compared to 35–40 percent in Belgium and the Netherlands.

Import Needs and Comparative Advantage

Korea's import requirements for reaching a high rate of economic growth is a further consideration. To begin with, Korea needs raw materials and foodstuffs that are not available domestically. At the same time, in view of its limited natural resources and changes in food consumption patterns noted below, the increment in Korea's consumption of foods and materials will increasingly come from abroad. In requiring larger imports of machinery, the expected rise in the share of investment in GNP will also raise import shares in Korea. Conversely, increases in the share of services would tend to reduce the ratio of imports to GNP.

Next, the possibilities for import substitution need to be considered. Such possibilities exist in machinery and equipment, where the human capital-intensity of the production process confers a comparative advantage on Korea which has a well-educated labor force. However, production costs in the machinery industry depend to a considerable extent on the scale of output and on the length of production runs, necessitating specialization in a relatively narrow range of products. Given the small size of the domestic market, then, Korea would need to export *and* to replace imports in some machinery productions while continuing to import others.

Expressed differently, at Korea's present stage of development, intraindustry specialization in technologically more sophisticated products would have to increasingly replace reliance on interindustry specialization in relatively simple manufactures such as plywood, textiles, and clothing. Intraindustry specialization, in turn, requires imports to grow more rapidly than GNP since, apart from the inputs necessary for domestic production, increased exports of manufactured goods would have to be accompanied by increased imports.

The prevalence of intraindustry specialization has contributed to the high growth elasticities for imports observed in developed countries. Among the smaller European countries, in the period 1960–75 this elasticity was 1.98 in Belgium and 1.71 in the Netherlands; it was 1.25 in Japan. Nor could the growth elasticity for imports in Korea fall from 2.10 in the period 1965–75 to 0.96 as projected in the preliminary plan document without jeopardizing rapid economic expansion.

This is not to say that the import elasticity could not decline in Korea over the next 15 years. Aside from the machinery sector, there are possibilities for backward integration in intermediate products that can be produced efficiently on a scale required by the needs of industries utilizing these products as inputs. This would permit producing for domestic markets and reducing the import content of exports.

At the same time, Korea should avoid establishing inefficient industries oriented towards import substitution. This may occur in the machinery industry if rather than by providing equal incentives to production for domestic use and for exports, production for the narrow domestic market is encouraged by protection. In industries producing intermediate goods, government-sponsored investments undertaken without adequate project evaluation may lead to inefficiencies and high costs. High-cost machinery and intermediate products, in turn, would reduce the competitiveness of Korean exports.

In this connection, particular attention needs to be given to the petrochemical and chemical industries, paper manufacturing, and primary metals, where net import substitution is relatively small, since the principal material needs to be imported, while capital requirements are high. Thus, physical capital per worker was estimated at $126.1 thousand for petroleum and coal products, $57.6 thousand for paper manufacturing, $41.4 thousand for chemical products and $32.9 thousand for primary metals. By contrast, in Korea's traditional exports, the capital-worker ratio was $2.0 thousand for clothing, $4.5

thousand for furniture, $5.7 thousand for miscellaneous manufactured products, and $5.9 thousand for leather and leather products.[13]

Apart from the traditional labor-intensive industries, physical-capital needs are relatively low in the skill-intensive industries where Korea's comparative advantage will increasingly lie. Thus, physical capital per worker was $7.1 thousand for electrical equipment, $9.1 thousand for fabricated metal products, $10.0 thousand for nonelectrical machinery, $11.1 thousand for instruments and related products, and $11.6 thousand for transportation equipment.

Given the scarcity of physical capital and the increased availability of skills in Korea, further interest attaches to intercommodity differences in regard to the ratio of physical to human capital. Using a more detailed product classification scheme, one finds that this ratio was the lowest, between 0.1 and 0.2, for canvas products, radio and TV equipment, aircraft, ships and boats optical instruments, and scientific instruments and control equipment. By contrast, the ratio of physical to human capital exceeded 1.5 for organic chemicals, cellulosic manmade fibers, dyeing and tanning extracts, fertilizers, carbon black, and petroleum products.[14]

Export Expansion and Vulnerability

It has been noted that export expansion has been an important factor contributing to economic growth and that exports have played an important role in the growth process in Korea as well as in other developing and developed countries. And, apart from the favorable direct and indirect effects of export expansion on economic growth, Korea needs the continued expansion of exports in order to provide for its growing import needs.

The question has been raised, however, if continued export orientation would make the Korean economy excessively vulnerable to foreign events. In addressing this question, it should be emphasized that the gross value of exports, whether expressed as a proportion of manufactured output or GNP, will provide an exaggerated measure of an economy's vulnerability to the foreign business cycle. This is because a decline in gross exports would be accompanied by a proportionate fall in imported inputs used in export production. Furthermore, as shown below, even under the alternative projections, Korea's 1991 export share in manufactured output would be lower, and the share of export value added in GNP higher, than the export shares of the smaller European countries whose 1975 GNP would be reached in Korea at the end of the 15-year plan period.

At any rate, one should not exaggerate the vulnerability of an economy with a high export share. Thus, during the 1974–75 world recession, export-oriented developing countries in general, and Korea in particular, fared relatively well, since they had more of a margin to spare as far as imports are concerned. By contrast, countries which went the farthest in import substitution, and limited imports to what appeared to be absolutely necessary inputs, suffered serious production setbacks because of their inability to procure these inputs as their balance-of-payments situation deteriorated.

Finally, as the author has elsewhere noted, the degree of instability of the world economic system should not be overstated. "This is because the confluence of the circumstances existing in 1974—the quadrupling of oil prices and the doubling of grain prices, together with a deep world recession, partly caused by reactions to the sudden oil price increase and partly the consequence of the super boom of the years 1972–73—cannot be expected to recur."[15]

Another aspect of vulnerability is the danger of the imposition of protective measures abroad. This danger may be reduced by upgrading and by diversifying exports. Korea has been successful in this regard as witnessed by the 82 percent increase in export volume between 1973 and 1976, involving a considerable degree of export diversification. As noted above, further diversification would involve the expansion of skill-intensive exports where Korea is evolving a comparative advantage.

In turn, a policy favoring import substitution would have adverse effects on economic growth and employment by raising capital-output and capital-labor ratios and hindering specialization in skill-intensive industries. Thus, the choice is essentially between low export–low growth–low employment and high export–high growth–high employment strategies.

Projections for the Manufacturing Sector

The above considerations call for the growth of exports to exceed that envisaged in the preliminary projections. This conclusion is supported by increases in exports that took place in 1976, the first year of the plan period. Thus, while the preliminary projections envisaged that manufactured exports would grow at an average annual rate of 22.5 percent between 1975 and 1981, the actual increase in terms of constant prices was 46 percent in 1976 alone.

Taking account of actual and expected increases in 1976 and in 1977, and assuming average annual increases of 20 percent during the remainder of the Fourth Five-Year Plan period, manufactured exports in 1981 may exceed the 1975 level four times, corresponding to an average annual rate of increase of 26.0 percent. In particular, actual increases may exceed the projections by a substantial margin in the case of leather and leather products; miscellaneous manufactures; metal products, and machinery and equipment. The preliminary projections and the alternative projections proposed here are shown in Table 15.2.

The preliminary projections of export growth for the period 1981–91 also need to be revised upwards. This is the case in particular for metal products, machinery and equipment, textiles, clothing, and footwear, leather and leather products, and miscellaneous manufactures. The proposed alternative projec-

TABLE 15.2
Export Projections for Korea, 1975–1991 (in 1975 prices)

| | Percent | | | | | Average Annual Growth Rate | | | | | | |
| | | | | | | | Preliminary Projections | | | Alternative Projections | | |
	Actual 1975	Preliminary Projections 1981	Alternative Projections 1981	Preliminary Projections 1991	Alternative Projections 1991	Actual 1975-6	1975-81	1981-91	1975-91	1975-81	1981-91	1975-91
All Manufacturing	100.0	100.0	100.0	100.0	100.0	45.9	22.5	10.5	14.8	26.0	14.4	18.6
Light Manufacturing	64.6	47.2	45.8	30.0	25.9	34.3	16.3	5.6	9.5	19.0	8.1	12.0
Food, Beverages & Tobacco	6.7	4.9	4.2	3.1	1.9	−11.5	16.5	5.5	9.5	16.6	5.5	9.5
Textiles, Clothing & Footwear	45.4	29.3	28.2	16.9	15.8	41.6	13.9	4.6	8.0	16.4	8.0	11.1
Wood, Wood Products & Furniture	5.5	5.5	5.1	3.7	2.4	30.6	22.3	6.3	12.0	24.2	6.3	12.7
Printing & Publishing	0.1	—	0.1	0.1	0.1	85.9	19.7	13.1	15.5	34.4	13.1	20.6
Leather & Leather Products	1.9	2.0	2.4	1.9	1.9	84.3	23.5	9.8	14.8	31.4	12.0	18.9
Rubber Products	1.9	2.3	2.2	2.0	1.3	31.1	26.4	9.0	15.2	28.6	9.0	16.0
Other Manufacturing	3.1	3.2	3.6	2.3	2.4	9.3	23.1	6.8	12.6	29.2	10.0	16.9
Heavy and Chemical Industries	35.4	52.8	54.2	70.0	74.1	69.8	31.0	13.6	19.8	35.3	18.0	24.2
Paper & Paper Products	0.7	0.8	1.0	1.0	0.8	68.5	24.7	12.9	17.2	31.5	12.9	19.5
Chemicals & Chemical Products	4.4	5.2	5.1	7.1	4.8	55.6	26.2	13.8	18.3	29.0	13.8	19.3
Coal & Petrolem Products	1.8	1.9	1.8	2.0	1.3	33.6	23.9	11.0	15.7	25.8	11.0	16.3
Nonmetallic Mineral Products	2.0	2.7	3.1	3.3	2.6	86.5	28.6	12.5	18.3	35.4	12.5	20.6
Basic Metals	4.5	8.0	7.7	13.0	8.9	53.9	35.0	16.0	22.8	38.0	16.0	23.8
Iron and Steel	4.3	7.7	7.4	12.7	8.6	52.9	35.2	16.1	22.9	38.2	16.1	23.9
Nonferrous	0.2	0.3	0.3	0.4	0.3	106.2	31.1	13.5	19.8	34.0	13.5	20.8
Metal Products	2.6	3.3	3.6	3.5	4.1	76.6	27.0	11.3	16.9	32.7	16.0	22.0
Machinery and Equipment	19.3	30.8	31.9	40.0	51.4	77.3	32.5	13.4	20.2	37.1	20.0	26.1
Machinery	4.8	7.5	8.4	10.6	13.6	—	32.0	14.4	20.7	38.5	20.0	26.6
Electronics	9.4	13.3	13.3	16.8	21.3	—	29.8	13.1	19.1	33.3	20.0	24.8
Transport Equipment	5.1	10.0	10.2	12.6	16.5	—	37.3	13.0	21.5	41.7	20.0	27.7

Source: See Table 15.1.

tions take cognizance of the changing pattern of Korea's comparative advantage, the experience of Japan, and possible market limitations abroad.

Korea's comparative advantage in skill-intensive products and its very small share in the world market for such products point to the possibilities of increasing the exports of machinery and equipment at a rapid rate. It may be assumed that these exports would rise at an average annual rate of 20.0 percent between 1981 and 1991 as compared to 13.4 percent a year in the preliminary projections.

The proposed alternative projections are still lower than Japan's export growth rates for these products, which averaged 26.0 percent in 1951–67 and 23.3 percent in 1967–75 (Table 17.5). Nevertheless, the share of machinery and equipment in Korea's manufactured exports would rise from 19.3 percent in 1975 and 21.2 percent in 1976 to 51.4 percent in 1991 while this product group surpassed the 50 percent mark in Japan's exports only in the early seventies.

Further interest attaches to comparisons of Korea's projected export composition for 1991 and Japan's export composition in 1963, when Japan reached the level of per capita incomes projected for 1991 in Korea.[17] Comparing the alternative projections for Korea with the Japanese figures shown in Table 17.5, it appears that Korea would have a lower share of the exports of chemicals and chemical products and of basic metals in 1991 (13.7 percent) than Japan had in 1963 (23.5 percent) while the share of the exports of machinery and equipment would be higher in Korea (51.4 percent) than it was in 1963 in Japan (32.3 percent). These differences may be explained in part by the larger size of the Japanese economy, which provided a domestic base for chemical industries and basic metals that are subject to economies of scale, and in part by the developments of electronics industries since 1963.

Korea's exports of light industrial products are also expected to rise at a rapid rate. In particular, although the exports of textiles, clothing, and shoes to the industrial countries are limited by international agreements, there are considerable possibilities for upgrading existing exports and for expanding the exports of these commodities to developing country markets. Expansion possibilities also appear favorable for leather and leather products, and export diversification promises further gains for miscellaneous manufactures.

All in all, the alternative projections call for increases in Korea's exports of manufactured goods averaging 14.4 percent a year between 1981 and 1991 as compared to the preliminary projections of 10.5 percent a year. For the entire 1975–91 period, the relevant figures are 18.6 percent and 14.8 percent. By comparison, Japan's manufactured exports grew at an average annual rate of 16.9 percent between 1951 and 1967, and 17.9 percent between 1967 and 1975.

Increases in export growth rates in the alternative projections would be necessary to attain the rate of growth of productivity in the manufacturing sector projected in the preliminary plan document. In fact, as noted below, the higher rate of growth of the manufacturing value added in the alternative projections of 12.6 percent a year between 1975 and 1991 as compared to 12.3 percent in the preliminary projections, would be entirely due to the assumed reallocation of the labor force towards manufacturing activities. Correspondingly, the share of exports in manufacturing output would approach 40 percent in the alternative projections as compared a share of 26.5 percent in the preliminary projections. Adjusted for differences in import content, however, this share would still be smaller than that for Belgium and the Netherlands in 1975.

Projections for the Agricultural Sector

In revising the projections contained in the preliminary plan document, the estimated sectoral productivity growth rates were not modified but the intersectoral allocation of labor was changed. This involved assuming that the labor force in agriculture, forestry, and fishing (for short, agriculture) would decline at an average annual rate of 2.0 percent and the manpower thus released would be reallocated to manufacturing and to services in proportion with their share in the labor force in 1975.

The reduced manpower in agriculture, coupled with projected productvity growth, would mean a decrease in the rate of growth of value added in agriculture for the period 1975–91 from 4.3 percent a year in the preliminary projections to 3.2 percent in the alternative projections. These estimates appear reasonable from the point-of-view of potential supply and demand.

To begin with, given the poor natural resource endowment of Korea, it would be difficult to maintain agricultural growth rates at the level reached in the 1965–75 period (4.0 percent a year). Such has also been the experience of Japan where, under similar natural conditions, postwar agricultural growth rates did not exceed 2–3 percent a year.

The Japanese example, as well as the application of Engel's Law, also point to the need for a downward revision of the projected growth rate for food consumption. The demand for food at the farm level will be further reduced by reason of the increased processing of foodstuffs and the shift towards a more import-intensive pattern of food consumption at higher income levels.

According to the preliminary projections, the consumption of food, beverages and tobacco would rise at an average annual rate of 7.4 percent a year as compared to 7.0 percent for the period 1965–75. Increases in the income elasticity of demand for food (0.58 in 1975–75 and 0.74 in 1975–91) would be even larger, given the assumed decline in the rate of growth of per capita incomes. By comparison, the income elasticity of demand for food, beverages, and tobacco in Japan declined from 0.57 during the 1953–67 period to 0.46 in 1967–74.[17]

Further interest attaches to changes in the consumption of various foodstuffs. Data reported in FAO *Production Yearbook* indicate that Korea's per capita food consumption levels at the end of the sixties were by-and-large comparable to those of Japan in the mid-fifties, except that the consumption of cereals reached higher levels at the expense of potatoes and other staple foods, and meat consumption was higher, and the consumption of oils and fats lower, than in Japan.

With the rising incomes, future changes in Korea's food consumption may also approximate the changes experienced in Japan at a comparable stage of its development. It is noteworthy, then, that the per capita consumption of cereals in Japan declined from 420 grams per day in the mid-fifties to 350 grams in 1970 while that of potatoes and starchy foods fell from 190 grams to 160 grams. These changes were accompanied by rapid increases in the consumption of meat (from 11 to 48 grams) and oils and fats (from 8 to 26 grams).[18]

At the same time, just as in Japan, cereals, potatoes, and starchy foods that have a negative income elasticity of demand are by-and-large domestically produced in Korea while those with a positive income elasticity have a higher import content. This explains why per capita food imports into Japan, valued in 1975 prices, increased from $14 in 1951 to $56 in 1967 and to $93 in 1975. By comparison, Korean food imports were $29 per head in 1975.

Given the slow growth of demand for domestically-produced foodstuffs and the existence of high production costs that makes exporting practially impossible, food production in Korea can hardly be expected to grow at a rate approaching 4 percent a year. These conclusions are not materially affected if account is taken of fisheries and forestry production, which are included with agriculture in the national accounts.

Employment, Productivity, and Economic Growth

As noted above, the preliminary projections of sectoral growth rates of labor productivity in Korea were utilized in deriving the alternative projections. The projections call for an increase of productivity growth in agriculture from 3.2 percent in 1965–75 to 5.3 percent in 1975–91, a decline of productivity growth in manufacturing from 8.4 percent to 4.9 percent, and a decrease of productivity growth in services from 5.6 percent to 4.7 percent (Table 15.3).

The projected growth of productivity in agriculture conforms to the experience of present-day industrial countries. It is also consistent with the alternative projections for agricultural employment, which would raise productivity by reducing the extent of underemployment in agriculture. The projected rise in service productivity, too, may be considered realistic.

While Korea is not expected to match the 8.4 percent annual rate of growth of labor productivity attained during the 1965–75 period when capacity utilization rates increased rapidly, continued export orientation promises substantial productivity improvements in the manufacturing sector also. Increases in labor productivity would, however, be smaller if the export and import growth rates assumed in the preliminary projections materialized. These projections envisaged a shift towards import substitution that has higher capital requirements and does not provide for the efficient use of Korea's scarce resources. Lower rates of productivity growth, together with the adverse employment effects of increased import substitution, then, would not permit attaining the rate of economic growth envisaged in the preliminary projections.

Apart from sectoral productivity growth, the rise of labor productivity on the national economy level is affected by the intersectoral movement of the labor force. Thus, a shift of labor from lower to higher productivity activities would raise the overall productivity level, even though sectoral productivities remained unchanged.

The intersectoral movement of labor importantly contributed to economic growth in Korea in the past and it is expected to do so during the period of projection also. In the 1965–75 period, the average annual rate of increase of labor productivity on the national economy level was 6.9 percent, as compared to increases of 5.2 percent calculated on the assumption that the intersectoral distribution of the labor force remained unchanged. Under the latter assumption, productivity on the national economy level would rise at an average annual rate of 4.9 percent a year between 1975 and 1991 as compared to increases of 6.1 percent in the preliminary projections and 6.2 percent in the alternative projections.

It follows that the growth of GNP would accelerate in Korea under the alternative projections that involve an additional reallocation of labor from low-productivity agriculture to high-productivity manufacturing and services. As shown in Table 15.3, the average annual rate of growth of GNP would reach 9.6 percent in 1975–91 as compared to 9.4 percent in the preliminary projections.

A final question concerns the share of exports in GNP. Accepting the preliminary projections for primary and for service exports, the alternative estimates for manufactured exports would entail raising projected growth rates of the exports of goods and services from 20.1 percent to 23.0 percent in the period 1975–81 and from 10.0 percent to 13.6 percent in the period 1981–91. As a result, the projected 1991 ratio of the exports of goods and services to GNP, measured in 1975 prices, would rise from 57.8 percent to 89.1 percent, Adjusting for increases in service prices, the change would be from 38.9 percent to 60.0 percent.

The latter figure exceeds the 45.8 percent share in Belgium and the 53.5 percent share in the Netherlands in the year 1975. However, the differences in the results disappear if adjustment is made for the import content of exports. Assuming that the import content of Korea's exports would decline from 45 percent to 40 percent during the period under consideration, the share of value added in exports in Korea's GNP would reach 36 percent as compared to 35–40 percent in Belgium and the Netherlands. Thus, Korea again would fit the pattern observed in the smaller industrial countries.

TABLE 15.3
Employment, Productivity and GNP in Korea, 1965–1991
(Average Annual Rates of Growth, in 1975 prices)

	1965-75 Actual			1975-91 Preliminary Projections			1975-91 Alternative Projections		
	Value Added	Employment	Productivity	Value Added	Employment	Productivity	Value Added	Employment	Productivity
Agriculture, Forestry and Fishery	4.0	0.5	3.2	4.3	−1.0	5.3	3.2	−2.0	5.3
Mining and Manufacturing	19.1	9.9	8.4	12.2	6.9	4.9	12.4	7.2	4.9
Services	11.0	4.6	5.6	9.3	4.4	4.7	9.7	4.7	4.7
Gross National Product	10.4	3.3	6.9	9.4	3.2	6.1	9.6	3.2	6.2

Source: *Korea Statistical Yearbook, 1976, Long-Term Social and Economic Development Plan for Korea, 1976-91* and text.

Conclusions

In this essay, recommendations have been made for revising the preliminary projections of the 15-year plan for Korea. The recommendations call for raising the projections for the service sector, reducing those for agriculture and, most importantly, setting higher export targets and lowering projections for import substitution in the manufacturing sector. This would entail retaining the export orientation of the Korean economy and eschewing a shift towards import substitution that underlies the preliminary projections.

Attaining rapid growth of exports and GNP would necessitate taking appropriate policy measures. Economic project evaluation would need to be introduced for investments in highly capital-intensive industries where the bulkiness of the investment often necessitates some form of government participation. In all other industries continued reliance should be placed on incentive measures.

At the same time, incentives to new industries should take the form of production subsidies and promotional measures rather than protection. This is of particular importance in the machinery industry, in part to ensure intra-industry specialization necessary to exploit economies of scale and long production runs and in part to avoid reducing the competitiveness of user industries through increased costs.

There is further need to reform the system of protection presently applied in Korea. This would involve reducing tariffs and rationalizing their structure as well as liberalizing import restrictions. The reforms of the system of protection should be carried out according to a predetermined time table, so as to prepare producers for the changes and induce them to make the necessary adjustments.

ESSAY 16

Inflation and Trade Liberalization in Korea

Introduction

The present essay follows the author's "The 15 Year Social and Economic Development Plan for Korea," published as Essay 15 in this volume. The preceding essay made recommendations for modifying the projections contained in *Long-Term Social and Economic Development Plan for Korea, 1976–91* and for maintaining an outward-oriented development strategy in Korea. It also briefly considered the policies necessary to pursue this strategy.

The essay will review the revised plan projections for the 1976-91 period, and compare them with the preliminary plan projections and the alternative projections proposed by the author. It will also examine the effects of Korea's balance of payments surplus on inflation and make recommendations for policies that aim at lowering the rate of inflation while pursuing objectives of efficient resource allocation and economic growth. The policy recommendations will concern the scope of import licensing, the system of tariffs, the coordination of incentives, the promotion of the automobile industry, and the reform of agricultural policies.

The Revised Fifteen Year Plan[1]

On the whole, the revised projections are more realistic than those of the preliminary version and reflect a greater degree of outward orientation that is the stated objective of the revised plan. Thus, the extent of import substitution envisaged for the plan period has been reduced, and export projections have been raised, although not as much as proposed by the author.

In turn, projected rates of economic growth have been raised to a greater extent than proposed in the alternative projections. While the revised plan adopts the author's projection of a 3.2 percent growth rate for agriculture, it goes beyond the author in raising projected growth rates for mining and manufacturing and for services to 12.7 percent and 10.0 percent, respectively.

All in all, GNP would rise at an average annual rate of 10.1 percent under the revised projections as compared to economic growth rates of 9.4 percent under the preliminary projections and 9.6 percent under the alternative projections proposed by the author. The higher GNP projection largely reflects the assumption of higher productivity growth rates in mining and manufacturing, where labor productivity is assumed to rise at an average annual rate of 6.0 percent between 1976 and 1981 as compared to a growth rate of 4.9 percent in the preliminary projections that were also adopted by the author (Table 16.1).

Korea experienced rapid rates of productivity growth in the past, with labor productivity in mining and manufacturing rising at an average annual rate of 8.4 percent between 1965 and 1975 (Table 15.3). However, these increases were attained from a low base and cannot be expected to continue in the future. And, future rate of productivity in growth will greatly depend on the rate of export expansion and on the investment and savings effort.

The revised projections have raised the preliminary estimate of export growth for the 1976–81 period from 12.4 percent to 14.6 percent while the alternative projections proposed by the author called for increases of 16.3 percent a year for the same period;[2] the corresponding figures are 10.3 percent, 13.0 percent and 14.2 percent for the 1981–91 period. Upward adjustments have been smaller in regard to the export elasticities (the ratio of the annual rate of growth of exports to that of GNP), which are affected by differences in GNP growth rates. For the 1976–91 period, this elasticity is 1.45 in the revised projections as compared to 1.36 in the preliminary projections and 1.87 in the alternative projections proposed by the author.

It is doubtful, however, that the projected rate of growth of GNP could be attained without further stepping up the export effort. As noted in Essay 15, exports contribute to the growth of GNP directly as well as indirectly, and rapid economic growth in Korea and elsewhere has entailed an export elasticity much exceeding the projected figure. This elasticity was 3.08 in Korea in the 1965–75 period; it was 1.70 in Japan and slightly exceeded 2.0 in Belgium and in the Netherlands.[3]

A more rapid expansion of Korean exports could take the form of across-the-board increases in the projected exports of various manufactured goods. In this connection, note that the composition of manufactured exports in the revised plan tends to conform to the author's estimates. In particular, the 1991 share of machinery and equipment is 50.4 percent in the revised projections as compared to 40.0 percent in the preliminary projections and 51.4 percent in the alternative projections proposed by the author (Table 16.2).

The principal exception is basic metals, almost entirely iron and steel, where the revised projections are substantially higher than the estimate put forward by the author. At the same time, given the relatively high capital-intensity of this industry and the expected continuation of world overcapacity for some time to come, these projections appear to be on the high side.

TABLE 16.1

Employment, Productivity and GNP in Korea: Revised Estimates (Average Annual Rates of Growth in Constant Prices)

	1975-91 Preliminary Projections			1975-91 Alternative Projections			1976-91 Revised Projections		
	Value Added	Employment	Productivity	Value Added	Employment	Productivity	Value Added	Employment	Productivity
Agriculture, Forestry and Fishery	4.3	−1.0	5.3	3.2	−2.0	5.3	3.2	−1.3	4.5
Mining and Manufacturing	12.2	6.9	4.9	12.4	7.2	4.9	12.7	6.3	6.0
Services	9.3	4.4	4.7	9.7	4.7	4.7	10.0	5.1	4.8
Gross National Product	9.4	3.2	6.1	9.6	3.2	6.2	10.1	3.3	6.6

Sources: Preliminary Projections: Korea Development Institute, Long-Term Social and Economic Development Plan for Korea, 1976-91. Alternative Projections: Bela Balassa, "The 15 Year Social and Economic Development Plan for Korea," Essay 15 in this volume. Revised Projections: Korea Development Institute, Long-Term Prospect for Economic and Social Development, 1977-91.

TABLE 16.2
The Composition of Korean Manufactured Exports, 1991

	Preliminary Projections	Alternative Projections	Revised Projections
All Manufacturing	100.0	100.0	100.0
Light Manufacturing	30.0	25.9	26.5
Food, Beverages, Tobacco	3.1	1.9	1.8
Textiles, Clothing and Footwear	16.9	15.9	14.9
Other Light Industrial Products	10.0	8.2	9.8
Heavy and Chemical Industries	70.0	74.1	73.5
Paper and Paper Products	1.0	0.8	0.4
Chemicals, Coal and Petroleum Products	9.1	6.1	5.5
Nonmetallic Mineral Products	3.3	2.7	1.8
Basic Metals	13.1	8.9	11.5
Metal Products	3.5	4.2	3.7
Machinery and Equipment	40.0	51.4	50.4

Sources: See Table 16.1.

The revised projections envisage an increased investment effort to support the acceleration of economic growth. Gross domestic investment would rise at an average annual rate of 12.4 percent between 1976 and 1991 as compared to a growth rate of 9.9 percent in the preliminary projections. As a result, the share of gross domestic investment in GNP, expressed in terms of 1975 prices, would rise from 28.9 percent in 1976 to 33.2 percent in 1981 and again to 38.0 percent in 1991.

According to the revised projections, the rise in the investment share would be accomplished by increases in domestic savings (in 1975 prices) from 24.3 percent of GNP in 1976 to 33.2 percent in 1981 and 39.0 percent in 1991; by contrast, net foreign savings, which accounted for a substantial share of capital formation in Korea during the postwar period and still equalled 4.6 percent of GNP in 1976, would be nil in 1981 and would amount to −1.0 percent of GNP in 1991. Thus, domestic savings would not only have to finance increased capital formation but would also have to bear the burden of Korea's shift from a capital importer to a capital exporter status.

The bulk of the increase in domestic savings would have to be provided by household savings that are projected to rise at an average annual rate of 15.0 percent between 1976 and 1981, raising their ratio to GNP from 6.7 percent in 1976 to 16.3 percent in 1981. Assuming that disposable income increased at the same rate as GNP, this projection corresponds to a marginal savings ratio of 48 percent in the 1976–91 period. By contrast, in the first half of the seventies, the marginal savings ratio was 7 percent. And while this ratio reached 38 percent in 1976, this was because consumption lagged behind the rapid growth of incomes in that year. The marginal savings ratio averaged 18 percent in the 1970–76 period taken as a whole.

It appears unlikely, therefore, that the domestic savings projections would be realized. Since neither public nor business savings could be realistically expected to fill the gap, it would have to be filled by foreign savings, transforming the projected net outflow of capital into a net inflow. In conjunction with the more rapid increase in exports, this inflow would also permit providing for the economy's import needs while avoiding costly import substitution, the substantial reduction of the import coefficient envisaged in the fifteen-year plan would entail.

At any rate, a capital-poor country, such as Korea, needs an inflow, rather than an outflow, of capital. For one thing, amounts borrowed abroad can be profitably invested domestically, with the marginal productivity of capital in Korea exceeding the real rate of interest on foreign borrowing by a substantial margin. For another thing, foreign direct investment is desirable in industries characterized by rapid technological change, such as machinery and equipment, in order to keep up with technological progress abroad and to provide marketing channels.

The projected surplus also tends to confirm the fears expressed in the United States and Western Europe that Korea would follow the example of Japan in accumulating surpluses, and thus increase the pressure for protection in the industrial countries. Finally, a balance of payments surplus contributes to domestic inflation as evidenced by the experience of Korea in the years 1977–78.

Balance-of-Payments Surplus, the Money Supply, and Inflation, 1977–78

In 1977–78, a close relationship is observed between changes in the money supply and in the wholesale price index in Korea, with price increases following the growth of the money supply with a lag of 3 to 6 months. This is apparent from Table 16.3 which shows that the rapid increase in the money supply between June 1977 and February 1978 was followed by an acceleration of inflation in the first half of 1978.

The growth of the money supply closely paralleled increases in the holdings of foreign assets in the monetary system. As shown in Table 16.3, the 34 percent increase in the money supply between June 1977 and February 1978 nearly matched the 31 percent rise in foreign asset holdings. In turn, the money supply and foreign asset holdings declined in a parallel fashion between February and May 1978 and both increased again in June.[4]

The close relationship between increases in foreign asset holdings and in the money supply is explained by the absence of open market operations through which the inflow of foreign assets could have been sterilized. In these circumstances, reductions in foreign asset holdings would contribute to the deceleration of inflation. Such a reduction in turn requires eliminating Korea's current account surplus and transformming it into a deficit.

The objective of eliminating the surplus on the current account, and transforming it into a deficit, may be accomplished through the revaluation of the exchange rate or through the liberalization of trade. The Korean

TABLE 16.3
Foreign Assets, Money Supply, Wholesale and Consumer Prices in Korea

	Foreign Assets		Money Supply			
	billion won	Index	billion won	Index	Wholesale Prices Index	Consumer Prices Index
1976 average	1076.6	100.0	1303.9	100.0	100.0	100.0
1977 average	1846.7	171.5	1811.9	139.0	109.0	110.1
1977 June	1774.1	164.8	1735.7	133.1	108.8	109.9
July	1850.1	171.8	1796.8	137.8	109.4	111.3
Aug.	1912.0	177.6	1808.1	138.7	110.2	112.7
Sept.	2050.5	190.5	2000.6	153.4	111.0	113.1
Oct.	2184.8	202.9	2040.3	156.5	111.3	112.7
Nov.	2153.6	200.0	2077.3	159.3	111.8	113.2
Dec.	2381.8	221.2	2172.6	166.6	113.3	114.2
1978 Jan.	2377.4	220.8	2241.8	171.9	115.9	117.5
Feb.	2326.1	216.0	2319.0	177.8	117.9	119.9
Mar.	2278.2	211.6	2189.4	167.9	118.3	121.5
Apr.	2072.3	192.5	2211.7	169.6	119.0	121.3
May	2077.9	193.0	2175.8	166.9	120.0	122.5
June	2180.2	202.5	2293.8	175.9	121.6	125.9

Source: Bank of Korea, *Monthly Economic Statistics,* various issues.

government apparently opted for the latter alternative. A multiannual plan for the liberalization of import restrictions was announced in April 1978, and in August 1978 it was decided to import an additional $500 million worth of restricted items. It was further decided to reduce tariffs and to eliminate prepayment requirements on imports.

The choice made for trade liberalization may be welcomed inasmuch as a revaluation of the won would have adversely affected exporters that already experienced a deterioration of their competitiveness vis-à-vis the United States. Thus, after increases in the early seventies, the real exchange rate (the nominal exchange rate adjusted for changes in relative prices) in terms of the U.S. dollar declined and it was 12 percent below the 1975 level in the first half of 1978 (Table 16.4).

Also, while the revaluation of the yen improved Korea's competitive position vis-à-vis Japan, the average real exchange rate in terms of the U.S. dollar and the Japanese yen fell by 6 percent between 1975 and the first half of 1978, reflecting the importance of the United States as an export market for Korea. At the same time, the figures do not allow for the fact that the large share of intermediate products and machinery imported from Japan raised the cost of Korean exports relative to production costs in the United States and in competing countries which, Taiwan excepted, rely to a much lesser extent on inputs imported from Japan.

An additional consideration is that, following reductions in export subsidies undertaken after 1970, the continued existence of import protection entails a bias against exports in Korea. Since it is not desirable to increase export

TABLE 16.4
Real Exchange Rates for Korean Exports

	1970	1971	1972	1973	1974	1975	1976	1977	1978 (I-VI)
Nominal Exchange Rates									
Won/dollar	310.6	347.7	392.9	398.3	404.5	484.0	484.0	484.0	484.0
Yen/dollar	358.1	348.0	303.1	271.2	291.5	296.8	296.5	268.5	229.2
Won/yen	.867	.999	1.296	1.469	1.388	1.631	1.632	1.803	2.112
Exchange Rate Indexes									
Won/dollar (W_u)	100.0	111.9	126.5	128.2	130.2	155.8	155.8	155.8	155.8
Yen/dollar (Y_u)	100.0	97.2	84.6	75.7	81.4	82.9	82.8	75.0	64.0
Won/yen (W_j)	100.0	115.1	149.5	169.3	160.0	187.9	188.2	207.7	243.4
Wholesale Price Indexes									
Korea (P_k)	100.0	108.5	123.5	132.1	187.6	237.5	266.3	290.3	316.0
Japan (P_j)	100.0	99.2	100.0	115.8	152.2	156.7	164.7	167.7	165.3
USA (P_u)	100.0	103.3	107.9	122.0	145.0	158.5	165.8	177.0	185.7
Index of Real Exchange Rates									
(a) Korea vs. Japan[a]	100.0	105.2	121.0	148.4	129.8	124.0	116.4	120.0	127.3
(b) Korea vs. USA[b]	100.0	106.5	110.5	118.4	100.6	104.0	97.0	95.0	91.6
(c) Korea vs. Japan, USA[c]	100.0	106.1	114.4	129.5	111.4	111.4	104.2	104.2	104.8

Sources: Bank of Korea, *Economic Statistical Yearbook* and *Monthly Economic Statistics*, various issues and International Monetary Fund, *International Financial Statistics*, May and August 1978.

Notes: The relevant formulas are: (a) $\dfrac{W_j}{P_k/P_j}$; (b) $\dfrac{W_u}{P_k/P_u}$; (c) a weighted average of (a) and (b), assigning weights of .37 and .63 to them respective-

ly. These weights are based upon the respective shares of Japan and USA in Korea's exports to these two countries in 1970.

subsidies because of the threat of countervailing action, trade liberalization should be relied upon to lessen this bias. Lowering the protection of final goods will reduce the attractiveness of production for domestic markets relative to exports while lowering the protection of inputs will reduce the cost of export production. At the same time, in lowering import prices, reductions in protection will have beneficial effects on inflation.

The liberalization of trade will thus lessen inflationary pressures through reductions in the rate of growth of the money supply and by lowering the domestic prices of imported goods, and it will further contribute to efficient resource allocation and economic growth by lessening the existing bias against exports and in favor of import substitution. In the following, plans for liberalizing import restrictions and reducing tariffs will be reviewed and recommendations made for further changes.

Liberalizing Import Restrictions

Under the four-year plan of import liberalization, banned items were abolished on May 1, 1978 and the share of automatic approval items in the total reached 63.5 percent by August 1978 as compared to 53.8 percent in January of the same year. This share would increase further to 67.1 percent in 1979–80 and 75.2 percent in 1981–82.

The preparation of a four-year plan of import liberalization represents a step towards the elimination of import restrictions in Korea. One may also welcome the publication of the list of items to be decontrolled each year as it provides advance information to affected firms. But, the plan is not sufficiently far-reaching. Thus, the remaining 25 percent of restricted items represent a substantial share of domestic production and of potential imports.

At the present stage of Korea's development, there is little justification for the continued use of import restrictions. The elimination of import restrictions is of particular importance in the machinery industry where production for domestic markets behind protection gives rise to small-scale operations at high costs that would be difficult to subsequently transform into export industries.

In order to accelerate the import liberalization process, it would be desirable to have the August 1978 import program followed by further programs during the Fourth Five Year Plan period that ends in 1981. The import programs should be integrated with the import liberalization plan by making the elimination of restrictions on the commodities involved permanent. It would further be desirable to coordinate the liberalization of import restrictions with the reform of the tariff structure.

Reforming the Tariff Structure

Tariffs were reduced in the framework of the 1977 reform.[5] The proposed reform of the system of tariffs, prepared by the Ministry of Finance, aims at further reducing tariffs and rationalizing their structure. Table 16.5 shows the "basic" tariff rates, the "actual" tariff rates which incorporate tariff reductions that have not yet been communicated to GATT in order to use them as a bargaining counter in trade negotiations, and the tariff rates proposed under the reform. The relevant comparison is with the actual rates since these affect producers' behavior.

TABLE 16.5
Changes in Korean Tariff Rates under the Proposed Reform

| | Present | | | | | |
	Basic	Share	Actual	Share	Reform	Share
0%	44	1.7	116	4.6	138	6.5
5%	—	—	44	1.7	62	3.0
10%	52	2.1	48	1.9	260	12.2
15%	—	—	30	1.2	220	10.4
20%	1,210	48.0	1,226	48.2	614	28.8
25%	—	—	7	0.3	83	4.0
30%	237	9.4	396	15.6	293	13.7
40%	411	16.4	347	13.7	193	9.1
50%	—	—	2	0.1	22	1.0
60%	292	11.6	259	10.1	196	9.2
80%	159	6.3	15	0.6	9	0.4
100%	82	3.2	27	1.1	13	0.6
150%	17	0.7	12	0.4	7	0.3
Specific Duty	15	0.6	15	0.6	17	0.8
Total	2,519	100.0	2,544	100.0	2,127	100.0

Source: Korean Ministry of Finance.

Under the reform proposal, the share of tariff rates of 10 percent and lower would rise from 8.2 percent of the total to 21.7 percent, with corresponding reductions in the relative shares of higher rates. Furthermore, in the application of the "product tree approach," the proposal aims to equalize tariffs on products at each level of fabrication using the same basic material and to reduce the degree of escalation of tariffs from lower to higher levels of fabrication. An example is provided by the automobile industry, where actual tariffs would be reduced from 100-150 percent to 80 percent on assembled cars; from 40–100 percent to 40 percent on body, chassis, transmission and similar items; from 30–40 percent to 30 percent on crankshaft, springs and other inputs used at the next higher level of fabrication; and from 10–30 percent to 10–20 percent on metal parts. Also, tariffs on machinery would be equalized at 15 percent as compared to the present 15 to 20 percent rates.

The tariff reform proposal is well thought-out and its early implementation can be recommended. At the same time, the proposed tariff rates continue to be overly high; thus, two-fifths of the rates would exceed 20 percent and one-tenth would exceed 50 percent. Tariffs are particularly high on luxury goods and on automobiles. It would be desirable to reduce tariffs on luxury goods, replacing them by excise taxes, lest the production of such goods be encouraged. It would further be desirable to reform the protection of the automobile industry in Korea. Proposals to this effect will be considered below.

More generally, there is need to lower the entire tariff structure. This has been done with beneficial effects in the smaller European countries, where tariffs now average about 5 percent. Lowering tariffs is of particular importance in Korea which has a relatively small domestic market for manufactured goods, since the gains from trade liberalization are negatively correlated with market size.[6]

Tariff reductions could be undertaken in the framework of a three-year plan for tariff reform, with 1981 as the terminal year, of which the present tariff reform would represent the first step. At the same time, one should consider the tariff rates set for 1981 as intermediate targets, to be followed by further reductions in the period of the next five-year plan.

The plan for tariff reform would provide an opportunity for the rationalization of the tariff structure. This should be done by moving towards the equalization of effective tariff rates on value added. And while additional protection may be provided to infant industries on a temporary basis, such additional protection should be eliminated according to a pre-established schedule in, say, five years. The plan for tariff reform should also be made public in advance, so as to prepare firms for future reductions in tariffs.

The Coordination of Incentives

In the present essay, note has been taken of the need to coordinate the liberalization of import restrictions and the reform of the tariff structure. This would permit avoiding a situation where the elimination of import restrictions is rendered ineffective by high tariffs or tariff reductions remain inoperative because of continued import restrictions. At the same time, large tariff reductions may increase resistance to abolishing import restrictions, which are the more undesirable form of protection because they practially exclude imports and allow protection without limitation.

It would be desirable to establish an interministerial committee to coordinate the liberalization of import restrictions and the tariff reform, which are the responsibility of different ministries. The committee should also assure the coordination of measures affecting imports and exports with the system of taxation and investment incentives.

Investment incentives are subject to a number of laws and regulations in Korea, including the Foreign Investment Law, the National Investment Law, Presidential decrees concerning industry rationalization and small-scale enterprises, as well as regulations on a variety of investment-related matters. Most of these laws and regulations are administered independently from each other and on the basis of different criteria.

In 1976, a proposal was made to replace existing laws and regulations by a single Investment Promotion Law. The proposed law was designed to simplify and unify existing incentives, to provide additional incentives for research and development and for the formation of skilled manpower, and to establish procedures for the evaluation of investments financed from public funds.

Since 1976, project evaluation machinery has been established in Korea but the proposal for the Investment Promotion Law has not been submitted to the legislature. Yet, the coordination of investment incentives is of high priority, since it would introduce greater rationality in decision-making. It would be desirable, therefore, to proceed with the preparation of the Investment Promotion Law. However, the earlier proposal would need to be revised in several respects.

To begin with, it would be desirable to replace the "positive" list with a "negative" list of activities eligible for investment incentives. Under the negative list, incentives would be provided to all activities except for those that encounter market limitations abroad. Through the general provision of investment incentives, one may avoid discrimination against potential export activities and prevent the application of countervailing measures against exports. Such measures have been invoked in the United States against the selective application of investment incentives, even though the incentives were not linked to exports.

Furthermore, given the need for small and medium size plants to produce parts, components, and accessories for machinery and transport equipment, provisions on minimum plant size as a requirement for investment incentives should be limited to industries producing standardized intermediate products. Finally, use should be made of reductions in corporate income taxes in the place of accelerated depreciation provisions, since the latter favor capital-intensive activities.

The Promotion of the Machinery and Automobile Industries

As noted above, particular importance attaches to eliminating import restrictions in the machinery industry, where domestic market orientation gives rise to high-cost operations on a small scale that would be difficult to subsequently transform into export industries. Rather than protection, whether by means of import restrictions or tariffs, use should be made of promotional measures that encourage production for both domestic and export markets. In this way, it can be assured that efficient-scale operations are established, which can enjoy economies of scale by exporting part of their output.

Apart from the investment incentives referred to above, infant industry considerations warrant taking additional measures to promote the machinery industry in Korea. These measures should aim at encouraging improvements in the organization of work, increasing the use of foreign technology, promoting research and development, and improving workers' training.

The government may usefully extend its technical assistance effort, involving the use of foreign engineering consultants, with a view to improving the organization of work in machinery-producing firms. It should also extend its efforts to establish research institutes and technical schools.

At the same time, in order to ensure that improvements in technology and skills are made by the firms themselves, it would be desirable to provide incentives supporting the actions taken by the firms. This may be done by granting tax concessions for the purchase of foreign patents and licenses, expenditures on research and product development, and the training of skilled labor.

The government has also made efforts to establish machinery complexes in Korea. While the establishment of such complexes permits capturing external economies, greater reliance on private initiative would be more desirable than has been the case heretofore. There would further be need to review domestic content regulations, which set minimum levels for the use of domestically-produced inputs in the case of some machinery products.

Domestic content regulations are applied in the entire automobile industry. These regulations have allowed the high-cost production of parts and components, in some cases even in excess of the high tariffs. In fact, available data show that the average price of automobile parts and components in Korea is 52 percent above the import price.[7] Given the 90 percent domestic content requirement, the high input prices have substantially raised the cost of Korean-produced automobiles.

Korea plans to rapidly expand its automobile industry, with emphasis given to exports. The production and the marketing characteristics of the automobile industry do not favor such a strategy, however. To begin with, the establishment of a full-scale automobile industry requires a large domestic market base. Also competitiveness on the world market presupposes the availability of a large network of suppliers of parts, components, and accessories, produced on an efficient scale. Finally, exporting involves a high cost of entry as it necessitates the establishment of marketing and repair facilities in foreign markets as well as brand name identification.[8]

In view of these considerations, an alternative strategy would appear more appropriate for Korea. This would involve concentrating on the production of relatively labor-intensive parts, components, and accessories and on assembly operations, in cooperation with foreign firms. In this connection, one may refer to overtures reportedly made by General Motors to establish a large-scale plant producing engines in Korea and by Toyota for a plant to assemble 500,000 vehicles a year, both destined for exports.

More generally, Korea would benefit from engaging in operations that require unskilled and skilled labor for domestic use and for export while importing parts, components, and accessories that are relatively capital intensive. Apart from exploiting Korea's comparative advantages, this strategy would permit the utilization of large-scale production methods.

Furthermore, the described pattern of trade would not necessitate high protection of domestic industry and would not require subsidies to exports. At present, the exportation of automobiles is heavily subsidized in Korea, by means of an export-import link system. Apart from its high cost to the national economy, such subsidization is subject to countervailing action and, once cars are exported in appreciable quantities, action would undoubtedly be taken.

Reforming Agricultural Policies

As a result of the policy of raising agricultural support prices, the price of rice, barley, and wheat are two times, and that of beef five times, the world market price in Korea. This policy aimed simultaneously at self-sufficiency in foodstuffs and at reducing income inequalities. But, high support prices in agriculture had adverse repercussions in the Korean economy.

To begin with, the high rice price gave rise to large surpluses and entailed storage costs. It further discouraged the production of alternative crops, in particular vegetables and fruits, for which demand increases rapidly at higher income levels, leading to a considerable rise in prices. The high support prices of cereals and beef also added to inflationary pressures.

In raising agricultural prices, the policy applied adversely affected export competitiveness as high food prices necessitated increases in nominal wages. By contrast, among Korea's main export competitors, Hong Kong and Singapore buy food at world market prices, and food prices exceed world market prices by a smaller margin in Taiwan than in Korea.

Nor is national selfsufficiency an appropriate objective in a country with a poor natural resource endowment. This has been recognized as far as beef is concerned and in 1978 for the first time imports have been allowed. However, the import allotment is small and it is unlikely to affect prices to an appreciable extent; rather, it may give rise to high profits for traders.

Correspondingly, it would be desirable to increase the importation of beef, as well as that of other foodstuffs, in order to lower the cost of living and the rate of inflation in Korea. The objective of selfsufficiency in rice would also need to be reconsidered. This objective was adopted at the time of world-wide shortages and high rice prices, which are not expected to recur.

Note further that the high price of rice, and high agricultural prices in general, tend to discourage the movement of labor from agriculture to industry which involves an economic cost, since Korea's comparative advantage lies in manufacturing industries. And, rural-urban migration apart, it would be more desirable to raise incomes in agricultural areas by creating off-farm employment rather than through high food prices which encourage inefficient production. Agricultural incomes could be raised further by providing inducements to the production of foodstuffs, such as fruits and vegetables, for which demand is rising rapidly and import possibilities are limited due to perishability. This may be done through agricultural extension services, the provision of improved seeds, and the establishment of storage facilities.

It is recognized that the proposed measures cannot be taken overnight. Rather, there would be need for a multiannual plan for agriculture, to encompass actions regarding prices, incentives, and industrial employment. One may, for example, envisage increases in agricultural support prices not exceeding one-half of the rise in the consumer price index over a period of several years, leading to a decline of agricultural prices in real terms. At the same time, the preparation of a multiannual plan for agriculture would provide an opportunity for examining the social profitability of alternative crops.

Conclusions

This essay has provided a review of the projections of the revised 15 year plan for Korea. While noting the intention expressed in the plan to continue with an outward-oriented development strategy, doubts have been expressed as to whether the projected export growth rates will suffice to reach the rate of economic growth envisaged in the revised plan document. Also, objections have been raised to the maintenance of the export surplus envisaged for the plan period. Rather, it has been suggested that this surplus be turned into a deficit by liberalizing trade that would also permit reducing the rate of inflation and assuring efficient resource allocation and rapid economic growth.

In particular, it has been suggested that the $500 million import program instituted for the period September 1978–March 1979 be followed by additional programs, and that these be integrated with the four-year import liberalization plan. It has further been recommended to reduce tariffs and to rationalize the tariff structure in the framework of a multiannual plan, of which the proposed 1979 reform would represent the first stage.

The liberalization of import restrictions and the reform of the tariff structure should be coordinated with tax policy and investment incentives. Investment incentives, in turn, would need to be simplified and rationalized, involving the replacement of the multiplicity of existing laws and regulations by a single Investment Promotion Law. This should be done by revising the present draft of the proposed law, with the aim to reduce the role of discretionary decision-making, eliminate discrimination against medium-size firms, and avoid encouragement of capital-intensive activities.

Recommendations have further been made to replace the protection of the domestic machinery industry by promotional measures that provide equal incentives to domestic and to export sales. The policy aimed at high domestic content of machinery should also be reconsidered. The latter conclusion applies, *a fortiori*, to the automobile industry, where increasing domestic content has led to substantial cost increases. Rather than attempting to produce and export cars with a high domestic content, the expansion of labor-intensive activities in the automobile industry for domestic use and for export should be encouraged.

It has also been suggested that the pricing policy in agriculture be revised so that the prices of the major foodstuffs decline over time in real terms. At the same time, it would be desirable to provide inducements to the production of foodstuffs, for which domestic demand is rising rapidly and perishability limits import possibilities. Finally, creating off-farm employment would simultaneously improve income distribution and contribute to continued industrialization.

ESSAY 17

Development Strategy and the Six Year Plan in Taiwan

Introduction

The performance of the Taiwanese economy following the reforms undertaken around 1960 has been remarkable. Between 1960 and 1975, Taiwan's gross national product grew at an average annual rate of 8.5 percent (Table 17.1). With population increasing 2.7 percent a year, per capita GNP rose at an annual annual rate of 5.7 percent, reaching $907 in 1975—more than double the level attained in 1960. In the same period, per capita GNP in the developing countries increased on the average 3.1 percent a year and, apart from some oil-producing countries, only Japan (7.8 percent) and Korea (6.7 percent) matched Taiwan's performance.[1]

Available data also indicate that in the mid-sixties Taiwan had a more equal income distribution than Japan and Korea, whether measured in terms of the relative income of high to low income households or the Gini coefficient of income distribution.[2] Income distribution improved further in the period 1964 to 1975: the ratio of average incomes in the highest to the lowest quintile fell from 5.3 to 4.2 and the Gini coefficient declined from 0.36 to 0.31.[3]

The results reflect the favorable effects of outward-looking policies. In conformity with Taiwan's comparative advantage, these policies led to the rapid expansion of labor-intensive exports. Between 1960 and 1975, the volume of commodity exports increased at an average annual rate of 18.7 percent, with manufactured exports (excluding food, beverages and tobacco) growing 28.9 percent a year and their share in the total rising from 29 to 83 percent.

Rapid increases in manufactured exports contributed to the expansion of manufacturing production, averaging 15.9 percent a year between 1960 and 1975, and to the rise of manufacturing employment at a rate of 9.9 percent a year. The contribution of exports to employment was estimated at 10 percent in 1961, 19 percent in 1966, and 24 percent in 1971,[4] to which indirect employment effects through higher incomes should be added.

The rise of manufacturing employment was associated with increased labor force participation rates, lower unemployment rates, and the intersectoral movement of the labor force. Labor participation rates of the population aged 15 and above rose from 55.3 percent in 1966 to 58.2 percent in 1975; unemployment rates declined from 3.1 percent in 1966 to 2.4 percent in 1975; and the share of manufacturing in total employment rose from 17.3 percent in 1966 to 27.2 percent in 1975, with an incremental share of 47.7 percent.

The movement of labor from low-productivity to high-productivity sectors contributed to overall productivity growth in Taiwan. Available data show that overall productivity growth in the period 1966-75 would have been 29 percent lower if sectoral shares of employment had remained unchanged. Increased capacity use and the exploitation of large-scale economies in export industries also contributed to the rapid growth of labor productivity (4.8 percent a year between 1960 and 1975), and to low incremental capital-output ratios (2.8 percent a year between 1960 and 1975), in the Taiwanese economy.

It appears, then, that exports were the engine of economic growth in Taiwan, with the export elasticity (the ratio of the rate of growth of exports to that of GNP) averaging 2.20 between 1960 and 1975. At the same time, the labor-intensive character of exports contributed to increases in employment and to improvements in the distribution of incomes.

Projections of the Six Year Plan

The preliminary version of the *Six Year Plan for Economic Development of Taiwan, 1976–1981* has envisaged certain changes in the orientation of the Taiwanese economy.[5] It projects and average annual rate of growth of 7.5 percent for GNP and 12.5 percent for commodity exports, entailing a decline in the export elasticity to 1.67 in 1975–81 (Table 17.1).[6] The lowering of the export elasticity would be attained largely through import substitution in the production of intermediate goods.

Given the high capital intensity of industries producing intermediate goods, the incremental capital-output ratio is projected to reach 4.3 in the 1976–81 period. Also, a slowdown is projected for the manufacturing sector, with an average annual rate of growth of 9.5 percent. Larger than average increases would take place in the so-called capital and technology intensive industries (13.0 percent), with slow expansion in labor-intensive industries (7.1 percent).

The events of the first two years of the plan period have shown that the preliminary projections of the Six Year Plan were unduly pessimistic. Taiwan's GNP rose by 11.5 percent and the volume of its commodity exports by 43.2 percent in 1976; estimated increases are 8.1 percent for GNP and 7.4 percent for export volume in 1977, when world market conditions were relatively unfavorable. Thus, in two years, more than one-half of the increase in exports projected for the six-year period has been attained.

These developments call for a reconsideration of the projections made for the six year plan period. There is further need for a reappraisal of the proposed

TABLE 17.1
Principal Economic Data for Taiwan, 1960–1981

	1960-75 Actual	1975-77 Actual	1975-81 Preliminary Projections	1975-81 Alternative Projections	1977-81 Preliminar Projections	1977-81 Alternative Projections
Annual Average Growth Rates						
(1) Gross National Product	8.5	9.8	7.5	8.8	6.4	8.3
(2) Population	2.7	2.1	1.8	1.9	1.6	1.8
(3) Per Capita GNP	5.7	7.5	5.6	6.8	4.7	6.4
(4) Agricultural Production	3.8	6.8	2.5	2.5	0.4	0.4
(5) Manufacturing Production	15.9	13.5	9.5	12.1	7.6	11.4
(6) Exports	18.7	24.0	12.5	17.3	7.2	14.1
(7) Export Elasticity (6):(1)	2.20	2.45	1.67	1.97	1.13	1.70
(8) Imports	15.1	14.0	10.9	15.5	9.4	16.3
(9) Import Elasticity (8):(1)	1.78	1.43	1.45	1.76	1.47	1.95
(10) Employment	3.6	3.0	3.0	3.0	3.0	3.0
(11) Labor Productivity	4.8	6.7	4.4	5.7	3.3	5.2
Ratios						
(12) GCF/GDP	23.7	27.3	31.4	30.8	33.2	32.2
(13) GDS/GDP	24.1	30.0	29.8	28.4	29.7	27.8
(14) ICOR	2.8	2.8	4.2	3.5	5.2	3.9

Sources: 1960-75: *Taiwan Statistical Data Book, 1977,* Taipai, 1977. 1975-77: Council for Economic Planning and Development, special communication. 1975-81: Economic Planning Council, Executive Yuan, *Six Year Plan for Economic Development of Taiwan, 1976–1981* and text.

Notes: GCF/GDP = ratio of gross capital formation to the gross domestic product. GDS/GDP = ratio of gross domestic savings to the gross domestic product. ICOR = incremental capital - output ratio.

strategy that would place emphasis on capital and technology intensive industries. In this connection, attention will be given to the internal and external constraints facing the Taiwanese economy. This will be followed by a brief discussion of incentive policies in Taiwan.

Internal Constraints: The Availability and the Cost of Labor

According to the preliminary plan document, "demand for labor has risen dramatically in recent years following the rapid development of labor-intensive industries, gradually causing a labor shortage, particularly among skilled personnel and unskilled workers. In addition, wages have risen at a rate exceeding that of productivity. These factors have not only caused a decline in export competitiveness but also threaten to slow the pace of industrial development and general economic growth."[7]

There is no evidence, however, that Taiwan's export competitiveness would have declined. Thus, the 54 percent increase in the volume of commodity exports between 1975 and 1977, far exceeding the performance of any country other than Korea, and the rising export surplus (3.0 percent of GNP in 1976 and 3.8 percent in 1977) in the face of rapid economic growth and increases in foreign exchange expenditures on petroleum, point to an improvement rather than a deterioration of Taiwan's competitiveness. And, while average manufacturing wages, expressed in US dollars, increased somewhat more in Taiwan (131 percent) than in Korea (116 percent) between 1971 and 1976, the increase was substantially less than in Japan (167 percent).

Also, Taiwanese wages are low in absolute terms. In 1976, the average manufacturing wage in Taiwan was 14 percent of wages in the United States and 20 percent of wages in Japan and, with labor productivity differences being much smaller than differences in wages, labor costs per unit of output were substantially lower than in the two countries.[8] Moreover, Taiwan's competitive position vis-à-vis Japan greatly improved in 1977 as the value of the yen per U.S. dollar fell from an average of 297 in 1976 to 241 in December 1977 while the exchange rate for the Taiwanese dollar remained unchanged. Finally, wages in Taiwan exceeded wages in Korea by 16 percent in 1976, with differences narrowing in 1977.

But what about the future? Will labor shortages develop during the plan period, hindering the expansion of the manufacturing sector that provides much of Taiwan's export earnings? To answer this question, one has to consider prospective changes in total employment as well as in its sectoral distribution.

The preliminary projections call for increases in total employment of 3.0 percent a year between 1975 and 1981 as compared to 4.5 percent between 1966 and 1975. The projected decline in employment growth rates would result from slower increases in the working age population (2.9 percent a year in 1975–81 as compared to 3.8 percent in 1966–75), lower labor force participation rates (a decline from 55.7 percent in 1975 to 55.4 percent in 1981), and relatively small decreases in the rate of unemployment (from 3.7 percent in 1975 to 3.0 percent in 1981).[9]

The preliminary projections of labor force participation rates and unemployment rates may be on the high side as both of these rates fell by a full percentage point between 1975 and 1976. However, the resulting overstatements in the two figures offset each other, and one may assume that total employment would rise by-and-large according to the preliminary plan projections between 1975 and 1981.

For the projected increase of total employment, the potential for the growth of manufacturing employment is largely determined by the possibilities for transferring labor from agriculture and by the labor needs of commerce and other services. The preliminary projections call for a small decline in agricultural employment, from 1652 thousand in 1975 to 1590 thousand in 1981, and for a substantial increase of employment in commerce and other services, from 1593 thousand in 1975 to 2196 thousand in 1981. The rate of growth of employment in commerce and other services is projected to rise from 4.7 percent in 1966–75 to 5.5 percent in 1975–81 as against a decline in the rate of growth of manufacturing employment from 9.9 percent to 3.6 percent (Table 17.2).

These projections require reconsideration. To begin with, the experience of the present-day developed countries indicates that possibilities exist for a larger decline in agricultural employment than envisaged in the preliminary plan document. Such a decline occurred in the nineteen-twenties and thirties in the United States, and in the postwar period in Western Europe, with agricultural employment decreasing at an average annual rate of 3 percent in Germany and in France during the fifties. The decline was 1.5 percent a year between 1953 and 1959 in Japan, whose 1953 per capital GNP was attained in Taiwan in 1975 and whose 1959 per capita would be reached in Taiwan by 1981.

Given the potential for productivity improvements, agricultural employment in Taiwan could decrease at a rate approximating that experienced in Japan at its comparable stage of development. Calculating with an average decline of 1.5 percent a year, agricultural employment would be 1508 thousand (22.9 percent of the total) in 1981 rather than 1590 thousand (24.2 percent) as projected.

The preliminary projections for commerce and other services also require modification. The projections call for an increase in the share of commerce and other services in total employment from 28.9 percent in 1975 to 33.4 percent in 1981. Yet this share decreased in recent years from a peak of 29.7 percent in 1972, and the decline continued into 1976 when the share of commerce and other services in total employment fell to 28.6 percent.

Separating the two components of commerce and other services, one finds

TABLE 17.2
Value Added, Employment, and Productivity in Taiwan, 1975–1981 (in 1975 prices)

Sector	1975 Actual	1981 Preliminary Projections	1981 Alternative Projections	1975-81 Preliminary Projections	1975-81 Alternative Projections
		(percent)		(growth rate)	
Agriculture					
Value Added	13.8	10.3	9.6	2.5	2.5
Employment	29.9	24.2	23.0	-0.6	-1.5
Productivity	46.0	43.0	42.0	3.1	4.1
Mining					
Value Added	1.1	0.8	0.7	1.0	1.0
Employment	1.3	0.9	0.9	-2.7	-2.7
Productivity	84.0	81.0	75.0	3.9	3.9
Manufacturing					
Value Added	35.2	39.2	42.1	9.5	12.1
Employment	27.2	28.2	32.5	3.6	6.1
Productivity	130.0	139.0	130.0	5.7	5.7
Construction					
Value Added	4.6	4.7	4.5	7.8	8.5
Employment	6.4	7.1	7.4	4.7	5.3
Productivity	72.0	66.0	61.0	3.0	3.0
Electricity, Gas, Water					
Value Added	2.8	2.9	2.7	8.3	8.3
Employment	0.6	0.4	0.4	-3.9	-3.9
Productivity	460.0	725.0	676.0	12.7	12.7
Transportation and Communication					
Value Added	6.1	6.6	7.3	8.9	11.9
Employment	5.7	5.8	6.8	3.2	6.1
Productivity	107.0	114.0	106.0	5.5	5.5
Commerce and Other Services					
Value Added	36.4	35.5	33.1	7.1	7.1
Employment	28.9	33.4	29.0	5.5	3.0
Productivity	126.0	106.0	114.0	1.5	3.9

Sources: See Table 17.1.

that the share of commerce in total employment reached a peak of 14.7 percent in 1970 and declined more-or-less continuously to 13.4 percent in 1975 and 13.3 percent in 1976. Given the existing overmanning, a further decrease can be anticipated, and it may be assumed that the share of commerce in total employment will not exceed 13 percent in 1981.

The miscellaneous group of other services, including a variety of private as well as public services, showed large fluctuations, with its share varying between 14.7 percent and 16.4 percent in total employment over the last decade. Demand for these services tends to rise more rapidly than per capita incomes and this may be offset only in part by increases in productivity. It may be assumed, then, that the employment share of this sector would reach 16 percent in 1981 as compared to 15.5 percent in 1975.

Under the alternative projection, the employment share of commerce and other services would reach 29.0 percent in 1981 as compared to a share of 33.4 percent projected in the preliminary plan document, and employment in this sector would rise 3.0 percent a year between 1975 and 1981 as against the plan projection of 5.5 percent. Adopting the 7.1 percent annual increase in value added envisaged in the preliminary projections, labor productivity in commerce and services would rise at an average annual rate of 3.9 percent rather than the projected figure of 1.5 percent. The latter figure, incidentally, is less than one-half of the productivity increase observed in the previous decade and it is low by the historical standards of present-day developed countries at similar stages of development.

The preliminary projections for mining and for electricity, gas and water do not require modification while value added in construction may rise at the same rate as gross fixed capital formation (8.5 percent a year), entailing an increase in its employment share from 6.4 percent in 1975 to 7.4 percent in 1981 under the productivity hypothesis adopted in the preliminary plan document. For the assumptions made, one is left with an employment share of 39.3 percent for manufacturing and for transportation and communication, taken together, in 1981, representing an average rate of growth of employment of 6.1 percent a year between 1975 and 1981 (Table 17.2).

Assuming that this growth rate applied to both sectors, the share of manufacturing in total employment would reach 32.5 percent in 1981 as compared to a share of 27.2 percent in 1975 and 28.4 percent in 1976, which already surpassed the preliminary projection of 28.2 percent for 1981. Notwithstanding the projected decrease in overall employment growth rates from 4.5 percent a year in 1966–75 to 3.0 percent in 1976–81, an accelerated decline of employment in agriculture and a lower than planned increase of employment in commerce and other services would thus permit employment in manufacturing to grow at an average rate of 6.1 percent a year between 1975 and 1981 as against a growth rate of 3.6 percent in the plan document.

Adopting the preliminary projections for productivity growth in manufacturing value added in this sector would rise at an average annual rate of 12.1

percent in the 1975–81 period. At the same time, more rapid productivity growth in agriculture and in commerce and services, and the transfer of labor from these sectors to manufacturing and to transportation and communication, which exhibit higher productivity, would raise overall productivity levels and hence the rate of growth of GNP in Taiwan. The alternative projections are an overall productivity growth of 5.7 percent a year as against 4.4 percent in the plan document and a GNP growth of 8.8 percent a year as against the preliminary projections of 7.5 percent (Table 17.2).

With more rapid increases of value added in manufacturing, the share of this sector in the gross domestic product, expressed in terms of 1975 prices, would reach 42.1 percent in 1981 as compared to a 39.2 percent share under the preliminary projections. In this connection, the question has been raised as to whether the share of manufacturing in GDP would not reach overly high levels in Taiwan. Such a query has little justification, however, as the share of manufacturing depends on the availability of natural resources and on the prices used in the calculations. Thus, in Singapore and Hong Kong, countries that have hardly any primary production, the share of manufacturing in GDP is substantially higher than projected figures for Taiwan, and this share exceeds 40 percent in Germany also. Moreover, calculation in terms of constant prices leads to an overestimation of the future share of manufacturing in Taiwanese GDP, since service prices tend to rise faster than the prices of manufactured goods.[10]

The issue of the sectoral composition of employment can also be posed in a different way. The experience of the present-day industrial countries at a comparable stage of their development points to the conclusion that through the creation of more productive employment the expansion of the manufacturing sector is the key to rapid economic growth, higher living standards, and improved income distribution. In fact, the transfer of labor from lower-productivity to higher-productivity sectors was an important factor contributing to growth in Continental Europe even during the fifties, accounting for one-fifth to one-third of the overall increase of labor productivity. By contrast, according to the preliminary projections, their contribution would be only 11 percent in the period 1975–81 in Taiwan. The alternative projections proposed here would raise this contribution to 19 percent if rates of productivity growth were those contained in the plan document and to 16 percent if account was taken of the revised higher rates of productivity growth for agriculture and for commerce and other services.

The question is, then, if the proposed orientation of the plan, entailing a rapid expansion of what has been termed "capital and technology intensive industries" would create a sufficient number of highly-productive jobs in the manufacturing sector for rapid economic growth. This question will be considered in the following, with reference made to the constraint due to the limited availability of capital in Taiwan.

Internal Constraints: The Availability of Capital and the Sectoral Composition of Manufacturing

The expression "capital and technology intensive industries" is a misnomer. It encompasses, on the one hand, industries producing intermediate goods which are highly capital-intensive but not technology-intensive as they embody the application of known techniques that are not susceptible to rapid change. It includes, on the other hand, industries producing machinery and equipment which have relatively low capital requirements per job created and embody modern and rapidly changing technology. Also, while the former group of industries create relatively few skilled jobs per dollar invested, the latter group have high skill requirements.

These statements are borne out by estimates for U.S. manufacturing. The estimates distinguish between physical capital, which is considered under the heading "capital" in the preliminary plan document, and human capital, which represents the value of investment in skills utilized in a particular industry.[11]

In a two-digit classification scheme, the amount of physical capital needed for creating a new job, expressed in thousands of U.S. dollars, is the highest for petroleum and coal products (126.1), followed by paper and paper products (57.6), chemicals (41.4), and primary metals (32.9). By contrast, physical capital needs per job created are only about one-half of the industrial average of 20.5 in nonelectrical machinery (10.0), electrical equipment (7.1), transport equipment (11.6), and instruments and related products (11.1). It is noteworthy that some of these industries have a lower capital requirement per job created than textiles (9.4), which also include synthetic materials. At the same time, the ratio is the lowest in clothing (2.0), a traditional unskilled-labor intensive industry.

In industries producing intermediate goods, the cost of creating skilled and technical jobs in terms of physical capital invested is also high. This is indicated by the fact that the industries in question have physical to human capital ratios ranging from 1.2 to 1.9 as compared to an overall average of 0.73 for the manufacturing sector. In turn, the skill-intensive machinery and equipment industries exhibit low ratios of physical to human capital, ranging from 0.27 to 0.43 (Table 6.6).

U.S. data on capital intensity exist in a 184 commodity-category breakdown. We have established three groups of product categories, representing (a) unskilled-labor intensive, (b) physical-capital intensive, and (c) human-capital intensive products. The first group in Table 17.3 includes nine product categories which have the lowest physical capital requirements per job created, ranging from 1.6 to 2.4. At the other extreme, physical capital requirements per job created range between 40.8 and 126.1 for the nine product categories that belong to the physical-capital intensive group. Finally, the ratio of physical capital per worker is relatively low (between 5.4 and 7.4) for the nine product categories in the machinery and equipment industries that are human-capital intensive. In the latter case, the ratio of physical to human capital ranges between .13 and .19 as compared to ratios of 1.2 to 1.9 for the physical capital intensive product categories. Thus, physical capital requirements per job created as well as the ratio of physical to human capital are about ten times as high for the group of intermediate products than for the machinery and equipment product categories in Table 17.3.[12]

The data presented in Tables 6.6 and 17.3 need to be appraised by reference to the scarcity of physical capital and the relative abundance of human capital in Taiwan. The scarcity of physical capital is indicated by the fact that the value of plant and equipment per worker in Taiwan does not reach one-tenth of that in the major industrial countries of North America and Western Europe and it is lower than in several developing countries.[13] In turn, Taiwan has a high educational level that contributes to the availability of skilled and technical labor. This is shown by the Harbison-Myers index, calculated as a weighted average of enrollment rates in secondary and university education, which is substantially higher in Taiwan (103.5) than in most developing countries and it is not much below that of several industrial countries.[14]

The scarcity of physical capital and the high educational level of the labor force points to the need for upgrading Taiwan's traditional unskilled-labor intensive exports, developing machinery and equipment industries that are highly skill-intensive, and de-emphasizing industries producing intermediate goods that have high physical capital requirements. At the same time, as noted below, efficiency requires that machinery and equipment industries be oriented towards exports.

These conclusions are supported by information on interindustry differences in capital-output ratios, expressed as the ratio of plant and equipment to value added created in particular industries. The data of Table 17.3 show that industries producing intermediate goods require investments in plant and equipment per value added 3 to 6 times greater than in industries producing machinery and equipment and 5 to 10 times greater than in unskilled-labor intensive industries other than woolen yarn.

The high physical capital requirements of intermediate products find expression in the projected rise of incremental capital-output ratios from 2.8 between 1960 and 1975 to 4.2 in 1975–81 (Table 17.1), reducing increments in GNP that can be obtained with a given savings effort. At the same time, the projected rise in the average ratio of private savings to disposable income from 13.7 percent in 1975 to 22.6 percent in 1981 (Table 17.4), corresponding to a marginal savings ratio of 37.6 percent, may not be realistically expected to occur. While the marginal savings ratio exceeded 35 percent in Taiwan in years of very high increases in incomes when consumption temporarily lagged behind, it invariably declined afterwards.

TABLE 17.3
Average Capital-Labor and Capital-Output Ratios in US Manufacturing:
Selected Products

	Physical capital per worker (1)	Human capital per worker (2)	Ratio of physical to human capital (1):(2) (3)	Capital-output ratio (4)
	(thousand US dollars)			
A. *Unskilled-labor intensive* (least physical capital-intensive)				
Woolen yarn and thread	1.6	1.6	1.02	0.80
Men's and boy's clothing	1.7	9.5	0.18	0.21
Leather clothing	1.9	7.8	0.24	0.23
Underwear	1.9	7.3	0.26	0.25
Ties, corsets and gloves	2.0	15.6	0.13	0.20
Hats and caps	2.1	11.2	0.18	0.24
Women's and girl's clothing	2.1	12.4	0.17	0.24
Footwear	2.2	1.6	1.41	0.25
Leather bags	2.4	3.1	0.76	0.27
B. *Physical-capital intensive*				
Petroleum refining and products	126.1	65.6	1.92	2.92
Woodpulp	88.0	47.5	1.85	3.24
Organic chemicals	75.5	48.7	1.55	2.03
Synthetic rubber	69.4	51.2	1.36	1.82
Carbon black	62.2	38.9	1.60	1.52
Inorganic chemicals	53.5	39.3	1.36	1.77
Paper	49.3	39.8	1.24	2.59
Paperboard	42.8	35.6	1.20	1.81
Synthetic fibers	40.8	28.9	1.41	1.75
C. *Human-capital intensive*				
Radio and television	5.5	43.0	0.13	0.36
X-ray apparatus	5.9	42.9	0.14	0.34
Optical instruments	6.6	43.4	0.15	0.42
Safes and vaults	6.1	38.5	0.16	0.26
Aircraft	6.8	41.5	0.16	0.39
Scientific instruments and control equipment	6.0	35.2	0.18	0.42
Ships and boats	5.7	32.2	0.18	0.52
Computers	7.4	41.6	0.18	0.37
Electrical measuring instruments	5.7	30.0	0.19	0.38

Source: Bela Balassa, "A 'Stages Approach' to Comparative Advantage," Essay 6 in this volume, Supplementary Tables.

Calculating with a marginal savings ratio of 30 percent for the 1975–81 period,[15] the average private savings ratio would be 19.8 percent in 1981 under the projected GNP growth rate of 7.5 percent.[16] For given public and foreign savings, the share of gross domestic investment in GNP in 1981 would then be 31.0 percent as compared to the projected figure of 32.9 percent. With lower

TABLE 17.4
Export-Import and Investment-Savings Balance in Taiwan, 1975 and 1981

	Actual 1975	Preliminary Projections 1981	Alternative Projections 1981	Average Annual Growth Rates	
				Preliminary Projections 1975-81	Alternative Projections 1975-81
	(billions of 1975 NT dollars)			(percent)	
A. Export-Import Balance					
Exports					
(1) Commodity	201.6	408.8	525.8	12.5	17.3
(2) Services	27.9	50.5	50.5	10.4	10.4
(3) Together	229.5	459.3	576.3	12.3	16.6
Imports					
(4) Commodity	211.2	393.0	501.8	10.9	15.5
(5) Services	35.7	64.0	84.8	10.2	15.5
(6) Together	246.9	457.0	586.6	10.8	15.5
(7) Commodity Trade Balance (1)—(4)	−9.6	+15.8	+24.0		
(8) Services Balance (2)—(5)	−7.8	−13.5	−34.3		
(9) Goods and Services Balances (3)—(6) = (7)—(8)	−17.4	+2.3	−10.3		
(10) Factor Income Payments	−3.3	−5.0	−5.0		
(11) Transfer Payments	+0.3	+0.3	+0.4		
(12) Foreign Capital (9)—(10)—(11)	−20.4	−2.4	−14.9		
B. Investment Savings Balance					
(1) Disposable Income	368.0	583.5	627.4	8.0	9.3
(2) Private Consumption	317.4	451.8	499.0	6.1	7.8
(3) Private Savings	50.6	131.7	128.4	17.3	16.8
(4) Average Savings Rate	13.7	22.6	20.5		
(5) Government Savings	39.2	63.0	64.2	8.2	8.6
(6) Savings by Public Enterprises	12.2	19.9	20.3	8.5	8.9
(7) Depreciation	40.8	67.6	68.5	8.8	9.0
(8) Cross Domestic Savings (3)—(5)—(6)—(7)	142.8	282.2	281.4	12.0	12.0
(9) Foreign Capital (A12)	20.4	2.4	14.9	−30.0	−5.1
(10) Gross Capital Formation (GCF)	163.2	284.6	296.3	9.8	10.5
(11) Gross Domestic Product (GDP)	560.0	864.9	928.9	7.5	8.8
(12) GCF/GDP (10)÷(11)	29.1	32.9	31.9		
(13) Foreign Capital/GDP (9)÷(11)	3.6	0.3	1.6		
(14) Gross Domestic Savings/GDP (8)÷(11)	25.5	32.6	30.3		
(15) Foreign Capital/GCF (9)÷(10)	12.5	0.8	5.0		

Source: See Table 17.1.

savings and investment ratios, then, projected rates of economic growth could not be reached under the planned industrial composition of GNP. This is, *a fortiori*, the case for attaining the 8.8 percent GNP growth rate envisaged under the alternative projections.

The above considerations indicate the undesirability of rapidly expanding industries producing intermediate goods, even if foreign savings were to provide for 5 percent of capital formation in 1981, instead of a share of 0.8 percent envisaged in preliminary projections, as proposed below. The reallocation of investment resources to industries with lower capital requirements, then, would permit reducing the projected incremental capital output ratio of 4.2 to 3.5 in the 1975–81 period (Table 17.1).

It has been suggested, however, that the expansion of industries producing intermediate products would be necessary in order to ensure the security of supplies. Such suggestions find their origin in the situation existing in 1973–74, when shortages of petrochemicals and fertilizers were experienced and there were few suppliers to choose from. But, rather than shortages, one can expect an oversupply of these products over the next decade. And, with the expansion of the production of petrochemicals and fertilizers in the industrial countries, as well as in several oil-exporting countries, there will be a diversity of suppliers in the future. At the same time, Taiwan is put at a disadvantage in the production of petrochemicals and fertilizers by reason of the high cost of capital and energy used both as a raw material and in processing, while these factors provide advantages especially to the oil-producing countries.

Limitations of domestic energy supplies should also discourage the expansion of the production of non-ferrous metals in Taiwan, where the high cost of transporting the raw material provides a further disadvantage. These considerations explain why few industrial countries produce nonferrous metals. Thus, copper is usually manufactured in countries where copper deposits are found, while aluminum is produced where cheap hydroelectricity is available. Also, small industrial countries do not produce petrochemicals and fertilizers or produce only certain varieties in order to exploit economies of scale. This contrasts with suggestions made for Taiwan to aim at self-efficiency in the principal petrochemicals and fertilizers used domestically as well as in nonferrous metals.

Apart from reducing the rate of economic growth, such a policy would not fail to have adverse effects on employment, the regionalization of industry, and income distribution. To begin with, industries producing physical-capital intensive intermediate goods create few jobs and would absorb only a small fraction of Taiwan's educated labor force. This would slow down the transfer of labor to industry as well as the upgrading of the labor, and it may give rise to unemployment among educated people. Also, the large investments necessary for producing physical-capital intensive intermediate products are less conducive to the regional dispersion of industry than the expansion of other industrial sectors. The slow upgrading of the labor force, the possible unemployment of educated people, the low rate of labor transfer to industry, and the lack of creation of industrial employment opportunities in agricultural areas would not fail to have adverse effects on income distribution in Taiwan.

Note further that foreign exchange savings in physical-capital intensive intermediate goods are small, since the basic materials have to be imported. At the same time, in order to make these industries profitable, they require protection that raises costs to domestic industries and ultimately discourages exports. The low or even negative profitability of the production of these commodities in terms of world market prices (social profitability) contrasts with rates of social profits of approximately 15 percent in other industries.[17]

External Constraints

It may be concluded that, rather than a shift towards import substitution in intermediate goods, continued outward orientation would be beneficial for Taiwan. This would involve the upgrading of traditional unskilled-labor intensive exports as well as the development of skill-intensive production and exports of machinery and equipment. Broadly defined, the latter also includes the production of parts, components, and accessories for assembly abroad.

Recommendations made for continued outward orientation raise questions as to the external constraints Taiwan may face in regard to particular commodities and markets. In this connection, it has been suggested that the possibilities for further expanding the exports of textiles, clothing, and shoes are poor in Taiwan, in part because of increased protection in the developed countries and in part because of the emergence of new competitors in the developing countries. Correspondingly, the preliminary plan document projects these exports to rise at an average annual rate of growth of 8.3 percent in terms of constant prices, representing an increase of 61 percent for the entire 1975–81 period (Table 17.5).[18] However, the exports of this category rose by 55 percent in terms of current prices in 1976 alone, when price increases were small. And, while the 1976 figure was apparently not fully matched in 1977 when world market conditions were poor, various considerations suggest that exports would increase further in the future.

To begin with, quantitative import restrictions on the products in question are set in volume rather than in value terms, thereby providing opportunities for upgrading exports. Furthermore, markets exist outside the developed countries, in particular in the Middle East, where Taiwanese exports could increase substantially. Finally, there are few signs as yet that new competitors would emerge among countries at lower income levels in the near future.

Taking account of these factors, the exports of textiles, clothing and footwear may increase at a rate substantially higher than that projected in the preliminary plan document. One may envisage a growth rate of 13.0 percent for 1975–81, corresponding to an export growth rate of about 8 percent between 1977 and 1981. This projection is slightly below that contained in the preliminary 1975–81 plan for Korea (13.9 percent) and it is substantively below the alternative projections proposed by the author (16.4 percent) (Table 17.5).

Higher export growth rates may also be envisaged for the group of miscellaneous light industrial products, where continued product diversification promises considerable possibilities of expansion. A growth rate of 20.0 percent is proposed here which exceeds the 15.0 figure in the plan document but it is lower than the actual growth rate between 1975 and 1977 in Taiwan and the planned growth rates for the constituent parts of this product category for Korea, none of which are below 23 percent.

The preliminary projections for wood, wood products, and furniture also need to be revised upwards. Given the possibilities for expanding the exports of furniture, it is recommended that the projected growth rate of 10.8 percent be raised to 15.0 percent. This compares with growth rates of 22.3 and 24.2 percent under the plan projections and the proposed revisions, respectively, for Korea.

The preliminary projections for food, beverages, and tobacco (an average annual rate of 3.9 percent) are also on the low side as the expansion of nontraditional exports between 1975 and 1977 can be expected to continue in the future. Calculating with a growth rate of 5.0 percent a year, the proposed revisions would entail raising projected export growth rates for light industrial products from 9.5 percent to 13.8 percent for the period 1977–81.

Within the heavy and chemical industries group, the export projections would need to be raised for the machinery and equipment industries. The average growth rate of 18.2 percent projected for these industries is not only substantially lower than the preliminary plan projections (32.5) and the proposed revisions (37.1) for Korea, but also falls below past growth rates in Japan.

Japanese exports of machinery and equipment rose at an average annual rate of 26.0 percent between 1951 and 1967 and 23.3 percent between 1967 and 1975 (Table 17.5). Considering that Taiwan would reach Japan's 1959 income level only in 1981, it could attain the 1951–67 Japanese export growth rates for machinery and equipment during the plan period, provided that appropriate policies are followed.

Correspondingly, the projected export growth rate for machinery and equipment has been raised from 18.2 percent to 25.0 percent for the 1975–81 period, with a greater than average adjustment made for the machinery category, where Taiwan made more rapid progress in recent years than Korea. Upward adjustments have also been made in the chemicals, coal and petroleum products, nonmetallic mineral products, and metal products categories, where the 1981 targets have in large part been reached by 1977.

With the proposed adjustments, the export growth rates projected for the 1975–81 period would be raised from 12.7 percent to 17.5 percent for manufactured exports, taken together (Table 17.5). These figures may still be

TABLE 17.5
The Growth and Composition of Manufactured Exports in Japan,
Korea, and Taiwan (in constant prices)

	Japan					
	1951	1963	1967	1975	1951-67	1967-75
	percent				growth rate	
Light Manufacturing	*48.3*	*34.9*	*28.5*	*12.4*	*13.0*	*5.8*
Food, Beverages, Tobacco	5.3	2.8	1.9	0.5	9.6	0.8
Textiles, Clothing, Footwear	35.3	20.1	15.8	6.1	11.2	4.7
Wood, Wood Products, Furniture	1.6	1.9	1.2	0.2	14.5	−6.8
Paper and Paper Products	1.5	1.2	0.9	0.8	13.6	15.5
Leather and Leather Products	0.2	0.0	0.0	0.0	n/a	n/a
Rubber Products	0.5	1.5	1.3	1.3	23.3	18.7
Other	3.9	7.3	7.5	2.5	22.0	7.2
Heavy and Chemical Industries	*51.7*	*65.1*	*71.5*	*87.6*	*19.1*	*20.9*
Chemicals and Chemical Products	2.8	6.2	8.2	7.3	12.5	16.1
Coal and Petroleum Products	0.1	0.3	0.4	0.3	30.7	15.1
Nonmetallic Mineral Products	6.3	4.4	2.8	1.4	11.8	7.7
Basic Metals	26.2	17.3	16.6	20.1	13.6	20.7
Iron and Steel	20.8	16.3	15.3	19.1	14.7	21.1
Nonferrous	5.4	1.0	1.3	1.0	6.8	14.5
Metal Products	4.8	4.6	4.9	3.4	16.9	12.6
Machinery and Equipment	11.6	32.3	38.6	55.2	26.0	23.3
Machinery	n/a	n/a	n/a	n/a	n/a	n/a
Electronics	n/a	n/a	n/a	n/a	n/a	n/a
Transport Equipment	n/a	n/a	n/a	n/a	n/a	n/a
Manufacturing, total	100.0	100.0	100.0	100.0	16.9	17.9

Sources: Japan: United Nations, *Yearbook of International Trade Statistics* and International
Monetary Fund, *International Financial Statistics.* Korea: A. *Long-Term Social and Eco-
nomic Development Plan for Korea, 1976-91.* B - Alternative Projections contained in Bela
Balassa, "The Fifteen-Year Social and Economic Development Plan for Korea" reprinted in
Essay 15 in this volume. Taiwan: A - *Six Year Plan for Economic Development of Taiwan,
1976–1981.* B - Alternative projections described in text.

Notes: Constant value figures for Taiwan's exports for the 1975-81 period have been derived by
assuming that the general export price deflator used in the plan applied equally to all commodity
groups. Furthermore, plastic shoes have been included in the textiles, clothing and footwear
category while other plastic products and other textile, leather, rubber, paper and allied products
have been consolidated with the other category and included among light industrial products for
comparability with Japanese and Korean data.

n/a = not available.

on the low side, however, if we consider that projected growth rates of Korean
manufactured exports are 22.5 percent under the preliminary plan for 1975–
81 and 26.0 percent under the proposed revisions, while the rate of export
expansion was about the same in the two countries between 1975 and 1977.

The plan figures for primary exports also require modification. As a result
of the rapid expansion of nontraditional exports, including vegetables and
feathers, primary exports rose by two-thirds in terms of current prices between
1975 and 1977 while the preliminary projections envisaged increases barely

Korea					Taiwan				
1975	1981A	1981B	1975-81		1975	1981A	1981B	1975-81	
	percent		growth rate A	B		percent		growth rate A	B
65.3	48.0	46.8	16.3	19.0	68.8	57.9	58.9	9.5	13.8
6.7	4.9	4.2	16.5	16.6	12.8	7.2	5.3	3.9	5.0
45.4	29.3	28.2	13.9	16.4	36.2	28.5	29.9	8.3	13.0
5.5	5.5	5.1	22.3	24.2	5.7	5.1	5.0	10.6	15.0
0.7	0.8	1.0	24.7	31.5	0.8				
1.9	2.0	2.4	23.5	31.4	n/a	17.1	18.1	15.0	20.0
1.9	2.3	2.2	26.4	28.6	0.9				
3.2	3.2	3.7	23.1	29.2	13.5				
34.7	52.0	53.2	31.0	35.3	31.2	42.1	42.9	18.5	24.0
4.4	5.2	5.1	26.2	29.0	2.1	3.4	3.0	22.1	25.0
1.8	1.9	1.8	23.9	25.8	1.1	1.3	1.3	17.1	20.0
2.0	2.7	3.1	28.6	25.4	1.2	1.7	1.7	20.0	24.0
4.5	8.0	7.7	35.0	38.0	2.4	3.4	2.4	19.1	19.1
4.3	7.7	7.4	35.2	38.2	n/a	n/a	n/a	n/a	n/a
0.2	0.3	0.3	31.1	34.0	n/a	n/a	n/a	n/a	n/a
2.6	3.3	3.6	27.0	32.7	2.7	3.3	3.1	16.1	20.0
19.3	30.8	31.9	32.5	37.1	21.7	29.0	31.4	18.2	25.0
4.8	7.5	8.4	32.0	38.5	8.3	10.1	11.7	16.2	24.4
9.4	13.3	13.4	29.8	33.3	11.0	15.6	16.3	19.4	25.5
5.1	10.0	10.2	37.3	41.7	2.4	3.3	3.4	19.3	25.0
100.0	100.0	100.0	22.5	26.0	100.0	100.0	100.0	12.7	17.5

exceeding one-half in terms of constant prices between 1975 and 1981. A volume increase of 125 percent in these exports is within the realm of possibilities.

All in all, the alternative projections would entail raising projected growth rates for the commodity exports of Taiwan in the 1975–81 period from 12.5 percent to 17.3 percent. The resulting export elasticity of 1.97 (Table 17.1) would exceed export elasticities of 1.78 for Japan in 1951–67 and 1.69 in 1967–75; it is comparable to the figure projected for Korea in the 1975–81 period (1.95 under the preliminary projections and 2.05 under the alternative projections) and to the corresponding elasticities for smaller European countries, such as Belgium (1.98) and the Netherlands (2.00), during the 1960–75 period. Nor would Taiwan exceed the share of exports in GNP observed in Belgium and the Netherlands in 1981 under the alternative projections if exports are expressed in value added terms and in current prices, with adjustments made for trends in relative prices.[9]

Note further that the average export elasticity was 2.20 in Taiwan between 1960 and 1975 and it exceeded 2 even during the 1970–75 period, which encompassed the 1974–75 world recession. And, the export elasticity was

2.45 in 1975–77, so that the alternative projections correspond to an export elasticity of 1.70 for 1977–81. The latter figure would result from an export growth rate of 14.1 percent and a GNP growth rate of 8.3 percent for the remaining four years of the plan period.

The higher export elasticity proposed for the 1975–81 period reflects the importance of exports in the process of economic growth. As shown in a comparative study of eleven developing countries, exports contribute to economic growth by permitting specialization according to comparative advantage, increasing the degree óf capacity utilization, allowing for economies of scale, and stimulating technological improvements.[20] These factors assume special importance in small countries such as Taiwan where the possibilities for rapid growth in the confines of domestic markets are severely circumscribed.

Domestic market limitations also call for specializing in narrow product ranges in machinery and equipment industries i.e., exporting some products and importing others, while the scarcity of physical capital should discourage import-substitution in intermediate products as noted above. Considering further the need for imported foods and raw materials that are unavailable in Taiwan, or are available only in limited quantities, imports would have to rise more rapidly than envisaged in the preliminary plan document.

Taking account of these factors, as well as the desirability to maintain the inflow of foreign capital as discussed below, it would be appropriate to raise the projected import growth rate from 10.9 percent to 15.5 percent a year for the 1975–81 period. With increases in the projected rate of growth of GNP from 7.5 percent to 8.8 percent, this would entail raising the import elasticity from 1.45 to 1.76, which roughly equals the elasticity of 1.78 for the 1960–75 period. For the remaining four years of the plan, the import elasticity would be 1.95, exceeding the average for the 1960–75 period but falling behind the 1965–70 figure of 2.20.

Incentive Policies for the Machinery Sector[21]

A study of the system of incentives in Taiwan shows that, in accordance with the outward-oriented policy followed, exports and import substitution received approximately equal incentives.[22] In recent years, however, import substitution in industries producing intermediate goods received preferential treatment. The measures used for this purpose included the provision of investment credit at low interest rates; exemptions from corporate income taxes for a five-year period or accelerated depreciation at the choice of the producer; deferment of the starting date of the period of tax exemption; reductions in corporate income tax rates after the end of the period of tax exemption; tax credits for purchasers of stocks and bonds of companies in these industries; tariff exemptions and access to low interest loans on imported machinery; and, in some cases, the provision of domestically produced materials below cost.

By raising rates of private profitability above social profitability, the described measures favor industries producing intermediate goods that are highly (physical) capital-intensive and do not conform to Taiwan's comparative advantage. At the same time, the measures applied encourage the use of physical capital that is scarce in Taiwan while reducing employment possibilities.

These considerations call for reducing the preferential treatment granted to the industries in question. The conclusion is reinforced if we consider that the infant industry argument has little relevance to industries producing intermediate goods, which generally utilize a well-known technology. In turn, the production of machinery and equipment often involves a long learning process and infant industry considerations warrant the application of promotional measures on a temporary basis. Various measures may be taken for this purpose.

To begin with, although credit facilities are supposed to be equally available for the production of machinery and equipment and for the manufacture of intermediate products, in practice the latter tend to receive more advantageous treatment. Public enterprises generally have first claim on investment credit; apart from a state-owned firm producing machinery, these enterprises are in intermediate goods industries. Also, large private firms manufacturing intermediate products have greater access to credit than the generally smaller firms producing machinery and equipment. Finally, the availability of credit is affected by the fact that there is less risk in lending to protected intermediate goods industries, which sell mostly in the domestic market, than in lending to firms producing machinery and equipment, whose profits greatly depend on success in exporting that involves considerable uncertainty.

Increasing the size of the relatively small Development Fund and channeling resources from the public to the private sector would improve the availability of capital to the machinery and equipment industries. This objective would further be served by establishing a separate bank to finance investment in these industries. Such a bank could be empowered to take greater risks by the judicious use of government guarantees.

Among producers of machinery and equipment, small and medium size firms in particular suffer discrimination in the provision of credit. Furthermore, the lower limit established for granting duty-free entry of machinery and equipment in Taiwan—a minimum of NT$100 million for a new firm as well as for an extension of an existing firm—excludes even medium size machinery producers. Thus, several machinery firms reported on by Larry Westphal, each of which exported more than $2 million a year and had a labor force of 300 to 500, had paid-in capital of less than this limit.[23]

Promotional efforts also tend to benefit large firms. The government provides support to enter the export market for large, world-scale turn-key plants without giving equal attention to exports of small plants. Yet, medium size firms have been successful in exporting small turn-key plants that fit the needs of developing countries. And, for some time to come, technological as well as marketing factors will continue to favor the exportation of such plants, utilizing intermediate technology, from Taiwan to the developing countries.

These considerations indicate the desirability of eliminating discrimination against medium size machinery producers in the provision of credit in government promotion, and in setting a lower limit of eligibility for the duty-free entry of machinery and equipment. Eligibility limits for capacity expansion would also need to be reduced in order to encourage the growth of existing producers.

It would further be desirable to decentralize the existing large research institute in Taiwan and to establish specialized institutes serving the needs of the principal machinery and equipment industries, so as to increase the relevance of research for the practical application of new technology. This objective would also be served by providing preferential treatment for the establishment of joint research facilities by private firms. Finally, the development of machinery and equipment industries would be promoted through the creation of specialized industrial parks and increases in the governments contribution to the cost of vocational training.

The proposed measures would have the effect of reducing the cost of production in Taiwan's fledgling machinery and equipment industries for sale in both domestic and export markets. These measures are preferable to protection which favors production for domestic markets over exports; limits the volume and thus raises the cost of production; and adversely affects the costs of user industries. In particular, subjecting machinery imports to licensing would have adverse economic effects, as governmental organizations are hardly able to evaluate differences in quality and specifications between domestically-produced and imported machinery and equipment in judging the merits of requests for import licenses.

Finally, the need to keep up with rapid technological change abroad in the machinery and equipment industries points to the desirability of attracting foreign investment to these industries. Such will be the case particularly if foreign investment involves joint ownership with the country's own nationals, thus contributing to the transfer of knowledge. And, apart from technology, the foreign partners bring marketing expertise, which is of particular importance in industries characterized by product differentiation, such as machinery and equipment.

Technological and marketing considerations also favor subcontracting arrangements under which Taiwanese firms produce parts, components and accessories for assembly elsewhere. Given its geographical proximity and the large difference in wage levels, Japan offers good prospects for such arrangements. There are some examples of subcontracting, e.g., in the automobile industry, but further encouragement on the part of the government would be desirable.

More generally, it would be desirable that the Taiwanese Government increases its efforts to attract foreign direct investment. Vigorous promotion and greater administrative simplicity in the treatment of foreign investment would be of particular usefulness in this regard.

Reforming Price Incentives

The proposed measures aim at the expansion of machinery and equipment industries where Taiwan has a comparative advantage and infant industry considerations are of considerable importance. At the same time, one should forego the preferential treatment of industries producing intermediate goods where these conditions are not fulfilled. Changes would also be desirable in incentives to other industries, including price setting by the government, export subsidies, import tariffs and import licensing.

Price setting by the government plays an important role in agriculture as well as in regard to natural gas and petroleum products. As to the former, the government purchase-price of rice was much below the market price during the fifties and the sixties, entailing the imposition of a "hidden rice tax." This, in turn, led to the expansion of the production of alternative crops, including sugar cane, fruit, and vegetables at the expense of rice.[24]

The hidden tax on rice was reduced in the late sixties and the situation was reversed a few years afterwards when, in response to worldwide shortages, the government purchase price of rice was substantially raised; this price now exceeds the world market price by over one-half. As a result, rice production has greatly expanded, leading to overproduction and inventory accumulation that has entailed a substantial cost for the Treasury.

In retrospect, it appears that the response to a temporary shortage of rice has been overdone. With increasing production in Southeast Asia, Taiwan can obtain rice at a low cost in years where its production does not meet domestic needs. At the same time, foreign exchange earned in the production of export crops, such as sugar, fruits, and vegetables, entails lower domestic resource costs than does the saving of foreign exchange in rice imports.

Increased incomes in export crops, then, may be attained at a lower cost (greater benefit) to the national economy. Correspondingly, a high rice price can hardly be an appropriate income distributional measure as it was suggested. This conclusion applies *a fortiori* to the creation of industrial employment that promises considerable benefits to Taiwan while a high rice price may slow down the transfer of labor to high-productivity industrial jobs.

Taking further account of relatively small expected increases in the demand for rice at higher income levels, it appears desirable to reduce the government purchase-price of rice below current levels. At the same time, security objectives could be served by stocking rice in an amount corresponding to one year's imports.

The pricing of foodgrains, too, would require reconsideration. There is a potential contradiction in the preliminary plan document that proposes "to lower import duties on food grains in the interest of promoting growth of the livestock industry"[25] while stating that "guaranteed prices will be set for feed crops".[26] Given the rapid rise of demand for meat and other livestock products, one would need to avoid setting overly high prices for domestically-produced feedgrains and to continue relying on cheap imported feedstocks.

Questions arise also concerning the price of natural gas and petroleum products. The price of gasoline is relatively low in Taiwan by comparison to the other countries of the region. And, the price of diesel oil is much below that of gasoline, which is not the case in the other countries. Differences are even larger for fuel oil, and the China Petroleum Company provides natural gas and certain petroleum products to domestic users for further transformation at prices lower than the world market prices.

The relatively low prices of gasoline, diesel oil, and fertilizer are not conducive to savings in fuel. Furthermore, the low price of natural gas and petroleum products provides a subsidy to domestic users, thereby contributing to the maintenance and expansion of energy-using production methods. The adoption of more realistic prices, in turn, would lead to import savings and discourage inefficient operations.

Incentives to Export and Import Substitution

Taiwan has long provided practically free trade treatment to exports, with some additional subsidies, while import protection has often been redundant. As noted above, exports and import substitution received, on the average, similar treatment in 1969. Since 1975, however, there has been a decline in export subsidies. Thus, the government has abolished income tax reductions for exports, preferential credit margins have been reduced,[27] and the schemes applied in several industries by manufacturers' associations to subsidize exports no longer exist.

The decline in export incentives has not been compensated by commensurate reductions in import protection, leading to a rise in the extent of the bias against exports. Tariff changes undertaken in 1970 were generally in the upward direction, and subsequent reductions in tariffs have been smaller in magnitude. And, while the number of products subject to import control was greatly reduced in the early sixties, import licensing requirements have subsequently been imposed on various products in conjunction with the objective of expanding industries producing intermediate goods and machinery.

Considerations of economic efficiency would require that exports receive equal treatment with production for domestic markets, since foreign exchange earned through exports has the same value to the national economy as foreign exchange saved through import substitution. Furthermore, new exports in the machinery and equipment industries would need preferential treatment, in part to support their early development and in part to increase their competitiveness vis-à-vis developed country producers that benefit from preferential credits and tied aid provisions.

These objectives would be served by increasing incentives to exports and reducing import protection. Export incentives can take the form of increasing the scope of export credits, reforming the system of export guarantees, and initiating additional export promotion measures.

While short-term preferential export credits have long been provided, they are not granted automatically as in the case of Korea. In fact, while under current regulations export credits could amount to one-fifth of the exports of the previous 12 months, in November 1977 the actual ratio was only 2.9 percent.[28] This result is indicative of the rather conservative banking practices in Taiwan and compares with a ratio of 12.3 percent in Korea. At the same time, the amount available for medium-term export credit is also limited in Taiwan, and export credits with a maturity of over 5 years will be provided only after the establishment of the proposed Export-Import Bank. And the initial capitalization of the Bank is rather low, with a total of NT$5 billion.

To further the expansion of exports, it would be desirable to liberalize requirements for export credit and to increase the amount made available for this purpose. This may involve, among other things, providing credits for working capital needs at the time the export contract is signed and increasing the size of the proposed Export-Import Bank. It would further be desirable to reform the existing system of export guarantees; the fact that such guarantees are costly and difficult to obtain may be one of the factors responsible for the low utilization of export credits.

Credit allocation has recently been liberalized for large trading firms, which also enjoy prior exemption from tariffs on important inputs without the need for Bank guarantees required from other importers. Consideration should be given to extending these benefits to smaller, specialized trading firms, which may be especially effective in exporting to developing countries. It would also be desirable to grant preferential income tax treatment on marketing expenditures in new export markets and new export products. Finally, an increased effort should be made to collect market information abroad.

There would further be need to reform the present tariff structure. A large proportion of tariffs are redundant but have nevertheless remained on the books. Nor do differences in tariffs on inputs and outputs exhibit a clear economic purpose, and recent changes in selected tariffs have done little to improve their rationality.

The rationalization of tariffs would require an overall reform rather than piecemeal changes. Such a reform could be accomplished by devising general rules that take protection of value added in processing as a point of departure.[29] This is referred to in the plan document that calls for adjusting the structure of import tariff rates, so "as to make the difference in rates for raw materials, semi-finished products and finished products more rational for promoting transformation of the industrial structure and protecting domestic industry".[30] At the same time, the proposed reduction or elimination of tariffs on raw materials[31] without commensurate changes in tariffs on products using these materials as inputs would increase the effective protection of user activities.

The reform of the tariff structure assumes particular importance as the Taiwanese economy become more sophisticated, and horizontal as well as vertical differences in tariffs create increasing distoritions in resource allocation. Reducing these distortions and lessening the bias against exports would also require lowering tariffs.

As it is recognized in the preliminary plan document[32] tariffs reductions would involve a loss in budgetary revenue. This may be recouped by increasing indirect taxes or raising income tax revenues. As regards the former, consideration should be given to introducing a value added tax to replace existing commodity and stamp taxes. A value added tax has the advantages of neutrality in its economic effects and of providing encouragement to exports through the use of tax rebates which are permissible under GATT. A value added tax could be combined with luxury taxes on selected items.

Reforming the tariff system could not be accomplished overnight. Rather, in order to limit disruptions in the national economy and to reduce uncertainty to producers, tariff reductions would need to be carried out over time according to a timetable made public in advance. This could be done by setting tariff targets for the end of the six-year plan period, together with tariff changes for intervening years. Provisions may also be made for additional infant industry protection on a temporary basis and on a degressive scale.

Reforming the tariff system would not suffice, however, as long as import licensing is used to exclude, or to limit, the imports of certain commodities that compete with domestic production.[33] The plan document calls for relaxing "unnecessary import controls."[34] This should be part of the application of a general reform of trade liberalization, to be coordinated with the reform of the structure of tariffs.

The liberalization of import control is desirable in order to improve the rationality of the system of protection. It could further be used as a bargaining tool since the maintenance of import restrictions increases the danger of limitations on Taiwanese exports. In this connection, it should be emphasized that, with manufactured imports exceeding $5 billion in 1977, Taiwan offers a substantial market for foreign goods.

Particular importance attaches to trade with the member countries of the European Common Market, which accounted for only 9.8 percent of Taiwanese imports in 1976 as compared to a share of 32.3 percent for Japan and 23.6 percent for the United States. At the same time, Taiwan had an export surplus with the Common Market that adds to protectionist pressures in the EEC countries.

Taiwan's balance-of-payments position would permit trade liberalization in the immediate future. At the same time, apart from fueling protectionist pressures abroad, a balance-of-payments surplus is undesirable since it involves a transfer of Taiwanese savings abroad while Taiwan needs to import foreign capital.

The desirability of capital imports is not sufficiently recognized in the preliminary plan document, which envisages a decline in net capital imports from NT20.4 billion in 1975 to NT2.4 billion in 1981 in terms of 1975 prices, i.e., from 12.5 percent to 0.8 percent of total capital requirements (Table 17.4).[35] Various considerations call for increasing this figure.

To begin with, as noted earlier, it does not appear likely that private savings would reach levels projected in the plan document. Furthermore, the development of machinery and equipment industries calls for foreign direct investment that brings with it new technology and marketing knowledge. Finally, the excess of the social profitability of capital in Taiwan over foreign interest rates points to the desirability of borrowing abroad.

It may be suggested that, as a minimum, Taiwan should aim at financing 5 percent of its total capital requirements by the inflow of foreign capital in 1981 (Table 17.4). The increased capital inflow would offset part of the shortfall in private savings as compared to the preliminary plan projections. This would be sufficient for reaching a growth rate of GNP of 8.8 percent as reductions in the share of physical-capital intensive intermediate goods industries would entail a lowering of incremental capital-output ratios (Table 17.1).

Conclusions

This essay has reviewed proposed policies and preliminary projections for the 1975–81 period covered by the Six Year Plan. It has been proposed that Taiwan should continue with its outward-oriented strategy, involving the upgrading of traditional manufactured exports and the development of machinery and equipment exports, and that it should avoid rapid expansion in industries producing intermediate goods.

This alternative would represent an efficient use of resources in the Taiwanese economy, given the actual and potential availability of skilled and technical labor, which are required to upgrade traditional exports and to expand the production of machinery and equipment, and the scarcity of physical capital and energy, which are used extensively in intermediate goods industries. The low physical-capital requirements of traditional and nontraditional export industries and the increased use of high-productivity labor in the manufacturing sector would also permit raising targets for economic growth in the 1975–81 period. At the same time, the transfer of labor from agriculture to manufacturing and the upgrading of industrial labor would lead to more equitable income distribution.

Continuing with outward orientation would require providing appropriate incentives as well as capital to export industries. Apart from reducing incentives and credit allocation to industries producing intermediate goods, recommendations have been made in this essay for the application of measures that would ensure the development of efficient machinery and equipment industries and the expansion of exports in general. Also, it has been proposed to prepare a comprehensive reform of the tariff structure and the system of import licensing.

Taiwan's export surplus in 1977 would permit liberalizing imports in the immediate future. In fact, it would be desirable to turn this surplus into a deficit, in part to reduce protectionist pressures abroad and in part to obtain the benefits of the inflow of foreign capital. As regards the former, Taiwan could enter into bilateral negotiations to ensure better treatment for its exports in exchange for liberalizing imports. Also, in view of the expected shortfall of private savings as compared to the preliminary projections, the technical and marketing know-how associated with foreign direct investments, and the high productivity of capital in Taiwan, it would be desirable to encourage foreign direct investment in Taiwan.

ESSAY 18
Incentives for Economic Growth in Taiwan

Introduction

This essay follows the author's "Development Strategy and the Six Year Plan in Taiwan," published as Essay 17 in this volume. The preceding essay made recommendations for modifying the projections of the *Six Year Plan for Economic Development of Taiwan, 1976–81* and for maintaining an outward-oriented development strategy in Taiwan. It also proposed measures for promoting the machinery industry, reforming incentives, and reducing discrimination against exports relative to import substitution.

The essay will review the revised plan projections pertaining to the years 1978 to 1981. It will further examine alternative ways to eliminate the actual and projected current account surplus of Taiwan and recommend establishing a program of trade liberalization for this purpose. Recommendations will also be made for coordinating incentive policies and reforming the Statute for Encouragement of Incentives. Finally, issues relating to the establishment of an automobile industry and the modernization of agriculture will be briefly considered.

The Revised Six Year Plan[1]

The revised Six Year Plan presents a realistic and consistent set of projections that appropriately reflect the potential of the Taiwanese economy. The revised growth projections for the 1978–81 period are substantially higher than those of the preliminary version and generally conform to the recommendations made by the author. Also, the revised plan recognizes the need for exports to continue their leading role in Taiwan's economic development. This represents the continuation of an outward-oriented strategy whereas the previous version envisaged a considerable degree of import substitution that was criticized by the author.

As shown in Table 18.1, variants A and B of the plan, respectively, call for GNP growth rates of 9.3 percent and 8.3 percent, equidistant from the 8.8 figure proposed by the author and substantially above the preliminary projection of 7.5 percent for the 1975–81 period. The following discussion will concentrate on Alternative A of the revised plan projections. This is in part because complete projections under Alternative B are not available and in part because the higher growth rate appears attainable.

With projected agricultural growth rates remaining unchanged at 2.5 percent a year, the higher rate of economic growth would largely reflect the direct and indirect (through demand for services) contribution of the more rapid expansion of manufacturing industries. The revised plan calls for manufacturing output to increase at an average annual rate of 12.0 percent, roughly equal to the 12.1 percent growth rate projected by the author and much exceeding the preliminary projection of 9.5 percent.

The more rapid expansion of manufacturing output is predicated on a high rate of growth of exports. Correspondingly, the projected rate of growth of commodity exports has been raised from 12.5 percent to 16.2 percent, and that of imports from 10.9 percent to 20.4 percent, in the revised plan. By comparison, the author recommended export and import growth rates of 17.3 percent and 15.5 percent.[2]

Greater export orientation would, in turn, permit a more rapid increase of the productivity of labor and the better use of capital. In fact, the projected rate of growth of labor productivity has been raised from 4.4 percent to 5.8 percent which compares with the author's projection of 5.7 percent. Furthermore, the projected marginal capital-output ratio has been reduced from 4.2 to 3.3; the author's projection was 3.5 (Table 18.1).

The rapid growth of labor productivity would be attained, in part, by an accelerated movement of labor from other sectors to manufacturing industries. The revised plan accepts the author's recommendation for reducing agricultural employment at an average annual rate of 1.5 percent, rather than at a rate of 0.6 percent a year as originally envisaged, with commensurate increases in agricultural productivity. It is also envisaged that employment in commerce and other services would rise at an average annual rate of 4.1 percent as compared to the earlier projection of 5.5 percent; the author's projection was 3.0 percent a year (Table 18.2).

With labor productivity in manufacturing being one-third above, and that of agriculture three-fifths below, the economy-wide average, the increased employment share of the former, and the reduced share of the latter, would contribute to economic growth in Taiwan. Assuming unchanged sectoral productivity growth rates, the changed distribution of employment alone would raise the average annual rate of growth of GNP from 7.5 percent to 8.0 percent, i.e. a differential of 0.5 percent a year. Additional influences contributing to the higher projected GNP growth rate of 9.3 percent are faster employment growth (3.2 percent instead of 3.0 percent a year) and higher

TABLE 18.1
Plan Projections for Taiwan, 1975–1981 (in constant prices)

	Preliminary Projections 1975-81	Alternative Projections 1975-81	Revised Projections 1978-81	
			Variant A	Variant B
Average Annual Growth Rates				
(1) Gross National Product	7.5	8.8	9.3	8.3
(2) Population	1.8	1.9	1.8	1.8
(3) Per Capita GNP	5.6	6.8	7.4	6.4
(4) Agricultural Production	2.5	2.5	2.5	2.5
(5) Manufacturing Production	9.5	12.1	12.0	10.5
(6) Exports	12.5	17.3	16.2	15.0
(7) Export Elasticity (6 ÷ 1)	1.67	1.97	1.76	1.81
(8) Imports	10.9	15.5	20.4	17.6
(9) Import Elasticity (8 ÷ 1)	1.45	1.76	2.19	2.12
(10) Employment	3.0	3.0	3.2	2.6
(11) Labor Productivity	4.4	5.7	5.8	5.6
Ratios				
(12) GCF/GDP	31.4	30.8	30.4	n/a
(13) GDS/GDP	29.8	28.4	31.3	n/a
(14) ICOR	4.2	3.5	3.3	n/a

Sources: Preliminary Projections: Economic Planning Council, Executive Yuan, *Six-Year Plan for Development of Taiwan,* 1976–1981. Essay 17 in this volume.

Revised Projections, Council for Economic Planning and Development, *Revised Economic Plan, 1979–1981* (special communication).

Alternative Projections, Bela Balassa, "Development Strategy and the Six-Year Plan in Taiwan" Essay 17 in this volume.

Notes: GCF/GDP = ratio of gross capital formation to the gross domestic product. GDS/GDP = ratio of gross domestic savings to the gross domestic product. ICOR = incremental capital-output ratio.

sectoral productivity growth rates (accounting for the remaining difference of 1.1 percent).[3]

The Composition of Exports and Manufacturing Output

A higher projected growth rate for commodity exports would not mean proportionate increases in all categories. Rather, in line with Taiwan's emerging comparative advantage in skill-intensive products, larger than average increases are projected for machinery and metal products: 23.2 percent a year between 1978 and 1981, much exceeding the original projection of 18.1 percent a year between 1975 and 1981 and only slightly below the 24.5 percent figure suggested by the author (Table 18.3).

Within the machinery and metal products category, exports are projected to rise at an average annual rate of 25 percent in the case of nonelectrical

TABLE 18.2
Value Added, Employment and Productivity in Taiwan, 1975-81 (in constant prices)

| | Preliminary Projections 1975-81 | | Alternative Projections, by 1975-81 | | Revised Projections, 1978-81 | | | |
| | | | | | Variant A | | Variant B | |
	growth rate	percent	growth rate	percent	growth rate	percent	growth rate	percent
Agriculture								
Value Added	2.5	10.3	2.5	9.6	2.5	9.0	2.5	9.2
Employment	−0.6	24.2	−1.5	23.0	−1.5	22.5	−1.5	22.9
Productivity	3.1	43.0	4.1	42.0	4.1	40.0	4.1	40.3
Mining								
Value Added	1.0	0.8	1.0	0.7	7.0	0.9	7.0	0.9
Employment	−2.7	0.9	−2.7	0.9	−1.3	1.1	−1.3	1.1
Productivity	3.9	81.0	3.9	75.0	8.3	81.5	8.3	82.1
Manufacturing								
Value Added	9.5	39.2	12.1	42.1	12.0	41.5	10.5	40.9
Employment	3.6	28.2	6.1	32.5	5.5	32.1	4.1	31.4
Productivity	5.7	139.0	5.7	130.0	6.0	129.5	6.0	130.4
Construction								
Value Added	7.8	4.7	8.5	4.5	12.0	5.2	10.0	5.2
Employment	4.7	7.1	5.3	7.4	5.7	7.5	4.7	7.5
Productivity	3.0	66.0	3.0	61.0	5.0	69.6	5.0	70.0
Electricity, Gas & Water								
Value Added	8.3	2.9	8.3	2.7	12.1	3.2	11.0	3.0
Employment	−3.9	0.4	−3.9	0.4	1.3	0.4	1.3	0.4
Productivity	12.7	725.0	12.7	676.0	10.6	822.5	9.6	769.5
Transport & Communications								
Value Added	8.9	6.6	11.9	7.3	9.9	6.4	8.8	6.4
Employment	3.2	5.8	6.1	6.8	5.0	6.6	4.0	6.5
Productivity	5.5	114.0	5.5	106.0	4.7	97.8	4.7	98.5
Commerce & Other Services								
Value Added	7.1	35.5	7.1	33.1	7.5	33.8	7.0	34.5
Employment	5.5	33.4	3.0	29.0	4.1	29.8	3.8	30.1
Productivity	1.5	106.0	3.8	114.0	3.3	113.1	3.1	113.5
Total								
Value Added	7.5	100.0	8.8	100.0	9.3	100.0	8.3	100.0
Employment	3.0	100.0	3.0	100.0	3.2	100.0	2.6	100.0
Productivity	4.4	100.0	5.7	100.0	5.8	100.0	5.6	100.0

Sources: See Table 18.1.

TABLE 18.3
The Growth and Composition of Exports in Taiwan, 1975-81 (in constant prices)

| | Actual | | Projected | | | | growth rate | |
	1975	1978	Preliminary Projections	Alternative Projections	Revised Projections	Preliminary Projections 1975-81	Alternative Projections 1975-81	Revised Projections 1975-81
			percent					
Commodity Exports, Total	100.0	100.0	100.0	100.0	100.0	12.5	17.3	16.2
Agriculture, Forestry and Fishing	5.2	3.1	3.9	4.2	2.2	7.5	13.3	3.6
Manufactures, Total	94.6	96.9	96.9	95.8	97.8	12.7	17.5	16.5
Food, Beverage & Tobacco	11.2	5.5	6.9	5.7	3.7	3.9	5.0	2.0
Textile, Leather, Timber,								
Paper & Related Products	37.6	38.9	31.4	32.4	33.1	9.1	13.7	10.0
Textile Products	30.5	29.0	24.2	25.4	25.3	8.2	13.0	11.1
Wood, Wood Products, Furniture	5.3	5.9	4.9	4.8	4.4	10.8	15.0	5.5
Others	1.8	4.0	2.3	2.0	3.4	17.6	20.0	8.9
Oil and Petroleum Products	1.0	1.2	1.3	1.2	1.2	17.1	20.0	16.6
Nonmetallic Mineral Products	1.1	1.5	1.7	1.6	1.5	20.0	24.0	13.3
Chemicals and Chemical Products	2.0	2.3	3.2	2.9	3.2	22.1	25.0	29.7
Basic Metals	2.3	1.5	3.3	2.3	1.3	19.1	19.1	12.5
Machinery & Metal Products	23.1	30.0	31.0	33.1	35.8	18.1	24.5	23.2
Nonelectrical Machinery	4.4	4.8	5.3	6.2	5.9	16.2	24.4	25.0
Transportation Equipment	2.2	2.5	3.2	3.3	2.8	19.3	25.0	20.0
Electrical Machinery & Apparatus	3.5	3.2	4.3	5.0	3.5	16.2	24.4	19.2
Electronics	10.4	14.9	15.0	15.6	18.5	19.4	25.5	25.0
Metal Products	2.6	4.6	3.2	3.0	5.1	16.1	20.0	19.9
Plastics Products	6.5	5.9	8.3	6.1	5.4	17.3	16.0	13.0
Plastic Shoes	5.8	3.2	3.2	3.1	2.7	8.9	13.0	9.4
Others	0.7	2.7	5.1	3.0	2.7	26.1	20.0	17.0
Other Manufactures	10.0	10.1	9.0	10.5	12.6	10.5	20.0	25.0

Sources: See Table 18.1.

machinery and electronics and approximately 20 percent for transportation equipment, electrical machinery and apparatus, and metal products. As a result, the share of the exports of machinery and metal products would rise from 30.0 percent in 1978 to 35.8 percent in 1981 as compared to the earlier projection of 31.0 percent and the 33.1 percent figure recommended by the author.

Among other commodity categories, the increase in the projected growth rates for textile products is noteworthy. In accordance with the views expressed by the author this reflects a more optimistic appraisal of the possibilities to upgrade textile production for export to developed country markets and to expand exports to developing country markets, in part by replacing Japanese exports. With a projected export growth rate of 11.1 percent, textile products would account for 25.3 percent of total exports in 1981, approximately equalling the target of 25.4 percent recommended by the author.

With the continued outward orientation of the Taiwanese economy, changes in the output of individual industries would by-and-large correspond to changes in exports. Projected increases are the largest, with average annual rates of growth of 20 to 25 percent, for the machinery and equipment industries which would experience the most rapid export growth. Projected output growth rates of 10 to 15 percent a year for chemicals and most metals and 7 percent a year for traditional industries also largely reflect interindustry differences in export growth rates.

On the whole, the export and output projections of the revised plan can be considered realistic. However, the investment requirements of the expanding industries appear to have been underestimated. This is because the method applied neglects the possibility of unfinished investments and the lack of full capacity use at the end of the plan period, both of which are likely to be important for rapidly growing industries.

Balance of Payments and Savings Projections

As noted above, projected export and import growth rates have been raised to a considerable extent in the revised plan, with larger increases projected for imports by reason of the existence of a substantial trade surplus in the base year, 1978. Notwithstanding the projected rapid rise in imports, however, a surplus in the current account balance is projected for 1981. This surplus, amounting to NT$6.1 billion, contrasts with a projected deficit of NT$2.4 billion in the preliminary plan and a deficit of NT$14.9 billion proposed by the author.[4]

The projected surplus in the current account balance, would contribute to a considerable accumulation of foreign exchange reserves. While in the preliminary plan, a reserve accumulation of $1.5 billion was projected for the entire 1975–81 period, according to the revised plan foreign exchange reserves would rise by $2.3 billion between 1978 and 1981.

The projected accumulation of foreign exchange reserves does not appear desirable. To begin with, Taiwan's foreign exchange reserves reached the equivalent of 8 months of imports in August 1978 and further increases would represent an unproductive use of resources. Also, as reserves are held in U.S. dollars, more rapid inflation in the United States than in Japan, Taiwan's main supplier, reduces the purchasing power of reserves over time. Yet, for international political reasons, a switch of reserves into other currencies may be difficult in practice.

More generally, it is not desirable to run a current account surplus that involves the outflow of capital from a capital-poor country to capital-rich countries. With the social marginal productivity of capital estimated at 15 percent, it much exceeds the rate at which Taiwan can borrow in international financial markets. Given its excellent credit rating, Taiwan can borrow at a rate only slightly above LIBOR that hardly exceeds zero in real terms, i.e., adjusted for inflation.

Furthermore, as discussed in some detail in Essay 17, Taiwan needs foreign direct investment in its machinery and equipment industries, where production and exports are projected to grow the most rapidly. While the need for foreign direct investment is recognized in the revised plan, substantial investment from abroad would lead to an accumulation of foreign exchange reserves even exceeding the projected figure.

The above considerations indicate the need for a current account deficit instead of a current account surplus in Taiwan. This conclusion is strengthened if we consider the investment requirements of the projected rate of growth of GNP. While, according to the revised plan, the additional investments made necessary by the faster growth of output would be financed largely by increased savings of the government and of public enterprises, the former would involve a considerable increase in the tax burden and the latter would adversely affect the competitiveness of exports by raising the cost of public services. Also, as noted above the investment requirements of expanding industries have been underestimated in the revised plan.

A current account surplus is also bound to give rise to adverse reactions, and may involve retaliation, on the part of Taiwan's major developed country trading partners. These considerations found expression in an article entitled "Taiwan—A Trade Surplus that Irks Washington" in the September 4, 1978 issue of *Business Week*. In fact, some Americans and Europeans see the spectre of a new Japan arising that will run current account surpluses to the detriment of the balance of payments of the developed countries, with adverse effects on employment in these countries.

Finally, rapid reserve accumulation has adverse effects on the domestic economy by creating inflationary pressures through increases in the money supply. Largely as a result of the accumulation of foreign exchange reserves, the money supply increased by 33 percent between July 1977 and July 1978. And although this increase did not immediately lead to the acceleration of inflation, the experience of the 1972–73 period illustrates the inflationary danger. As the money supply increased by 38 percent and 49 percent in 1972 and 1973, respectively, when Taiwan ran large export surpluses, the rise in prices followed with a time lag. Thus, whereas wholesale prices increased at an average annual rate of 2 percent during the sixties and were unchanged in 1971, they rose by 4 percent in 1972, 23 percent in 1973 and 41 percent in 1974. (In the latter year, however, the quadrupling of oil prices also affected the results.)

The Need for Trade Liberalization

Reducing the accumulation of foreign exchange reserves may be accomplished in two ways: revaluing the currency or liberalizing trade. The first of these alternatives is equivalent to the imposition of export taxes matched by reductions in import tariffs; it would not affect, however, industries protected by import restrictions. In turn, trade liberalization entails lowering tariffs and/or reducing import restrictions and it would benefit exports by reducing the cost of imported inputs.

Taiwan's choice was basically for the first alternative as the NT dollar was revalued from 38 to 36 per U.S. dollar in July 1978 while trade liberalization measures undertaken at the time have been of limited scope. Thus, tariffs were reduced by only 3 percent and transfers from the controlled to the automatic list for import licensing concerned relatively unimportant items.

By contrast, Korea maintained its exchange rate vis-à-vis the U.S. dollar unchanged and employed trade liberalization measures. Following the 1977 tariff reform, a new proposal was prepared for reducing tariffs. Furthermore, Korea adopted a four-year plan for liberalizing import restrictions and, in August 1978, it decided to import an additional $500 million worth of items on the restricted list.

Various considerations support the choice of trade liberalization to eliminate Taiwan's balance-of-payments surplus. As discussed in detail in Essay 17, Taiwan needs a shift from unskilled and labor-intensive to skilled labor-intensive exports. In order to accomplish this shift, it is necessary to ensure that the new exports are profitable.

The profitability of exports was adversely affected by the 16 percent increase in manufacturing wages between July 1977 and July 1978, coupled with the 4 percent revaluation. Placing reliance on trade liberalization would permit avoiding future revaluations and lower the cost of exports through reduced prices of imported machinery and intermediate inputs.

While adverse reactions to the July 1978 revaluation on the part of exporters were widely reported, few complaints were voiced in industries competing with imports. This may be explained by the existence of redundant tariff protection in various Taiwanese industries. This was documented in a detailed study for 1969 for industries experiencing rapid productivity improvements and it is likely to have increased since that time, as more industries have entered this category.[5]

The experience of the present-day developed countries also supports the case for trade liberalization. Tariffs have been the lowest in the small countries of Scandinavia and the Benelux, and these countries have also foregone the use of import restrictions. This is because, given their limited market size, small countries benefit the most from international specialization.[6]

Given Taiwan's small domestic market, it should gain from following the example of the small European countries in liberalizing trade. Trade liberalization would further be necessary in order to obtain better treatment for Taiwanese exports in foreign markets. While European and American producers are often blamed in Taiwan for not making an effort to sell in Taiwanese markets, relatively high tariffs and import licensing have provided a disincentive for such efforts. Domestic protection, and Taiwan's large export surplus with the United States and European countries,[7] in turn, appear to have contributed to the application of protectionist measures against Taiwanese goods in the United States and Western Europe.

Import Restrictions

While import restrictions on a number of goods were eliminated over the last two decades, 378 items continue to be subject to import control in Taiwan. For these items, the availability of domestic substitutes of adequate quality serves as the principle decision criterion. There are also 17 items, the imports of which are prohibited for public security or health reasons.

Among so-called permissible imports, import requests for another 4,000 items are channeled through the same process as are controlled items. While the purpose is to direct sources of the supply of imports from Japan to the United States and Western Europe, the existence of an administrative process contributes to arbitrariness in decision-making and creates uncertainty for the exporter. In turn, import licenses are issued automatically for 12,000 items.

As a first step in the liberalization of imports restrictions, it would be desirable to transfer all permissible import items to the automatic category where authorized banks can issue licenses. At the same time, a program of import liberalization should be prepared for the remaining three years of the Six Year Plan with the view to eliminate practically all import restrictions by 1981.

Reforming the System of Tariffs

The tariff schedule in effect in Taiwan is the result of decisions taken at different points of time and it does not reflect an economic rationale. This result may be explained by the fact that the tariff schedule presently applied was initially destined for revenue purposes and has not since undergone a major revision. At the same time, revenue considerations continue to be of importance as customs duties account for about one-fourth of government income.

While in the early seventies tariffs were lower in Taiwan than in Korea, following the 1973 and 1977 tariff reforms in Korea the situation has been reversed. Thus, in 1978, the ratio of tariff revenue to the cif value of dutiable items was 13 percent in Korea as compared to 20 percent in Taiwan,[8] and an item-by-item comparison of the tariff structure of the two countries shows tariffs to be generally higher in the former than in the latter, the principal exception being automobiles. Furthermore, under the new tariff proposal, tariffs in Korea would be reduced by about 25 percent, on the average.[9]

It is recommended that Taiwan follow the example of Korea in lowering tariffs. It would further be desirable to eliminate the possibility of setting tariffs retroactively on the basis of domestic sales prices, which creates uncertainty and conflicts with GATT rules. Finally, there is need for rationalizing the tariff structure. While this has been attempted in the case of textiles, tariffs exhibit little economic rationale in other industries. For one thing, substantial differences are shown among items at the same level of fabrication and entering the same production process. For another thing, the relationship between input and output tariffs varies to a considerable extent among industries.

The Coordination of Incentive Policies

It would be desirable to carry out the reform of the tariff structure on the basis of a program made public in advance, so as to permit firms to prepare for tariff reductions. Also, one should coordinate reductions in tariffs with the liberalization of import restrictions, lest tariff reductions be used as an argument against the liberalization of imports which is the more objectionable of the two.

Tariff reductions would also need to be coordinated with tax policy. At the same time, one can hardly object to tariff reductions on account of revenue considerations. Tariff receipts have been rising rapidly and exceeded budgetary estimates by nearly one-fifth in fiscal year 1978. At the same time, the increase in the share of customs revenue in government income from 19 percent in the early sixties to 24 percent in the mid-seventies conflicts with the experience of other countries where customs revenue as a proportion of government income has declined in the process of economic development.

The modernization of the tax system would require increasingly replacing customs revenue with revenue derived from other taxes in Taiwan. Apart from raising indirect tax rates and introducing a value added tax as proposed in Essay 17, revenue from income taxes could be used for this purpose. While it would not be desirable to raise the upper bracket rate of 50 percent, one may increase the lower limit that is presently about NT$100,000 for a family with two children. Thus, such a family does not pay an income tax as long as its income does not exceed the double of average per capita GNP of $1400.

The reform of import licensing, tariffs, and taxation should further be coordinated with measures of export promotion and with investment incentives. While Chapter 17 contains recommendations for export promotion measures, in the following consideration will be given to reforming the Statute for Encouragement of Investment.

Statute for Encouragement of Investment

The Statute for Encouragement of Investment, promulgated on September 10, 1960 and amended several times since, will expire on December 31, 1980. It would be desirable to prepare the new Statute at an early date, so as to reduce uncertainty in business decision on new investments and to permit coordination with tariffs, licensing, and tax policy, as proposed above.

The stated purpose of the Statute is to encourage investment and to accelerate economic development in Taiwan. Apart from Article 6 that applies to new and old firms alike, incentives are provided to new firms and to firms undertaking expansion. The incentives take the form of a five-year exemption[10] from corporate income taxes or accelerated depreciation at the choice of the firm (Article 6); the lowering of the corporate tax rate from 25 to 22 percent (Article 10); and the duty-free entry of machinery and equipment (Article 27). Since July 1977, possibilities have been provided to postpone the start of the period of tax exemptions by up to three years.

Investment incentives are granted on a selective basis. Under Articles 10 and 27, incentives are accorded to firms producing iron and steel (smelting, rolling, and electroplating), aluminum, copper, electrical machinery, electronics, nonelectrical machinery, and transport equipment, while Article 10 only applies to petrochemicals and Article 27 to selected chemicals, organic fertilizers, textile dyeing and finishing. The granting of incentives is subject to additional limitations as regards minimum capacity or the amount invested and, in some instances, the manufacturing process; in several cases, it requires decisions by the Ministry of Economic Affairs.

Tax exemptions (or accelerated depreciation) under Article 6 are provided in a larger number of industries. Apart from the industries listed above, they include processed food, pulp and paper, rubber processing, various nonmetallic minerals, textiles, prefabricated housing units, and several miscellaneous items. However, within particular industries, the benefits are granted only to firms producing commodities specifically listed, and there are a number of instances where a decision on the part of the Ministry of Economic Affairs is required.

In appraising the provision of the Statute for Encouragement of Investment, the first question relates to the freedom of choice of the firm as between income tax exemptions and accelerated depreciation. Thus far, most firms have made use of the former rather than the latter the exceptions being iron and steel and petrochemicals. The exceptions indicate the advantages capital-intensive industries derive from accelerated depreciation provision. While income tax exemptions are neutral in their effects on the use of capital and labor, accelerated depreciation provisions discriminate in favor of capital-intensive operations. In view of the existing capital scarcity in Taiwan, such discrimination is not desirable and one should rather place reliance on income tax exemptions.

Revisions allowing firms to postpone the start of the period of exemption from corporate income taxes also require comment. There is the danger that such provisions give rise to evasion as firms may attempt to show losses in the first few years of their operation, thereby postponing profits to other years when income tax exemptions will apply. And, at any rate, a total of eight years of tax exemptions does not appear to be warranted. Exempting firms from income taxes for a substantial part of the life of the investment provides benefits in excess of those obtained in other developing countries, and reduces the effects of other incentives that involve income tax reductions. Among the latter, mention may be made of tax incentives to research and training that are of importance for promoting technology-intensive industries.

Further questions arise concerning the minimum limits imposed on the size of capacity and the amount of investment as a condition for benefiting from the principal provisions of the Statute. While such limits may serve a useful purpose in industries producing standardized intermediate products, where economies of scale are well-defined, this is not the case for differentiated products, where optimal size depends on the extent of horizontal and vertical specialization. For one thing, optimal size will be small if the firm narrows product variety (horizontal specialization) that permits the use of specialized machinery and is conducive to learning-by-doing. For another thing, vertical specialization through the production of parts, components, and accessories in different establishments permits efficient operations in small- and medium-size plants.

These considerations apply in particular to the machinery industry (electrical as well as nonelectrical), where duty exemptions on imported machinery are subject to a lower limit of NT$100,000. This limitation excludes several Taiwanese producers of machinery and machine tools that had a labor force of 300 to 500 and exported more than $2 million a year.[11] Also, it has been reported that in France 95 percent of firms in the machinery industry have less than 300 workers.

It would further be desirable to simplify existing regulations on investment incentives and to reduce the scope of discretionary action. In particular, the "positive list" for providing such incentives should be replaced by a "negative" list, which would only exclude products to which foreign export limitations apply.

In this connection, note that the list of activities eligible for tax exemptions in the nonelectrical and electrical machinery and electronics industries is not all-inclusive at present, so that worthwhile activities may not receive exemptions. Similar considerations apply to a variety of miscellaneous products, where export possibilities may exist. Also, one unduly restricts the tax exemptions by limiting eligibility to firms designated by the Ministry of Economic Affairs in industrial branches producing machine tools and precision machinery. Finally, the application of a "negative" instead of a "positive" list would reduce the chances of countervailing action that was initiated by the United States in a case where an industry exporting to the U.S. benefited from investment incentives.

The Statute for Encouragement of Investment also grants incentives to savers in the form of tax credits for the purchase of shares and bonds by individuals (Article 10); tax exemptions on interest income derived from savings held for more than two years (Article 21); and tax exemptions on the first NT$24,000 of divident income (Article 14, as amended in July 1977). It further permits firms that come under Article 10 to retain profits up to 100 percent as compared to the 50 percent limitation applying to all other firms (Amendment, July 1977).

Several of these provisions require comment. To begin with, by imposing a limit on the tax deductibility of dividends, existing regulations discriminate against investment in the stock market in favor of savings deposits to which such limitations do not apply. Yet, banks relend savings deposits on rather conservative principles, mostly requiring real estate as security, while venture capital is provided through the stock market.

Given the importance of venture capital in technology-intensive industries, it would be desirable to eliminate existing discrimination against dividends. This may be done by establishing an identical limit for the deductibility of interest and dividends for income tax purposes. In order to promote savings and investment, the limit should be set higher than the present limit on dividends.

The same objective would be served by eliminating existing limitations on retained earnings for all firms or, alternatively, integrating corporate and personal income taxes. Given the possibilities of tax evasion under the former alternative, it would be preferable to employ the latter which is utilized by most European countries in order to encourage savings and investment by reducing the total tax burden on income derived from capital.

The Establishment of an Automobile Industry

Following a consideration of desirable changes in incentives, attention will be given to the proposal made by five noted economists of Chinese origin that Taiwan establish a full-scale automobile industry, which would serve as an outlet for its metal-working and machinery industries.[12] This recommendation is open to a variety of objections.

To begin with, the establishment of a full-scale automobile industry requires a large domestic market base. Also, a precondition of competitiveness on the world market is the availability of a large network of suppliers of parts, components, and accessories, all of which produce on an efficient scale. Finally, exporting involves a high cost of entry as it necessitates the establishment of marketing and repair facilities in foreign markets as well as brand name identification.

The need for a home market base and for economies of scale in the production of parts, components, and accessories, in marketing, and in servicing explain the absence of national automobile manufacturing in the Benelux and in Scandinavian countries other than Sweden. And, in the larger countries of Western Europe, a movement towards concentration has gathered momentum, the apparent survivors being Peugeot-Citroen-Chrysler-Europe, Fiat, Volkswagen, Ford-Europe, Renault, and a British grouping, each of which produces over one-and-a-half million cars a year. Production levels are similar in Japan which, incidentally, began exporting automobiles only after total domestic sales approached 2 million a year. Finally, in the United States unit costs are the lowest in General Motors, indicating the importance of economies of scale even at very high production levels.

Low unit costs in General Motors are explained by the presence of a large network of several thousand subcontractors, each of which enjoys economies of scale. The importance of economies of scale in the production of parts, components, and accessories is also reflected by the international division of the production process in automobile production. Swedish producers, for example, have subcontractors in Denmark, Finland and Norway.

Given its relatively small domestic market and the high cost of entry into work markets, it would not be desirable for Taiwan to aim at the establishment of a full-scale automobile industry. Rather, Taiwan would be well-advised to follow the example of the smaller European countries in attracting the production of parts, components and accessories as well as assembly operations of international firms. Such possibilities exist in cooperation with U.S. firms (e.g., world-wide sourcing by Ford) and, in particular, with Japanese firms which have the advantages of geographical proximity and lack of extensive commitments in other countries.

The Modernization of Agriculture

Following the land reform of the nineteen-fifties that transferred ownership from landlords to tenants, rapid increases in agricultural productivity occurred in Taiwan. Industrialization gave further impetus to agricultural productivity growth by absorbing the surplus population in rural areas with an absolute decline in the agricultural labor force occurring after 1969.

As noted in Essay 17, further increases in agricultural productivity are necessary to ensure the continued rapid transformation of the Taiwanese economy. Agriculture still accounts for 27 percent of the labor force, the double of that of Japan. This ratio is projected to decline below 23 percent under the revised Six Year Plan. To realize this goal, and to attain further reductions in the agricultural labor force, it would be desirable to modernize agriculture in Taiwan.

The modernization of agriculture requires, first of all, the consolidation of land holdings. Rather than increasing, the size of farms decreased in Taiwan during the seventies. At the same time, the fragmentation of land holdings represents an obstacle to mechanization and to the improved organization of production.

Land consolidation may be promoted by the use of positive as well as negative measures. They comprise the provision of credit for land purchases, the increased availability of off-farm employment, the introduction of a retirement scheme for farmers, and the linking of particular forms of assistance to farmers to the size of the cultivated area. At the same time, the program of land consolidation would need to be accompanied by measures that increase productivity on larger land holdings, in particular increased mechanization and advice on organizational improvements that are necessary to make mechanization effective.

The government's land policy would also need to be revised. In order to encourage the owners of small farms to rent their land, it would be desirable to end the "land to the tiller program" as far as small landholdings are concerned. Furthermore, decisions would need to be reached on the future industrial use of land in particular regions, as, in the absence of such a decision, there is a tendency to "hoard" land in the hope of obtaining a capital gain from increases in land prices in the future.

As proposed in Essay 17, it would further be desirable to reduce the government purchase price of rice in real terms. Apart from contributing to surplus production, the high rice price discourages farmers from shifting land to socially profitable crops and from engaging in industrial occupations, which provide greater benefits to the national economy.

Conclusions

This essay has provided a review of the revised version of the Six Year Plan for Economic Development of Taiwan for the period 1975–1981. It has been concluded that the revised plan presents a realistic and consistent set of projections that reflect the potential of the Taiwanese economy. In contradistinction with the preliminay version where there is a tendency towards import substitution in industries producing intermediate goods, the revised version of the plan has endorsed the continuation of the outward-oriented strategy successfully followed by Taiwan in the preceding one-and-a-half decades.

In this essay exception has been taken, however, to the planned current account surplus and the resulting accumulation of foreign exchange reserves in Taiwan. Such a surplus contributes to inflation and invites retaliation on the part of Taiwan's trade partners while reducing the availability of investment funds. Among possible ways of eliminating the surplus, it has been suggested that reliance be based on trade liberalization, including tariff reductions as well as the elimination of import restrictions.

Tariff reductions and the elimination of import restrictions should be carried out according to multi-annual programs, with provisions made for their coordination. They should also be coordinated with tax policy and with the Statute for Encouragement of Investment. As regards the Statute, recommendations have been made for limiting the scope of discretionary action and increasing the scope of automatic rules. Finally, desirable policies for the automobile industry and for agricultural modernization have been briefly outlined.

NOTES

Notes To Reader's Guide

1. Pergamon Press, Oxford, 1977, ix, 175; Chinese translation (partial text), Council for Economic Planning and Development, Taipei, 1978; Spanish translation, Centro de Estudios Monetarios Latinoamericanos, Mexico City, 1979.

2. The data originate in the *1979 World Bank Atlas* (Washington, D.C., 1980) and *World Development Report,* 1979 (Washington, D.C., 1979). Following the practice of various international organizations, the group of newly-industrializing countries includes Israel, with per capita incomes of $4120, and excludes Ireland, with per capita incomes of $3476.

3. The lecture was published as Essay No. 141 in *Essays in International Finance,* International Finance Section, Department of Economics, Princeton University, Princeton, N.J., December 1980. It will also appear in the Proceedings of the U.S.-China Conference on Alternative Strategies, organized by the Committee on Scholarly Communication with the People's Republic of China and held in Racine, Wisconsin, in November 1980.

4. Essay 2 appeared in *Weltwirtschaftliches Archiv,* Band 117, 1981 and, in Portuguese translation, in *Pesquisa e Planejamento Econômico,* April, 1981; Spanish translation is scheduled to be published in *Integración Latinoamericana.* Essay 3 was presented at the NBER/FINE/BEBR Conference on Trade Prospects among the Americas: Latin American Export Expansion and Diversification held in Sao Paulo, Brazil in March 1980, and published simultaneously in the Proceedings of the Conference, in the Summer 1981 issue of the *Quarterly Review of Economics and Business,* and, in Portuguese translation, in *Estudos Econômicos,* June 1981.

5. Essays 4 and 5 appeared in the *Journal of World Trade Law* in September-October 1978 and March-April 1980, respectively. Essay 4 was also published in *World Trade: Constraints and Opportunities in the 80s* (Bela Balassa, *et al.*), *The Atlantic Papers,* No. 36, Paris, 1978 and, in a slightly abbreviated form, under the title "The New Protectionism: Evaluation and Prospects for Reform" in *Challenges to a Liberal International Economic Order,* Proceedings of a Conference sponsored by the American Enterprise Institute for Public Policy Research and held in Washington, D.C. in December 1977 (Ryan C. Amacher, Gottfried Haberler, and Thomas D. Willett, eds.), Washington, D.C., American Enterprise Institute for Public Policy Research, 1979; Italian translation in *Il Nuovo Assetto del Comercio Internazionale el i Problemi di Finanziamento delle Esportazioni,* Supplement to the review *Thema,* 1978; Spanish translation in *Integración Latinoamericana,* May 1979. Essay 5 was published in Spanish translation in the November 1980 issue of *Integración Latinoamericana.*

6. Essay 6 was presented at the Fifth World Congress of the International Economic Association, held in Tokyo in September 1977, and published in the Proceedings of the Congress, *Economic Growth of Resources,* Volume 4, National and International Issues (Irma Adelman, ed.), London, Macmillan, 1979; it was published in an abbreviated form under the title "The Changing Pattern of Comparative Advantage in Manufactured Goods" in the May 1979 issue of *Review of Economics and Statistics.* Essay 7 appeared in the September 1978 issue of the *Banca Nazionale de Lavoro, Quarterly Review;* it was published in French translation in *Annales*

Economiques, 1981, in Hungarian translation in *Gazdaság,* 1980(1), and in Spanish translation in *Integración Latinoamericana,* May, 1980.

7. Essays 8 and 9 were presented at the Symposium on Industrial Policies for the 80's, organized by the Ministry of Industry and Energy of the Government of Spain and held in Madrid in May 1980. Essay 8 was published in the March 1981 issue of *World Development;* Essay 9 appeared in the October 1980 issue of the *Journal of Policy Modeling.* The two essays are scheduled to be published together under the title "Structural Change in Trade in Manufactured Goods between Industrial and Developing Countries" in the Proceedings of the Symposium and, in French translation, in the *Revue Economique,* September, 1981.

8. This essay was published simultaneously in *World Development,* November-December, 1979 and, in Portuguese translation, in *Pesquisa e Planejamento Economico,* December 1979. It was published in Spanish translation in the December 1980 issue of *Integración Latinoamericana.*

9. This essay was presented at the IInd International Conference on the Portuguese Economy, held in Lisbon in September 1979; it was published in 1980 in the Proceedings of the Conference. Recommendations for policy changes were earlier made in the author's "Industrial and Trade Policy in Portugal," published in 1977 in the Proceedings of the International Conference on the Portuguese Economy, organized by the Gulbenkian Foundation and the German Marshall Fund and held in Lisbon in October 1976; the paper was republished in Essay 7 in Bela Balassa, *Policy Reform in Developing Countries.*

10. This essay, originally written under the title "The 1978–1982 Five Year Plan in Greece," was prepared at the request of the Ministry of Coordination, Center of Planning and Economic Research in June 1978.

11. An earlier version of this paper was presented under the title "Policies for Stable Economic Growth in Turkey" at the Seminar of the Role of Foreign Exchange Rate in Achieving the Outward-Orientation of the Turkish Economy, organized by Meban Securities and held in Istanbul in July 1979 and, in a revised form, under the present title at a Conference on "The Security of Turkey and Its Allies," organized by the European-American Institute for Security Research and held in Istanbul in September 1979. It is scheduled to be published in the Proceedings of the Seminar and of the Conference.

12. Published in *European Economic Review,* December 1978 and, in Hugarian translation, in *Valóság.* 1978(7).

13. The two advisory reports on Korea were prepared at the request of Economic Planning Bureau in September 1977 and October 1978, respectively. They follow earlier advisory reports by the author, published as Essays 8 and 9 in *Policy Reform in Developing Countries.*

14. The two advisory reports on Taiwan were prepared at the request of the Council for Economic Planning and Development in February 1978 and September 1978, respectively.

Essay 2

1. Organization for Economic Co-operation and Development, *The Impact of the Newly Industrializing Countries on Production and Trade in Manufactures* Paris, OECD, 1979.

2. The data have been derived from the World Bank, *World Development Report* 1979 (Washington, D.C., 1979), and *1978 World Bank Atlas* (Washington, D.C., 1979).—The newly-industrialized developing country category overlaps with the upper ranges of the group of middle-income countries as defined in the *World Development Report,* that also includes newly-industrializing countries which are members of the OECD, the international economic organization of developed countries (Greece, Portugal, Spain and Turkey).

3. The findings of the study have been reported in the author's "Export Incentives and Export Performance in Developing Countries," *Weltwirtschaftliches Archiv* 114 (1978), 24–61; "Exports and Economic Growth: Further Evidence," *Journal of Developmental Economics,* 5 (1978), 181–189; and *Development Strategies in Semi-Industrial Countries,* Baltimore, Md., The Johns Hopkins University Press, 1981, Chapter 3.

4. All coefficients are significant at the one percent level. Results obtained by the use of alternative methods and for the subperiods 1960–65 and 1966–73 are reported in the publications cited above. Correlations for output net of exports have not been calculated in the case of agriculture. All the calculations exclude Uruguay.

5. The index numbers reported in United Nations, *Monthly Bulletin of Statistics* (December 1971 and June 1977) are 103 including, and 93 excluding, fuels in 1971–73 on a 1970 basis; the comparable averages for the 1961–70 period are 101 and 98 respectively.

6. Traditional exports have been defined to include commodities that accounted for at least 1.5 percent of the country's merchandise exports in the years 1971–73, on the average. Manufactured goods have been defined as SITC categories 5 to 8 less 68; fuels as SITC category 3; nontraditional primary exports other than fuels include the remainder.

7. Estimates of balance-of-payments effects pertaining to individual years are shown on a "1972" basis. Changes between individual years can be derived as the difference between the reported estimates for consecutive years.

8. More detailed estimates of the balance-of-payments effects of external shocks, and of policy reponses to external shocks in three Latin American countries (Brazil, Mexico and Uruguay) are contained in Bela Balassa, "Policy Responses to External Shocks in Selected Latin American Countries," Essay 3 in this volume. Detailed results for the other nine countries are available from the author.

9. Exporters continued to benefit from the duty free entry of these inputs. While officially the prior exemption system on imported inputs was transformed into a drawback system, involving the payment and the subsequent rebate of duties, in practice payments were not made.

10. The real exchange rate vis-a-vis the U.S. dollar was 84 percent of its "1972" level in 1977 and 81 percent in 1978; in the two years, the real value of the money supply increased by 29 percent and 12 percent, respectively.

11. The high value of the resource gap reflects the fact that the "1972" trade deficit would have increased further if import and export trends observed in the preceding decade continued.

12. Table 5 also provides information on the net debt service ratio, derived by deducting interest receipts from debt service obligations, and the net external debt ratio, obtained by adjusting gross external debt for the net values of reserves. These ratios will be referred to in cases when they show results substantially different from the gross ratios.

13. Apart from a small decline in 1974, the real value of the money supply increased at rates ranging from 4 percent to 15 percent between 1971 and 1976.

14. The money supply increased by 10 percent in 1976, 3 percent in 1977, and 6 percent in 1978 in real terms.

15. Under the methodology applied, the latter appears as a loss in market shares in traditional exports that in part offset the gains Uruguay made in nontraditional exports.

16. It should be recalled that, in calculating these ratios, the gross national product and the average value of exports and imports (average value of trade) have been expressed in "1972" prices.

17. The only exception is Brazil where the share of exports increased, notwithstanding the rise in the anti-export bias due to higher protection. But, export shares declined towards the end of the period and a number of industrial firms were subjected to contractual export obligations, giving rise to exports below cost.

18. External shocks and ratios of policy responses to external shocks, including additional net external financing, increases in export market shares, import substitution, and lowering the rate of economic growth are averages for the years 1974–1978, calculated on a 1971–73 basis. The relevant data are shown in Table 7.

19. Extrapolating the value of statistical significance calculated for ten observations, a Spearman rank correlation coefficient of 0.29 or higher will be significant at the one percent level in the case of twelve observations.

20. The results are not appreciably affected if the share of gross domestic investment, or that of gross domestic fixed investment, is used in the calculation in the place of the domestic savings ratio. (Data on the share of investment in aggregate expenditure are shown in Table 6.)

21.   Michael Hopkins and Ralph van der Hooven, "Basic Needs and Economic Theory," Geneva, International Labor Office, August 1980 (mimeo).

22.   Explanation of symbols: y = average annual rate of growth of GNP; I = gross domestic investment, S/Y = gross domestic savings ratio; t-values are shown in parenthesis.

Essay 3

1.   Estimates of balance-of-payments effects pertaining to individual years are shown on a "1972" basis. Changes between individual years can be derived as the difference between the reported estimates for consecutive years.

2.   It should be recalled that developments in particular years are derived as differences in the estimates for consecutive years.

3.   It should be noted, however, that the outcome is affected by efforts made by developing countries to increase export supply.

4.   As export shortfalls are shown with a positive sign, a negative sign denotes an improvement in Table 3.2.

5.   The latter result is, however, affected by the choice of "1972" as the base period. This is because the high GNP growth rate in 1973 raised the average for the "1972"–1978 period.

6.   We did not net out interest receipts on the grounds that these relate largely to holdings of foreign exchange reserves. Such is the case in Brazil, Uruguay, and to a lesser extent in Mexico.

7.   A ratio of 60 percent means that actual imports were 37 percent lower than what they would have been in the absence of import substitution.

8.   Net reserves were defined as the sum of foreign exchange holdings, gold reserves as valued by the national authorities, SDR holdings, reserve position in the International Monetary Fund, less the use of Fund credit. Changes in the valuation of gold are reflected in the reserve figures in Table 2.6 but are not included with changes in reserves in Table 2.3.

9.   The gross debt service ratio was 49 percent in 1974, when debt repayments were postponed on account of Mexico's balance-of-payments deficit.

10.   As elsewhere in the essay, exports are defined to include merchandise exports only. The inclusion of tourism would add $3.2 billion to exports in 1978, reducing the gross debt service ratio to 75 percent and the net debt service ratio to 72 percent. However, against this figure there is a debit item of $2.3 billion on account of tourism by Mexicans abroad. (In Brazil tourist expenditures abroad exceeded the small tourist receipts.)

11.   The gross debt service ratio was only 16.5 percent in 1974, when loan repayments were postponed due to Uruguay's large balance-of-payments deficit.

12.   Gold accounted for two-thirds of reserve holdings at the end of 1978. Increases in the national valuation of gold holdings, from $149 million at the end of 1973 to $562 million at the end of 1978, largely reflect increases in the price of gold. But reserves other than gold also increased from $52 million at the end of 1973 to $287 million at the end of 1978, offsetting the rise in the gross external debt as a proportion of GNP.

Essay 4

1.   While the ratio of tariffs to dutiable imports does not appropriately measure the extent of protection, it may be used to indicate general trends. In the United States, this ratio averaged 38 percent in 1922-29; it was 53 percent in 1930-33 under the Hawley-Smoot law; and it decreased to 25 percent by 1957 (Sidney Ratner, *The Tariff in American History,* New York, Van Nostrand, 1972, 52-57). The ratio of U.S. tariffs to dutiable imports declined further following the Dillon-round (1960-61) and the Kennedy-round (1963-67) negotiations and reached 8 percent in 1974, U.S. Department of Commerce, *Statistical Abstract of the United States, 1975,* 22).

2. Cf. J. M. Finger, "Tariff Provisions for Offshore Assembly and the Exports of Developing Countries," *Economic Journal*, 85 (1975), 365-72 and "Effects of the Kennedy Round Tariff Concessions on the Exports of Developing Countries," *Ibid.*, 86 (1976), 87-95.

3. Cf. Bela Balassa, *European Economic Integration*, Amsterdam, North Holland, 1975, ch. 2.

4. Manufactured goods will be defined as UN Standard International Trade Classification commodity classes 5 to 8 less nonferrous metals (68).

5. Ragnar Nurkse, "Patterns of Trade and Development," in *Equilibrium and Growth in the World Economy*, Cambridge, Mass., Harvard University Press, 1961, 283.

6. *Ibid*, 289.

7. *Ibid*, 310.

8. Gunnar Myrdal, *Economic Theory and Underdeveloped Regions*, London, Duckworth, 1957.

9. Raul Prebisch, "Commercial Policy in the Underdeveloped Countries," *American Economic Review Papers and Proceedings*, 49 (1959), 251-73.

10. United Nations, *Yearbook of International Trade Statistics*, 1962 and Bela Balassa, *Trade Prospects for Developing Countries*, Homewood, Ill. R. D. Irwin, 1964, 7, 10. — All data have been expressed in terms of constant prices.

11. *Trade Prospects for Developing Countries*, 9–10.

12. Irving B. Kravis, "Trade as a Handmaiden of Growth: Similarities between the Nineteenth and the Twentieth Centuries," *Economic Journal*, 80 (1970), 850–72; R. C. Porter, "Some Implications of Primary-Product Trends," *Journal of Political Economy*, 78 (1970), 586–97; and Bela Balassa, *The Structure of Protection in Developing Countries*, Baltimore, Md., Johns Hopkins Press, 1971, ch. 2 and 4.

13. United Nations, *Monthly Bulletin of Statistics*, October 1977 — Developed countries are defined to include the industrial countries of North America, Western Europe, and Japan, as well as Australia, New Zealand, Israel, and South Africa. All other market economies are classified as developing.

14. "Trade and Development: Trends, Needs and Policies, Part I" in United Nations, *World Economic Survey*, 1963, New York, 1965, 31, and United Nations, *Monthly Bulletin of Statistics*, June 1977.

15. Bela Balassa, "Export Incentives and Export Performance in Developing Countries: A Comparative Analysis," *Weltwirtschaftliches Archiv*, 114 (1978), 24–61.

16. United Nations, *Monthly Bulletin of Statistics*, June 1977 and February 1978.

17. Donald B. Keesing, "World Trade and Output of Manufactures: Structural Trends and Developing Countries' Exports," World Bank Staff Working Paper No. 316, Washington, D.C. January 1979.

18. United Nations, *Monthly Bulletin of Statistics*, August 1976.

19. On this point, see Jan Tumlir, "The New Protectionism, Cartels, and the International Order," *Challenges to a Liberal International Economic Order*, (Ryan C. Amacher, Gottfried Haberler, and Thomas D. Willett, ed.). Proceedings of a Conference held in Washington, D.C. in November 1977, Washington, D.C., American Enterprise Institute for Public Policy Research, 1979, 239–58.

20. *The Economist*, December 24, 1977.

21. *Ibid*, May 13, 1978.

22. *The Wall Street Journal*, February 23, 1978.

23. The Treasury countervailed the imports of bromide and bromide products from Israel that benefit from regional aids, although only 3 percent of total production is exported to the U.S.

24. *Business Week*, November 14, 1977.

25. It was reported, for example, that ITC found the Japanese steel producers guilty of "predatory pricing" which has been defined in a similar way as dumping violations that are ruled on by the Treasury (*Washington Post*, January 15, 1978). It was also reported that the White House objected to the ITC negotiating consent orders between domestic and foreign color TV

makers on its own initiative (*The Wall Street Journal*, November 25, 1977). Note further that the Message from the Chairman, introducing the 1976 report of the ITC, spoke of "an innovative approach to our substantive and administrative duties and . . . considerable progess in meeting the objectives which the Commission had set as a result of its increased role in international trade."

26.   *The Wall Street Journal*, November 25, 1977.

27.   December 29, 1977.

28.   In this connection, a statement made following the December 1977 AFL-CIO Convention may deserve quotation - "Although organized labor lost its last big fight for import protection only three year ago, [when the Burke-Hartke bill went down in defeat], AFL-CIO officials say that much has changed since then. The steel, electronics, shoe, textile, and apparel industries have been badly hurt by imports, unemployment has soared, and multinational operations have suffered a black eye for overseas bribery. The 'new reality' says a union economist is that the public no longer perceives protectionism as a bad thing." (*Business Week*, December 26, 1977).

29.   In response to these pressures the House of Representatives organized a 150-member steel caucus and a 229-member fiber caucus to defend the interests of the steel and textile industries (*The Wall Street Journal*, Dec. 29, 1977). More recently, in a joint appeal, business and labor "called on the Carter Administration and Congress to take 'strong and immediate' action to counteract a 'stunning increase' in textile, apparel and fiber imports" (*Washington Post*, June 30, 1978).

30.   A case in point is the imposition of anti-dumping duties amounting to $46 million in March 1978 on Japanese-made television sets imported in 1972 and 1973.

31.   An example of apparent harassment of foreign exporters is the simultaneous initiation of countervailing, anti-dumping, and escape clause action against imports of bicycle tires and tubes from Korea.

32.   Cf. e.g. *Le Monde*, April 4, 1978 and *The Wall Street Journal*, April 24, 1978.

33.   On the latter, see the favorable reactions in the Italian press to the author's speech on the "new protectionism" on March 31, 1978.

34.   *The Economist* (December 24, 1977) reports on the increasing number of anti-dumping cases in the EEC and the increase in the "Commission's anti- dumping staff from three to 10 to cope with the burgeoning work load."

35.   *The New York Times*, September 23, 1977.

36.   January 14, 1978.

37.   *The Economist*, October 15 and December 31, 1977.

38.   *Ibid.*, December 31, 1977.

39.   *Ibid.*, October 15, 1977.

40.   According to the *New York Times*, (April 2, 1978), these include "fast writeoffs when companies develop new facilities to serve export markets, tax credits for those that establish foreign sales offices, a new tax program on exports tailored principally for medium-sized companies, a system of information-exchange to promote greater exports, a Government loan program for companies that introduce a new product line for exports, and a beefed-up operation (in money and personnel) for the existing Commerce State export-development activities."

41.   It was reported, for example, that "when the fast-growing computer firms in Japan began to have difficulties with their cash flow situation, the Japanese government organized a leasing company to buy computers and handle the leasing, thus providing a fast injection of cash and reducing the ongoing capital burden." (H. B. Malmgren, "International Order for Public Subsidies," *Thames Essay No. 11*, London, Trade Policy Research Centre, 1977, 24.)

42.   Statement made at the National Press Club in Washington on September 16, 1977 and quoted in the press release of the French Embassy.

43.   Foreign Trade Minister André Rossi in *Le Monde*, July 27, 1977 and Raymond Barre in the *Journal de Genève*, September 15, 1977.

44.   *Journal de Genève*, September 15, 1977 — As noted above, the negotiations of the last 20 years led to a considerable expansion of trade and economic growth through trade.

45. According to Raymond Barre, "when a country develops a sector that is indispensable to the structural equilibrium of its economy but unable to meet normal competition until it reaches a sufficient size, that country may rightfully take such steps as are necessary to protect this activity from being destroyed while it is vulnerable" (*Journal de Genève,* September 15, 1977).

46. As Raymond Barre expressed it, "France cannot allow international competition to develop under conditions that would throw its economic structures into confusion, bring about the sudden collapse of whole sections of its industry or agriculture, put thousands of workers out of work, and jeopardize its independence by eliminating essential activities" (*L'Aurore,* March 25, 1977).

47. *Business Week,* December 5, 1977.

48. *Ibid.,* November 28, 1977.

49. *The Economist,* April 29, 1978.

50. These conclusions also apply to the use of reference prices as an instrument to limit imports, as evidenced by the 5.5 percent increase in trigger prices on steel as of July 1, 1978 and the demands for the imposition of trigger prices on wire products in the United States. It suggested that steel-using industries will also request increased protection, since "distortions arising in steel affect the international competitive position of all steel users—from producers of nuts and bolts to manufacturers of sophisticated machinery" (*New York Times,* May 11, 1978).

51. *Business Week,* December 26, 1977.

52. *Barron's,* April 24, 1978.

53. R. N. Cooper, *The Economics of Interdependence: Economic Policy in the Atlantic Community,* New York, McGraw Hill, 1962.

54. Assar Lindbeck, "Economic Dependence and Interdependence in the Industrialized World," in *From Marshall Plan to Global Interdependence,* (L. Gordon, ed.) Organization for Economic Co-Operation and Development, Paris, 1978, 82.

55. *Business Week,* March 27, 1978 and *The Economist,* May 27, 1978.

56. In this connection, note that prices paid for steel, as opposed to list prices, reportedly increased by 7 to 20 percent in the EEC between November 1977 and April 1978 while there was little change in sales (*The Economist,* May 13, 1978).

57. For an excellent discussion, see Jan Tumlir, "The New Protectionism, Cartels, and the International Economic Order," *op. cit.*

58. *The Economist,* February 12, 1977.

59. Between 1926–29 and 1931–35 world trade in manufactured goods fell by 28 percent (League of Nations, *Industrialization and Foreign Trade,* Geneva, 1945, 157) — As beforehand data are expressed in constant prices.

60. P. W. Bidwell, *The Invisible Tariff,* New York, Council on Foreign Relations, 1939, chs. IV and V.

61. Cf. e.g. G. W. Stocking and M. W. Watkins, *Cartels in Action,* New York, Twentieth Century Fund, 1946.

62. Frederick Haussman and Daniel Ahearn, "International Cartels and World Trade, an Explanatory Estimate," *Thought,* Fordham University Quarterly 5 (1944), 429.

63. League of Nations, *International Cartels,* Lake Success, N.Y., 1947, 3.

64. Cf. e.g. D. Edwards, "International Cartels as Obstacles to International Trade, *American Economic Review,* 34 (1944), 330–39 and B. F. Hoselitz, "International Cartel Policy," *Journal of Political Economy,* 55 (1947), 1–28.

65. Between 1973 and 1976 the trade surplus of the developed countries with the oil-importing developing countries increased from $2.8 billion to $5.3 billion in the United States, from $11.2 billion to $16.3 billion in the European Common Market, and from $7.5 billion to $12.7 billion in Japan (GATT *International Trade, 1977/78* Geneva, 1978).

66. For a detailed discussion, see Essay 7 in this volume.

67. Cf. Bela Balassa, "Resolving Policy Conflicts for Rapid Growth in the World Economy," *Banca Nazionale del Lavoro Quarterly Review,* 126 (1978), 271–82.

68. For a detailed discussion, cf. *Ibid.*

69. On this point see Richard Blackhurst, Nicolas Marian, and Jan Tumlir, "Trade Liberalization, Protectionism and Interdependence," *GATT Studies in International Trade No. 5,* Geneva, November 1977.

70. Cf. Bela Balassa, "A 'Stages' Approach to Comparative Advantage," Essay 6 in this volume.

71. OECD Development Research Centre, *Adjustment for Trade: Studies on Industrial Adjustment Problems and Policies,* Paris, 1975, 9, 11.

72. For a detailed discussion, see Essay 5 in this volume.

Essay 5

1. Essay 4 in this volume.

2. " 'Tokyo Round' Hopes Fading—Talks May be Abandoned" *(The Journal of Commerce,* February 2, 1977), "The Growing Threat to the Tokyo Round" *(Business Week,* March 13, 1978), and "A World Trade Time Bomb Ticks in Congress" *(The Christian Science Monitor,* September 22, 1978).

3. Cf. e.g. "Too Many Goodies to the Trade Sharks?" *(The Washington Post,* June 14, 1979).

4. For an earlier, and more pessimistic, appraisal see Robert E. Baldwin "The Multilateral Trade Negotiations: Towards Greater Liberalization?" *AEI Special Analysis,* Washington, D.C., American Enterprise Institute for Public Policy Research, 1978, 6.

5. James Riedel and Linda M. Gard, "Recent Changes in Protectionism," World Bank, International Trade and Capital Flows Division, Economic Analysis and Projections Department, Development Policy Staff, Working Paper No. 3, Washington, D.C., October 1979, 9.

6. Office of the Special Representative for Trade Negotiations, *Trade Actions Monitoring System Report,* various issues.

7. *The Wall Street Journal,* November 9, 1978 and *Trade Actions Monitoring System Report,* October 1979.

8. *OAS-CECON Trade News,* Washington, D.C. Secretariat of American States, August, 1979, 5.

9. *The New York Times,* October 31, 1979.

10. *Ibid.,* November 21, 1979.

11. Riedel and Gard, *op. cit.,* Table 2.

12. "Rapport sur les principales options due VIIIème Plan," *Journal Officiel,* July 12, 1979, 7.

13. International Monetary Fund, *Annual Report on Exchange Arrangements and Exchange Restrictions 1979,* Washington, D.C., 1979, 6, 239–40.

14. Between 1977 and 1978, the dollar value of Japanese imports of all commodities and of manufactured products, respectively, increased by 42.7 and 53.8 percent from Hong Kong, 22.8 and 43.4 percent from Korea, 26.5 and 43.7 percent from Singapore, and 35.7 and 56.7 percent from Taiwan. Increases were even larger in the first nine months of 1979, for which only data on total imports from the four Far Eastern countries are available. The relevant figures are: Hong Kong, 49.4 percent, Korea, 40.6 percent, Singapore, 53.2 percent; and Taiwan, 54.9 percent. (The author is indebted to Susan MacKnight of the United States-Japan Trade Council for providing him with the relevant information.)

15. Cf. the declaration made by President Giscard D'Estaing in *Le Monde,* October 18, 1978, as well as subsequent statements by Prime Minister Raymond Barre.

16. *Business Week,* August 6, 1979. See also the article in the October 16, 1979 issue of *The Wall Street Journal,* entitled "Going Private: Western Europe Acts to Take More Firms Off the Public Dole."

17. *The Economists,* July 29, 1978.

18. Essay 4.

19. GATT, *International Trade 1977/78,* Geneva, 1978, 7.
20. GATT, *International Trade 1978/79,* Geneva, 1979, 8.
21. *Ibid.,* 9.
22. GATT, *The Tokyo Round of Multilateral Trade Negotiations,* Geneva, General Agreement on Tariffs and Trade, April 1979, 120–22 (to be cited as the GATT Report). It should be recalled that weighting by imports entails a downward bias as low tariffs leading to increased imports have a large weight and highly protective tariffs a low weight.
23. UNCTAD V, *Multilateral Trade Negotiations: Evaluation and Further Recommendations Arising Therefrom,* Manila, United Nations Conference on Trade and Development, May 7, 1979, 12–13—to be cited as the UNCTAD Report.
24. *Ibid.,* 14–15—The estimates have been made on the basis of 1976 trade flows.
25. Peter J. Ginman, Thomas A. Pugel, and Ingo Walter, "Implications of the Tokyo Round of Trade Negotiations for Exports from the Developing Countries," August 1979 (mimeo).
26. W. R. Cline et al., *Trade Negotiations in Tokyo Round: A Quantitative Assessment* Washington, D.C., The Brookings Institution, 1978, 58.
27. The decline in exports due to reductions in preference margins has been estimated as the difference between trade diversion vis-à-vis competing developed countries under (a) pre-Tokyo round and (b) post-Tokyo round tariffs.

$$DTD = \sum_i M_{N_i} \eta_i (\Delta t_i \ 1 + t_i) - \sum_i M_{N_i} \eta_i (\Delta t_i \ 1 + t_i),$$

where DTD is the decrease in trade diversion, M_{N_i} the 1976 level of the imports of preference-giving countries from competing exporters, t_i and t_i' the nonpreferential tariffs before and after the Tokyo Round, Δt_i and $\Delta t_i'$ the preferential margins and η_i the relevant elasticity. In turn, trade creation in non-GSP products (TC) is estimated as

$$TC = \sum_i M_{b_i} \eta_i (\Delta t_i \ 1 + t_i)$$

where M_{b_i} denotes the 1976 imports of non-GSP products from developing countries, t_i the pre-Tokyo Round tariff, and Δt_i the reduction in the tariff.
28. *Ibid.,* 5.
29. In this connection, note that in the European Common Market extra-area imports account for only about 10 percent of the consumption of industrial goods and the comparable figures for the United States and Japan are 9 percent and 6 percent, respectively (United Nations, *Commodity Trade Statistics and* World Bank *World Development Report, 1979).* Note further that, excluding duty-free exports under MFN, the industrial exports of the developing countries to developed countries amounted to $28.9 billion in 1976, of which $10.4 billion were non-GSP products (GATT Report, 123), and these proportions have changed at the expense of GSP products following the reclassification effected by the United States in 1979.
30. Robert E. Baldwin and Tracy Murray, "MFN Tariff Reductions and Developing Country Trade Benefits under the GSP," *Economic Journal,* 87 (1977), 30–46—The non-beneficiary developing countries include most Southern European countries in the U.S. and EEC scheme, Taiwan in the EEC scheme, and, partially, Hong Kong in the Japanese scheme.
31. Tracy Murray, "The 'Tokyo Round' and Latin America" paper presented at the Annual Meeting of the Eastern Economics Association held in Washington, D.C., May 1979.
32. Thomas B. Birnberg, "Tariff Reform Options: Economic Effects on Developing and Developed Countries" in *Policy Alternatives for a New International Economic Order* (William R. Cline, ed.), New York, Praeger Publications to the Overseas Development Council, 1979, 237–39.
33. In the immediate postwar years, the OEEC, later transformed into the OECD, was, however, instrumental in liberalizing quantitative restrictions on manufactured imports in Western Europe.
34. Essay 4—In the following, the expression "non-tariff measures" will be used to refer to non-tariff barriers to trade, government aids to industry, and administrative measures that affect the conduct of international trade.

35. The discussion will not cover the agricultural codes on beef and dairy products that concern few developing countries, the code on anti-dumping that basically aims at securing conformity with the Code on Subsidies and Countervailing Measures, and the code on safeguards on which no agreement has been reached. The latter will be considered in Section IV below.

36. In extending the application of countervailing action to products that enter duty free, however, the 1974 Trade Act has introduced an injury test in such cases.

37. GATT provides for a dispute settlement mechanism under Article XXIII, whenever subsidization has the effect of "nullifying and impairing" the benefit from tariff reductions accruing to a contracting party, but this provision has remained practically unused.

38. For such an interpretation, cf. *MTN Studies 6, Part 1*. A Report prepared at the Request of the Committee on Finance, United States Senate, Washington, D.C., August, 1979, 195, 212.—However, as noted below, export subsidies are subject to countervailing action if the injury test is met.

39. Cf. *MTN Studies 6, Part 1*, 152.

40. On possible challenges to the failure of the United States to apply the injury test to the case of a country that is a contracting party in GATT but is not a signatory to the Code, see *MTN Studies 6, Part 1*, 220–23.

41. *MTN Studies 6, Part 2*, 3.

42. *Ibid.,* 21.

43. *Ibid.,* 303, 307.

44. "The Multilateral Trade Negotiations: Toward Greater Liberalization?" *op. cit.,* 18.

45. Cf. Ingo Walter and Jae W. Chung, "Non-tariff Distortions and Trade Preference for Developing Countries," *Kyklos,* 24 (1971), 733–752.

46. The Code covers services only to the extent that these are involved in the purchase of products—The list of governmental entities subject to the Code is provided in an annex appended to it.

47. *New York Times,* November 21, 1979.

48. Cf. George Alvares Maciel, "Brazil's Proposals for the Reform of the GATT System" *The World Economy,* 2 (1979), 163–76.

49. The following discussion will not cover the proposed Understanding Regarding Export Restrictions and Charges on which no agreement has been reached.

50. *Op. cit.,* 33.

51. For a similar view, see *MTN Studies 6,* Part 4. 165.

52. Cf. Bela Balassa, "A 'Stages' Approach to Comparative Advantage" Essay 6 in this volume.

53. For a detailed discussion of the "graduation" issue, followed by recommendations for dealing with it, see Isaiah Frank, "The 'Graduation' Issue on Trade Policy Towards LDCs" World Bank Staff Working Paper No. 334, Washington, D.C., June 1979.

54. For such a proposal, see UNCTAD Report, 37–38.

Essay 6

1. Hal B. Lary, *Imports of Manufactures from Less-Developed Countries,* New York, Columbia University Press, National Bureau of Economic Research, 1968; K. Kojima, "Structure of Comparative Advantage in Industrial Countries: A Verification of the Factor-Proportions Theorem," *Hitotsubashi Journal of Economics,* 11 (1970), 1–29; Gerhard Fels, "The Choice of Industry Mix in the Division of Labor Between Developed and Developing Countries," *Weltwirtschaftliches Archiv,* 108 (1972), 71–121; A. Mahfuzur Rahman, *Exports of Manufactures from Developing Countries,* Rotterdam, Center for Development Planning, Rotterdam University Press, 1973.

2. Gary C. Hufbauer, "The Impact of National Characteristics and Technology on the Commodity Composition of Trade in Manufactured Goods" in *The Technology Factor in*

International Trade, (R. Vernon, ed.), New York, Columbia University Press for the National Bureau of Economic Research, 1970, 145–232.

3. Bohuslav Herman and Jan Tinbergen, "Planning of International Development," *Proceedings of the International Conference on Industrial Economics,* Budapest, April 15–17, 1970; Bohuslav Herman, *The Optimal International Division of Labor,* Geneva, International Labor Office, 1975.

4. Seev Hirsch, "Capital or Technology? Confronting the Neo-Factor Proportions and the Neo-Technology Accounts of International Trade," *Weltwirtschaftliches Archiv.* 110 (1974), 535–63.

5. Harry G. Johnson, "The State of Theory in Relation to Empirical Analysis" in *The Technology Factor in International Trade, op. cit.,* 17.

6. William H. Branson, "Factor Inputs, U.S. Trade, and the Heckscher-Ohlin Model," Seminar Paper No. 27, Institute for International Economic Studies, University of Stockholm, 1973. On the complementarity of physical and human capital, see P. R. Fallon and P. R. G. Layard, "Capital-Skill Complementarity, Income Distribution, and Output Accounting," *Journal of Political Economy,* 83 (1975), 279–302.

7. Physical and human capital have also been separated in a recent article by Hirsch, which has come to the author's attention after this study was completed. Hirsch makes a distinction between high-skill and low-skill industries, further separating (physical) capital and (unskilled) labor-intensive industries within each. For each group, export performance is related to incomes per head, taken as a proxy for physical *and* human capital (Seev Hirsch, "The Product Cycle Model of International Trade—A Multi-Country Cross Section Analysis," *Oxford Bulletin of Economics and Statistics,* November, 27 (1975), 305–17). Thus, in contradistinction with the present study, an aggregated commodity classification scheme is used and capital endowment variables are not introduced in the analysis. Also, the human capital intensity of the different product categories is defined in terms of skill intensity, the usefulness of which will be questioned below.

8. Robert F. Baldwin, "Determinants of the Commodity Structure of U.S. Trade," *American Economic Review Papers and Proceedings,* 61 (1961), 126–46; J. F. Morall, *Human Capital, Technology and the Role of the U.S. in International Trade,* Gainesville, University of Florida Press, 1972; William H. Branson and Helen Junz, "Trends in U.S. Comparative Advantage," *Brookings Papers on Economic Activity,* 2 (1971), 285–345; Bernard Goodman and Fikret Ceyhun, "U.S. Export Performance in Manufacturing Industries: An Empirical Investigation," *Weltwirtschaftliches Archiv.* 112 (1976), 525–55.

9. Peter Kenen, "Nature, Capital and Trade," *Journal of Political Economy,* 73 (1965), 437–460; Gerhard Fels, *op. cit.;* William Branson, *op. cit.*

10. Fels has employed both measures in correlating net German exports with capital intensity in a nineteen industry sample *(op. cit.,* Table 3). In turn, Lary has used Hufbauer's data to calculate the rank correlation coefficient between country averages of value added per employee in exports and per capita incomes *(op. cit.).*

11. Lary, *op. cit.,* Appendix D.

12. A. B. Cornwall, "Influence of the Natural Resource Factor on the Comparative Advantage of Less-Developed Countries," *Inter-mountain Economic Review,* 3 (1972), 61–72.

13. Information on the capital intensity of the 184 product categories chosen, using the stock as well as the flow measure of capital, and further separating physical and human capital, is available from the author.

14. This is in between the discount rates of 9.0 and 12.7 percent used by Kenen *(op. cit.);* the same discount rate was used by Fels *(op. cit.)* and by Branson *(op. cit.).*

15. On the use of per capita incomes as one of the explanatory variables, see Section III below.

16. Hufbauer, *op. cit.,* 157.

17. This choice can be rationalized on the grounds that, *ex ante,* capital can be allocated to manufacturing as well as to other sectors. And while adjustments would need to be made if there

was complementary between capital and natural resources in certain uses, such as mining, information on the sectoral composition of investment was not available for a number of the countries under study.

18.   "Capital or Technology? Confronting the Neo-Factor Proportions and the Neo-Technology Accounts of International Trade," *op. cit.*, 542.

19.   Hofbauer, *op. cit.*, 158.

20.   This index has also been used in a study of world trade flows by William H. Gruber and Raymond Vernon, "The Technology Factor in a World Trade Matrix" in *The Technology Factor in International Trade, op. cit.*, 233–72.

21.   It is derived as the secondary school enrollment rate plus five times the university enrollment rate in the respective age cohorts.

22.   Frederick H. Harbison, Jan Maruhnic and Jane R. Resnick, *Quantitative Analyses of Modernization and Development*, Princeton, N.J., Industrial Relations Section, Dept. of Economics, Princeton University, 1970, 175–76.

23.   Bela Balassa, "Trade Liberalization and Revealed Comparative Advantage,"*Manchester School*, 33 (1965), 99–123.

24.   An alternative measure would involve relating exports to output in each country. In the absence of output figures, however, this measure could not be utilized in the present investigation. At any rate, it would require adjusting the country size (Bela Balassa, "Country Size and Trade Patterns: Comment," *American Economic Review*, 59 (1969), 201–04) while the measure used here does not require such an adjustment.

25.   Since the logarithm of zero is undefined, in the estimating equations an important ratio of .001 has been used to represent cases when the exports of a country in a particular product category were nil. We have also experimented with the use of a .01 ratio and have obtained practically the same results. Nor are the results materially affected if we drop the zero observations from the regressions. This and other estimates not reported in the paper are available from the author on request.

26.   Alternatively, use may be made of non-parametric tests involving the calculation of the Spearman rank correlation coefficient between the "revealed" comparative advantage ratio and the individual factor intensity measures. This test has the disadvantage, however, that it cannot handle more than one explanatory variable and that it does not permit indicating the implications of the intercountry results for a country's future comparative advantage (on the last point, see Section IV).

27.   The results contrast with those obtained by Helleiner who found total (physical and human) capital intensity to have lower explanatory power than skill intensity alone. But, Helleiner's results pertain to the trade of the developing countries taken as a group; he did not employ a stock measure of capital; and he used the average wage as a measure of skill intensity. (Gerald K. Helleiner, "Industry Characteristics and the Competitiveness of Manufactures from Less-Developed Countries," *Weltwirtschaftliches Archiv*, 112 (1976), 507–24).

Helleiner also used some additional variables, of which scale economies was statistically significant in trade between developing and developed countries. However, comparative advantage in products subject to scale economies is related to the size of the domestic market ("Country Size and Trade Patterns: Comment," *op. cit.*) and, with developing countries having smaller markets, Helleiner's results raise problems of identification.

28.   Note that, with variations in the standard errors of the β coefficients derived in equation (4), the regression results obtained in equation (5) will be subject to heteroscedasticity which increases the standard error of the coefficients. However, the estimates are little affected if we weigh the data for the individual countries by the inversion of the standard error of the β coefficients to reduce heteroscedasticity.

29.   Regressing the rank correlation coefficients calculated as between the "revealed" comparative advantage ratio and the factor intensity measures on factor endowment variables has generally confirmed the reported results, although the level of statistical significance of the coefficients was somewhat lower.

30. Hufbauer, *op. cit.,* 169.

31. The relevant regression results with t-values in parentheses are

$$\beta_j^s = -1.36 + .14 \text{ GNPCAP} + 1.39 \text{ GDICAP} + .33 \text{ HMIND} \quad R^2 = .65$$
$$\quad (8.46)\ (.06) \qquad\qquad (1.20) \qquad\qquad (1.52)$$

$$\beta_j^f = -2.70 + 1.66 \text{ GNPCAP} + 1.79 \text{ GDICAP} + .68 \text{ HMIND} \quad R^2 = .78$$
$$\quad (12.06)\ (.51) \qquad\qquad (1.11) \qquad\qquad (2.25)$$

32. Some major exceptions are various textile fabrics, reclaimed rubber, aluminum castings, ball bearings, and railroad cars where the stock measure, and toilet articles, paints, electric housewares, electric lamps, and motor vehicles where the flow measure shows a considerably higher degree of capital intensity than the other measure of capital intensity.

33. The results obtained by the use of the flow measure of capital intensity are broadly comparable, although they differ in regard to particular commodities.

34. The expression "stages" is used here to denote changes over time that occur more-or-less continuously, rather than to discrete, stepwise changes. It is thus unrelated to economic stages described by Marx, the exponents of the German historical school, and Rostow.

35. Peter S. Heller, "Factor Endowment Change and Comparative Advantage," *Review of Economics and Statistics,* 58 (1976), 283–92.

36. In 1974, average wages in manufacturing in Korea were 9 percent, and in the Philippines 6 percent, of U.S. wages (ILO, *Yearbook of Labor Statistics*).

37. The difference in the cost of capital has been estimated at 43.3 percent under the assumption that value added in the manufacturing sector and the absolute difference between skilled and unskilled wages were the same in the two cases. It has further been assumed that pre-tax returns and depreciation amount to 30 percent of the gross value of physical capital in the United States.

38. As elsewhere in the essay, the calculations do not allow for factor substitution in response of intercountry differences in factor prices.

39. In line with the stages approach to comparative advantage, this is done on the assumption that new countries exporting manufactured goods will enter at the lower end of the spectrum. It is further assumed that the relative importance of capital-intensive goods in world exports will continue to increase over time.

40. These projections further need to be adjusted in cases when observed values of the β coefficients differ from values estimated from the intercountry regression. The results are also subject to the usual projection error and may be biased to the extent that high protection in countries with poor capital endowment affects the slope of the intercountry regression.

Essay 7

1. The volumnous statistical work underlying the estimates of the section was undertaken by Kishore Nadkarni.

2. Robert E. Baldwin, "Trade and Employment Effects in the United States Multilateral Tariff Reductions," *American Economic Review, Papers and Proceedings,* 66 (1976), 146.

3. *Ibid.,* 148.

4. William Cline et. al., *Trade Negotiations in the Tokyo Round: A Quantitative Assessment,* Washington, D.C., the Brookings Institution, 1978, 63.

5. *Ibid.,* 125–26.

6. *Ibid.,* 232.

7. Cline, et al., however, also estimated the direct employment effects of multilateral trade liberalization in textiles. These are −37 thousand jobs in the United States, −6 in Canada, −17 in EEC, and −41 in Japan (132–35).

8. Anne O. Krueger, "Impact of LDC Exports on Employment in American Industry,"

Paper presented to the Annual Conference of the International Economic Study Group, White House, Isle of Thorns, Sussex, England, 1978, 2 (mimeo).

9. Errol Grinols and Erik Thorbecke, "The Effects of Trade between the U.S. and Developing Countries in U.S. Employment," Working Paper No. 171, Department of Economics, Cornell University, 1978, 11.

10. *Ibid.,* 36.

11. *Ibid.,* 11. The cited estimates exclude processed food that is not part of manufactured goods under the definition used in this paper.

12. P. De Grauwe, W. Kennes, T. Peeters, and R. Van Straelen, "Trade Liberalization with the Less Developed Countries: A Case Study of Belgium," *Bulletin de l'IRES,* 44 (1977), 9.

13. D. Schumacher, "Verstärkter Handel mit der Dritten Welt: Eher Umsetzung als Freisetzung deutscher Arbeitskräfte," *DIW Wochenbericht,* February 3, 1977, 39.

14. U. Hiemenz and K.W. Schatz, *Trade in Place of Migration,* Geneva, International Labor Office, 1979, 48–49.

15. H.F. Lydall, *Trade and Employment,* Geneva, International Labor Office, 1975, 110–11.

16. Thomas Birnberg, "Economic Effects of Changes in Trade Relations between Developed and Less Developed Countries," NIEO Monograph Series, Overseas Development Council, Summer 1978, 66.

17. Bela Balassa, "A 'Stages Approach' to Comparative Advantage," Essay 6 in this volume.—We have excluded from our purview primary products where the availability of natural resources affects the outcome. At any rate, in public discussions attention has been concentrated on the employment effects of trade in manufactured goods.

18. H.F. Lydall, *op. cit.,* 87.

19. The OECD includes the industrial countries (the United States, Canada, the EEC, EFTA, and Japan) as well as the countries of Southern Europe (Greece, Spain, and Turkey), Australia and New Zealand.

20. D. Schumacher, "Beschäftigungswirkungen von Importen aus Entwicklungslandern nicht dramatisieren," *DIW Wochenbericht,* January 1978, 10. Schumacher's more recent estimates do not report direct labor-input coefficients alone. Also, there seems to be a conflict between estimates of direct plus indirect employment effects in Schumacher's estimates reported in his 1977 and 1978 articles as well as between the results shown in two of the tables in his 1978 paper.

21. Labor-input coefficients are the same for exports and for imports in the case of furniture and petroleum products where, due to data limitations, further disaggregation was not feasible.

22. In all cases, we have taken one-tenth of the sum of positive and negative employment balances shown in Table 7.2. It is apparent from the table that the net employment effects for particular industries were generally of the same sign in the individual developed countries and country groups as for the OECD as a whole.

23. Results for the individual occupational groups have been obtained by utilizing U.S. statistics on Occupation by Industry for the year 1970.

24. Exceptions are clerical workers in Japan and workers in construction, transportation, and material handling in the United States.

25. Donald B. Keesing, "Labor Skills and International Trade: Evaluating Many Trade Flows with a Single Measuring Device," *Review of Economics and Statistics,* 47 (1965), 291.

26. Robert E. Baldwin and Wayne E. Lewis, "The U.S. Tariff Effects on Trade and Employment in Detailed SIC Industries," *The Impact of International Trade and Investment in Employment,* Proceedings of a Conference on the Department of Labor Research results, held on December 2 and 3, 1976, Washington, D.C., U.S. Department of Labor, 1978, 253.

27. Donald B. Keesing, *op. cit.,;* "Labor Skills and the Structure of Trade in Manufactures," in *The Open Economy* (Peter B. Kenen and Robert Lawrence, ed.), New York, Columbia University Press, 1968, 3–18; "Different Countries' Labor Skill Coefficients and the Skill Intensity of International Trade Flows," *Journal of International Economics,* 1 (1971), 443–52.

In the first two papers, Keesing also used U.S. labor input coefficients for examining the occupational effects of the exports of various industrial countries. In the third paper, Keesing has made use of data obtained for the individual industrial countries. This has not been done in the present investigation for lack of comparable data in the appropriate breakdown.

28. Peter B. Kenen, "Nature, Capital, and Trade," *Journal of Political Economy*, 73 (1965), 437–60.

29. P. De Grauwe, et. al., *op. cit.,* 8.

30. The calculations reported in this section were performed by Joung-Yong Lee.

31. World Bank, *World Development Report, 1978*, Washington, D.C., 1978—to be cited as WDR I.

32. WDR I, 29.

33. *Ibid.*

34. *Ibid.,* 28.

35. Donald B. Keesing, "World Trade and Output of Manufactures: Structural Trends and Developing Countries' Exports," World Bank Staff Working Paper, No. 316, Washington, D.C., January 1979.

36. WDR I, 32.

37. Estimated by regression analysis for data published in United Nations, *Monthly Bulletin of Statistics and Yearbook of National Accounts of Statistics.*

38. Nevertheless, in this study the rate of GNP growth has been taken as exogenous and estimates of the effects of trade on economic growth have not been made.

39. Table 7.6b and OECD, Labor Force Statistics, 1978.

40. WDR I, 28.

41. Results based on trade data and on information provided in WDR I (28).

42. In the case of Germany, one-fifth of the projected job loss would be compensated by a decline in immigration (Hiemenz and Schatz, *op. cit.,* 50).

Essay 8

1. Belgium, Denmark, France, Germany, Ireland, Italy, Luxemburg, Netherlands, and the United Kingdom.

2. Austria, Finland, Iceland, Norway, Portugal, Sweden, and Switzerland.

3. Algeria, Ecuador, Gabon, Indonesia, Iran, Iraq, Kuwait, Libya, Nigeria, Qatar, Saudi Arabia, United Arab Emirates.

4. The countries of Latin American and the Caribbean, Africa (other than South Africa), Asia (other than Japan), Oceania (other than Australia and New Zealand), excluding centally planned economies and the OPEC countries.

5. General Agreements on Tariffs and Trade, *International Trade, 1978/79,* Geneva, 1979, Table B to F—The data for 1978 are preliminary.

6. GATT, *International Trade, 1978/79* and Table 8.1.

7. United Nations, *Yearbook of National Accounts Statistics, 1978* and World Bank Data Base.

8. "The Changing International Division of Labor in Manufactured Goods," Essay 7 in this volume.

9. GATT, *International Trade, 1978/79,* Table G.

10. On the relevant methodology and its application to three developing countries, see Bela Balassa, "Policy Responses to External Shocks in Selected Latin American Countries," Essay 3 in this volume.

11. Bela Balassa, "The Tokyo Round and the Developing Countries," Essay 5 in this volume.

12. GATT, "International Trade in 1979 and Present Prospects: Fist Assessment by the GATT Secretariat," Geneva, February 15, 1980.

13. Cf. Bela Balassa, "The Newly-Industrializing Countries After the Oil Crisis," Essay 2 in this volume.

14. The differences are larger if comparison is made with Canada and, as far as the share of developing countries in total manufactured imports is concerned, with EFTA. In the case of Canada, protection against LDC products affected the outcome. In turn, the results for the EFTA countries reflect the importance of the United States as supplier.

15. "The Tokyo Round and the Developing Countries," Essay 5 in this volume.

16. For sources, see Table 8.1.

17. "A 'Stages Approach' to Comparative Advantage," Essay 6 in this volume.

18. The capital-labor ratios themselves have been derived from the data of the U.S. Industrial Census. Their use in the present context assumes equal substitution elasticities between capital and labor across industries.

19. In addition to these "stock" coefficients, in the earlier paper "flow" coefficients are also reported, representing profits per worker in the case of physical capital and the average wage in the case of human capital. The stock coefficients are preferred, however, in view of fluctuations in profit rates over time and the inclusion of the unskilled wage in the average wage figures.

20. The OPEC countries have been excluded from these comparisons as they export practically no manufactured goods.

21. For lack of price indices on a commodity group basis, export ratios have been expressed in terms of current prices.

22. Table 8.3 and the sources sited therein.

23. Data for the gross domestic product pertain to the year 1975 and have been expressed in 1975 prices and exchange rates. Import data have been derived from the trade statistics of the industrial countries and overestimate the shares of Hong Kong and Singapore by including their re-exports.

24. Bela Balassa, "Prospects for Trade in Manufactured Goods between Industrial and Developing Countries, 1978-1990," Essay 9 in this volume.

25. *Ibid.*

Essay 9

1. On the composition of the various country groups, see "Trade in Manufactured Goods: Patterns of Change," Essay 8 in this volume.

2. Commodity classes 5 to 8 in the UN Standard International Trade Classification less nonferrous metals (68).

3. World Bank, *World Development Report, 1979,* Washington, D.C., 1979, 18 (to be cited as WDR II)— Compared to the definition of industrial countries used in this study, the estimates include Australia and New Zealand and exclude Portugal. Making adjustments for these countries would not modify the results, however. The same conclusion applies to the estimated GDP growth rate of 4.1 percent a year for the 1978-90 period.

4. Wasily, Leontief, Anne P. Carter, and Peter A. Petri, *The Future of the World Economy,* A United Nations Study, New York, Oxford University Press, 1977, Annex VI. (To be cited as Leontief et. al. Unless otherwise noted, all references relate to Annex VI.)—The cited estimates pertain to the same group of countries as in the present study, except that they exclude Portugal.

5. Interfutures, *Facing the Future,* Paris, Organization for Economic Co-Operation and Development, 1979, 121, 131, and 328 (to be cited as Interfutures)—The estimates pertain to the entire OECD, thus including Southern Europe, Australia, and New Zealand as well. The exclusion of these countries would hardly affect the results, however, as they account for only 7 percent of OECD GDP.

Interfutures also provides additional scenarios, involving changes in social values in the industrial countries, with a consensus on slowing down economic growth; a rift between the industrial countries and the developing countries; and mounting protection on trade among the industrial countries, together with preferential ties between particular industrial countries and developing countries. The assumptions underlying these scenarios may be considered less realistic, however, and they are not reported here.

6. Interfutures, 89—Under the rapid convergent growth scenario, Interfutures postulates a long-run productivity growth rate of 1.84 percent for the United States on the basis of an estimate of the Council of Economic Advisors. This is raised to 2.2 percent in the period 1975-2000 because of the assumed catch-up to the pre-recession productivity trend (p. 121).

7. Interfutures, 89—The source for data in 1975 prices and exchange rates is the *1978 World Bank Atlas,* Washington, D.C., 1979, 28–29.

8. Interfutures, 13 and 89—In the calculations, population growth rates estimated for the period 1975-2000 (United States 0.6 percent; Common Market, 0.1 percent; and Japan 0.7 percent) have been assumed to apply to the 1975-90 period as well.

9. *Ibid.,* 138.

10. The estimates include the countries of Southern Europe (Cyprus, Greece, Israel, Malta, Portugal, Spain, Turkey and Yogoslavia) and exclude the capital-surplus oil exporters (Kuwait, Libya, Oman, Qatar, Saudi Arabia, and the United Arab Emirates). Adjusting for these countries would not affect the results, however.

11. For empirical evidence on the latter point, cf. Bela Balassa, "Exports and Economic Growth: Further Evidence," *Journal of Development Economics,* 5 (1978), 181–89.

12. United Nations, *Yearbook of National Accounts Statistics,* various issues; OECD, *National Accounts of the OECD Countries, 1979* and *Economic Outlook,* December 1979.

13. WDR II, 18.

14. United Nations, *Yearbook of National Accounts Statistics 1978* and World Bank data base.

15. WDR II, 5.

16. While the former estimate pertains to exports to all destinations and the latter to exports to the industrial countries alone, from WDR II it would appear that, if anything, the projected rate of growth of manufactured exports to the industrial countries is lower than the average. (*Ibid.,* 5, 27–28).

17. The relevant figures are 7.6 percent for 1977 and 15.5 percent for 1978 (Bela Balassa. "Trade in Manufactured Goods: Patterns of Change," *op. cit.)*

18. WDR II, 5.

19. Comparable estimates are not available in the Interfutures study.

20. United Nations Industrial Development Organization, *Industry 2000—New Perspectives,* New York, United Nations, 1979, 219–20 (to be cited as the UNIDO Report)—Data for the industrial countries include Southern Europe, Australia, and New Zealand.

21. Table 8.1—Estimates of the apparent income elasticity of import demand in the developing countries for manufactured imports originating in the industrial countries, cited below, derive from the same source.

22. The projections in WDR II are 15.3 for machinery and transport equipment and 9.0 percent for other manufactures for the period 1976-90 (p. 5); the differences are smaller, with growth rates of 9.5 and 8.2 percent, in the estimates by Leontief et. al. for the period 1980-90.

23. Bela Balassa, "A 'Stages Approach' to Comparative Advantages," Essay 6 in this volume.

24. UNIDO Report, 220.

25. *Ibid.*

26. In interpreting these figures, emphasis should be given to changes in the ratios rather than the ratios themselves as the Interfuture figure for 1970 represents an underestimate.

27. The difference in the results were due in part to statistical discrepancy and in part to the cif valuation of imports in the EEC, EFTA, and Japan.

28.   GATT, *International Trade, 1978-79,* Tables B to F.

29.   United Nations, *Monthly Bulletin of Statistics,* June 1979 and *Yearbook of National Accounts Statistics, 1978.*

30.   Landsberg, Hans H., Leonard L. Fischman and Joseph L. Fisher, *Resources in America's Future,* Baltimore, Md., the Johns Hopkins Press, 1963, 556–58, 561–63.

31.   Houthakker, H. S. and Lester D. Taylor, *Consumer Demand in the United States: Analysis and Projections,* Cambridge, Mass., Harvard University Press, 1970, 1974–75.

32.   Deaton, Angus S., *Models and Projections of Demand in Postwar Britain,* London, Chapman and Hill, 1975.

33.   Berner, Richard B., "A General Equilibrium Model of International Discrimination" Ph.D. dissertation submitted to the University of Pennsylvania, 1976.

34.   It should be emphasized that the consumption as well as the production estimates are expressed in terms of gross values rather than value added.

35.   United Nations, *Yearbook of National Accounts Statistics, 1978* and national statistics.

Essay 10

1.   Joel Bergsman and Pedro S. Malan, "The Structure of Protection in Brazil," in Bela Balassa and Associates, *The Structure of Protection in Developing Countries,* Baltimore, Md., The Johns Hopkins University Press, 1977, 103–36. Further references to protection in 1966 also originate in this study.

2.   Nathaniel H. Leff, "Export Stagnation and Autarkic Development in Brazil, 1947-1962," *Quarterly Journal of Economics,* 81 (1967), 286–301.

3.   Traditional exports have been defined to include products that accounted for at least 2 percent of exports in 1953. Cf. Bela Balassa, "Export Incentives and Export Performance in Developing Countries: A Comparative Analysis," *Weltwirtschaftliches Archiv,* 114 (1978), 24–61.

4.   Nathaniel H. Leff, *op. cit.*

5.   José Augusto A. Savasini, *Export Promotion: The Case of Brazil,* New York, Praeger, 1978, 30–39. —The same source provides estimates of export subsidies on an industry-by-industry basis.

6.   William G. Tyler, *Manufactured Exports Expansion and Industrialization in Brazil,* Kieler Studien, 134, Tubingen, J.C.B. Mohr, 1976, 239.

7.   Antonio C. Lemgruber, "Inflation in Brazil," in Lawrence B. Krause and Walter S. Salant, ed. *Worldwide Inflation, Theory and Recent Experience,* Washington, D.C., The Brookings Institution, 1977, 395–442.

8.   Argentina, Brazil, Chile, Colombia, India, Israel, Korea, Mexico, Singapore, Taiwan, and Yugoslavia.

9.   Edmar Bacha, "Issues and Evidence on Recent Brazilian Economic Growth," *World Development,* 5 (1977), 47–48.

10.   Pedro S. Malan and Regis Bonelli, "The Brazilian Economy in the Seventies: Old and New Developments," *World Development,* 5 (1977), 35. —In referring to the periods 1968-74 and 1968-73, respectively, Bacha and Malan-Bonelli take the relatively slow growth year of 1967 as a basis. In the present paper, 1966 is used as the base year. This choice has entailed lowering average measured growth rates for the period considered as the policy changes made were in large part in effect in 1967.

11.   W. Suzigan, et. al., "Crecimento industrial no Brasil—incentivos a desempenho recente," IPEA, *Coleção Relatórios de Pesquisa,* 26 (1974), and Regis Bonelli, "Growth and Technological Change in Brazilian Manufacturing Industries During the 1960s," unpublished Ph.D. dissertation, Berkeley, Cal., University of California, 1975.

12.   José L. Carvalho and Claudio L. S. Haddad, "A promoçao de exportacoes: experiência brasileira até 1974," *Revista Brasileira do Economia,* 32, (1978), Table 11.

13. Pedro S. Malan and Regis Bonelli, *op. cit.*, 29.

14. José L. Carvalho and Claudio L. S. Haddad, *op. cit.*, 131.

15. William G. Tyler, *Manufactured Exports Expansion and Industrialization in Brazil, op. cit.*, 262.

16. Mauricio Barata de Paula Pinto, "Brazilian Manufactured Exports: Growth Change in Structure," unpublished Ph.D. dissertation, Baltimore, Md., The Johns Hopkins University, 1979, ch. 5.

17. Pedro S. Malan and Regis Bonelli, *op. cit.*, 21.

18. Organization for Economic Cooperation and Development, *National Accounts of OECD Countries*, various issues.

19. *Conjuntura Econômica*, November 1978. Unless otherwise noted, all data relating to Brazil originate in this publication. For comparability with other countries, different sources are used in Essays 2 and 3 of this volume, resulting in some differences in the estimates for later years.

20. João Paul dos Reis Velloso, *Brasil: A Soluçcão Positiva*, São Paulo, Abril-Tec Editora, 1978, 115.

21. For year-end data on the money supply and annual averages of the wholesale price index and government revenue and expenditure, see Table 3.3. —The expenditure data include the federal government only. According to one estimate, the combined deficit of the public sector, including state and local governments and public enterprises as well, reached 6 percent of GNP in 1976. Note finally that the rate of inflation was underestimated in 1973.

22. Edmar Bacha, "Brazil's Balance of Payments Before and After the Oil Crisis," paper prepared for an UNCTAD/UNDP project on the Impact of the Oil Crisis on the Balance of Payments of Developing Countries, July 1978, 34.

23. Other contributing factors were the poor agricultural harvest and increased protection; on the latter point, see below.

24. Annual data are shown in Table 3.4. Quarterly data for 1978 and 1979 and estimates using industrial prices rather than the general price index are reported in Bela Balassa, "Incentive Policies in Brazil," *World Development*, 7 (1979), 1023–42.

25. D. Munhoz, "Importações—Etapas da politica do controle," *Conjuntura Economica*, (1976), 76–80.

26. World Bank data bank.

27. Pedro S. Malan and Regis Bonelli, *op cit.*, 33.

28. On the question of inventory accumulation, see also below.

29. While the estimates are subject to a considerable error, according to various calculations the marginal productivity of capital is about 15 percent in Brazil (Carlos Langoni, "A Study in Economic Growth: The Brazilian Case," unpublished Ph.D. dissertation, Chicago, Ill., University of Chicago, 1970, and Edmar Bacha, "Case Studies in the Estimation of National Economic Parameters in Less Developed Countries: Brazil," *Social and Economic Dimensions of Project Evaluation*, (Hugh Schwartz and Richard Barney ed.), Washington, D.C., Interamerican Development Bank, 1977).

30. The increases are even larger if we consider that the consumption figures reported in 1973 included a considerable amount of stockpiling.

31. Edmar Bacha, "Brazil's Balance of Payments Before and After the Oil Crisis," *op cit.*, 36.

32. D. Munhoz, "Inflação—impulsos de custos reversíveis a nao reversíveis e a taxa dé inflação de equilíbrio," Brasilia Department of Economics, University of Brasília, 1978 (mimeo).

33. William R. Cline, "World Inflation and the Brazilian Economy," in *Worldwide Inflation and the Developing Countries*, Washington, D.C., The Brookings Institution, 1979, 26–29 (mimeo).

34. José Augusto A. Savasini and Honorio Kume, "Análise da política de promoção de exportações segundo o custo dos recursos domésticos por unidade de divisa gerada," *Fundacão Centro de Estudos do Comércio Exterior*, Projeto II, Subprojeto II—Relatório Final (Versão Preliminar), Rio de Janeiro, 1978, 60. The benchmark for the DRC ratios is the ratio of the shadow

exchange rate to the actual exchange rate, which the authors assumed to be in the range of 1.25 and 1.35.

35. William G. Tyler, "Brazil: Protection and Competition of the Capital Goods Producing Industries," Washington, D.C., World Bank, April 1979 (mimeo), 13–14.

36. *Ibid.,* 12, 27.

37. *Ibid.,* 27–40.

38. The exchange rate at which capital originally was imported does not affect this conclusion; it will be relevant only for the repatriation of capital.

39. Affonso Celso Pastore, José Augusto A. Savasini, and Joal de Azambuja Rosa, "Quantificaçào dos incentivos ás exportaçòes," *Fundacào Centro de Estudos do Comércio Exterior,* Projeto I—Relatorio Final, (Versào Preliminar), Rio de Janeiro, 1977, 31–32.

40. *Ibid.*

41. *Ibid.*, 37–41.

42. William G. Tyler, "Brazil: Protection and Competition of the Capital Goods Producing Industries," *op cit.,* 13.

43. In 1975, the subsidy equivalent of credit preferences was estimated to average 2.6 percent, and the net burden of indirect taxes 3.1 percent, of the fob value of total exports other than coffee (Pastore, Savasini and Rosa, *op. cit.*). No estimate is available on the subsidy element of the BEFIEX system.

Essay 11

1. World Bank data bank.

2. Unless otherwise noted, all data on Portugal originate from the Banco de Portugal, *Relatorio do Conselho de Administracao*, various issues or special communications, while international data derive from International Monetary Fund, *International Financial Statistics.*

3. In practice, this meant the government taking over the management of the firms in question.

4. World Bank, *Portugal: Current and Prospective Economic Trends*, Washington, D.C., November 1978, 38.

5. The index of production costs has been calculated by weighting the index of wage costs, the index of the prices of purchased inputs, represented by wholesale price index for home and import goods, and the cost of capital goods, represented by a weighted average of price indices for machinery and construction. The relevant weights have been derived from the 1970 input-output table for Portugal: G.E.B.E.I. *Sistema de Matrices Multisectoriais para o Continente Portugues*, Vol. V, Lisbon, 1975.

6. United Nations, *Commodity Trade Statistics*, various issues.

7. Increases in labor productivity, however, partly reflect the increased share of capital-intensive industries.

8. World Bank data bank.

9. European Communities, Commission, "Opinion on Portuguese Application for Membership," *Bulletin of the European Communities,* 12 (1978), Supplement No. 5.

10. Organization for Economic Cooperation and Development, *Portugal,* Paris, OECD Economic Surveys, 1979.

11. European Communities, Commission, *Economic and Sectoral Aspects; Commission Analyses Supplementing its View on Enlargement,* COM (78) 200 final, Brussels, 1978, 22.

12. World Bank, *Portugal: Agricultural Sector Survey,* Washington, D.C., November 1978, 3.

13. *Portugal: Agricultural Sector Survey, op. cit.,* 138.

14. In 1974, yields in Portugal, expressed as a percentage of yields in Greece and Spain were 48 and 79 percent for wheat, 35 and 44 percent for barley, 40 and 50 percent for oats, 39 and 41 percent for maize, and 78 and 65 percent for rice (*Ibid,* 34).

15. Hyung M. Kim, "Agricultural Prices and Subsidies—Portugal Case Study," Washington, D.C., World Bank, 1978, 73–87 (mimeo).

16. In the case of beef, veal, and wine, the orientation price, in the case of pork, the base price is relevant.

17. On May 14, 1979, the MCAs were 10.8 percent in Germany, 3.3 percent for the Benelux countries, nil for Denmark and Ireland, —5.3 percent for France, —15.7 percent for Italy, and —20.0 percent for the United Kingdom (*The Economist,* May 19, 1979). For the calculations, the assumption was made that the MCA for Portugal would be set at zero.

18. Kim, *op cit.,* 79–81.

19. R. D. Hunt, "Fruit and Vegetable Exports from the Mediterranean Area to the EEC," World Bank Staff Working Paper, No. 321, March 1979, 32.

20. *Portugal: Agricultural Sector Survey, op. cit.,* 6.

21. *Ibid.*

22. Kim, *op. cit.*

23. Data from the municipalities of Evora and Viana show that in the collective sector of farming, 72 percent of credit goes for salaries while in the private sector (mainly small farms) only 4 percent is so used (Earl O. Heady, "An Analysis of Agricultural Development and Agrarian Reform Possibilities in Portugal," Lisbon, 1979 [mimeo]).

24. U.S. data for the years 1969–70 show capital expenditures per job in thousand dollars of 126 for petroleum refining and products, 75 for other petrochemicals, and 40 for fertilizers, as compared to 9 for textiles, 2 for clothing, 1 for leather and leather products, 12 for stone, clay and glass products, 9 for fabricated metal products and 7 for electrical equipment and supplies (Bela Balassa, "A 'Stages' Approach to Comparative Advantage," Essay 6 in this volume).

25. OECD, *op. cit.,* 35.

26. *Ibid.*

27. On the Hungarian experience, see Bela Balassa, "The Economic Reform in Hungary Ten Years After," Essay 14 in this volume.

28. Bela Balassa. "A 'Stages' Approach to Comparative Advantage," *op. cit.*

29. Bela Balassa, "Planning and Programming in the European Common Market," *European Economic Review,* 4 (1973), 217–33. For a more detailed discussion of issues relevant to planning in Portugal, see Bela Balassa, "Proposals for Economic Planning in Portugal," *Economia,* 2 (1978), 117–24.

30. For instance, an agreement reached in early 1979 permitting the Portuguese subsidiary of ITT to discharge 270 workers was overturned by the subsequent government.

31. Self-investment will be privately profitable and socially unprofitable if its rate of return exceeds the rate obtainable on savings deposits but falls short of returns in alternative investments.

32. For the relevant data, see Manuel P. Barbosa and Luis Miguel P. Beleza, "External Disequilibrium in Portugal: 1975–78," paper prepared for the IInd International Conference on Portuguese Economy, Lisbon, September 1979, Table 6. This paper, as well as the paper by Maxwell J. Fry, "Money, Interest and Growth," prepared for the IInd International Conference on the Portuguese Economy, Lisbon, September 1979, also provides a good analysis of the adverse economic effects of low interest rates in Portugal.

33. OECD, *op. cit.,* 34.

34. Erik Lundberg, "Economic Policies in Portugal," Lisbon, Banco de Portugal, 1978 (mimeo).

35. *Ibid.,* 13.

Essay 12

1. Unless otherwise noted, all data have been expressed in terms of constant domestic prices.

2. World Bank, *Atlas,* Washington, D.C., 1975.

3. United Nations, *Yearbook of International Trade Statistics*, 1962 and 1976.

4. World Bank, *World Tables*, 1976 and United Nations, *Yearbook of National Account Statistics*, 1975.

5. United Nations, *Yearbook of Industrial Statistics,* 1975.

6. Ministry of Coordination, National Accounts Service, *Provisional National Accounts of Greece, Year 1977*, Athens, 1978, Table 18. Unless otherwise stated, all national accounts data originate from this source.

7. The preliminary plan document, *Macro-Economic Evaluations*, Athens, June 1968, was prepared by the Center of Planning and Economic Research, known after its initials in Greek KEPE. Several of the tables of this document have been reproduced in an abbreviated form in this essay, with alternative projections by the author added.

8. Xenophon Zolotas, "Inflation and the Monetary Target in Greece," *Papers and Lectures No. 38*, Athens, Bank of Greece, 1978, 22; Bank of Greece, special communication; and U.K. *National Institute Economic Review*, May 1978.

9. International Monetary Fund, *International Financial Statistics,* June 1980.

10. Xenophon Zolotas, *op. cit.*

11. *Macro-Economic Evaluations, op. cit.*, 43.

12. Organisation for Economic Cooperation and Development, *Greece*, Paris, OECD Economic Surveys, June 1977, 19.

13. The calculations have been made on the basis of data published in United Nations Educational, Scientific, and Cultural Organization, *Statistical Yearbook*, 1975.

14. International Labour Office, *Yearbook of Labour Statistics,* and International Monetary Fund, *International Financial Statistics*; data for Turkey are not available.

15. On the skill intensity of these industries, see Bela Balassa, "A 'Stages' Approach to Comparative Advantage," Essay 6 in this volume.

16. Calculated from data in United Nations, *Yearbook of National Accounts Statistics*, and *Yearbook of International Trade Statistics*.

17. World Bank, *World Development Report, 1978*, Washington, D.C., 29.

18. The difference between the two figures reflects the assumption that exports would have to rise more than proportionately in order to secure additional increases in manufacturing output.

19. In other words, the proposed low projections for the national economy, as well as for individual sectors, coincide with the estimates shown under Assumption B of the preliminary plan document.

20. The years cited refer to the investment data while output data are lagged by one year.

21. *Provisional National Accounts of Greece, Year 1977*, Tables 2 and 20.

22. The ratio of the rate of growth of imports to that of GDP.—In Essays 8 and 9 of this volume, the expression "apparent" income elasticity of import demand has been used to refer to this ratio.

23. Bela Balassa, "L'économie francaise sous la Cinquième République, 1958–1978," *Revue Economique*, 6 (1979), 939–72.

24. Data provided by KEPE.

25. The corresponding growth rates for total exports are shown in Table 12.2.

26. Bank of Greece, special communication and U.K. *National Institute Economic Review, op. cit.*

27. International Monetary Fund, *International Financial Statistics*, June 1978.

28. *Provisional National Accounting of Greece, Year 1977*, 92. In June 1978, a U.S. dollar equaled 36.9 drachmas.

29. Estimates prepared at KEPE indicate the existence of a positive relationship between real interest rates and private savings.

30. Wilhelm Hummen, *Greek Industry in the European Community: Prospects and Problems*, Berlin: German Development Institute, 1977, 43.

31. Cf. Bela Balassa, "L'économie francaise sous la Cinquième République, 1958–1978," *op. cit.*

32. Xenophon Zolotas, *op. cit.*, 18.

Essay 13

1. Cf. Bela Balassa, "Incentive Policies in Brazil," Essay 10 in this volume. Other Latin American countries with a similar experience include Argentina and Colombia; in turn, Chile and India provide examples of countries where inward-looking policies continued after 1966, with adverse effects on economic growth. For a detailed discussion, see Bela Balassa, "Export Incentives and Export Performance in Developing Countries: A Comparative Analysis," *Weltwirtschaftliches Archiv,* 114 (1978), 24–61, which examines the experience of eleven newly-industrializing developing countries, classified according to the policies followed in the 1953–73 period.

2. Unless otherwise noted, the data originate from International Monetary Fund, *International Financial Statistics.* In the following, the expressions "exports" and "imports" will be used to refer to merchandise exports and imports.

3. On recommendations made for continuing with an outward-oriented strategy, see Bela Balassa, "Korea's Development Strategy for the Fourth Five-Year Plan Period (1977–81)," Essay 8 in *Policy Reform in Developing Countries,* Oxford, Pergamon Press, 1977, 119–37.

4. The nominal exchange rate adjusted for changes in wholesale prices at home and abroad. See further p. 311 below.

5. Anne O. Krueger, *Foreign Trade Regimes and Economic Development: Turkey,* New York, Columbia University Press, National Bureau of Economic Research, 1974, 259.

6. *Ibid.,* 260.

7. Merih Celasun, "Sources of Industrial Growth and Structural Change: The Case of Turkey (1953–1973)," Ankara, October 1978, (mimeo), Tables III.8 and III.9. Similar results were reached for the same time periods by Tansu Ciller, "Industrial Incentives in Turkey," Appendix B, Import Regime in Turkey, Istanbul, 1978, (mimeo), Table 3.5, and for the periods 1963–67 and the 1967–71 by Hasan Olgun, "The Structure of Protection and the Policy of Industrialization in the Turkish Manufacturing Industries, 1963–1971," unpublished Ph.D. dissertation, Baltimore, Md., The Johns Hopkins University, 1973, Tables 3.5 and 3.6.

8. Anne O. Krueger, "Some Economic Costs of Exchange Control: The Turkish Case," *Journal of Political Economy,* 74 (1966), 473.

9. This may be represented by the decline in labor force participation rates, shown by official data, from 80.0 percent in 1962 to 75.0 percent in 1967, 70.6 percent in 1972, and 67.7 percent in 1977.

10. The increase in the number of workers abroad also reduced unemployment rates.

11. Tansu Ciller, *op cit.,* 16.

12. Kemal Dervis and Sherman Robinson, *Planning Models in Development Policy,* Cambridge, Cambridge University Press, 1980 (forthcoming), Table 6.8. Under the definition used by the authors, "normal" foreign borrowing would have amounted to $940 million in 1977, i.e. approximately 2 percent of GNP (chapters 6, 19).

13. In the years 1956–73, net foreign borrowing averaged 0.3 percent of GNP. The average figure is 0.5 percent if we exclude the years 1972 and 1973 that were characterized by the accumulation of foreign exchange reserves, which is considered a capital outflow in the account.

14. This is due in part to the use of a time trend of total factor productivity (technical change), unaffected by changes in the availability of foreign exchange, in the calculations and in part to the assumption of continuous substitution between capital and labor (i.e. lack of discontinuity in the form of bulky investments).

15. Kemal Dervis and Sherman Robinson, *op. cit.,* Figure 6.3.

16. These rates were increased more or less steadily between 1973 and 1977; they were reduced on the occasion of the March 1978 devaluation, and raised again subsequently, averaging about 15 percent of the fob value of manufactured exports, including processed foods, in early 1979. Exports of fruits and vegetables too received rebates. Note further that the rebates were supposed to provide compensation for the payment of indirect taxes but there were numerous cases of over- and under-compensation.

17. TÜSIAD, *Turkey's Industrial Sector in Foreign Trade with Special Reference to EEC Relations,* Istanbul, Turkish Industrialists and Businessmen's Association, April 1978, 32–33.

18. However, between July 1978 and April 1979 exporters could retain 25 percent of their foreign exchange earnings to finance the importation of inputs, and this ratio was raised to 50 percent in April 1979, when the use of such foreign exchange was extended to the domestic suppliers of the exporters.

19. TÜSIAD, *The Turkish Economy: Prospects for Growth Within Stability,* Istanbul, Turkish Industrialists and Businessmen's Association, July 1978, 204.

20. Tansu Ciller, *op. cit.,* 16.

21. A case in point is that of an importer who contracted to sell tractors at a given price only to find that the June 1979 devaluation raised its input costs by nearly three-fourths.

22. Between April 1978 and May 1979, interest rates in Turkey were in the 8 to 20 percent range for savings deposits and 16 percent on non-preferential loans as compared to increases in consumer and wholesale prices of 50–60 percent a year. At the same time, the transaction tax and various bank charges may have raised the lending rate to 23–25 percent.

23. Maxwell J. Fry, "Alternative Stabilization Strategies from a Model of Short Run Price and Output Fluctuations in Turkey," *Studies in Development,* 5 (1978), 21–33.

24. Istanbul Chamber of Industry, *Foreign Currency Shortage in 1978 and Effects on Manufacturing Industry,* Istanbul, 1979, 5.

25. *Ibid.,* 9–10.

26. *Ibid.,* 12–13.

27. The current account deficit equals the net inflow of capital, including changes in foreign exchange reserves. During the eighteen year period preceding the oil crisis, for which data are available, it exceeded 2.0 percent of GNP only in 1963.

28. Seedless raisins, hazelnuts, pistachio, dried figs, cotton, rice in husk, lentil, mohair, livestock, oil cake, and molasses.

29. Estimates of this elasticity for developing countries range between 3 and 7; the latter figure has been obtained for the devaluation of 1959 in Spain that was at the time in a similar situation as Turkey is at present as far as tourism is concerned (Andrias S. Gerakis, "Effects of Exchange-Rate Devaluations and Revaluations on Receipts of Tourism," *International Monetary Fund Staff Papers,* 12 (1965), 365–83).

30. Government imports, chiefly petroleum and military equipment, could be financed from the proceeds of agricultural exports and foreign loans. However, the objective of energy conservation would necessitate imposing additional taxes on fuel.

31. While traditionally the principal sources of Turkey's oil imports were Iraq, Libya, and Iran, it is planned to increase imports from Saudi Arabia in the future.

32. The calculations do not take account of the possibility that oil-producing countries would limit the price increases applicable to Turkey. They further assume unchanged transportation costs.

33. According to estimates of the Ministry of Finance, about $10 billion of repayment, amortization, and interest are due during the period of the Fourth Five-Year Plan (1979–83), of which nearly one-half represents the repayment of short-term debt.

34. For the conditions of this integration, see the following discussion of the system of protection.

35. Tansu Ciller, *op. cit.,* Table 2.2.

36. *The Turkish Economy: Prospects for Growth Within Stability, op. cit.,* 133.

37. Tansu Ciller, *op cit.,* Table 2.6.

38. Other commodities in the intermediate products category include forest products, paper and printing, leather, rubber, plastics, chemicals, fertilizers, cement and its products, glass, and ceramics.

39. State Planning Organization, "Turkey's Fourth Five Year Plan (1979–83)," preliminary version, Ankara, 1978, Table 142.

40. *Ibid.,* Table 141.

41. *Ibid.*, Tables 139 and 142.

42. Bela Balassa, "A 'Stages' Approach to Comparative Advantage," Essay 6 in this volume.

43. State Planning Organization, *op. cit.,* Table 123.

44. According to estimates of the Ministry of Finance, in 1978 the financing requirements of state economic enterprises amounted to TL90 billion, of which TL57 billion represented investment expenditures and TL33 billion the oeprating deficit. In the same year, the total financing requirements of the public sector were TL106 billion, i.e. over 8 percent of GNP. About one-sixth of the total was financed through the issue of debt obligations, reportedly exceeding private corporate issues ten times (Statement by Mehmet Gun Calika in *The Wall Street Journal,* May 31, 1979), one-sixth by foreign borrowing, three-fifths by borrowing from the Central Bank, and the remainder from other domestic sources.

45. State Planning Organization, *op. cit.,* Tables 25, 122, 123.

46. Erol Manisali, *Foreign Economic Relations of Turkey,* Istanbul, Güryay Madbaasi, 1979, 105.

47. *Ibid,* 96.

48. *The Turkish Economy: Prospects for Growth Within Stability, op. cit.,* Tables 21 and 22.

49. *Ibid.,* 26.

50. *Ibid.,* 47.

51. TÜSIAD, *The Turkish Economy, 1979,* Istanbul, Turkish Industrialist and Businessmen's Association, July 1979, 104.

52. Shigeyuki Abe, Maxwell J. Fry, Byoung Kyun Min, Pairoj Vongvipanond and Teh-Pei Yu, "Financial Liberalization and Domestic Saving in Economic Development: An Empirical Test for Six Countries," *Pakistan Development Review,* 16 (1977), 298–308.

53. Ronald McKinnon, *Money and Capital in Economic Development,* Washington, D.C., The Brookings Institution, 1973.

54. Seventy-three production activities from tomato paste to motorcycle and bicycle tires were deleted from the list in 1979 while a number of activities from mushrooms and asparagus for export to various motor vehicle parts and components were added (*The Turkish Economy, 1979, op. cit.,* 75).

55. According to a recent study of state manufacturing enterprises in Turkey, "crucial constraints are imposed by the institutional framework: political appointments, political interference in management, low pay to executives, poorly defined objectives, and poor performance audit." (Bertil Walstedt, "State Manufacturing Enterprise in a Mixed Economy: The Turkish Case," A World Bank Research Publication, Baltimore, Md., The Johns Hopkins University Press, 1980, 49.

56. *Ibid.,* 182, 144.

57. *The Turkish Economy: Prospects for Growth Within Stability, op. cit.,* 38.

58. *Ibid.,* 39–41.

59. Cf. Bela Balassa, "The Economic Reform in Hungary Ten Years After," Essay 14 in this volume.

60. The latter figure represents an average of sectoral productivity growth rates (agriculture, 3.7 percent; industry, 3.7 percent; and services, 1.0 percent), the weights being the sectoral composition of the labor force in the base year, 1967.

61. Simon Kuznets, *Modern Economic Growth: Rate, Structure and Spread,* New Haven, Conn., Yale University Press, 1966, 402–03.

62. Hasan Olgun, *op. cit.,* Table 6.16. Even higher protection rates for manufacturing industries were obtained by Tansu Ciller (*op cit.,* Table 2.4), whose results could not, however, be used for present purposes because of the lack of aggregation for the manufacturing sector.

63. The same assumption has been made in regard to gas, electricity, and water, which are combined with manufacturing in the table. The industry sector further includes mining, for which Olgun estimated the ratio of domestic to world market value added at 1.20 (Hasan Olgun, *op. cit.,*

Table 6.16). With mining accounting for 7.9 percent, and electricity, gas and water for 5.6 percent, of value added in the manufacturing sector (OECD, *National Accounts of the OECD Countries, 1975*, Vol. II, Paris, 1977), the ratio of domestic to world market value added is estimated at 3.68 for industry as a whole.

64.   The 0.5 percentage points difference between estimates made at domestic and at world market prices exceeds similar estimates made by the author for other developing countries, Pakistan excepted, by a considerable margin. The estimated differences in terms of percentage points are: Brazil, 0.1; Mexico, 0.1; Pakistan, 0.5; and the Philippines, 0.1. No differences are shown for Chile and Malaysia while for Norway there is a 0.1 percentage point difference in the opposite direction (Bela Balassa and Associates, *The Structure of Protection in Developing Countries*, Baltimore, Md., Johns Hopkins University Press, 1971, 34).

65.   *Foreign Trade Regimes and Economic Development: Turkey, op. cit.,* 259.

66.   Public consumption increased at an average annual rate of 11 percent between 1967 and 1977 while private consumption grew by only 5 percent (*The Turkish Economy, 1979, op. cit.,* 101).

Essay 14

1.   A description of the reform measures is provided in Friss (1969). For an early appraisal, see Balassa (1960).

2.   The deterioration in the efficiency of resource use is reflected by the fact that unit increases in consumption necessitated increasing efforts in the form of resources devoted to new investments. Thus, between 1958 and 1966, the volume of investments increased by 177 percent, while the net material product rose by 62 percent, and total consumption (private and public) by 46 percent. Correspondingly, despite the increased share of resources devoted to investment, the average annual rate of growth of the net material product declined from 7.1 percent in 1957–60 to 5.5 percent in 1960–63, and again to 4.6 percent in 1963–66. (Unless otherwise noted, all data relating to the Hungarian economy originate from the *Statistical Yearbook* and the *Foreign Trade Statistical Yearbook,* both published by the Hungarian Statistical office. The former publication is available in Hungarian and in English, the latter in Hungarian only.)

3.   Hungarian Socialist Workers' (Communist) Party.

4.   Béla Csikós-Nagy, ("A Gazdasági Kalkulációról" (On Economic Calculations), *Közgazdasági Szemle*, 23 (1976), 644), the President of the Hungarian Materials and Prices Board, reports that, in 1974, 70 percent of increases in world market prices were neutralized through subsidies to imports.

5.   According to József Bognár, (*Világgazdasági Korszakváltás (Changes in an Era of the World Economy)*, Budapest, Közgadasági és Jogi Könyvkiadó, 1976, 17), one of the architects of the reform, "we know from experience that the correct solution to all fundamental problems of the Hungarian economy (growth, development, rate of expansion, rational economic structure, equilibrium conditions, technological development, living standards, etc.) depends primarily on the effectiveness of adapting to world market conditions."

6.   László Akar, "Az Exportösztönzes Egyes Kérdései" (Some Questions Concerning Export Incentives), *Pénzügyi Szemle*, 20 (1976), 483.

7.   Ottó Gadó, *The Economic Mechanism in Hungary—How It Works,* Budapest, A.W. Sijthoff, Leyden, and Akadémiai Kiadó, 1976, 16, 26—27.

8.   Bela Balassa, *The Firm in the New Economic Mechanism in Hungary,* in M. Bornstein, ed., *Plan and Market,* New Haven, Yale University Press, 1973, 349–56. The role of profit incentives is downplayed by David Granick (*Enterprise Guidance in Eastern Europe,* Princeton, N.J., Princeton University Press, 1975), whose conclusions are based on interviews with five firms. By contrast, the results cited by the author are based on a survey of 152 firms.

9.   These conclusions differ from those of Granick (*op. cit.,* 305–09) based on the experience of the first 3–4 years of the reform. The differences may be explained by the transitional difficulties experienced in the first few years following the reform's introduction.

10. Data on exports and GDP in market economies originate from the *International Financial Statistics*, published by the International Monetary Fund.

11. However, GDP increased at an average annual rate of 8.8 percent in Korea where this was supported by the rapid expansion of exports.

12. The amount of Hungary's debts in convertible currencies, adjusted for Eurocurrency deposits in Western banks, reportedly reached $2.4 billion at the end of 1976 (*The Economist*, October 29, 1977), approximately equalling its foreign exchange earnings in these currencies. Hungary also had a deficit in its trade with the rouble area.

13. On this point, see Section II below.

14. Data on export composition originate in United Nations *Commodity Trade Statistics*, except for Taiwan for which the *Taiwan Statistical Data Book* has been used.—Note further that while Korea and Taiwan are at a lower level of economic development than Hungary, their manufactured exports reached $2.7 billion and $3.7 billion, respectively, in 1973 as compared to Hungarian exports of $0.8 billion to market economies, and $2.3 billion to socialist countries. The differences increased further between 1973 and 1976.

15. For discussion of the situation existing at the time of reform, see Imre Vajda, "External Equilibrium, Neo-techniques and Economic Reform," *Acta Oeconomica*, 4 (1967), 291–307.

16. Basic manufactures and machinery and transport equipment dominate Hungary's exports to developing countries, which accounted for 15 percent of exports to developed and developing market economies, taken together, in 1973.

17. World Bank Atlas, 1975.

18. Imre Vajda, "Müszaki Fejlödés és Külkereskedelem" (Technological Development and Foreign Trade), *Külkereskedelem*, 5 (1966), 1–15.

19. In this connection, note that in 1976 already the Soviet Union reportedly exported more crude oil to market economies than to socialist countries (*International Herald Tribune*, June 13, 1977).

20. As Lajos Faluvégi ("Development of Financial Regulators and the New Hungarian Five-Year Plan," *Acta Oeconomica*, 16 (1976), 28), the Hungarian Minister of Finance, noted: "A part of Hungarian enterprises could augment their exports to socialist markets at a faster rate, but, if imports cannot be increased, the increase of exports is not justified either. All the more so, because it is a basic issue of improving the balance of trade, whether exports to capitalist markets can be increased to such extent as laid down in the plan."

21. Emil Nyúl, *Arpolitikánk az Ötödik Ötéves Tern Idöszakában (Our Price Policy in the Period of the Fifth Five Year Plan)*, Budapest, Kossuth Konyvkiadó, 1977, 108.

22. In 1974, net subsidies averaged 19 percent of food prices and 32 percent of service prices: in turn, on the average, clothing was subject to a 21 percent tax (Béla Csikós-Nagy, "Árpolitikank az V. Ötéves Terv Inditásakor" (Our Price Policy at the Start of the Fifth Five Year Plan), *Pénzügyi Szemle*, 20 (1976), 13).

23. Emil Nyúl, *op. cit.*, 89.

24. "A Gazdasági Kalkulációról" *op. cit.*, 639.

25. In accordance with the devaluation of the U.S. dollar vis-à-vis most major currencies, the average revaluation of the forint was smaller in regard to the currencies of Hungary's trading partners.

26. In the same year, the ratios of the import price to the domestic price were 3.1 for caustic soda, 1.8 for polyethylene, 1.3 for cellulose-base fiber, and 1.2 for cotton yarn (Gadó, *op cit.*, 29).

27. In fact, the Materials and Prices Board has begun to use forward-looking pricing.

28. Imre Farkas, "A Nyereségadózás és az Érdekeltsegi Alapképzés a Körülmények és a Célok Oldaláról" (The Taxation of Profits and the Formation of Distribution Fund from the Point of View of Existing Conditions and Objectives), *Pénzügyi Szemle*, 19 (1975), 901.

29. László Akar, *op. cit.*, 489.

30. Subsidies are provided, albeit to a lesser extent, for exports to the rouble area as well.

31. In this connection, note that in 1972 the ratio of direct plus indirect imports to production value in manufacturing varied between 23 percent in clothing and 53 percent in organic and inorganic chemicals (Gyula Kovács, "Külkereskedelmúnk és Külkereskedelmi Politikánk

Feladatairól" (On the Tasks of Our Foreign Trade and Our Foreign Trade Policy), *Gazdaság,* 10 (1976), 84.

32.　It has been suggested, for example, that "in the situation developed in 1974–75 the enterprises were interested in successful negotiations with the state organs responsible for taxes and subsidies rather than in adaptation to the market tendencies" (Márton Tardos, "Impact of World Economic Changes on the Hungarian Economy," *Acta Oeconomica,* 15 (1975), 287).

33.　Bela Balassa, "Export Incentives and Export Performance in Developing Countries: A Comparative Analysis," *Weltwirtschaftliches Archiv,* 114 (1978), 24–61. Value added is defined here in terms of world market prices. It thus equals net exchange earnings.

34.　Ferenc Vissi, "Az Adórendszer és a Kétszintü Árrendszer" (The Tax System and the Two-Level System of Prices), *Közgazdasági Szemle,* 23 (1976), 819–32.

35.　The unweighted average of tariffs was 24 percent in 1975 (Ottó Gadó, *op. cit.*, 115), but the tariff structure exhibits a considerable degree of escalation from raw materials to manufactures (Janos Nyerges, "A Vámok Hatása Magyarországon" (The Effects of Duties in Hungary), *Pénzügyi Szemle,* 18 (1974), 795–806). In turn, according to data reported in the *Statistical Yearbook*, subsidies averaged 12 percent of industrial exports in 1974.

36.　Such subsidies have been successfully applied in Greece and Israel.

37.　Bela Balassa, *op. cit.*

38.　This was apparent in the 1972–74 period, when the trading companies did not fully exploit the opportunities created by booming world markets for raising prices.

39.　On price differences in trade among socialist countries, see the interesting work by Sándor Ausch, *Theory and Practice of CMEA Cooperation,* Budapest, Akadémiai Kiadó, 1972.

40.　According to official statistics, the average number of plants per firm was ten in food processing, eight in textiles, clothing and shoe manufacturing, and seven in the machinery industry.

41.　On this point, see László Horváth, "A Szocialista Iparvállalatok Mérete, Tulajdonosi Integráciok" (The Size of Socialist Firms and Their Integration), *Közgazdasági Szemle,* 23 (1976), 509–22. In turn, György Varga, "Vállalati Nagyság és Rugalmas Akalmazkodás" (Size of the Enterprise and Flexible Adaptation), *Gazdaság,* 11 (1977), 51–64, considers the possibility of diseconomies of scale in some large Hungarian firms.

42.　Lajos Faluvégi, "Gazdasági Fejlettség, a Gazdasági Szerkezet, a Külgazdaság uj Jelenségei" (The Level of Economic Development, Economic Structure, and New Developments in External Trade), *Gazdaság,* 9 (1975), 14.

43.　"The Firm in the New Economic Mechanism in Hungary," *op. cit.*, 352.

44.　Further recommendations for improving the process of wage determination have been put forward by Sándor Balázsy, "A Keresetszabályozás 'Megoldhatalan' Dilemmája" (The 'Unsolvable' Dilemma of Regulating Earnings), *Közgazdasági Szemle,* 24 (1978), 154–73.

45.　Béla Csikós-Nagy, "Price Mechanism and Trade in the Means of Production in Hungary," *Acta Oeconomica,* 16 (1976), 43.

46.　"Gazdasági Fejlettség, a Gazdasági Szerkezet, a Külgazdaság uj Jelenségei," *op. cit.*, 17.

47.　The following two paragraphs are based on Andrea Deák, "A Vállalatok Beruházási Döntési Lehetöségeiröl" (On the Possibilities for Investment Decisions by the Firms), *Közgazdasági Szemle,* 22 (1975), 97–103.

48.　Andrea Deák, "A Vállalati Beruházások Allami Támogatása" (The State Support of Firm Investments), *Pénzügyi Szemle,* 20 (1976), 245.

49.　Bela Balassa, Essay 6 in this volume.

50.　For one thing, the transformation of crude oil into petroleum products tends to diminish pressure on oil prices; for another, these countries can utilize in their petrochemical industries natural gas that would otherwise be flared off.

51.　While Hungary's geographical position is not conducive for constructing sea-faring ships, Romania has entered into an agreement with Western firms for the production of airplanes as noted below.

52. Supplementary material to Essay 6.

53. In this connection, reference may be made to the figures originating in György Szakolczay, "A Termelés és as Export Reális Költségei és a Szelektivgazdaságfejlesztés Kriteriumréndszere" (The Real Cost of Production and Export and Criteria for Selective Economic Development), *Gazdaság,* 11 (1977), 7–29.

54. Márton Tardos, "Commodity Pattern of Hungarian Trade," *Acta Oeconomica,* 17 (1976), 285–300.

55. According to Mihály Simai, "Külgazdasági Stratégiánk Néhány Nemzetközi Összefüggéséröl," *Közgazdasági Szemle,* 24 (1977), 502–03, "the increasing importance of capitalist countries in our foreign trade during the next 10–15 years will greatly depend on the extent to which use will be made of new methods serving the needs and the concrete objectives of the partners, such as joint enterprises, industrial–technical cooperation, and joint operations in third markets, etc."

56. Between 1965 and 1976, two hundred and twenty-five cooperation contracts were signed with Western firms, of which 21 percent involved product specialization and 29 percent the division of the production process (Gyula Kovács, "Role of International Cooperation in Hungarian Economic Growth," *Acta Oeconomica,* 17 (1976), 58).

57. *New York Herald Tribune,* June 7, 1977.

58. According to József Bognár, "Epochenwechsel in der Weltwirtschaft und Die Ungarisch Wirtschaft," *Europaische Rundschau,* 5 (1977), 65, "all problems of our economic development should be solved in a way which makes it possible to increase our export and to make this more economical."

59. According to Lajos Faluvégi, "Az Ország Pénze" (The Money of the Country), *Valóság,* 11 (1977), 23, "it is increasingly understood in the government that we restrain the development of firms and cooperatives, and at the same time increase the bureaucracy, with the actual, excessively detailed regulations. Our determination is thus greater than it has been in the last several years to strengthen the role of general regulations, leaving to those executing them."

60. Hungarian language periodicals cited, with English translation in parentheses *Gazdaság (Economy), Külkereskedelem (Foreign Trade), Közgazdásagi Szemle (Economic Review), Pénzügyi Szemle (Financial Review), and Valóság (Reality).*

Essay 15

1. Korea Development Institute, *Long Term Social and Economic Development Plan for Korea, 1976–91,* Seoul, 1977. We depart from Korean custom which does not show the base year in reporting growth rates, i.e., data for the period 1975–91. Unless otherwise noted, all figures are expressed in 1975 prices and exchange rates.

2. The method applied involves expressing GNP in domestic prices of the year 1964 and converting domestic values into U.S. dollars at the 1964 exchange rate.—Unless otherwise noted, for countries other than Korea, all data cited in this essay derive from the International Monetary Fund, *International Financial Statistics.*

3. In the comparisons, no account is taken of the possibility that GNP deflators and exchange rates change at different rates.

4. Hollis Chenery and Tsunehiko Watanabe, "The Role of Industrialization in Japanese Development, 1914–1965," Washington, D.C., World Bank, 1977, (mimeo).

5. The projections for the service sector exclude the balance on factor incomes with the rest of the world, which is, however, included in the service total in the 1975 figures reported in the plan projections. Services including and excluding the factor income balance are shown in rows I and II of Table 15.1.

In 1975, the base year of the projections, Korea had a negative net balance of factor incomes with the rest of the world. To the extent that this balance would improve during the period of the 15 year plan, the growth of domestic service items is overstated in the preliminary projections.

However, for lack of explicit projections of the factor income balance, an adjustment could not be made on this count.

6. Bela Balassa, "Exports and Economic Growth: Further Evidence," *Journal of Development Economics*, 5 (1978), 181–89.

7. Cf. Larry E. Westphal and Kwang Suh Kim, "Industrial Policy and Development in Korea," World Bank Staff Working Paper No. 263, August 1977.

8. "Exports and Economic Growth: Further Evidence," *op. cit.*

9. H. B. Chenery and Moises Syrquin, *Patterns of Development, 1950–1970*, London, Oxford University Press, 1975, 212.

10. The comparable figure for Japan was 13.9 percent in 1975.

11. United Nations, *Yearbook of Industrial Statistics*, New York, 1976—Data on the gross output of the manufacturing sector are not available for Belgium; we have assumed that the ratio of gross output to value added in this country was equal to the ratio in the Netherlands.

12. Office Statistique des Communautés Européennes, *Tableaux Entrées–Sorties*, Luxembourg, 1970.

13. Bela Balassa, "A 'Stages' Approach to Comparative Advantage," Essay 6 in this volume, Table 6.6.—The estimates have been derived by utilizing the "stock" measure of capital intensity; they pertain to the United States and to 1969–70.

14. *Ibid.*, Supplementary Tables.

15. Bela Balassa, "Korea's Development Strategy for the Fourth Five-Year Plan Period (1977–81)," published as Essay 8 in Bela Balassa, *Policy Reform in Developing Countries*, Pergamon Press, 1977, 121.

16. Table 17.3 shows estimates for Japan, Korea, and Taiwan on a comparative basis. The classification scheme used in this table is slightly different from that of Table 15.2. Printing and publishing is not shown separately, and paper and paper products are included with light manufacturing rather than with the heavy and chemical industries.

17. This result is not affected whether calculations are made in 1964 or in 1975 prices and exchange rates. At the same time, we did not follow the preliminary projections in making adjustments for presumed changes in the ratio of GNP deflators to the exchange rate.

18. United Nations, *Yearbook of National Accounts Statistics*, 1976.

19. Korean 1969 daily consumption levels were cereals, 572 grams; potatoes and other staple foods, 150 grams; meat, 22 grams; and oils and fats, 4 grams. Comparable figures for more recent years are not published in the FAO, *Production Yearbook*.

Essay 16

1. Korea Development Institute, *Long-Term Prospect for Economic and Social Development, 1977–91*, Seoul, 1977.

2. A projection of 17.4 percent for 1975–81, adjusted for actual increases in exports between 1975 and 1976.

3. The data cited for Japan, Belgium, and the Netherlands relate to the 1965–75 period; they referred to different periods in Essay 15.

4. With smaller but parallel variations in foreign liabilities, changes in net foreign assets were greater in relative, and smaller in absolute, terms.

5. Bela Balassa, "Incentives for Economic Growth in Korea," published as Essay 9 in Bela Balassa, *Policy Reform in Developing Countries*, Oxford, Pergamon Press, 1977.

6. Cf. Bela Balassa, *Trade Liberalization Among Industrial Countries: Objectives and Alternatives*, New York, McGraw Hill, 1967, ch. 7.

7. Chuck Kuo Kim and Chul Hee Lee, "The Growth of the Automobile Industry in Korea," Working Paper 2809, Seoul, Korea Development Institute, August 1978, 50–51.

8. For a more detailed discussion, see Bela Balassa, "Incentives for Economic Growth in Taiwan," Essay 18 in this volume.

Essay 17

1. Unless otherwise noted, data for Taiwan originate in the *Taiwan Statistical Yearbook*, 1977 and, for the years 1976 and 1977, they have been provided by the Council for Economic Planning and Development; for other countries the sources are the International Monetary Fund, *International Financial Statistics*, and national statistical publications.

2. Shail Jain, *Size Distribution of Incomes, A Compilation of Data*, Washington, D.C., World Bank, 1975.

3. Directorate-General of Budget, Accounting & Statistics, Executive Yuan, *A Report on Personal Income Distribution in Taiwan Area, Republic of China, 1964–1975*, Taipei, 1976.

4. Shirley W.Y. Kuo, "Labor Absorption in Taiwan, 1954–1971." *Economic Essays*, 7 (1977), Taipei Graduate Institute of Economics, National Taiwan University.

5. Economic Planning Council, Executive Yuan, *Six Year Plan for Economic Development in Taiwan, 1976–1981*, Taipei, October 1976.

6. Following customary usage, reference will be to the 1975–81 period in presenting the projections of the six year plan, the base of which is 1975.

7. *Ibid*, 4.

8. In 1976 the share of wage costs in the value of gross output in Taiwan was 8.3 percent in textiles, 16.2 percent in apparel, and 11.3 percent in communication equipment. Comparable figures for 1967 in the United States were 21.2, 30.2, and 36.4 percent. Maurice Scott, "Foreign Trade" in *The Economic Development of Taiwan, 1945–75*, (forthcoming).

9. Estimates of labor force participation and unemployment rates reported in the preliminary plan projection for 1975 are not comparable with those cited earlier, because of changes in definitions.

10. On this point, see "The 15 Year Social and Economic Development Plan for Korea," Essay 15 in this volume, where estimates for Korea are provided in terms of both constant and current prices.

11. Bela Balassa, "A 'Stages' Approach to Comparative Advantage," Essay 6 in this volume.—Investment in human capital has been calculated as the discounted value of the difference between the actual remuneration of labor and its remuneration calculated at unskilled wage rates. The assumption underlying the calculations is that the entire excess over the unskilled wage can be attributed to investment in skills. The data refer to the years 1969–70.

12. Physical to human capital ratios are low also in the case of several unskilled labor-intensive product categories, including ties, corsets, and gloves (0.13), women and girls' clothing (0.17), men's and boys' clothing (0.18), and hats and caps (0.18), as well as in some additional textile and clothign products, such as fur goods (0.11), canvas products (0.12), and lace and embroidery (0.16), which are not included in Table 17.3.

13. In 1972, the value of plant and equipment per worker was estimated at $630 in Taiwan, $752 in Colombia, $1016 in Brazil, $1067 in Mexico, $2049 in Spain, $2196 in Greece, $7102 in Germany, $7211 in France, $7616 in the United States and $7806 in Norway (Bela Balassa, "A 'Stages' Approach to Comparative Advantage," *op. cit.*, Table 6.1) on the assumption that operating plant and equipment includes that established in the preceding fifteen years. This assumption, if anything, overstates the availability of physical capital in Taiwan as compared to the industrial countries since the latter have a large proportion of old equipment.

14. The relevant indices are: Brazil, 29.3; Colombia, 32.3; Mexico, 41.1; Spain, 63.4; Greece, 93.7; Norway, 107.4; Germany, 114.3; and France, 138.8 (Frederick H. Harbison, Jan Maruhnic, and Jane R. Resnick, *Quantitative Analyses of Modernization and Development*, Princeton, N.J., Industrial Relations Section, Department of Economics, Princeton University, 1970, 175–76). The estimates refer to 1965 and can be used to indicate the educational level of the labor force in subsequent periods.

15. This figure is double the marginal savings ratio observed in the 1960–75 period, and while it is lower than the 38 percent ratio attained between 1975 and 1977, the latter is hardly sustainable for a longer period.

16.   As shown in Table 17.4, the average private savings ratio would be 20.5 percent if the rate of growth of GNP reached 8.8 percent in 1975–81.

17.   Maurice Scott, *op. cit.*

18.   Constant price data for individual commodity categories have been derived from the current price data provided in the plan document by assuming that the overall export price deflator applied to each category.

19.   For similar calculations on Korea, and a discussion of the question of vulnerability to foreign events, see Essay 15 in this volume.

20.   Bela Balassa, "Export Incentives and Export Performance: A Comparative Analysis," *Weltwirtschaftliches Archiv*, 114 (1978), 24–61.

21.   For a detailed discussion of the existing system of incentives, in particular as it relates to the machinery sector, see Larry E. Westphal, "Industrial Incentives in Taiwan," Washington, D.C., World Bank, March 1978 (mimeo).

22.   T.H. Lee and Kuo-shu Liang, "Incentive Policies and Economic Development in Taiwan," in Bela Balassa, et.al., *Development Strategies in Semi-Industrial Countries*, Baltimore, Md., Johns Hopkins University Press, 1981.

23.   "Industrial Incentives in Taiwan," *op. cit.*

24.   Shirley W.Y. Kuo, "Effects of Land Reform, Agricultural Princing Policy and Economic Growth in Multiple-Crop Diversification in Taiwan," *Economic Essays*, 8 (1977), Taipei Graduate Institute of Economics, National Taiwan University.

25.   Economic Planning Council, Executive Yuan, *op. cit.*, 39.

26.   *Ibid.*, 6.

27.   In 1969 the interest rate paid on short-term export credits was 0.56 percent per month as compared to 1.17 percent charged for unsecured loans, representing a preference margin of 8 percentage points on an annual basis. This margin was 5.8 percentage points in May 1975 and has since declined to 4.0 percentage points; by comparison, the preferential margin on export credits in 7.0 percentage points in Korea (T.H. Lee and Kuo-Shu Liang, "Incentive Policies and Economic Development in Taiwan," *op. cit.*).

28.   This figure has been calculated by assuming that all export orders are accompanied by letters of credit and that export credits have an average maturity of 3 months (Larry E. Westphal, "Industrial Incentives in Taiwan," *op. cit.*).

29.   Cf. Bela Balassa, "Reforming the System of Protection in Developing Countries," *World Development*, 3 (1975), 365–82; republished as Essay 1 in Bela Balassa, *Policy Reform in Developing Countries*, Oxford, Pergamon Press, 1977.

30.   Economic Planning Council, Executive Yuan, *op. cit.*, 18.

31.   *Ibid.*, 17.

32.   *Ibid.*

33.   The list includes petrochemical and machinery products as well as various chemicals, textiles and clothing products imported from major Asian producing countries.

34.   Economic Planning Council, Executive Yuan, *op. cit.*, 17.

35.   The exchange rate has been 38NT$ to the U.S. dollar since 1974.

Essay 18

1.   Council for Economic Planning and Development, *Revised Economic Plan, 1979–1981*, Taipei, 1978 (special communication).

2.   In interpreting the import projections, it should be noted that they are affected by the choice of 1978, with a substantial export surplus, as the base year for the projections. The question of the desirability of an export surplus will be taken up below.

3.   By comparison, the author accepted the employment projections of the preliminary version of the Six Year Plan and calculated with a 0.5 percent differential due to the redistribution of labor towards manufacturing and a 0.8 percent differential due to higher sectoral productivity growth rates.

4.   The exchange rate was NT$38 to the U.S. dollar until July 1978 when it was reduced by 5 percent.

5.   T.H. Lee and Kuo-Shu Liang, "Incentive Policies and Economic Development in Taiwan," Chapter 10 in Bela Balassa, et.al., *Development Strategies in Semi-Industrial Countries,* Baltimore, Md., Johns Hopkins University Press, 1981.

6.   Bela Balassa, *Trade Liberalization Among Industrial Countries: Objectives and Alternatives*, New York, McGraw Hill, 1966, ch. 3.

7.   In 1977, Taiwanese exports and imports, respectively, were $3.6 billion and $2.0 billion in trade with the United States and $1.3 billion and $0.8 billion in trade with Western Europe.

8.   The data for Taiwan include the 20 percent surcharge and the 4 percent harbor tax that are added to tariffs (Larry E. Westphal, "Industrial Incentives in Taiwan," Washington, D.C., World Bank, March 1978, (mimeo)). At the same time, it should be noted that, notwithstanding recent efforts at import liberalization, Korea has import restrictions to a greater extent than Taiwan (cf. Bela Balassa, "Inflation and Trade Liberalization in Korea," Essay 16 in this volume).

10.   Four years in the case of expansion.

11.   Cf. Bela Balassa, "Development Strategy and the Six Year Plan in Taiwan," *op. cit.*, that also provides a detailed discussion of incentives affecting the machinery industry.

12.   *China News*, September 5, 1978.

Index

Japan used a variety of formal and informal measures to limit the imports of manufactured goods, in particular from developing countries. These measures were liberalized in 1978.[15] As a result, the volume of manufactured imports from the developing countries increased by more than one-fourth between 1977 and 1978,[16] following a decline in the 1973–77 period.

A consideration of the imports of all manufactured goods originating in the developing countries does not suffice, however, to appraise the effects of the trade policies followed by the industrial countries. For this purpose, it is further necessary to examine the commodity composition of imports, since some products encounter non-tariff barriers in the industrial countries while others are subject only to tariffs. This question will be taken up in Section II below.

II. Comparative Advantage and the Commodity Composition of Trade in Manufactured Goods

In an earlier paper,[17] the author has shown that the pattern of world exports of manufactured goods can be explained in terms of intercommodity differences in capital-labor ratios and intercountry differences in capital endowments. The indicators of comparative advantage derived in that paper will be utilized in the following to analyze the pattern of export-import ratios in manufactured trade between the industrial and the non-OPEC developing countries in 1973. Subsequent changes in the commodity composition of this trade will further be examined, with consideration given to the factors that influenced the observed results. Finally, the role of the newly-industrializing countries in the exports of manufactured goods from the developing countries will be noted.

The Structure of Comparative Advantage

In order to examine the comparative advantages of the industrial and the developing countries in their mutual trade in manufactured goods, the capital-labor ratios reported in the earlier paper have been averaged in the eleven commodity category breakdown employed in GATT statistics, using U.S. production data as weights.[18] The estimated ratios pertain to physical as well as to human capital. The former has been obtained as the ratio of the (physical) capital stock to employment; the latter has been estimated as the discounted value of the difference between the average and the unskilled wage, taken to represent the return on investment in human capital. The relevant data are shown in Table 8.3.[19]

Although the eleven commodity category scheme involves a considerable degree of aggregation, substantial differences are observed in capital-labor ratios among the individual categories. The ratio of physical capital per worker (expressed in thousand U.S. dollars per worker) is the highest for iron and steel (27.7) and for chemicals (21.4); it is the lowest for clothing (2.4) and for other

TABLE 8.3
Comparative Advantage Ratios and Trade in Manufactured Goods between Industrial and Developing Countries

	Capital per Worker $ thousand			Export Surplus[2] $ billion		Export-Import Ratio[3]		Ratio of 1978 to 1973 Trade[b]			Ratio of NICs[c] in imports from non-OPEC LDCs
	Physical	Human	Total	1973	1978	1973	1978	Export non-OPEC LDC	Import non-OPEC LDC	Export OPEC	
Iron & Steel	27.71	28.15	55.85	3.00	5.73	6.45	5.82	1.95	2.16	3.45	76
Chemicals	21.37	25.51	46.88	5.43	12.02	6.90	7.91	2.26	2.53	3.38	47
Other Semimanufactures	19.59	24.21	43.80	-0.11	0.58	1.00	1.10	2.57	2.34	5.17	58
Engineering Products, subtotal	9.61	29.38	38.99	18.52	45.16	6.01	4.61	2.59	3.38	5.74	83
Machinery for Specialized Industries	9.44	28.34	37.79	6.81	16.79	53.98	29.46	2.50	4.54	5.01	90
Office & Telecommunication Equipment	7.91	35.22	43.15	1.13	2.31	1.88	1.62	2.50	2.91	5.09	75
Road Motor Vehicles	12.89	25.40	38.39	3.39	8.76	38.67	21.37	2.64	4.78	5.31	91
Other Machinery & Transport Equipment	9.66	30.27	39.93	6.62	16.80	7.07	5.20	2.70	3.67	6.81	77
Household Appliances	8.29	39.09	47.38	0.47	0.31	1.42	1.08	2.56	3.36	5.43	95
Textiles	10.00	16.62	26.62	0.32	0.05	1.16	1.01	1.58	1.81	2.50	55
Clothing	2.37	11.00	13.37	-3.03	-8.75	0.11	0.09	2.18	2.81	5.88	81
Other Consumer Goods	6.73	25.99	32.72	-0.86	-3.70	0.80	0.49	2.55	3.22	7.24	90
Manufactured Goods, total	11.89	26.11	38.00	23.29	51.14	2.50	2.20	2.41	2.74	5.04	75

Sources: Capital per Worker: Bela Balassa, "A 'Stages' Approach to Comparative Advantage" *op. cit.* Exports and Imports: GATT, *International Trade 1978/79* and GATT tapes.

Notes: (a) Industrial countries' exports to, and imports from, the non-OPEC developing countries. (b) Ratio of the industrial countries' exports and imports, respectively, in trade with developing countries. (c) Newly industrializing countries, defined to include Argentina, Brazil, Chile, Mexico, Uruguay, Israel, Hong Kong, Korea, Singapore and Taiwan.

consumer goods (6.7). The ratio of human capital per worker is also the lowest for clothing (11.0), followed by textiles (16.6); it is the highest for household appliances (39.1) and for office and telecommunication equipment (35.2). Combining physical and human capital, iron and steel (55.9), household appliances (47.4) and chemicals (46.9) are at the upper, clothing (13.4) textiles (26.6) and other consumer goods (32.7) at the lower, end of the range (Table 8.3).

If engineering products are considered as a single group, 1973 export-import ratios in trade between the industrial countries and the non-OPEC developing countries largely correspond to the pattern of comparative advantage as represented by capital-labor ratios, the only exception being semimanufactures.[20] As shown in Table 8.4, iron and steel and chemicals with the highest overall capital-labor ratios also had the highest export-import ratios (6.5 and 6.9 respectively) in 1973. Apart from semimanufactures, engineering products placed next in terms of overall capital-output ratios (39.0) as well as export-import ratios (6.0).

At the other extreme, the exports of the industrial countries to the non-OPEC developing countries hardly reached one-tenth of their imports in the case of clothing that exhibits by far the lowest capital-labor ratio. The next lowest export-import ratio (0.8) is shown for the other consumer goods category, including shoes, travel goods, toys, sports goods, and a variety of miscellaneous products, which exhibit the second-lowest capital intensity.

A seemingly aberrant result is observed in the case of other semi-manufactures that had an export-import ratio of 1.0 in 1973, notwithstanding their relatively high capital-labor ratio (43.8). However, several of the commodities included in this category are natural resource products, which in fact provides an advantage to developing countries that possess the resources in question. Also, the category is rather heterogeneous as it includes capital-intensive products, such as pulp and paper, as well as labor-intensive products, such as leather and rubber manufactures, when weighting by U.S. production imparts an upward bias to the estimated average capital-labor ratio for the group as a whole.

Apart from their above-average capital intensity, the sophistication of the production process and the need for the availability of precision-engineered parts, components, and accessories limited the export possibilities of the developing countries in a variety of engineering products. These factors in large part explain the very high export-import ratios in the trade of the industrial countries with the non-OPEC developing countries in the case of machinery for specialized industries (54.0) and road motor vehicles (38.7). In turn, the export-import ratio was 7.1 for the other machinery and transport equipment category, which also includes some relatively simple products, such as bicycles.

Finally, 1973 export-import ratios were relatively low for office and telecommunication equipment (1.9) and for household appliances (1.4). In both instances, physical capital-labor ratios are substantially lower than for the average, although relatively high human capital intensity raises their overall capital-labor ratio. At the same time, within the first category, developing countries exported chiefly electronic components that are highly labor intensive while a large share of exports in the second category were radios that are produced by relatively simple techniques.

We have further calculated weighted averages of capital-labor ratios for the exports and the imports of the industrial countries in their trade in manufactured goods with the non-OPEC developing countries, the weights being the value of exports and imports in the eleven commodity-group breakdown. In 1973, the relevant ratios for exports (expressed in thousand U.S. dollars per worker) were 13.8 for physical capital and 27.5 for human capital, totalling 41.3. In turn, average capital-labor ratios for the manufactured imports of the industrial countries from the non-OPEC developing countries were 9.8, 25.1, and 34.8, respectively.

The results indicate the comparative advantages of the industrial countries in capital-intensive commodities vis-à-vis the non-OPEC developing countries. This conclusion applies also to the industrial countries and country groups, taken individually, with percentage differences in average capital-labor ratios for their exports and imports in trade in manufactured goods with the non-OPEC developing countries ranging between 18 percent in the United States to 36 percent in Canada. At the same time, for the industrial countries, taken together, as well as for the individual countries and country groups, the extent of comparative advantage vis-à-vis the non-OPEC developing countries appears to be greater in regard to physical than for human capital.

Changes in the Commodity Composition of Trade, 1973–1978

Industrial Country Exports.   In the exports of the industrial countries to OPEC in the 1973–1978 period, above-average increases are shown for consumer goods; the ratio of 1978 to 1973 exports was 5.3 for motor vehicles, 5.4 for household appliances, 5.9 for clothing and 7.2 for other consumer goods as against an overall average of 5.0.[21] In turn, the lowest ratios are observed in the case of iron and steel (3.5), chemicals (3.4), and textiles (2.5). Finally, machinery and equipment exhibited average ratios (5.0 to 5.1), except for the high ratio shown for the "other machinery and transport equipment" category (6.8) where aircraft and other military equipment are of importance.

Given the limited domestic production of manufactured goods in most of the OPEC countries, these results tend to reflect patterns of domestic use. It would then appear that, on the whole, increases in oil earnings were used more to increase consumption and military expenditure than to raise investment levels.

Iron and steel, chemicals, and textiles also experienced smaller than average increases in industrial country exports of manufactured goods to the non-